# The Value of a Dollar

1600 - 1865

# The Value
# of a Dollar

## Colonial Era to the Civil War

## 1600 – 1865

**Scott Derks and Tony Smith**

A UNIVERSAL REFERENCE BOOK

Grey House
Publishing

|                      |                        |
|----------------------|------------------------|
| PUBLISHER:           | Leslie Mackenzie       |
| EDITORIAL DIRECTOR:  | Laura Mars-Proietti    |
| AUTHORS:             | Scott Derks, Tony Smith |
| COPYEDITOR:          | Elaine Alibrandi       |
| COMPOSITION:         | Q2A Solutions          |
| MARKETING DIRECTOR:  | Jessica Moody          |

A Universal Reference Book
Grey House Publishing, Inc.
185 Millerton Road
Millerton, NY 12546
518.789.8700
FAX 518.789.0545
www.greyhouse.com
e-mail: books @greyhouse.com

Publisher's Cataloging-In-Publication Data
(Prepared by The Donohue Group, Inc.)


The value of a dollar, 1600-1865 : the colonial era to the civil war / by Scott Derks/Tony Smith

  p. : 450
Includes bibliographical references and index.
ISBN: 1-59237-094-2

1. Prices--United States--History. 2. Wages--United States--History. 3. Purchasing power--United States--History. 4. Cost and standard of living--United States--History. I. Derks, Scott. 2. Smith, Tony

HB235.U6 V358 2005
338.5/2/0973

To our wives, Ellen and Ingrid,
for their loving patience and silent understanding

# Acknowledgments

Without the work of many this book would not have been possible. The authors wish to thank and acknowledge the contributions of many friends and family who found joy in helping us dig out these intriguing bits of obscure information. The first tip of the hat is awarded to Ingrid Smith for research assistance and initial draft editing. Thanks must also be lavished on contributors Bill Gaillard, Jan Brown, Brian Stanley, David Lavoie, Lucia Derks, Ellen Hanckel and Sonny Howell. As always, we also celebrate the work of copyeditor Elaine Alibrandi and editorial director Laura Mars-Proietti, who always know how to make the words run in the same direction. And thanks to publisher Leslie Mackenzie who continues to believe in the importance of these books.

In celebration of librarians everywhere, the bulk of the praise for this edition goes to Stephanie Philbrick, Maine Historical Society; Rachel Roberts, Dallas Historical Society; Staff at South Carolina Department of Archives and History; Staff at the Massachusetts State Archives; Staff at the Richland County Public Library, Columbia, South Carolina; Staff at Virginia Historical Society; Staff at the Free Library of Philadelphia; Staff at the Library of Virginia; and the staff of the Blue Ridge Regional Library, Martinsville, Virginia. We are also indebted to the probate research conducted by Gunston Hall Plantation, Old Sturbridge Village, Gary Stanton at the University of Mary Washington's Department of Historic Preservation, Richard E. Stevens at the University of Delaware, Sue Patterson's work on Collins County, Texas and Patricia Scott Deetz, Christopher Fennell & J. Eric Deetz's The Plymouth Colony Archive Project. Thanks too for Robert Sahr of Oregon State University and his research and information on historical Consumer Price Indexing and Louis Jordan's work on The Coins of Colonial and Early America. Finally, appreciation to Professor Charles M. Dobbs, at Iowa State University, for his thoughtful comments. God bless you all.

# Contents

# Chapter 4
## 1800-1824: Another War, Manufacturing, Self-Sufficiency and Prosperity

# Chapter 5
## 1825-1849: Western Expansion, Canal Transportation and American Confidence

# Chapter 6
## 1850-1865: Railroads, Slavery and a Nation at War with Itself

# Introduction

Welcome to the first edition of *The Value of a Dollar, 1600-1865*. This book both parallels and complements its popular older brother *The Value of a Dollar, 1860-2004, now in its third edition*. Starting with the founding of America and extending through the Colonial Era to the Civil War, this volume of *The Value of a Dollar* focuses on what things cost and how much workers made. Its coverage is diverse, including the cost of everything from clothing to cows, from treatment of a snake bite to nervousness, from the passage of a young female slave to a clothing trunk. Efforts have been made to include nearly every item necessary for everyday life so students, historians and the simply curious can explore the wage and price structure of early America. Also illustrated are commodity values, investment data and income opportunities. There is no other publisher's work that contains the range of years covered, and the comprehensiveness of items and services compiled.

This easy-to-use reference book will allow researchers -- including genealogists and antique collectors -- to determine the original cost of a finely made mahogany chest or calculate the financial burden of buying a horse-drawn carriage large enough to take a farm family to church. Under the best of circumstances, pricing is an inexact science. The value of a given item fluctuates from year-to-year, season-to-season. Often pricing decisions are based upon a variety of issues including scarcity, the storekeeper's need for cash or consumer demand. The price of a shovel -- even today -- might vary in price from region to region, store to store or even month to month. Exploring these questions during the 1600s, 1700s and 1800s creates its own set of complexities, including the availability and quality of sources, the wide variance of prices from region to region, type of currency used, the high cost of transportation or political issues such as boycotts, tariffs, taxes or war. Though many studies abound on wholesale prices, few studies define the value of a dollar at the point of purchase. Thus the authors made extensive use of primary documents such as probate inventories, account records, newspapers, magazines, letters and posters. In addition, rural America was wedded to the barter system during this period, exchanging a pig for an oil lamp, further complicating efforts to establish a fixed price on goods and services.

Unique to this book is the availability of currency conversion tables for the reader. To grasp the monetary value of the price expressed during the period, one can calculate the price equivalent in 2002 dollars – the most reliable year available for British Sterling conversions. It is easier to understand the value of an item in the past by knowing its worth its worth in the present. Though economic indexes were not established until the 20th Century, many historians have complied information on prices and attempted to develop a measure for statistical analysis. Because data is limited, values in the conversion tables are approximate. Such values may vary greatly and might exceed a margin of error of +/-25%.

## Arrangement

The book is divided into six chapters which, after the first on the era of early colonial settlement to 1749, follows a standard format. This broad coverage provides a good overview of when the colonies and commerce, both domestic and international, were just forming, and records few. Subsequent chapters cover the periods from 1750-1774; 1775-1799; 1800-1824; 1825-1849; 1850-1865. Each chapter begins with a background essay describing the major social and economical focus of the period.

Unlike The *Value of a Dollar, 1865-2004*, which drew heavily upon commercial sources such as newspaper or magazine advertisements, nationally distributed catalogues or sales fliers, this volume of *The Value of a Dollar, 1600-1865*, musters much of its credibility from public sources such as probate records, land sale documents, store ledgers, governmental statutes and publications which faithfully record key issues of commerce during this period of America's history; refer to the Bibliography at the back of this volume for a list of titles used. Prices recorded for a set of fine English china incorporates the sale price of the dinnerware, but also the tariffs, transportation and broker fees on both sides of the Atlantic. These records do not, however, record its comparative quality or scarcity in that market, its age and condition at time of evaluation, only its value on the market that day. These sources provided incredible variety and depth, although the actual description of an axe or tea set might be scant. Thus great effort has been made to show the source, location and year of the transaction. In this way the reader has greater insight into understanding everyday costs. When possible similar items, such as tools or tables, have been listed multiple times for perspective and comparison.

Information has been provided using the original spelling and capitalization found in the official records. While this may occasionally cause confusion or give the appearance of a misspelled word, the authors believe the richness of the material is better conveyed in this manner. At the suggestion of librarians nationwide, this volume is filled with conversion tables that are repeated throughout each chapter, so the reader can readily calculate the current value of a fee, income or selected price, for any given year covered, into modern dollars. In the first three chapter the conversion chart is expressed in British pounds, shillings and pence -- the most recognized medium of exchange during those periods. Later chapters are appropriately shown in U.S. dollars.

## Content

Each chapter contains the following elements:

> **Historical Snapshots:** A chronology of key economic and historical events from each year.

> **Selected Incomes:** A selection of jobs listed from data compiled from primary sources, such as governmental records, diaries, newspapers, state statues and payroll accounts. Many secondary sources were used from various historical publications and US Department of Labor - Bureau of the Census' *Historical Statistics of the United States, Colonial Times to 1970*. Also, comprehensive, modern studies have been drawn upon to document the wages of specialized jobs such as cabinet makers, glass blowers or gunsmiths in their exploration of a particular craft. During the years covered in this book, the majority of workers were farmers whose income and wages often came though crops, barter or labor

exchanges with neighbors that conceal the real earnings of this essential group. Efforts have also been made to differentiate the wages of men, women, children, slaves who were hired out, and freedmen.

**Services & Fees:** To provide a more accurate look at the cost of doing business in early America, the book incorporates a new section embracing the often hidden cost of managing a household budget --fees and services. Within this field can be found the tolls charged by Indian tribes for wagon trains to pass through their area, the cost to have the local doctor treat a snake bite, the fines levied on those who fell asleep in church or hotel fees for weary travelers. The source of this information was frequently found in specialized publications that focused on medicine, furniture making, taverns or even the invoices of storekeepers

**Financial Rates & Exchanges:** Financial information is limited during the early American colonial period. Material within this category arrived from a number of sources, primarily the Economic Historical research provided by EH.Net, US Department of Labor - Bureau of the Census' *Historical Statistics of the United States, Colonial Times to 1970* and Sidney Homer & Richard Sylla's, *A History of Interest Rate.*

**Slave Trade:** A section dedicated to the price traded for slaves imported to the Americas by British merchants. The prices within the first two chapters provides an average price of purchasing a slave within Africa and the amount of purchasing one in North America from a merchant. Chapters 3 and 4 only cover an average price of slaves imported into America by the British until the slave trade legally ended in 1807. Information was gathered by the US Department of Labor - Bureau of the Census' *Historical Statistics of the United States, Colonial Times to 1970* and Stanley Engerman & Eugene Genovese's, *Race and Slavery in the Western Hemisphere*

**Commodities:** A report of the wholesale commodities traded within Philadelphia only in the first two chapters, and within several major American cities in the later chapters. The commodities expressed are food items, agricultural products and manufactured goods. In the first half of the book, values are expressed in silver dollars currently traded in the city noted. The second half of the book is in United States Dollars. Much of this information was acquired from the primary research conducted by Arthur Harrison Cole found within his book *Wholesale Commodity Prices in the United States 1700-1861.*

**Selected Prices:** A selection of priced items typically found in public records such as probate inventories during the period. These items are typically valued based upon their value, condition and scarcity, but may be worth more depending upon the availability within the market. A gold watch may be appraised at a less value than what a consumer is willing to purchase. Prices were also acquired from other primary sources, such as a storekeeper's account books and inventories, which reflect the actual price paid by the consumer. Other sources include newspapers, advertisements and written accounts during the period. Sources also include secondary historical publications.

**Miscellany:** A selection of fascinating insights into early America drawn from diaries, advertisements, letters, speeches and books of the times. Many feature financial issues of the day; all are provided to explore the lifestyle, culture and emotions of the period.

## Audience

As with the last edition of *The Value of Dollar, 1860-2004*, this book has been prepared for people curious about social history: students studying the topics that require knowledge abut everyday life in America; teachers who seek information to enliven classroom discussions while broadening their students' understanding of the quality of American life; writers who need access to the basic facts of American commerce; business historians seeking data to establish a framework of salary and price information during a specific period; reporters seeking to enhance a story with economic details. *The Value of a Dollar* series is for the both the user who simply wants to know what life was like during the time in the his or her American ancestors and the serious historical researcher.

# 1600-1749

# The Development of the Colonies

The colonization of North America from the early 1600s through the first half of the 1700s was an extremely difficult, ambitious, foolhardy, rewarding and often deadly process. To Europeans, this untamed land of few people and plentiful resources represented a cornucopia of opportunities. While the reasons for coming to the New World were many and varied, including religious freedom and fundamental values, the settling of America was economic development at its best and worst. The religious Pilgrims also talked of marketing fish; Virginians fell in love with growing tobacco. The British Navy wanted to harvest tall virgin timber for building sailing ships; English weavers needed potash. The Spanish, like many, wanted gold. The Dutch traded with the Indians for beaver pelts and the French shipped deerskins by the thousands. In the end, settlers came to the new continent for vastly different reasons, and thus they created colonies with very different social, religious, political and economic structures-an economic fact that indelibly marked each region's future.

America's early growth was closely linked to European turmoil, government-led oppression of minorities and economic downturns. In Pennsylvania alone, the waves of impoverished Scotch-Irish and German emigrants flooding that state caused its population to explode from 18,000 in 1700 to 120,000 in 1750. When too many poor people were chasing too few jobs in Europe, the colonies offered the ideal safety value to Germans or English or Swedes. Many clung to old customs and native languages while harboring new dreams. Seaport records indicate that indigent English servants comprised three-quarters of the early 120,000 emigrants to the Chesapeake area. Most were young, unmarried laborers-the census included only 15 percent women-who owned nothing, or journeymen artisans who possessed some skills but no shop. Too poor to afford the £6 cost of the transatlantic passage, most mortgaged four to seven years of their lives for the opportunity to escape a life of unrelenting poverty. Many lost their lives in the pursuit of wealth in the nearly classless society of America. And

when their debts were paid, most immediately sought one thing: land of their own. Liberal land ownership laws proved effective. The Virginia Company, for example, was teetering on bankruptcy after transporting 1,700 people, at a cost of 50,000 pounds, before it changed its structure to allow colonists to own and work land as their private property. Nearly everyone wanted uncultivated land for agricultural purposes. So much existed that colonists indulged themselves in often wasteful and short-sighted practices. Land-strapped Englishmen wrote often about girdled trees left rotting in the fields or the tendency of farmers to simply abandon exhausted fields. This same land lust also crowded the Indian population out of their traditional lands, invariably transforming the natives into an intractable foe, forced by the waves of new settlers to fight for their very survival.

Investors quickly found that America was a land of varied attitudes and motivations. For example, while many settlers were poor, the emigrants to New England were "middling sorts" who preserved their freedom by paying their own way across the Atlantic. The group known as Puritans espoused a rigorous faith that set them apart from Anglican England, where the crown often dictated the very content of sermons. These colonists' values helped them prosper in a demanding land by developing an entrepreneurial and independent view. Unlike other parts of the colonies which relied on indentured servants or imported slaves, in New England, farmers looked to their own families for labor, which led to a more egalitarian distribution of property and wealth. By contrast, in the Southern colonies, slave labor dominated. During the eighteenth century, the British colonies imported 1.5 million slaves, or three times the number of free immigrants. The average price of an African slave in 1710 was £17.

At its core, though, the American colonial economy was export-driven, encouraged by investors who wanted to turn rice, indigo, lumber or furs into huge profits. Notwithstanding the English navigation laws, which restricted American manufacturing and mandated where the crops could be sold, colonists sought self-sufficiency. They not only grew most of their own food, but also made many of the crude tools they used in production. But because goods such as nails or glass were cheaper to buy from England than to manufacture, the colonial economy remained dependent on the Motherland. Real economic growth should be seen as the result of both the quality of foreign commerce and the dynamics of expanding local economies.

In many ways, settling America was a noble experiment. England did not have a single, successful colony in the New World in 1603, when James Stuart ascended the throne. Yet England was endowed with new confidence after its defeat of Spain and ready for a new role in international affairs. America was viewed as a place to find riches, sell manufactured goods, buy crops and to send the nation's "valiant rogues and sturdy beggars" who had been displaced by expanding sheep farms. The colonies were to be an extension of European life. But in class-driven England, the role and position of the aristocracy was clear, whereas in America, most of the leading men lacked the mystique of a traditional ruling class. Hard-driving merchants and planters of middling origins aggressively battled to create fortunes and claim high office. Thus, this period was marked with dozens of rebellions as unqualified or insensitive ruling-class British tried to snare the reins of prosperity from the colonists.

While land was plentiful and disease ever present, hard money of all types was scarce. Barter ruled the day. When a marriage was arranged in early Virginia, the groom was required to pay the London Company 120 pounds of tobacco for the bride's transportation. In New York, among the Dutch, beaver pelts held sway. And for the French traders and southern trappers, the availability of deerskins helped create the concept of a "buck" having a specified value. (Between 1699 and 1715, South Carolina alone exported an average 53,000 deerskins a year.) Throughout the colonies, farmers swapped surplus grain for needed tools. Barter worked well as long as the exchange was local. By the middle of the eighteenth century, however, paper notes became an important part of commerce, creating a regional flavor to capital values. South Carolina established the first public bank in 1712, followed by the other colonies. Unfortunately, each had different values and could not be exchanged easily. As a result, salt or wheat would command a variety of apparent prices based on the monetary exchange rate in Massachusetts or Pennsylvania, not on the quality of the commodity. England acted in 1741 to halt the chaotic system by forbidding private individuals and companies from issuing paper money. It was one of dozens of laws England used to rein in the increasingly unruly colonies. These efforts to control wealth would eventually lead to the Revolutionary War and its theme of no taxation without representation.

# HISTORICAL SNAPSHOTS
# 1600-1749

## 1600–1609

### 1600

♦ William Shakespeare's *Hamlet* was first performed

♦ At a time when the corsets of European women were usually made of whalebone, Marie de Medici unsuccessfully tried to introduce metal corsets into fashion

### 1601

♦ Dutch navigator Olivier van Noort returned after three years at sea circumnavigating the world

♦ England abolished monopolies

♦ Shakespeare wrote *Troilus and Cressida*

♦ Jesuit missionary Matteo Ricci was admitted to Peking, China

♦ The Earl of Essex led a revolt against Queen Elizabeth I; he was tried for treason and executed

♦ England passed the Elizabethan Poor Law under which each parish was responsible for looking after its own poor

### 1602

♦ Ben Johnson wrote the comedy *The Poetaster*

♦ Shakespeare wrote *All's Well That Ends Well*

♦ The Ambrosian Library of Milan, Italy, was founded; the Bodleian Library of Oxford, England, opened

♦ The Dutch East India Company was founded and capitalized in Batavia to become the first modern public company

♦ Galileo investigated the laws of gravitation and oscillation

♦ Spanish traders were admitted to eastern Japan

### 1603

♦ England experienced an outbreak of the plague

♦ Queen Elizabeth I of England died and was succeeded by her cousin James VI of Scotland, who became James I

♦ Fabricio di Acquapendente discovered valves in veins

♦ Carlo Maderna built the façade at St. Peter's cathedral in Rome, Italy

### 1604

♦ Peace was declared between Spain and England

♦ The Spanish captured Ostend from the Dutch after a three-and-a-half-year siege

♦ Shakespeare wrote *Measure for Measure*

♦ King James I issued his "Counterblast to Tobacco"

### 1605

♦ Cervantes published *Don Quixote, Part 1*

♦ Santa Fe, New Mexico, was founded

♦ Shakespeare wrote both *King Lear* and *Macbeth*

♦ Guy Fawkes was arrested and accused of trying to blow up the Houses of Parliament

### 1606

♦ Galileo Galilei invented the proportional compass

♦ The Virginia Company of London granted a royal charter and 120 colonists were sent to Virginia

♦ The first open air opera was held in Rome

### 1607

♦ Jamestown, Virginia, the first English settlement in the American mainland, was founded

♦ The Union of England and Scotland was rejected by Parliament

♦ The Bank of Genoa failed after the announcement of national bankruptcy in Spain

### 1608

♦ Thomas Middleton wrote the satirical comedy, *A Mad World, My Masters*

♦ The first checks, known as cash letters, came into use in The Netherlands

♦ The Dutch scientist Johann Lippershey invented the telescope

### 1609

♦ Tea from China was shipped for the first time to Europe by the Dutch East India Company

♦ Delft created the first tin-enameled dinnerware

♦ Henry Hudson explored Delaware Bay and the Hudson River

C Smith taketh the King of Pamavnkee prisoner 1608

## 1610–1619

### 1610

- King James said in a speech to Parliament that "kings are not only God's lieutenants upon earth, and sit upon God's throne, but even by God himself they are called gods"
- Galileo first observed the moons of Jupiter
- Thomas Harriott was one of the first to observe sunspots

### 1611

- The Official (King James or Authorized) version of the Bible in English was published
- The University of Rome was established
- Marco de Dominis published a scientific explanation of rainbows

### 1612

- Tobacco was planted in the Virginia colony

- William Shakespeare wrote *Henry VIII*
- The German mathematician Bartholomew Pitiscus introduced the decimal point in a trigonometrical table
- The Dutch used Manhattan as a fur-trading post for the first time

### 1613

- Francisco de Suarez, a Spanish Catholic theologian, published *Defensio Fidei Catholicae,* which criticized James 1's theory of the divine right of kings
- Copper coins first came into use
- Samuel de Champlain explored the Ottawa River to Alumette Island

### 1614

- The glass-making industry began to develop in England
- North American Indian princess Pocahontas married John Rolfe

- Virginia colonists attempted to prevent French settlements in Maine and Nova Scotia

### 1615

- Cervantes published *Don Quixote, Part 2*
- Galileo Galilei stood before the Inquisition for the first time
- The British company Merchants Adventurers was granted a monopoly for the export of English cloth to the colonies

### 1616

- American Indian Pocahontas was baptized under the name of Rebecca and taken to England
- The works of Ben Johnson, the first folio edition of its kind, was published
- William Shakespeare died
- Galileo Galilei was prohibited by the Catholic Church from further scientific study

**1617**

♦ "Stuart collars" came into fashion for both men and women
♦ Pocahontas died at age 22
♦ John Calvin's collected *Works* was published in Geneva

**1618**

♦ The Puritans objected to the playing of popular sports in the American colonies
♦ The Thirty Years War began in central Europe
♦ Van Dyck became a member of the Antwerp guild of painters

**1619**

♦ Slavery was introduced into Virginia
♦ The Virginia House of Burgesses was formed-the beginning of representative government in North America
♦ William Harvey first announced his discovery of how blood circulates in the body

## 1620–1629

**1620**

♦ **The Mayflower** landed in Plymouth, Massachusetts as winter began, with 102 passengers
♦ The Mayflower Compact was signed, creating "just and equal laws"
♦ Francis Bacon published *Novum Organum*
♦ Oliver Cromwell was denounced in England because he partici-pated in the "disreputable game of cricket"

**1621**

♦ Potatoes were planted in Germany for the first time
♦ The English attempted to colonize Newfoundland and Nova Scotia
♦ The Huguenots began a rebellion against French ruler Louis XIII
♦ Sir Francis Wyatt arrived in Virginia as its new governor

**1622**

♦ New England town meetings began
♦ James I dissolved the English Parliament
♦ William Bradford was named governor of Plymouth Colony

♦ The papal chancellery adopted January 1 as the beginning of the year instead of March 25

**1623**

♦ The first English settlement was established in New Hampshire by David Thomas at Little Harbor
♦ Patent laws were introduced in England to protect inventors
♦ New Netherlands in America was formally organized as a province

**1624**

♦ The Dutch settled in the area later known as New Amsterdam
♦ England declared war on Spain
♦ Captain John Smith issued *A General Historie of Virginia, New England and the Summer Isles*

**1625**

♦ A colonial office was established in London
♦ Full-bottomed wigs were introduced in Europe
♦ The Order of Sisters of Mercy was founded in Paris
♦ Charles I was named king of England and Scotland upon the death of James I

**1626**

♦ John Donne published *Five Sermons*
♦ A French royal edict condemned anyone to death who killed an adversary in a duel
♦ The Dutch colony of New Amsterdam was founded on the Hudson River

**1627**

♦ Rembrandt painted *The Money-Changer*
♦ Spanish sailors visited Hawaii
♦ Johanne Kepler compiled the Rudolphine Tables, giving the location of 1,005 stars
♦ James Morton of Merrymount organized a trading company to compete with Plymouth for the Indian trade in beaver pelts
♦ Japan banned contact with foreigners and closed its ports

**1628**

♦ The Alexandrian Codex was pre-sented to Charles I by Cyril Lucaris, patriarch of Constantinople

♦ The Huguenot town of **La Rochelle**, France, surrendered to Cardinal Richelieu's Catholic forces
♦ John Ford staged the premiere of his play *Lover's Melancholy* in London
♦ The Reformed Protestant Dutch Church was established by settlers in New York

**1629**

♦ England's King Charles I dissolved Parliament
♦ John Endicott became governor of the Massachusetts Bay Colony
♦ The Dutch West India Company granted religious freedom in the West Indies
♦ In Japan, women performers were banned in Kabuki theaters

## 1630–1639

**1630**

♦ Indians introduced the Pilgrims to popcorn
♦ The Puritans landed at Salem, forming the Massachusetts Bay Colony
♦ The first American legislation prohibiting gambling was enacted in Boston
♦ The fork was introduced to American colonial dining by John Winthrop
♦ New Amsterdam's governor bought Gull Island from the Indians and renamed it Oyster Island, which was later known as Ellis Island

**1631**

♦ The English colony of Massachusetts Bay granted Puritan men voting rights and John Winthrop was elected the first governor of Massachusetts
♦ In Italy, Mount Vesuvius erupted, destroying six villages and killing 3,400 people
♦ Barker and Lucas, the king's printers in England, were fined 300 pounds for their Bible misprint that omitted "not" from the seventh commandment, "thou shalt not commit adultery"
♦ England granted Lord Baltimore rights to the Chesapeake Bay area

## 1632

- King Gustavus II Adolphus of Sweden died in battle
- Rembrandt van Rijn painted his work *Europa* and *Portrait of a Lady Aged 62*
- Galileo's book *Dialogue Concerning the Two Chief World Systems* was published with the full backing of the church censors
- The French explorer Etienne Brule was killed by the Huron Indians

## 1633

- The tobacco laws of Virginia were codified, limiting tobacco production to reduce dependence on a single-crop economy
- Galileo was tortured and ordered by the Inquisition to "abjure, curse, and detest" his Copernican heliocentric views asserting that Earth orbits the sun
- Rembrandt painted the *Portrait of a Bearded Man in a Red Coat*
- René Descartes wrote *Le Monde*, in which he upheld the theories of Copernicus

## 1634

- Samuel Cole opened the first tavern in Boston, Massachusetts
- The Academie Française was established to preserve the purity of the French language
- The Catholic colony of Maryland was founded by English colonists sent by Cecil Calvert
- Massachusetts Bay Colony annexed the Maine Colony
- The Dutch tulip craze known as the "tulipomania" began when a futures market was created for tulip bulbs in Dutch taverns and prices became dramatically inflated

## 1635

- Boston Public Latin School was founded in Massachusetts
- Virginia Governor John Harvey was accused of treason and removed from office
- Cardinal Richelieu of France intervened in the great conflict in Europe by declaring war on the Hapsburgs in Spain
- The French colony of Guadeloupe was established in the Caribbean

- Religious dissident Roger Williams was banished from the Massachusetts Bay Colony
- The City of Providence, Rhode Island, was founded

## 1636

- Harvard College, the first college in America, was founded as Cambridge College
- The Massachusetts Plymouth Company drafted its first law
- Peter Paul Rubens painted *Aurora and Cephalus*
- Westerners in Japan were sequestered as the government cracked down on all things foreign

## 1637

- Cardinal Richelieu of France popularized the table knife
- The English and their Mohegan allies killed as many as 600 Pequot Indians in the area of Connecticut
- King Charles of England handed over the American colony of Massachusetts to Sir Fernando Gorges
- James Morton published *New English Canaan*, a satiric book describing his encounters with the New England Pilgrims
- French mathematician René Descartes began using the final letters of the alphabet to represent unknowns

## 1638

- Anne Hutchinson was banished from the Massachusetts Bay Colony for teaching that salvation could come through grace rather than through good works
- Swedish Lutherans who settled in Delaware built some of the first log cabins in America
- Galileo smuggled his book *Dialogue Concerning Two New Sciences* to a publisher in Holland

## 1639

- Virginia became the first colony to order surplus crops (tobacco) destroyed
- Representatives from three Connecticut towns wrote the first constitution in the New World

- William Coddington founded Newport, Rhode Island
- Dorchester, Massachusetts, formed the first school funded by local taxes
- The first printing press in America began operating
- The first post office in the colonies opened in Massachusetts
- Descartes published his *Discourse on Method*, which included the statement, "I think; therefore, I am"

# 1640–1649

## 1640

- Belgian physician Jan van Helmont coined the word gas, later termed carbon dioxide
- The Indian War in New England ended
- English King Charles I signed a peace treaty with Scotland
- In Connecticut, Roger Williams prepared the first primer of the Algonquian Indian language
- The Massachusetts Bay Company sent 300,000 codfish to market

## 1641

- Spain lost control of Portugal
- Catholics in Ireland, under Phelim O'Neil, rose against the Protestants and massacred at least 40,000 men, women and children
- Massachusetts became the first colony to give statutory recognition to slavery
- Puritans wrote a statute that enjoined husbands not to beat their wives

## 1642

- In New Netherland Dutch settlers killed hundreds of lower Hudson Valley Indians who were seeking refuge from Mohawk attackers
- Georgeana (York), Maine, became the first American city to incorporate
- Christian Huygens discovered the Martian south polar cap
- Civil war in England began as Charles I declared war on the Puritan Parliament at Nottingham
- London's Globe Theater was closed as the Puritan-controlled British Parliament suppressed theaters and other forms of popular entertainment

- In France, Blaise Pascal invented a calculating machine

**1643**

- Delegates from four New England colonies, Massachusetts Bay, Plymouth, Connecticut and New Harbor, met in Boston to form a confederation, the United Colonies of New England
- Ann Radcliffe established the first scholarship at Harvard College
- The first livestock branding law was passed by Connecticut
- Roger Williams was granted a charter to colonize Rhode Island
- Florentine scientist Evangelista Torricelli invented the barometer

**1644**

- Seven General Baptist churches issued the *London Confession* which said that men must be allowed to obey their own conscience and understanding
- The Globe Theater in London was dismantled
- The Manchu emperors of China ordered all male subjects to shave the tops of their heads and wear the rest of their hair in a braid
- Settlers in New Amsterdam established peace with the Indians after conducting talks with the Mohawks

**1645**

- Capuchin monks sailed up the Congo River
- Preliminary meetings undertaken by London scientists led to the foundation of the Royal Society
- John Milton produced *L'Allegro*

**1646**

- George Fox began following the "inner light," which formed the basis of the Religious Society of Friends, also known as Quakers
- Roger Scott was tried in Massachusetts for sleeping in church
- Joseph Jenkes received the first colonial machine patent
- The first Protestant church assembly for Indians was established in Massachusetts
- A treaty with Virginia Indians required the state to protect the

Mattaponi from "enemies," but only on the reservation in King William County

**1647**

- The Scottish Army handed King Charles I over to the English Parliament
- Peter Stuyvesant arrived in New Amsterdam to become governor and head the Dutch trading colony
- A new law banned Catholic priests from the colony of Massachusetts; the penalty was banishment or death for a second offense
- In Salem, Massachusetts, Achsah Young became the first recorded American woman to be executed for witchcraft
- Massachusetts passed the first compulsory school attendance law in the colonies

**1648**

- Peter Stuyvesant established the first volunteer firemen unit in the American colonies
- The shoemakers of Boston were unionized
- Thomas Pride prevented 96 Presbyterians from sitting in the English Parliament

**1649**

- King Charles I of England was beheaded for treason; the Prince of Wales became King Charles II upon the death of his father
- The Maryland Toleration Act, which provided for freedom of worship for all Christians, was passed by the Maryland assembly
- Poussin created his painting *Moses Striking the Rock*
- Iroquois attacks and starvation had decimated the Huron nation from some 12,000 people to a few hundred
- In Seville, Spain, one in three people died of the Black Plague

# 1650–1659

**1650**

- The Colonial population was estimated at 50,400; the world's population was about 500 million
- Tea was introduced into England

- The English Parliament declared its right to rule over the fledgling American colonies
- Archbishop James Usher's *Years of the Old and New Testaments* dated the events in the Bible; the creation was fixed at 4004 BC, and Noah's landing on Mt. Ararat in 2348 BC
- In Massachusetts, the Puritans ordered Obadiah Holmes to be "well whipped" for holding a Baptist service

**1651**

- Thomas Hobbes's *Leviathan* was published in London
- Charles II (Stuart) was crowned king of Scotland
- Laws were passed in Massachusetts forbidding the poor to adopt excessive styles of dress
- The General Court of Boston levied a five-shilling fine on anyone caught "observing any such day as Christmas"
- Under the "Liberty Tree," a tulip poplar at St. John's College campus in Annapolis, Maryland, Virginia Puritans were welcomed as colonists by Lord Baltimore, and smoked peace pipes with the Susquehanna Indians

**1652**

- War broke out between The Netherlands and England
- The Dutch established a settlement at Cape Town, South Africa
- Massachusetts declared itself an independent commonwealth

**1653**

- Izaak Walton wrote *The Compleat Angler*
- To protect the Dutch settlers from the Indians, New Netherland Governor Peter Stuyvesant ordered a wall built, which gave New York's Wall Street its name
- The Iroquois League signed a peace treaty with the French, vowing not to wage war with other tribes under French protection
- Oliver Cromwell took on dictatorial powers with the title of "Lord Protector" of England, Scotland and Ireland

## 1654

- Jacob van Loo painted *An Allegory of Venus and Cupid as Lady World and Homo Bulla*
- The Taj Mahal was completed
- A bridge in Rowley, Massachusetts charged a toll for animals, while people crossed for free
- Louis XIV was crowned King of France in Rheims

## 1655

- Johannes Vermeer painted his *Saint Praxedis*
- The first slave auction was held in New Amsterdam
- Puritans jailed Governor Stone after a military victory over Catholic forces in the colony of Maryland
- New Amsterdam and Peter Stuyvesant barred Jews from military service
- English Lord Protector Cromwell banned Anglicans

## 1656

- Massachusetts Bay Colony Puritans imprisoned and banished the first Quakers to arrive in the colony
- A all-woman jury in Maryland, a first in the colonies, acquitted Judith Catchpole on charges of murdering her unborn child
- John Hammond published *Lea and Rachel, or The Two Fruitfull Sisters, Virginia and Maryland*
- In the colony of Virginia, suffrage was extended to all free men regardless of their religion

## 1657

- Christiaan Huygens first began to regulate clocks with a pendulum
- Fountain pens were manufactured in Paris
- France and England formed an alliance against Spain
- The first autopsy and coroner's jury verdict was recorded in the colony of Maryland
- English Admiral Robert Blake fought his last battle when he destroyed the Spanish fleet in Santa Cruz Bay

## 1658

- Legislation in Massachusetts Bay Colony barred the Quakers from holding their services, called "meetings"
- The British Parliament invoked a law that made it a crime, punishable by burning at the stake, to forecast the weather
- Oliver Cromwell, Lord Protector of the New Commonwealth, and ruler over England's Puritan Parliament died

## 1659

- Quakers William Robinson and Marmaduke Stephenson were hanged for refusing to leave Massachusetts
- Samuel Pepys began his *Diary*
- Peter Stuyvesant of New Netherland forbade tennis playing during religious services
- Christiaan Huygens of Holland discovered that the length of a Martian day is similar that of an Earth day

# 1660–1669

## 1660

- Quaker Mary Dyer was hanged in Massachusetts after defying an expulsion order by returning to Boston
- The Dutch crafted an early version of a boat they called a "yacht"
- The British began to dominate the trade in port wine from Portugal
- Charles II, who had fled to France, was restored to the English throne
- Asser Levy was granted a butcher's license for kosher meat in New Amsterdam

## 1661

- White Virginians, who wanted to keep their servants, legalized the enslavement of African immigrants
- The Paris Opera Ballet was founded

## 1662

- British law established that mourning clothes had to be made of English wool
- Englishman Christopher Merret presented a paper to the Royal Society on making sparkling wine
- Governor William Berkeley of Virginia failed in his attempts to repeal the Navigation Acts
- Michael Wigglesworth wrote "The Day of Doom," an immensely popular poem that sold 1,800 copies in its first year

## 1663

- New France in Canada was established as a French colony
- Charles II of England awarded lands known as Carolina in North America to eight members of the nobility who had assisted in his restoration
- King Charles II granted a charter to Rhode Island guaranteeing freedom of worship
- British Parliament passed a second Navigation Act, requiring all goods bound for the colonies to be sent in British ships from British ports
- The first serious American slave conspiracy occurred in Virginia
- Turnpike tolls were introduced in England

## 1664

- The English seized New Amsterdam from the Dutch and renamed it New York
- Stephen Blake wrote The Compleat Gardeners Practices
- Litigation was suspended in London, England, because of the severity of the Black Plague
- New Jersey became a British colony
- A charter to colonize Rhode Island was granted to Roger Williams
- Wealthy non-church members in Massachusetts were given the right to vote
- Maryland passed the first law to stop the interracial marriage of English women and black men

## 1665

- Even though English law provided that slaves may be freed if they converted to Christianity and established legal residence, Maryland, New York, New Jersey, North Carolina, South Carolina, and Virginia passed laws which allowed conversion and residence without freedom from slavery

- The Great Plague of London killed more than 68,000 people
- One of the first horse racing tracks in America was laid out on Long Island
- Johannes Vermeer painted his *Girl with a Pearl Earring*
- England installed a municipal government in New York, formerly the Dutch settlement of New Amsterdam

### 1666

- Molière wrote his play *The Misanthrope* that condemned the falseness and intrigue of French aristocratic society
- Newton formulated his law of universal gravitation
- The Great Fire of London demolished about four-fifths of the city; approximately 13,200 houses, 90 churches and 50 livery company halls burned down
- Samuel Pepys reported on the first blood transfusion, which was performed using dogs

### 1667

- John Milton wrote *Paradise Lost*
- Connecticut adopted America's first divorce law
- The War of Devolution was fought between France and Spain
- The Dutch fleet sailed up the Thames and threatened London

### 1668

- The Spaniards established a permanent settlement on Guam
- The Netherlands, England and Sweden concluded an alliance directed against Louis XIV of France
- Three colonists were expelled from Massachusetts for being Baptists
- Jews of Barbados were forbidden to engage in retail trade

### 1669

- Nils Steensen's *Prodromus* explained the successive order of Earth strata
- Designed by Christopher Wren, the semicircular Sheldonian Theater at Oxford, England, was completed
- Phosphorus was prepared for the first time by alchemist Henning Brand of Hamburg, Germany

# 1670–1679

### 1670

- John Ray printed a book of aphorisms such as "blood is thicker than water" and "haste makes waste"
- Café Procope in Paris began serving ice cream
- Minute hands on watches first appeared
- Colonists landed on the western bank of the Ashley River in South Carolina, five miles from the sea, and named their settlement Charles Town in honor of Charles II, King of England
- The Hudson Bay Company was chartered by King Charles II to exploit the resources of the Hudson Bay area

### 1671

- Samuel Danforth wrote *A Brief Recognition of New Englands Errand into the Wilderness*
- Newton constructed the reflecting telescope
- Rice was imported into South Carolina from Madagascar
- In Germany, Gottfried Wilhelm Leibniz devised a mechanical calculator to add, subtract, multiply and divide

### 1672

- Christiaan Huygens of Holland discovered white polar caps on Mars
- The Royal African Company was granted a charter to expand the slave trade and supply English sugar colonies with 3,000 slaves annually
- King Louis XIV of France invaded The Netherlands
- New York Governor Francis Lovelace announced monthly mail service between New York and Boston
- England and France declared war on the Dutch

### 1673

- French explorers Louis Joliet and Jacques Marquette discovered the headwaters of the Mississippi River
- The French Blue Diamond was cut into a 67-carat stone

- James Needham returned to Virginia after exploring the land to the west, which would become Tennessee
- The Mitsui family's trading house in Japan was founded

### 1674

- The Treaty of Westminster recognized inhabitants of New York and New Sweden as British subjects
- Father Jacques Marquette built the first dwelling at what is now Chicago

### 1675

- The Royal Greenwich Observatory was established in England by Charles II
- King Philip's War began when Indians, in retaliation for the execution of three of their people who had been charged with murder by the English, massacred colonists at Swansea, Plymouth Colony
- Christiaan Huygens patented a pocket watch

### 1676

- Bacon's Rebellion began after Virginia tobacco planters, led by Nathan Bacon, requested and were denied permission to attack the Susquehannock Indians; enraged at Governor William Berkeley's refusal, the colonists burned Jamestown and killed many Indians
- Increase Mather published *A Brief History of the War with the Indians in New England*
- Danish astronomer Ole Christensen Roemer discovered that light travels at a finite, but very high speed; his calculation estimated the speed at 140,000 miles per second
- Indian Chief King Philip, also known as Metacom, was killed by English soldiers, ending the war between the Indians and the colonists

### 1677

- In direct defiance of the Crown, Virginia Governor William Berkeley executed 23 of the rebels from Bacon's Rebellion

- King Charles II and 12 Virginia Indian chiefs signed a treaty that established a three-mile non-encroachment zone around Indian land
- John and Nicolaas van der Heyden patented a fire extinguisher

### 1678

- Louis XIV claimed the region of Alsace from Germany
- The Godiva procession, commemorating Lady Godiva's legendary naked ride, became part of the Coventry Fair
- *A Pilgrim's Progress* by John Bunyan was published
- England's King Charles II accused his wife, Catherine of Braganza, of treason because she had yet to bear him children
- Roman Catholics were banned from the English Parliament

### 1679

- The British Crown claimed New Hampshire as a royal colony
- René Robert Cavelier, Sieur de la Salle, and Father Louis Hennepin, found Niagara Falls while exploring Canada
- New Hampshire was separated from Massachusetts by royal decree

# 1680–1689

### 1680

- John Locke completed *The Second Treatise on Civil Government* that concerned the interconnection of three great ideas: property, government, and revolution
- In Hamburg, Germany, a cymbal was used for the first time in an orchestra
- Maryland colonists ran out of supplies and survived by eating oysters
- The first American tall case clock, later called a "grandfather clock," was built
- War began when the Spanish were expelled from Santa Fe, New Mexico, by Pueblo Indians under Chief Pope

### 1681

- Nehemiah Grew described the sloth in his catalog of specimens

- The dodo bird, last seen on Mauritius, was declared extinct
- England's King Charles II granted a charter to William Penn for an area of land that became Pennsylvania
- England declared war on France

### 1682

- Frenchman Sieur de la Salle claimed the land at the mouth of the Mississippi for France and called it Louisiana
- Louis XIV established Versailles as his royal residence in France

- English astronomer Edmund Halley saw his namesake comet
- William Penn founded Philadelphia, Pennsylvania, as a "Holy Experiment" based on Quaker principles

### 1683

- The New York Chapter of Liberties gave freeholders the right to vote
- William Penn and Native Americans negotiated a peace treaty at Shackamaxon under the Treaty Elm
- Antonie van Leeuwenhoek reported the existence of bacteria
- King Louis XIV expelled all Jews from French possessions in America
- Encouraged by William Penn's offer of 5,000 acres of land and the freedom to practice their religion, 13 Mennonite families from Krefeld, Germany, founded Germantown, Pennsylvania

### 1684

- The charter for Massachusetts Bay Colony was revoked because the colony had frequently violated the terms of the charter and consistently ignored royal orders; this ended the requirement of church membership for voting
- Efforts were made in London to light the streets
- The Bermudas became a British colony

### 1685

- Charles II barred Jews from settling in Stockholm, Sweden
- New York was made a royal province
- William Penn was given jurisdiction over Delaware
- The number of French Huguenot immigrants to the American colonies accelerated after French King Louis XIV revoked the Edict of Nantes that protected their religious freedom
- Increase Mather was named president of Harvard College
- Dutch mapmaker Johannes van Keulen produced a map of New York and Long Island
- In Canada, a shortage of currency required that playing cards be assigned monetary values for use as money

## 1686

♦ Sir Edmund Andros, as governor general of the Dominion of New England, dissolved the assemblies of New York and Connecticut, limited the number of town meetings in New England to one per year, placed the militia under his direct control, and forced Puritans and Anglicans to worship together in the Old South Church

♦ The first volume of Isaac Newton's *Mathematical Principles of Natural Philosophy* was published in Latin explaining his invention of differential and integral calculus

♦ Soldiers of the Roman Catholic faith were readmitted into the English army

## 1687

♦ William Penn published *The Excellent Privilege of Liberty and Property*

♦ French explorer Robert Cavelier, Sieur de La Salle was murdered while searching for the mouth of the Mississippi along the coast of the Gulf of Mexico

## 1688

♦ Governor Edmund Andros placed the militia of New England under his direct control

♦ The Quakers at Germantown, Pennsylvania, issued the earliest known antislavery tract in the colonies

♦ Joseph de la Vega published his work *Confusion de Confusiones*, which offered trading strategies to speculators

♦ Edward Lloyd opened a London coffee shop where shipping insurance was bought and sold

♦ In France, a blind Benedictine monk called Dom Perignon discovered the fermentation process that led to the creation of champagne

## 1689

♦ William (III) of Orange and Mary II were officially named King and Queen of England

♦ The Toleration Acts were passed by Parliament giving limited freedom of religion to citizens

♦ A Bill of Rights was passed by Parliament as a statute

♦ Rebellious New England American colonists ousted Governor Edmond Andros

♦ Cotton Mather published *Memorable Providences, Related to Witchcrafts and Possessions*, contributing to the hysteria that led to the Salem witch trials

♦ Racine wrote a drama based on the Book of Esther

♦ The Iroquois took Montreal

♦ Peter the Great became Tsar of Russia

# 1690–1699

## 1690

♦ The series of wars began with King William's War, in which Schenectady, New York, and other areas were burned by French and Native Americans; Massachusetts colonists captured Port Royal, Nova Scotia; and Canadian forces destroyed Casco, Maine

♦ The first paper mill in the American colonies was established in Pennsylvania

♦ The clarinet was invented in Germany

♦ The first paper money in America was issued by Massachusetts and was used to pay soldiers fighting a war against Quebec

♦ One of the earliest American newspapers, *Publick Occurrences,* published its first-and last-edition in Boston

♦ The population of Charles Town, South Carolina, reached 1,200, making it the fifth-largest city in North America.

## 1691

♦ Delaware formed a government separate from Pennsylvania

♦ Maryland was declared a royal province, thus removing Lord Baltimore from political power

♦ The salt tax was doubled in England

♦ Father Eusebio Kino founded the Tumacacori mission 45 miles south of Tucson, Arizona

♦ The Massachusetts Bay Company along with Plymouth Colony and Maine were incorporated into the Massachusetts Bay Colony

♦ The first directory of addresses was published in Paris

## 1692

♦ Pennsylvania was named a royal colony

♦ The Salem witchcraft trials occurred; 20 persons were executed before the trials ended

♦ Deodat Lawson wrote *A Brief and True Narrative of Some Remarkable Passages Relating to Sundry Persons Afflicted by Witchcraft*

♦ The English naturalist John Ray noted that whales had more in common with four-legged mammals than with fish

## 1693

♦ The College of William and Mary was founded in Williamsburg, Virginia

♦ China required that European ships be forbidden to land anywhere except Canton

♦ The Amish sect was formed

♦ Carolina colony was divided into North Carolina and South Carolina

## 1694

♦ Colonists signed a peace treaty with the Iroquois to keep them from forming any future alliances with the French

♦ Freedom of the press was assured in England

♦ The Bank of England received a royal charter as a commercial institution

♦ Queen Mary II of England died after five years of joint rule with her husband, King William III

## 1695

♦ Portugal established colonial rule in the eastern half of Timor Island

♦ New York Jews petitioned the governor for religious liberty

♦ English botanist Nehemiah Grew isolated magnesium sulfate, also known as Epsom salts

## 1696

♦ The Navigation Acts of 1696 were passed by the English Parliament that limited all colonial trade to English-built vessels

♦ Peter the Great became czar of Russia

♦ Duke Eberhard Ludwig of Wurttemberg, Germany, banned all lead-based wine additives

## 1697

- The Treaty of Ryswick ended King William's War and restored all colonial possessions to prewar ownership
- The Massachusetts general court expressed official repentance for the witchcraft trials
- Charles Perrault published *Mother Goose Tales*
- Hannah Duston of New Hampshire was declared a hero after she managed to kill 10 of the 12 Indians who attacked her; she took home their scalps for bounty money
- St. Paul's Cathedral opened in London

## 1698

- Paper manufacturing began in North America
- In an effort to move his people away from Asian customs, Russian Tsar Peter I imposed a tax on beards
- Thomas Bray wrote *A General View of English Colonies in America with Respect to Religion*, which supported the establishment of the Anglican Church in Maryland and the need for missionaries in the colonies

## 1699

- The peace treaty at Casco Bay, Maine, ended hostilities between the Abenaki Indians and the Massachusetts Bay Colony
- Pirate Captain Kidd was captured and sent to England where he was sentenced to be executed in 1701
- The Wool Act forbidding the export of wool from the American colonies was passed by Parliament to protect the British wool industry
- The King of Spain banned the production of wine in the Americas, except for that made by the Church
- Peter the Great ordered the Russian New Year changed from September 1 to January 1

# 1700–1709

## 1700

- Massachusetts required all Roman Catholic priests to leave the colony within three months or be arrested
- The overall population of the colonies numbered around 275,000; the largest city, Boston, boasted 7,000 people, and New York, 5,000
- Judge Samuel Sewall published *The Selling of Joseph*, an anti-slavery tract
- The English slave ship *Henrietta Marie* sank near Key West, Florida
- Germany adopted the Gregorian calendar, first established in 1582
- In Spain, bullfighting emerged in its modern form
- Thomas Sheraton, an English furniture maker, introduced twin beds

## 1701

- Jethro Tull created a horse-drawn mechanical drill to plant evenly distributed seeds in a row
- Antoine de la Mothe Cadillac established Fort Pontchartrain for France in Detroit, Michigan, to halt the advance of the English into the western Great Lakes region
- England, Austria, and The Netherlands formed an alliance against France
- Yale University was founded as The Collegiate School of Killingworth, Connecticut, by Congregationalists who considered Harvard College too liberal

## 1702

- On the death of William III of Orange, Anne Stuart, sister of Mary II, succeeded to the throne of England, Scotland and Ireland
- Lord Cornbury, Queen Anne's cousin, was made governor of New York
- The first regular English newspaper, *The Daily Courant*, was published
- The War of Spanish Succession arose from the disputed succession to the Spanish throne following the death of Charles II, the last of the Spanish Habsburgs

- English troops plundered the Spanish-held St. Augustine, Florida

## 1703

- Johann Sebastian Bach obtained his first position as organist for the city of Arnstadt, Thuringia, Germany
- In Russia, Peter the Great laid the foundations of St. Petersburg
- English novelist Daniel Defoe was punished for offending the government and church with his satire *The Shortest Way With Dissenters*
- Delaware formally separated from Pennsylvania and became a colony

## 1704

- Deerfield, Massachusetts, was destroyed and 100 residents were abducted by Indians, a consequence of Queen Anne's War between France and England
- In an English prison, Daniel Defoe began publishing his weekly newspaper, *The Review*
- Britain seized the colony of Gibraltar from Spain
- The first successful newspaper in the American colonies, the *Boston News-Letter*, was established

## 1705

- Joseph Addison wrote the poem "The Campaign" for the Duke of Marlborough to commemorate the military victory over France and Spain at the Battle of Blenheim
- The first steam engine was built
- George Frederic Handel's first opera "Almira," premiered in Hamburg
- Queen Anne of England knighted Isaac Newton at Trinity College
- Nicholas Rowe's "Ulysses" premiered in London

## 1706

- Bishop White Kennet printed his *Complete History of England with the Lives of All the Kings and Queens Thereof, Vol. 3* in London
- The First Presbyterian Church was organized in Philadelphia

- Isaac Newton published the results of his 40 years of experiments with light in *Opticks*
- English engineer Henry Mill constructed carriage springs
- The San Felipe Church in Albuquerque was founded

## 1707

- Settlers in Charles Town, South Carolina, successfully defended their town against an attack by French and Spanish colonists
- Billiards were introduced in Berlin coffeehouses
- French engineer Denis Papin invented the high-pressure boiler
- John Williams wrote *The Redeemed Captive*, a bestselling narrative recounting his abduction by Indians during the Deerfield, Massachusetts, raid three years earlier
- Sir John Floyer promoted the value of counting pulse beats

## 1708

- The German Baptist Brethren emigrated to America
- Haverhill, Massachusetts, was destroyed by the French and Indians
- Peter the Great divided Russia into eight government districts to ease administration

## 1709

- Augustus the Strong, Elector of Saxony, imprisoned alchemist Johann Friedrich Bottger until he discovered how to re-create the formula for oriental porcelain
- The postage rates in England were regulated by mileage
- Britain passed its first Copyright Act
- The first major group of Swiss and German colonists reached the Carolinas
- Japanese magnolias were introduced into England

# 1710–1719
## 1710

- Three thousand German refugees from the Palatinate first settled at the Hudson River in New York, then in eastern Pennsylvania

- The original Chapel of San Miguel in Santa Fe, New Mexico, was erected
- Jakob Christoph Le Blon invented three-color printing
- Baron Johann Bottger invented the Meissen hard-paste porcelain at the Meissen factory
- Umbrellas became popular in London
- British troops occupied Port Royal, Nova Scotia

## 1711

- A British attempt to invade Canada by sea failed
- The Tuscarora Indian War began with a massacre of settlers in North Carolina, sparked by white encroachment that included the enslaving of Indian children
- French troops occupied Rio de Janeiro
- The clarinet was used for the first time in an orchestra

## 1712

- The Carolina Slave Code was created to regulate slave life
- Handel composed his operas "Il Pastor Fido" and "Teseo"
- In Mexico, Maria de Ortiz Espejo was convicted by the Inquisition for telling women that hummingbirds and earthquakes could help them get pregnant
- A slave insurrection in New York City was suppressed by the militia and ended with the execution of 21 slaves
- The Pennsylvania Assembly banned the importation of slaves

## 1713

- England's South Sea Company was allowed to transport 4,800 slaves per year into the Spanish colonies of North America
- Bach composed his "Brandenburg Concerto No. 3"
- Andrew Robinson built the first schooner in New England, where "to scoon" meant "to skim"
- The Peace of Utrecht was signed in which France ceded the colony of Acadia to Great Britain; the Acadians who would not

swear allegiance to the crown were deported, and many went to the bayou country of Louisiana
- Spain ceded the 2.5-square-mile Gibraltar in perpetuity to Britain under the Treaty of Utrecht

## 1714

- Cotton Mather preached a sermon that supported the Copernican theory of the universe
- Henry Mill received a patent for a typewriter in England
- Queen Anne of England died and was succeeded by George Louis of Hanover, who was crowned George I of England
- French surgeon Dominique Anel invented the fine-pointed syringe for surgical purposes
- Daniel Gabriel Fahrenheit constructed a mercury thermometer with a temperature scale

## 1715

- Yamasee tribes attacked and killed several hundred Carolina settlers
- King Louis XIV, "the Sun King," died of gangrene
- A French manufacturer debuted the first folding umbrella
- The Riot Act went into effect in England, making it a crime for 12 or more people to refuse to disperse within an hour of being ordered to by a magistrate
- England granted the first patent to an American, Sybilla Masters, who had created a corn processing device

## 1716

- South Carolina settlers and their Cherokee allies attacked and defeated the Yamassee
- In France, Scottish economist John Law established a private bank called Law & Co. with the promise that his notes were redeemable on demand for coin
- The Virginia Colonial Assembly passed a law that required every householder to plant at least 10 grapevines
- The first lighthouse in the American colonies was built in Boston

13

## 1717

- Scots-Irish immigration in America began, with most settling in western Pennsylvania
- Handel composed "Water Music," played for George I on the occasion of a royal barge trip on the Thames
- A freeze on the value of the gold guinea was established in England to create an appropriate ratio between the prices of gold and silver and their supply
- Thomas Coke, the first Earl of Leicester, purchased the manuscript made by Leonardo da Vinci that came to be known as the Codex Leicester

## 1718

- British inventor James Puckle patented a multi-shot rifle that utilized a revolving block for firing square bullets
- Jean Baptiste Le Moyne, Sieur de Bienville, French-Canadian explorer, founded New Orleans
- Edward Teach, aka Blackbeard, began to pillage settlements along the Atlantic coast; he was captured by a force of British troops during a battle off the Virginia coast and was beheaded

## 1719

- In New Hampshire, the first potato in America was planted
- The French government gave the Law company the right of coinage, which controlled the mint, public finances, the bank, the sea trade, Louisiana, and tobacco
- Daniel Defoe's novel *Robinson Crusoe* was published in London, based on the story of Alexander Selkirk, a man who was voluntarily put ashore on a desert island
- Thomas Fleet of Boston published *Mother Goose's Melodies For Children*
- France declared war on Spain

# 1720–1729

## 1720

- The estimated population of the American colonies was 474,000
- The French built forts on the Mississippi, the St. Lawrence, and the Niagara rivers

- England prohibited the emigration of skilled craftsmen and the export of machinery, models and plans to the colonies to prevent competition
- German Dunkers founded their communal society Amish country near Philadelphia
- Timothy Hanson took the seeds of a European perennial grass known as hay from New York to the Carolinas
- Wallpaper became fashionable in England
- Speculators in London bid up the price of the South Sea Co. before the South Sea bubble burst and London markets crashed
- In France, John Law's bank closed

## 1721

- A smallpox epidemic in Boston prompted Cotton Mather and Zabdiel Boylston to experiment with inoculation against the disease
- Samuel Johnson published his *Dictionary of the English Language*
- In Germany, Johann Sebastian Bach published the six Brandenburg Concertos
- South Carolina was formally incorporated as a royal colony
- Swiss immigrants introduced rifles into the American colonies

## 1722

- Daniel Defoe wrote his novel *Moll Flanders*
- Jonathon Swift, author and pamphleteer, urged his fellow countrymen to boycott English goods and "burn everything that comes from England, except their people and their coals"
- A French Jesuit sent home detailed letters on porcelain production that allowed France to develop its own porcelain plant at Sèvres
- Czar Peter the Great capped his reforms in Russia with the "Table of Rank," which decreed a commoner could climb on merit to the highest positions
- French C. Hopffer patented the fire extinguisher

## 1723

- Voltaire published *La Henriade*
- Gin drinking became popular in England
- J.S. Bach wrote "St John Passion"

## 1724

- The Carpenter's Company of Philadelphia was chartered to assist in carpenters' instruction and well-being
- Jewish settlers were exiled from the Louisiana colony
- Captain Samuel Johnson's *General History of the Pirates* was published
- George Frederic Handel composed his opera "Giulio Cesare"
- Benjamin Franklin arrived in London

## 1725

- The first fossilized salamander was found in Germany
- The *New York Gazette* was first issued
- The St. Petersburg Academy of Science was founded by Catherine I
- Alexander Pope translated *The Odyssey* by Homer

## 1726

- Georg Philipp Telemann published his collection of 72 sacred cantatas: "Der Harmonischer Gottesdienst," a pietistic paraphrase of Biblical verse set to music
- George Frederic Handel became a British subject
- The first circulating library was established in Edinburgh in

## 1727

- Brazil planted its first coffee
- George II of England was crowned
- The New York General Assembly permitted Jews to omit the phrase "upon the faith of a Christian" from an abjuration oath
- Quakers demanded the abolition of slavery
- Racing Calendar in England was published for the first time
- James Bradley discovered the aberration of light of fixed stars

## 1728

♦ Prospective brides arrived in Louisiana for the French settlers there; the women were known as "casket girls" because they had received dresses in small trunks, or caskets, as an incentive for immigration

♦ "The Beggar's Opera," a ballad opera sung in English, full of satire addressed against the Walpole administration, had its premiere in London

♦ The first constitution of American Presbyterianism was adopted

♦ Opium smoking was banned in China

♦ The city of Baltimore was founded

♦ Natchez Indians killed most of the 300 French settlers and soldiers at Fort Rosalie, Louisiana

## 1730–1739

### 1730

♦ Stephen Hales learned to measure blood pressure by using a horse as a subject

♦ Edward Scarlett, a London optician, began anchoring eyeglasses to the ears with rigid side pieces called temples

♦ In Germany, Franz Anton Ketterer invented the cuckoo clock

♦ The Hudson Bay Company built a stone fortress on the western shore of the Hudson Bay in Canada to support the Chipewyan fur trade

♦ Nine German gun makers located in Pennsylvania began producing the Kentucky rifle, so named because it was intended for use on the Kentucky frontier

### 1731

♦ Franklin's Junto Club established the Library Company of Philadelphia, the first circulating library in the American colonies

♦ Fort Vincennes, later Fort Sackville, was built by the French near present-day Vincennes, Indiana

### 1732

♦ Benjamin Franklin began publishing *Poor Richard's Almanac*

♦ Pope Clement XII renewed anti-Jewish laws of Rome

♦ Professional librarian, Louis Timothee, was hired in Philadelphia

### 1733

♦ John Kay invented the flying shuttle

♦ Voltaire authored his *Lettres Anglaises* in which he hailed England as a "nation of philosophers" and recognized the English Enlightenment

♦ Handel's opera "Orlando" was first performed

♦ The Pennsylvania city of Reading became one of America's first producers of iron

♦ English colonists led by James Oglethorpe founded Savannah, Georgia, to produce an ideal colony where silk and wine would be created

### 1734

♦ John Peter Zenger, editor of the *New York Weekly Journal, was* imprisoned in New York, accused of libeling New York Governor William Cosby

♦ Holkham Hall in Norfolk, England, was begun by Thomas Coke, an agricultural reformer who pioneered farming techniques that increased yields

♦ Charles III was crowned king of the Two Sicilies

### 1735

♦ Newspaper editor John Peter Zenger was acquitted of libel when his attorney showed that the charges could not be libelous because the accusations were true

♦ Jonathan Edwards began preaching fiery sermons to crowds in Northampton, Massachusetts, the beginning of the religious revival movement known as the Great Awakening

### 1736

♦ Robert Walpole became the first British prime minister to live at 10 Downing Street

♦ Early expansion of American Presbyterianism was spurred by the founding of "log colleges"

♦ British and Chickasaw Indians defeated the French at the Battle of Ackia in northwestern Mississippi, opening the region to English settlement

### 1737

♦ Richmond, Virginia, was founded

♦ London officials worried about the large number of British government bonds held by Dutch investors

♦ Rev. Andrew Le Mercier, a Huguenot living in Boston, set the first horses out to graze on Sable Island

♦ Antonio Stradivari, renowned violin maker, died in Cremona, Italy; he made about 1,200 violins

### 1738

♦ British preacher George Whitefield arrived in Savannah; his sermons helped spread the "Great Awakening" throughout the 1740s

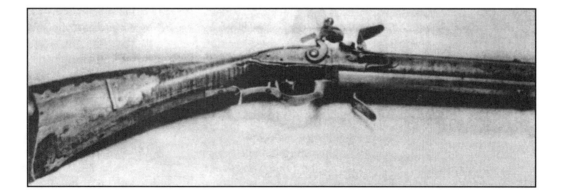

- Daniel Bernoulli, Swiss physicist and mathematician, explained how lift was created by a difference of air pressures
- The Methodist Church was established

### 1739

- A slave revolt in Stono, South Carolina, led by an Angolan named Jemmy, killed 25 whites; it was one of three slave rebellions that year
- Handel composed his oratorio "Israel in Egypt" using text taken from the book of Exodus and the Psalms
- England declared war on Spain over borderlines in Florida

## 1740–1749

### 1740

- Frederick the Great was awarded the first medal for combat bravery, the Pour le Merite, nicknamed the Blue Max
- Antonio de Solis, a Spanish priest, found the ruins of Palenque, Mexico, while planting a field
- Thomas Arne's song "Rule Britannia" was performed for the first time
- The first mention of an African American doctor in the colonies was made in the *Pennsylvania Gazette*

### 1741

- Jonathan Edwards delivered *Sinners in the Hands of an Angry God*
- A slave revolt in New York led to a panic that resulted in the conviction of 101 blacks, the hanging of 18 blacks and four whites, the burning alive of 13 blacks and the banishment from the city of 70
- Andrew Bradford of Pennsylvania published the first American magazine called *The American Magazine, or A Monthly View of the Political State of the British Colonies*
- Handel finished the "Messiah" oratorio, after working on it non-stop for 23 days
- Astronomer Anders Celsius introduced the centigrade temperature scale

### 1742

- General James Edward Oglethorpe fought with the Spanish on

16

St. Simons Island off the coast of Georgia
- Edmund Hoyle popularized the card game later called bridge
- Edmond Hoyle published his *Short Treatise* on the card game whist
- Faneuil Hall in Boston opened to the public
- Empress Elisabeth ordered the expulsion of all Jews from Russia

### 1743

- In France, Louis XV had the first elevator installed at Versailles
- The British warship *Centurion* engaged and overcame the Spanish treasure galleon *Nuestra Señora de Covadonga* to capture over one million Spanish silver dollars and 500 pounds of native silver
- England's King George defeated the French at Dettingen, Bavaria

### 1744

- The Iroquois sachem Cannasatego advised the American colonists to form a union like that of the Iroquois
- The Royal Porcelain Manufactory of Vienna began to use an upside-down shield, resembling a beehive, as its emblem
- In Britain, Elizabeth Robinson of Middlesex and two other women were tried and convicted on a charge of stealing from a grocer's warehouse 104 oranges imported from China with the intent to sell them

### 1745

- The French attacked and burned Saratoga, New York, during King George's War
- William Hogarth made his print series *Marriage à la Mode* in which he made fun of the new social mobility
- Louisbourg, the French fortress on Cape Breton Island in Nova Scotia was captured by a ragtag army of New Englanders
- Georges Louis Leclerc suggested that a giant comet had hit the sun, releasing the matter that formed the planets
- Edinburgh was occupied by Jacobites under Bonnie Prince Charlie, the Young Pretender, claimant to the British throne

- Bonnie Prince Charlie's troops occupied Carlisle
- French troops attacked the Indians at Saratoga, New York

### 1746

- The American Presbyterian College of New Jersey was founded
- The first lectures on electricity in the American colonies were given by John Winthrop IV at Harvard
- King George II won the battle of Culloden, a crushing defeat for Bonnie Prince Charlie and the Highlander clans that backed him

### 1747

- Mark Catesby, the English naturalist, published *The Natural History of Carolina, Florida and the Bahama Islands* using 220 watercolors for etchings in his work on the flora and fauna of North America
- A Scottish chemist discovered that beets contained sugar
- In Britain, a tax was imposed on carriages
- England and The Netherlands signed a military treaty
- Benjamin Franklin began his experiments in electricity

### 1748

- Samuel Richardson wrote his novel *Clarissa*
- British Commodore George Anson published an account of his trip to China
- The city of Pompeii, buried by an eruption of Mt. Vesuvius in 79 AD, was discovered

### 1749

- The first American repertory acting company was established in Philadelphia
- King George II commissioned Handel's "Music for the Royal Fireworks" to highlight the end of the War of the Austrian Succession
- George II granted a charter to the Ohio Company to settle Ohio Valley
- The Georgia Colony reversed itself and ruled slavery to be legal
- The English Ohio Trade Company formed its first trading post

# Currency in Colonial America

For the early colonists, the most significant business issue was money, or, more accurately, the lack of a "hard currency" (e.g., gold or silver). For most of the colonial period, currency was scarce, thus encouraging individuals to conduct business through barter. This system may have been successful in large transactions, but hindered the typical daily transactions for services. Bartering goods depreciated the value of property many colonists owned. In 1640, John Winthrop wrote in his journal:

*The scarcity of money made a great change in all commerce. Merchants would sell no wares but for ready money, men could not pay their debts though they had enough [i.e., capital], prices of lands and cattle fell soon to the one half and less . . .*

Colonial governments received numerous reports of this limited commerce, such as ferry operators refusing transportation to those unable to pay in advance. Some farmers were forced to sell livestock at reduced prices in order to access hard currency to pay for servants. At times, it was easier and cheaper for some to dismiss servants than to sell livestock at reduced market values.

To remedy the lack of a hard currency, individuals developed numerous ways to overcome this obstacle. Many would receive a short-term credit, typically known as a book credit, to fulfill a payment obligation. The buyer would acquire a good or service and it would be recorded as an obligation by the seller. The debt would be forgiven when the buyer paid the seller in hard currency, or more typically, in acceptable goods and services. A storekeeper may have sold an item and in return received a pig or a day's work acceptable to the storekeeper to satisfy the obligation. Many account books during the period testify to this form of barter, referred to by historians as "bookkeeping barter." This was not the best system to encourage commerce and other methods developed out of market demand.

Trade became more of a necessity for colonies to thrive and commerce to grow. Out of this growth, colonies placed values on commodities, such as tobacco, rice, sugar, Indian corn, salted beef and beaver skins, to serve as a currency. Colonial governments would legislate a value, typically on a barrel or bushel basis, and permit individuals to use the valued commodity to service a debt obligation. These obligations may have been owed to the colonial government or to private individuals. This form of currency was referred to as "county pay."

Sometimes legislatures overvalued the county pay, which would be disadvantageous to the debtor. To contend with this disadvantage, the debtor would select the commodity and its quality to service a debt, typically to his advantage. This would occur if there was an oversupply grown by farmers, causing a weak demand and undervaluing the commodity. Because of annual price fluctuations, it was not unusual for individuals to disagree on terms of payment and argue over the acceptance of county pay over hard currency.

The most common hard currency in the colonies was the Spanish American eight reales, (also known as the Spanish piece of eight or "Spanish dollar"). The mints in Mexico and Peru minted these crude "cobs" without a standard shape for quick inventorying and shipment to Spain. As these cobs worked their way into the American colonies by British traders in the West Indies, they filled a void of hard currency in the colonies and created new commerce problems.

Because of the irregular shape of the Spanish reale, holders often clipped small pieces of silver and passed them off in full value. As the coins circulated, they became lighter in weight and their value questionable. The irregular shape also permitted individuals to counterfeit the coin with less of a silver content and pass them off in circulation. With the number of coins in circulation in Massachusetts, the colony required silver coins to be counterstamped with the true value based upon weight. Unfortunately, this did not resolve the purity issue or the possibility of the coin being snipped after being stamped.

Many states were having issues with the limited quality of hard currency. In 1652, the Massachusetts legislature authorized a facility in Boston to melt silver bullion and foreign coins for the purpose of minting coins at a standard weight and fineness. Referred to as the Boston shilling, the coins were intended to expand trade within the colony. The legislature required the coin minted at a lower silver rate than the British shilling to prevent the coined silver leaving the colony. Because of the scarcity of hard currency, the coin was traded on par or greater than the British shilling in colonies as far south as Virginia. By 1682, the king of England prohibited the minting of coins in all colonies because it damaged the value of the British sterling and hurt London merchants accepting the Boston shilling.

With hard currency still in demand, colonies developed paper money, known as "bills of credit." Massachusetts was first in establishing the bills of credit in 1690, with other colonies following similar paths in the early eighteenth century. This paper currency was issued in a number of ways that made it attractive to the public. One method was for the colony to issue paper bills into circulation for debts owed and to levy taxes over a period of time. Once sufficient funds were raised, the bills would be exchanged for hard currency and the paper bills destroyed. The other method was for the colony to issue bills that yielded interest and were secured with land. Once the land was sold with sufficient funds raised, these bills would be collected. Bill holders would receive hard currency based upon the bill's value, plus accrued interest. This method is typically referred to as the land bank system.

Most bills of credit were issued with a set denomination value inscribed on the bill indicating an express sum in silver. Even with this value expressed on the bill, it was only backed by the authority of the government and not with silver. The colonial treasurer would exchange these bills for hard currency, but typically there was no legal provision indicating that the bill holders had a legal claim to silver or other valued currency. At times, colonies failed to keep promises on their bills of credit. When that happened, many often spoke negatively upon the colony. When the province of Massachusetts Bay failed to keep its promise in 1748, some ministers condemned the colony in their sermons.

# British Currency

The British currency system covered in this book is different than then the decimal systems of today's American currency. One will encounter different denominations and names associated with each coin. When reviewing the earlier periods of American history, a majority of the values are based upon British units during that period. The intent of this section is to provide a review of the currency system and clarify the monetary units.

The farthing is the smallest denomination followed by the penny, or pence in the plural form. In between these currencies is the halfpenny. Two farthings equal a halfpenny while two halfpennies equal one penny. Typical references abbreviated the penny with the symbol "d" for record keeping. Thus a penny was record as 1d, a halfpenny as ½d, and a farthing as ¼d.

The shilling, equal to twelve pence, is the next currency in value in the British System and base for larger denominations. A crown equal 5 shillings, while a half crown equal to two shillings six pence. During colonial times, the values are not uncommonly expressed in crowns.

The pound, equal to twenty shillings (or four crowns), is the next basic unit for measure. A gold sovereign is equivalent to a pound and a gold guinea is valued at one pound and one shilling.

Methods of recording the three primary denominations (pound, shilling and penny) through abbreviations made accounting notations simpler. The pound may be expressed using the symbol "£" derived from the Latin word libra" (Latin for pound). For the shilling, symbol "s" may be used for this unit of measure. The "s" abbreviation is derived from the roman coin solidus which was derived from 12 units. Finally, the penny may utilize the letter "d" from the word denarius (a small denomination roman coin).

During this period, many methods of recording British units were utilized. One may encounter the abbreviations, periods "." or back-slashes "/". For example, four pound five shillings and 3 pence may be noted as "£4 5s 3d", "4.5.3" or "4/5/3". (To assist the reader of this book, most British units have been expressed in pounds, shillings and pence unless otherwise expressed)

The following chart expresses the value of the units to each other:

| 1 Gold Guinea | 1 Pound, 1 Shilling | 21 Shillings | 252 Pence |
|---|---|---|---|
| 1 Gold Sovereign | 1 Pound | 20 Shillings | 240 Pence |
| 1 Pound | | 20 Shillings | 240 Pence |
| 1 Crown | | 5 Shillings | 60 Pence |
| 1 Shilling | | | 12 Pence |
| 1 Penny | | | 1 Penny |
| Halfpence | | | ½ Pence or 2 Farthings |
| Farthing | | | ¼ Pence |

# SELECTED INCOMES 1600-1749

| Occupation | Data Source | Description | Price |
|---|---|---|---|
| Bricklayer | US Census (1976) | Daily wages of a mason paid in local currency without board furnished in Virginia, 1621 | 4 shillings |
| Bricklayer | US Census (1976) | Daily wages of a bricklayer paid in local currency without board furnished in Massachusetts, 1631 | 2 shillings |
| Bricklayer | US Census (1976) | Daily wages of a bricklayer paid in local currency without board furnished in New Haven, 1640 | 2 shillings 6 pence |
| Bricklayer | US Census (1976) | Daily wages of a bricklayer paid in local currency without board furnished in New Haven, 1641 | 2 shillings |
| Bricklayer | US Census (1976) | Daily wages of a bricklayer paid in local currency without board furnished in Massachusetts, 1670 | 2 shillings |
| Bricklayer | US Census (1976) | Daily wages of a bricklayer paid in local currency without board furnished in South Carolina, 1710 | 6 shillings |
| Carpenter | US Census (1976) | Daily wages of a carpenter paid in local currency without board furnished in Virginia, 1621 | 4 shillings |
| Carpenter | US Census (1976) | Daily wages of a carpenter paid in local currency without board furnished in Massachusetts, 1631 | 2 shillings |
| Carpenter | US Census (1976) | Daily wages of a carpenter paid in local currency without board furnished in New Haven, 1640 | 2 shillings 6 pence |
| Carpenter | US Census (1976) | Daily wages of a carpenter paid in local currency without board furnished in New Haven, 1641 | 2 shillings |
| Carpenter | US Census (1976) | Daily wages of a carpenter paid in local currency without board furnished in Massachusetts, 1670 | 2 shillings |

## Based Upon the British Currency System

| Year | Pound in 2002 US Dollars | Shilling in 2002 US Dollars | Pence in 2002 US Dollars |
|---|---|---|---|
| 1650 | $120.00 | $6.00 | $0.50 |
| 1660 | $144.00 | $7.20 | $0.60 |
| 1670 | $120.00 | $6.00 | $0.70 |
| 1680 | $120.00 | $6.00 | $0.70 |
| 1690 | $120.00 | $6.00 | $0.80 |
| 1700 | $168.00 | $8.40 | $0.70 |
| 1710 | $144.00 | $7.20 | $0.60 |
| 1720 | $168.00 | $8.40 | $0.70 |
| 1730 | $192.00 | $9.60 | $0.80 |
| 1740 | $144.00 | $7.20 | $0.60 |
| 1749 | $192.00 | $9.60 | $0.80 |

*Calculations are approximate values based upon economic historical data*

| Occupation | Data Source | Description | Price |
|---|---|---|---|
| Carpenter | US Census (1976) | Daily wages of a carpenter paid in local currency without board furnished in South Carolina, 1710 | 4 shillings |
| Clerk | Executive Journals, Council of Colonial Virginia, Vol. IV (1930) | Annual salary of the Clerk of the Executive Council in Virginia, 1724 | 100 pounds |
| Clerk | Colonial Records of South Carolina - Journal of the Commons House of Assembly 1744-1745 (1955) | Clerk of the Committee of Correspondence in South Carolina, 1744 | 50 pounds |
| College President | Massachusetts Colony Order (1747) | Annual income of the President of Harvard College, Reverend Edward Holyoke, 1747 | 300 pounds |
| College Professor | Massachusetts Colony Order (1742) | Annual income of the Professor of Divinity, Reverend Edward Wigglesworth Hollinan, at Harvard College,1742 | 25 pounds |
| Commander | Colonial Records of South Carolina - Journal of the Commons House of Assembly 1744-1745 (1955) | Commander for Fort Moore in South Carolina, 1744 | 300 pounds |
| Commissioner | Colonial Records of South Carolina - Journal of the Commons House of Assembly 1744-1745 (1955) | Annual salary to the Commissioner of the Indian Trade in South Carolina, 1744 | 100 pounds |
| Cooper | US Census (1976) | Daily wages of a cooper paid in local currency without board furnished in Virginia, 1621 | 4 shillings |
| Cooper | US Census (1976) | Daily wages of a cooper paid in local currency without board furnished in New Haven, 1640 | 2 shillings 6 pence |
| Cooper | US Census (1976) | Daily wages of a cooper paid in local currency without board furnished in New Haven, 1641 | 2 shillings |
| Cooper | US Census (1976) | Daily wages of a cooper paid in local currency without board furnished in Massachusetts, 1670 | 2 shillings 8 pence |
| Cooper | US Census (1976) | Daily wages of a cooper paid in local currency without board furnished in South Carolina, 1710 | 4 shillings |
| Coroner | Colonial Records of South Carolina - Journal of the Commons House of Assembly 1744-1745 (1955) | Payment to Alexander Stewart, Coroner of Berkeley County, South Carolina | 155 pounds |
| Governor | Executive Journals, Council of Colonial Virginia, Vol. IV (1930) | Annual salary of the Governor of Virginia, 1724 | 2,000 pounds |
| Governor | Colonial Records of South Carolina - Journal of the Commons House of Assembly 1744-1745 (1955) | Annual salary of the Governor of South Carolina, 1745 | 3,500 pounds |
| Joiner | US Census (1976) | Daily wages of a joiner paid in local currency without board furnished in Virginia, 1621 | 5 shillings |
| Joiner | US Census (1976) | Daily wages of a joiner paid in local currency without board furnished in Massachusetts, 1631 | 2 shillings |
| Joiner | US Census (1976) | Daily wages of a joiner paid in local currency without board furnished in New Haven, 1640 | 2 shillings 6 pence |
| Joiner | US Census (1976) | Daily wages of a joiner paid in local currency without board furnished in New Haven, 1641 | 2 shillings |
| Joiner | US Census (1976) | Daily wages of a joiner paid in local currency without board furnished in South Carolina, 1710 | 5 shillings |

| Occupation | Data Source | Description | Price |
|---|---|---|---|
| Laborer | US Census (1976) | Daily wages of a laborer paid in local currency without board furnished in Virginia, 1621 | 3 shillings |
| Laborer | US Census (1976) | Daily wages of a laborer paid in local currency without board furnished in Massachusetts, 1631 | 1 shilling 6 pence |
| Laborer | US Census (1976) | Daily wages of a laborer paid in local currency without board furnished in New Haven, 1640 | 2 shillings |
| Laborer | US Census (1976) | Daily wages of a laborer paid in local currency without board furnished in New Haven, 1641 | 1 shilling 6 pence |
| Laborer | US Census (1976) | Daily wages of a laborer paid in local currency without board furnished in Massachusetts, 1670 | 1 shilling 3 pence |
| Laborer | US Census (1976) | Daily wages of a laborer paid in local currency without board furnished in South Carolina, 1710 | 1 shilling 2 pence |
| Lieutenant | Colonial Records of South Carolina - Journal of the Commons House of Assembly 1744-1745 (1955) | Monthly wages of the Lieutenant of the Rangers in South Carolina, 1744 | 20 pounds |
| Mason | US Census (1976) | Daily wages of a bricklayer paid in local currency without board furnished in Virginia, 1621 | 4 shillings |
| Mason | US Census (1976) | Daily wages of a mason paid in local currency without board furnished in Massachusetts, 1631 | 2 shillings |
| Mason | US Census (1976) | Daily wages of a mason paid in local currency without board furnished in New Haven, 1640 | 2 shillings 6 pence |
| Mason | US Census (1976) | Daily wages of a mason paid in local currency without board furnished in New Haven, 1641 | 2 shillings |
| Mason | US Census (1976) | Daily wages of a mason paid in local currency without board furnished in Massachusetts, 1670 | 2 shillings |
| Mason | US Census (1976) | Daily wages of a mason paid in local currency without board furnished in South Carolina, 1710 | 6 shillings |

## Based Upon the British Currency System

| Year | Pound in 2002 US Dollars | Shilling in 2002 US Dollars | Pence in 2002 US Dollars |
|---|---|---|---|
| 1650 | $120.00 | $6.00 | $0.50 |
| 1660 | $144.00 | $7.20 | $0.60 |
| 1670 | $120.00 | $6.00 | $0.70 |
| 1680 | $120.00 | $6.00 | $0.70 |
| 1690 | $120.00 | $6.00 | $0.80 |
| 1700 | $168.00 | $8.40 | $0.70 |
| 1710 | $144.00 | $7.20 | $0.60 |
| 1720 | $168.00 | $8.40 | $0.70 |
| 1730 | $192.00 | $9.60 | $0.80 |
| 1740 | $144.00 | $7.20 | $0.60 |
| 1749 | $192.00 | $9.60 | $0.80 |

*Calculations are approximate values based upon economic historical data*

| Occupation | Data Source | Description | Price |
|---|---|---|---|
| Patrol Commander | White Servitude in Colonial South Carolina, Warren B. Smith (1961) | Annual income for the district commander to provide safety in the region | 100 pounds |
| Patrolman | White Servitude in Colonial South Carolina, Warren B. Smith (1961) | Annual income for a district patrol man to provide safety in the region | 60 pounds |
| Rigger | US Census (1976) | Daily wages of a rigger paid in local currency without board furnished in Virginia, 1621 | 5 shillings |
| Rigger | US Census (1976) | Daily wages of a rigger paid in local currency without board furnished in Massachusetts, 1631 | 2 shillings |
| Rigger | US Census (1976) | Daily wages of a rigger paid in local currency without board furnished in New Haven, 1640 | 2 shillings 6 pence |
| Rigger | US Census (1976) | Daily wages of a rigger paid in local currency without board furnished in New Haven, 1641 | 2 shillings |
| Rigger | US Census (1976) | Daily wages of a rigger paid in local currency without board furnished in South Carolina, 1710 | 3 shillings |
| Sergeant | Colonial Records of South Carolina - Journal of the Commons House of Assembly 1744-1745 (1955) | Monthly pay of the Sergeant at Fort Johnson, South Carolina, 1744 | 12 pounds |
| Schoolmaster | Fourth Report of the Boston Record Commissioners (1651) | Annual salary for Mr. Butler for his teaching in Dorchester, Massachusetts, 1651 | 30 pounds |
| Schoolmaster | Dedham Records, Vol. III (1651) | Annual salary of a schoolmaster in Dedham, Massachusetts, 1651 | 20 pounds |
| Schoolmaster | Records of the Town of Braintree (1679) | Annual salary for a schoolmaster in Braintree, Massachusetts, 1679 | 30 pounds |
| Schoolmaster | The Records of the Town of Cambridge (1692) | Annual salary of a schoolmaster in Cambridge, Massachusetts, 1692 | 20 pounds |
| Sheriff | Virginia Assembly (1634) | Fee paid to a sheriff in Virginia for an arrest made in 1634 | 10 pounds of tobacco |
| Sheriff | Virginia Assembly (1634) | Fee paid to a sheriff in Virginia for taking someone to the pillory in 1634 | 20 pounds of tobacco |
| Tailor | US Census (1976) | Daily wages of a tailor paid in local currency without board furnished in Virginia, 1621 | 3 shillings |
| Tailor | US Census (1976) | Daily wages of a tailor paid in local currency without board furnished in Massachusetts, 1670 | 1 shilling 8 pence |
| Tailor | US Census (1976) | Daily wages of a tailor paid in local currency without board furnished in South Carolina, 1710 | 5 shillings |

# SERVICES & FEES 1600-1749

| Service/Fee | Data Source | Description | Price |
|---|---|---|---|
| Cure | Executive Journals, Council of Colonial Virginia, Vol. IV (1930) | Annual pension paid to James Pappaw by the Virginia colonial government for cure of certain diseases, 1730 | 20 pounds current money |
| Dwelling house | Inventory of Caleb Coy (1723) | Unfinished dwelling house in Beverly, MA | 20 pounds |
| Fine | Billings, The Old Dominion in the Seventeenth Century (1975) | Fine by county for failing to send two burgesses to the House of Burgesses every session, Virginia 1670 | 10,000 pounds of tobacco |
| Fine | | Fine for observing the Christmas holiday in Massachusetts | 5 shillings |
| Grinding | John Hall Day Book (1688) | Income earned from grinding one bushel of wheat in Boston 1866 | 1 shilling |
| Horse hire | Colonial Records of South Carolina - Journal of the Commons House of Assembly 1744-1745 (1955) | Payment to John Cart for the hire of a horse for the public service in South Carolina, 1744 | 8 pounds |

| Service/Fee | Data Source | Description | Price |
|---|---|---|---|
| Port duties | Executive Journals, Council of Colonial Virginia, Vol. IV (1930) | Duty on each hogshead in Virginia, 1730 | 2 shillings |
| Repairing arms | Colonial Records of South Carolina - Journal of the Commons House of Assembly 1744-1745 (1955) | Payment to John Scott, Gun Smith, for cleaning and repairing the Public Arms in South Carolina, 1744 | 43 pounds 15 shillings |
| Supplying liquor | Colonial Records of South Carolina - Journal of the Commons House of Assembly 1744-1745 (1955) | Payment to John Hanbury for supplying liquor to the Creek Indians in South Carolina, 1744 | 4 pounds |
| Tax | Quint Rent Rolls of Virginia 1704 | Tax on 50 acres of land in Virginia that goes directly to the English Crown | 1 shilling |
| Tuition | Dedham Records, Vol. III (1652) | Annual tuition of Male Children or servants betwixt the age of 4 and 14 years, Dedham, Massachusetts, 1652 | 5 shillings |
| Tuition | Records of the Town of Braintree (1700) | Quarterly charge for pupils to attend school in Braintree, Massachusetts, 1700 | 1 shilling |
| Wearing clothes | Inventory of John Colby (1674) | Set of clothing in Amesbury, MA | 1 pound, 10 shillings |

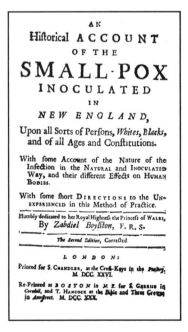

# FINANCIAL RATES & EXCHANGES
## 1600-1749

| Year | British Official Price of Gold (per Ounce) | Inflation Rate in Colonial America | Yield of Long-Term British Government Securities | Average Price per Pound of Maryland Tobacco (Pence) | Exchange Rate: Pennsylvania Currency for Pound Sterling |
|------|------|------|------|------|------|
| 1670 | £4.05 | −1.82% | — | 1.15 | — |
| 1671 | £4.05 | 1.85% | — | 1.05 | — |
| 1672 | £4.05 | −0.91% | — | 1.00 | — |
| 1673 | £4.05 | −4.59% | — | 1.00 | — |
| 1674 | £4.05 | 7.69% | — | 1.00 | — |
| 1675 | £4.05 | −13.39% | — | 1.00 | — |
| 1676 | £4.05 | 1.03% | — | 1.05 | — |
| 1677 | £4.05 | 1.02% | — | 1.15 | — |
| 1678 | £4.05 | −2.02% | — | 1.15 | — |
| 1679 | £4.05 | −1.03% | — | 1.05 | — |
| 1680 | £4.05 | 14.58% | — | 1.00 | — |
| 1681 | £4.05 | 2.73% | — | 0.90 | — |
| 1682 | £4.05 | −18.58% | — | 0.80 | — |
| 1683 | £4.05 | 0.00% | — | 0.80 | — |
| 1684 | £4.05 | 0.00% | — | 0.80 | — |
| 1685 | £4.05 | 7.61% | — | 1.00 | — |
| 1686 | £4.05 | −6.06% | — | 1.00 | — |
| 1687 | £4.05 | 0.00% | — | 0.85 | — |
| 1688 | £4.05 | −8.60% | — | 0.75 | — |
| 1689 | £4.05 | 2.35% | — | 0.70 | — |

## Based Upon the British Currency System

| Year | Pound in 2002 US Dollars | Shilling in 2002 US Dollars | Pence in 2002 US Dollars |
|------|------|------|------|
| 1650 | $120.00 | $6.00 | $0.50 |
| 1660 | $144.00 | $7.20 | $0.60 |
| 1670 | $120.00 | $6.00 | $0.70 |
| 1680 | $120.00 | $6.00 | $0.70 |
| 1690 | $120.00 | $6.00 | $0.80 |
| 1700 | $168.00 | $8.40 | $0.70 |
| 1710 | $144.00 | $7.20 | $0.60 |
| 1720 | $168.00 | $8.40 | $0.70 |
| 1730 | $192.00 | $9.60 | $0.80 |
| 1740 | $144.00 | $7.20 | $0.60 |
| 1749 | $192.00 | $9.60 | $0.80 |

*Calculations are approximate values based upon economic historical data*

| Year | British Official Price of Gold (per Ounce) | Inflation Rate in Colonial America | Yield of Long-Term British Government Securities | Average Price per Pound of Maryland Tobacco (Pence) | Exchange Rate: Pennsylvania Currency for Pound Sterling |
|---|---|---|---|---|---|
| 1690 | £4.05 | 2.30% | — | 0.80 | — |
| 1691 | £4.05 | 4.49% | — | 0.80 | — |
| 1692 | £4.05 | −5.38% | — | 0.80 | — |
| 1693 | £4.05 | −5.68% | — | 0.75 | — |
| 1694 | £4.05 | 6.02% | — | 0.75 | — |
| 1695 | £4.05 | −7.95% | — | 0.75 | — |
| 1696 | £4.45 | 17.28% | — | 0.85 | — |
| 1697 | £4.45 | −2.11% | — | 0.90 | — |
| 1698 | £4.45 | −5.38% | — | 1.00 | — |
| 1699 | £4.35 | 9.09% | — | 1.05 | — |
| | | | | | |
| 1700 | £4.35 | −3.13% | — | 1.00 | — |
| 1701 | £4.35 | 5.38% | — | 0.95 | — |
| 1702 | £4.35 | −8.16% | — | 1.00 | — |
| 1703 | £4.35 | −1.11% | — | 0.85 | — |
| 1704 | £4.35 | 13.48% | — | 0.90 | — |
| 1705 | £4.35 | −9.90% | — | 0.80 | — |
| 1706 | £4.35 | 7.69% | — | 0.80 | — |
| 1707 | £4.35 | −4.08% | — | 0.90 | — |
| 1708 | £4.35 | −21.28% | — | 0.90 | — |
| 1709 | £4.35 | 20.27% | — | 0.90 | — |
| | | | | | |
| 1710 | £4.35 | −10.11% | — | 0.85 | — |
| 1711 | £4.35 | −1.25% | — | 0.97 | — |
| 1712 | £4.35 | −5.06% | — | 1.00 | — |
| 1713 | £4.35 | 6.67% | — | 1.00 | — |
| 1714 | £4.35 | −8.75% | — | 0.71 | — |
| 1715 | £4.35 | 12.33% | — | 0.72 | — |
| 1716 | £4.35 | −6.10% | — | 0.80 | — |
| 1717 | £4.25 | 6.49% | — | 0.79 | — |
| 1718 | £4.25 | −6.10% | — | 0.89 | — |
| 1719 | £4.25 | 6.49% | — | 1.04 | — |
| | | | | | |
| 1720 | £4.25 | −7.32% | — | 1.19 | 1.33 |
| 1721 | £4.25 | −6.58% | — | 0.97 | 1.33 |
| 1722 | £4.25 | 5.63% | — | 0.86 | 1.33 |
| 1723 | £4.25 | 1.33% | — | 1.07 | — |
| 1724 | £4.25 | 3.95% | — | 0.90 | — |
| 1725 | £4.25 | 13.92% | — | 1.05 | — |
| 1726 | £4.25 | −7.78% | — | 0.91 | — |
| 1727 | £4.25 | 3.61% | — | 0.82 | 1.50 |
| 1728 | £4.25 | −5.81% | — | 0.67 | 1.50 |
| 1729 | £4.25 | −1.23% | 3.07% | 0.70 | 1.50 |
| | | | | | |
| 1730 | £4.25 | 0.00% | 2.97% | 0.67 | 1.52 |
| 1731 | £4.25 | −11.25% | 3.04% | 0.65 | 1.53 |
| 1732 | £4.25 | −7.04% | 2.92% | 0.74 | 1.61 |
| 1733 | £4.25 | 3.03% | 2.92% | 0.84 | 1.65 |
| 1734 | £4.25 | −2.94% | 3.11% | 0.97 | — |
| 1735 | £4.25 | 3.03% | 3.02% | 0.93 | 1.63 |

| Year | British Official Price of Gold (per Ounce) | Inflation Rate in Colonial America | Yield of Long-Term British Government Securities | Average Price per Pound of Maryland Tobacco (Pence) | Exchange Rate: Pennsylvania Currency for Pound Sterling |
|------|------|------|------|------|------|
| 1736 | £4.25 | −4.41% | 2.74% | 1.02 | 1.65 |
| 1737 | £4.25 | 3.08% | 2.71% | 0.93 | 1.68 |
| 1738 | £4.25 | 4.48% | 2.73% | 1.02 | 1.65 |
| 1739 | £4.25 | −11.43% | 2.83% | 1.01 | 1.70 |
| 1740 | £4.25 | 6.45% | 2.87% | 0.80 | 1.64 |
| 1741 | £4.25 | 37.88% | 2.90% | 0.62 | 1.45 |
| 1742 | £4.25 | −10.99% | 2.85% | 0.67 | 1.60 |
| 1743 | £4.25 | −12.35% | 2.82% | 0.67 | 1.60 |
| 1744 | £4.25 | −7.04% | 3.06% | 0.63 | 1.67 |
| 1745 | £4.25 | −3.03% | 3.23% | 0.56 | 1.76 |
| 1746 | £4.25 | 1.56% | 3.48% | 0.61 | 1.79 |
| 1747 | £4.25 | 10.77% | 3.42% | 0.45 | 1.85 |
| 1748 | £4.25 | 13.89% | 3.33% | 0.67 | 1.74 |
| 1749 | £4.25 | 2.44% | 2.92% | 0.76 | 1.72 |

## Based Upon the British Currency System

| Year | Pound in 2002 US Dollars | Shilling in 2002 US Dollars | Pence in 2002 US Dollars |
|------|------|------|------|
| 1650 | $120.00 | $6.00 | $0.50 |
| 1660 | $144.00 | $7.20 | $0.60 |
| 1670 | $120.00 | $6.00 | $0.70 |
| 1680 | $120.00 | $6.00 | $0.70 |
| 1690 | $120.00 | $6.00 | $0.80 |
| 1700 | $168.00 | $8.40 | $0.70 |
| 1710 | $144.00 | $7.20 | $0.60 |
| 1720 | $168.00 | $8.40 | $0.70 |
| 1730 | $192.00 | $9.60 | $0.80 |
| 1740 | $144.00 | $7.20 | $0.60 |
| 1749 | $192.00 | $9.60 | $0.80 |

*Calculations are approximate values based upon economic historical data*

# SLAVE TRADES 1600-1749

### Average Price of British American and West African Slaves
*Price in Pounds Sterling*

| Year | Price Paid for Slave by Traders in West Africa | Price Paid for Slave by British Colonists in America | Year | Price Paid for Slave by Traders in West Africa | Price Paid for Slave by British Colonists in America |
|---|---|---|---|---|---|
| 1638 | 3.91 | 16.50 | 1678 | 3.28 | 19.32 |
| 1639 | 3.91 | 16.50 | 1679 | 3.28 | 19.32 |
| 1640 | 3.91 | 16.50 | 1680 | 3.28 | 19.32 |
| 1641 | 3.91 | 16.50 | 1681 | 3.28 | 19.32 |
| 1642 | 3.91 | 16.50 | 1682 | 3.28 | 19.32 |
| 1643 | 1.87 | 20.20 | 1683 | 3.92 | 19.95 |
| 1644 | 1.87 | 20.20 | 1684 | 3.92 | 19.95 |
| 1645 | 1.87 | 20.20 | 1685 | 3.92 | 19.95 |
| 1646 | 1.87 | 20.20 | 1686 | 3.92 | 19.95 |
| 1647 | 1.87 | 20.20 | 1687 | 3.92 | 19.95 |
| 1648 | 6.72 | 27.70 | 1688 | 3.37 | 23.85 |
| 1649 | 6.72 | 27.70 | 1689 | 3.37 | 23.85 |
| 1650 | 6.72 | 27.70 | 1690 | 3.37 | 23.85 |
| 1651 | 6.72 | 27.70 | 1691 | 3.37 | 23.85 |
| 1652 | 6.72 | 27.70 | 1692 | 3.37 | 23.85 |
| 1653 | 11.38 | 24.09 | 1693 | 4.19 | 26.02 |
| 1654 | 11.38 | 24.09 | 1694 | 4.19 | 26.02 |
| 1655 | 11.38 | 24.09 | 1695 | 4.19 | 26.02 |
| 1656 | 11.38 | 24.09 | 1696 | 4.19 | 26.02 |
| 1657 | 11.38 | 24.09 | 1697 | 4.19 | 26.02 |
| 1658 | 3.01 | 21.12 | 1698 | 5.21 | 23.68 |
| 1659 | 3.01 | 21.12 | 1699 | 5.21 | 23.68 |
| 1660 | 3.01 | 21.12 | 1700 | 5.21 | 23.68 |
| 1661 | 3.01 | 21.12 | 1701 | 5.21 | 23.68 |
| 1662 | 3.01 | 21.12 | 1702 | 5.21 | 23.68 |
| 1663 | 5.41 | 21.14 | 1703 | 8.87 | 26.37 |
| 1664 | 5.41 | 21.14 | 1704 | 8.87 | 26.37 |
| 1665 | 5.41 | 21.14 | 1705 | 8.87 | 26.37 |
| 1666 | 5.41 | 21.14 | 1706 | 8.87 | 26.37 |
| 1667 | 5.41 | 21.14 | 1707 | 8.87 | 26.37 |
| 1668 | 3.03 | 21.14 | 1708 | 8.75 | 24.37 |
| 1669 | 3.03 | 21.14 | 1709 | 8.75 | 24.37 |
| 1670 | 3.03 | 21.14 | 1710 | 8.75 | 24.37 |
| 1671 | 3.03 | 21.14 | 1711 | 8.75 | 24.37 |
| 1672 | 3.03 | 21.14 | 1712 | 8.75 | 24.37 |
| 1673 | 2.04 | 21.92 | 1713 | 9.88 | 25.67 |
| 1674 | 2.04 | 21.92 | 1714 | 9.88 | 25.67 |
| 1675 | 2.04 | 21.92 | 1715 | 9.88 | 25.67 |
| 1676 | 2.04 | 21.92 | 1716 | 9.88 | 25.67 |
| 1677 | 2.04 | 21.92 | 1717 | 9.88 | 25.67 |

| Year | Price Paid for Slave by Traders in West Africa | Price Paid for Slave by British Colonists in America | Year | Price Paid for Slave by Traders in West Africa | Price Paid for Slave by British Colonists in America |
|---|---|---|---|---|---|
| 1718 | 11.13 | 24.11 | 1734 | 15.37 | 18.50 |
| 1719 | 11.13 | 24.11 | 1735 | 15.37 | 18.50 |
|  |  |  | 1736 | 15.37 | 18.50 |
| 1720 | 11.13 | 24.11 | 1737 | 15.37 | 18.50 |
| 1721 | 11.13 | 24.11 | 1738 | 17.43 | 26.64 |
| 1722 | 11.13 | 24.11 | 1739 | 17.43 | 26.64 |
| 1723 | 11.87 | 23.92 |  |  |  |
| 1724 | 11.87 | 23.92 | 1740 | 17.43 | 26.64 |
| 1725 | 11.87 | 23.92 | 1741 | 17.43 | 26.64 |
| 1726 | 11.87 | 23.92 | 1742 | 17.43 | 26.64 |
| 1727 | 11.87 | 23.92 | 1743 | 11.21 | 31.04 |
| 1728 | 12.86 | 24.91 | 1744 | 11.21 | 31.04 |
| 1729 | 12.86 | 24.91 | 1745 | 11.21 | 31.04 |
|  |  |  | 1746 | 11.21 | 31.04 |
| 1730 | 12.86 | 24.91 | 1747 | 11.21 | 31.04 |
| 1731 | 12.86 | 24.91 | 1748 | 14.01 | 27.12 |
| 1732 | 12.86 | 24.91 | 1749 | 14.01 | 27.12 |
| 1733 | 15.37 | 18.50 |  |  |  |

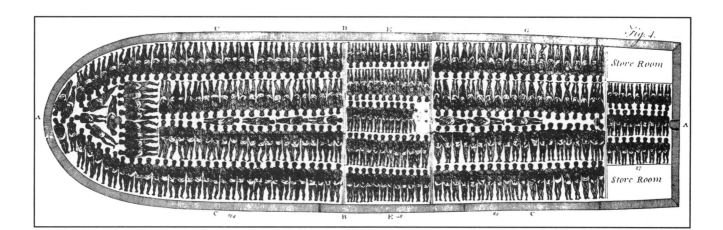

# COMMODITIES 1600-1749

| Commodity | Year | Philadelphia | Year | Philadelphia |
|---|---|---|---|---|
| Beef, per barrel | 1720 | 4.00 | 1735 | 3.73 |
| | 1721 | 4.00 | 1736 | 4.27 |
| | 1722 | 4.13 | 1737 | 4.67 |
| | 1723 | 4.33 | 1738 | 5.33 |
| | 1724 | 3.40 | 1739 | 4.67 |
| | 1725 | 4.27 | 1740 | 4.67 |
| | 1726 | 4.00 | 1741 | 6.00 |
| | 1727 | 4.27 | 1742 | 4.67 |
| | 1728 | 5.33 | 1743 | 7.00 |
| | 1729 | 4.67 | 1744 | 5.33 |
| | 1730 | 4.00 | 1745 | 4.67 |
| | 1731 | 4.69 | 1746 | 5.33 |
| | 1732 | 3.73 | 1747 | 5.17 |
| | 1733 | 5.67 | 1748 | 6.00 |
| | 1734 | 3.96 | 1749 | 5.33 |
| Bread, per hundredweight | 1720 | 1.73 | 1735 | 2.00 |
| | 1721 | 1.73 | 1736 | 1.73 |
| | 1722 | 1.60 | 1737 | 1.93 |
| | 1723 | 1.53 | 1738 | 2.27 |
| | 1724 | 1.60 | 1739 | 1.67 |
| | 1725 | 1.60 | 1740 | 1.67 |
| | 1726 | 1.87 | 1741 | 2.67 |
| | 1727 | 1.75 | 1742 | 2.00 |
| | 1728 | 1.73 | 1743 | 1.83 |
| | 1729 | 1.80 | 1744 | 1.71 |
| | 1730 | 2.00 | 1745 | 1.67 |
| | 1731 | 1.49 | 1746 | 1.87 |
| | 1732 | 1.57 | 1747 | 2.13 |
| | 1733 | 1.67 | 1748 | 2.27 |
| | 1734 | 1.80 | 1749 | 3.69 |
| Corn, per bushel | 1720 | 0.23 | 1729 | 0.27 |
| | 1721 | 0.26 | 1730 | 0.25 |
| | 1722 | 0.23 | 1731 | 0.24 |
| | 1723 | 0.23 | 1732 | 0.22 |
| | 1724 | 0.28 | 1733 | 0.27 |
| | 1725 | 0.28 | 1734 | 0.27 |
| | 1726 | 0.29 | 1735 | 0.20 |
| | 1727 | 0.26 | 1736 | 0.24 |
| | 1728 | 0.32 | 1737 | 0.27 |

Values are expressed in Silver Dollars, the most common currency in the colony for trade

| Commodity | Year | Philadelphia | Year | Philadelphia |
|---|---|---|---|---|
| | 1738 | 0.33 | 1744 | 0.22 |
| | 1739 | 0.17 | 1745 | 0.19 |
| | 1740 | 0.18 | 1746 | 0.21 |
| | 1741 | 0.30 | 1747 | 0.27 |
| | 1742 | 0.34 | 1748 | 0.29 |
| | 1743 | 0.30 | 1749 | 0.38 |
| | | | | |
| Cotton, per pound | 1731 | 0.16 | 1741 | 0.16 |
| | 1732 | 0.11 | 1742 | 0.14 |
| | 1733 | 0.16 | 1743 | 0.13 |
| | 1734 | 0.13 | 1744 | 0.15 |
| | 1735 | 0.15 | 1745 | 0.18 |
| | 1736 | 0.13 | 1746 | 0.23 |
| | 1737 | 0.16 | 1747 | 0.26 |
| | 1738 | 0.14 | 1748 | 0.27 |
| | 1739 | 0.18 | 1749 | 0.22 |
| | 1740 | 0.18 | | |
| | | | | |
| Flour, per hundredweight | 1700 | 2.53 | 1726 | 1.60 |
| | 1701 | 2.93 | 1727 | 1.55 |
| | 1702 | 2.67 | 1728 | 1.28 |
| | 1703 | 2.40 | 1729 | 1.20 |
| | 1704 | 1.93 | 1730 | 1.60 |
| | 1705 | 2.00 | 1731 | 1.04 |
| | 1708 | 2.53 | 1732 | 1.07 |
| | 1709 | 1.49 | 1733 | 1.07 |
| | 1710 | 1.47 | 1734 | 1.29 |
| | 1711 | 1.40 | 1735 | 1.67 |
| | 1712 | 1.60 | 1736 | 1.20 |
| | 1713 | 1.87 | 1737 | 1.33 |
| | 1714 | 2.32 | 1738 | 1.60 |
| | 1715 | 1.31 | 1739 | 1.00 |
| | 1716 | 0.96 | 1740 | 0.97 |
| | 1717 | 1.13 | 1741 | 1.80 |
| | 1718 | 1.27 | 1742 | 1.37 |
| | 1719 | 1.33 | 1743 | 1.07 |
| | 1720 | 1.17 | 1744 | 0.97 |
| | 1721 | 1.10 | 1745 | 0.93 |
| | 1722 | 1.17 | 1746 | 1.07 |
| | 1723 | 1.20 | 1747 | 1.22 |
| | 1724 | 1.40 | 1748 | 1.57 |
| | 1725 | 1.53 | 1749 | 2.32 |

Values are expressed in Silver Dollars, the most common currency in the colony for trade

| Commodity | Year | Philadelphia | Year | Philadelphia |
|---|---|---|---|---|
| Indigo, per pound | 1731 | 0.67 | 1741 | 1.33 |
| | 1732 | 0.50 | 1742 | 1.07 |
| | 1733 | 0.60 | 1743 | 1.00 |
| | 1734 | 0.87 | 1744 | 0.93 |
| | 1735 | 1.33 | 1745 | 0.87 |
| | 1736 | 1.07 | 1746 | 0.80 |
| | 1737 | 0.80 | 1747 | 0.93 |
| | 1738 | 0.73 | 1748 | 0.73 |
| | 1739 | 0.93 | 1749 | 0.74 |
| | 1740 | 0.80 | | |
| Iron - Bar, per ton | 1738 | 80.00 | 1745 | 58.67 |
| | 1740 | 73.33 | 1746 | 52.00 |
| | 1741 | 80.00 | 1747 | 66.67 |
| | 1742 | 66.67 | 1748 | 70.40 |
| | 1743 | 66.67 | 1749 | 74.67 |
| Molasses, per gallon | 1700 | 0.33 | 1725 | 0.19 |
| | 1701 | 0.33 | 1726 | 0.20 |
| | 1702 | 0.33 | 1727 | 0.18 |
| | 1703 | 0.29 | 1728 | 0.20 |
| | 1704 | 0.31 | 1729 | 0.21 |
| | 1705 | 0.27 | 1730 | 0.20 |
| | 1706 | 0.27 | 1731 | 0.19 |
| | 1707 | 0.30 | 1732 | 0.19 |
| | 1708 | 0.27 | 1733 | 0.19 |
| | 1709 | 0.22 | 1734 | 0.20 |
| | 1710 | 0.33 | 1735 | 0.22 |
| | 1711 | 0.33 | 1736 | 0.20 |
| | 1712 | 0.33 | 1737 | 0.20 |
| | 1713 | 0.29 | 1738 | 0.22 |
| | 1714 | 0.27 | 1739 | 0.20 |
| | 1715 | 0.20 | 1740 | 0.21 |
| | 1716 | 0.20 | 1741 | 0.22 |
| | 1717 | 0.20 | 1742 | 0.29 |
| | 1718 | 0.22 | 1743 | 0.24 |
| | 1719 | 0.21 | 1744 | 0.22 |
| | 1720 | 0.18 | 1745 | 0.28 |
| | 1721 | 0.17 | 1746 | 0.33 |
| | 1722 | 0.17 | 1747 | 0.36 |
| | 1723 | 0.17 | 1748 | 0.39 |
| | 1724 | 0.16 | 1749 | 0.29 |
| Pork, per barrel | 1720 | 6.00 | 1725 | 5.67 |
| | 1721 | 6.00 | 1726 | 6.67 |
| | 1722 | 6.00 | 1727 | 6.13 |
| | 1723 | 5.67 | 1728 | 8.67 |
| | 1724 | 4.69 | 1729 | 6.83 |

Values are expressed in Silver Dollars, the most common currency in the colony for trade

| Commodity | Year | Philadelphia | Year | Philadelphia |
|---|---|---|---|---|
| | 1730 | 7.84 | 1740 | 5.33 |
| | 1731 | 6.67 | 1741 | 6.40 |
| | 1732 | 6.67 | 1742 | 6.33 |
| | 1733 | 5.73 | 1743 | 9.67 |
| | 1734 | 6.00 | 1744 | 7.84 |
| | 1735 | 4.00 | 1745 | 5.67 |
| | 1736 | 5.00 | 1746 | 7.49 |
| | 1737 | 6.00 | 1747 | 7.67 |
| | 1738 | 7.00 | 1748 | 7.67 |
| | 1739 | 7.13 | 1749 | 8.00 |
| Rice, per hundredweight | 1720 | 2.13 | 1736 | 2.13 |
| | 1721 | 2.13 | 1737 | 2.13 |
| | 1722 | 1.93 | 1738 | 2.80 |
| | 1723 | 2.01 | 1739 | 2.13 |
| | 1724 | 1.80 | 1740 | 1.87 |
| | 1725 | 2.67 | 1741 | 2.13 |
| | 1726 | 2.93 | 1742 | 2.40 |
| | 1728 | 2.40 | 1743 | 1.49 |
| | 1729 | 2.40 | 1744 | 1.33 |
| | 1730 | 2.13 | 1745 | 1.00 |
| | 1731 | 2.00 | 1746 | 0.93 |
| | 1732 | 2.13 | 1747 | 1.33 |
| | 1733 | 1.60 | 1748 | 2.13 |
| | 1734 | 2.40 | 1749 | 2.40 |
| | 1735 | 2.40 | | |
| Rum, per gallon | 1700 | 0.60 | 1721 | 0.27 |
| | 1701 | 0.63 | 1722 | 0.31 |
| | 1702 | 0.83 | 1723 | 0.27 |
| | 1703 | 0.50 | 1724 | 0.26 |
| | 1705 | 0.39 | 1725 | 0.33 |
| | 1706 | 0.40 | 1726 | 0.40 |
| | 1707 | 0.38 | 1727 | 0.33 |
| | 1708 | 0.43 | 1728 | 0.31 |
| | 1709 | 0.33 | 1729 | 0.32 |
| | 1710 | 0.30 | 1730 | 0.31 |
| | 1711 | 0.33 | 1731 | 0.31 |
| | 1712 | 0.47 | 1732 | 0.31 |
| | 1713 | 0.60 | 1733 | 0.32 |
| | 1714 | 0.73 | 1734 | 0.32 |
| | 1715 | 0.38 | 1735 | 0.29 |
| | 1716 | 0.38 | 1736 | 0.29 |
| | 1717 | 0.33 | 1737 | 0.29 |
| | 1718 | 0.37 | 1738 | 0.28 |
| | 1719 | 0.40 | 1739 | 0.27 |
| | 1720 | 0.27 | 1740 | 0.22 |

Values are expressed in Silver Dollars, the most common currency in the colony for trade

| Commodity | Year | Philadelphia | Year | Philadelphia |
|---|---|---|---|---|
| | 1741 | 0.28 | 1746 | 0.37 |
| | 1742 | 0.36 | 1747 | 0.50 |
| | 1743 | 0.29 | 1748 | 0.47 |
| | 1744 | 0.32 | 1749 | 0.34 |
| | 1745 | 0.33 | | |
| Salt, per bushel | | | | |
| | 1700 | 0.33 | 1726 | 0.20 |
| | 1703 | 0.60 | 1727 | 0.27 |
| | 1704 | 0.53 | 1728 | 0.22 |
| | 1705 | 0.60 | 1729 | 0.25 |
| | 1706 | 0.43 | 1730 | 0.38 |
| | 1707 | 0.59 | 1731 | 0.40 |
| | 1708 | 0.32 | 1732 | 0.33 |
| | 1709 | 0.40 | 1733 | 0.21 |
| | 1710 | 0.40 | 1734 | 0.24 |
| | 1711 | 0.31 | 1735 | 0.22 |
| | 1712 | 0.67 | 1736 | 0.27 |
| | 1713 | 0.33 | 1737 | 0.27 |
| | 1714 | 0.36 | 1738 | 0.28 |
| | 1715 | 0.33 | 1739 | 0.22 |
| | 1716 | 0.24 | 1740 | 0.22 |
| | 1717 | 0.33 | 1741 | 0.20 |
| | 1718 | 0.33 | 1742 | 0.40 |
| | 1719 | 0.27 | 1743 | 0.31 |
| | 1720 | 0.27 | 1744 | 0.20 |
| | 1721 | 0.20 | 1745 | 0.33 |
| | 1722 | 0.18 | 1746 | 0.40 |
| | 1723 | 0.22 | 1747 | 0.43 |
| | 1724 | 0.40 | 1748 | 0.40 |
| | 1725 | 0.33 | 1749 | 0.33 |
| Staves, per 1200 units | 1721 | 6.00 | 1740 | 6.67 |
| | 1722 | 6.00 | 1741 | 10.00 |
| | 1723 | 6.00 | 1742 | 9.17 |
| | 1724 | 5.33 | 1743 | 8.35 |
| | 1728 | 4.67 | 1744 | 7.33 |
| | 1734 | 8.00 | 1745 | 7.33 |
| | 1735 | 6.88 | 1746 | 8.00 |
| | 1736 | 5.68 | 1747 | 9.68 |
| | 1737 | 8.00 | 1748 | 14.21 |
| | 1738 | 8.67 | 1749 | 15.33 |
| | 1739 | 8.13 | | |
| Sugar, per hundredweight | 1700 | 6.83 | 1704 | 7.67 |
| | 1701 | 8.63 | 1705 | 7.47 |
| | 1702 | 10.67 | 1707 | 4.40 |
| | 1703 | 6.67 | 1709 | 6.00 |

Values are expressed in Silver Dollars, the most common currency in the colony for trade

| Commodity | Year | Philadelphia | Year | Philadelphia |
|---|---|---|---|---|
| | 1710 | 4.80 | 1730 | 4.00 |
| | 1711 | 5.20 | 1731 | 4.67 |
| | 1712 | 7.47 | 1732 | 4.67 |
| | 1713 | 9.96 | 1733 | 4.00 |
| | 1714 | 7.47 | 1734 | 3.56 |
| | 1715 | 5.33 | 1735 | 5.33 |
| | 1716 | 6.00 | 1736 | 4.80 |
| | 1717 | 5.00 | 1737 | 4.00 |
| | 1718 | 6.23 | 1738 | 4.67 |
| | 1719 | 4.67 | 1739 | 5.07 |
| | 1720 | 5.00 | 1740 | 4.67 |
| | 1721 | 4.67 | 1741 | 5.20 |
| | 1722 | 4.00 | 1742 | 4.67 |
| | 1723 | 5.00 | 1743 | 4.67 |
| | 1724 | 3.07 | 1744 | 6.51 |
| | 1725 | 4.00 | 1745 | 5.67 |
| | 1726 | 5.33 | 1746 | 6.00 |
| | 1727 | 4.27 | 1747 | 7.49 |
| | 1728 | 4.67 | 1748 | 7.33 |
| | 1729 | 4.67 | 1749 | 5.56 |
| Tea, per pound | 1720 | 6.67 | 1724 | 2.33 |
| | 1721 | 3.73 | 1725 | 2.40 |
| | 1722 | 3.67 | 1726 | 2.67 |
| | 1723 | 2.67 | | |
| Tobacco, per hundredweight | 1721 | 1.27 | 1736 | 2.13 |
| | 1722 | 1.40 | 1738 | 2.13 |
| | 1724 | 2.29 | 1739 | 2.00 |
| | 1725 | 5.23 | 1740 | 2.00 |
| | 1726 | 2.31 | 1741 | 1.87 |
| | 1727 | 2.55 | 1742 | 2.27 |
| | 1728 | 2.20 | 1743 | 2.16 |
| | 1729 | 2.40 | 1744 | 1.60 |
| | 1730 | 1.33 | 1745 | 1.53 |
| | 1731 | 1.47 | 1746 | 1.73 |
| | 1732 | 1.73 | 1747 | 2.43 |
| | 1733 | 1.87 | 1748 | 2.33 |
| | 1734 | 2.67 | 1749 | 1.77 |
| | 1735 | 1.87 | | |
| Turpentine, per hundredweight | 1721 | 1.07 | 1729 | 1.07 |
| | 1722 | 1.27 | 1730 | 1.60 |
| | 1726 | 1.87 | 1731 | 1.33 |

Values are expressed in Silver Dollars, the most common currency in the colony for trade

| Commodity | Year | Philadelphia | Year | Philadelphia |
|---|---|---|---|---|
| Wheat, per bushel | 1700 | 0.67 | 1726 | 0.53 |
| | 1703 | 0.53 | 1727 | 0.48 |
| | 1704 | 0.61 | 1728 | 0.45 |
| | 1705 | 0.59 | 1729 | 0.48 |
| | 1706 | 0.50 | 1730 | 0.51 |
| | 1707 | 0.47 | 1731 | 0.29 |
| | 1708 | 0.73 | 1732 | 0.34 |
| | 1709 | 0.43 | 1733 | 0.38 |
| | 1710 | 0.45 | 1734 | 0.47 |
| | 1711 | 0.42 | 1735 | 0.56 |
| | 1712 | 0.46 | 1736 | 0.40 |
| | 1713 | 0.51 | 1737 | 0.44 |
| | 1714 | 0.58 | 1738 | 0.51 |
| | 1715 | 0.31 | 1739 | 0.36 |
| | 1716 | 0.37 | 1740 | 0.39 |
| | 1717 | 0.33 | 1741 | 0.60 |
| | 1718 | 0.42 | 1742 | 0.47 |
| | 1719 | 0.40 | 1743 | 0.34 |
| | 1720 | 0.40 | 1744 | 0.31 |
| | 1721 | 0.39 | 1745 | 0.31 |
| | 1722 | 0.39 | 1746 | 0.37 |
| | 1723 | 0.36 | 1747 | 0.40 |
| | 1724 | 0.44 | 1748 | 0.57 |
| | 1725 | 0.48 | 1749 | 0.84 |

Values are expressed in Silver Dollars, the most common currency in the colony for trade

| Commodity | Year | Philadelphia | Year | Philadelphia |
|-----------|------|--------------|------|--------------|
| Wine, per pipe | 1720 | 48.00 | 1739 | 58.67 |
|  | 1721 | 48.00 | 1740 | 56.00 |
|  | 1722 | 54.67 | 1741 | 64.00 |
|  | 1723 | 54.67 | 1742 | 64.00 |
|  | 1724 | 56.00 | 1743 | 69.87 |
|  | 1733 | 56.00 | 1744 | 67.20 |
|  | 1734 | 56.00 | 1745 | 73.33 |
|  | 1735 | 56.00 | 1746 | 58.67 |
|  | 1736 | 53.33 | 1747 | 66.67 |
|  | 1737 | 56.00 | 1748 | 66.67 |
|  | 1738 | 58.67 | 1749 | 80.00 |

Values are expressed in Silver Dollars, the most common currency in the colony for trade

# SELECTED PRICES 1600-1749

| Item | Data Source | Description | Price |
|---|---|---|---|
| **Alcohol** | | | |
| Ale | Inventory of Jesse Ball (1742) | Dozen bottles of ale in Lancaster, Virginia, 1747 | 2 shillings |
| Bottles | Inventory of Jesse Ball (1742) | Empty Qt Bottles in Lancaster, Virginia, 1747 | 2 shillings |
| Brandy | Inventory of A. Pearce (1690) | Quart of Brandy in Suffolk County, Massachusetts, 1690 | 2 shillings 3 pence |
| Cask | Inventory of Henry Fitzhugh (1742) | Old Cyder Cask in Stafford County, Virginia, 1742 | 2 shillings 4 pence |
| Cider | Inventory of Jesse Ball (1742) | Gallon of Cyder in Lancaster, Virginia, 1747 | 4 pence |
| Rum | Inventory of Samuel Hanson (1741) | Gallon of rum in Charles County, Maryland, 1741 | 5 shillings |
| Spirits | Inventory of A. Pearce (1690) | Gallon of Spirits in Suffolk County, Massachusetts, 1690 | 3 shillings |
| Still | Inventory of Henry Fitzhugh (1742) | Copper still in Stafford County, Virginia, 1742 | 30 pounds 10 shillings |
| Wine | Inventory of Nicholas Mardin (1696) | Pipe of madera wine in Charles Town, 1696 | 20 pounds |
| Wine | Inventory of Jesse Ball (1742) | Dozen bottles of wine in Lancaster, Virginia, 1747 | 1 pound |
| **Apparel - Children** | | | |
| Cap | Inventory of Johnathan Newell (1672) | Childs sattin capp in York County, Virginia, 1672 | 6 pence |
| Coat | Inventory of Johnathan Newell (1672) | Small wast coat for children in York County, Virginia, 1672 | 10 pence |
| Gloves | Inventory of Johnathan Newell (1672) | Pair of Children yarne Gloves in York County, Virginia, 1672 | 3 pence |
| Hat | Inventory of Josias Du Pre (1692) | Childrens hatt in Charleston, South Carolina, 1692 | 5 shillings |
| Shoes | Inventory of Johnathan Newell (1672) | Pair of Chidrens shooes in York County, Virginia, 1672 | 1 pound 4 pence |
| Stockings | Inventory of Johnathan Newell (1672) | Pair of Boys Stockens in York County, Virginia, 1672 | 10 pence |
| **Apparel - Men** | | | |
| Boots | Cressy, Coming Over (1987) | A pair of boots in New England during 1630 | 9 shillings |
| Boots | Inventory of Captian Arthur Dunn (1724) | Pair Old Boots in Middlesex, Massachusetts, 1724 | 10 shillings |
| Britches | Inventory of Jesse Ball (1742) | Pair of Leather Breeches in Lancaster, Virginia, 1747 | 13 shillings |
| Britches | Inventory of Roger Annadowne (1673) | A paire of Cloth breiches in Plymouth, Massachusetts, 1673 | 12 shillings |
| Buckle | Inventory of Zephaniah Wade (1746) | Silver Stock buckle in Fairfax, Virginia, 1746 | 5 shillings |
| Buckles | Inventory of Peter Perdriau (1692) | Payre Silver Shoes buckles in Charleston, South Carolina, 1692 | 2 shillings 6 pence |
| Buttons | Inventory of Captian Arthur Dunn (1724) | Pair Gold Buttons in Middlesex, Massachusetts, 1724 | 7 pounds 2 shillings 6 pence |
| Buttons | Inventory of Zephaniah Wade (1746) | Pair Silver Sleeve buttons in Fairfax, Virginia, 1746 | 1 shilling 6 pence |
| Cap | Billings, The Old Dominion in the Seventeenth Century (1975) | Manmouth Cap in Virginia, 1611 | 1 shilling 10 pence |

| Item | Data Source | Description | Price |
|------|-------------|-------------|-------|
| Cap | Inventory of John Jay (1678) | Satin cap in Suffolk, Massachusetts, 1678 | 3 shillings 6 pence |
| Clasps | Inventory of Jesse Ball (1742) | Pair of Silver Neck Clasps in Lancaster, Virginia, 1747 | 2 shillings 5 pence |
| Cloak | Inventory of James Lindale (1652) | A stuffe cloake in Plymouth, Massachusetts, 1652 | 10 shillings |
| Cloak | Inventory of John Vansusteren (1694) | Camlett Cloake in Charles Towne, South Carolina, 1694 | 2 pounds |
| Coat | Inventory of Captian Arthur Dunn (1724) | Lapell Bever Coat in Middlesex, Massachusetts, 1724 | 13 pounds 10 shillings |
| Doublet | Inventory of William Kemp (1641) | A leather Dublet wth silvr buttons in Plymouth, Massachusetts, 1641 | 1 pound |
| Drawers | Inventory of John Jay (1678) | Paire Red cotten drawers in Suffolk, Massachusetts, 1678 | 3 shillings 9 pence |
| Falling bands | Cressy, Coming Over (1987) | Three falling bands in New England during 1630 | 1 shilling 3 pence |
| Garters | Billings, The Old Dominion in the Seventeenth Century (1975) | Paire of garters in Virginia, 1611 | 10 pence |
| Gloves | Inventory of Josias Du Pre (1692) | Pair of perfund mans gloves in Charleston, South Carolina, 1692 | 5 shillings |
| Gloves | Inventory of Henry Fitzhugh (1742) | Pair of kid skin Gloves in Stafford County, Virginia, 1742 | 1 shilling 6 pence |
| Handkerchief | Inventory of William Kemp (1641) | Holland handkerchiefs in Plymouth, Massachusetts, 1641 | 1 shilling |
| Handkerchief | Inventory of Samuel Hanson (1741) | Silk Handerchief in Charles County, Maryland, 1741 | 3 shillings 6 pence |
| Hat | Inventory of Josias Du Pre (1692) | Felte hatt in Charleston, South Carolina, 1692 | 15 shillings |
| Hat | Inventory of Jesse Ball (1742) | Man's fine hat in Lancaster, Virginia, 1747 | 18 shillings 2 pence |
| Hat band | Inventory of Josias Du Pre (1692) | Silver twisted hatt band in Charleston, South Carolina, 1692 | 1 shilling 3 pence |
| Hose | Inventory of Captian Arthur Dunn (1724) | Pair New Worsted Hose in Middlesex, Massachusetts, 1724 | 18 shillings |

**Based Upon the British Currency System**

| Year | Pound in 2002 US Dollars | Shilling in 2002 US Dollars | Pence in 2002 US Dollars |
|------|--------------------------|-----------------------------|--------------------------|
| 1650 | $120.00 | $6.00 | $0.50 |
| 1660 | $144.00 | $7.20 | $0.60 |
| 1670 | $120.00 | $6.00 | $0.70 |
| 1680 | $120.00 | $6.00 | $0.70 |
| 1690 | $120.00 | $6.00 | $0.80 |
| 1700 | $168.00 | $8.40 | $0.70 |
| 1710 | $144.00 | $7.20 | $0.60 |
| 1720 | $168.00 | $8.40 | $0.70 |
| 1730 | $192.00 | $9.60 | $0.80 |
| 1740 | $144.00 | $7.20 | $0.60 |
| 1749 | $192.00 | $9.60 | $0.80 |

*Calculations are approximate values based upon economic historical data*

| Item | Data Source | Description | Price |
|------|-------------|-------------|-------|
| Hose | Inventory of Captian Arthur Dunn (1724) | Pair Silk Hose in Middlesex, Massachusetts, 1724 | 1 pound 2 shillings 6 pence |
| Jacket | Inventory of John Vansusteren (1694) | Flanell Jackett in Charles Towne, South Carolina, 1694 | 10 shillings |
| Jacket | Inventory of Captian Arthur Dunn (1724) | Old Velvett Jackett in Middlesex, Massachusetts, 1724 | 2 pounds 5 shillings |
| Jacket | Inventory of Captian Arthur Dunn (1724) | Black Sattin Jackett in Middlesex, Massachusetts, 1724 | 5 pounds |
| Jerkin | Inventory of William Kemp (1641) | A frize jerkine in Plymouth, Massachusetts, 1641 | 8 shillings |
| Leather | Cressy, Coming Over (1987) | Cost of one pound of leather to mend shoes in New England during 1630 | 1 shilling 3 pence |
| Mittens | Inventory of Captian Arthur Dunn (1724) | Pair Old Yarn Mittons in Middlesex, Massachusetts, 1724 | 2 shillings 6 pence |
| Pants | Billings, The Old Dominion in the Seventeenth Century (1975) | Doozen of pants in Virginia, 1611 | 3 pence |
| Scarf | Inventory of Peter Perdriau (1692) | Old red Silck Scarffe in Charleston, South Carolina, 1692 | 1 shilling |
| Sea Cape | Cressy, Coming Over (1987) | One sea cape or gown, of coarse cloth in New England during 1630 | 16 shillings |
| Shirt | Inventory of Captian Arthur Dunn (1724) | Check Shirts in Middlesex, Massachusetts, 1724 | 15 shillings |
| Shirt | Inventory of Henry Fitzhugh (1742) | Negro Shirt in Stafford County, Virginia, 1742 | 3 shillings 7 pence |
| Shoes | Billings, The Old Dominion in the Seventeenth Century (1975) | Paire of shooes in Virginia, 1611 | 2 shillings 2 pence |
| Shoes | Inventory of Henry Fitzhugh (1742) | Pair negro shoes in Stafford County, Virginia, 1742 | 3 shillings 6 pence |
| Silk Outfit | Inventory of Nicholas Mardin (1696) | Silk weascoate & britches in Charles Town, South Carolina, 1696 | 5 pounds |
| Stockings | Billings, The Old Dominion in the Seventeenth Century (1975) | Paire of Irish stockings in Virginia, 1611 | 1 shilling 4 pence |
| Stockings | Inventory of Peter Perdriau (1692) | Payre old Silck Stockins in Charleston, South Carolina, 1692 | 5 shillings |
| Stockings | Inventory of John Vansusteren (1694) | Paire of Course Stockins in Charles Towne, South Carolina, 1694 | 3 shillings |
| Studs | Inventory of Henry Fitzhugh (1742) | Pair of gold studs in Stafford County, Virginia, 1742 | 1 pound |
| Suit | Billings, The Old Dominion in the Seventeenth Century (1975) | Sute of Cloth in Virginia, 1611 | 10 shillings |
| Suit | Inventory of Samuell Palmer (1676) | A serge suite in Plymouth, Massachusetts, 1676 | 1 pound 10 shillings |
| Suit | Inventory of Jesse Ball (1742) | Best suit of Cloth in Lancaster, Virginia, 1747 | 2 pounds |
| Waist | Cressy, Coming Over (1987) | A man's waist in New England during 1630 | 2 shillings 6 pence |
| Waistcoat | Inventory of John Jay (1678) | Tuffted holand waistcoate in Suffolk, Massachusetts, 1678 | 6 shillings |
| Wig | Inventory of Jesse Ball (1742) | Wigg & puff in Lancaster, Virginia, 1747 | 1 pound 10 shillings |

## Apparel - Women

| | | | |
|------|-------------|-------------|-------|
| Apron | Inventory of Mary Ring (1631) | A black Say apron in Plymouth, Massachusetts, 1631 | 7 shillings |
| Bodice | Inventory of Johnathan Newell (1672) | Womens Bodice in York County, Virginia, 1672 | 2 shillings 4 pence |

| Item | Data Source | Description | Price |
|------|-------------|-------------|-------|
| Cloak | Inventory of Godbert Godbertson & Zarah (1633) | Cloake in Plymouth, Massachusetts, 1633 | 1 pound 10 shillings |
| Gloves | Inventory of Josias Du Pre (1692) | Pair of white womans gloves in Charleston, South Carolina, 1692 | 5 shillings |
| Gown | Inventory of Godbert Godbertson & Zarah (1633) | A Gowne in Plymouth, Massachusetts, 1633 | 2 pounds |
| Gown | Inventory of Margaret Howland (1684) | A green Cloth Gowne in Plymouth, Massachusetts, 1684 | 10 shillings |
| Handkerchief | Inventory of Mary Ring (1631) | A fine kerchief in Plymouth, Massachusetts, 1631 | 2 shillings 8 pence |
| Handkerchief | Inventory of Martha Nelson (1684) | Necke handkerchife in Plymouth, Massachusetts, 1684 | 12 shillings |
| Hat | Inventory of Mary Ring (1631) | Hatt in Plymouth, Massachusetts, 1631 | 5 shillings |
| Hat | Inventory of Martha Nelson (1684) | A hatt in Plymouth, Massachusetts, 1684 | 2 pounds 13 shillings |
| Petticoat | Inventory of Mary Ring (1631) | Red petticote in Plymouth, Massachusetts, 1631 | 16 shillings |
| Petticoat | Inventory of Margaret Howland (1684) | A homspon petticoat in Plymouth, Massachusetts, 1684 | 8 shillings |
| Shoes | Inventory of Mary Ring (1631) | Pair of Shoes in Plymouth, Massachusetts, 1631 | 1 shilling |
| Shoes | Inventory of Jesse Ball (1742) | Pair of womens shoes in Lancaster, Virginia, 1747 | 10 shillings |
| Stockings | Inventory of Mary Ring (1631) | Pair white Irish stockings in Plymouth, Massachusetts, 1631 | 1 shilling 6 pence |
| Stockings | Inventory of John Vansusteren (1694) | Pair of red silk stockings in Charles Towne, South Carolina, 1694 | 1 pound |
| Waistcoat | Inventory of Mary Ring (1631) | A violet coloured Wastcoate in Plymouth, Massachusetts, 1631 | 8 shillings |
| Wig | Inventory of Zephaniah Wade (1746) | Wigg in Fairfax, Virginia, 1746 | 10 shillings |

## Commodities

| Item | Data Source | Description | Price |
|------|-------------|-------------|-------|
| Barley | University of Notre Dame Libraries (2004) | Bushel of barley in the Massachusetts colony, 1690 | 4 shillings |
| Beef | University of Notre Dame Libraries (2004) | Barrel of beef in the Massachusetts colony, 1690 | 1 pound 12 shillings 6 pence |

| Item | Data Source | Description | Price |
|---|---|---|---|
| Beaver pelt | Don Taxay, Money of the American Indians and other Primitive Currencies of the Americas (1970) | 3 bever pelts in New York, 1688 | 2 pounds |
| Board | Inventory of Wilson Dunston (1692) | Thousand foot of pine boards in Charleston, South Carolina, 1692 | 2 pounds |
| Bone | Inventory of Johnathan Newell (1672) | Pound of whale bone in York County, Virginia, 1672 | 2 shillings |
| Brass | Inventory of Nicholas Townsend (1694) | Per pound price for brass in Charles Towne, South Carolina, 1694 | 7½ pence |
| Corn | Inventory of William Kemp (1641) | Bushell of Indian Corne in Plymouth, Massachusetts, 1641 | 2 shillings 6 pence |
| Cotton | Inventory of Nicholas Townsend (1694) | Per pound of Spone Cotton in Charles Towne, South Carolina, 1694 | 1 shillings 9 pence |
| Cotton | Inventory of Henry Fitzhugh (1742) | Pound of picked Cotton in Stafford County, Virginia, 1742 | 2 shillings |
| Feathers | Inventory of Nicholas Townsend (1694) | Per pound price for feathers and ticken in Charles Towne, South Carolina, 1694 | 6 pence |
| Indigo | Inventory of Jesse Ball (1742) | Pound of indigo in Lancaster, Virginia, 1747 | 2 shillings 6 pence |
| Iron | Inventory of John Haill (1646) | Pound of New Iron in Suffolk, Massachusetts, 1646 | 1 pound 8 shillings |
| Iron | Inventory of Sarah Ball (1742) | Per pound cost of Barr Iron in Lancaster, Virginia, 1742 | 2½ pence |
| Lead | Inventory of Wilson Dunston (1692) | Pound of Lead pigge in Charleston, South Carolina, 1692 | 1 pound 5 shillings |
| Leather | Inventory of William Ball, Junr. (1742) | Side of Leather in Tan in Lancaster County, Virginia, 1742 | 2 shillings 6 pence |
| Lumber | Inventory of William Ball, Junr. (1742) | One foot of walnut inch plant board in Lancaster County, Virginia, 1742 | 1 pence |
| Lumber | Inventory of Jesse Ball (1742) | 100 foot oak plank in Lancaster, Virginia, 1747 | 6 shillings |
| Molasses | Inventory of James B. Joyner (1694) | Gallon of mallases found in the estate's Dary in South Carolina, 1694 | 2 shillings |
| Oats | University of Notre Dame Libraries (2004) | Bushel of oats in the Massachusetts colony, 1690 | 1 shilling 6 pence |
| Oats | Inventory of Samuel Hanson (1741) | Bushel of oats in Charles County, Maryland, 1741 | 2 shillings |
| Peas | University of Notre Dame Libraries (2004) | Bushel of peas in the Massachusetts colony in 1642 | 3 shillings 4 pence |
| Pewter | Inventory of Stephen North (1720) | Pound of old pewter in Suffolk County, Massachusetts, 1720 | 1 shilling 10 pence |
| Pine boards | University of Notre Dame Libraries (2004) | Value of a cord of pine boards in New Hapmpshire, 1707 | 25 shillings |
| Plank | Inventory of Wilson Dunston (1692) | Popler Plank in Charleston, South Carolina, 1692 | 1 shilling 4 pence |
| Pork | University of Notre Dame Libraries (2004) | Barrel of pork in the Massachusetts colony, 1690 | 3 pounds |
| Pork | Don Taxay, Money of the American Indians and other Primitive Currencies of the Americas (1970) | Trade for 10 pound of pork between Indians and colonists in New York | 1 beaver pelt |
| Post | Inventory of John Vansusteren (1694) | Ceader Post in Charles Towne, South Carolina, 1694 | 9½ pence |
| Rice | Inventory of of Barnard Schencking (1692) | Bushel of Rice in Colleton County, South Carolina, 1692 | 2 shillings |

| Item | Data Source | Description | Price |
|---|---|---|---|
| Rye | University of Notre Dame Libraries (2004) | Bushel of rye in the Massachusetts colony in 1642 | 3 shillings 4 pence |
| Salt | Inventory of Godbert Godbertson & Zarah (1633) | Bushel of salt in Plymouth, Massachusetts, 1633 | 4 shillings 7 pence |
| Salt | Inventory of Rawleigh Traverse (1749) | Bushel of salt in Stafford, Virginia, 1749 | 2 shillings |
| Shingles | Inventory of John Vansusteren (1694) | 100 Shingles in Charles Towne, South Carolina, 1694 | 1 shilling 3 pence |
| Steel | Inventory of John Haill (1646) | Pound of steele in a blacksmith shop in Suffolk, Massachusetts, 1646 | 8 pence |
| Stock | Billings, The Old Dominion in the Seventeenth Century (1975) | Share of stock in the London Company, 1610 | 25 pounds |
| Tar | Inventory of James Samford (1742) | Barrell Tarr in Richmond County, Virginia, 1742 | 6 shillings |
| Tobacco | University of Notre Dame Libraries (2004) | Value per pound of the best grade of tobacco in Virginia, 1619 | 3 shillings |
| Wheat | Inventory of William Kemp (1641) | A thrane of sumer wheat in Plymouth, Massachusetts, 1641 | 5 shillings |
| Wheat | University of Notre Dame Libraries (2004) | Bushel of wheat in New Hampshire,1707 | 4 shillings 6 pence |
| Wheat | Inventory of Samuel Hanson (1741) | Bushel of wheat in Charles County, Maryland, 1741 | 4 shillings |
| Wood | Inventory of James B. Joyner (1694) | Value of 200 foote of cedar board found in the estate's Coockerome in South Carolina in 1694 | 18 shillings 4 pence |
| Wool | Inventory of Martha Nelson (1684) | Pound of woole in Plymouth, Massachusetts, 1684 | 7 shillings |
| Wool | Inventory of Henry Fitzhugh (1742) | Pound of Washed wool in Stafford County, Virginia, 1742 | 10 pence |

## Entertainment

| | | | |
|---|---|---|---|
| Backgammon table | Inventory of Jesse Ball (1742) | Bagamon Table in Lancaster, Virginia, 1747 | 10 shillings |

### Based Upon the British Currency System

| Year | Pound in 2002 US Dollars | Shilling in 2002 US Dollars | Pence in 2002 US Dollars |
|---|---|---|---|
| 1650 | $120.00 | $6.00 | $0.50 |
| 1660 | $144.00 | $7.20 | $0.60 |
| 1670 | $120.00 | $6.00 | $0.70 |
| 1680 | $120.00 | $6.00 | $0.70 |
| 1690 | $120.00 | $6.00 | $0.80 |
| 1700 | $168.00 | $8.40 | $0.70 |
| 1710 | $144.00 | $7.20 | $0.60 |
| 1720 | $168.00 | $8.40 | $0.70 |
| 1730 | $192.00 | $9.60 | $0.80 |
| 1740 | $144.00 | $7.20 | $0.60 |
| 1749 | $192.00 | $9.60 | $0.80 |

*Calculations are approximate values based upon economic historical data*

| Item | Data Source | Description | Price |
|------|-------------|-------------|-------|
| **Fabrics & Sewing Materials** | | | |
| Buttons | Inventory of Johnathan Newell (1672) | Gross of leather buttons in York County, Virginia, 1672 | 3 shillings |
| Buttons | Inventory of John Vansusteren (1694) | One gross of gold buttons in Charles Towne, South Carolina, 1694 | 1 pound 13 shillings 6 pence |
| Buttons | Inventory of John Vansusteren (1694) | One gross of silver buttons in Charles Towne, South Carolina, 1694 | 1 pound 16 shillings |
| Cloth | Inventory of Mary Ring (1631) | Yard gray kersey in Plymouth, Massachusetts, 1631 | 2 shillings |
| Cloth | Inventory of Mary Ring (1631) | Peece of red moll 1 yrd in Plymouth, Massachusetts, 1631 | 1 shilling 6 pence |
| Cloth | Inventory of Thomas Richards (1650) | One yard of Italian Cloth in Suffolk, Massachusetts, 1650 | 5 shillings 4 pence |
| Fabric | Inventory of Henry Fitzhugh (1742) | Yard of fine tartan in Stafford County, Virginia, 1742 | 3 shillings 9 pence |
| Fabric | Inventory of Henry Fitzhugh (1742) | Yard of Damask Silk in Stafford County, Virginia, 1742 | 6 shillings 6 pence |
| Lace | Inventory of Thomas Richards (1650) | Bone Lace per yard in Suffolk, Massachusetts, 1650 | 10 shillings 6 pence |
| Lace | Inventory of John Vansusteren (1694) | Yard of Silk Gimp Lase in Charles Towne, South Carolina, 1694 | 7¾ pence |
| Linen | John Hall Day Book (1688) | Cost for one yard of printed linnen in Boston (value in 1688) | 10 pence |
| Lining | Inventory of John Vansusteren (1694) | Yard of Cullered Lining in Charles Towne, South Carolina, 1694 | 1 shilling 9 pence |
| Mohair | Inventory of Samuel Hanson (1741) | Pound of Mohair in Charles County, Maryland, 1741 | 12 shillings |
| Muslin | Inventory of Wilson Dunston (1692) | Muslin neck cloath in Charleston, South Carolina, 1692 | 1 shilling 3 pence |
| Needles | Inventory of Wilson Dunston (1692) | Thousand Glovers needles in Charleston, South Carolina, 1692 | 2 pounds |
| Needles | Inventory of William Ball, Junr. (1742) | 30 brass Knitting Kneedles in Lancaster County, Virginia, 1742 | 1 shilling 10 pence |
| Pins | Inventory of Samuel Hanson (1741) | Thousand pins in Charles County, Maryland, 1741 | 1 shilling 6 pence |
| Ribbon | Inventory of John Vansusteren (1694) | Peice of Tafaty riband in Charles Towne, South Carolina, 1694 | 8 shillings 9 pence |
| Serge | Inventory of Thomas Richards (1650) | One piece of serge in Suffolk, Massachusetts, 1650 | 5 shillings 15 shillings |
| Silk | Inventory of John Jay (1678) | One ounce of Sewing silke in Suffolk, Massachusetts, 1678 | 1 shilling 6 pence |
| Silk | Inventory of Peter Perdriau (1692) | One yard of black silk in Charleston, South Carolina, 1692 | 3 shillings |
| Skin | Inventory of Wilson Dunston (1692) | Tanned deare Skin in Charleston, South Carolina, 1692 | 2 shillings 6 pence |
| Tape | Inventory of Johnathan Newell (1672) | Yard of Manchester binding in York County, Virginia, 1672 | ½ pence |
| Thimble | Inventory of Wilson Dunston (1692) | Woman's thimble in Charleston, South Carolina, 1692 | 2 pence |
| Thimble | Inventory of Jesse Ball (1742) | Dozen thimbles in Lancaster, Virginia, 1747 | 3 pence |
| Thread | Inventory of Peter Perdriau (1692) | Ounce of fine threed in Charleston, South Carolina, 1692 | 6 pence |
| Wrapper | Inventory of Sarah Ball (1742) | Yard of wrapper in Lancaster, Virginia, 1742 | 6 pence |
| Yarn | Inventory of Sarah Ball (1742) | Pound of negroe Yarn in Lancaster, Virginia, 1742 | 1 shilling 4 pence |

| Item | Data Source | Description | Price |
|------|-------------|-------------|-------|
| **Farm Equipment & Tools** | | | |
| Auger | Cressy, Coming Over (1987) | Price for a auger in New England during 1630 | 6 pence |
| Axe | Inventory of Godbert Godbertson & Zarah (1633) | A broade Axe in Plymouth, Massachusetts, 1633 | 6 pence |
| Axe | Inventory of Sarah Ball (1742) | New narrow axe in Lancaster, Virginia, 1742 | 4 shillings |
| Barrow | Inventory of Sarah Ball (1742) | Best barrow in Lancaster, Virginia, 1742 | 6 shillings |
| Bee Hive | Inventory of Nicholas Townsend (1694) | A hive of beese in Charles Towne, South Carolina, 1694 | 6 shillings |
| Bucket | Inventory of Zephaniah Wade (1746) | Tin Garden Water Bucket in Fairfax, Virginia, 1746 | 2 shillings 6 pence |
| Cart | Inventory of Zephaniah Wade (1746) | Old cart in Fairfax, Virginia, 1746 | 10 shillings |
| Chain | Inventory of Johnathan Newell (1672) | Plow Chaine in York County, Virginia, 1672 | 5 shillings |
| Cheese press | Inventory Captian Thomas Southworth (1669) | Chees Presse in Plymouth, Massachusetts, 1669 | 3 shillings |
| Chisel & auger | Inventory of Godbert Godbertson & Zarah (1633) | A chisell & Auger in Plymouth, Massachusetts, 1633 | 6 pence |
| File | Inventory of Wilson Dunston (1692) | Whip saw file in Charleston, South Carolina, 1692 | 10 pence |
| Grinding Stone | Inventory of Joseph Elliott (1697) | Grinding stoone in Charles Town, South Carolina, 1697 | 12 shillings 6 pence |
| Hammer | Cressy, Coming Over (1987) | Value of a hammer in New England during 1630 | 1 shilling |
| Hatchet | Cressy, Coming Over (1987) | Price of a hatchet in New England during 1630 | 1 shilling 9 pence |
| Hoe | Inventory of Roger Annadowne (1673) | Old broad hoe in Plymouth, Massachusetts, 1673 | 1 shilling 6 pence |
| Hoe | Inventory of Rawleigh Traverse (1749) | Hilling hoe in Stafford, Virginia, 1749 | 2 shillings 6 pence |
| Hook | Inventory of Samuel Hanson (1741) | Reap Hook in Charles County, Maryland, 1741 | 1 shilling |
| Hooks | Inventory of Godbert Godbertson & Zarah (1633) | Hay hooks in Plymouth, Massachusetts, 1633 | 6 pence |
| Ladder | Inventory of William Kemp (1641) | Ladder in Plymouth, Massachusetts, 1641 | 2 shillings |

**Based Upon the British Currency System**

| Year | Pound in 2002 US Dollars | Shilling in 2002 US Dollars | Pence in 2002 US Dollars |
|------|--------------------------|------------------------------|---------------------------|
| 1650 | $120.00 | $6.00 | $0.50 |
| 1660 | $144.00 | $7.20 | $0.60 |
| 1670 | $120.00 | $6.00 | $0.70 |
| 1680 | $120.00 | $6.00 | $0.70 |
| 1690 | $120.00 | $6.00 | $0.80 |
| 1700 | $168.00 | $8.40 | $0.70 |
| 1710 | $144.00 | $7.20 | $0.60 |
| 1720 | $168.00 | $8.40 | $0.70 |
| 1730 | $192.00 | $9.60 | $0.80 |
| 1740 | $144.00 | $7.20 | $0.60 |
| 1749 | $192.00 | $9.60 | $0.80 |

*Calculations are approximate values based upon economic historical data*

| Item | Data Source | Description | Price |
|------|-------------|-------------|-------|
| Mill | Inventory of William Kemp (1641) | A steele Mill in Plymouth, Massachusetts, 1641 | 10 shillings |
| Nails | Inventory of William Kemp (1641) | A prcell of 6d nayles in Plymouth, Massachusetts, 1641 | 3 shillings |
| Nails | Inventory of Sarah Ball (1742) | Hundred four-penny nails in Lancaster, Virginia, 1742 | 3 shillings 4 pence |
| Pan | Inventory of James Samford (1742) | Milk pan in the Dairy in Richmond County, Virginia, 1742 | 6 pence |
| Pitchfork | Inventory of William Kemp (1641) | A pitche fork pronges in Plymouth, Massachusetts, 1641 | 8 pence |
| Pliers | Inventory of Samuel Hanson (1741) | Pair plyers in Charles County, Maryland, 1741 | 6 pence |
| Plow | Inventory of John Millard, Jr. (1684) | A Cart & plow with their Irons in Plymouth, Massachusetts, 1684 | 1 pound 10 shillings |
| Pot | Inventory of James Samford (1742) | Cream Pott in Richmond County, Virginia, 1742 | 6 pence |
| Rake | Inventory of Martha Nelson (1684) | Iron rake in Plymouth, Massachusetts, 1684 | 1 shilling |
| Rake head | Inventory of William Kemp (1641) | Rake head in Plymouth, Massachusetts, 1641 | 2 pence |
| Rope | Inventory of Samuel Hanson (1741) | Fathom Rope in Charles County, Maryland, 1741 | 8 pence |
| Saw | Cressy, Coming Over (1987) | A whipsaw priced in New England during 1630 | 10 shillings |
| Saw | Inventory of Rawleigh Traverse (1749) | Croscut Saw in Stafford, Virginia, 1749 | 15 shillings |
| Scythe | John Hall Day Book (1688) | Cost for one Scythe found in the records of John Hall of Boston in 1688 | 3 shillings |
| Scythe stone | John Hall Day Book (1688) | Cost for one Scythe stone found in the records of John Hall of Boston in 1688 | 2 shillings |
| Share | Cressy, Coming Over (1987) | One plowshare for crops in New England during 1630 | 2 shillings 11 pence |
| Shears | Inventory of Martha Nelson (1684) | Pair of sheep shears in Plymouth, Massachusetts, 1684 | 1 shilling |
| Shovel | Inventory of William Kemp (1641) | A iron shovell in Plymouth, Massachusetts, 1641 | 3 shillings |
| Shovel | Inventory of Robert Osborn (1744) | Shovel in Fairfax, Virginia, 1744 | 6 pence |
| Sickle | Inventory of Godbert Godbertson & Zarah (1633) | A sickle in Plymouth, Massachusetts, 1633 | 6 pence |
| Sieve | Inventory of William Kemp (1641) | Sieve in Plymouth, Massachusetts, 1641 | 4 pence |
| Sieve | Inventory of Henry Fitzhugh (1742) | Wheat Sive in Stafford County, Virginia, 1742 | 2 shillings |
| Spade | Inventory of John Sutton (1672) | Spade in Plymouth, Massachusetts, 1672 | 1 shilling |
| Tray | Inventory of James B. Joyner (1694) | Leaden milke Tray found in the estate's Dary in South Carolina, 1694 | 3 shillings 3 pence |
| Trough | Inventory of Roger Annadowne (1673) | Apple Trough in Plymouth, Massachusetts, 1673 | 2 shillings |
| Vise | Cressy, Coming Over (1987) | One hand vise in New England during 1630 | 2 shillings 6 pence |
| Water pot | Inventory of William Kemp (1641) | A latin water port for a garden in Plymouth, Massachusetts, 1641 | 8 pence |
| Wedge | Inventory of Godbert Godbertson & Zarah (1633) | Wedge in Plymouth, Massachusetts, 1633 | 9 pence |
| Wheelbarrow | Cressy, Coming Over (1987) | Wooden Wheelbarrow | 6 shillings |

| Item | Data Source | Description | Price |
|---|---|---|---|
| Wheels | Cressy, Coming Over (1987) | One pair wooden wheels for a cart | 14 shillings |
| Wimble | Cressy, Coming Over (1987) | One wimble with six piercer bits | 1 shilling 6 pence |

**Firearms & Supplies**

| Item | Data Source | Description | Price |
|---|---|---|---|
| Armor | Billings, The Old Dominion in the Seventeenth Century (1975) | Armour compleat, light in Virginia, 1611 | 17 shillings |
| Bandoleer | Billings, The Old Dominion in the Seventeenth Century (1975) | Bandallere in Virginia, 1611 | 1 shilling 6 pence |
| Bullets | Inventory of Samuell Palmer (1676) | Pound of bulletts in Plymouth, Massachusetts, 1676 | 4 pence |
| Cutlass | Inventory of Josias Du Pre (1692) | Cutlasin Charleston, South Carolina, 1692 | 1 pound 10 shillings |
| Dagger | Inventory of William Kemp (1641) | Dagger in Plymouth, Massachusetts, 1641 | 1 shilling |
| Flint | Arnade, The Siege of St. Augustine in 1702. (1959) | Flint valued at St Augustine, 1702 | 8 Reales |
| Flintlock | Arnade, The Siege of St. Augustine in 1702. (1959) | Brand new flintlocks provided to the Spanish at St Augustine, 1702 | 10 Pesos |
| Gun | Inventory of Captian Arthur Dunn (1724) | French Gun in Middlesex, Massachusetts, 1724 | 8 pounds |
| Gun | Inventory of Robert Osborn (1744) | Gun in Fairfax, Virginia, 1744 | 1 pound |
| Gun barrel | Inventory of John Haill (1646) | Gun Barrel made in a blacksmith shop in Suffolk, Massachusetts, 1646 | 5 shillings |
| Gun lock | Inventory of Wilson Dunston (1692) | Lock for Gun in Charleston, South Carolina, 1692 | 2 shillings 6 pence |
| Gunpowder | Billings, The Old Dominion in the Seventeenth Century (1975) | Twentie pound of Powder in Virginia, 1611 | 18 shillings |
| Gunpowder | Don Taxay, Money of the American Indians and other Primitive Currencies of the Americas (1970) | Two pints of powder when traded between Indians and colonist in New York | 1 beaver pelt |
| Gunpowder | Arnade, The Siege of St. Augustine in 1702. (1959) | One Thousand pounds of excellent gunpowder provided to the Spanish at St Augustine, 1702 | 500 Pesos |

**Based Upon the British Currency System**

| Year | Pound in 2002 US Dollars | Shilling in 2002 US Dollars | Pence in 2002 US Dollars |
|---|---|---|---|
| 1650 | $120.00 | $6.00 | $0.50 |
| 1660 | $144.00 | $7.20 | $0.60 |
| 1670 | $120.00 | $6.00 | $0.70 |
| 1680 | $120.00 | $6.00 | $0.70 |
| 1690 | $120.00 | $6.00 | $0.80 |
| 1700 | $168.00 | $8.40 | $0.70 |
| 1710 | $144.00 | $7.20 | $0.60 |
| 1720 | $168.00 | $8.40 | $0.70 |
| 1730 | $192.00 | $9.60 | $0.80 |
| 1740 | $144.00 | $7.20 | $0.60 |
| 1749 | $192.00 | $9.60 | $0.80 |

*Calculations are approximate values based upon economic historical data*

| Item | Data Source | Description | Price |
|------|-------------|-------------|-------|
| Horn | Inventory of Rawleigh Traverse (1749) | A powder horn & Shot bagg in Stafford, Virginia, 1749 | 1 shilling |
| Molds | Inventory of Rawleigh Traverse (1749) | Pair of Bullet molds in Stafford, Virginia, 1749 | 1 shilling 6 pence |
| Musket | Inventory of John Sutton (1672) | Muskett in Plymouth, Massachusetts, 1672 | 15 shillings |
| Pistol | Inventory of Godbert Godbertson & Zarah (1633) | A pistoll in Plymouth, Massachusetts, 1633 | 1 shilling |
| Pistols | Inventory of John Jay (1678) | One paire of pistolls & holdsters in Suffolk, Massachusetts, 1678 | 1 pound 15 shillings |
| Powder horn | Inventory of Samuell Palmer (1676) | A pouder horne in Plymouth, Massachusetts, 1676 | 1 shilling |
| Scouring rod | Inventory of Robert Osborn (1744) | Gun Scouring rod in Fairfax, Virginia, 1744 | 1 shilling |
| Shot | Billings, The Old Dominion in the Seventeenth Century (1975) | Sixtie pound of shot or lead, Pistoll and Goose shot in Virginia, 1611 | 5 shillings |
| Sword | Billings, The Old Dominion in the Seventeenth Century (1975) | Sword in Virginia, 1611 | 5 shillings |
| Sword | Inventory of John Jay (1678) | Sword and belt in Suffolk, Massachusetts, 1678 | 14 shillings |
| Sword | Inventory of Henry Fitzhugh (1742) | Silver hilted small sword in Stafford County, Virginia, 1742 | 3 pounds 10 shillings |

## Food Products

| Item | Data Source | Description | Price |
|------|-------------|-------------|-------|
| Alum | Inventory of Sarah Ball (1742) | Pound of Allom in Lancaster, Virginia, 1742 | 4 pence |
| Aquavitæ | Billings, The Old Dominion in the Seventeenth Century (1975) | Gallon of Aquavitæ in Virginia, 1611 | 3 shillings 6 pence |
| Bacon | Cressy, Coming Over (1987) | One pound of bacon in New England during 1630 | 4 pence |
| Beef | Cressy, Coming Over (1987) | One Hunderweight of beef in New England during 1630 | 18 shillings |
| Bread | Inventory of Nicholas Mardin (1696) | Cask of bread in Charles Town, 1696 | 5 pounds 5 shillings |
| Butter | Cressy, Coming Over (1987) | One unit of butter in New England during 1630 | 8 pence |
| Butter | Inventory of John Harris (1694) | One pound of butter in Charles Towne, South Carolina, 1694 | 4 pence |
| Cheese | Cressy, Coming Over (1987) | Price for half a hundred weight in New England during 1630 | 12 shillings |
| Corn | Inventory of Godbert Godbertson & Zarah (1633) | Bushell of Corne in Plymouth, Massachusetts, 1633 | 6 shillings |
| Corn | Inventory of Roger Annadowne (1673) | Bushel of Indian Corn in Plymouth, Massachusetts, 1673 | 3 shillings |
| Honey | Inventory of John Jay (1678) | One paile of honey in Suffolk, Massachusetts, 1678 | 12 shillings |
| Honey | Inventory of Sarah Ball (1742) | Gallon of honey in Lancaster, Virginia, 1742 | 4 shillings |
| Malt | Cressy, Coming Over (1987) | One hogshead of malt in New England during 1630 | 1 pound |
| Meal | Cressy, Coming Over (1987) | One hogshead of meal in New England during 1630 | 2 pounds |
| Molasses | Inventory of Martha Nelson (1684) | Gallon of mallasses in Plymouth, Massachusetts, 1684 | 1 shilling 4 pence |
| Oatmeal | Billings, The Old Dominion in the Seventeenth Century (1975) | Bushel of Oatmeale in Virginia, 1611 | 4 shillings 6 pence |
| Oil | Billings, The Old Dominion in the Seventeenth Century (1975) | Gallon of Oyle in Virginia, 1611 | 2 shillings |
| Peas | Billings, The Old Dominion in the Seventeenth Century (1975) | Bushel of Pease in Virginia, 1611 | 3 shillings |
| Pork | Cressy, Coming Over (1987) | One hundred pounds of pickled pork in New England during 1630 | 1 pound 5 shillings |
| Rice | Inventory of Samuel Hanson (1741) | Pound of rice in Charles County, Maryland, 1741 | 4 pence |

| Item | Data Source | Description | Price |
|------|-------------|-------------|-------|
| Salt | Cressy, Coming Over (1987) | One hogshead of salt to save fish in New England during 1630 | 1 pound |
| Salt | Inventory of William Ball, Junr. (1742) | Bushel of salt in Lancaster County, Virginia, 1742 | 1 shilling |
| Spice | Inventory of Wilson Dunston (1692) | Pound of Nut megg in Charleston, South Carolina, 1692 | 15 shillings |
| Spice | Inventory of Wilson Dunston (1692) | Ounce of mace in Charleston, South Carolina, 1692 | 2 shillings |
| Spice | Inventory of Sarah Ball (1742) | Ounce of Cinnamon in Lancaster, Virginia, 1742 | 1 shilling |
| Spice | Inventory of Sarah Ball (1742) | Ounce of nutmegs in Lancaster, Virginia, 1742 | 1 shilling |
| Spice | Inventory of Sarah Ball (1742) | Ounce of cloves in Lancaster, Virginia, 1742 | 1 shilling |
| Spice | Inventory of Jesse Ball (1742) | Pound of ginger in Lancaster, Virginia, 1747 | 1 shilling 3 pence |
| Spice | Inventory of Jesse Ball (1742) | Pound of pepper in Lancaster, Virginia, 1747 | 1 shilling 2 pence |
| Sugar | Inventory of Rawleigh Traverse (1749) | Box of bor Sugar in Stafford, Virginia, 1749 | 5 shillings |
| Tea | Inventory of William Ball, Junr. (1742) | Pound of green tea in Lancaster County, Virginia, 1742 | 8 shillings |
| Vinegar | Billings, The Old Dominion in the Seventeenth Century (1975) | Gallon of vinegar in Virginia, 1611 | 1 shilling |
| Wheat | Inventory of William Kemp (1641) | A bushell of wheate brann in Plymouth, Massachusetts, 1641 | 4 pence |
| Wheat | Inventory of Sarah Ball (1742) | Bushel of wheat in Lancaster, Virginia, 1742 | 3 shillings |

## Household Furniture

| Item | Data Source | Description | Price |
|------|-------------|-------------|-------|
| Bed | Inventory of Mary Ring (1631) | A ffetherbed & bolster in Plymouth, Massachusetts, 1631 | 2 pounds 10 shillings |
| Bed | Inventory of Roger Annadowne (1673) | Childrens bed and bed stead in Plymouth, Massachusetts, 1673 | 7 shillings |
| Bed | Inventory of A. Pearce (1690) | Small bed for a negro boy lay upon in Suffolk County, Massachusetts, 1690 | 10 shillings |
| Bed Set | Inventory of Zephaniah Wade (1746) | Feather bed with bolster, 2 pillows, blanket and old quilt in Fairfax, Virginia, 1746 | 4 pounds 5 shillings |

### Based Upon the British Currency System

| Year | Pound in 2002 US Dollars | Shilling in 2002 US Dollars | Pence in 2002 US Dollars |
|------|--------------------------|------------------------------|--------------------------|
| 1650 | $120.00 | $6.00 | $0.50 |
| 1660 | $144.00 | $7.20 | $0.60 |
| 1670 | $120.00 | $6.00 | $0.70 |
| 1680 | $120.00 | $6.00 | $0.70 |
| 1690 | $120.00 | $6.00 | $0.80 |
| 1700 | $168.00 | $8.40 | $0.70 |
| 1710 | $144.00 | $7.20 | $0.60 |
| 1720 | $168.00 | $8.40 | $0.70 |
| 1730 | $192.00 | $9.60 | $0.80 |
| 1740 | $144.00 | $7.20 | $0.60 |
| 1749 | $192.00 | $9.60 | $0.80 |

*Calculations are approximate values based upon economic historical data*

| Item | Data Source | Description | Price |
|------|-------------|-------------|-------|
| Bedding set | Inventory of A. Pearce (1690) | Bedding curtains, a small Rug blanket and small pillow in Suffolk County, Massachusetts, 1690 | 3 pounds 10 shillings |
| Bedding set | Inventory of Stephen North (1720) | Bedstead with curtains and coverings in Suffolk County, Massachusetts, 1720 | 6 pounds, 19 shillings |
| Bedstead | Inventory of William Kemp (1641) | Hanging bedstead in Plymouth, Massachusetts, 1641 | 2 shillings 4 pence |
| Bedstead | Inventory of Henry Fitzhugh (1742) | High bedstead & furniture with 2 beds & callico Curtains in Stafford County, Virginia, 1742 | 12 pounds |
| Bookcase | Inventory of Henry Fitzhugh (1742) | Bookcase in Stafford County, Virginia, 1742 | 3 pounds 16 shillings |
| Cabinet | Inventory of William Kemp (1641) | Cabbanett in Plymouth, Massachusetts, 1641 | 4 shillings |
| Case of drawers | Inventory of Captian Cratey (1695) | Olive Wood case of drawers in Boston, Massachusetts in 1695 | 8 pounds |
| Chair | Inventory of Dr. Thomas Pemberton (1693) | One cane chair in Boston, Massachusetts in 1693 | 17 shillings |
| Chair | Inventory of Stephen North (1720) | Leather dining room chair in Suffolk County, Massachusetts, 1720 | 10 shillings |
| Chair | Inventory of Jesse Ball (1742) | Red Leather Chair in Lancaster, Virginia, 1747 | 8 shillings |
| Chair frame | Inventory of Robert Osborn (1744) | Chair frame in Fairfax, Virginia, 1744 | 1 shilling |
| Chest | Inventory of Captian Arthur Dunn (1724) | Chest in Middlesex, Massachusetts, 1724 | 1 pound 2 shillings 6 pence |
| Chest of drawers | Inventory of Timothy Lindall (1698) | One chist of drawers with doors in Salem, Massachusetts in 1698 | 20 shillings |
| Clock | Inventory of Captian Cratey (1695) | Working clock in Boston, Massachusetts in 1695 | 10 pounds |
| Clock | Inventory of Samuel Hanson (1741) | Eight Days Clock out of Repair in Charles County, Maryland, 1741 | 8 pounds |

| Item | Data Source | Description | Price |
|---|---|---|---|
| Couch | Inventory of Captian Cratey (1695) | Lackered cane couch in Boston, Massachusetts in 1695 | 1 pound |
| Couch | Inventory of Sarah Ball (1742) | Couch in Lancaster, Virginia, 1742 | 1 pound |
| Cradle | Inventory of William Kemp (1641) | Cradle in Plymouth, Massachusetts, 1641 | 4 shillings |
| Cupboard | Inventory of James Samford (1742) | Cupboard in Richmond County, Virginia, 1742 | 3 shillings |
| Curtains | Inventory of Stephen North (1720) | Pair of window curtains in Suffolk County, Massachusetts, 1720 | 15 shillings |
| Desk | Inventory of Wilson Dunston (1692) | Ceader Desk with Lock in Charleston, South Carolina, 1692 | 10 shillings |
| Desk | Inventory of William Ball, Junr. (1742) | Black walnut Desk in Lancaster County, Virginia, 1742 | 3 pounds 15 shillings |
| Dressing glass | Inventory of Henry Fitzhugh (1742) | Dressing Glass & Table in Stafford County, Virginia, 1742 | 2 pounds |
| Looking glass | Inventory of James Samford (1742) | Small looking glass in Richmond County, Virginia, 1742 | 4 shillings |
| Pillow | Inventory of Stephen North (1720) | Pillow bear in Suffolk County, Massachusetts, 1720 | 5 shillings, 1 pence |
| Rug | Inventory of William Kemp (1641) | A blew Rugg in Plymouth, Massachusetts, 1641 | 1 pound |
| Screen | Inventory of Captian Cratey (1695) | Gilded leather screen in Boston, Massachusetts in 1695 | 3 pounds |
| Screen | Inventory of Stephen North (1720) | Dressing screen in Suffolk County, Massachusetts, 1720 | 8 shillings |
| Stand | Inventory of Jesse Ball (1742) | Wooden stand for a candle in Lancaster, Virginia, 1747 | 1 shilling |
| Stand | Inventory of Rawleigh Traverse (1749) | Wash stand in Stafford, Virginia, 1749 | 2 shillings |
| Stool | Inventory of William Kemp (1641) | A brodred stool in Plymouth, Massachusetts, 1641 | 1 shilling |
| Stool | Inventory of Zephaniah Wade (1746) | Stool in Fairfax, Virginia, 1746 | 2 pence |
| Stool pan | Inventory of John Vansusteren (1694) | Children close Stole pan in Charles Towne, South Carolina, 1694 | 7½ pence |

**Based Upon the British Currency System**

| Year | Pound in 2002 US Dollars | Shilling in 2002 US Dollars | Pence in 2002 US Dollars |
|---|---|---|---|
| 1650 | $120.00 | $6.00 | $0.50 |
| 1660 | $144.00 | $7.20 | $0.60 |
| 1670 | $120.00 | $6.00 | $0.70 |
| 1680 | $120.00 | $6.00 | $0.70 |
| 1690 | $120.00 | $6.00 | $0.80 |
| 1700 | $168.00 | $8.40 | $0.70 |
| 1710 | $144.00 | $7.20 | $0.60 |
| 1720 | $168.00 | $8.40 | $0.70 |
| 1730 | $192.00 | $9.60 | $0.80 |
| 1740 | $144.00 | $7.20 | $0.60 |
| 1749 | $192.00 | $9.60 | $0.80 |

*Calculations are approximate values based upon economic historical data*

| Item | Data Source | Description | Price |
|------|-------------|-------------|-------|
| Table | Inventory of Obadiah Walker (1676) | A square table of black walnutt in Suffolk, Massachusetts in 1676 | 1 pound 5 shillings |
| Table | Inventory of Dr. Thomas Pemberton (1693) | Slate table in Boston, Massachusetts in 1693 | 1 pound |
| Table | Inventory of Henry Fitzhugh (1742) | Wild Cherry tree table in Stafford County, Virginia, 1742 | 2 pounds 5 shillings |
| Tea chest | Inventory of Henry Fitzhugh (1742) | Tea chest & Canisters in Stafford County, Virginia, 1742 | 18 shillings |
| Trunk | Inventory of William Kemp (1641) | A trunk covered wth seale skins in Plymouth, Massachusetts, 1641 | 1 pound |

### Household Products

| Item | Data Source | Description | Price |
|------|-------------|-------------|-------|
| Basket | Inventory of Henry Fitzhugh (1742) | Indian basket in Stafford County, Virginia, 1742 | 1 shilling |
| Basin | Inventory of Nicholas Mardin (1696) | Pewter bason in Charles Town, South Carolina, 1696 | 2 shillings 6 pence |
| Basin | Inventory of Sarah Ball (1742) | Earthen bason in Lancaster, Virginia, 1742 | 3 pence |
| Bed cord | Inventory of Jesse Ball (1742) | Bed cords in Lancaster, Virginia, 1747 | 1 shilling 6 pence |
| Bedding | Cressy, Coming Over (1987) | Seven Ells canvas to make bed and bolster in New England during 1630 | 5 shillings |
| Bedtick | Inventory of Rawleigh Traverse (1749) | A new Bedtick in Stafford, Virginia, 1749 | 12 shillings 6 pence |
| Bellows | Inventory of Mary Ring (1631) | Pair of Bellowes in Plymouth, Massachusetts, 1631 | 1 shilling 4 pence |
| Bellows | Inventory of Stephen North (1720) | Pair of chamber bellows in Suffolk County, Massachusetts, 1720 | 6 shillings |
| Blanket | Inventory of Mary Ring (1631) | Blanket in Plymouth, Massachusetts, 1631 | 4 shillings |
| Blanket | Inventory of Henry Fitzhugh (1742) | Pair of old blankets in Stafford County, Virginia, 1742 | 8 shillings |
| Bolster | Inventory of Roger Annadowne (1673) | Feather bolster in Plymouth, Massachusetts, 1673 | 12 shillings |
| Bottle | Inventory of William Ball, Junr. (1742) | Quart bottle in Lancaster County, Virginia, 1742 | 2 pence |
| Bottles | Inventory of Wilson Dunston (1692) | Dozen half-pint bottles in Charleston, South Carolina, 1692 | 2 shillings 6 pence |
| Bottles | Inventory of Henry Fitzhugh (1742) | Gross of Bottles in Stafford County, Virginia, 1742 | 5 pounds 5 shillings |
| Bowl | Inventory of Sarah Ball (1742) | Lignum Vitae punch Bowl in Lancaster, Virginia, 1742 | 6 pence |

| Item | Data Source | Description | Price |
|------|-------------|-------------|-------|
| Bowl | Inventory of Zephaniah Wade (1746) | China Bowl in Fairfax, Virginia, 1746 | 8 pence |
| Box | Inventory of Godbert Godbertson & Zarah (1633) | Rownd box in Plymouth, Massachusetts, 1633 | 2 shillings 6 pence |
| Box | Inventory of Peter Perdriau (1692) | Old Ceder box in Charleston, South Carolina, 1692 | 6 shillings 3 pence |
| Box | Inventory of Jesse Ball (1742) | A flowered Sugar box in Lancaster, Virginia, 1747 | 2 shillings 6 pence |
| Brush | Inventory of Wilson Dunston (1692) | Cloath brush in Charleston, South Carolina, 1692 | 6½ pence |
| Brush | Inventory of Sarah Ball (1742) | Hat brush in Lancaster, Virginia, 1742 | 3 pence |
| Can | Inventory of Jesse Ball (1742) | Glass can in Lancaster, Virginia, 1747 | 2 shillings |
| Candle | Inventory of Sarah Ball (1742) | Pound of candles in Lancaster, Virginia, 1742 | 6 pence |
| Candlesnuffer | Inventory of William Ball, Junr. (1742) | Candle snufrs in Lancaster County, Virginia, 1742 | 6 pence |
| Candlestick | Inventory of Wilson Dunston (1692) | Hanging Candlestick in Charleston, South Carolina, 1692 | 6 pence |
| Candlestick | Bartholomew Gedney (1699) | Large Iron Candlestick in Salem, Massachusetts in 1699 | 18 shillings |
| Candlestick | Inventory of Stephen North (1720) | Brass candlestick in Suffolk County, Massachusetts, 1720 | 2 shillings, 3 pence |
| Candlestick | Inventory of Jesse Ball (1742) | Tin candlestick in Lancaster, Virginia, 1747 | 7½ pence |
| Canister | Inventory of William Ball, Junr. (1742) | Tea cannister in Lancaster County, Virginia, 1742 | 6 pence |
| Card | Inventory of Wilson Dunston (1692) | Paire of woole Cards in Charleston, South Carolina, 1692 | 1 shilling 6 pence |
| Carpet | Inventory of William Kemp (1641) | An old tapstry carpett in Plymouth, Massachusetts, 1641 | 4 shillings |
| Case | Inventory of Henry Fitzhugh (1742) | Watch case in Stafford County, Virginia, 1742 | 7 shillings 6 pence |
| Case & bottles | Inventory of Henry Fitzhugh (1742) | Old case with six bottles in Stafford County, Virginia, 1742 | 5 shillings |
| Cask | Inventory of William Ball, Junr. (1742) | Large Cyder cask in Lancaster County, Virginia, 1742 | 5 shillings |

---

### Based Upon the British Currency System

| Year | Pound in 2002 US Dollars | Shilling in 2002 US Dollars | Pence in 2002 US Dollars |
|------|--------------------------|-----------------------------|--------------------------|
| 1650 | $120.00 | $6.00 | $0.50 |
| 1660 | $144.00 | $7.20 | $0.60 |
| 1670 | $120.00 | $6.00 | $0.70 |
| 1680 | $120.00 | $6.00 | $0.70 |
| 1690 | $120.00 | $6.00 | $0.80 |
| 1700 | $168.00 | $8.40 | $0.70 |
| 1710 | $144.00 | $7.20 | $0.60 |
| 1720 | $168.00 | $8.40 | $0.70 |
| 1730 | $192.00 | $9.60 | $0.80 |
| 1740 | $144.00 | $7.20 | $0.60 |
| 1749 | $192.00 | $9.60 | $0.80 |

*Calculations are approximate values based upon economic historical data*

| Item | Data Source | Description | Price |
|------|-------------|-------------|-------|
| Chamber pot | Inventory of Wilson Dunston (1692) | Pewter Chamber Pott in Charleston, South Carolina, 1692 | 2 shillings 6 pence |
| Chest | Inventory of William Kemp (1641) | A great chest in Plymouth, Massachusetts, 1641 | 8 shillings |
| Chest | Inventory of James Samford (1742) | Small Chest in Richmond County, Virginia, 1742 | 1 shilling |
| Cistern | Inventory of Jesse Ball (1742) | Water Cistern in Lancaster, Virginia, 1747 | 13 shillings |
| Clock | Inventory of Jesse Ball (1742) | Clock in Lancaster, Virginia, 1747 | 8 pounds |
| Close stool | Inventory of Rawleigh Traverse (1749) | Close Stool in Stafford, Virginia, 1749 | 15 shillings |
| Coffee mill | Inventory of Rawleigh Traverse (1749) | Coffee mill in Stafford, Virginia, 1749 | 5 shillings |
| Coffee roaster | Inventory of Henry Fitzhugh (1742) | Coffee roaster in Stafford County, Virginia, 1742 | 10 shillings |
| Comb | Inventory of Margaret Howland (1684) | New Iuory Combe & Combe Case in Plymouth, Massachusetts, 1684 | 1 shilling 3 pence |
| Comb case | Inventory of Wilson Dunston (1692) | Leather Combe Case in Charleston, South Carolina, 1692 | 2 pence |
| Corkscrew | Inventory of Samuel Hanson (1741) | Corkscrew in Charles County, Maryland, 1741 | 3 pence |
| Cruet | Inventory of Zephaniah Wade (1746) | Flint Glass Cruet in Fairfax, Virginia, 1746 | 8 pence |
| Cup | Inventory of James Lindale (1652) | A pewter cupp in Plymouth, Massachusetts, 1652 | 2 shillings 6 pence |
| Cup | Inventory of John Vansusteren (1694) | Custerd cup in Charles Towne, South Carolina, 1694 | 4 pence |
| Cup | Inventory of Sarah Ball (1742) | Chocolat Cup in Lancaster, Virginia, 1742 | 1 pence |
| Curtains | Inventory of Nicholas Mardin (1696) | Windo curtain in Charles Town, South Carolina, 1696 | 3 shillings 7 pence |
| Curtains | Inventory of Henry Fitzhugh (1742) | Suit of Callico window Curtians in Stafford County, Virginia, 1742 | 15 shillings |
| Decanter | Inventory of Sarah Ball (1742) | Decanter in Lancaster, Virginia, 1742 | 6 pence |
| Dish | Inventory of John Sutton (1672) | Brasse Chaffing dish in Plymouth, Massachusetts, 1672 | 5 shillings |
| Dish | Inventory of Nicholas Mardin (1696) | Pewter dish in Charles Town, South Carolina, 1696 | 5 shillings |
| Dish | Inventory of William Ball, Junr. (1742) | Fine flowered Earthen dish in Lancaster County, Virginia, 1742 | 6 pence |
| Fire tongs | Inventory of William Ball, Junr. (1742) | Pair of fire tongs in Lancaster County, Virginia, 1742 | 2 shillings 6 pence |
| Fork | Inventory of William Ball, Junr. (1742) | Flesh fork in Lancaster County, Virginia, 1742 | 1 shilling 6 pence |
| Hand irons | Inventory of William Kemp (1641) | A paire of bras brandirions in Plymouth, Massachusetts, 1641 | 12 shillings |
| Hone | Inventory of Zephaniah Wade (1746) | Hone in Fairfax, Virginia, 1746 | 2 shillings |
| Ink Horn | Inventory of Wilson Dunston (1692) | Inke horne in Charleston, South Carolina, 1692 | 5 pence |
| Iron dogs | Inventory of Zephaniah Wade (1746) | Pair Cast Iron Doggs in Fairfax, Virginia, 1746 | 10 shillings |
| Jar | Inventory of Jesse Ball (1742) | Bread Jarr in Lancaster, Virginia, 1747 | 1 shilling |
| Jug | Inventory of William Kemp (1641) | A jugg pott tipt wth silvr in Plymouth, Massachusetts, 1641 | 10 shillings |
| Jug | Inventory of William Ball, Junr. (1742) | Stone jug in Lancaster County, Virginia, 1742 | 1 shilling 6 pence |

| Item | Data Source | Description | Price |
|---|---|---|---|
| Knife | John Hall Day Book (1688) | Cost for one knife found in invoice book of John Hall of Boston in 1688 | 6 pence |
| Knife | Inventory of Jesse Ball (1742) | Black table knife in Lancaster, Virginia, 1747 | 2¾ pence |
| Ladle | Inventory of Rawleigh Traverse (1749) | Punch ladle in Stafford, Virginia, 1749 | 1 shilling 3 pence |
| Lantern | Cressy, Coming Over (1987) | Priced of a lattern in New England during 1630 | 1 shilling 3 pence |
| Linen wheel | Inventory of Jesse Ball (1742) | Linnen wheel in Lancaster, Virginia, 1747 | 15 shillings |
| Lock | Inventory of Jesse Ball (1742) | Iron bound Locks in Lancaster, Virginia, 1747 | 8 shillings 4 pence |
| Mug | Inventory of Henry Fitzhugh (1742) | A quart Mug in Stafford County, Virginia, 1742 | 10 pence |
| Napkin | Inventory of Rawleigh Traverse (1749) | Coarse Linnen Napkin in Stafford, Virginia, 1749 | 9½ pence |
| Napkin | Inventory of Nicholas Mardin (1696) | Plane napkin in Charles Town, 1696 | 1 shilling |
| Pail | Inventory of John Sutton (1672) | Paile in Plymouth, Massachusetts, 1672 | 1 shilling 6 pence |
| Pail | Inventory of William Ball, Junr. (1742) | Water pail in Lancaster County, Virginia, 1742 | 1 shilling 3 pence |
| Pan | Inventory of James Lindale (1652) | Warming pan in Plymouth, Massachusetts, 1652 | 6 shillings |
| Pan | Inventory of Sarah Ball (1742) | Milk pan in Lancaster, Virginia, 1742 | 6 pence |
| Paper | Inventory of Wilson Dunston (1692) | Ream writting paper in Charleston, South Carolina, 1692 | 12 shillings |
| Pen knife | Inventory of Wilson Dunston (1692) | Ivory Screw pen knife in Charleston, South Carolina, 1692 | 1 shilling 8 pence |
| Pie mold | Inventory of William Ball, Junr. (1742) | Earthern pye mold in Lancaster County, Virginia, 1742 | 2 pence |
| Pillow | Inventory of William Kemp (1641) | Feather pillow in Plymouth, Massachusetts, 1641 | 2 shillings |
| Pillow bear | Inventory of Zephaniah Wade (1746) | Pillow bear in Fairfax, Virginia, 1746 | 4 pence |

| Item | Data Source | Description | Price |
|------|-------------|-------------|-------|
| Pillowcase | Inventory of William Kemp (1641) | A pillow case in Plymouth, Massachusetts, 1641 | 1 shilling 6 pence |
| Pillowcase | Inventory of Rawleigh Traverse (1749) | White Linen pillow Case in Stafford, Virginia, 1749 | 1 shilling |
| Plate | Inventory of John Harris (1694) | Pewter plate in Charles Towne, South Carolina, 1694 | 9½ pence |
| Plate | Inventory of William Ball, Junr. (1742) | Fine flowered soop plate in Lancaster County, Virginia, 1742 | 4 pence |
| Plate warmer | Inventory of Rawleigh Traverse (1749) | Plate warmer in Stafford, Virginia, 1749 | 1 pound 5 shillings |
| Platter | Inventory of Mary Ring (1631) | A erthen platter in Plymouth, Massachusetts, 1631 | 3 pence |
| Platter | Inventory of Martha Nelson (1684) | Pewter platter in Plymouth, Massachusetts, 1684 | 5 shillings |
| Pot | Inventory of William Kemp (1641) | Earthen old oyle pott in Plymouth, Massachusetts, 1641 | 2 pence |
| Pot | Inventory of Sarah Ball (1742) | Butter pott in Lancaster, Virginia, 1742 | 9 pence |
| Powder | Inventory of Josias Du Pre (1692) | Pound of Sented Powder in Charleston, South Carolina, 1692 | 10 shillings |
| Quilt | Inventory of Captian Arthur Dunn (1724) | Small Beld Quilt in Middlesex, Massachusetts, 1724 | 2 pounds |
| Razor | Inventory of Joseph Elliott (1697) | Rasor & hone in Charles Town, South Carolina, 1697 | 2 shillings 6 pence |
| Razor | Inventory of Zephaniah Wade (1746) | Razor in Fairfax, Virginia, 1746 | 6 pence |
| Rug | Billings, The Old Dominion in the Seventeenth Century (1975) | Rug for a bed serving for two men in Virginia, 1611 | 8 shillings |
| Rug | Inventory of Nicholas Townsend (1694) | A green Ruge in Charles Towne, South Carolina, 1694 | 10 shillings |
| Rug | Inventory of Henry Fitzhugh (1742) | New rugg in Stafford County, Virginia, 1742 | 8 shillings 3 pence |
| Salt box | Inventory of James Lindale (1652) | Salt box in Plymouth, Massachusetts, 1652 | 6 pence |
| Salt cellar | Inventory of Nicholas Mardin (1696) | Value of one Salt Seller in Charles Town, South Carolina, 1696 | 15 shillings |
| Saucer | Inventory of John Vansusteren (1694) | Earthen sawser in Charles Towne, South Carolina, 1694 | 3 pence |
| Sheets | Billings, The Old Dominion in the Seventeenth Century (1975) | Paire of Canvase sheets in Virginia, 1611 | 8 shillings |
| Sheets | Inventory of Rawleigh Traverse (1749) | Pair Coarse Sheets in Stafford, Virginia, 1749 | 9 shillings |
| Shovel & tongs | Inventory of Rawleigh Traverse (1749) | Shovel & tongs in Stafford, Virginia, 1749 | 4 shillings |
| Spinning wheel | Inventory of William Kemp (1641) | Spinning wheel in Plymouth, Massachusetts, 1641 | 3 shillings |
| Spinning wheel | Inventory of Jesse Ball (1742) | Spinning wheel in Lancaster, Virginia, 1747 | 10 shillings |
| Spoon | Inventory of William Kemp (1641) | Silver spoon in Plymouth, Massachusetts, 1641 | 4 shillings 2 pence |
| Spoons | Inventory of William Ball, Junr. (1742) | Dozen pewter spoons in Lancaster County, Virginia, 1742 | 1 shilling 6 pence |
| Spyglass | Inventory of Henry Fitzhugh (1742) | A spy Glass in Stafford County, Virginia, 1742 | 13 shillings |
| Stand | Inventory of Rawleigh Traverse (1749) | Ink Stand in Stafford, Virginia, 1749 | 1 shilling 3 pence |
| Table | Inventory of William Ball, Junr. (1742) | Square walnut table in Lancaster County, Virginia, 1742 | 10 shillings |
| Tablecloth | Inventory of Mary Ring (1631) | Diapr Tablecloath in Plymouth, Massachusetts, 1631 | 5 shillings |

| Item | Data Source | Description | Price |
|------|-------------|-------------|-------|
| Tablecloth | Inventory of Sarah Ball (1742) | Linnen Table Cloath in Lancaster, Virginia, 1742 | 2 shillings 6 pence |
| Tallow | Inventory of Rawleigh Traverse (1749) | Pound of tallow in Stafford, Virginia, 1749 | 6 pence |
| Tankard | Inventory of Nicholas Mardin (1696) | Silver Tankard weighing 23 ounces in Charles Town, South Carolina, 1696 | 8 pounds 4 shillings 6 pence |
| Tea & coffee set | Inventory of Henry Fitzhugh (1742) | Set of tea & Coffee ware in Stafford County, Virginia, 1742 | 10 shillings |
| Towel | Inventory of William Kemp (1641) | Hand towel in Plymouth, Massachusetts, 1641 | 2 shillings |
| Towel | Inventory of William Ball, Junr. (1742) | Fine towel in Lancaster County, Virginia, 1742 | 1 shilling 3 pence |
| Tray | Inventory of Godbert Godbertson & Zarah (1633) | Tray in Plymouth, Massachusetts, 1633 | 6 pence |
| Tray | Inventory of Roger Annadowne (1673) | A small Indian tray in Plymouth, Massachusetts, 1673 | 6 pence |
| Trivet | Inventory of Wilson Dunston (1692) | Trivett in Charleston, South Carolina, 1692 | 1 shilling 3 pence |
| Trunk | Inventory of Godbert Godbertson & Zarah (1633 | A trunck in Plymouth, Massachusetts, 1633 | 6 shillings |
| Trunk | Inventory of Thomas Richards (1650) | Trunke in Suffolk, Massachusetts, 1650 | 14 shillings |
| Tub | Inventory of William Ball, Junr. (1742) | Washing tub in Lancaster County, Virginia, 1742 | 2 shillings |
| Tumbler | Inventory of Robert Osborn (1744) | Silver Tumbler in Fairfax, Virginia, 1744 | 18 shillings |
| Twine | Inventory of Wilson Dunston (1692) | Pound of twine in Charleston, South Carolina, 1692 | 2 shillings 6 pence |
| Utensils | Inventory of Zephaniah Wade (1746) | Shagreen Case with 11 knives & 12 forks Ivory in Fairfax, Virginia, 1746 | 1 pound 5 shillings |
| Utensils | Inventory of Rawleigh Traverse (1749) | Dozen Ivory handl knives & forks in Stafford, Virginia, 1749 | 3 shillings |
| Wash balls | Inventory of Wilson Dunston (1692) | Dozen wash Balls in Charleston, South Carolina, 1692 | 7½ pence |

| Item | Data Source | Description | Price |
|------|-------------|-------------|-------|
| Wax | Inventory of Johnathan Newell (1672) | Pound of sealing wax in York County, Virginia, 1672 | 3 shillings |
| Wine glass | Inventory of William Ball, Junr. (1742) | Wine glass in Lancaster County, Virginia, 1742 | 3 pence |
| Writing book | Inventory of Wilson Dunston (1692) | Writing Booke of paper in folio in Charleston, South Carolina, 1692 | 5 shillings |

## Jewelry

| Item | Data Source | Description | Price |
|------|-------------|-------------|-------|
| Buttons | Inventory of Rawleigh Traverse (1749) | Three dozen of Gold washt Buttons in Stafford, Virginia, 1749 | 5 shillings |
| Ring | Inventory of Samuel Hanson (1741) | Gold Ring wt - 94 ¾ in Charles County, Maryland, 1741 | 14 shillings |
| Ring | Inventory of William Kemp (1641) | A gould ringe in Plymouth, Massachusetts, 1641 | 18 shillings |
| Watch | Inventory of Josias Du Pre (1692) | One watch with a Silver kaese, Silver Chaine in Charleston, South Carolina, 1692 | 4 pounds |
| Watch | Inventory of Henry Fitzhugh (1742) | Silver watch in Stafford County, Virginia, 1742 | 10 pounds |

## Kitchen Items

| Item | Data Source | Description | Price |
|------|-------------|-------------|-------|
| Box | Inventory of Henry Fitzhugh (1742) | Brass pepper box in Stafford County, Virginia, 1742 | 2 shillings |
| Bread grater | Inventory of William Kemp (1641) | Bread grater in Plymouth, Massachusetts, 1641 | 1 shilling 6 pence |
| Butcher's knife | Inventory of Wilson Dunston (1692) | Butchers knive in Charleston, South Carolina, 1692 | 7 shillings 6 pence |
| Canister | Inventory of Henry Fitzhugh (1742) | Tin canister in Stafford County, Virginia, 1742 | 2 shillings |
| Churn | Inventory of Henry Fitzhugh (1742) | Earthern Churn in Stafford County, Virginia, 1742 | 1 shilling 6 pence |
| Cleaver | Inventory of Henry Fitzhugh (1742) | Iron cleaver in Stafford County, Virginia, 1742 6 pence | 2 shillings |
| Clock | Inventory of Henry Fitzhugh (1742) | Kitchen Clock in Stafford County, Virginia, 1742 | 1 pound |
| Coffee pot | Inventory of Zephaniah Wade (1746) | Copper Coffee Pott in Fairfax, Virginia, 1746 | 4 shillings 6 pence |
| Colander | Inventory of William Ball, Junr. (1742) | Cullender in Lancaster County, Virginia, 1742 | 1 shilling 6 pence |
| Dish | Inventory of William Ball, Junr. (1742) | Brass chafing Dish in Lancaster County, Virginia, 1742 | 2 shillings 6 pence |
| Egg slice | Inventory of Samuel Hanson (1741) | Tin Egg Slice in Charles County, Maryland, 1741 | 6 pence |
| Fork | Inventory of Zephaniah Wade (1746) | Flesh fork in Fairfax, Virginia, 1746 | 9 pence |
| Frying pan | Inventory of Nicholas Mardin (1696) | Copper frying Pann in Charles Town, South Carolina, 1696 | 7 shillings 6 pence |
| Frying pan | Inventory of Robert Osborn (1744) | Frying pan in Fairfax, Virginia, 1744 | 6 shillings |
| Funnel | Inventory of Wilson Dunston (1692) | Two-quart funnel in Charleston, South Carolina, 1692 | 1 shilling |
| Funnel | Inventory of Henry Fitzhugh (1742) | Tin funnel in Stafford County, Virginia, 1742 | 1 shilling |
| Grater | Inventory of Samuel Hanson (1741) | Old Chocolate Grater in Charles County, Maryland, 1741 | 3 pence |
| Gridiron | Cressy, Coming Over (1987) | A gridiron in New England during 1630 | 2 shillings |

| Item | Data Source | Description | Price |
|---|---|---|---|
| Gridiron | Inventory of Henry Fitzhugh (1742) | One grid iron in Stafford County, Virginia, 1742 | 1 shilling 8 pence |
| Hooks | Inventory of Sarah Ball (1742) | Pair of pot hooks in Lancaster, Virginia, 1742 | 10 pence |
| Kettle | Inventory of Mary Ring (1631) | Old brasse kettle in Plymouth, Massachusetts, 1631 | 10 pence |
| Kettle | Inventory of William Kemp (1641) | Iron kettle in Plymouth, Massachusetts, 1641 | 10 shillings |
| Kettle | Inventory of Henry Fitzhugh (1742) | Fish kettle in Stafford County, Virginia, 1742 | 3 pounds |
| Knife | Inventory of Henry Fitzhugh (1742) | Choping knife in Stafford County, Virginia, 1742 | 1 pound 6 shillings |
| Mill | Inventory of Jesse Ball (1742) | Pepper mill in Lancaster, Virginia, 1747 | 5 shillings |
| Mortar | Cressy, Coming Over (1987) | A brass mortar in New England during 1630 | 3 shillings |
| Mortar & pestle | Inventory of Robert Osborn (1744) | Iron mortar & pestle in Fairfax, Virginia, 1744 | 2 shillings |
| Mortar | Inventory of Henry Fitzhugh (1742) | Marble Morter & pestle in Stafford County, Virginia, 1742 | 2 pounds 10 shillings |
| Mortar | Inventory of Stephen North (1720) | Wooden mortor and pestle in Suffolk County, Massachusetts, 1720 | 9 shillings |
| Nutmeg grater | Inventory of Wilson Dunston (1692) | Nut megg graters in Charleston, South Carolina, 1692 | 4½ pence |
| Pan | Cressy, Coming Over (1987) | One large frying pan in New England during 1630 | 2 shillings 8 pence |
| Pan | Inventory of Henry Fitzhugh (1742) | Stew pan in Stafford County, Virginia, 1742 | 18 shillings |
| Pan | Inventory of Henry Fitzhugh (1742) | Pewter milk pan in Stafford County, Virginia, 1742 | 3 shillings |
| Pot | Inventory of Mary Ring (1631) | A brasse pott in Plymouth, Massachusetts, 1631 | 7 shillings 4 pence |
| Pot | Inventory of Roger Annadowne (1673) | Pewter pott in Plymouth, Massachusetts, 1673 | 1 shilling 6 pence |
| Pot | Inventory of Samuel Hanson (1741) | Coffy pot in Charles County, Maryland, 1741 | 6 shillings 6 pence |
| Pot | Inventory of Henry Fitzhugh (1742) | Butter pot in Stafford County, Virginia, 1742 | 3 shillings |

### Based Upon the British Currency System

| Year | Pound in 2002 US Dollars | Shilling in 2002 US Dollars | Pence in 2002 US Dollars |
|---|---|---|---|
| 1650 | $120.00 | $6.00 | $0.50 |
| 1660 | $144.00 | $7.20 | $0.60 |
| 1670 | $120.00 | $6.00 | $0.70 |
| 1680 | $120.00 | $6.00 | $0.70 |
| 1690 | $120.00 | $6.00 | $0.80 |
| 1700 | $168.00 | $8.40 | $0.70 |
| 1710 | $144.00 | $7.20 | $0.60 |
| 1720 | $168.00 | $8.40 | $0.70 |
| 1730 | $192.00 | $9.60 | $0.80 |
| 1740 | $144.00 | $7.20 | $0.60 |
| 1749 | $192.00 | $9.60 | $0.80 |

*Calculations are approximate values based upon economic historical data*

| Item | Data Source | Description | Price |
|------|-------------|-------------|-------|
| Pot | Inventory of Jesse Ball (1742) | Chocolate pott in Lancaster, Virginia, 1747 | 10 shillings |
| Pot hooks | Inventory of Zephaniah Wade (1746) | Pair of Pot hooks in Fairfax, Virginia, 1746 | 1 shilling 6 pence |
| Pot rack | Inventory of Robert Osborn (1744) | Iron pot rack in Fairfax, Virginia, 1744 | 5 shillings |
| Salt cellar | Inventory of Wilson Dunston (1692) | Pewter Salt Seller in Charleston, South Carolina, 1692 | 1 shilling |
| Skillet | Inventory of John Sutton (1672) | Iron skillett in Plymouth, Massachusetts, 1672 | 3 shillings |
| Skillet | Inventory of Roger Annadowne (1673) | A brasse skillett in Plymouth, Massachusetts, 1673 | 6 shillings 6 pence |
| Snuffer | Inventory of Zephaniah Wade (1746) | Snuffer in Fairfax, Virginia, 1746 | 2 pence |
| Spit | Cressy, Coming Over (1987) | One spit for roasting in New England during 1630 | 2 shillings |
| Spit | Inventory of Henry Fitzhugh (1742) | Spit in Stafford County, Virginia, 1742 | 5 shillings |
| Spoon | Inventory of Jesse Ball (1742) | Larding spoon in Lancaster, Virginia, 1747 | 3 pence |
| Toaster | Inventory of Henry Fitzhugh (1742) | Toaster in Stafford County, Virginia, 1742 | 7 shillings 6 pence |
| Tray | Inventory of Henry Fitzhugh (1742) | Breading Tray in Stafford County, Virginia, 1742 | 10 pence |
| Utensils | Inventory of Stephen North (1720) | Flesh fork in Suffolk County, Massachusetts, 1720 | 1 shilling |
| Utensils | Inventory of Stephen North (1720) | Chaffing knife in Suffolk County, Massachusetts, 1720 | 2 shillings, 6 pence |

## Livery Animals & Tools

| Item | Data Source | Description | Price |
|------|-------------|-------------|-------|
| Bell | Inventory of Johnathan Newell (1672) | Cow bell in York County, Virginia, 1672 | 6 pence |
| Brand | Cressy, Coming Over (1987) | Brand to brand beasts in New England during 1630 | 6 pence |
| Bridle | Inventory of James Samford (1742) | Mans Saddle Bridle & housing in Richmond County, Virginia, 1742 | 1 pound 1 shilling 6 pence |
| Carriage | Inventory of Henry Fitzhugh (1742) | Old Chaize Carriage with 4 wheels & Chair whip in Stafford County, Virginia, 1742 | 8 pounds 13 shillings |
| Cart | Inventory of Robert Osborn (1744) | Cart & hames in Fairfax, Virginia, 1744 | 2 pounds |
| Comb | Cressy, Coming Over (1987) | Curry Comb used in New England during 1630 | 6 pence |
| Harness | Inventory of Jesse Ball (1742) | Sett Cart Harness in Lancaster, Virginia, 1747 | 15 shillings |
| Horse | Inventory of Roger Annadowne (1673) | Horse in Plymouth, Massachusetts, 1673 | 3 pounds |
| Horse | Inventory of Zephaniah Wade (1746) | Horse in Fairfax, Virginia, 1746 | 4 pounds |
| Jack | Inventory of A. Pearce (1690) | Jack in Suffolk County, Massachusetts, 1690 | 8 shillings |
| Jack | Inventory of Stephen North (1720) | Jack in Suffolk County, Massachusetts, 1720 | 3 pounds, 7 shillings |
| Lock | Inventory of Wilson Dunston (1692) | Horse lock in Charleston, South Carolina, 1692 | 2 shillings |
| Riding chair | Inventory of Henry Fitzhugh (1742) | Riding Chair & harness in Stafford County, Virginia, 1742 | 15 pounds |
| Saddle | Inventory of of Barnard Schencking (1692) | Old Sadle 2 Snafles & one bitt in Colleton County, South Carolna, 1692 | 2 shillings 6 pence |
| Saddle | Inventory of Henry Fitzhugh (1742) | Woman's side saddle & slip cover in Stafford County, Virginia, 1742 | 3 pounds |
| Saddlebags | Inventory of Rawleigh Traverse (1749) | Pair of Saddlebags in Stafford, Virginia, 1749 | 2 shillings 6 pence |

| Item | Data Source | Description | Price |
|------|-------------|-------------|-------|
| Spurs | Inventory of Wilson Dunston (1692) | Spurres in Charleston, South Carolina, 1692 | 1 shilling |
| Spurs | Inventory of Jesse Ball (1742) | Pair of Silver Spurrs in Lancaster, Virginia, 1747 | 1 pound 10 shillings |
| Switch | Inventory of Jesse Ball (1742) | Horse switch in Lancaster, Virginia, 1747 | 7 shillings 6 pence |
| Whip | Inventory of Wilson Dunston (1692) | Whip in Charleston, South Carolina, 1692 | 1 shilling 8 pence |

### Livestock

| Item | Data Source | Description | Price |
|------|-------------|-------------|-------|
| Bull | Inventory of James Lindale (1652) | Young bull in Plymouth, Massachusetts, 1652 | 2 pounds |
| Bull | Inventory of Rawleigh Traverse (1749) | Bull in Stafford, Virginia, 1749 | 1 pound 5 shillings |
| Calf | Inventory of James Lindale (1652) | Calf in Plymouth, Massachusetts, 1652 | 1 pound 7 shillings 6 pence |
| Calf | Inventory of William Ball, Junr. (1742) | Motherless calf in Lancaster County, Virginia, 1742 | 2 shillings 6 pence |
| Cattle | Inventory of William P. Marriner (1694) | Head of cattle in Berkeley County, South Carolina, 1693 | 7 pence |
| Colt | Inventory of William Kemp (1641) | Coult in Plymouth, Massachusetts, 1641 | 6 pounds |
| Cow | Inventory Captian Thomas Southworth (1669) | Cow in Plymouth, Massachusetts, 1669 | 2 pounds 8 shillings |
| Cow | Inventory of William Ball, Junr. (1742) | Barren Cow in Lancaster County, Virginia, 1742 | 1 pound 2 shillings 6 pence |
| Cow | Inventory of Rawleigh Traverse (1749) | Fatten'd cow in Stafford, Virginia, 1749 | 2 pounds 10 shillings |
| Duck | Inventory of Zephaniah Wade (1746) | Old Duck in Fairfax, Virginia, 1746 | 6 pence |
| Ewe | Inventory of Francis Hammersley (1745) | Ewe in Charles County, Maryland, 1745 | 10 shillings |
| Goat | Inventory of William Kemp (1641) | Ewe goat in Plymouth, Massachusetts, 1641 | 6 shillings 8 pence |

| Based Upon the British Currency System | | | |
|------|------|------|------|
| Year | Pound in 2002 US Dollars | Shilling in 2002 US Dollars | Pence in 2002 US Dollars |
| 1650 | $120.00 | $6.00 | $0.50 |
| 1660 | $144.00 | $7.20 | $0.60 |
| 1670 | $120.00 | $6.00 | $0.70 |
| 1680 | $120.00 | $6.00 | $0.70 |
| 1690 | $120.00 | $6.00 | $0.80 |
| 1700 | $168.00 | $8.40 | $0.70 |
| 1710 | $144.00 | $7.20 | $0.60 |
| 1720 | $168.00 | $8.40 | $0.70 |
| 1730 | $192.00 | $9.60 | $0.80 |
| 1740 | $144.00 | $7.20 | $0.60 |
| 1749 | $192.00 | $9.60 | $0.80 |

*Calculations are approximate values based upon economic historical data*

| Item | Data Source | Description | Price |
|------|-------------|-------------|-------|
| Goose | Inventory of Sarah Ball (1742) | Goose in Lancaster, Virginia, 1742 | 1 shilling |
| Heifer | Inventory of William Kemp (1641) | Heiffer 2 yere old in Plymouth, Massachusetts, 1641 | 3 pounds |
| Heifer | Inventory of Sarah Ball (1742) | Three year old heifers in Lancaster County, Virginia, 1742 | 1 pound |
| Hog | Inventory of William Kemp (1641) | Hog in Plymouth, Massachusetts, 1641 | 1 pound |
| Hog | Inventory of Rawleigh Traverse (1749) | Fatten'd hog in Stafford, Virginia, 1749 | 12 shillings |
| Lamb | Inventory of William Kemp (1641) | Ewe lamb in Plymouth, Massachusetts, 1641 | 3 shillings |
| Ox | Inventory of James Lindale (1652) | Ox prised in Plymouth, Massachusetts, 1652 | 6 pounds |
| Oxen | Inventory of Rawleigh Traverse (1749) | Yoak of Oxen in Stafford, Virginia, 1749 | 7 pounds |
| Pig | Inventory of Martha Nelson (1684) | Pig in Plymouth, Massachusetts, 1684 | 4 shillings |
| Poultry | Inventory of James Lindale (1652) | Poultrey in Plymouth, Massachusetts, 1652 | 6 pence |
| Sheep | Inventory of Rawleigh Traverse (1749) | Sheep in Stafford, Virginia, 1749 | 5 shillings |
| Shoat | Inventory Captian Thomas Southworth (1669) | Shoat in Plymouth, Massachusetts, 1669 | 1 shilling 3 pence |
| Shoat | Inventory of William Ball, Junr. (1742) | Shoat in Lancaster County, Virginia, 1742 | 2 shillings |
| Sow | Inventory of James Lindale (1652) | Sow in Plymouth, Massachusetts, 1652 | 1 pound 10 shillings |
| Sow | Inventory of William Ball, Junr. (1742) | Breeding sows in Lancaster County, Virginia, 1742 | 6 shillings |
| Steer | Inventory of William Kemp (1641) | Steare 2 yere old in Plymouth, Massachusetts, 1641 | 3 pounds |
| Steer | Inventory of James Lindale (1652) | Steer in Plymouth, Massachusetts, 1652 | 2 pounds 15 shillings |
| Steer | Inventory of Rawleigh Traverse (1749) | Large Stear in Stafford, Virginia, 1749 | 1 pound 10 shillings |
| Turkey | Inventory of Zephaniah Wade (1746) | Old Turkeys in Fairfax, Virginia, 1746 | 1 shilling 3 pence |

## Medicine

| Item | Data Source | Description | Price |
|------|-------------|-------------|-------|
| Elixir | Inventory of Sarah Ball (1742) | Pint of Squire's grand Elixir in Lancaster, Virginia, 1742 | 4 shillings |
| Surgeon's instruments | Inventory of Sarah Ball (1742) | Chirurgeons Instruments in Lancaster, Virginia, 1742 | 6 pounds 6 shillings |

| Item | Data Source | Description | Price |
|------|-------------|-------------|-------|
| **Music** | | | |
| Drum | Inventory of Henry Fitzhugh (1742) | Drum in Stafford County, Virginia, 1742 | 1 pounds 6 shillings |
| Fiddle | Inventory of Rawleigh Traverse (1749) | Fiddle in Stafford, Virginia, 1749 | 10 shillings |
| Flute | Inventory of Jesse Ball (1742) | Flute in Lancaster, Virginia, 1747 | 15 shillings |
| Trumpet | Inventory of Henry Fitzhugh (1742) | Silver Trumpet in Stafford County, Virginia, 1742 | 20 pounds |
| Violin | Inventory of Jesse Ball (1742) | Violin & Case in Lancaster, Virginia, 1747 | 1 pound |
| **Other** | | | |
| Bell | Inventory of William Kemp (1641) | Bell in Plymouth, Massachusetts, 1641 | 8 pence |
| Bird cage | Inventory of Johnathan Newell (1672) | Bird cage in York County, Virginia, 1672 | 4 shillings |
| Bolster tick | Inventory of William Kemp (1641) | Bolster tick in Plymouth, Massachusetts, 1641 | 4 shillings |
| Cane | Inventory of Mary Ring (1631) | Canne in Plymouth, Massachusetts, 1631 | 4 pence |
| Cane | Inventory of Jesse Ball (1742) | Brass head cane in Lancaster, Virginia, 1747 | 7 shillings |
| Cart | Inventory of Wilson Dunston (1692) | Hand Carte in Charleston, South Carolina, 1692 | 1 pound |
| Cider press | Inventory of John Millard, Jr. (1684) | An old Sider press in Plymouth, Massachusetts, 1684 | 1 pound 6 shillings |
| Ear picker | Inventory of John Vansusteren (1694) | One gold ring and eare picker in Charles Towne, South Carolina, 1694 | 1 pound |
| Fishing line | Inventory of Mary Ring (1631) | Fishing line in Plymouth, Massachusetts, 1631 | 8 pence |
| Fishing reel | Inventory of Henry Fitzhugh (1742) | Fishing reel in Stafford County, Virginia, 1742 | 12 shillings |
| Flower box | Inventory of Wilson Dunston (1692) | Flower box in Charleston, South Carolina, 1692 | 6 pence |
| Glass | Inventory of Samuel Hanson (1741) | Pane Sash Glass in Charles County, Maryland, 1741 | 1 shilling |
| Hat case | Inventory of William Kemp (1641) | Leather hat case in Plymouth, Massachusetts, 1641 | 3 shillings |

### Based Upon the British Currency System

| Year | Pound in 2002 US Dollars | Shilling in 2002 US Dollars | Pence in 2002 US Dollars |
|------|--------------------------|------------------------------|---------------------------|
| 1650 | $120.00 | $6.00 | $0.50 |
| 1660 | $144.00 | $7.20 | $0.60 |
| 1670 | $120.00 | $6.00 | $0.70 |
| 1680 | $120.00 | $6.00 | $0.70 |
| 1690 | $120.00 | $6.00 | $0.80 |
| 1700 | $168.00 | $8.40 | $0.70 |
| 1710 | $144.00 | $7.20 | $0.60 |
| 1720 | $168.00 | $8.40 | $0.70 |
| 1730 | $192.00 | $9.60 | $0.80 |
| 1740 | $144.00 | $7.20 | $0.60 |
| 1749 | $192.00 | $9.60 | $0.80 |

*Calculations are approximate values based upon economic historical data*

| Item | Data Source | Description | Price |
|------|-------------|-------------|-------|
| Hinges | Inventory of William Kemp (1641) | A paire of hinges in Plymouth, Massachusetts, 1641 | 9 pence |
| Hour glass | Inventory of Martha Nelson (1684) | A houre Glasse in Plymouth, Massachusetts, 1684 | 1 shilling |
| Ink powder | Inventory of Samuel Hanson (1741) | Paper of Ink powder in Charles County, Maryland, 1741 | 10 pence |
| Ink stand | Inventory of Samuel Hanson (1741) | Leaden Inkstand in Charles County, Maryland, 1741 | 1 shilling |
| Latch | Inventory of Rawleigh Traverse (1749) | Iron latch in Stafford, Virginia, 1749 | 6 pence |
| Lock | Inventory of Wilson Dunston (1692) | Sea Chest Lock in Charleston, South Carolina, 1692 | 1 shilling 6 pence |
| Lock and fetter | Cressy, Coming Over (1987) | For shackling a foot used in New England during 1630 | 2 shillings |
| Money scales | Inventory of Wilson Dunston (1692) | Paire of money Scalls box & Weights in Charleston, South Carolina, 1692 | 10 shillings |
| Oyster shell | Inventory of Zephaniah Wade (1746) | Bushel of Oster Shells in Fairfax, Virginia, 1746 | 2 pence |
| Paper | Inventory of Henry Fitzhugh (1742) | One rem fine paper in Stafford County, Virginia, 1742 | 12 shillings 6 pence |
| Pen | Inventory of Jesse Ball (1742) | Fountian pen in Lancaster, Virginia, 1747 | 11 pence |
| Pen engine | Inventory of Samuel Hanson (1741) | Pen Engine in Charles County, Maryland, 1741 | 2 shillings 6 pence |
| Pen knife | Inventory of John Vansusteren (1694) | Pen knife in Charleston, South Carolina, 1694 | 1 shilling |
| Pen knife | Inventory of Jesse Ball (1742) | Pen knife with a seal in Lancaster, Virginia, 1747 | 5 pence |
| Press | Inventory of Jesse Ball (1742) | Paper press in Lancaster, Virginia, 1747 | 15 shillings |
| Purse | Inventory of Zephaniah Wade (1746) | Silk purse in Fairfax, Virginia, 1746 | 1 shilling 6 pence |
| Scales | Inventory of Martha Nelson (1684) | A payer of Scales in Plymouth, Massachusetts, 1684 | 6 pence |
| Scales | Inventory of Robert Osborn (1744) | Pair money Scales in Fairfax, Virginia, 1744 | 5 shillings |
| Slate | Inventory of Godbert Godbertson & Zarah (1633) | A writing table of slate in Plymouth, Massachusetts, 1633 | 4 pence |
| Slate | Inventory of Rawleigh Traverse (1749) | Slate in Stafford, Virginia, 1749 | 2 shillings |
| Spectacles | Inventory of Nicholas Townsend (1694) | A paire of Speckteckles & turkle Shell Casse | 2 shillings 6 pence |
| Spectacles | Inventory of Jesse Ball (1742) | Pair of Spectacles in Lancaster, Virginia, 1747 | 6 pence |
| Still | Inventory of Rawleigh Traverse (1749) | A Copper Still & Tub in Stafford, Virginia, 1749 | 25 pounds |
| Trap | Inventory of Wilson Dunston (1692) | Steele fox trape in Charleston, South Carolina, 1692 | 4 shillings |
| Umbrella | Inventory of Josias Du Pre (1692) | Ombrello in Charleston, South Carolina, 1692 | 1 pound |
| Wallet | Inventory of Samuel Hanson (1741) | Linnen Wallet in Charles County, Maryland, 1741 | 1 shilling |
| Whale bone | Inventory of James Lindale (1652) | Pound of whalebone in Plymouth, Massachusetts, 1652 | 6 pence |
| Window glass | Inventory of Rawleigh Traverse (1749) | Pane of window glass in Stafford, Virginia, 1749 | 1 shilling |

## Publications

| Item | Data Source | Description | Price |
|------|-------------|-------------|-------|
| Bible | Inventory of Godbert Godbertson & Zarah (1633) | A great bible in Plymouth, Massachusetts, 1633 | 10 shillings |

| Item | Data Source | Description | Price |
|------|-------------|-------------|-------|
| Bible | Inventory of Nicholas Townsend (1694) | Great Bible in Charles Towne, South Carolina, 1694 | 5 shillings |
| Bible | Inventory of Robert Osborn (1744) | Large Bible in Fairfax, Virginia, 1744 | 1 pound |
| Book | Inventory of Godbert Godbertson & Zarah (1633) | Communion of Sts in french in Plymouth, Massachusetts, 1633 | 6 pence |
| Book | Inventory of Samuel Hanson (1741) | English Dictionary in Charles County, Maryland, 1741 | 9 shillings |
| Book | Inventory of Samuel Hanson (1741) | The History of the World by Sr Walter Raleigh in Charles County, Maryland, 1741 | 1 shilling 6 pence |
| Catechism | John Hall Day Book (1688) | Cost for Chathachism in Boston (value in 1688) | 6 pence |

**Real Estate**

| Item | Data Source | Description | Price |
|------|-------------|-------------|-------|
| County development | Acts of Assembly 1720 | Monies provided by the Virginia colonial assembly to use as "Christian tithables" to settle new terriorty and purchase arms and ammunition | 1,000 pounds |
| House | Inventory of John Haill (1646) | Dwelling house and ground both before & behind the house in Suffolk, Massachusetts, 1646 | 120 pounds |
| House | Inventory of John Millard, Jr. (1684) | The house & homestead with ye Orchard Containig 5 acres & a halfe: more or less in Plymouth, Massachusetts, 1684 | 45 pounds |
| House | Inventory of Godbert Godbertson & Zarah (1633) | Dwelling house & fence & garden in Plymouth, Massachusetts, 1633 | 14 pounds |
| Island | American Heritage (1959) | Value of items, such as knives, axes, clothing and beads, offered to the Canarsee tribe for Manhattan Island by the Dutch, 1626 | 60 gilders |
| Island | The Islands of Boston Harbor (1999) | Yearly lease of Spectacle Island to the Town of Boston from Nathan Ward, 1634 | 1 shilling |
| Land | Diary of Sameul Sewall (1689) | Orchard lot on the "Broad Street" - Boston, Massachusetts in 1689 | 60 pounds |
| Property | Maud Carter Clement, History of Pittsylvania County Virginia | Purchase of land in Pittsylvania, Virginia for 400 acres on Bye Creek of Banister River in 1746 | 1 Spanish pistol |
| Windmill | Inventory of John Haill (1646) | Wynd mill and the ground on wynd mill hill in Suffolk, Massachusetts, 1646 | 66 pounds 15 shillings 4 pence |

### Based Upon the British Currency System

| Year | Pound in 2002 US Dollars | Shilling in 2002 US Dollars | Pence in 2002 US Dollars |
|------|--------------------------|-----------------------------|--------------------------|
| 1650 | $120.00 | $6.00 | $0.50 |
| 1660 | $144.00 | $7.20 | $0.60 |
| 1670 | $120.00 | $6.00 | $0.70 |
| 1680 | $120.00 | $6.00 | $0.70 |
| 1690 | $120.00 | $6.00 | $0.80 |
| 1700 | $168.00 | $8.40 | $0.70 |
| 1710 | $144.00 | $7.20 | $0.60 |
| 1720 | $168.00 | $8.40 | $0.70 |
| 1730 | $192.00 | $9.60 | $0.80 |
| 1740 | $144.00 | $7.20 | $0.60 |
| 1749 | $192.00 | $9.60 | $0.80 |

*Calculations are approximate values based upon economic historical data*

| Item | Data Source | Description | Price |
|------|-------------|-------------|-------|
| **Servant** | | | |
| Indentured servant | Inventory of Richard Phillyps (1695) | Indian Wooman and Child in Charleston, South Carolina, 1695 | 25 pounds |
| Indentured servant | Inventory of Thomas Lynch (1736) | Servant Alex Agnen and wife for one years Serv in South Carolina, 1736 | 50 pounds |
| Indentured servant | Inventory of Sarah Ball (1742) | Negro man Tommy about 5 years to serve in Lancaster, Virginia, 1742 | 8 pounds |
| Indentured servant | Inventory of Francis Hammersley (1745) | Jess a young man 14 years to Serve in Charles County, Maryland, 1745 | 30 pounds |
| Indentured servant | Inventory of Zephaniah Wade (1746) | Thomas Paine 1 Year & 7 months to Serve in Fairfax, Virginia, 1746 | 5 pounds |
| Indentured servant | Inventory of Col. Barnwell (1724) | 13 Years of a bought Servant in Charlestown, South Carolina, 1724 | 50 pounds |
| Indentured servant | Inventory of James St. John (1743) | A Dutch servant man named Gaspor a shoemaker to serve upward a year and half in Charlestown, South Carolina, 1743 | 50 pounds |
| Indentured servant | Inventory of John Horton (1682) | One sick servt maid in Charlestown, South Carolina, 1682 | 6 pounds 6 shillings |
| Public incentive | White Servitude in Colonial South Carolina, Warren B. Smith (1961) | Colonial Incentive by South Carolina to inport healthy men between the ages of twelve and thirity as servants | 14 pounds |
| Public incentive | White Servitude in Colonial South Carolina, Warren B. Smith (1961) | Colonial incentive by South Carolina to import white servants for plantation owners who have no white servants | 5 pounds |
| Slave | Inventory of James B. Joyner (1694) | One negro girell Sarah in South Carolina, 1694 | 14 pounds |
| Slave | Inventory of Joseph Elliott (1697) | One negrow boy in Charles Town, South Carolina, 1697 | 33 pounds |
| Slave | Inventory of Stephen North (1720) | Negro Women named Bess in Suffolk County, Massachusetts in 1720 | 45 pounds, 16 shillings, 4 pence |
| Slave | Inventory of Francis Hammersley (1745) | Negro Harry Carpenter in Charles County, Maryland, 1745 | 50 pounds |
| Slave | Inventory of Zephaniah Wade (1746) | Indian Tom in Fairfax, Virginia, 1746 | 40 pounds |
| Slave | Inventory of Jesse Ball (1742) | Old Dick in Lancaster, Virgina, 1747 | 8 pounds |
| Slave | Inventory of Rawleigh Traverse (1749) | Dinah & Child in Stafford, Virginia, 1749 | 45 pounds |
| **Tobacco Products** | | | |
| Box | Inventory of Samuel Hanson (1741) | Leaden Tobacco Box in Charles County, Maryland, 1741 | 1 shilling |
| Snuff box | Inventory of Josias Du Pre (1692) | Snoff Cabos box with a Brase pompe in Charleston, South Carolina, 1692 | 5 shillings |
| Tobacco box | Inventory of James Lindale (1652) | Tobacco box in Plymouth, Massachusetts, 1652 | 2 pence |
| **Trade Equipment & Tools** | | | |
| Adze | Inventory of Wilson Dunston (1692) | Coopers adze in Charleston, South Carolina, 1692 | 2 shillings 6 pence |
| Adze | Inventory of Henry Fitzhugh (1742) | Coopers Adz in Stafford County, Virginia, 1742 | 1 shilling |
| Anvil | Inventory of John Haill (1646) | Great Anvill in a blacksmith shop in Suffolk, Massachusetts, 1646 | 9 pounds |
| Auger | Inventory of Jesse Ball (1742) | ½ inch auger in Lancaster, Virginia, 1747 | 10 pence |
| Axletree | Cressy, Coming Over (1987) | Wooden Axletree | 8 pence |

| Item | Data Source | Description | Price |
|------|-------------|-------------|-------|
| Barrel | John Hall Day Book (1688) | One barrel that can hold 4 bushels of salt | 2 shillings 6 pence |
| Bevel | Inventory of William Ball, Junr. (1742) | Bevel in Lancaster County, Virginia, 1742 | 3 pence |
| Cart | Cressy, Coming Over (1987) | Wooden Cart | 10 shillings |
| Cheese press | Inventory of James B. Joyner (1694) | Cheese press found in the estate's Buttry in South Carolina, 1694 | 10 shillings |
| Chisel | Inventory of William Ball, Junr. (1742) | Small chizell and gouge in Lancaster County, Virginia, 1742 | 2 pence |
| Compass | Inventory of Johnathan Newell (1672) | Pare large Compasses in York County, Virginia, 1672 | 1 shilling |
| Compass | Inventory of William Ball, Junr. (1742) | Commpass in Lancaster County, Virginia, 1742 | 4½ pence |
| Cooper's tools | Inventory of Rawleigh Traverse (1749) | Parcel of Coopers Tools in Stafford, Virginia, 1749 | 1 pound |
| Fasts | Inventory of William Ball, Junr. (1742) | Joyner's hold fasts in Lancaster County, Virginia, 1742 | 5 shillings |
| Fenner | Inventory of William Howell (1717) | Joiner's walnut fenere in Suffolk, Massachusetts in 1717 | 8 pounds 18 shillings |
| File | Inventory of Wilson Dunston (1692) | Square file in Charleston, South Carolina, 1692 | 5 pence |
| Files | Inventory of William Ball, Junr. (1742) | Dozen blacksmith files in Lancaster County, Virginia, 1742 | 4 shillings |
| Fishing line | Inventory of Jesse Ball (1742) | Five fishing lines in Lancaster, Virginia, 1747 | 3 shillings 5½ |
| Frow | Cressy, Coming Over (1987) | Frow to cleave pail in New England during 1630 | 1 shilling 6 pence |
| Froze | Inventory of Wilson Dunston (1692) | Coopers froze in Charleston, South Carolina, 1692 | 1 shilling 10½ pence |
| Gimlet | Cressy, Coming Over (1987) | A gimlet in New England during 1630 | 2 pence |
| Gimlet | Inventory of James B. Joyner (1694) | Gimlet in South Carolina, 1694 | 4 pence |
| Hammer | Inventory of William Ball, Junr. (1742) | Blacksmith's riviting hammer in Lancaster County, Virginia, 1742 | 10 shillings |
| Hand bill | Cressy, Coming Over (1987) | Cost of a Hand Bill in New England during 1630 | 1 shilling 8 pence |

### Based Upon the British Currency System

| Year | Pound in 2002 US Dollars | Shilling in 2002 US Dollars | Pence in 2002 US Dollars |
|------|--------------------------|------------------------------|---------------------------|
| 1650 | $120.00 | $6.00 | $0.50 |
| 1660 | $144.00 | $7.20 | $0.60 |
| 1670 | $120.00 | $6.00 | $0.70 |
| 1680 | $120.00 | $6.00 | $0.70 |
| 1690 | $120.00 | $6.00 | $0.80 |
| 1700 | $168.00 | $8.40 | $0.70 |
| 1710 | $144.00 | $7.20 | $0.60 |
| 1720 | $168.00 | $8.40 | $0.70 |
| 1730 | $192.00 | $9.60 | $0.80 |
| 1740 | $144.00 | $7.20 | $0.60 |
| 1749 | $192.00 | $9.60 | $0.80 |

*Calculations are approximate values based upon economic historical data*

| Item | Data Source | Description | Price |
|---|---|---|---|
| Hatchet | Inventory of Wilson Dunston (1692) | Carpenders axe in Charleston, South Carolina, 1692 | 4 shillings |
| Hatchet | Inventory of William Ball, Junr. (1742) | Hatchet in Lancaster County, Virginia, 1742 | 1 shilling 6 pence |
| Hinge | Inventory of Wilson Dunston (1692) | Dove taile hinge in Charleston, South Carolina, 1692 | 3 pence |
| Hook | Cressy, Coming Over (1987) | Cost for one cod hook - sold in units of 12 for 2 shillings | 2 pence |
| Hooks | Inventory of Jesse Ball (1742) | Dozen fishing hooks in Lancaster, Virginia, 1747 | 5½ pence |
| Howell | Inventory of Wilson Dunston (1692) | Coopers howells in Charleston, South Carolina, 1692 | 2 shillings |
| Irons | Inventory of Wilson Dunston (1692) | Coopers Joynter Iron in Charleston, South Carolina, 1692 | 1 pound |
| Knife | Inventory of Zephaniah Wade (1746) | Fro & drawing knife in Fairfax, Virginia, 1746 | 2 shillings |
| Knife | Inventory of Jesse Ball (1742) | Shoemakers knife in Lancaster, Virginia, 1747 | 1 shilling |
| Leather | Inventory of Wilson Dunston | Pound of sole leather in Charleston, South Carolina, 1692 | 4 pence |
| Line | Cressy, Coming Over (1987) | One line for fishing | 1 shilling |
| Line | Cressy, Coming Over (1987) | One mackerel line and 12 hooks | 10 pence |
| Locks | Inventory of James B. Joyner (1694) | Two Locks and paire of Dove tailes in South Carolina, 1694 | 7 shillings |
| Loom | Inventory of William Ball, Junr. (1742) | Weaver's loom & gear in Lancaster County, Virginia, 1742 | 1 pound |
| Mallet | Inventory of Roger Annadowne (1673) | Calkeing mallett in Plymouth, Massachusetts, 1673 | 8 pence |
| Nails | Inventory of Wilson Dunston (1692) | Thousand six-penny nails in Charleston, South Carolina, 1692 | 4 shillings |
| Nails | Inventory of Wilson Dunston (1692) | Hundred four penny-nails in Charleston, South Carolina, 1692 | 3 pence |
| Pinchers | Inventory of Samuel Hanson (1741) | Pair of Shoemakers pinchers in Charles County, Maryland, 1741 | 1 shilling 6 pence |
| Plane iron | Inventory of James B. Joyner (1694) | Plaine iron in South Carolina, 1694 | 3 pence |
| Pot | Inventory of William Ball, Junr. (1742) | Glue pot in Lancaster County, Virginia, 1742 | 2 shillings 6 pence |
| Rasp | Inventory of Jesse Ball (1742) | Shoemakers Rasp in Lancaster, Virginia, 1747 | 5½ pence |
| Rule | Inventory of Nicholas Townsend (1694) | Joynted rule in Charles Towne, South Carolina, 1694 | 7½ pence |
| Saw | Inventory of Samuel Hanson (1741) | Old Handsaw in Charles County, Maryland, 1741 | 1 shilling 6 pence |
| Scoop | Cressy, Coming Over (1987) | One scoop made of wood | 9 pence |
| Screws | Inventory of James B. Joyner (1694) | Parcell of bed scrues in South Carolina, 1694 | 2 pounds 6 pence |
| Sea instruments | Inventory of William P. Marriner (1694) | Parcel of sea instruments in Berkeley County, South Carolina, 1693 | 1 pound 6 shillings 3 pence |
| Shave | Inventory of Wilson Dunston (1692) | Coopers round shave in Charleston, South Carolina, 1692 | 1 shilling |
| Shoe thread | Inventory of Jesse Ball (1742) | Pound of shoe thread in Lancaster, Virginia, 1747 | 1 shilling 2 pence |
| Shoemaker's tools | Inventory of Rawleigh Traverse (1749) | Set of Shoemakers tools in Stafford, Virginia, 1749 | 7 shillings 6 pence |
| Shovel | Cressy, Coming Over (1987) | Wooden casting shovel | 10 pence |
| Skin | Inventory of James B. Joyner (1694) | Drest dear Skin in South Carolina, 1694 | 2 shillings 3 pence |
| Skin | Inventory of John Harris (1694) | Tan Calfe Skin in Charles Towne, South Carolina, 1694 | 1 shilling 2½ pence |

| Item | Data Source | Description | Price |
|---|---|---|---|
| Skin | Inventory of Wilson Dunston (1692) | Racoone skin in Charleston, South Carolina, 1692 | 5 pence |
| Skin | Inventory of Wilson Dunston (1692) | Cat Skin in Charleston, South Carolina, 1692 | 10 pence |
| Skin | Inventory of Wilson Dunston (1692) | Beare Skin in Charleston, South Carolina, 1692 | 4 shillings |
| Surveyors instrument | Inventory of Henry Fitzhugh (1742) | Set of surveyors Instrument in Stafford County, Virginia, 1742 | 4 pounds 10 shillings |
| Thimble | Inventory of Wilson Dunston (1692) | Taylors thimble in Charleston, South Carolina, 1692 | 2 pence |
| Thread | Inventory of Sarah Ball (1742) | Pound of shoe thread in Lancaster, Virginia, 1742 | 6 pence |
| Tools | Inventory of William Ball, Junr. (1742) | Small parcel of sliversmith's tools in Lancaster County, Virginia, 1742 | 10 shillings |
| Tools | Inventory of Sarah Ball (1742) | Parsell of cooper's Tools in Lancaster, Virginia, 1742 | 10 shillings |
| Trowel | Inventory of Jesse Ball (1742) | Trowel in Lancaster, Virginia, 1747 | 1 shilling 6 pence |
| Vise | Inventory of Wilson Dunston (1692) | Coopers vice in Charleston, South Carolina, 1692 | 5 pence |
| Vise | Inventory of John Haill (1646) | Vise in a blacksmith shop in Suffolk, Massachusetts, 1646 | 10 shillings |
| Vise | Inventory of William Ball, Junr. (1742) | Silversmith's small hand vise in Lancaster County, Virginia, 1742 | 4 shillings |

## Travel & Transportation

| Item | Data Source | Description | Price |
|---|---|---|---|
| Boat | Inventory of William P. Marriner (1694) | Solid boat in Berkeley County, South Carolina, 1693 | 2 pounds |
| Boat | Inventory of James Samford (1742) | Old boat in Richmond County, Virginia, 1742 | 5 shillings |
| Canoe | Inventory of Godbert Godbertson & Zarah (1633) | A Canoe & sayle in Plymouth, Massachusetts, 1633 | 10 pounds |
| Fare | American Heritage (1959) | Fare charged by Cornelis Dircksen - New York to Brooklyn (1638) | 3 Stivers Wampum |
| Freight | Billings, The Old Dominion in the Seventeenth Century (1975) | Fraight of provisions for a man, will be about half a Tun to Virginia, 1611 | 1 pound 10 shillings |
| Freight | Colonial Records of South Carolina - Journal of the Commons House of Assembly 1744-1745 (1955) | Payment to John Tucker for Freight of great Guns and Carriages to Stono Inlet, South Carolina (1744) | 15 pounds |
| Passage | Billings, The Old Dominion in the Seventeenth Century (1975) | Passage for each man from England to Virginia, 1611 | 6 pounds |
| Passage | Annie L. Jester, Domestic Life in Virginia in the Seventeeth Century. | Cost for passage from England to the Virginia colony with freight | 20 pounds |

# MISCELLANY 1600-1749

## Early Settlement Attire

The Virginia Company in London advised each emigrant to provide himself with the following articles of dress:

- *A Monmouth cap*
- *Three shirts*
- *One suit of canvas*
- *One pair of garters*
- *Four pair of shoes*
- *Three falling bands*
- *One waistcoat*
- *One suit of frieze*
- *One suit of broadcloth*
- *Three pairs of silk stockings*
- *One dozen pairs of pants*

In 1623, the Massachusetts Bay Company provided each man with a suitable outfit of the following:

- *Four pairs of shoes*
- *Four pairs of stockings*
- *A pair of Norwich gaiters*
- *Four shirts*
- *Two suits of doublet and hose of leather lined with oil skin*
- *A woolen suite lined with leather*
- *Four bands*
- *Two handkerchiefs*
- *A green cotton waistcoat*
- *A leather belt*
- *A woolen cap*
- *A black hat*
- *Two red knit caps*
- *Two pair of gloves*
- *A mandollion or cloak lined with cotton*
- *Extra pair of breeches*

*Source: History of American Costume 1607- 1870,*
Elisabeth McClellan (1969)

## Headright System in Virginia

In the early settlement of Virginia, the Virginia Company stipulated that no individual assignment of land would be granted - thus creating a communal plan. This plan was terminated in 1616 and granted to those who came prior to 1616 one-hundred acres to every individual intended upon settling the region. Those who arrived after 1616 were entitled to fifty acres if they paid their own passage and an additional fifty acres for each person whose passage he paid. This system of granting land was known as the Headright system.

*Source: Domestic Life in Virginia in the Seventeenth Century,* Annie L. Jester (1957)

## Incentive for Indentured Servants

South Carolina enacted an article that encouraged the importation of servants on June 7, 1712, and provided cash incentives to individuals. The first article of the act states the following:

The "*publick Receiver for the time being . . . during the Term of Four Years, after the Ratification of this Act, [to] pay out of the publick Treasury of this Province, the Sum of Fourteen Pounds Current Money to the Owners or Importers of each healthy Male British Servant, betwixt the Age of Twelve and Thirty Years, as soon as the Said Servant or Servants are assigned over into his Hands by him or them to whom they belong.*"

*Source:* White Servitude in Colonial South Carolina, Warren B. Smith (1961)

## Advertisement of Escaped Servants, 1749

"Whreas the fubfcriber has not been able to get intelligence of two *Palatine* fervants, who came in the fhip *Griffin*, capt. Arthur, from *London*, and deferted from the fick quarters in *Charles Town*, one call'd *Jahannes Schollar*, aged about 23 years, a fhort thick perfon, and *Philip Schaffer* (a huffar) . . . Early enquiry having been made in *Saxe-Gotha, Congorer, &c.* where 'twas imagined they were gone, it's now fufpected they may be harbour'd at fome plantation not fo diftant as thofe townfhips. If they, or either of them will return, or procure payment of their paffage, it will be accepted: 10 *l.* reward for intelligence where one or both may be found . . . ."

*Source: South Carolina Gazette,*
November 27, 1749

## Bacon's Declaration in the Name of the People
## July 30, 1676
## The Declaracon of the People.

1. For haveing upon specious pretences of publiqe works raised greate unjust taxes upon the Comonality for the advancement of private favorites and other sinister ends, but noe visible effects in any measure adequate, For not haveing dureing this long time of his Gouvernement in any measure advanced this hopefull Colony either by fortificacons Townes or Trade.
2. For haveing abused and rendred contemptable the Magistrates of Justice, by advanceing to places of Judicature, scandalous and Ignorant favorites.
3. For haveing wronged his Majesties prerogative and interest, by assumeing Monopoly of the Beaver trade, and for haveing in that unjust gaine betrayed and sold his Majesties Country and the lives of his loyall subjects, to the barbarous heathen.
4. For haveing, protected, favoured, and Imboldned the Indians against his Majesties loyall subjects, never contriveing, requireing, or appointing any due or proper meanes of sattisfaction for theire many Invasions, robbories, and murthers comitted upon us.
5. For haveing when the Army of English, was just upon the track of those Indians, who now in all places burne, spoyle, murther and when we might with ease have distroyed them: who then were in open hostillity, for then haveing expressly countermanded, and sent back our Army, by passing his word for the peaceable demeanour of the said Indians, who imediately prosecuted theire evill intentions, comitting horred murthers and robberies in all places, being protected by the said ingagement and word past of him the said Sir William Berkeley, haveing ruined and laid desolate a greate part of his Majesties Country, and have now drawne themselves into such obscure and remote places, and are by theire success soe imboldned and confirmed, by theire confederacy soe strengthned that the cryes of blood are in all places, and the terror, and constimation of the people soe greate, are now become, not onely a difficult, but a very formidable enimy, who might att first with ease have beene distroyed.

6. And lately when upon the loud outcryes of blood the Assembly had with all care raised and framed an Army for the preventing of further mischeife and safeguard of this his Majesties Colony.
7. For haveing with onely the privacy of some few favorites, without acquainting the people, onely by the alteracon of a figure, forged a Comission, by we know not what hand, not onely without, but even against the consent of the people, for the raiseing and effecting civill warr and distruction, which being happily and without blood shed prevented, for haveing the second time attempted the same, thereby calling downe our forces from the defence of the fronteeres and most weekely exposed places.
8. For the prevencon of civill mischeife and ruin amongst ourselves, whilst the barbarous enimy in all places did invade, murther and spoyle us, his majesties most faithfull subjects.

Of this and the aforesaid Articles we accuse Sir William Berkeley as guilty of each and every one of the same, and as one who hath traiterously attempted, violated and Injured his Majesties interest here, by a loss of a greate part of this his Colony and many of his faithfull loyall subjects, by him betrayed and in a barbarous and shamefull manner exposed to the Incursions and murther of the heathen, And we doe further declare these the ensueing persons in this list, to have beene his wicked and pernicious councellours Confederates, aiders, and assisters against the Comonality in these our Civill comotions.

Sir Henry Chichley William Claiburne Junior
Lieut. Coll. Christopher Thomas Hawkins
Wormeley William Sherwood
Phillip Ludwell John Page Clerke
Robert Beverley John Cluffe Clerke
Richard Lee John West
Thomas Ballard Hubert Farrell
William Cole Thomas Reade
Richard Whitacre Matthew Kempe
Nicholas Spencer
Joseph Bridger

And we doe further demand that the said Sir William Berkeley with all the persons in this list be forthwith delivered up or surrender themselves within fower days after the notice hereof, Or otherwise we declare as followeth.

That in whatsoever place, howse, or ship, any of the said persons shall reside, be hidd, or protected, we declaire the owners, Masters or Inhabitants of the said places, to be confederates and trayters to the people and the estates of them is alsoe of all the aforesaid persons to be confiscated, and this we the Comons of Virginia doe declare, desiering a firme union amongst our selves that we may joyntly and with one accord defend our selves against the common Enimy, and lett not the faults of the guilty be the reproach of the inocent, or the faults or crimes of the oppressours devide and separate us who have suffered by theire oppressions.

These are therefore in his majesties name to command you forthwith to seize the persons above mentioned as Trayters to the King and Country and them to bring to Midle plantacon, and there to secure them untill further order, and in case of opposition, if you want any further assistance you are forthwith to demand itt in the name of the people in all the Counties of Virginia.

*Nathaniel Bacon*
*Generall by Consent of the people.*

## The "Starving Time, 1609-1610

*Arber and Bradley, eds Travels and Works of John Smith, II, 498-499.*

Nay, so great was our famine, that a Salvage we slew and buried, the poorer sort tooke him up againe and eat him, and so did divers one another boyled and stewed with roots and herbs: And one amongst the rest did kill his wife, powdered [i.e., salted] her, and had eatern part of her before it was knowne; for which hee was executed, as hee well deserved: now whether shee was better roasted, boyled or carbonado'd [i.e., grilled], I know not; but of such a dish as powdered wife I never heard of.

*Source: The Old Dominion in the Seventeenth Century,*
Edited by Warren M. Billings (1975)

## An Act Fining Counties for Failing to Elect Burgesses, October, 1670

*Hening, ed., Statutes at Large, II, 282-283*

Whereas the act for electing two burgesses for each county for want of a Fine hath not had that due observance it ought, *It is enacted* that every county not sending to every session of assembly two burgesses shall be fined ten thousand pounds of tobacco to the use of the publique.

*Source: The Old Dominion in the Seventeenth Century,*
Edited by Warren M. Billings (1975)

## Roger Jones's Indenture, 1688

*Middlesex County Order Book, 1680-1694, 343.*

Roger Jones Servant to Mr. William Churchill Comes and acknowledges that hee is freely Willing to Serve his Master Seaven yeares from his Arival, The said Churchill promising that hee will imploy his said Servant in the Stoar and other his occasions and not imploy him in Common working in the Ground.

*Source: The Old Dominion in the Seventeenth Century,*
Edited by Warren M. Billings (1975)

## Richard Frethorne's Account of his Plight in Virginia (1623), Excerpt

Richard Frethorne to his parents, March 20, April 2, 3, 1623, in Susan Myra Kingsbury, ed., *The Records of the Virginia Company of London* (Washington, D.C., 1906-1935), IV, 58-59, 62.

*. . . I have nothing at all, no not a shirt to my backe, but two Ragges nor no Clothes, but one poore suite, nor but one paire of shooes, but one paire of stockins, but one Capp, but two bands, my Cloke is stolen by one of my owne fellows, and to his dying hower would not tell mee what he did with it . . . . but I am not halfe a quarter so strong as I was in England, and all is for want of victualls, for I doe protest unto you, that I have eaten more in a day at home than I have allowed me here for a Weeke . . . .*

*Source: The Old Dominion in the Seventeenth Century,*
Edited by Warren M. Billings (1975)

# 1750-1774

# The Run up to the War of American Independence

During the 25-year period preceding the Revolutionary War, the vast majority of American colonists were consumed by the variable elements of agriculture and weather. Making a living in colonial America was a difficult and often uncertain occupation, plagued by crop failures, uncertain money supply, rising taxation, rumors of war and a plethora of economic boycotts. By 1750, the east coast of North America was home to approximately 900,000 European settlers, 240,000 African slaves, and 200,000 Native Americans. This was still a new world, dominated less by human beings than by the natural environment. Towering forests of pine, oak, maple, elm, beech, and chestnut still covered most of eastern North America. These forests were home to tens of thousands of deer and other wildlife. Large numbers of saltwater fish and shellfish inhabited the relatively shallow waters off the northeastern coast of the continent. These fish and animals, which had long provided food and fur clothing for Native Americans, yielded valuable exports for the European inhabitants.

It was also a region experiencing exceptional growth. The economic opportunities of the New World led couples to marry younger and raise larger families. The wide open environment, unlike the sometimes crowded conditions in Europe, reduced the impacts of infectious childhood diseases. Benjamin Franklin extrapolated that the birthrate alone was doubling the population every 25 years, creating enormous consumer demand and prosperity for merchants and manufacturers on both sides of the Atlantic. Yet, a vast majority of the families possessed one dream: the hope of having land of their own independent of the landlords they had known in Germany, England or elsewhere. This produced a people largely unwilling to work for others, virtually starving manufacturing facilities of the labor necessary to be successful. Those not tied to the land were mostly entrepreneurial-minded tradesmen eager to peddle to their neighbors the best goods-most of which came from England-at the best price.

Despite the enduring myth of self-sufficiency and opposition to England, for most of this period, the colonists enjoyed a flourishing trade and a high level of interest in British products. Import records and store receipts show that the rapidly growing American colonies were highly dependent on the mother country for finished goods. Virtually no facilities for the manufacture of paper, glass, china, firearms and many types of cloth existed in the colonies. Early efforts to establish manufacturing facilities suffered from both an inadequate supply of skilled labor and intense competition from British merchants. From 1740 to 1760 alone, the value of imports from England to America increased 130 percent. During the 1750 to 1775 period, the people who were soon to fight England for the right to be independent purchased half the ironware, earthenware, silk goods, printed cotton goods and flannels that English merchants sold abroad. And because the British had imposed the Navigation Acts of the 1660s-more than a century before-the colonies were essentially a closed, captive market of England. American crops such as tobacco, rice or timber conveyed to European markets could only be transported in English ships, cutting out most competitors. And most goods going to the colonies had to pass through an English port, effectively eliminating France, the Netherlands and Spain from the emerging market. Although this promoted organized smuggling by some country, America's dependence on Britain commerce was well established.

The American tide of taxation angst bloomed fullest after the French and Indian War. In 1763 Britain stood triumphant in the western world. After a century of war, it had finally defeated France; its kingdom was spread from Detroit to Calcutta. All of North America east of the Mississippi and north of Florida was British. The colonists were as jubilant in victory as Britain's King George III, who was celebrated as a hero. A hero, that is, until the British Parliament passed the Proclamation of 1763, restricting westward expansion and Sugar Act of 1765, which increased duties on non-British goods shipped to the colonies. The French and Indian War had been a long, costly conflict and King George was determined to prevent further territorial conflicts and recoup the costs of fighting the hated French in America. The Sugar Act was the first law specifically aimed at raising colonial money for the crown, but not the last.

The act increased the duties on imported sugar and other items such as textiles, coffee, wines and indigo (dye), and doubled the duties on foreign goods reshipped from England to the colonies. Thus, for the first time in the 150-year history of the British colonies in America, the Americans were told they would pay tax not to their own local legislatures in America, but directly to England. By the winter of 1765 a boycott of British goods was initiated over the equally onerous Stamp Act, whose proceeds were exclusively designated for the defense of the colonies. Daily business and legal transactions in the colonies diminished. In New York City, violence broke out as a mob burned the royal governor in effigy, harassed British troops, and looted houses. Five months later, the English Parliament repealed some of the tax acts, but declared that the British government had total power to legislate any laws governing the American colonies.

This back-and-forth chess match between the colonies and the mother country set the pattern for an eventual declaration of independence a decade later. In the interim, the Americans attempted hundreds of boycotts against British goods, delivered thousands of speeches and witnessed dozens of riots. Violence broke out in New York between British soldiers and armed colonists as a result of the continuing refusal of New York colonists to comply with the Quartering Act, which required the colonies to provide barracks and supplies to British troops. In response, the New York legislature was suspended by the English Crown. The exasperated English Parliament then passed-despite warnings about a possible revolt-the Townsend Revenue Acts, imposing a new series of taxes on the colonists to offset the costs of administering and protecting the American colonies. Items taxed included imports such as paper,

tea, glass, lead and paints. This led to further merchant boycotts in the bustling trade centers of Boston and Philadelphia.

In the southern colony of Virginia, when the House of Burgesses formally opposed taxation without representation and British plans to possibly send American agitators to England for trial, the royal governor of Virginia dissolved the House of Burgesses. This action triggered further boycotts of trade goods, luxury items and slaves obtained and sold by Great Britain. Smuggling goods to and from other countries, eager supply the colonies, increased and loyalty to England was weakened.

This mishmash of efforts to stage boycotts was haphazard, inconsistent, and infuriating to the British. Pressure built on both sides of the Atlantic. For the colonists, Britain was the only source of some manufactured goods. In 1771, when well-organized boycotts of British goods collapsed, the colonial markets were again flooded with goods including nails, axes, firearms, coaches, clocks, saddles, handkerchiefs and buttons. Half of all woolen cloth in the colonies came from England. Despite highly visible protests against the hated Stamp Act and other laws, consumers continued to buy.

As the conflicts continued, the 13 separate colonies began to find unity in their opposition to English domination, particularly the power to tax. The colonies had developed in relative isolation from each other, each with its own distinctive character and government. In response to the Boston Tea party in 1774, Britain passed a series of five laws that came to be known in America as the Intolerable Acts. These laws aroused pronounced opposition that surpassed any previous action taken by the British government. Initially most of the colonies did not initially seek revolution, only the economic freedom of being left alone. The Declaration of Rights and Grievances drawn up by the First Continental Congress only asserted the colonists tights based on the "the immutable laws of nature, the principles of the English constitution," and the various compacts and charters previously approved. After all, how could 13 separately controlled colonies battle mighty England's army, which had so recently defeated the French?

# HISTORICAL SNAPSHOTS
# 1750-1774

## 1750–1759

### 1750

- The population of Europe was estimated to be 140 million
- The American colonies were home to approximately 900,000 European settlers, 240,000 African slaves, and 200,000 Native Americans
- French astronomer Nicolas Louis de Lacaille led an expedition to the Cape of Good Hope to determine solar and lunar parallax
- John Gay's *The Beggar's Opera* was performed for the first time in New York
- Jonathan Edwards was dismissed from his Northampton, Massachusetts church when he rejected the liberal "halfway covenant," which stated that adults who had been baptized, but who had were not full members of the church, could nevertheless have their children baptized
- The word "bluestocking" entered the language after naturalist and intellectual Benjamin Stillingfleet wore blue rather than white stockings

### 1751

- Benjamin Franklin published *New Experiments and Observations on Electricity*
- David Hume published *Enquiry concerning the Principles of Morals;* Carolus Linnaeus completed *Philosophia Botania*
- The British calendar was altered by an Act of Parliament making January 1, not March 25, the beginning of the New Year
- The first mental asylums were established in London
- American colonists ordered the Liberty Bell from England

### 1752

- Benjamin Franklin proved that lightning was electricity using a kite

- Pennsylvania Hospital, the first general hospital in the American colonies, opened in Philadelphia
- The British Empire adopted the Gregorian calendar, eliminating eleven days; September 2 was followed directly by September 14 that year
- English scientist Lord John Davies first observed a respiratory collapse
- British novelist Fanny Burney broke literary ground by writing about the experiences of young girls entering society

### 1753

- French troops from Canada seized the Ohio Valley region
- George Washington explored western Pennsylvania and ordered the French to leave
- Carolus Linnaeus's *Species plantarum* standardized the use of binary nomenclature in botany
- In Scotland, Charles Morrison proposed the construction of a telegraph consisting of 26 electrical lines, each corresponding to a letter of the alphabet
- Zinnias and marigolds, both plants native to Mexico, were first imported into England
- *Treatise on Scurvy* by James Lind described the curative dietary effect of oranges and lemons on scurvy

### 1754

- Benjamin Franklin issued the Albany Plan of Union, under which each colonial legislature would elect delegates to an American continental assembly presided over by a royal governor
- French and Indian War erupted over land disputes in the Ohio River Valley
- Major George Washington lost the battle of Fort Necessity in the Ohio territory after being attacked by numerically superior French forces

- Thomas Chippendale issued *The Gentleman and Cabinetmakers Directory*
- The St. Andrews Royal and Ancient Golf Club was founded in Scotland
- The nutritional value of plants was described in Charles Bonnet's *Recherches sur l'usage des feuilles des plantes (Study of the use of plant leaves)*
- A rugged marine chronometer for routine shipboard use was developed by France's Ferdinand Berthoud

### 1755

- Nine hundred French and Indian soldiers were defeated by an army of 2,000 troops led by English Commander-in-chief General Edward Braddock and Lt. Col. George Washington in the Ohio territories
- Immanuel Kant's doctoral thesis observed that nebulae were large star systems similar to the Milky Way and that the solar system originated from a dust cloud
- Scottish chemist Joseph Black wrote that carbonates are compounds of a base and of a gas that he termed "fixed air," known today as carbon dioxide
- French playwright Pierre-Augustin Caron de Beaumarchais invented a clock that could be wound by turning a ring on the clock's face
- Samuel Johnson published *Dictionary of the English Language*

### 1756

- The French and Indian War in the colonies spread to Europe as England declared war on France
- Wolfgang Amadeus Mozart was born
- The first chocolate factory was built in Germany
- Joseph Black's publication *Experiments upon Magnesia, Quicklime, and Other Alkaline Substances* became the first detailed examination of chemical action

- The first cotton velvets were made at Bolton, Lancashire, England
- Philipp Pfaff wrote the first description of how to mold false teeth
- Charles Augustin Coulomb reinvented the diving bell

### 1757

- Daniel P. Custis died and left his White House plantation to his wife Martha, the future wife of George Washington
- Martha Wadsworth Brewster of Lebanon, Connecticut, wrote *Poems on Divers Subjects* which discussed military events and the brutality of war
- A monthly magazine, *The American Magazine and Monthly Chronicle,* began publication to showcase the talent of the colonies

### 1758

- Jonathon Edwards became president of the College of New Jersey, later named Princeton University
- Benjamin Franklin published *The Way to Wealth*
- French troops were victorious at a battle at Fort Ticonderoga, New York
- A machine to knit hosiery was invented by Jedediah Strutt
- Halley's Comet appeared in the sky on December 25
- Rudjer Boscovich published his atomic theory
- The first English manual on guitar playing was published

### 1759

- George Washington wed Martha Custis and honeymooned at her home, the White House
- Francis Hopkinson wrote the song "My Days Have Been So Wondrous Free," considered the earliest song written by a native-born American
- Samuel Hopkins published *Sin, Thro' Divine Interpretation,* a defense of the existence of sin in the world as part of God's divine plan for humanity's salvation
- The colonies' first life insurance company was incorporated in Philadelphia

- Ferdinand VI of Spain was succeeded by his half-brother Carlos III
- French Canada fell to British forces outside Quebec; both the French commander and the British general were fatally wounded in the fighting
- Adam Smith published *Theory of Moral Sentiments*

# 1760–1769

### 1760

- Pennsylvania-born painter Benjamin West traveled to Italy to study art
- The new English king, George III, ruled over a colonial population of 1.6 million people
- Josiah Wedgwood founded his English pottery works factory
- The commercial production of pencils was started by German cabinetmaker Konrad Faber
- Benjamin Franklin published *The Interest of Great Britain Considered with Regard to Her Colonies,* which advocated that England treat the colonies as vital and equal partners
- John Michell theorized that earthquakes were waves produced when one layer of rock rubbed against another
- Russian scientist Mikhail Lomonosov explained the formation of icebergs

### 1761

- The Society of Arts in London opened the first exhibition of agricultural machines
- The atmosphere of the planet Venus was discovered by Mikhail Lomonosov
- French astronomer Nicolas Louis de Lacaille accurately measured the distance from Earth to the moon
- Joseph Kölreuter showed how wind and insects promote pollination in plants
- The song, "Twinkle, Twinkle, Little Star" was published in France
- Nathaniel Evans wrote his poetic *Ode on the Prospect of Peace*

### 1762

- Benjamin Franklin redesigned the harmonica to make it a practical musical instrument

- Spain acquired Louisiana from France
- The St. Cecilia Music Society became active in Charleston, South Carolina
- Robert Lowth published his influential book, *A Short Introduction to English Grammar*
- John Roebuck converted cast iron into malleable iron in Stirlingshire, Scotland
- South Carolinian Christopher Gadsden defended the honor of colonial militiamen in *Observations on Two Campaigns Against the Cherokees*
- Abolitionist John Woolson appealed to all Christians to voluntarily end slavery in *Some Considerations on the Keeping of Negroes*
- William Goddard established the first printing shop in Providence and printed the first issue of the *Providence Gazette*
- Britain declared war on Spain and Naples
- Catherine II (the Great) became empress of Russia upon the murder of Peter III of Russia
- The British East India Company seized the port city of Manila, Philippines, from the Spaniards

### 1763

- The Treaty of Paris ended the Seven Years War, also known as the French and Indian War; France gave England all French territory east of the Mississippi River, except New Orleans; the Spanish gave up east and west Florida to the English in exchange for Cuba
- The Proclamation of 1763, signed by King George III of England, attempted to ease tensions with Native Americans by prohibiting any English settlement west of the Appalachian Mountains, and demanded that current settlers return east
- After the British refused to supply trade goods and ammunition, the Ottawas under Chief Pontiac destroyed western British garrisons, among them Fort Duquesne
- Patrick Henry presented the theory of a mutual compact between the governed and the ruler

- Vigilantes known as the Paxton Boys massacred a peaceful Susquehanna Indian village in Conestoga

**1764**

- Boston lawyer James Otis published *The Rights of the British Colonies Asserted and Proved*
- British Parliament passed the Sugar Act, which increased duties on imported sugar, textiles, coffee, wines and indigo, and doubled the duties on foreign goods reshipped from England to the colonies
- Parliament passed the Currency Act which prohibited American colonies from issuing their own currency
- Colonists in Massachusetts refused to use imported English goods to protest Parliament's Sugar Act and Currency Acts
- British weaver James Hargreaves invented the spinning jenny, named after his daughter
- Mozart wrote his first symphony at the age of eight

**1765**

- American colonists showed opposition to the British Quartering Act, which required the colonies to provide barracks and supplies to British troops
- Parliament passed the Stamp Act, a direct tax on newspapers, almanacs, pamphlets, broadsides, legal documents, dice, and playing cards to raise money for Britain
- The American-based Stamp Act Congress passed a "Declaration of Rights and Grievances," which claimed colonial equality with British citizens and stated that without colonial representation, Parliament could not tax colonists
- A network of secret organizations known as the Sons of Liberty formed in the colonies to intimidate the stamp agents who collected Parliament's taxes
- Organized as an auxiliary of the Sons of Liberty, the Daughters of Liberty was the first society of working women
- The potato was the most popular European foodstuff

**1766**

- The Stamp Act was repealed and the colonies abandoned their ban on imported British goods

- The Declaratory Act, passed by Parliament on the same day the Stamp Act was repealed, stated that Parliament could make laws binding the American colonies "in all cases whatsoever"
- When the New York Assembly refused to assist in quartering troops, Parliament threatened to suspend the Assembly's powers
- Surveyors Charles Mason and Jeremiah Dixon established the boundary line between Maryland and Pennsylvania that would be used to separate the country's free and slave regions
- *On Factitious Airs* by English chemist Henry Cavendish announced the discovery of hydrogen, which he termed "inflammable air"
- Backwoods minister Charles Woodmason wrote *The Carolina Backcountry on the Eve of the Revolution: The Journal and Other Writings of Charles Woodmason, Anglican Itinerant,* which depicted the Carolina backcountry as an impoverished, disease-ridden land filled with crude, lazy men and women bordering on barbarism

## 1767

- Daniel Boone traveled to the Kentucky territory through the Cumberland Gap
- The British Parliament passed the Townshend Acts, which taxed glass, lead, paint and paper
- John Dickinson's 12 *Letters from a Farmer in Pennsylvania,* published in the *Pennsylvania Chronicle,* urged his fellow countrymen to oppose arbitrary taxation by legal petition, boycott or armed resistance
- The New York Assembly was suspended for refusing to quarter British troops

## 1768

- Samuel Adams wrote the Massachusetts Circular Letter that attacked Parliament's taxation policies
- In response to the Massachusetts Circular Letter, the British governor of Massachusetts dissolved the state's legislature
- British troops arrived in Boston
- Treaties with the Iroquois and Creek Indians extended the western frontier
- The *Encyclopedia Britannica* began publication as a weekly edition
- New York Chamber of Commerce was established

## 1769

- The Virginia House of Burgesses passed resolutions that allowed only Virginia's governor and legislature to tax the colony's citizens
- Father Junipero Serra founded the Mission at San Diego to begin the colonization of California
- Colonial merchants began a non-importation movement of British goods
- James Watt was granted a patent for his separate condenser steam engine
- John Robison showed that the repulsion between two charged bodies is inversely proportional to the distance between the two bodies
- Englishman Richard Arkwright received a patent for the hydraulic, or water-frame, spinning machine, instrumental to the creation of centralized factories

# 1770–1774

## 1770

- In response to the colonial boycott of imported British goods, Parliament withdrew all of the Townshend Act taxes except for the tax on tea

- A riot erupted between citizens and soldiers in New York over the Quartering Act, which required the colonies to provide barracks and supplies to British troops
- British troops in Boston opened fire on an unfriendly crowd of colonists, killing three and fatally wounding two more
- Robert Munford published his satirical play "The Candidates; or, The Humours of A Virginia Election," concerning the conducting of elections
- The newspaper *The Massachusetts Spy* began publication
- Thomas Jefferson designed and built his first house at Monticello
- Visiting cards were introduced in England

## 1771

- North Carolina passed the "Bloody Act" resulting in a skirmish between British and colonial soldiers on the western frontier
- *The Letters of Freeman* by Charlestonian William Henry Drayton defended British authority in America
- Spain ceded the Falkland Islands to England
- The first bound edition of the *Encyclopaedia Britannica* was published in three volumes

- Italian physician Luigi Galvani discovered the electrical nature of nervous impulse in animals

**1772**

- The Boston Assembly demanded the rights of the colonies and threatened secession
- Samuel Adams formed the Committees of Correspondence of Massachusetts to communicate its concerns to the other colonies and call for action against England
- Of the 3,500 physicians practicing in the colonies, only 400 were medical doctors by formal training and degree
- The London firm of Flight and Kelly produced the first barrel organ
- World explorer James Cook left England on his second voyage
- George Frederic Handel's *Messiah* was first performed in Germany

**1773**

- To save the nearly bankrupt East India Company, Parliament passed the Tea Act which gave the British East India Company a virtual monopoly on the importation of tea in America, resulting in a colonial boycott of tea
- About 8,000 Bostonians heard Samuel Adams announce that Royal Governor Hutchinson would not allow ships out of the harbor until the tea taxes were paid
- That night, the Boston Tea Party occurred as colonial activists, disguised as Mohawk Indians, dumped all 342 containers of tea into the harbor
- William Bartram began his travels throughout the Southeast which he later chronicled in his book *Travels*
- America's first female black poet, Phillis Wheatley, published *Poems on Various Subjects, Religious and Moral*
- The Philadelphia Museum was founded
- The waltz became fashionable in Vienna

**1774**

- In response to the Boston Tea Party, Parliament closed Boston Harbor, banning the loading or unloading of any ships
- Parliament offered protection to royal officials in Massachusetts, allowing them to transfer to England all court cases against them involving riot suppression or revenue collection
- Fifty-one women in Edenton, North Carolina, publicly pledged to no longer drink tea or wear English manufactured clothing
- Parliament broadened its previous Quartering Act to include the quartering of British troops in any occupied dwelling
- Twelve of the 13 colonies sent delegates to the First Continental Congress, formed to enforce a ban on using English goods
- Concerned about an uprising, British troops fortified Boston and seized ammunition belonging to the colony of Massachusetts
- Groups of colonial militia, known as Minute Men, were organized to be ready for instant action
- British Quaker and writer Thomas Paine emigrated to America

# Currency, War & the Economy

Hard currency, or the lack of it, continued to be a primary issue for individuals in the American colonies. The limited supply impacted commerce and created hardships on many. That is why several colonial legislatures continued to issue bills of credit to resolve this problem, especially during times of war. When military conflicts developed, colonial governments lacked the gold or silver in their treasuries to pay for necessary expenditures such as food, munitions and soldiers' pay. It became more of a necessity to meet the obligations and fulfill any outstanding ones. Bills of credit tended to be the most effective method.

During the French and Indian War (1755-1763), the colonies of New York and Pennsylvania had a sizable number of bills of credit in circulation. The total bills in circulation exceeded 250% compared to the number in circulation prior to the war. The expanded circulation, with British funds flowing in to finance the war, caused Benjamin Franklin to write in 1756:

*New York is growing immensely rich, by Money brought into it from all Quarters for the Pay and Subsistence of the Troops.*

The expanded circulation of paper currency in these colonies created additional purchasing power within the population, thus stimulating imports from England for various goods. It was New York's and Pennsylvania's good fortune that Britain provided financial support during the French and Indian War. The inflow of hard currency to finance the war's effort in the colonies diminished the prospect of inflation. This was not the case for all the colonies.

Virginia was one of the last colonies to issue bills of credit, but was required to offset the cost developing from the French and Indian War. Virginia issued its bills by 1755, but agreed to exchange the bills in the treasury at face value each year. This annual exchange, coupled with increasing currency in circulation, poor tobacco crops and little hard currency in the treasury created inflation on Virginia's bills of credit. Virginia saw the exchange rate of its bills of credit with the British sterling rise over 25% between 1755 and 1764. New York and Pennsylvania saw exchange rates with the British sterling fall during the war.

Maryland's bills of credit were more unique than those of the other colonies during this period. The colony gave the holder of the paper currency a legal claim to a valuable asset. By levying a tax and investing the proceeds in England, Maryland promised to

the holders a determined sum in sterling at predetermined exchange dates. The proceeds would be drawn from the colony's balance in London and paid in full. In reality, the bills of credit were more of a promissory note than currency. Regardless, this structure was considered stable and attractive to most holders.

By the end of the French and Indian War, the British government began to observe issues with the colonial currency system. There was no standard value on which to base the notes and the exchange system was confusing to British merchants. Many English creditors and merchants supported a return to a hard currency system for currency stability reasons when colonial notes rapidly depreciated. In September of 1764, Parliament passed the Currency Act which prohibited the use of paper money as legal tender. In addition, the act required existing bills of credit to retire in a prescribed timetable.

Passage of the Act enraged the American colonists because it entirely eliminated the colonial bills of credit, thus impacting the availability of currency for trade and creating severe monetary problems. Many in the colonies would have preferred to have a system that regulated the colonial bills instead of the return of a hard currency system. The Currency Act severely limited trade, thereby causing a trade deficit with Great Britain. Historians noted that the effects of this act reminded colonists that the economy of the colonies was subordinate to the economic well-being of Britain.

The return to hard currency proved difficult for traders, especially when little of it existed and its value fluctuated due to demand. To contend with this currency issue, it was not uncommon for a colony's merchants to meet and agree upon the value of various grades of hard currency present in the market. These meetings typically contradicted the laws enacted by Parliament in London, but also violated statutes set by colonial legislatures. Interestingly enough, there were usually no ramifications on the colonial merchants for setting these values, as many of the judges and legislatures of the day were their peers. By the late 1760s, hard currency exchange rates were published in almanacs after merchant discussions in New York's Chamber of Commerce.

From 1764 to 1775, Britain continued to legislate a number of acts affecting the colonies that impacted commerce. The Sugar Act, the Stamp Act and the Townsend Act all were vehicles for Britain to control the colonial economy and repay debts incurred during the recent wars. The passage of these acts further incensed the colonial population. The parliamentary restrictions increased the fears that England was conspiring to impact the American colonies' economic liberties. Many merchants initially saw this issue with the passage of the Sugar Act.

The Sugar Act contained a number of trade requirements that made colonial commerce complicated, difficult and costly. It increased Britain's efforts to enforce the tax of British West Indian molasses while prohibiting trade with foreign countries and their colonies, most notably the French West Indies. Besides molasses, the Act placed restrictions on lumber and other commodities from the American colonies. This reduced the number of markets that the American colonists could sell. The increased cost and restrictions made trade less profitable and threatened to impact trade negatively for the American colonies.

The diminishing prospects of economic prosperity, in tandem with infringement of other liberties the colonists developed, helped spark discussions of revolution within the population. Most of the colonial conflict centered on who was responsible for determining the long-term economic future of the colonies and the prospect of foreign trade. It wasn't until April of 1775 that the heated debate developed into a military conflict.

# SELECTED INCOMES 1750-1774

| Occupation | Data Source | Description | Price |
|---|---|---|---|
| Agent | The Journal of the Commons House of Assembly (1759) | Annual salary of the Agent in Great Britain for South Carolina, 1759 | 1081 pounds 12 shillings 11 pence |
| Attorney General | Executive Journals of the Council of Colonial Virginia, Vol. VI (1966) | Half a year's salary to the Council of Colonial Virginia's Attorney General, 1771 | 135 pounds |
| Cabinetmaker | Brock Jobe, New England Furniture: The Colonial Era (1984) | Approximate annual income earned by Lemuel Tobey for furniture making in Dartmouth, Massachusetts, 1774 | 115 pounds 6 shillings |
| Clerk | The Journal of the Commons House of Assembly (1759) | Annual salary of The Clerk of the Council of South Carolina, 1759 | 231 pounds 15 shillings 7 pence |
| Clerk | Vestry Book of Camden Parish (1767) | Payment to clerk of the vestry for six months work in Camden Parish, Virginia | 500 lbs. of Tobacco |
| Clerk | Executive Journals of the Council of Colonial Virginia, Vol. VI (1966) | Half a year's salary to the Council of Colonial Virginia's Clerk of the Council, 1771 | 75 pounds |
| Collector | Vestry Book of Camden Parish (1767) | Payment to collector for collecting 14,920 lbs of tobacco for Camden Parish, Virginia | 250 lbs. of Tobacco |
| College President | Massachusetts Colony Order (1750) | Annual income of the President of Harvard College, Reverend Edward Holyoke, 1750 | 250 pounds |
| College Professor | Massachusetts Colony Order (1753) | Annual income for the Professor of Hebrew, Reverand Judah Monis, at Harvard College, 1753 | 25 pounds |
| College Professor | Massachusetts Colony Order (1757) | Annual income for the Professor of Hebrew, Reverand Judah Monis, at Harvard College,1757 | 18 pounds |
| Commander | Statutes at Large of South Carolina, Vol. Fourth (1838) | Annual salary of the commander at Fort Johnson in South Carolina, 1758 | 200 pounds |
| Commander | The Journal of the Commons House of Assembly (1759) | Annual salary to the Commander of Fort Johnson in South Carolina, 1759 | 200 pounds |
| Commissioner for Indian affairs | Statutes at Large of South Carolina, Vol. Fourth (1838) | Annual salary to the Commissioner for Indian affars in South Carolina, 1758 | 100 pounds |
| Construction | Maud Carter Clement, History of Pittsylvania County Virginia (1929) | Constuction of two prisions in 1770, on to be 14x12 feet and the other 10 x 12 feet in Pittsylvania, Virginia, 1782 | 75 pounds |
| Governor | Statutes at Large of South Carolina, Vol. Fourth (1838) | To his Excellency the Governor for allowances to public officers in South Carolina, 1758 | 3500 pounds |
| Governor | The Journal of the Commons House of Assembly (1759) | Annual salary of His Excellency the Governor of South Carolina in 1759 | 2704 pounds 2 shillings 2 pence |
| Gunner | Statutes at Large of South Carolina, Vol. Fourth (1838) | Monthly salary of the gunner at Fort Johnson in South Carolina, 1758 | 18 pounds |
| Gunner | Statutes at Large of South Carolina, Vol. Fourth (1838) | Monthly salary of the gunner at Fort Moore in South Carolina, 1758 | 14 pounds |
| Gunner | The Journal of the Commons House of Assembly (1759) | Monthly salary to the gunner at Fort Johnson in South Carolina, 1759 | 18 pounds |

| Occupation | Data Source | Description | Price |
|---|---|---|---|
| Gunner | Executive Journals of the Council of Colonial Virginia, Vol. VI (1966) | Half a year's salary to the Gunners of the Batteries in Virginia, 1771 | 12 pounds 10 shillings |
| Lookout | Statutes at Large of South Carolina, Vol. Fourth (1838) | Monthly income for a Lookout, South Carolina, 1758 | 12 pounds |
| Military Service | General Assembly of Virginia (1758) | Pay to Lieut Thomas Green and a party of militia under his command in Halifax, as by muster rolls | 43 pounds |
| Military Service | General Assembly of Virginia (1758) | Pay to Thomas Spragin as a lieutenant and a party of militia under his command, as by muster rolls | 5 pounds 10 shillings |
| Military Service | General Assembly of Virginia (1758) | Pay to Captian Robert Wooding and a party of militia under his command as per muster rolls | 32 pounds |
| Military Service | General Assembly of Virginia (1758) | To Nathaniel Terry, the balance of his pay for attending the militia and building three forts | 29 pounds |
| Military Service | General Assembly of Virginia (1758) | To Colonel Abraham Maury for 28 days service in riding to the Forts and settling townships | 14 pounds |
| Minister | Statutes at Large of South Carolina, Vol. Fourth (1838) | Annual salary to the rector or minister of St Stephen parish, South Carolina, 1758 | 100 pounds |
| Overseer | John Duffy, The Healers, The Rise of the Medical Establishment (1976) | Annual service of an overseer at St David's Parish in Marlboro, South Carolina in 1774 | 27 pounds |
| Pastor | Vestry Book of Camden Parish (1767) | Payment to Rev Alexander Gordon of Halifax County, Virginia to preach | 16,000 lbs. of tobacco |
| Pension | Maud Carter Clement, History of Pittsylvania County Virginia (1929) | Yearly pension for the wife of Col Andrew Lewis by Virginia General Assembly in 1774 | 20 pounds |
| President | Executive Journals of the Council of Colonial Virginia, Vol. VI (1966) | Half a year's salary to the Council of Colonial Virginia's President, 1771 | 1,000 pounds |
| Quarter Gunner | Statutes at Large of South Carolina, Vol. Fourth (1838) | Monthly salary of the quarter gunner at Fort Johnson in South Carolina, 1758 | 8 pounds |
| Reader | Vestry Book of Camden Parish 1767 | Payment as a laymen reading the church service for six months at different points in Camden Parish, Virginia | 50 lbs. of Tobacco |

### Based Upon the British Currency System

| Year | Pound in 2002 US Dollars | Shilling in 2002 US Dollars | Pence in 2002 US Dollars |
|---|---|---|---|
| 1750 | $216.00 | $10.80 | $0.90 |
| 1755 | $216.00 | $10.80 | $0.90 |
| 1760 | $192.00 | $ 9.60 | $0.80 |
| 1765 | $168.00 | $ 8.40 | $0.70 |
| 1770 | $168.00 | $ 8.40 | $0.70 |
| 1774 | $144.00 | $ 7.20 | $0.60 |

*Calculations are approximate values based upon economic historical data*

| Occupation | Data Source | Description | Price |
|---|---|---|---|
| Scout Boat Commander | Statutes at Large of South Carolina, Vol. Fourth (1838) | Annual income for Scout Boat commander, South Carolina, 1758 | 300 pounds |
| Scout Boat Crewman | Statutes at Large of South Carolina, Vol. Fourth (1838) | Monthly income of Scout Boat crewman, South Carolina, 1758 | 10 pounds |
| Sexton | Vestry Book of Camden Parish 1767 | Payment to sexton for six months work in Camden Parish, Virginia | 200 lbs. of tobacco |

# SERVICES & FEES 1750-1774

| Services/Fees | Data Source | Description | Price |
|---|---|---|---|
| Ammunition | The Journal of the Commons House of Assembly (1754) | Payment to John Buckles and John Tanner for Ammunition supplied the Chickesaws when they were attacked by the French and Chactaws in South Carolina, 1754 | 426 pounds 11 shillings 3 pence |
| Beef casks | The Journal of the Commons House of Assembly (1759) | Payment to Richard Coytmore for making 33 Beef Casks for the Use of Fort Loudoun, South Carolina, 1759 | 24 pounds 15 shillings |
| Binding journals | Statutes at Large of South Carolina, Vol. Fourth (1838) | To Robert Wells, for binding journals in South Carolina, 1758 | 33 pounds 10 shillings |
| Boarding officers | Statutes at Large of South Carolina, Vol. Fourth (1838) | Fee charged by Barnard Keeman for quartering officers in South Carolina, 1758 | 22 pounds 10 shillings |
| Boarding prisoners | Statutes at Large of South Carolina, Vol. Fourth (1838) | Fee charged by Judith Postell for boarding several prisoners of war in South Carolina, 1758 | 680 pounds 17 shillings 6 pence |
| Boat & Indians | The Journal of the Commons House of Assembly (1754) | Payment to George Smith for use of Indians and the Scout Boats in South Carolina, 1754 | 78 pounds 2½ pence |
| Boat repair | The Journal of the Commons House of Assembly (1759) | Payment to Joseph Maxey for Repairs of a Boat belonging to Fort Johnson in South Carolina, 1759 | 27 pounds 19 shillings 9 pence |
| Canoe | Statutes at Large of South Carolina, Vol. Fourth (1838) | Fee charged by Ephraim Ellis for 2 canoes for the garrisons at Fort Prince George & Fort Lowdoun in the Cherokees in South Carolina, 1758 | 27 pounds |
| Chief Justice | Statutes at Large of South Carolina, Vol. Fourth (1838) | Fees to South Carolina's Chief Justice for prosecuting criminals at March and October sessions, 1758 | 208 pounds 15 shillings |
| Clerk of the Crown | Statutes at Large of South Carolina, Vol. Fourth (1838) | Fees to South Carolina's Clerk of the Crown for prosecuting criminals at March and October sessions, 1758 | 169 pounds 10 shillings |
| Cure | Statutes at Large of South Carolina, Vol. Fourth (1838) | Annuity to the negro Sampson, for discovering a cure for the bites of rattlesnakes, South Carolina, 1758 | 2 pounds 10 shillings |

### Based Upon the British Currency System

| Year | Pound in 2002 US Dollars | Shilling in 2002 US Dollars | Pence in 2002 US Dollars |
|---|---|---|---|
| 1750 | $216.00 | $10.80 | $0.90 |
| 1755 | $216.00 | $10.80 | $0.90 |
| 1760 | $192.00 | $ 9.60 | $0.80 |
| 1765 | $168.00 | $ 8.40 | $0.70 |
| 1770 | $168.00 | $ 8.40 | $0.70 |
| 1774 | $144.00 | $ 7.20 | $0.60 |

*Calculations are approximate values based upon economic historical data*

| Service/Fee | Data Source | Description | Price |
|---|---|---|---|
| Driving cattle | Statutes at Large of South Carolina, Vol. Fourth (1838) | Fee charged by Isham Clayton for driving cattle to military forces in South Carolina, 1758 | 6 pounds |
| Entertainment | The Journal of the Commons House of Assembly (1754) | Payment to Mary Russell for the entertainment of Cherokee Indians in South Carolina, 1754 | 30 pounds 17 shillings 6 pence |
| Entertainment | The Journal of the Commons House of Assembly (1754) | Payment to John Wheeler for the entertainment of Catawba Indians in South Carolina, 1754 | 7 pounds 10 shillings |
| Entertainment | The Journal of the Commons House of Assembly (1754) | Payment to John Gordon for entertaining Ensign Turner and Men employed in bringnig down Indian Prisoners taken by Virtue of the Governours Proclamation in South Carolina, 1754 | 49 pounds |
| Executions | Statutes at Large of South Carolina, Vol. Fourth (1838) | Fees to John Geissendanner, for (criminal) slaves executed in South Carolina, 1758 | 200 pounds |
| Fee | Executive Journals of the Council of Colonial Virginia, Vol. VI (1966) | Fee charged to the Account of his Majesty's Revenue for each hogshead within Virginia, 1771 | 2 shillings |
| Ferriage | The Journal of the Commons House of the Assembly (1754) | Payment to George Livingston for Ferriage and Liquor for Indians in South Carolina, 1754 | 3 pounds 8 shillings 9 pence |
| Flag Making | The Journal of the Commons House of Assembly (1759) | Payment to Jane Duthy for making Flaggs in South Carolina, 1759 | 18 pounds |
| Flag Making | The Journal of the Commons House of Assembly (1754) | Payment to Margaret Boone for making Flags for Indians in South Carolina, 1754 | 12 pounds |
| Government expense | Kitman, George Washington's Expense Account (1970) | Expenditures reported by the colony of New York for governmental operations 1774 | 5000 pounds |
| Horse Hire | The Journal of the Commons House of Assembly (1759) | Payment to Serjeant Thomas Harrision for Horse-hire at Fort Prince George in South Carolina, 1759 | 15 pounds |
| Interpreter | Statutes at Large of South Carolina, Vol. Fourth (1838) | Fee charged by William Shorey as interpreter for the garrisons at Fort Prince George & Fort Lowdoun, in the Cherokees, South Carolina, 1758 | 150 pounds |
| Medicine | Statutes at Large of South Carolina, Vol. Fourth (1838) | Fee chared by John Channing for medicines for prisoners of war in South Carolina, 1758 | 17 pounds 10 shillings |
| Medicine | The Journal of the Commons House of Assembly (1754) | Payment to Dr George Milligen for Medecines administred to sick Criminals and Indians in South Carolina, 1754 | 46 pounds 5 shillings |
| Minister | Executive Journals of the Council of Colonial Virginia, Vol. VI (1966) | Minister Attending one General Court in Virginia, 1771 | 8 pounds |
| Painter | Kitman, George Washington's Expense Account (1970) | Fee charged by Mr Peale for painting George Washington's picture, 1772 | 18 pounds 4 shillings |
| Pasturage | The Journal of the Commons House of Assembly (1754) | Payment to Hoyland and Harris for pasturage of Indian Horse in South Carolina, 1754 | 40 pounds |
| Repair | Executive Journals of the Council of Colonial Virginia, Vol. VI (1966) | Payment for services to repair the Governor's House in Virginia, 1771 | 34 pounds 9 shillings 6 pence |
| Repairs | Statutes at Large of South Carolina, Vol. Fourth (1838) | To Robert Hume, for repairs to the parsonage of St James, Goose Greek, South Carolina, 1758 | 50 pounds 4 shillings 7 pence |

| Service/Fee | Data Source | Description | Price |
| --- | --- | --- | --- |
| Reward | The Pennsylvania Gazette (1754) | Reward offered for two English servant who ran away from their master in Yorktown, Pennsylvania, 1754 | 6 pounds |
| Reward | The Pennsylvania Gazette (1762) | For a run away indentured servant from Philadelphia, Pennsylvania, 1762 | 2 pounds |
| Reward | The Pennsylvania Gazette (1762) | Reward for missing purse with over seven British Pounds in currency and notes 1762 | 15 shillings |
| Stabling | Alan D. Watson, Society In Early North Carolina (2000) | Stabling a horse 24 hours with plenty of Hay or Fodder and if of Common woods hay in Rowan County, North Carolina, 1774 | 8 pence |
| Summoning | The Journal of the Commons House of Assembly (1759) | Payment for service to Adam Wood, Provost Marshal, for serving Writts of Election, Summoning Jurors, & attending the Courts in South Carolina, 1759 | 115 pounds 17 shillings 9 pence |
| Surveying | Executive Journals of the Council of Colonial Virginia, Vol. VI (1966) | Payment to George Washington, Lieut Colonel of the first Virginia Regiment for surveying territory in Virginia, 1771 | 15,000 acres |
| Surveying | Executive Journals of the Council of Colonial Virginia, Vol. VI (1966) | Payment to a private of the first Virginia Regiment for surveying terriority in Virginia, 1771 | 400 acres |
| Tailoring | Statutes at Large of South Carolina (1754) | Payment to Andrew Taylor for making six Suits of Indian Cloaths in South Carolina, 1754 | 36 pounds |
| Tax | Tax Invoice of John Smith to Sheriff of Halifax (1756) | Tax owed per slave in the colony in Halifax, Virginia | 2 shillings |
| Transport | Statutes at Large of South Carolina, Vol. Fourth (1838) | Fee charged by Captain John Stuart for carrying of two swivel guns to Fort Loudon in South Carolina, 1758 | 40 pounds |

# FINANCIAL RATES & EXCHANGES
## 1750-1774

| Year | British Official Price of Gold (per Ounce) | Inflation Rate in Colonial America | Yield of Long-Term British Government Securities | Average Price per Pound of Maryland Tobacco (Pence) | Exchange Rate: Pennsylvania Currency for Pound Sterling |
|---|---|---|---|---|---|
| 1750 | £4.25 | 0.00% | 3.00% | 1.16 | 1.71 |
| 1751 | £4.25 | 1.19% | 3.03% | 1.16 | 1.71 |
| 1752 | £4.25 | 1.18% | 2.86% | 1.48 | 1.67 |
| 1753 | £4.25 | −2.33% | 2.86% | 1.16 | 1.68 |
| 1754 | £4.25 | −3.57% | 2.91% | 1.04 | 1.68 |
| 1755 | £4.25 | −2.47% | 3.14% | 0.85 | 1.69 |
| 1756 | £4.25 | −2.53% | 3.37% | 1.07 | 1.83 |
| 1757 | £4.25 | 5.19% | 3.39% | 1.16 | 1.66 |
| 1758 | £4.25 | 7.41% | 3.21% | 1.26 | 1.59 |
| 1759 | £4.25 | 13.79% | 3.59% | 2.05 | 1.55 |
| 1760 | £4.25 | −3.03% | 3.77% | 1.6 | 1.60 |
| 1761 | £4.25 | −8.33% | 3.90% | 1.54 | 1.74 |
| 1762 | £4.25 | 7.95% | 4.29% | 1.39 | 1.76 |
| 1763 | £4.25 | 0.00% | 3.37% | 1.1 | 1.73 |
| 1764 | £4.25 | −7.37% | 3.61% | 1.26 | 1.72 |
| 1765 | £4.25 | 1.14% | 3.41% | 1.33 | 1.72 |
| 1766 | £4.25 | 8.99% | 3.39% | 1.45 | 1.65 |
| 1767 | £4.25 | −2.06% | 3.37% | 1.63 | 1.66 |
| 1768 | £4.25 | −5.26% | 3.31% | 1.81 | 1.66 |
| 1769 | £4.25 | 3.33% | 3.47% | 2.23 | 1.58 |
| 1770 | £4.25 | 7.53% | 3.64% | 2.06 | 1.54 |
| 1771 | £4.25 | −4.00% | 3.55% | 1.9 | 1.66 |
| 1772 | £4.25 | 14.58% | 3.30% | 1.64 | 1.61 |
| 1773 | £4.25 | −7.24% | 3.47% | 1.33 | 1.66 |
| 1774 | £4.25 | −4.90% | 3.43% | 1.41 | 1.70 |

# SLAVE TRADES 1750-1774

### Average Price of British American and West African Slaves
*Price in Pounds Sterling*

| Year | Price Paid for Slave by Traders in West Africa | Price Paid for Slave by British Colonists in America | Year | Price Paid for Slave by Traders in West Africa | Price Paid for Slave by British Colonists in America |
|------|------|------|------|------|------|
| 1750 | 14.01 | 27.12 | 1763 | 15.91 | 34.74 |
| 1751 | 14.01 | 27.12 | 1764 | 15.91 | 34.74 |
| 1752 | 14.01 | 27.12 | 1765 | 15.91 | 34.74 |
| 1753 | 13.66 | 33.10 | 1766 | 15.91 | 34.74 |
| 1754 | 13.66 | 33.10 | 1767 | 15.91 | 34.74 |
| 1755 | 13.66 | 33.10 | 1768 | 17.72 | 38.39 |
| 1756 | 13.66 | 33.10 | 1769 | 17.72 | 38.39 |
| 1757 | 13.66 | 33.10 | | | |
| 1758 | 13.71 | 35.61 | 1770 | 17.72 | 38.39 |
| 1759 | 13.71 | 35.61 | 1771 | 17.72 | 38.39 |
| | | | 1772 | 17.72 | 38.39 |
| 1760 | 13.71 | 35.61 | 1773 | 14.04 | 44.08 |
| 1761 | 13.71 | 35.61 | 1774 | 14.04 | 44.08 |
| 1762 | 13.71 | 35.61 | | | |

### Based Upon the British Currency System

| Year | Pound in 2002 US Dollars | Shilling in 2002 US Dollars | Pence in 2002 US Dollars |
|------|------|------|------|
| 1750 | $216.00 | $10.80 | $0.90 |
| 1755 | $216.00 | $10.80 | $0.90 |
| 1760 | $192.00 | $ 9.60 | $0.80 |
| 1765 | $168.00 | $ 8.40 | $0.70 |
| 1770 | $168.00 | $ 8.40 | $0.70 |
| 1774 | $144.00 | $ 7.20 | $0.60 |

*Calculations are approximate values based upon economic historical data*

# COMMODITIES 1750-1774

| Commodity | Year | Philadelphia | Year | Philadelphia |
|---|---|---|---|---|
| Beef, per barrel | 1750 | 4.67 | 1763 | 8.00 |
| | 1751 | 6.51 | 1764 | 8.00 |
| | 1752 | 7.67 | 1765 | 8.67 |
| | 1753 | 6.27 | 1766 | 7.33 |
| | 1754 | 6.25 | 1767 | 7.43 |
| | 1755 | 6.00 | 1768 | 6.67 |
| | 1756 | 7.33 | 1769 | 7.41 |
| | 1757 | 5.67 | 1770 | 6.67 |
| | 1758 | 6.67 | 1771 | 6.77 |
| | 1759 | 6.43 | 1772 | 7.56 |
| | 1760 | 7.56 | 1773 | 7.33 |
| | 1761 | 8.00 | 1774 | 6.67 |
| | 1762 | 7.33 | | |
| Bread, per hundredweight | 1750 | 3.07 | 1763 | 4.00 |
| | 1751 | 3.07 | 1764 | 2.67 |
| | 1752 | 2.92 | 1765 | 3.73 |
| | 1753 | 2.76 | 1766 | 2.93 |
| | 1754 | 2.87 | 1767 | 3.73 |
| | 1755 | 2.67 | 1768 | 3.60 |
| | 1756 | 2.80 | 1769 | 2.67 |
| | 1757 | 2.80 | 1770 | 3.77 |
| | 1758 | 2.93 | 1771 | 3.73 |
| | 1759 | 2.83 | 1772 | 3.93 |
| | 1760 | 3.20 | 1773 | 4.09 |
| | 1761 | 3.33 | 1774 | 4.27 |
| | 1762 | 3.64 | | |
| Corn, per bushel | 1750 | 0.32 | 1763 | 0.51 |
| | 1751 | 0.39 | 1764 | 0.33 |
| | 1752 | 0.33 | 1765 | 0.38 |
| | 1753 | 0.38 | 1766 | 0.47 |
| | 1754 | 0.32 | 1767 | 0.40 |
| | 1755 | 0.27 | 1768 | 0.33 |
| | 1756 | 0.37 | 1769 | 0.38 |
| | 1757 | 0.20 | 1770 | 0.46 |
| | 1758 | 0.22 | 1771 | 0.44 |
| | 1759 | 0.42 | 1772 | 0.53 |
| | 1760 | 0.39 | 1773 | 0.41 |
| | 1761 | 0.30 | 1774 | 0.36 |
| | 1762 | 0.47 | | |

Values are expressed in Silver Dollars, the most common currency in the colony for trade

| Commodity | Year | Philadelphia | Year | Philadelphia |
|---|---|---|---|---|
| Cotton, per pound | 1750 | 0.27 | 1762 | 0.29 |
| | 1751 | 0.30 | 1763 | 0.20 |
| | 1752 | 0.27 | 1764 | 0.29 |
| | 1753 | 0.20 | 1767 | 0.28 |
| | 1754 | 0.22 | 1768 | 0.23 |
| | 1755 | 0.21 | 1769 | 0.18 |
| | 1756 | 0.20 | 1770 | 0.18 |
| | 1757 | 0.22 | 1771 | 0.19 |
| | 1758 | 0.17 | 1772 | 0.18 |
| | 1759 | 0.21 | 1773 | 0.20 |
| | 1760 | 0.17 | 1774 | 0.18 |
| | 1761 | 0.18 | | |
| Flour, per hundredweight | 1750 | 1.49 | 1763 | 2.47 |
| | 1751 | 1.51 | 1764 | 1.47 |
| | 1752 | 1.71 | 1765 | 1.68 |
| | 1753 | 1.62 | 1766 | 1.90 |
| | 1754 | 1.87 | 1767 | 2.22 |
| | 1755 | 1.70 | 1768 | 2.35 |
| | 1756 | 1.67 | 1769 | 1.92 |
| | 1757 | 1.43 | 1770 | 1.97 |
| | 1758 | 1.60 | 1771 | 2.34 |
| | 1759 | 1.83 | 1772 | 2.66 |
| | 1760 | 1.88 | 1773 | 2.45 |
| | 1761 | 1.90 | 1774 | 2.47 |
| | 1762 | 1.97 | | |

Values are expressed in Silver Dollars, the most common currency in the colony for trade

| Commodity | Year | Philadelphia | Year | Philadelphia |
|---|---|---|---|---|
| Indigo, per pound | 1750 | 1.00 | 1757 | 1.32 |
| | 1751 | 1.03 | 1758 | 1.33 |
| | 1752 | 1.87 | 1759 | 1.10 |
| | 1753 | 1.47 | 1760 | 1.07 |
| | 1754 | 1.53 | 1761 | 0.93 |
| | 1755 | 1.60 | 1762 | 1.03 |
| | 1756 | 1.57 | 1763 | 1.07 |
| | | | | |
| Iron - Bar, per ton | 1750 | 72.00 | 1763 | 77.33 |
| | 1751 | 66.67 | 1764 | 66.67 |
| | 1753 | 64.00 | 1765 | 69.33 |
| | 1754 | 61.33 | 1766 | 66.67 |
| | 1755 | 60.00 | 1767 | 64.00 |
| | 1756 | 58.40 | 1768 | 64.00 |
| | 1757 | 60.00 | 1769 | 64.00 |
| | 1758 | 61.33 | 1770 | 61.33 |
| | 1759 | 72.00 | 1771 | 64.00 |
| | 1760 | 85.33 | 1772 | 70.67 |
| | 1761 | 90.67 | 1773 | 69.33 |
| | 1762 | 90.67 | 1774 | 69.33 |
| | | | | |
| Molasses, per gallon | 1750 | 0.20 | 1763 | 0.28 |
| | 1751 | 0.24 | 1764 | 0.21 |
| | 1752 | 0.27 | 1765 | 0.21 |
| | 1753 | 0.27 | 1766 | 0.29 |
| | 1754 | 0.27 | 1767 | 0.21 |
| | 1755 | 0.26 | 1768 | 0.25 |
| | 1756 | 0.26 | 1769 | 0.22 |
| | 1757 | 0.31 | 1770 | 0.26 |
| | 1758 | 0.31 | 1771 | 0.24 |
| | 1759 | 0.38 | 1772 | 0.23 |
| | 1760 | 0.44 | 1773 | 0.23 |
| | 1761 | 0.31 | 1774 | 0.24 |
| | 1762 | 0.31 | | |
| | | | | |
| Pork, per barrel | 1750 | 8.67 | 1760 | 9.24 |
| | 1751 | 9.23 | 1761 | 9.67 |
| | 1752 | 9.89 | 1762 | 12.67 |
| | 1753 | 8.23 | 1763 | 11.60 |
| | 1754 | 7.67 | 1764 | 13.33 |
| | 1755 | 10.00 | 1765 | 8.67 |
| | 1756 | 8.33 | 1766 | 9.67 |
| | 1757 | 8.00 | 1767 | 10.09 |
| | 1758 | 7.00 | 1768 | 9.27 |
| | 1759 | 8.87 | 1769 | 10.00 |

Values are expressed in Silver Dollars, the most common currency in the colony for trade

| Commodity | Year | Philadelphia | Year | Philadelphia |
|---|---|---|---|---|
| | 1770 | 10.67 | 1773 | 12.07 |
| | 1771 | 10.67 | 1774 | 11.33 |
| | 1772 | 12.52 | | |
| Rice, per hundredweight | 1750 | 2.67 | 1763 | 1.87 |
| | 1751 | 2.13 | 1764 | 1.87 |
| | 1752 | 1.87 | 1765 | 1.87 |
| | 1753 | 3.67 | 1766 | 2.33 |
| | 1754 | 1.96 | 1767 | 2.28 |
| | 1755 | 2.27 | 1768 | 2.40 |
| | 1756 | 1.97 | 1769 | 2.40 |
| | 1757 | 2.00 | 1770 | 2.20 |
| | 1758 | 1.80 | 1771 | 2.00 |
| | 1759 | 2.67 | 1772 | 3.33 |
| | 1760 | 2.67 | 1773 | 2.40 |
| | 1761 | 2.07 | 1774 | 2.27 |
| | 1762 | 1.87 | | |
| Rum, per gallon | 1750 | 0.31 | 1763 | 0.38 |
| | 1751 | 0.32 | 1764 | 0.28 |
| | 1752 | 0.32 | 1765 | 0.27 |
| | 1753 | 0.33 | 1766 | 0.32 |
| | 1754 | 0.33 | 1767 | 0.27 |
| | 1755 | 0.32 | 1768 | 0.29 |
| | 1756 | 0.30 | 1769 | 0.28 |
| | 1757 | 0.38 | 1770 | 0.31 |
| | 1758 | 0.40 | 1771 | 0.29 |
| | 1759 | 0.47 | 1772 | 0.28 |
| | 1760 | 0.51 | 1773 | 0.29 |
| | 1761 | 0.41 | 1774 | 0.29 |
| | 1762 | 0.37 | | |
| Salt, per bushel | 1750 | 0.20 | 1763 | 0.20 |
| | 1751 | 0.17 | 1764 | 0.27 |
| | 1752 | 0.16 | 1765 | 0.18 |
| | 1753 | 0.27 | 1766 | 0.18 |
| | 1754 | 0.22 | 1767 | 0.20 |
| | 1755 | 0.18 | 1768 | 0.20 |
| | 1756 | 0.24 | 1769 | 0.20 |
| | 1757 | 0.31 | 1770 | 0.24 |
| | 1758 | 0.31 | 1771 | 0.22 |
| | 1759 | 0.32 | 1772 | 0.20 |
| | 1760 | 0.37 | 1773 | 0.21 |
| | 1761 | 0.40 | 1774 | 0.27 |
| | 1762 | 0.33 | | |

Values are expressed in Silver Dollars, the most common currency in the colony for trade

| Commodity | Year | Philadelphia | Year | Philadelphia |
|-----------|------|--------------|------|--------------|
| Staves, per 1200 units | 1750 | 13.33 | 1762 | 24.00 |
| | 1751 | 12.08 | 1763 | 14.67 |
| | 1752 | 10.13 | 1764 | 16.00 |
| | 1753 | 11.68 | 1765 | 13.33 |
| | 1754 | 11.60 | 1766 | 16.00 |
| | 1755 | 12.35 | 1767 | 19.33 |
| | 1756 | 9.81 | 1768 | 13.33 |
| | 1757 | 9.01 | 1769 | 12.67 |
| | 1758 | 14.67 | 1770 | 15.33 |
| | 1759 | 12.83 | 1771 | 16.45 |
| | 1760 | 13.55 | 1772 | 17.33 |
| | 1761 | 20.00 | 1773 | 15.20 |
| 1774     16.00 | 1750 | 6.67 | 1757 | 6.33 |
| | 1751 | 6.00 | 1758 | 6.51 |
| Sugar, per hundredweight | 1752 | 6.16 | 1759 | 6.00 |
| | 1753 | 6.76 | 1760 | 6.67 |
| | 1754 | 7.08 | 1761 | 6.00 |
| | 1755 | 6.67 | 1762 | 6.83 |
| | 1756 | 6.67 | 1763 | 7.33 |

Values are expressed in Silver Dollars, the most common currency in the colony for trade

| Commodity | Year | Philadelphia | Year | Philadelphia |
|-----------|------|--------------|------|--------------|
| | 1764 | 6.67 | 1770 | 7.17 |
| | 1765 | 6.33 | 1771 | 6.33 |
| | 1766 | 6.67 | 1772 | 6.69 |
| | 1767 | 6.80 | 1773 | 6.51 |
| | 1768 | 6.19 | 1774 | 7.33 |
| | 1769 | 7.17 | | |
| Tea, per pound | 1752 | 0.68 | 1764 | 0.90 |
| | 1753 | 0.72 | 1765 | 0.93 |
| | 1754 | 0.67 | 1766 | 0.83 |
| | 1755 | 0.70 | 1767 | 0.72 |
| | 1756 | 0.60 | 1768 | 0.58 |
| | 1757 | 0.87 | 1769 | 0.46 |
| | 1758 | 0.91 | 1770 | 1.00 |
| | 1759 | 1.00 | 1771 | 0.70 |
| | 1760 | 0.78 | 1772 | 0.53 |
| | 1761 | 0.73 | 1773 | 0.53 |
| | 1762 | 1.07 | 1774 | 0.73 |
| | 1763 | 0.84 | | |
| Tobacco, per hundredweight | 1750 | 2.40 | 1762 | 2.83 |
| | 1751 | 2.53 | 1763 | 2.67 |
| | 1752 | 2.65 | 1764 | 2.33 |
| | 1753 | 2.56 | 1765 | 2.33 |
| | 1754 | 2.59 | 1766 | 2.67 |
| | 1755 | 2.00 | 1767 | 2.97 |
| | 1756 | 1.96 | 1768 | 3.00 |
| | 1757 | 2.33 | 1769 | 3.00 |
| | 1758 | 2.47 | 1770 | 4.16 |
| | 1759 | 2.83 | 1771 | 4.33 |
| | 1760 | 3.33 | 1772 | 4.33 |
| | 1761 | 2.33 | | |
| Wheat, per bushel | 1750 | 0.54 | 1763 | 0.90 |
| | 1751 | 0.53 | 1764 | 0.57 |
| | 1752 | 0.57 | 1765 | 0.63 |
| | 1753 | 0.59 | 1766 | 0.83 |
| | 1754 | 0.61 | 1767 | 0.82 |
| | 1755 | 0.59 | 1768 | 0.95 |
| | 1756 | 0.64 | 1769 | 0.70 |
| | 1757 | 0.53 | 1770 | 0.76 |
| | 1758 | 0.53 | 1771 | 0.93 |
| | 1759 | 0.64 | 1772 | 1.05 |
| | 1760 | 0.64 | 1773 | 1.02 |
| | 1761 | 0.62 | 1774 | 1.03 |
| | 1762 | 0.70 | | |

Values are expressed in Silver Dollars, the most common currency in the colony for trade

| Commodity | Year | Philadelphia | Year | Philadelphia |
|---|---|---|---|---|
| Wine, per pipe | 1750 | 80.00 | 1763 | 146.67 |
| | 1751 | 82.13 | 1764 | 106.67 |
| | 1752 | 82.13 | 1765 | 120.00 |
| | 1753 | 82.67 | 1766 | 133.33 |
| | 1754 | 82.67 | 1767 | 133.33 |
| | 1755 | 66.67 | 1768 | 133.33 |
| | 1756 | 82.67 | 1769 | 133.33 |
| | 1757 | 104.00 | 1770 | 133.33 |
| | 1758 | 106.67 | 1771 | 133.33 |
| | 1759 | 118.40 | 1772 | 133.33 |
| | 1760 | 128.80 | 1773 | 146.67 |
| | 1761 | 122.67 | 1774 | 166.67 |
| | 1762 | 133.33 | | |

Values are expressed in Silver Dollars, the most common currency in the colony for trade

# SELECTED PRICES 1750-1774

| Item | Data Source | Description | Price |
|---|---|---|---|
| **Alcohol** | | | |
| Ale | Inventory of John Fendall (1763) | Gallon of ale in Charles County, Maryland, 1763 | 4 shillings |
| Ale | Inventory of John Fendall (1763) | Bottle port ale in Charles County, Maryland, 1763 | 8 pence |
| Bottle | Inventory of Thomas Lewis (1750) | Quart bottle in Fairfax County, Virginia, 1750 | 3 pence |
| Brandy | Inventory of William Eilbeck (1765) | Gallon Brandy in Charles County, Maryland, 1765 | 2 shillings 6 pence |
| Cask | Inventory of Thomas Lewis (1750) | Cyder cask in Fairfax County, Virginia, 1750 | 5 shillings |
| Cider | Inventory of Joseph Galloway (1753) | Gallon Cyder in Anne Arundel County, Maryland, 1753 | 4 pence |
| Cider | Inventory of Thomas Lewis (1750) | Gallon of Cyder in Fairfax County, Virginia, 1750 | 4 pence |
| Cider | Alan D. Watson, Society In Early North Carolina (2000) | Quart of Cyder Royal in Rowan County, North Carolina, 1774 | 1 shilling 4 pence |
| Hops | Inventory of Daniel Dulany (1754) | One pound of hops in Annapolis, Maryland, 1754 | 8 pence |
| Port | Inventory of Daniel Dulany (1754) | Bottle old Bad Port in Annapolis, Maryland, 1754 | 15 shillings 7½ pence |
| Rum | Inventory of William Air (1754) | Gallon of Jamaica Rum in Beaufort County, South Carolina, 1754 | 20 shillings |
| Rum | Inventory of William Air (1754) | Gallon of Barbadoes Rum in Beaufort County, South Carolina, 1754 | 15 shillings |
| Rum | Inventory of William Shepard (1756) | Gallon of New England Rum in Charles Town, South Carolina, 1756 | 11 shillings |
| Rum | Inventory of John Fendall (1763) | Gallon of West India Rum in Charles County, Maryland, 1763 | 3 shillings 6 pence |
| Rum | Alan D. Watson, Society In Early North Carolina (2000) | Gallon of West India Rum sold in a tavern in Rowan County, North Carolina, 1774 | 16 shillings |
| Spirits | Inventory of Daniel Dulany (1754) | Half gallon bottle of Cane Spirits in Annapolis, Maryland, 1754 | 4 shillings 4 pence |

## Based Upon the British Currency System

| Year | Pound in 2002 US Dollars | Shilling in 2002 US Dollars | Pence in 2002 US Dollars |
|---|---|---|---|
| 1750 | $216.00 | $10.80 | $0.90 |
| 1755 | $216.00 | $10.80 | $0.90 |
| 1760 | $192.00 | $ 9.60 | $0.80 |
| 1765 | $168.00 | $ 8.40 | $0.70 |
| 1770 | $168.00 | $ 8.40 | $0.70 |
| 1774 | $144.00 | $ 7.20 | $0.60 |

*Calculations are approximate values based upon economic historical data*

| Item | Data Source | Description | Price |
|------|-------------|-------------|-------|
| Spirits | Inventory of John Fendall (1763) | Gallon of Spirits in Charles County, Maryland, 1763 | 5 shillings |
| Spirits | Inventory of John Brice (1767) | Quart of Cane Sperits in Ann Arundel, Maryland, 1767 | 2 shillings |
| Spirits | Inventory of Doctor Adam Thomson (1768) | One gallon of spirits in Prince George, Maryland, 1768 | 4 shillings |
| Still | Inventory of William Eilbeck (1765) | One Still & Worm about 40 Gallons in Charles County, Maryland, 1765 | 15 pounds |
| Whiskey | Alan D. Watson, Society In Early North Carolina (2000) | Gallon of whiskey sold in a tavern in Rowan County, North Carolina, 1774 | 10 shillings |
| Wine | Inventory of John Fendall (1763) | Bottle port wine in Charles County, Maryland, 1763 | 2 shillings |
| Wine | Inventory of John Fendall (1763) | Gallon white Wine in Charles County, Maryland, 1763 | 4 shillings 4 pence |
| Wine | Inventory of John Brice (1767) | Quart of sweet wine in Ann Arundel, Maryland, 1767 | 2 shillings 6 pence |
| Wine | Inventory of Doctor Adam Thomson (1768) | One bottle of Maderia Wine in Prince George, Maryland, 1768 | 1 shilling 9 pence |
| Wine | Alan D. Watson, Society In Early North Carolina (2000) | Gallon of Maderia wine sold in a tavern in Rowan County, North Carolina, 1774 | 16 shillings |

## Apparel - Children

| Item | Data Source | Description | Price |
|------|-------------|-------------|-------|
| Hat | Inventory of Daniel Dulany (1754) | Boys Castor Hatt in Annapolis, Maryland, 1754 | 1 shilling 6 pence |
| Mitts | Inventory of John Fendall (1763) | Pair of Boys worsted Mitts in Charles County, Maryland, 1763 | 10 pence |
| Shoes | Inventory of Samuel Kennastons (1754) | Pair of Children Lear Shoes in Charles Town, South Carolina, 1754 | 9 pence |
| Stockings | Inventory of Charles Pury (1756) | Pair of boys Knit worsted Stockings in the Town of Beaufort, South Carolina, 1756 | 18 shillings 7 pence |
| Stockings | Inventory of Charles Pury (1756) | Pair of Boys Thread Stockings in the Town of Beaufort, South Carolina, 1756 | 10 shillings 10 pence |

## Apparel - Men

| Item | Data Source | Description | Price |
|------|-------------|-------------|-------|
| Belt | Inventory of Thomas Lewis (1750) | Leather belt in Fairfax County, Virginia, 1750 | 1 shilling 3 pence |
| Bind | Inventory of Samuel Kennastons (1754) | Piece of stripped Cotton Binding in Charles Town, South Carolina, 1754 | 10 pence |
| Boots | Inventory of Thomas Lewis (1750) | Pair of old Boots in Fairfax County, Virginia, 1750 | 3 shillings |
| Boots | Inventory of Charles Pury (1756) | Pair of boots in the Town of Beaufort, South Carolina, 1756 | 3 pounds 10 shillings |
| Boots | Inventory of John Fendall (1763) | Pair Jockey Boots in Charles County, Maryland, 1763 | 1 pound 15 shillings |
| Breeches | Inventory of Thomas Lewis (1750) | Pair of black Cotton Plush Breeches in Fairfax County, Virginia, 1750 | 1 pound |
| Breeches | Inventory of Thomas Lewis (1750) | Pair of Cloath Breeches in Fairfax County, Virginia, 1750 | 10 shillings |
| Breeches | Inventory of Samuel Kennastons (1754) | Pair of Breeches in Charles Town, South Carolina, 1754 | 3 pounds 14 shillings |
| Buckles | Inventory of Samuel Kennastons (1754) | Pair of Silver shoe Buckles Bristol Stones in Charles Town, South Carolina, 1754 | 9 shillings 8 pence |
| Buckles | Inventory of Samuel Kennastons (1754) | Pair of silver shoe & knee Buckles in Charles Town, South Carolina, 1754 | 5 pounds |
| Buckles | Inventory of Jeremiah Chase (1755) | One pair Bristol Stone shoe Buckles in Charles County, Maryland, 1755 | 3 pounds 5 shillings |

| Item | Data Source | Description | Price |
|------|-------------|-------------|-------|
| Buttons | Inventory of Joseph Fox (1756) | Pair of gold sleeve buttons in Charles Town, South Carolina, 1756 | 9 pounds |
| Cap | Inventory of Thomas Lewis (1750) | Linen cap in Fairfax County, Virginia, 1750 | 8 pence |
| Cap | Inventory of Samuel Kennastons (1754) | Worsted Cap in Charles Town, South Carolina, 1754 | 4 pence |
| Cap | Inventory of Charles Pury (1756) | Velvet Cap in the Town of Beaufort, South Carolina, 1756 | 1 pound 10 shillings |
| Cap | Inventory of John Brice (1767) | Velvet cap in Ann Arundel, Maryland, 1767 | 2 shillings 6 pence |
| Cloak | Inventory of Daniel Dulany (1754) | Scarlet Duffle Cloak in Annapolis, Maryland, 1754 | 19 shillings 4 pence |
| Clogs | Inventory of Daniel Dulany (1754) | Pair Toed Clogs in Annapolis, Maryland, 1754 | 8 shillings |
| Coat | Inventory of Thomas Lewis (1750) | Linnen Coat in Fairfax County, Virginia, 1750 | 18 shillings |
| Coat | Inventory of Thomas Lewis (1750) | Lindsey woolsey Coat in Fairfax County, Virginia, 1750 | 1 pound 5 shillings |
| Coat | Inventory of Charles Pury (1756) | Mens great Coat in the Town of Beaufort, South Carolina,1756 | 3 pounds |
| Coat | Inventory of Samuel Kennastons (1754) | Great Coat in Charles Town, South Carolina, 1754 | 2 pounds |
| Gloves | Account Invoice of S. Ames (1764) | Pair of gloves purchased by a Harvard student, 1764 | 2 shillings |
| Handkerchief | Inventory of Daniel Dulany (1754) | Silk handkerchief in Annapolis, Maryland, 1754 | 4 shillings 6 pence |
| Hat | Inventory of Leroy Griffin (1750) | Fine hatt in Richmond County, Virginia, 1750 | 15 shillings |
| Hat | Inventory of Daniel Dulany (1754) | Mens Felts Hatt in Annapolis, Maryland, 1754 | 1 shilling 6 pence |
| Hat | Inventory of S. Hall (1757) | Beaver hat inventoried by a student at Harvard, 1757 | 12 shillings |
| Hat | Inventory of John Fendall (1763) | Mens Castor Hatt sold in Charles County, Maryland, 1763 | 15 shillings |
| Hat girdle | Inventory of Sam. Barrnard (1764) | Hat Girdle & Buckle inventoried by a Harvard student, 1764 | 3 shillings 4 pence |
| Hose | Unknown Harvard Student Account (approx. 1760) | Pair of Worsted Hose in Cambridge, Massachusetts, 1760 | 6 shillings |

## Based Upon the British Currency System

| Year | Pound in 2002 US Dollars | Shilling in 2002 US Dollars | Pence in 2002 US Dollars |
|------|--------------------------|-----------------------------|--------------------------|
| 1750 | $216.00 | $10.80 | $0.90 |
| 1755 | $216.00 | $10.80 | $0.90 |
| 1760 | $192.00 | $ 9.60 | $0.80 |
| 1765 | $168.00 | $ 8.40 | $0.70 |
| 1770 | $168.00 | $ 8.40 | $0.70 |
| 1774 | $144.00 | $ 7.20 | $0.60 |

*Calculations are approximate values based upon economic historical data*

| Item | Data Source | Description | Price |
|---|---|---|---|
| Hose | Inventory of John Brice (1767) | Pair of worsted hose in Ann Arundel, Maryland, 1767 | 2 shillings 4 pence |
| Jacket | Inventory of Samuel Kennastons (1754) | Jacket in Charles Town, South Carolina, 1754 | 2 pounds 4 shillings |
| Jacket | Inventory of S. Hall (1757) | Men's jacket inventoried by a student at Harvard in 1757 | 10 shillings |
| Jacket | Inventory of Sam. Barrnard (1764) | A Snuff colour'd Jacket inventoried by a Harvard student, 1764 | 12 shillings |
| Mitts | Inventory of John Fendall (1763) | Pair of Mens worsted Mitts in Charles County, Maryland, 1763 | 1 shilling |
| Neck buckle | Inventory of Joseph Fox (1756) | Silver neck buckle in Charles Town, South Carolina, 1756 | 2 pounds |
| Neckcloth | Inventory of Sam. Barrnard (1764) | Black Neckcloth inventoried by a Harvard Student, 1764 | 5 shillings |
| Shirt | Inventory of Thomas Lewis (1750) | Holld Shirt in Fairfax County, Virginia, 1750 | 1 pound |
| Shirt | Inventory of Thomas Lewis (1750) | White shirt in Fairfax County, Virginia, 1750 | 8 shillings |
| Shirt | Inventory of Samuel Kennastons (1754) | Shirt in Charles Town, South Carolina, 1754 | 1 pound 9 pence |
| Shoe buckles | Inventory of Samuel Kennastons (1754) | Pair of silver shoe buckles in Charles Town, South Carolina, 1754 | 8 shillings |
| Shoes | Inventory of Charles Pury (1756) | Pair of Negro Shoes in the Town of Beaufort, South Carolina, 1756 | 5 shillings |
| Shoes | Inventory of Leroy Griffin (1750) | Pair of new shoes in Richmond County, Virginia, 1750 | 8 shillings |
| Shoes | Inventory of William Air (1754) | Pair of Marocco shoes in Beaufort County, South Carolina, 1754 | 7 shillings 6 pence |
| Shoes | Inventory of Charles Pury (1756) | Pair of leather shoes in the Town of Beaufort, South Carolina, 1756 | 12 shillings 6 pence |
| Shoes | Inventory of John Fendall (1763) | Pair old Country made Callimanco Shoes in Charles County, Maryland, 1763 | 4 shillings |
| Spatter dash | Inventory of Charles Pury (1756) | Pair of spatter dashes in the Town of Beaufort, South Carolina, 1756 | 2 pounds |
| Stockings | Inventory of Daniel Dulany (1754) | One pair Mens Course worsted Stockings in Annapolis, Maryland, 1754 | 1 shilling 6 pence |
| Stockings | Inventory of Charles Pury (1756) | Pair of Mens Cotton Stockings in the Town of Beaufort, South Carolina, 1756 | 1 pound |
| Stockings | Inventory of Charles Pury (1756) | Pair of Mens thread stockings in the Town of Beaufort, South Carolina, 1756 | 16 shillings 8 pence |
| Suit | Inventory of Thomas Lewis (1750) | Suit of Duroy in Fairfax County, Virginia, 1750 | 1 pound 15 shillings |
| Suit | Inventory of Thomas Lewis (1750) | Suit of Brown Holland in Fairfax County, Virginia, 1750 | 15 shillings |
| Suit | Inventory of Willian Shepard (1756) | Blue Coat Westcoat and Britches in Charles Town, South Carolina, 1756 | 6 pounds |
| Trousers | Inventory of Thomas Lewis (1750) | Pair of stript Trowsers in Fairfax County, Virginia, 1750 | 2 shillings 6 pence |
| Vest | Inventory of Leroy Griffin (1750) | Velvet vest in Richmond County, Virginia, 1750 | 2 shillings 6 pence |
| Wig | Inventory of Thomas Lewis (1750) | Wigg in Fairfax County, Virginia, 1750 | 11 shillings 8 pence |
| Wig | Inventory of S. Hall (1757) | Men's wig inventoried by a student at Harvard, 1757 | 12 shillings |

| Item | Data Source | Description | Price |
|------|-------------|-------------|-------|
| **Apparel - Women** | | | |
| Bonnet | Inventory of Charles Pury (1756) | Silk Bonnett in the Town of Beaufort, South Carolina, 1756 | 1 pound 10 shillings |
| Cap | Inventory of Samuel Kennastons (1754) | Womens Sattin dressing Cap in Charles Town, South Carolina, 1754 | 10 shillings |
| Girdle | Inventory of Samuel Kennastons (1754) | Girdle in Charles Town, South Carolina, 1754 | 9 pence |
| Gloves | Inventory of Daniel Dulany (1754) | Pair Cotton Gloves in Annapolis, Maryland, 1754 | 7 shillings 2½ pence |
| Gloves | Inventory of Daniel Dulany (1754) | Pair of White Kid Gloves in Annapolis, Maryland, 1754 | 3 shillings 2½ pence |
| Handkerchief | Inventory of Samuel Kennastons (1754) | Silk Handkerchieft in Charles Town, South Carolina, 1754 | 3 shillings |
| Mittens | Inventory of Samuel Kennastons (1754) | Pair of Silk Mittens in Charles Town, South Carolina, 1754 | 5 shillings 7 pence |
| Mittens | Inventory of Daniel Dulany (1754) | Pair Colored Silk Mittings in Annapolis, Maryland, 1754 | 8 shillings |
| Shoes | Inventory of Samuel Kennastons (1754) | Pair of Womens & Girles Calaco shoes in Charles Town, South Carolina, 1754 | 3 shillings 1 pence |
| Shoes | Inventory of William Air (1754) | Pair of womans Silk Shoes in Beaufort County, South Carolina, 1754 | 3 pounds |
| Shoes | Inventory of William Air (1754) | Pair of womans Callimanco Shoes in Beaufort County, South Carolina, 1754 | 2 pounds 4 shillings |
| Shoes | Inventory of Daniel Dulany (1754) | Pair Silk Shoes in Annapolis, Maryland, 1754 | 19 shilling 3½ pence |
| Stockings | Inventory of Daniel Dulany (1754) | Pair Womens Silk Cloak Stockings in Annapolis, Maryland, 1754 | 6 shillings 10 pence |
| Stockings | Inventory of Charles Pury (1756) | Pair of Womens Cotton Stockings in the Town of Beaufort, South Carolina, 1756 | 1 pound 5 shillings |
| Stomager | Inventory of Samuel Kennastons (1754) | Stomager in Charles Town, South Carolina, 1754 | 1 shillings 5 pence |
| Straps | Inventory of Samuel Kennastons (1754) | Set of stay straps in Charles Town, South Carolina, 1754 | 2 shillings |
| **Commodities** | | | |
| Board | Inventory of Daniel Huger (1755) | 100 foot of board in Beaufort, South Carolina, 1755 | 1 pound 10 shillings |
| Bread | Inventory of Charles Pury (1756) | Bushell Bread in the Town of Beaufort, South Carolina, 1756 | 7 shillings 6 pence |

## Based Upon the British Currency System

| Year | Pound in 2002 US Dollars | Shilling in 2002 US Dollars | Pence in 2002 US Dollars |
|------|--------------------------|------------------------------|---------------------------|
| 1750 | $216.00 | $10.80 | $0.90 |
| 1755 | $216.00 | $10.80 | $0.90 |
| 1760 | $192.00 | $ 9.60 | $0.80 |
| 1765 | $168.00 | $ 8.40 | $0.70 |
| 1770 | $168.00 | $ 8.40 | $0.70 |
| 1774 | $144.00 | $ 7.20 | $0.60 |

*Calculations are approximate values based upon economic historical data*

| Item | Data Source | Description | Price |
|------|-------------|-------------|-------|
| Coal | Kitman, George Washington's Expense Account (1970) | Bushel of coal in Virginia, 1774 | 2 shillings |
| Coffee | Inventory of Samuel Kennastons (1754) | Pound of coffee in Charles Town, South Carolina, 1754 | 6 pence |
| Corn | Inventory of Paul Lepear (1756) | Bushel of corn in Charles Town, South Carolina, 1756 | 7 shillings 6 pence |
| Corn | Inventory of Thomas Holman (1756) | Bushel of Corn in St Andrews, South Carolina, 1756 | 10 shillings |
| Cotton | Inventory of John Fendall (1763) | Pound of Cotton in Charles County, Maryland, 1763 | 2 shillings 6 pence |
| Feathers | Inventory of Doctor Gustavus Brown (1762) | Pound of new feathers in Charles County, Maryland, 1762 | 22 shillings |
| Flour | Inventory of Charles Pury (1756) | Pound of Flower in the Town of Beaufort, South Carolina, 1756 | 4 pounds |
| Flour | Inventory of Charles Pury (1756) | Pound of Bread Flower in the Town of Beaufort, South Carolina, 1756 | 4 pounds 10 shillings |
| Indigo | Inventory of Willian Shepard (1756) | Pound of indigo in Charles Town, South Carolina, 1756 | 7 shillings |
| Indigo | Inventory of John Brice (1767) | Pound of indigo in Ann Arundel, Maryland, 1767 | 10 shillings |
| Indigo seed | Inventory of Paul Lepear (1756) | Bushel of indigo seed in Charles Town, South Carolina, 1756 | 8 pounds |
| Lead | Inventory of Daniel Dulany (1754) | One pound of lead in Annapolis, Maryland, 1754 | 3 pence |
| Lead | Inventory of William Edings (1756) | Pound of lead in Tooboodoe, South Carolina, 1756 | 2 shillings |
| Molasses | Inventory of Thomas Lewis (1750) | Gallon of molasses in Fairfax County, Virginia, 1750 | 2 shillings 6 pence |
| Molasses | Inventory of John Brice (1767) | Gallon of molasses in Ann Arundel, Maryland, 1767 | 1 shilling |
| Peas | Inventory of Daniel Huger (1755) | Bushel of Black Eyed pease in Beaufort, South Carolina, 1755 | 10 shillings |
| Peas | Inventory of Daniel Huger (1755) | Bushel of Pease in Beaufort, South Carolina, 1755 | 10 shillings |
| Rice | Inventory of Daniel Huger (1755) | Bushel of Rough Rice in Beaufort, South Carolina, 1755 | 10 shillings |
| Rice | Inventory of Daniel Huger (1755) | Barrel of small Rice in Beaufort, South Carolina, 1755 | 1 pound 5 shillings |
| Rice seed | Inventory of Daniel Huger (1755) | Bushel of Rice Seed in Beaufort, South Carolina, 1755 | 10 shillings |
| Salt | Inventory of Daniel Huger (1755) | Bushel of Salt in Beaufort, South Carolina, 1755 | 5 shillings |
| Salt | Inventory of John Brice (1767) | Bushell of salt in Ann Arundel, Maryland, 1767 | 1 shilling 1¼pence |
| Saltpeter | Inventory of John Brice (1767) | Pound of salt petre in Ann Arundel, Maryland, 1767 | 1 shilling 3 pence |
| Shells | Inventory of Thomas Lewis (1750) | Bushel of Oyster shels in Fairfax County, Virginia, 1750 | 2 pence |
| Tea | Inventory of Samuel Kennastons (1754) | Pound of tea in Charles Town, South Carolina, 1754 | 8 shillings 10 pence |
| Tea | Inventory of Samuel Kennastons (1754) | Pound of green tea in Charles Town, South Carolina, 1754 | 8 shillings 10 pence |
| Tea | Inventory of Samuel Kennastons (1754) | Pound of Bohea Tea in Charles Town, South Carolina, 1754 | 3 shillings |
| Vinegar | Inventory of Willian Shepard (1756) | Gallon of vinegar in Charles Town, South Carolina, 1756 | 4 shillings 7 pence |

| Item | Data Source | Description | Price |
|---|---|---|---|
| Wheat | Inventory of Leroy Griffin (1750) | Bushell of wheat in Richmond County, Virginia, 1750 | 3 shillings |
| Wool | Inventory of John Brice (1767) | Pound of wool in Ann Arundel, Maryland, 1767 | 4¾ pence |
| Yarn | Inventory of Doctor Adam Thomson (1768) | One pound of yarn in Prince George, Maryland, 1768 | 1 shilling |

### Entertainment

| Item | Data Source | Description | Price |
|---|---|---|---|
| Lottery | The Pennsylvania Gazette (1754) | Lottery with 5,000 tickets for raising 562 Pounds, 10 Shillings in monies for a lot in Germantown for a Dutch Lutheran Congregation's minister, a school house and other needs Multiple winnings with top prize valued at 400 Pieces of Eight Philadelphia, Pennsylvania 1754 | Two Pieces of Eight |
| Playing cards | Inventory of John Fendall (1763) | Pack playing Cards in Charles County, Maryland, 1763 | 6 pence |

### Fabrics & Sewing Materials

| Item | Data Source | Description | Price |
|---|---|---|---|
| Binding | Inventory of Samuel Kennastons (1754) | Peice worsted Binding in Charles Town, South Carolina, 1754 | 2 shillings |
| Bobbin | Inventory of John Brice (1767) | Bobbin in Ann Arundel, Maryland, 1767 | 1¼ pence |
| Bodkin | Inventory of Samuel Kennastons (1754) | Bodkin in Charles Town, South Carolina, 1754 | 1 shilling |
| Buttons | Inventory of Samuel Kennastons (1754) | Ten 2 oz Brest Buttons in Charles Town, South Carolina, 1754 | 6 pence |
| Buttons | Inventory of Samuel Kennastons (1754) | Value of 12 shirt buttons in Charles Town, South Carolina, 1754 | 1 pence |
| Buttons | Inventory of Thomas Lewis (1750) | Dozen thread buttons in Fairfax County, Virginia, 1750 | 3 pence |
| Buttons | Inventory of John Brice (1767) | Dozen waist buttons in Ann Arundel, Maryland, 1767 | 2½ pence |
| Cloth | Inventory of Thomas Lewis (1750) | Yard of Broad cloath in Fairfax County, Virginia, 1750 | 7 shillings |
| Cloth | Inventory of William Edings (1756) | Yard of Negro Cloth in Edisto Island, South Carolina, 1756 | 9 shillings |
| Cord | Inventory of Samuel Kennastons (1754) | Piece of union cord in Charles Town, South Carolina, 1754 | 1 shilling 7 pence |
| Fabric | Inventory of Joseph Galloway (1753) | Yard Irish Linnen in Anne Arundel County, Maryland, 1753 | 4 shillings 6 pence |

## Based Upon the British Currency System

| Year | Pound in 2002 US Dollars | Shilling in 2002 US Dollars | Pence in 2002 US Dollars |
|---|---|---|---|
| 1750 | $216.00 | $10.80 | $0.90 |
| 1755 | $216.00 | $10.80 | $0.90 |
| 1760 | $192.00 | $ 9.60 | $0.80 |
| 1765 | $168.00 | $ 8.40 | $0.70 |
| 1770 | $168.00 | $ 8.40 | $0.70 |
| 1774 | $144.00 | $ 7.20 | $0.60 |

*Calculations are approximate values based upon economic historical data*

| Item | Data Source | Description | Price |
|------|-------------|-------------|-------|
| Fabric | Inventory of Samuel Kennastons (1754) | Yard of Calamanco in Charles Town, South Carolina, 1754 | 10 pence |
| Fabric | Inventory of Samuel Kennastons (1754) | Yard of blue Stripped Holland in Charles Town, South Carolina, 1754 | 1 shilling 1 pence |
| Fabric | Inventory of Samuel Kennastons (1754) | Yard of Jeans in Charles Town, South Carolina, 1754 | 1 shilling 5 pence |
| Fabric | Inventory of William Air (1754) | One piece of Cotton Holland in Beaufort County, 1754 | 14 pounds 8 shillings |
| Fabric | Inventory of Daniel Dulany (1754) | One yard best wht Persian in Annapolis, Maryland, 1754 | 3 shillings 2½ pence |
| Fabric | Inventory of Charles Pury (1756) | Yard of Muslin in the Town of Beaufort, South Carolina, 1756 | 17 shillings 6 pence |
| Fabric | Inventory of Charles Pury (1756) | Yard of Persian Silk in the Town of Beaufort, South Carolina, 1756 | 7 shillings 6 pence |
| Fabric | Inventory of John Brice (1767) | Yard of flowd Damask in Ann Arundel, Maryland, 1767 | 1 shilling 6 pence |
| Fabric | Inventory of John Brice (1767) | Yard of blue Sattin in Ann Arundel, Maryland, 1767 | 8 shillings 7 pence |
| Fringe | Inventory of Samuel Kennastons (1754) | Yard of Fringe in Charles Town, South Carolina, 1754 | 2 shillings 4 pence |
| Gimp | Inventory of John Brice (1767) | Yard of gimp in Ann Arundel, Maryland, 1767 | 1½ pence |
| Lace | Inventory of Daniel Dulany (1754) | One yard Bed Lace in Annapolis, Maryland, 1754 | 1 shilling |
| Lace | Inventory of John Brice (1767) | Yard of Silver Lace in Ann Arundel, Maryland, 1767 | 6 shillings 2 pence |
| Lace | Inventory of Samuel Kennastons (1754) | Silk Lace in Charles Towne, South Carolina, 1754 | 2½ pence |
| Needles | Inventory of Samuel Kennastons (1754) | Value for 25 needles in Charles Town, South Carolina, 1754 | 1 pence |
| Needles | Inventory of Charles Pury (1756) | One thousand needles in the Town of Beaufort, South Carolina, 1756 | 2 pounds |
| Pattern | Inventory of Samuel Kennastons (1754) | Breeches Pattern in Charles Town, South Carolina, 1754 | 5 shillings 11 pence |
| Pattern | Inventory of Charles Pury (1756) | Cotton & silk pattern for gowns in the Town of Beaufort, South Carolina, 1756 | 4 pounds |
| Pattern | Inventory of John Brice (1767) | Waistcoat pattern in Ann Arundel, Maryland, 1767 | 6 shillings 14 pence |
| Pincushion | Inventory of Samuel Kennastons (1754) | One Silk Pinchusian in Charles Town, South Carolina, 1754 | 1 pence |
| Pins | Inventory of William Air (1754) | Pound of pound pins in Beaufort County, South Carolina, 1754 | 1 pound |
| Quilting | Inventory of John Brice (1767) | Yard of quilting in Ann Arundel, Maryland, 1767 | 2 shillings |
| Sewing silk | Inventory of Charles Pury (1756) | Pound of Sewing Silk in the Town of Beaufort, South Carolina, 1756 | 8 pounds 10 shillings |
| Tape | Inventory of Samuel Kennastons (1754) | Manchester Tape in Charles Towne, South Carolina, 1754 | 7½ pence |
| Tapestry | Inventory of Samuel Kennastons (1754) | Manchester Tape in Charles Town, South Carolina, 1754 | 8 pence |
| Thread | Inventory of Samuel Kennastons (1754) | Pound of Quilting Cotton thread in Charles Town, South Carolina, 1754 | 3 shillings 2 pence |
| Thread | Inventory of William Air (1754) | Pound of Nuns Thread in Beaufort County, South Carolina, 1754 | 1 pound 15 shillings |
| Thread | Inventory of Charles Pury (1756) | Pound of Shoe Thread in the Town of Beaufort, South Carolina, 1756 | 8 shillings |

| Item | Data Source | Description | Price |
|------|-------------|-------------|-------|
| Thread | Inventory of Charles Pury (1756) | Pound of Coloured thread in the Town of Beaufort, South Carolina, 1756 | 10 shillings |
| Thread | Inventory of Charles Pury (1756) | Ounce of Fine Thread in the Town of Beaufort, South Carolina, 1756 | 1 pound 10 shillings |

### Farm Equipment & Tools

| Item | Data Source | Description | Price |
|------|-------------|-------------|-------|
| Auger & chisel | Inventory of Paul Lepear (1756) | Auger and Chisell in Charles Town, South Carolina, 1756 | 5 shillings |
| Ax | Inventory of Joseph Fox (1756) | Broad Ax in Charles Town, South Carolina, 1756 | 15 shillings |
| Ax | Inventory of Paul Lepear (1756) | Falling axe in Charles Town, South Carolina, 1756 | 1 shilling 1 pence |
| Axe | Inventory of Leroy Griffin (1750) | Axe in Richmond County, Virginia, 1750 | 1 shilling |
| Axe | Inventory of Daniel Dulany (1754) | Old narrow Axe in Annapolis, Maryland, 1754 | 1 shilling |
| Axe | Inventory of Daniel Dulany (1754) | Broad Axe in Annapolis, Maryland, 1754 | 3 shillings |
| Axe | Inventory of Charles Pury (1756) | Broad Axe in the Town of Beaufort, South Carolina, 1756 | 1 pound |
| Axe | Inventory of John Brice (1767) | Axe in Ann Arundel, Maryland, 1767 | 3 shillings 8½ pence |
| Chain | Inventory of Thomas Lewis (1750) | 21 lb Iron chain in Fairfax County, Virginia, 1750 | 17 shillings 6 pence |
| Chain | Inventory of William Eilbeck (1765) | Old Chain for measuring Land in Charles County, Maryland, 1765 | 5 shillings |
| Cheese press | Inventory of William Edings (1756) | Cheese press in Edisto Island, South Carolina, 1756 | 2 pounds 10 shillings |
| Dung fork | Inventory of Charles Pury (1756) | Dung Fork in the Town of Beaufort, South Carolina, 1756 | 1 pound |
| File | Inventory of Daniel Dulany (1754) | Dutch File in Annapolis, Maryland, 1754 | 1½ pence |
| Hammer | Inventory of Charles Pury (1756) | Leithing Hammer in the Town of Beaufort, South Carolina, 1756 | 7 shillings 6 pence |
| Hammer | Inventory of Charles Pury (1756) | Claw Hammer in the Town of Beaufort, South Carolina, 1756 | 5 shillings |
| Hammer | Inventory of Charles Pury (1756) | Sledge Hammer in the Town of Beaufort, South Carolina, 1756 | 1 pound |
| Hatchet | Inventory of Charles Pury (1756) | Hatchet in the Town of Beaufort, South Carolina, 1756 | 1 pound |

## Based Upon the British Currency System

| Year | Pound in 2002 US Dollars | Shilling in 2002 US Dollars | Pence in 2002 US Dollars |
|------|--------------------------|-----------------------------|--------------------------|
| 1750 | $216.00 | $10.80 | $0.90 |
| 1755 | $216.00 | $10.80 | $0.90 |
| 1760 | $192.00 | $ 9.60 | $0.80 |
| 1765 | $168.00 | $ 8.40 | $0.70 |
| 1770 | $168.00 | $ 8.40 | $0.70 |
| 1774 | $144.00 | $ 7.20 | $0.60 |

*Calculations are approximate values based upon economic historical data*

| Item | Data Source | Description | Price |
|------|-------------|-------------|-------|
| Hoe | Inventory of Daniel Dulany (1754) | Grubbing hoe in Annapolis, Maryland, 1754 | 5 shillings |
| Hoe | Inventory of Daniel Dulany (1754) | Weeding hoe in Annapolis, Maryland, 1754 | 1 shilling 10½ pence |
| Hoe | Inventory of Daniel Dulany (1754) | Narrow hoe in Annapolis, Maryland, 1754 | 2 shillings |
| Hoe | Inventory of Paul Lepear (1756) | Grubbing Hoe in Charles Town, South Carolina, 1756 | 4 shillings |
| Hook | Inventory of Daniel Huger (1755) | Reaping Hook in Beaufort, South Carolina, 1755 | 1 shilling 5 pence |
| Ladder | Inventory of William Edings (1756) | Ladder in Edisto Island, South Carolina, 1756 | 10 shillings |
| Mill | Inventory of Daniel Huger (1755) | Steel corn mill in Beaufort, South Carolina, 1755 | 10 pounds |
| Nails | Inventory of William Edings (1756) | Cask of nails in Tooboodoe, South Carolina, 1756 | 5 pounds |
| Nails | Inventory of Charles Pury (1756) | One thousand 4 pence nails in the Town of Beaufort, South Carolina, 1756 | 12 shillings 6 pence |
| Nails | Inventory of Charles Pury (1756) | One thousand 8 pence nails Lenthened in the Town of Beaufort, South Carolina, 1756 | 1 pound 5 shillings |
| Pitch Fork | Inventory of John Fendall (1763) | Pitch Fork in Charles County, Maryland, 1763 | 1 shilling |
| Pot | Inventory of Joseph Galloway (1753) | Gallon pot located in the Milk House - Anne Arundel County, Maryland, 1753 | 7 shillings |
| Quern stones | Inventory of Daniel Huger (1755) | Pair of Quern Stones for Grinding Corn in Beaufort, South Carolina, 1755 | 12 pounds |
| Reaping hook | Inventory of Paul Lepear (1756) | Reaping hook in Charles Town, South Carolina, 1756 | 10 pence |
| Rice hook | Inventory of Daniel Huger (1755) | Rice hook in Beaufort, South Carolina, 1755 | 1 shilling 3 pence |
| Saw | Inventory of William Air (1754) | Cross Cut Saw in Beaufort County, South Carolina, 1754 | 1 pound 10 shillings |
| Saw | Inventory of Daniel Dulany (1754) | Steel Plate Hand Saw in Annapolis, Maryland, 1754 | 7 shillings 6 pence |
| Saw | Inventory of Daniel Huger (1755) | Whip cut saw in Beaufort, South Carolina, 1755 | 2 pounds |
| Saw | Inventory of Paul Lepear (1756) | Hand saw in Charles Town, South Carolina, 1756 | 2 shillings 6 pence |
| Scythe | Inventory of John Brice (1767) | Scythe in Ann Arundel, Maryland, 1767 | 3 shillings |
| Shears | Inventory of Leroy Griffin (1750) | Sheep shears in Richmond County, Virginia, 1750 | 3 pence |
| Shears | Inventory of Charles Pury (1756) | Pair of Shears in the Town of Beaufort, South Carolina, 1756 | 5 shillings |
| Sickle | Inventory of John Brice (1767) | Sickle in Ann Arundel, Maryland, 1767 | 6 pence |
| Sieve | Inventory of Leroy Griffin (1750) | Wire Sieve in Richmond County, Virginia, 1750 | 2 shillings 3 pence |
| Sieve | Inventory of Paul Lepear (1756) | Rice Sive in Charles Town, South Carolina, 1756 | 10 shillings |
| Spade | Inventory of Daniel Dulany (1754) | Garden Spade in Annapolis, Maryland, 1754 | 2 shillings 3¼ pence |
| Steelyards | Inventory of Daniel Huger (1755) | Pair of Steelyards in Beaufort, South Carolina, 1755 | 1 pound |
| Stone mill | Inventory of James Boisseau (1756) | Stone mill in Charles Town, South Carolina, 1756 | 14 pounds |
| Tar | Inventory of William Eilbeck (1765) | One Barrell Tar in Charles County, Maryland, 1765 | 10 shillings |
| Tub | Inventory of Leroy Griffin (1750) | Cyprus Tubb in Richmond County, Virginia, 1750 | 2 shillings 6 pence |

| Item | Data Source | Description | Price |
|------|-------------|-------------|-------|
| Whip | Inventory of Charles Pury (1756) | Whip in the Town of Beaufort, South Carolina, 1756 | 1 pound |

### Firearms & Supplies

| Item | Data Source | Description | Price |
|------|-------------|-------------|-------|
| Cutlass | Inventory of Doctor Adam Thomson (1768) | A cutlass and belt in Prince George, Maryland, 1768 | 1 pound 10 shillings |
| Gun | Inventory of Leroy Griffin (1750) | Gun in Richmond County, Virginia, 1750 | 1 pound 5 shillings |
| Gun | Inventory of Samuel Kennastons (1754) | Gun in Charles Town, South Carolina, 1754 | 9 pounds |
| Gun | Inventory of William Edings (1756) | Plantation gun in Tooboodoe, South Carolina, 1756 | 1 pound |
| Gun | Kitman, George Washington's Expense Account (1970) | Gun and bayonet purchased in Massachusetts, 1774 | 3 pounds |
| Gun | Kitman, George Washington's Expense Account (1970) | Gun and bayonet purchased in Virginia, 1774 | 5 pounds |
| Gun hammer | Inventory of Charles Pury (1756) | Gun hammer in the Town of Beaufort, South Carolina, 1756 | 5 shillings |
| Gunpowder | Inventory of William Air (1754) | Pound of Fine Gun Powder in Beaufort County, South Carolina, 1754 | 5 shillings |
| Gunpowder | Inventory o f William Shepard (1756) | Kegg Gun Powder about 20 pounds in Charles Town, South Carolina, 1756 | 6 pounds 17 shillings |
| Gunpowder | Inventory of Charles Pury (1756) | Pound of Gun Powder in the Town of Beaufort, South Carolina, 1756 | 6 shillings |
| Pistols | Inventory of Daniel Dulany (1754) | Case of Screw Barrelled Pistolls in Annapolis, Maryland, 1754 | 2 pounds |
| Pistols | Inventory of Daniel Dulany (1754) | Case of Pistols Brass mounted in Annapolis, Maryland, 1754 | 1 pound 5 shillings |
| Pistols | Inventory of Daniel Dulany (1754) | Case of Pistols Horsemans mounted in Annapolis, Maryland, 1754 | 10 shillings |
| Shot | Inventory of William Air (1754) | Pound of Small Shott in Beaufort County, South Carolina, 1754 | 1 shilling |
| Shot | Inventory of Charles Pury (1756) | Pound of Shott in the Town of Beaufort, South Carolina, 1756 | 1 shilling |
| Sword | Inventory of Daniel Huger (1755) | Silver Thilted Sword in Beaufort, South Carolina, 1755 | 15 pounds |
| Sword | Inventory of Jeremiah Chase (1755) | Mourning Sword in Charles County, Maryland, 1755 | 5 shillings |

### Based Upon the British Currency System

| Year | Pound in 2002 US Dollars | Shilling in 2002 US Dollars | Pence in 2002 US Dollars |
|------|--------------------------|-----------------------------|--------------------------|
| 1750 | $216.00 | $10.80 | $0.90 |
| 1755 | $216.00 | $10.80 | $0.90 |
| 1760 | $192.00 | $ 9.60 | $0.80 |
| 1765 | $168.00 | $ 8.40 | $0.70 |
| 1770 | $168.00 | $ 8.40 | $0.70 |
| 1774 | $144.00 | $ 7.20 | $0.60 |

*Calculations are approximate values based upon economic historical data*

| Item | Data Source | Description | Price |
|---|---|---|---|
| **Food Products** | | | |
| Allspice | Inventory of William Air (1754) | Pound of all Spice in Beaufort County, South Carolina, 1754 | 4 shillings |
| Alum | Inventory of William Eilbeck (1765) | Pound of Alum in Charles County, Maryland, 1765 | 6 pence |
| Alum | Inventory of John Brice (1767) | Pound of Allom in Ann Arundel, Maryland, 1767 | 3 pence |
| Bacon | Inventory of Daniel Dulany (1754) | Pound of bacon in Annapolis, Maryland, 1754 | 4 pence |
| Bacon | Inventory of Jeremiah Chase (1755) | Pound of bacon in Charles County, Maryland, 1755 | 5 pence |
| Beans | Inventory of Thomas Lewis (1750) | Bushel of beans in Fairfax County, Virginia, 1750 | 2 shillings |
| Beans | Inventory of Jeremiah Chase (1755) | Bushel of beans in Charles County, Maryland, 1755 | 3 shillings |
| Beef | Inventory of Jeremiah Chase (1755) | Pound of dryed beef in Charles County, Maryland, 1755 | 2½ pence |
| Beef | Inventory of John Fendall (1763) | Pound fresh Beef in Charles County, Maryland, 1763 | 2½ pence |
| Chocolate | Inventory of Charles Pury (1756) | Pound of old chocolate in the Town of Beaufort, South Carolina, 1756 | 7 shillings 6 pence |
| Chocolate | Inventory of John Fendall (1763) | Pound of chocolate in Charles County, Maryland, 1763 | 1 shilling 6 pence |
| Citron | Inventory of John Brice (1767) | Pound of citron in Ann Arundel, Maryland, 1767 | 1 shilling 6 pence |
| Coffee | Inventory of William Eilbeck (1765) | Pound of coffee in Charles County, Maryland, 1765 | 1 shilling 2 pence |
| Coffee | Inventory of John Brice (1767) | Pound of coffee in Ann Arundel, Maryland, 1767 | 1 shilling |
| Corn | Inventory of Thomas Lewis (1750) | Barrel of corn in Fairfax County, Virginia, 1750 | 6 shillings |
| Corn | Inventory of Jeremiah Chase (1755) | Barrell of Corn in Charles County, Maryland, 1755 | 10 shillings |
| Corn | Inventory of John Fendall (1763) | Barrell Indian Corn in Charles County, Maryland, 1763 | 12 shillings 6 pence |
| Fat | Inventory of Joseph Galloway (1753) | Pound Fatt in Anne Arundel County, Maryland, 1753 | 2 pounds |
| Honey | Inventory of Charles Pury (1756) | Bottle of honey in the Town of Beaufort, South Carolina, 1756 | 2 shillings 6 pence |
| Molasses | Inventory of William Air (1754) | Gallon of Melasses in Beaufort County, South Carolina, 1754 | 10 shillings |
| Molasses | Inventory of John Fendall (1763) | Gallon of Molasses in Charles County, Maryland, 1763 | 2 shillings |
| Mustard | Inventory of Samuel Kennastons (1754) | Bottle of mustard in Charles Town, South Carolina, 1754 | 4 pence |
| Oats | Inventory of Thomas Lewis (1750) | Bushel of oats in Fairfax County, Virginia, 1750 | 1 shilling |
| Oats | Inventory of William Eilbeck (1765) | Bushel of Oats in Charles County, Maryland, 1765 | 1 shilling 2 pence |
| Olives | Inventory of John Fendall (1763) | One jar Olives in Charles County, Maryland, 1763 | 15 shillings |
| Onions | Inventory of Samuel Kennastons (1754) | Bottle of Pickles onions in Charles Town, South Carolina, 1754 | 2 shillings 3 pence |
| Pork | Inventory of Daniel Dulany (1754) | Barrell of Pork in Annapolis, Maryland, 1754 | 2 pounds 5 shillings |
| Pork | Inventory of John Brice (1767) | Per pound of pork in Ann Arundel, Maryland, 1767 | 1 pence |
| Powder | Inventory of Samuel Kennastons (1754) | Box of Almond Powder in Charles Town, South Carolina, 1754 | 16 shillings 8 pence |

| Item | Data Source | Description | Price |
|------|-------------|-------------|-------|
| Raisins | Inventory of John Fendall (1763) | Pound of raisins in Charles County, Maryland, 1763 | 2 shillings |
| Salt | Inventory of John Fendall (1763) | Bushell Salt in Charles County, Maryland, 1763 | 3 shillings |
| Spice | Inventory of Samuel Kennastons (1754) | Ounce of cloves in Charles Town, South Carolina, 1754 | 5 pence |
| Spice | Inventory of Samuel Kennastons (1754) | Pound of ginger in Charles Town, South Carolina, 1754 | 3 pence |
| Spice | Inventory of Samuel Kennastons (1754) | Pound of nutmegs in Charles Town, South Carolina, 1754 | 7 shillings 4 pence |
| Spice | Inventory of Samuel Kennastons (1754) | Pound of Peper in Charles Town, South Carolina, 1754 | 1 shilling |
| Spice | Inventory of William Air (1754) | Pound of Cinnimon in Beaufort County, South Carolina, 1754 | 2 pounds |
| Spice | Inventory of Daniel Dulany (1754) | One pound of ginger in Annapolis, Maryland, 1754 | 4 pence |
| Spice | Inventory of Daniel Dulany (1754) | One pound All Spice in Annapolis, Maryland, 1754 | 1 shilling |
| Sugar | The Pennsylvania Gazette (1763) | Single refined sugar provided by William Wallace and Company in Philadelphia, Pennsylvania, 1763 | 1 shilling ½ pence |
| Sugar | The Pennsylvania Gazette (1763) | Double refined sugar provided by William Wallace and Company in Philadelphia, Pennsylvania, 1763 | 1 shilling 6 pence |
| Sugar | Inventory of Samuel Kennastons (1754) | Loaf of sugar in Charles Town, South Carolina, 1754 | 5 shillings |
| Sugar | Inventory of William Air (1754) | Pound of Muscovado Sugar in Beaufort County, South Carolina, 1754 | 2 shillings |
| Sugar | Inventory of William Eilbeck (1765) | Pound of brown sugar in Charles County, Maryland, 1765 | 7 pence |
| Tea | Inventory of Daniel Dulany (1754) | One pound of Hyson Tea in Annapolis, Maryland, 1754 | 1 pound 5 shillings 8 pence |
| Tea | Inventory of John Brice (1767) | Pound of Congo Tea in Ann Arundel, Maryland, 1767 | 14 shillings |
| Tea | Inventory of John Brice (1767) | Pound of Bohea Tea in Ann Arundel, Maryland, 1767 | 6 shillings |
| Vinegar | Inventory of John Fendall (1763) | Gallon of Vinegar in Charles County, Maryland, 1763 | 2 shillings |
| Wheat | Inventory of John Fendall (1763) | Bushell Wheat in Charles County, Maryland, 1763 | 4 shillings |

## Based Upon the British Currency System

| Year | Pound in 2002 US Dollars | Shilling in 2002 US Dollars | Pence in 2002 US Dollars |
|------|--------------------------|-----------------------------|--------------------------|
| 1750 | $216.00 | $10.80 | $0.90 |
| 1755 | $216.00 | $10.80 | $0.90 |
| 1760 | $192.00 | $ 9.60 | $0.80 |
| 1765 | $168.00 | $ 8.40 | $0.70 |
| 1770 | $168.00 | $ 8.40 | $0.70 |
| 1774 | $144.00 | $ 7.20 | $0.60 |

*Calculations are approximate values based upon economic historical data*

| Item | Data Source | Description | Price |
|------|-------------|-------------|-------|
| **Household Furniture** | | | |
| Bed | Inventory of Thomas Lewis (1750) | Chaff bed in Fairfax County, Virginia, 1750 | 5 shillings |
| Bed | Inventory of Paul Lepear (1756) | Bed and bolster in Charles Town, South Carolina, 1756 | 30 pounds |
| Bed | Harvard Student Inventory (1760) | Feather bed bolster and two pillows inventoried by a Harvard student, 1760 | 5 pounds 6 shillings 8 pence |
| Bed bolster | Unknown Harvard Student Account (approx. 1760) | Feather Bed Bolster and two Pillows & under Tick, Cambridge, Massachusetts, 1760 | 5 pounds 6 shillings 8 pence |
| Bed cord | Inventory of Jeremiah Chase (1755) | Small feather Bed in Charles County, Maryland, 1755 | 2 pounds |
| Bedstead | Unknown Harvard Student Account (approx. 1760) | Bed Steed in Cambridge, Massachusetts, 1760 | 8 shillings |
| Bookcase | Inventory of William Edings (1756) | Book case with glass doors in Charles Town, South Carolina, 1756 | 35 pounds |
| Bookcase | Inventory of Daniel Dulany (1754) | Black Walnut Book Case in Annapolis, Maryland, 1754 | 2 pounds 15 shillings |
| Bookcase | Account Invoice of E. Man (1764) | Student's bookcase at Harvard, 1764 | 6 shillings |
| Bureau | Inventory of William Air (1754) | Mahogany Beariau in Beaufort County, South Carolina, 1754 | 25 pounds |
| Carpet | Brock Jobe, New England Furniture: The Colonial Era (1984) | Wilton Bedside carpet purchased by a Poutsmouth merchant from Samuel Walker, a London craftsman, 1760 | 15 shillings |
| Chair | Inventory of Leroy Griffin (1750) | Spanish leather botton chair in Richmond County, Virginia, 1750 | 15 shillings |
| Chair | Inventory of Daniel Dulany (1754) | Silk damask bottom'd Mohogony Chair with Linnen Cover in Annapolis, Maryland, 1754 | 1 pound 10 shillings |
| Chair | Inventory of Daniel Dulany (1754) | Back walnut rush bottom'd chair in Annapolis, Maryland, 1754 | 6 shillings |
| Chair | Inventory of Jeremiah Chase (1755) | Armed Chair with Leather Seat in Charles County, Maryland, 1755 | 1 pound |
| Chair | Brock Jobe, New England Furniture: The Colonial Era (1984) | Mohogany Chair with seat covers purchased by a Poutsmouth merchant from Samuel Walker, a London craftsman, 1760 | 1 pound 2 shillings |
| Chair | Inventory of Doctor Gustavus Brown (1762) | One old Cane chear in Charles County, Maryland, 1762 | 2 shillings |
| Chair | Inventory of Doctor Adam Thomson (1768) | Old Windsor Arm Chair & cushion in Prince George, Maryland, 1768 | 4 shillings |
| Chair | Inventory of Doctor Adam Thomson (1768) | Mahogany Chairs with red Damask bottoms in Prince George, Maryland, 1768 | 15 shillings |
| Chamber glass | Inventory of William Holman (1756) | Chamber glass and table in Colleton, South Carolina, 1756 | 2 pounds 10 shillings |
| Chest | Inventory of William Edings (1756) | Tea chest in Charles Town, South Carolina, 1756 | 1 pound 5 shillings |
| Chest | Inventory of William Edings (1756) | Large painted chest in Tooboodoe, South Carolina, 1756 | 5 pounds |
| Chest of drawers | Inventory of Daniel Huger (1755) | Mahogany Chest of Drawers in Beaufort, South Carolina, 1755 | 40 pounds |
| Clock | Inventory of Daniel Dulany (1754) | Eight day clock in Annapolis, Maryland, 1754 | 10 pounds |
| Clock | Inventory of Daniel Dulany (1754) | Spring Clock in Annapolis, Maryland, 1754 | 10 shillings |

| Item | Data Source | Description | Price |
|------|-------------|-------------|-------|
| Cradle | Inventory of William Edings (1756) | Value of one cradle in Tooboodoe, South Carolina, 1756 | 1 pound 5 shillings |
| Desk | Inventory of Daniel Dulany (1754) | Cherry Tree Desk and Book Case in Annapolis, Maryland, 1754 | 12 pounds 10 shillings |
| Desk | Inventory of Daniel Dulany (1754) | Black walnut Writing Desk in Annapolis, Maryland, 1754 | 2 pounds 10 shillings |
| Desk | Inventory of William Edings (1756) | Read Bay Desk in Tooboodoe, South Carolina, 1756 | 20 pounds |
| Dining table | Inventory of William Edings (1756) | Small Red Bay Dineing Table in Charles Town, South Carolina, 1756 | 3 pounds 10 shillings |
| Dressing glass | Inventory of Leroy Griffin (1750) | Mohogony dressing Glass and Stool in Richmond County, Virginia, 1750 | 12 shillings 6 pence |
| Dressing table | Inventory of Daniel Huger (1755) | Dressing Table & Glass in Beaufort, South Carolina, 1755 | 5 pounds |
| Dumb waiter | Inventory of Jeremiah Chase (1755) | Dumb Waiter in Charles County, Maryland, 1755 | 1 pound 2 shillings 6 pence |
| Ink stand | Inventory of Daniel Dulany (1754) | Mahogony Ink Stand & Office Seal in Annapolis, Maryland, 1754 | 5 shillings |
| Looking glass | Inventory of John Brice (1767) | Parlour Looking Glass in Ann Arundel, Maryland, 1767 | 7 pounds |

| Item | Data Source | Description | Price |
|------|-------------|-------------|-------|
| Looking glass | Inventory of Charles Pury (1756) | Small Looking Glass Indian in the Town of Beaufort, South Carolina, 1756 | 7 shillings 6 pence |
| Screen | Inventory of Daniel Dulany (1754) | Mohogany round Screen Table in Annapolis, Maryland, 1754 | 1 pound 5 shillings |
| Screen | Inventory of John Brice (1767) | Parlour Screen in Ann Arundel, Maryland, 1767 | 7 shillings 6 pence |
| Side board | Inventory of William Edings (1756) | Mahogany side board in Tooboodoe, South Carolina, 1756 | 5 pounds |
| Stool | Inventory of Leroy Griffin (1750) | Close stool in Richmond County, Virginia, 1750 | 10 shillings |
| Stool | Inventory of Daniel Dulany (1754) | Leather Bottomed Stool in Annapolis, Maryland, 1754 | 2 shillings 6 pence |
| Table | Inventory of Daniel Dulany (1754) | Fineer'd Walnut table in Annapolis, Maryland, 1754 | 1 pound |
| Table | Inventory of Daniel Dulany (1754) | Mahogony dressing Table in Annapolis, Maryland, 1754 | 4 pounds |
| Table | Inventory of Daniel Dulany (1754) | Small Oval Black Walnut Table in Annapolis, Maryland, 1754 | 10 shillings |
| Table | Inventory of Daniel Dulany (1754) | Japan Tea Table in Annapolis, Maryland, 1754 | 10 shillings |
| Table | Inventory of Daniel Huger (1755) | Large Cedar Table in Beaufort, South Carolina, 1755 | 1 pound 10 shillings |
| Table | Inventory of Jeremiah Chase (1755) | One square Mahogany Table with Globe & Clawed feet in Charles County, Maryland, 1755 | 3 pounds 10 shillings |
| Table | Inventory of Jeremiah Chase (1755) | Back Gammn Table in Charles County, Maryland, 1755 | 10 shillings |
| Table | Inventory of William Edings (1756) | Black walnut table in Charles Town, South Carolina, 1756 | 4 pounds |
| Table | Inventory of William Edings (1756) | Poplar table in Tooboodoe, South Carolina, 1756 | 1 pound 10 shillings |
| Table | Brock Jobe, New England Furniture: The Colonial Era (1984) | Mohogany wrtiting table purchased by a Poutsmouth merchant from Samuel Walker, a London craftsman, 1760 | 4 pounds 4 shillings |
| Table | Inventory of Doctor Adam Thomson (1768) | Mahogany Card Table in Prince George, Maryland, 1768 | 3 pounds |

| Item | Data Source | Description | Price |
|---|---|---|---|
| Table | Inventory of Doctor Adam Thomson (1768) | Marble Table in Frame in Prince George, Maryland, 1768 | 2 pounds 10 shillings |
| Table | Inventory of Doctor Adam Thomson (1768) | Cherry Tree Tea table in Frame in Prince George, Maryland, 1768 | 1 pound |
| Table | Inventory of Doctor Adam Thomson (1768) | Large Mahogany Dining Table in Prince George, Maryland, 1768 | 2 pounds |
| Table & chair | Account Invoice of E. Man (1764) | Small round table and chair for a student attending Harvard, 1764 | 10 shillings |
| Tea board | Inventory of John Brice (1767) | Tea Board in Ann Arundel, Maryland, 1767 | 2 shillings |
| Tea chest | Inventory of Jeremiah Chase (1755) | Tea Chest and Cannisters in Charles County, Maryland, 1755 | 12 shillings 6 pence |
| Tea chest | Inventory of John Brice (1767) | Tea Chest in Ann Arundel, Maryland, 1767 | 10 shillings |
| Tea table | Inventory of Daniel Huger (1755) | Mahogany Table for Tea in Beaufort, South Carolina, 1755 | 5 pounds |
| Trunk | Inventory of Jeremiah Chase (1755) | Trunk made in the Year 1668 in Charles County, Maryland, 1755 | 2 shillings 6 pence |

## Household Products

| Item | Data Source | Description | Price |
|---|---|---|---|
| Basin | Inventory of William Eilbeck (1765) | Pewter Bason, approximately 2¾ lbs in Charles County, Maryland, 1765 | 3 shillings 7 pence |
| Basket | Inventory of Thomas Lewis (1750) | Straw Basket in Fairfax County, Virginia, 1750 | 2 shillings |
| Basket | Inventory of Doctor Adam Thomson (1768) | Japand Bread Baskett in Prince George, Maryland, 1768 | 2 shillings |
| Basin | Inventory of Charles Pury (1756) | White Bason in the Town of Beaufort, South Carolina, 1756 | 2 shillings 6 pence |
| Bed cord | Unknown Harvard Student Account (approx. 1760) | Bed Cord in Cambridge, Massachusetts, 1760 | 3 shillings |
| Bed cord | Inventory of John Brice (1767) | One set of bed cords in Ann Arundel, Maryland, 1767 | 1 shilling |
| Bed cover | Inventory of Jeremiah Chase (1755) | Stampt Cotton Bead Covers in Charles County, Maryland, 1755 | 10 shillings |
| Bed tick | Inventory of Charles Pury (1756) | Bed Tick in in the Town of Beaufort, South Carolina, 1756 | 7 pounds 10 shillings |
| Bedstead | Harvard Student Inventory (1760) | Bedstead used by a Harvard student, 1760 | 8 shillings |
| Bell | Inventory of Charles Pury (1756) | House bell in the Town of Beaufort, South Carolina, 1756 | 7 shillings 6 pence |

### Based Upon the British Currency System

| Year | Pound in 2002 US Dollars | Shilling in 2002 US Dollars | Pence in 2002 US Dollars |
|---|---|---|---|
| 1750 | $216.00 | $10.80 | $0.90 |
| 1755 | $216.00 | $10.80 | $0.90 |
| 1760 | $192.00 | $9.60 | $0.80 |
| 1765 | $168.00 | $8.40 | $0.70 |
| 1770 | $168.00 | $8.40 | $0.70 |
| 1774 | $144.00 | $7.20 | $0.60 |

*Calculations are approximate values based upon economic historical data*

| Item | Data Source | Description | Price |
|------|-------------|-------------|-------|
| Bellows | Inventory of Jeremiah Chase (1755) | Pair of Bellows with Brass Nose in Charles County, Maryland, 1755 | 4 shillings |
| Bellows | Inventory of William Eilbeck (1765) | Pair small Chamber Bellows in Charles County, Maryland, 1765 | 1 shilling 3 pence |
| Blanket | Inventory of Thomas Lewis (1750) | Negro Blanket in Fairfax County, Virginia, 1750 | 1 shilling 6 pence |
| Blanket | Harvard Student Inventory (1760) | Bed blanket used by a Harvard student, 1760 | 7 shillings 2 pence |
| Bottle | Inventory of Daniel Dulany (1754) | Empty quart bottle in Annapolis, Maryland, 1754 | 3 pence |
| Bowl | Inventory of Jeremiah Chase (1755) | China bowl in Charles County, Maryland, 1755 | 10 shillings |
| Bowl | Inventory of Charles Pury (1756) | Earthen Bowl in the Town of Beaufort, South Carolina, 1756 | 3 shillings |
| Bowl | Inventory of John Fendall (1763) | China chocolate Bowl in Charles County, Maryland, 1763 | 1 shilling |
| Box | Inventory of Leroy Griffin (1750) | Painted Sugar Boxes in Richmond County, Virginia, 1750 | 4 shillings |

| Item | Data Source | Description | Price |
|------|-------------|-------------|-------|
| Box | Inventory of Thomas Lewis (1750) | Box with 5 Drawers in Fairfax County, Virginia, 1750 | 2 shillings |
| Box | Inventory of Thomas Lewis (1750) | Flowered Tin Candle Box in Fairfax County, Virginia, 1750 | 9 pence |
| Broom | Inventory of Samuel Kennastons (1754) | Hair Broom in Charles Town, South Carolina, 1754 | 11 pence |
| Broom head | Inventory of John Brice (1767) | Broom head in Ann Arundel, Maryland, 1767 | 1 shilling |
| Brush | Inventory of Leroy Griffin (1750) | Cloaths Brush in Richmond County, Virginia, 1750 | 8 pence |
| Brush | Inventory of Samuel Kennastons (1754) | Scrubing Brush in Charles Town, South Carolina, 1754 | 10 pence |
| Brush | Inventory of Daniel Dulany (1754) | Hearth Brush in Annapolis, Maryland, 1754 | 1 shilling |
| Brush | Inventory of Daniel Dulany (1754) | Cloth Brush in Annapolis, Maryland, 1754 | 1 shilling |
| Brush | Inventory of John Brice (1767) | Shoe brush in Ann Arundel, Maryland, 1767 | 2 pence |
| Brush | Inventory of John Brice (1767) | White wash brush in Ann Arundel, Maryland, 1767 | 5½ pence |
| Candle mold | Inventory of Samuel Kennastons (1754) | Candle Mould in Charles Town, South Carolina, 1754 | 1 shilling 3 pence |
| Candles | Inventory of S. Hall (1757) | Pound of candles inventoried by a student at Harvard in 1757 | 1 shilling |
| Candles | Inventory of John Brice (1767) | Pound of Dript Candles in Ann Arundel, Maryland, 1767 | 9 pence |
| Candles | Inventory of John Brice (1767) | Pound of Mould Candles in Ann Arundel, Maryland, 1767 | 10 pence |
| Candlestick | Inventory of Daniel Dulany (1754) | Brass Candlestick in Annapolis, Maryland, 1754 | 3 shillings 9 pence |
| Candlestick | Inventory of Daniel Dulany (1754) | Iron Candlestick in Annapolis, Maryland, 1754 | 8 pence |
| Candlestick | Inventory of Doctor Gustavus Brown (1762) | One large Brass Candlestick in Charles County, Maryland, 1762 | 12 shillings 6 pence |
| Carpet | Inventory of William Eilbeck (1765) | Kilmarnock Carpet for floors in Charles County, Maryland, 1765 | 2 pounds 10 shillings |
| Chamber pot | Inventory of Doctor Gustavus Brown (1762) | White Stone Chamber Pott in Charles County, Maryland, 1762 | 2 shillings |
| China | Inventory of Charles Pury (1756) | Parcel China borked & Crackt in the Town of Beaufort, South Carolina, 1756 | 10 pounds 10 shillings |

## Based Upon the British Currency System

| Year | Pound in 2002 US Dollars | Shilling in 2002 US Dollars | Pence in 2002 US Dollars |
|------|--------------------------|-----------------------------|--------------------------|
| 1750 | $216.00 | $10.80 | $0.90 |
| 1755 | $216.00 | $10.80 | $0.90 |
| 1760 | $192.00 | $ 9.60 | $0.80 |
| 1765 | $168.00 | $ 8.40 | $0.70 |
| 1770 | $168.00 | $ 8.40 | $0.70 |
| 1774 | $144.00 | $ 7.20 | $0.60 |

*Calculations are approximate values based upon economic historical data*

| Item | Data Source | Description | Price |
|------|-------------|-------------|-------|
| China set | Inventory of Jeremiah Chase (1755) | Broken Set of Red & White China in Charles County, Maryland, 1755 | 1 pound 2 shillings 6 pence |
| Churn | Inventory of William Eilbeck (1765) | Wooden Churn in Charles County, Maryland, 1765 | 2 shillings 6 pence |
| Clamp | Inventory of Daniel Dulany (1754) | Scrubing Brush Clamp in Annapolis, Maryland, 1754 | 1 shilling |
| Coffee cups & saucers | Inventory of William Edings (1756) | Dozen coffee cups and saucers in Charles Town, South Carolina in 1756 | 3 pounds |
| Coffee mill | Inventory of Leroy Griffin (1750) | Coffee mill in Richmond County, Virginia, 1750 | 4 shillings |
| Coffee pot | Inventory of William Edings (1756) | Coffee pot in Tooboodoe, South Carolina, 1756 | 1 pound |
| Corkscrew | Inventory of Samuel Kennastons (1754) | Cork screw in Charles Town, South Carolina, 1754 | 3 pence |
| Coverlet | Harvard Student Inventory (1760) | Coverlet used by a Harvard student, 1760 | 14 shillings 8 pence |
| Cup | Inventory of Daniel Dulany (1754) | China Custard Cup in Annapolis, Maryland, 1754 | 10½ pence |
| Cups & saucers | Inventory of Doctor Gustavus Brown (1762) | Dozen Chaney cups & Saucers in Charles County, Maryland, 1762 | 1 pound 10 shillings |
| Cups & saucers | Inventory of Doctor Adam Thomson (1768) | Half dozen of Breakfast cups and saucers in Prince George, Maryland, 1768 | 5 shillings |
| Curtains | Inventory of Daniel Dulany (1754) | Pair of Sattin Window Curtians in Annapolis, Maryland, 1754 | 13 shillings 4 pence |
| Cutlery | Inventory of John Brice (1767) | Dozen knives and folks in Ann Arundel, Maryland, 1767 | 1 pound 10 shillings |
| Decanter | Inventory of Charles Pury (1756) | Glass Decanter in the Town of Beaufort, South Carolina, 1756 | 10 shillings |
| Dish | Inventory of Daniel Dulany (1754) | China dish in Annapolis, Maryland, 1754 | 8 shillings |
| Dish | Inventory of Daniel Dulany (1754) | Brass Chaffing Dish in Annapolis, Maryland, 1754 | 3 shillings |
| Dish | Inventory of Doctor Gustavus Brown (1762) | Gilted chaney dish in Charles County, Maryland, 1762 | 4 shillings |
| Dish | Inventory of William Eilbeck (1765) | New pewter plate, over 2½ lbs weight in Charles County, Maryland, 1765 | 4 shillings 6 pence |
| Dish | Inventory of John Brice (1767) | Cheese dish in Ann Arundel, Maryland, 1767 | 2 shillings |
| Fork | Inventory of Daniel Dulany (1754) | Ivory handled fork in Annapolis, Maryland, 1754 | 6 pence |
| Glass | Inventory of William Edings (1756) | Large peer Glass in Tooboodoe, South Carolina, 1756 | 10 pounds |
| Glass | Inventory of Doctor Gustavus Brown (1762) | Wine glass in Charles County, Maryland, 1762 | 9 pence |
| Glass | Inventory of William Eilbeck (1765) | Beer glass in Charles County, Maryland, 1765 | 6½ pence |
| Glasses | Inventory of Leroy Griffin (1750) | Dozen wine glasses in Richmond County, Virginia, 1750 | 5 shillings |
| Glasses | Inventory of William Edings (1756) | Two Mahogany pear Glasses in Charles Town, South Carolina, 1756 | 50 pounds |
| Grate | Inventory of Daniel Dulany (1754) | Iron stove grate in Annapolis, Maryland, 1754 | 5 shillings |
| Hair powder | Inventory of Samuel Kennastons (1754) | Pound of Scented Hair Powder in Charles Town, South Carolina, 1754 | 4 pence |
| Hearth | Inventory of William Edings (1756) | Brass Hearth with one pair of Dogs Shovel and Tongs in Charles Town, South Carolina in 1756 | 10 pounds |

| Item | Data Source | Description | Price |
|------|-------------|-------------|-------|
| Jar | Inventory of Daniel Dulany (1754) | Oyl Jar in Annapolis, Maryland, 1754 | 3 shillings 9 pence |
| Jar | Inventory of John Brice (1767) | Quart jar in Ann Arundel, Maryland, 1767 | 2¼ pence |
| Jug | Inventory of Leroy Griffin (1750) | Stone gallon water jugg in Richmond County, Virginia, 1750 | 2 shillings |
| Jug | Inventory of Doctor Adam Thomson (1768) | Three-gallon stone jug in Prince George, Maryland, 1768 | 2 shillings |
| Knife | Inventory of Daniel Dulany (1754) | Ivory handled knife in Annapolis, Maryland, 1754 | 6 pence |
| Knocker | Inventory of Daniel Dulany (1754) | Brass knocker in Annapolis, Maryland, 1754 | 7 shillings 6 pence |
| Ladle | Inventory of Leroy Griffin (1750) | Silver punch Ladle in Richmond County, Virginia, 1750 | 18 shillings |
| Lime squeezer | Inventory of William Edings (1756) | Lime Squeaser in Tooboodoe, South Carolina, 1756 | 1 pound |
| Lock | Inventory of Daniel Dulany (1754) | Closet Lock with Brass nobs and Cap staples in Annapolis, Maryland, 1754 | 1 shilling 8 pence |
| Mug | Inventory of Leroy Griffin (1750) | Black glaz'd pint mugg in Richmond County, Virginia, 1750 | 1 shilling 6 pence |
| Mug | Inventory of Daniel Dulany (1754) | White mug - one pint in Annapolis, Maryland, 1754 | 4 pence |
| Mug | Inventory of S. Hall (1757) | Stone mug inventoried by a student at Harvard, 1757 | 1 shilling 8 pence |
| Napkin | Inventory of Jeremiah Chase (1755) | Damask Napkin in Charles County, Maryland, 1755 | 3 shillings |
| Oil | Inventory of Daniel Dulany (1754) | One flask of Oyl in Annapolis, Maryland, 1754 | 3 shillings |
| Pan | Inventory of William Air (1754) | Earthen Pan in Beaufort County, South Carolina, 1754 | 3 shillings 9 pence |
| Pan | Inventory of Daniel Dulany (1754) | China Patty Pan in Annapolis, Maryland, 1754 | 1 shilling 3 pence |
| Paper | Inventory of Charles Pury (1756) | Ream of Small Writing Paper in the Town of Beaufort, South Carolina, 1756 | 2 pounds |
| Picture | Inventory of Daniel Dulany (1754) | Picture of fruit Annapolis, Maryland, 1754 | 8 shillings |
| Picture | Inventory of Daniel Dulany (1754) | Picture of flowers Annapolis, Maryland, 1754 | 4 shillings |

## Based Upon the British Currency System

| Year | Pound in 2002 US Dollars | Shilling in 2002 US Dollars | Pence in 2002 US Dollars |
|------|--------------------------|------------------------------|---------------------------|
| 1750 | $216.00 | $10.80 | $0.90 |
| 1755 | $216.00 | $10.80 | $0.90 |
| 1760 | $192.00 | $ 9.60 | $0.80 |
| 1765 | $168.00 | $ 8.40 | $0.70 |
| 1770 | $168.00 | $ 8.40 | $0.70 |
| 1774 | $144.00 | $ 7.20 | $0.60 |

*Calculations are approximate values based upon economic historical data*

| Item | Data Source | Description | Price |
|------|-------------|-------------|-------|
| Picture | Inventory of Daniel Dulany (1754) | Picture, Marriage a-al-Mode in Frames and Covered with Glass in Annapolis, Maryland, 1754 | 6 shillings |
| Picture | Inventory of Jeremiah Chase (1755) | Small Needle work Picture in Charles County, Maryland, 1755 | 1 shilling 3 pence |
| Pillow | Inventory of Leroy Griffin (1750) | Pillow in Richmond County, Virginia, 1750 | 3 shillings |
| Pillowcase | Inventory of Daniel Huger (1755) | New Pillow Case in Beaufort County, South Carolina, 1755 | 7 shillings 6 pence |
| Pillowcase | Inventory of Daniel Dulany (1754) | Irish Linnen Pillow Case in Annapolis, Maryland, 1754 | 3 shillings |
| Pillowcase | Inventory of Daniel Dulany (1754) | Holland Pillow Case in Annapolis, Maryland, 1754 | 5 shillings |
| Pitcher | Inventory of Leroy Griffin (1750) | Pottle Pitcher in Richmond County, Virginia, 1750 | 6 pence |
| Pitcher | Inventory of Doctor Gustavus Brown (1762) | One Stone Picher in Charles County, Maryland, 1762 | 2 shillings |
| Plate | Inventory of Daniel Dulany (1754) | China plate in Annapolis, Maryland, 1754 | 2 shillings |
| Plate | Inventory of Joseph Fox (1756) | Stone plate in Charles Town, South Carolina, 1756 | 5 shillings |
| Plate | Inventory of James Boisseau (1756) | Flat pewter plate in Charles Town, South Carolina, 1756 | 10 shillings |
| Plate | Inventory of Charles Pury (1756) | Per pound value of a pewter plate in the Town of Beaufort, South Carolina, 1756 | 6 shillings |
| Plate | Inventory of Doctor Gustavus Brown (1762) | One Chaney butter plate in Charles County, Maryland, 1762 | 2 shillings |
| Plate warmer | Inventory of Daniel Dulany (1754) | Brass Plate Warmer in Annapolis, Maryland, 1754 | 1 pound |
| Plate warmer | Inventory of Daniel Dulany (1754) | Iron Plate Warmer in Annapolis, Maryland, 1754 | 7 shillings 6 pence |
| Plates | Inventory of Leroy Griffin (1750) | Dozen china plates in Richmond County, Virginia, 1750 | 12 shillings |
| Plates | Inventory of Doctor Gustavus Brown (1762) | Dozen Gilted Chaney plates in Charles County, Maryland, 1762 | 1 pound 16 shillings |
| Pot | Inventory of Daniel Dulany (1754) | Large China cream pot in Annapolis, Maryland, 1754 | 2 shillings 6 pence |
| Pot | Inventory of Daniel Dulany (1754) | Earthen Stone Pot in Annapolis, Maryland, 1754 | 6 pence |
| Pot | Inventory of Doctor Gustavus Brown (1762) | One Chamey cream pott in Charles County, Maryland, 1762 | 2 shillings |
| Pot | Inventory of Doctor Gustavus Brown (1762) | One stone butter pot in Charles County, Maryland, 1762 | 2 shillings 6 pence |
| Pot | Inventory of Doctor Gustavus Brown (1762) | One small pickle pot in Charles County, Maryland, 1762 | 2 shillings |
| Punch bowl | Inventory of Daniel Dulany (1754) | China punch bowl in Annapolis, Maryland, 1754 | 9 shillings |
| Quilt | Inventory of Leroy Griffin (1750) | New Callico Quilt in Richmond County, Virginia, 1750 | 1 pound 10 shillings |
| Quilt | Inventory of Daniel Dulany (1754) | One old Quilt in Annapolis, Maryland, 1754 | 1 shilling |
| Razor | Inventory of S. Hall (1757) | Rasor & case inventoried by a student at Harvard, 1757 | 3 shillings |
| Razor strap | Inventory of Samuel Kennastons (1754) | Razor Strap in Charles Town, South Carolina, 1754 | 1 shilling 8 pence |
| Rug | Inventory of Leroy Griffin (1750) | Silk rug in Richmond County, Virginia, 1750 | 1 pound |

| Item | Data Source | Description | Price |
|------|-------------|-------------|-------|
| Rug | Inventory of Daniel Dulany (1754) | Spotted Yarn Rugg in Annapolis, Maryland, 1754 | 6 shillings |
| Shaving box | Inventory of Samuel Kennastons (1754) | Shaving Box in Charles Town, South Carolina, 1754 | 1 shilling 8 pence |
| Sheets | Inventory of Daniel Dulany (1754) | Oznabriggs Sheet in Annapolis, Maryland, 1754 | 3 shillings 3 pence |
| Sheets | Harvard Student Inventory (1760) | Pair of cotton sheets used by a Harvard student, 1760 | 1 pound 12 shillings |
| Sheets | Inventory of Daniel Dulany (1754) | Corse Sheets in Annapolis, Maryland, 1754 | 7 shillings |
| Sifter | Inventory of Daniel Dulany (1754) | Old Lawn Sifter in Annapolis, Maryland, 1754 | 6 pence |
| Silverware & case | Inventory of Jeremiah Chase (1755) | Shagreen Case with 1 doz Silver handled knives and forks in Charles County, Maryland, 1755 | 9 pounds 12 shillings |
| Slider | Inventory of Leroy Griffin (1750) | Mohogony bottle Slider in Richmond County, Virginia, 1750 | 3 shillings |
| Soap | Inventory of Samuel Kennastons (1754) | Pound of Castile Soap in Charles Town, South Carolina, 1754 | 6 pence |
| Soap | Inventory of Charles Pury (1756) | Pound of Ordinary Soap in the Town of Beaufort, South Carolina, 1756 | 2 shillings |
| Soap | Inventory of Doctor Gustavus Brown (1762) | One pound of Irish Sope in Charles County, Maryland, 1762 | 1 shilling |
| Spoon | Inventory of Daniel Dulany (1754) | Pewter Spoon in Annapolis, Maryland, 1754 | 2 pence |
| Spoons | Inventory of Charles Pury (1756) | Dozen pewter spoons in the Town of Beaufort, South Carolina, 1756 | 10 shillings |
| Spoons | Inventory of Charles Pury (1756) | Dozen Tea Spoons in the Town of Beaufort, South Carolina, 1756 | 5 shillings |
| Steelyards | Inventory of John Brice (1767) | Pair of Steelyards in Ann Arundel, Maryland, 1767 | 5 shillings |
| Stool pan | Inventory of William Eilbeck (1765) | Pewter close Stool Pan in Charles County, Maryland, 1765 | 5 shillings |
| Sugar box | Inventory of Joseph Fox (1756) | Tin sugar box in Charles Town, South Carolina, 1756 | 15 shillings |
| Tablecloth | Account Invoice of E. Man (1764) | Cost of a table cloth purchased by a student attending Harvard, 1764 | 3 shillings |
| Tablecloth | Inventory of Daniel Huger (1755) | Damask Table Cloth in Beaufort County, South Carolina, 1755 | 2 pounds |
| Tankard | Inventory of William Edings (1756) | Silver Tankard weighing 37 ounces in Charles Town, South Carolina in 1756 | 55 pounds 10 shillings |

## Based Upon the British Currency System

| Year | Pound in 2002 US Dollars | Shilling in 2002 US Dollars | Pence in 2002 US Dollars |
|------|--------------------------|-----------------------------|--------------------------|
| 1750 | $216.00 | $10.80 | $0.90 |
| 1755 | $216.00 | $10.80 | $0.90 |
| 1760 | $192.00 | $ 9.60 | $0.80 |
| 1765 | $168.00 | $ 8.40 | $0.70 |
| 1770 | $168.00 | $ 8.40 | $0.70 |
| 1774 | $144.00 | $ 7.20 | $0.60 |

*Calculations are approximate values based upon economic historical data*

| Item | Data Source | Description | Price |
|---|---|---|---|
| Tea chest | Inventory of William Eilbeck (1765) | Shagreen Tea Chest with Silver Cannisters in Charles County, Maryland, 1765 | 20 pounds |
| Tea kettle | Inventory of Joseph Fox (1756) | Tea Kittle in Charleson, South Carolina, 1756 | 1 pound 15 shillings |
| Teapot | Inventory of Charles Pury (1756) | Stone Tea Pot in the Town of Beaufort, South Carolina, 1756 | 2 shillings 6 pence |
| Teapot | Inventory of S. Hall (1757) | Tea pot inventoried by a student at Harvard in 1757 | 1 shilling 4 pence |
| Teapot | Inventory of Doctor Gustavus Brown (1762) | One Chaney Tea Pott in Charles County, Maryland, 1762 | 6 shillings |
| Tea set | Inventory of Leroy Griffin (1750) | Sixteen china cups and 12 Saucers coloured red with tea pot & Tray in Richmond County, Virginia, 1750 | 1 pound |
| Teaspoons | Inventory of Thomas Holman (1756) | Silver teaspoons in St Andrews, South Carolina, 1756 | 10 shillings |
| Teaspoons | Inventory of Sam. Barrnard (1764) | Silver Tea Spoons inventoried by a Harvard student, 1764 | 3 shillings 3 pence |
| Tinder box | Inventory of Charles Pury (1756) | Tinder Box in the Town of Beaufort, South Carolina, 1756 | 18 shillings 9 pence |
| Toaster | Inventory of Daniel Dulany (1754) | Cheese Toaster in Annapolis, Maryland, 1754 | 6 pence |
| Tongs & shovel | Inventory of William Edings (1756) | Pair of Brass headed Dogs Tongs and Shovel in Tooboodoe, South Carolina, 1756 | 7 pounds |
| Towel | Inventory of S. Hall (1757) | Towel inventoried by a student at Harvard, 1757 | 1 pound 3 shillings |
| Towels | Inventory of Joseph Galloway (1753) | Dozen Towalls Sorted in Anne Arundel County, Maryland, 1753 | 1 pound 10 shillings |
| Traps | Inventory of William Edings (1756) | Two Mouse Traps foiles and Chizells in Tooboodoe, South Carolina, 1756 | 10 shillings |
| Trunk | Inventory of Samuel Kennastons (1754) | Hair Trunk in Charles Town, South Carolina, 1754 | 4 shillings |
| Trunk | Inventory of Samuel Kennastons (1754) | Small Black Trunk in Charles Town, South Carolina, 1754 | 5 pounds |
| Waiter | Inventory of William Edings (1756) | Dum Waiter in Charles Town, South Carolina, 1756 | 2 pounds |
| Warming pan | Inventory of Daniel Huger (1755) | Warming pan in Beaufort, South Carolina, 1755 | 2 pounds 10 shillings |
| Warming pan | Inventory of John Brice (1767) | Warming pan in Ann Arundel, Maryland, 1767 | 1 pence |
| Wash ball | Inventory of Samuel Kennastons (1754) | Wash Ball in Charles Town, South Carolina, 1754 | 7 shillings 4 pence |
| Wash ball box | Inventory of Samuel Kennastons (1754) | Wash Ball Box in Charles Town, South Carolina, 1754 | 12 shillings 6 pence |
| Wash basin | Inventory of Joseph Fox (1756) | Wash Bason and Cullender in Charles Town, South Carolina, 1756 | 1 shilling |
| Wig block | Inventory of Leroy Griffin (1750) | Wigg block in Richmond County, Virginia, 1750 | 1 shilling |
| Yarn winder | Inventory of Doctor Adam Thomson (1768) | A yarn winder in Prince George, Maryland, 1768 | 1 pound 15 shillings |

### Jewelry

| Item | Data Source | Description | Price |
|---|---|---|---|
| Beads | Inventory of Charles Pury (1756) | Pound of beads in the Town of Beaufort, South Carolina, 1756 | 3 shillings |
| Earrings | Inventory of Samuel Kennastons (1754) | Pair of earings in Charles Town, South Carolina, 1754 | 1 pound 10 shillings |
| Necklace | Inventory of Daniel Dulany (1754) | French Necklace in Annapolis, Maryland, 1754 | 1 pound 1 pence |

| Item | Data Source | Description | Price |
|---|---|---|---|
| Ring | Inventory of Samuel Kennastons (1754) | Gold ring in Charles Town, South Carolina, South Carolina, 1756 | 1 pound 10 shillings |
| Watch | Inventory of Leroy Griffin (1750) | Silver watch in Richmond County, Virginia, 1750 | 2 shillings 3 pence |
| Watch | Inventory of Samuel Kennastons (1754) | Childs watch & Equipage in Charles Town, South Carolina, 1754 | 15 pounds |
| Watch | Inventory of Jeremiah Chase (1755) | Gold watch and seale in Charles County, Maryland, 1755 | 30 pounds |
| Watch string | Inventory of Samuel Kennastons (1754) | Watch string in Charles Town, South Carolina, 1754 | 3 pence |

### Kitchen Items

| Item | Data Source | Description | Price |
|---|---|---|---|
| Bowl | Inventory of Leroy Griffin (1750) | Milk bowl in Richmond County, Virginia, 1750 | 5 shillings |
| Butter pot | Inventory of Joseph Fox (1756) | Butter pot in Charles Town, South Carolina, 1756 | 10 pence |
| Canister | Inventory of Samuel Kennastons (1754) | Glass canister in Charles Town, South Carolina, 1754 | 2 shillings 6 pence |
| Canister | Inventory of Charles Pury (1756) | Large tin canister in the Town of Beaufort, South Carolina, 1756 | 3 shillings |
| Coffee mill | Inventory of Samuel Kennastons (1754) | Coffee mill in Charles Town, South Carolina, 1754 | 3 shillings 6 pence |
| Coffee pot | Inventory of Jeremiah Chase (1755) | Copper coffee Pot in Charles County, Maryland, 1755 | 10 shillings |
| Coffee roaster | Inventory of Daniel Dulany (1754) | Coffee Roaster in Annapolis, Maryland, 1754 | 4 shillings |
| Cruet stand | Inventory of Samuel Kennastons (1754) | Crewit stand in Charles Town, South Carolina, 1754 | 2 shillings |
| Fork | Inventory of Joseph Galloway (1753) | Scimmer Fork in Anne Arundel County, Maryland, 1753 | 2 shillings |
| Fork | Inventory of Joseph Galloway (1753) | Flesh Fork in Anne Arundel County, Maryland, 1753 | 15 shillings |
| Frying pan | Inventory of Joseph Fox (1756) | Frying pan in Charles Town, South Carolina, 1756 | 4 pence |
| Funnel | Inventory of Jeremiah Chase (1755) | Tin funnell in Charles County, Maryland, 1755 | 6 pence |
| Hooks | Inventory of John Fendall (1763) | Pair pot hooks in Charles County, Maryland, 1763 | 2 pounds 18 shillings 9 pence |
| Iron pot | Inventory of John Brice (1767) | A 299 pound iron kitchen pot in Ann Arundel, Maryland, 1767 | 6 shillings 3 pence |

### Based Upon the British Currency System

| Year | Pound in 2002 US Dollars | Shilling in 2002 US Dollars | Pence in 2002 US Dollars |
|---|---|---|---|
| 1750 | $216.00 | $10.80 | $0.90 |
| 1755 | $216.00 | $10.80 | $0.90 |
| 1760 | $192.00 | $9.60 | $0.80 |
| 1765 | $168.00 | $8.40 | $0.70 |
| 1770 | $168.00 | $8.40 | $0.70 |
| 1774 | $144.00 | $7.20 | $0.60 |

*Calculations are approximate values based upon economic historical data*

| Item | Data Source | Description | Price |
|------|-------------|-------------|-------|
| Jug | Inventory of Joseph Fox (1756) | Small jug in Charles Town, South Carolina, 1756 | 1 pound 7 shillings 6 pence |
| Kettle | Inventory of Leroy Griffin (1750) | Old Copper Kettle 33 lb in Richmond County, Virginia, 1750 | 10 shillings |
| Kettle | Inventory of Jedathan Ball (1750) | Brass Kettle 32 lb in King George County, Virginia, 1750 | 3 pounds |
| Kettle | Inventory of Jeremiah Chase (1755) | Copper fish Kettle in Charles County, Maryland, 1755 | 1 shilling |
| Knife | Inventory of Daniel Dulany (1754) | Choping knife in Annapolis, Maryland, 1754 | 7 shillings 6 pence |
| Measure | Inventory of John Fendall (1763) | Copper Gallon Measure in Charles County, Maryland, 1763 | 1 pound 10 shillings |
| Mortar | Inventory of Thomas Holman (1756) | Brass mortor in St Andrews, South Carolina, 1756 | 2 pence |
| Nutmeg grater | Inventory of Samuel Kennastons (1754) | Nutmeg grater in Charles Town, South Carolina, 1754 | 7 shillings 6 pence |
| Oven | Inventory of Nathenial Chapman (1761) | Dutch Oven of Cast Iron in Charles County, Maryland, 1761 | 3 shillings 9 pence |
| Pan | Inventory of Joseph Galloway (1753) | Frying pan in Anne Arundel County, Maryland, 1753 | 4½ pence |
| Pan | Inventory of Daniel Dulany (1754) | Cake Tin Pan in Annapolis, Maryland, 1754 | 3 pence |
| Pan | Inventory of Daniel Dulany (1754) | Large Tin Sauce Pan in Annapolis, Maryland, 1754 | 8 pence |
| Pan | Inventory of Jeremiah Chase (1755) | Copper Sauce pan in Charles County, Maryland, 1755 | 9 shillings |
| Pan | Inventory of Charles Pury (1756) | Large Copper Stew Pan in the Town of Beaufort, South Carolina, 1756 | 8 shillings |
| Pans | Inventory of Daniel Dulany (1754) | Tin pudding Pans in Annapolis, Maryland, 1754 | 2 shillings |
| Plates | Inventory of Leroy Griffin (1750) | Dozen best Plates in Richmond County, Virginia, 1750 | 6 pence |
| Pot | Inventory of Daniel Dulany (1754) | Butter Pot with Cover in Annapolis, Maryland, 1754 | 2 pounds |
| Pot | Inventory of Daniel Huger (1755) | Gallon Pot in Beaufort, South Carolina, 1755 | 7 shillings 6 pence |
| Pot | Inventory of Nathenial Chapman (1761) | Chocolate Pott in Charles County, Maryland, 1761 | 5 shillings |
| Rack | Inventory of William Eilbeck (1765) | Iron pott rack in Charles County, Maryland, 1765 | 12 shillings 6 pence |
| Skillet | Inventory of Leroy Griffin (1750) | Bell mettle Skillet Large in Richmond County, Virginia, 1750 | 3 shillings |
| Spit | Inventory of Leroy Griffin (1750) | Iron Spitt in Richmond County, Virginia, 1750 | 4 shillings |
| Spit | Inventory of Joseph Galloway (1753) | Spitt in Anne Arundel County, Maryland, 1753 | 2 pence |
| Spoon | Inventory of John Fendall (1763) | Brass Soop Spoon in Charles County, Maryland, 1763 | 6 shillings |
| Tea kettle | Inventory of Jeremiah Chase (1755) | Copper Tea Kettle in Charles County, Maryland, 1755 | 1 pound |
| Tea kettle | Inventory of Charles Pury (1756) | Brass tea kettle in the Town of Beaufort, South Carolina, 1756 | 6 pence |
| Toaster | Inventory of Jeremiah Chase (1755) | Tin Toaster in Charles County, Maryland, 1755 | 12 shillings |

| Item | Data Source | Description | Price |
|------|-------------|-------------|-------|
| **Livery Animals & Tools** | | | |
| Bell | Inventory of William Brunston (1756) | Horse bell in Charles Town, South Carolina, 1756 | 2 shillings 6 pence |
| Bell | Inventory of Charles Pury (1756) | Horse bell in the Town of Beaufort, South Carolina, 1756 | 12 pounds |
| Cart | Inventory of Daniel Huger (1755) | Ox Cart in Beaufort, South Carolina, 1755 | 4 pounds 10 shillings |
| Collar | Inventory of Thomas Lewis (1750) | Old horse collar in Fairfax County, Virginia, 1750 | 10 pounds |
| Harness | Inventory of William Eilbeck (1765) | Old Chaise & Harness in Charles County, Maryland, 1765 | 7 pounds |
| Horse | Inventory of Leroy Griffin (1750) | Bay riding horse in Richmond County, Virginia, 1750 | 20 pounds |
| Horse | Inventory of Joseph Fox (1756) | Sorrel horse in Charles Town, South Carolina, 1756 | 30 pounds |
| Horse | Inventory of William Brunston (1756) | Gray Stallion in Charles Town, South Carolina, 1756 | 12 pounds |
| Horse | Inventory of William Eilbeck (1765) | Bay horse very old in Charles County, Maryland, 1765 | 16 pounds |
| Horse | Inventory of William Eilbeck (1765) | Chestnut Horse in Charles County, Maryland, 1765 | 10 pounds |
| Horse | Inventory of William Eilbeck (1765) | Grey Mare in Charles County, Maryland, 1765 | 8 pounds |
| Horse | Inventory of William Eilbeck (1765) | Roan Mare in Charles County, Maryland, 1765 | 9 pounds |
| Horse | Inventory of William Eilbeck (1765) | Sorrel Mare Colt in Charles County, Maryland, 1765 | 2 pounds 17 shillings |
| Horse | Inventory of Thomas Lewis (1750) | Sorrell Stallion in Fairfax County, Virginia, 1750 | 6 pence |
| Lace | Inventory of Samuel Kennastons (1754) | One Gross of Saddle Lace in Charles Towne, South Carolina, 1754, | 16 shillings 2 pence |
| Ox yoke | Inventory of Daniel Huger (1755) | Ox Yoke in Beaufort, South Carolina, 1755 | 120 pounds |
| Riding chair | Inventory of Daniel Huger (1755) | New Riding Chair in Beaufort, South Carolina, 1755 | 1 pound 10 shillings |
| Saddle | Inventory of Daniel Dulany (1754) | Side Saddle and Cloth Covering in Annapolis, Maryland, 1754 | 3 pounds |

## Based Upon the British Currency System

| Year | Pound in 2002 US Dollars | Shilling in 2002 US Dollars | Pence in 2002 US Dollars |
|------|--------------------------|------------------------------|---------------------------|
| 1750 | $216.00 | $10.80 | $0.90 |
| 1755 | $216.00 | $10.80 | $0.90 |
| 1760 | $192.00 | $ 9.60 | $0.80 |
| 1765 | $168.00 | $ 8.40 | $0.70 |
| 1770 | $168.00 | $ 8.40 | $0.70 |
| 1774 | $144.00 | $ 7.20 | $0.60 |

*Calculations are approximate values based upon economic historical data*

| Item | Data Source | Description | Price |
|------|-------------|-------------|-------|
| Saddle | Inventory of William Screven (1755) | One mans Riding Saddle in Beaufort, South Carolina, 1755 | 25 pounds |
| Saddle | Inventory of William Brunston (1756) | Woman's saddle in Charles Town, South Carolina, 1756 | 6 pounds |
| Saddle | Inventory of William Edings (1756) | Saddle and bridle in Tooboodoe, South Carolina, 1756 | 3 pounds 10 shillings |
| Saddle | Inventory of Charles Pury (1756) | Boys Saddle old in the Town of Beaufort, South Carolina, 1756 | 7 shillings 6 pence |
| Saddle | Inventory of William Eilbeck (1765) | Old Mans Saddle in Charles County, Maryland, 1765 | 5 shillings |
| Saddle bag | Inventory of William Eilbeck (1765) | Pair old Saddle Baggs in Charles County, Maryland, 1765 | 2 shillings 6 pence |
| Spurs | Inventory of Charles Pury (1756) | Pair of spurs in the Town of Beaufort, South Carolina, 1756 | 3 shillings |
| Spurs | Inventory of John Brice (1767) | Spurs and buckles in Ann Arundel, Maryland, 1767 | 8 pounds |
| Stirrup | Inventory of Thomas Lewis (1750) | Brass stirrup in Fairfax County, Virginia, 1750 | 1 shilling 6 pence |
| Whip | Inventory of John Fendall (1763) | Horse Whip in Charles County, Maryland, 1763 | 7 pounds |
| Yearling | Inventory of James Boisseau (1756) | Mare yearling in Charles Town, South Carolina, 1756 | 5 pounds |
| Yearling | Inventory of James Boisseau (1756) | Grey horse yearling in Charles Town, South Carolina, 1756 | 4 shillings |
| Yoke | Inventory of Thomas Lewis (1750) | Yoke in Fairfax County, Virginia, 1750 | 7 shillings |

## Livestock

| Item | Data Source | Description | Price |
|------|-------------|-------------|-------|
| Buck | Inventory of John Fendall (1763) | Buck in Charles County, Maryland, 1763 | 2 pounds 10 shillings |
| Bull | Inventory of John Fendall (1763) | Large Bull in Charles County, Maryland, 1763 | 14 shillings |
| Calf | Inventory of John Brice (1767) | One calf in Ann Arundel, Maryland, 1767 | 4 pounds 10 shillings |
| Cattle | Inventory of William Screven (1755) | One head of cattle in Beaufort, South Carolina, 1755 | 5 pounds 6 shillings 8 pence |
| Cattle | Inventory of Joseph Fox (1756) | Head of cattle in Charles Town, South Carolina, 1756 | 4 pounds 15 shillings |
| Cattle | Inventory of William Edings (1756) | Head of cattle in Edisto Island, South Carolina, 1756 | 1 shilling 3 pence |
| Chicken | Inventory of William Edings (1756) | Chicken in Edisto Island, South Carolina, 1756 | 1 pound 5 shillings |
| Cow | Inventory of Leroy Griffin (1750) | Cow in Richmond County, Virginia, 1750 | 10 pounds 1 shilling |
| Cow | Inventory of William Brunston (1756) | Dry cow in Charles Town, South Carolina, 1756 | 12 pounds |
| Cow | Inventory of William Edings (1756) | Cow in Charles Town, South Carolina in 1756 | 1 pound 13 shillings 4 pence |
| Cow | Inventory of Doctor Gustavus Brown (1762) | One cow in Charles County, Maryland, 1762 | 2 pounds |
| Doe | Inventory of John Fendall (1763) | Doe in Charles County, Maryland, 1763 | 5 shillings |
| Duck | Inventory of William Screven (1755) | One duck in Beaufort, South Carolina, 1755 | 5 shillings |

| Item | Data Source | Description | Price |
|------|-------------|-------------|-------|
| Ewe | Inventory of John Fendall (1763) | Ewe in Charles County, Maryland, 1763 | 3 shillings 9 pence |
| Fowl | Inventory of William Edings (1756) | Grown Fowle in Edisto Island, South Carolina, 1756 | 7 shillings 6 pence |
| Goose | Inventory of William Screven (1755) | One goose in Beaufort, South Carolina, 1755 | 2 shillings 6 pence |
| Gosling | Inventory of William Edings (1756) | Goseling in Edisto Island, South Carolina, 1756 | 3 pounds 12 shillings |
| Heifer | Inventory of John Fendall (1763) | Heiffer in Charles County, Maryland, 1763 | 7 shillings |
| Hog | Inventory of Leroy Griffin (1750) | One old hogg in Richmond County, Virginia, 1750 | 2 pounds 10 shillings |
| Hog | Inventory of Paul Lepear (1756) | Hog in Charles Town, South Carolina, 1756 | 1 pound |
| Hog | Inventory of Doctor Gustavus Brown (1762) | One two year old hog in Charles County, Maryland, 1762 | 15 pounds |
| Ox | Inventory of James Boisseau (1756) | Working ox in Charles Town, South Carolina, 1756 | 3 pounds 10 shillings |
| Oxen | Inventory of Leroy Griffin (1750) | One yoke of oxen in Richmond County, Virginia, 1750 | 12 pounds |
| Oxen | Inventory of Daniel Huger (1755) | Head of Oxen in Beaufort, South Carolina, 1755 | 12 pounds |
| Oxen | Inventory of John Fendall (1763) | Ox in Charles County, Maryland, 1763 | 5 shillings |
| Pig | Inventory of Daniel Huger (1755) | Pig in Beaufort, South Carolina, 1755 | 7 shillings 6 pence |
| Ram | Inventory of John Fendall (1763) | Ram in Charles County, Maryland, 1763 | 4 shillings |
| Sheep | Inventory of Leroy Griffin (1750) | Sheep in Richmond County, Virginia, 1750 | 7 shillings |
| Sheep | Inventory of Joseph Galloway (1753) | Sheep in Anne Arundel County, Maryland, 1753 | 1 pound 10 shillings |
| Sheep | Inventory of Thomas Holman (1756) | Value of a sheep in St Andrews, South Carolina, 1756 | 2 pounds 5 shillings |
| Shoat | Inventory of Doctor Gustavus Brown (1762) | One shoat in Charles County, Maryland, 1762 | 10 shillings |
| Shoat | Inventory of John Fendall (1763) | Shoat in Charles County, Maryland, 1763 | 7 shillings 6 pence |

## Based Upon the British Currency System

| Year | Pound in 2002 US Dollars | Shilling in 2002 US Dollars | Pence in 2002 US Dollars |
|------|--------------------------|-----------------------------|--------------------------|
| 1750 | $216.00 | $10.80 | $0.90 |
| 1755 | $216.00 | $10.80 | $0.90 |
| 1760 | $192.00 | $9.60 | $0.80 |
| 1765 | $168.00 | $8.40 | $0.70 |
| 1770 | $168.00 | $8.40 | $0.70 |
| 1774 | $144.00 | $7.20 | $0.60 |

*Calculations are approximate values based upon economic historical data*

| Item | Data Source | Description | Price |
|------|-------------|-------------|-------|
| Sow | Inventory of Doctor Gustavus Brown (1762) | One sow in Charles County, Maryland, 1762 | 1 pound 7 shillings |
| Steer | Inventory of Leroy Griffin (1750) | Steer in Richmond County, Virginia, 1750 | 1 pound 5 shillings |
| Steer | Inventory of Jeremiah Chase (1755) | Three year old Steer in Charles County, Maryland, 1755 | 2 pounds 5 shillings |
| Steer | Inventory of John Fendall (1763) | Steer in Charles County, Maryland, 1763 | 4 pounds |
| Steer | Inventory of William Eilbeck (1765) | Young Steer in Charles County, Maryland, 1765 | 2 pounds 1 shilling 6¼ pence |
| Turkey | Inventory of William Edings (1756) | Turkey in Edisto Island, South Carolina, 1756 | 1 shillings 6 pence |

**Medicine**

| Item | Data Source | Description | Price |
|------|-------------|-------------|-------|
| Balsam | Inventory of Samuel Kennastons (1754) | Value of Turlingtons Balsam in Charles Town, South Carolina, 1754 | 7 pence |
| Drops | Inventory of Samuel Kennastons (1754) | Value of one Stoutons drop in Charles Town, South Carolina, 1754 | 10 pence |
| Drops | Inventory of Samuel Kennastons (1754) | Value of one Batemans drops in Charles Town, South Carolina, 1754 | 5 shillings |
| Elixir | Inventory of John Brice (1767) | Bottle of James Elixer in Ann Arundel, Maryland, 1767 | 9 pence |
| Elixir | Inventory of Samuel Kennastons (1754) | Daffys Elixir in Charles Town, South Carolina, 1754 | 4 shillings |
| Medicine | Inventory of John Brice (1767) | Bottle of Turlington in Ann Arundel, Maryland, 1767 | 9½ pence |
| Pills | Inventory of Samuel Kennastons (1754) | Andersons pills in Charles Towne, South Carolina, 1754 | 1 shillings 11 pence |
| Powder | Inventory of Samuel Kennastons (1754) | Package of James's Powder in Charles Town, South Carolina, 1754 | 4 shillings |
| Smelling salts | Inventory of Samuel Kennastons (1754) | Bottle of smelling salts in Charles Town, South Carolina, 1754 | 1 shilling |
| Tincture | Inventory of Samuel Kennastons (1754) | Value of one Greenoughs Tincture in Charles Town, South Carolina, 1754 | 10 pence |

**Music**

| Item | Data Source | Description | Price |
|------|-------------|-------------|-------|
| Violin | Inventory of Paul Lepear (1756) | Violin and case in Charles Town, South Carolina, 1756 | 10 pounds |
| Violin | Account Invoice of E. Man (1764) | An exquisite violin presented… for its intrinsic worth with a complete tutor - item on an account of an Harvard student, 1764 | 1 pound 8 shillings |

**Other**

| Item | Data Source | Description | Price |
|------|-------------|-------------|-------|
| Book | Account Invoice of E. Man (1764) | A Large Demy clean paper Book - purchase of student attending Harvard, 1764 | 6 shillings 8 pence |
| Cage | Inventory of Daniel Dulany (1754) | Old Parrot Cage in Annapolis, Maryland, 1754 | 2 pounds 9 shillings |
| Cards | Inventory of William Air (1754) | Parcell of Playing Cards in Beaufort County, South Carolina, 1754 | 10 shillings |
| Cards | Inventory of Joseph Fox (1756) | Value of 2 pair of cards, 1756 | 1 pound 15 shillings |
| Chalk | Inventory of Leroy Griffin (1750) | Parcell of Chalk in Richmond County, Virginia, 1750 | 5 shillings |
| Compass | Inventory of William Eilbeck (1765) | Small pocket Compass in Charles County, Maryland, 1765 | 1 shilling |
| Corks | Inventory of William Air (1754) | Gross of Corks in Beaufort County, South Carolina, 1754 | 3 shillings 9 pence |

| Item | Data Source | Description | Price |
|---|---|---|---|
| Fan | Inventory of Jeremiah Chase (1755) | Super fine fan and Case in Charles County, Maryland, 1755 | 15 pounds |
| Fan | Inventory of William Holman (1756) | Winnow Fan in Colleton, South Carolina, 1756 | 5 pounds |
| Flower box | Inventory of Daniel Dulany (1754) | Brass Flower Box in Annapolis, Maryland, 1754 | 12 shillings |
| Gift box | Inventory of Samuel Kennastons (1754) | Xmas Box in Charles Towne, South Carolina, 1754 | 1½ pence |
| Glass pane | Inventory of Daniel Dulany (1754) | Pane of glass 9 by 11 in Annapolis, Maryland, 1754 | 1 shilling 4 pence |
| Glasses | Inventory of Samuel Kennastons (1754) | Pair of Small Shew Glasses in Charles Town, South Carolina, 1754 | 10 pence |
| Glasses | Inventory of Samuel Kennastons (1754) | Pair of Large Shew Glasses in Charles Town, South Carolina, 1754 | 3 shillings 9 pence |
| Hair powder | Inventory of Samuel Kennastons (1754) | Pound of hair powder in Charles Towne, South Carolina, 1754 | 2½ pence |
| Hinges | Inventory of Thomas Lewis (1750) | Pair Large Door Hinges in Fairfax County, Virginia, 1750 | 2 shillings 6 pence |
| Hook & hinge | Inventory of Samuel Kennastons (1754) | Hook and hinge in Charles Town, South Carolina, 1754 | 1 shilling 2 pence |
| Ink pot | Inventory of S. Hall (1757) | Ink pot inventoried by a student at Harvard, 1757 | 1 shilling 8 pence |
| Ink powder | Inventory of Daniel Dulany (1754) | Ink Powder in Annapolis, Maryland, 1754 | 4 pence |
| Ink stand | Inventory of Samuel Kennastons (1754) | Ink stand in Charles Town, South Carolina, 1754 | 2 shillings 6 pence |
| Knife | Inventory of William Eilbeck (1765) | Pen knife in Charles County, Maryland, 1765 | 6 pence |
| Laces | Inventory of Samuel Kennastons (1754) | Ferret Laces in Charles Towne, South Carolina, 1754 | 1 shilling ½ pence |
| Lock | Inventory of Charles Pury (1756) | Lock Ordinary in the Town of Beaufort, South Carolina, 1756 | 7 shillings 6 pence |
| Lock | Harvard Student Inventory (1760) | Cleft and lock inventoried by a Harvard student, 1760 | 10 shillings 8 pence |
| Lock | Harvard Student Inventory (1760) | Lock for a student's study door at Harvard, 1760 | 2 shillings |
| Maps | Inventory of Daniel Dulany (1754) | Large Map of America & 4 small maps in Annapolis, Maryland, 1754 | 1 pound 15 shillings |

## Based Upon the British Currency System

| Year | Pound in 2002 US Dollars | Shilling in 2002 US Dollars | Pence in 2002 US Dollars |
|---|---|---|---|
| 1750 | $216.00 | $10.80 | $0.90 |
| 1755 | $216.00 | $10.80 | $0.90 |
| 1760 | $192.00 | $ 9.60 | $0.80 |
| 1765 | $168.00 | $ 8.40 | $0.70 |
| 1770 | $168.00 | $ 8.40 | $0.70 |
| 1774 | $144.00 | $ 7.20 | $0.60 |

*Calculations are approximate values based upon economic historical data*

| Item | Data Source | Description | Price |
|------|-------------|-------------|-------|
| Mill | Inventory of Paul Lepear (1756) | Steel mill in Charles Town, South Carolina in 1756 | 5 pounds |
| Mouse trap | Inventory of Samuel Kennastons (1754) | Mouse trap in Charles Town, South Carolina, 1754 | 2 shillings |
| Nails | Inventory of Samuel Kennastons (1754) | Cask of 20 pence nails in Charles Town, South Carolina, 1754 | 3 pounds 10 shillings |
| Nonsprettie | Inventory of Samuel Kennastons (1754) | Nonsprettie in Charles Town, South Carolina, 1754 | 5 pence |
| Padlock | Inventory of Charles Pury (1756) | Padlock in the Town of Beaufort, South Carolina, 1756 | 3 shillings 9 pence |
| Paper | Inventory of Samuel Kennastons (1754) | Rheam of Brown Rapping paper in Charles Town, South Carolina, 1754 | 1 shilling |
| Paper | Inventory of Daniel Dulany (1754) | Ream Fine Kings Arm Paper in Annapolis, Maryland, 1754 | 15 shillings |
| Paper | Inventory of Daniel Dulany (1754) | Ream Ordinary Paper in Annapolis, Maryland, 1754 | 10 shillings |
| Paper | Inventory of Samuel Kennastons (1754) | Quier of Paper in Charles Towne, South Carolina, 1754 | 5½ pence |
| Pencils | Inventory of John Brice (1767) | Dozen lead Pencils in Ann Arundel, Maryland, 1767 | 1 shilling 6¼ pence |
| Pettiagua | Inventory of William Holman (1756) | Moiety of a Pettiagua in Colleton, South Carolina, 1756 | 100 pounds |
| Pipe | Inventory of Thomas Lewis (1750) | Clister pipe in Fairfax County, Virginia, 1750 | 6 pence |
| Purse | Inventory of Thomas Lewis (1750) | Green silk purse in Fairfax County, Virginia, 1750 | 3 shillings |
| Scales | Inventory of Daniel Dulany (1754) | Pair old Brass Scales & Weights Lead Wts in Annapolis, Maryland, 1754 | 3 shillings 6 pence |
| Scales & weights | Inventory of Samuel Kennastons (1754) | Pair of gold scales & weights in Charles Town, South Carolina, 1754 | 5 shillings |
| Scales & weights | Inventory of Samuel Kennastons (1754) | Pair of money Scales & Weights in Charles Town, South Carolina, 1754 | 1 pound |
| Shingles | Inventory of Daniel Huger (1755) | 100 Cyprus Shingles in Beaufort, South Carolina, 1755 | 2 shillings 6 pence |
| Sieve | Inventory of William Eilbeck (1765) | Wire Wheat Sive in Charles County, Maryland, 1765 | 6 shillings |
| Slate | Inventory of S. Hall (1757) | Slate inventoried by a student at Harvard in 1757 | 1 shilling 6 pence |
| Spectacles | Inventory of Doctor Adam Thomson (1768) | Pair of spectacles and steel case in Prince George, Maryland, 1768 | 1 shilling |
| Spy Glass | Inventory of Leroy Griffin (1750) | Spie Glass in Richmond County, Virginia, 1750 | 2 shillings 6 pence |
| Starch | Inventory of Samuel Kennastons (1754) | Barrel of starch in Charles Town, South Carolina, 1754 | 1 pound 10 pence |
| Starch | Inventory of William Air (1754) | Pound of Starch in Beaufort County, South Carolina, 1754 | 1 shilling 6 pence |
| Stone Step | Inventory of Leroy Griffin (1750) | Stone step in Richmond County, Virginia, 1750 | 1 shilling |
| Sword | Inventory of James Boisseau (1756) | Cutlash and Cartouch Box in Charles Town, South Carolina, 1756 | 1 pound |
| Tape | Inventory of Charles Pury (1756) | One dozen Beggers Tape in the Town of Beaufort, South Carolina, 1756 | 1 pound 5 shillings |
| Toothbrush | Inventory of Samuel Kennastons (1754) | Tooth Brush in Charles Town, South Carolina, 1754 | 2 pence |

| Item | Data Source | Description | Price |
|---|---|---|---|
| Twine | Inventory of Samuel Kennastons (1754) | Pound of twine in Charles Town, South Carolina, 1754 | 9 pence |
| Umbrella | Inventory of Charles Pury (1756) | Umbrelloe in the Town of Beaufort, South Carolina, 1756 | 2 pounds |
| Water | Inventory of Samuel Kennastons (1754) | Bottle of Rose Water in Charles Town, South Carolina, 1754 | 7 pence |
| Water | Inventory of John Fendall (1763) | Bottle Orange flower Water in Charles County, Maryland, 1763 | 1 shilling |
| Water engine | Inventory of Daniel Dulany (1754) | Old Water Engine & Earthen Pipes in Annapolis, Maryland, 1754 | 3 pounds |
| Wax | Inventory of Charles Pury (1756) | Pound of Sealing Wax in the Town of Beaufort, South Carolina, 1756 | 14 shillings |
| Wax | Inventory of Charles Pury (1756) | Pound of Myrtle Wax in the Town of Beaufort, South Carolina, 1756 | 3 shillings 9 pence |
| Wax | Inventory of John Brice (1767) | One pound sealing wax in Ann Arundel, Maryland, 1767 | 5 shillings |
| Weights | Inventory of Daniel Dulany (1754) | Set of Brass Weights in Annapolis, Maryland, 1754 | 2 pounds 6 pence |
| Wig ribbon | Inventory of Samuel Kennastons (1754) | Piece of wig ribbon in Charles Town, South Carolina, 1754 | 3 shillings 4 pence |
| Wig rose | Inventory of Samuel Kennastons (1754) | Rose for Wig in Charles Town, South Carolina, 1754 | 7 pence |

## Publications

| Item | Data Source | Description | Price |
|---|---|---|---|
| Bible | Inventory of Doctor Gustavus Brown (1762) | One large Quaker bible in Charles County, Maryland, 1762 | 1 pound |
| Book | Inventory of Leroy Griffin (1750) | Arabian knights 6 vol in Richmond County, Virginia, 1750 | 5 shillings |
| Book | Inventory of Leroy Griffin (1750) | Nature display'd 4 vol in Richmond County, Virginia, 1750 | 12 shillings |
| Book | Inventory of Leroy Griffin (1750) | History of birds 2 vol in Richmond County, Virginia, 1750 | 4 shillings |
| Book | Inventory of Leroy Griffin (1750) | Dickes spelling book in Richmond County, Virginia, 1750 | 1 shilling |
| Book | Inventory of Leroy Griffin (1750) | Buckhannans Latin history in Richmond County, Virginia, 1750 | 3 shillings |
| Book | Inventory of Leroy Griffin (1750) | Blands Military discipline in Richmond County, Virginia, 1750 | 5 shillings |

### Based Upon the British Currency System

| Year | Pound in 2002 US Dollars | Shilling in 2002 US Dollars | Pence in 2002 US Dollars |
|---|---|---|---|
| 1750 | $216.00 | $10.80 | $0.90 |
| 1755 | $216.00 | $10.80 | $0.90 |
| 1760 | $192.00 | $9.60 | $0.80 |
| 1765 | $168.00 | $8.40 | $0.70 |
| 1770 | $168.00 | $8.40 | $0.70 |
| 1774 | $144.00 | $7.20 | $0.60 |

*Calculations are approximate values based upon economic historical data*

| Item | Data Source | Description | Price |
|------|-------------|-------------|-------|
| Book | Inventory of Leroy Griffin (1750) | Salmons modern history 2 vol in Richmond County, Virginia, 1750 | 8 shillings |
| Book | Inventory of Leroy Griffin (1750) | Miltons Paradise lost in Richmond County, Virginia, 1750 | 3 shillings |
| Book | Inventory of Leroy Griffin (1750) | Shaws Justice 2 vol in Richmond County, Virginia, 1750 | 7 shillings |
| Book | Inventory of Leroy Griffin (1750) | History of Jamaica in Richmond County, Virginia, 1750 | 4 shillings 6 pence |
| Book | Inventory of Leroy Griffin (1750) | Gullivers travels in Richmond County, Virginia, 1750 | 1 shilling 6 pence |
| Book | Inventory of Leroy Griffin (1750) | Rollins Roman History 10 vol in Richmond County, Virginia, 1750 | 1 pound 5 shillings |
| Book | Inventory of Leroy Griffin (1750) | Historical Dictionary 2 vol in Richmond County, Virginia, 1750 | 8 shillings |
| Book | Inventory of Leroy Griffin (1750) | Stiths History of Virginia in Richmond County, Virginia, 1750 | 5 shillings |
| Book | Inventory of Samuel Kennastons (1754) | Primmer in Charles Town, South Carolina, 1754 | 2 pence |
| Book | Inventory of Samuel Kennastons (1754) | Spelling Book in Charles Town, South Carolina, 1754 | 7 pence |
| Book | Inventory of Samuel Kennastons (1754) | Devout Book in Charles Town, South Carolina, 1754 | 4 pence |
| Book | Inventory of Samuel Kennastons (1754) | Reading made easie in Charles Town, South Carolina, 1754 | 4 pence |
| Book | Inventory of Samuel Kennastons (1754) | Testament in Charles Town, South Carolina, 1754 | 10 pence |
| Book | Inventory of Samuel Kennastons (1754) | Leather Pocket Book in Charles Town, South Carolina, 1754 | 5 pence |
| Book | Inventory of Samuel Kennastons (1754) | Prayer Book in Charles Town, South Carolina, 1754 | 2 shillings 4 pence |
| Book | Inventory of Daniel Dulany (1754) | History of the World in Annapolis, Maryland, 1754 | 15 shillings |
| Book | Inventory of Daniel Dulany (1754) | Drydens Virginll in Annapolis, Maryland, 1754 | 15 shillings |
| Book | Inventory of Daniel Dulany (1754) | The Bible with the Common Prayer in Annapolis, Maryland, 1754 | 1 pound |
| Book | Inventory of Daniel Dulany (1754) | Nelsons Festivals and Feats in Annapolis, Maryland, 1754 | 5 shillings |
| Book | Inventory of Daniel Dulany (1754) | Whole Duty of Man in Annapolis, Maryland, 1754 | 3 shillings |
| Book | Inventory of Daniel Dulany (1754) | Black Man on the Creation in Annapolis, Maryland, 1754 | 3 shillings 6 pence |
| Book | Inventory of Daniel Dulany (1754) | Nelsons lively Oracles in Annapolis, Maryland, 1754 | 1 shilling 6 pence |
| Book | Inventory of Daniel Dulany (1754) | Nelsons Government of the Tongue in Annapolis, Maryland, 1754 | 2 shillings 6 pence |
| Book | Inventory of Daniel Dulany (1754) | Nelsons Art of Contentment in Annapolis, Maryland, 1754 | 2 shillings |
| Book | Inventory of Daniel Dulany (1754) | Nelsons Ladys Colling in Annapolis, Maryland, 1754 | 2 shillings 6 pence |
| Book | Inventory of Daniel Dulany (1754) | Burnetts Reformation of the Church in Annapolis, Maryland, 1754 | 2 shillings |
| Book | Inventory of Daniel Dulany (1754) | Sherlock on Death in Annapolis, Maryland, 1754 | 1 shilling 6 pence |

| Item | Data Source | Description | Price |
|------|-------------|-------------|-------|
| Book | Inventory of Daniel Dulany (1754) | Tate and Broadleys Version of the Psalms in Annapolis, Maryland, 1754 | 1 shilling |
| Book | Inventory of Daniel Dulany (1754) | Langleys Architect of Prices of work in Annapolis, Maryland, 1754 | 5 shillings |
| Book | Inventory of Daniel Dulany (1754) | Crosby Mariners Guide in Annapolis, Maryland, 1754 | 2 shillings 6 pence |
| Book | Inventory of Daniel Dulany (1754) | Spelling Book in Annapolis, Maryland, 1754 | 8 pence |
| Book | Inventory of Daniel Dulany (1754) | Blank Book 4 qr in Annapolis, Maryland, 1754 | 6 shillings |
| Book | Inventory of Daniel Dulany (1754) | Ricants Lives of the Popes in Annapolis, Maryland, 1754 | 2 shillings 6 pence |
| Book | Inventory of Daniel Dulany (1754) | Latin Bible in Annapolis, Maryland, 1754 | 10 shillings |
| Book | Inventory of Charles Pury (1756) | 13 Vols Tillotsons Sermons - value in the Town of Beaufort, South Carolina, 1756 | 10 pounds |
| Book | Inventory of Charles Pury (1756) | 2 Vols Ecclesiase History of England - Damaged - value in the Town of Beaufort, South Carolina, 1756 | 5 pounds |
| Book | Inventory of Charles Pury (1756) | Burket on the New Testament - value in the Town of Beaufort, South Carolina, 1756 | 10 pounds |
| Book | Inventory of Charles Pury (1756) | Comber on the Common prayer - value in the Town of Beaufort, South Carolina, 1756 | 2 pounds 10 shillings |
| Book | Inventory of Charles Pury (1756) | 3 Vols Arguments on the Bible - value in the Town of Beaufort, South Carolina, 1756 | 1 pound 10 shillings |

| Item | Data Source | Description | Price |
|------|-------------|-------------|-------|
| Book | Inventory of Charles Pury (1756) | Blairs Sermons 2 Vols - value in the Town of Beaufort, South Carolina, 1756 | 1 pound |
| Book | Inventory of Charles Pury (1756) | Lennards wisdom - value in the Town of Beaufort, South Carolina, 1756 | 7 shillings 6 pence |
| Book | Inventory of Charles Pury (1756) | Coles Gods Sovereignty - value in the Town of Beaufort, South Carolina, 1756 | 5 shillings |
| Book | Inventory of Charles Pury (1756) | Coles on the Holy Communion - value in the Town of Beaufort, South Carolina, 1756 | 5 shillings |
| Book | Inventory of Charles Pury (1756) | Paragraph on St Pauls Epistles - value in the Town of Beaufort, South Carolina, 1756 | 10 shillings |
| Book | Inventory of Charles Pury (1756) | Goodwin on Hell - value in the Town of Beaufort, South Carolina, 1756 | 2 shillings 6 pence |
| Book | Inventory of Charles Pury (1756) | Short method with the Deist - value in the Town of Beaufort, South Carolina, 1756 | 12 shillings 6 pence |
| Book | Inventory of Charles Pury (1756) | History of Society Propagating the Gospel - value in the Town of Beaufort, South Carolina, 1756 | 10 shillings |
| Book | Inventory of Charles Pury (1756) | Boyers Dictionary - value in the Town of Beaufort, South Carolina, 1756 | 3 pounds |
| Book | Inventory of Charles Pury (1756) | Shakespears Works 7 Vols - value in the Town of Beaufort, South Carolina, 1756 | 5 pounds |
| Book | Harvard Student Inventory (1760) | Bible purchased by a student attending Harvard | 3 shillings 6 pence |
| Book | Harvard Student Inventory (1760) | The Spritual Warfare inventoried by a Harvard student prior to vacation | 1 shilling |
| Book | Harvard Student Inventory (1760) | Greek Lexicion inventoried by a Harvard student, 1760 | 9 shillings 4 pence |
| Book | Harvard Student Inventory (1760) | Greek Catechism inventoried by a Harvard student, 1760 | 1 shilling |
| Book | Harvard Student Inventory (1760) | Brattle's Logic - inventoried by a Harvard student, 1760 | 1 shilling 6 pence |
| Book | Unknown Harvard Student Account (approx. 1760) | Spiritual Warfare | 1 shilling |
| Book | Unknown Harvard Student Account (approx. 1760) | Greek Lexicion in Cambridge, Massachusetts, 1760 | 9 shillings 4 pence |
| Book | Unknown Harvard Student Account (approx. 1760) | Brattles Logic | 1 shilling 6 pence |
| Book | Inventory of Nathenial Chapman (1761) | Bissetts Abridgement of the Maryland Law | 2 shillings 6 pence |
| Book | Inventory of Nathenial Chapman (1761) | One Vol of Shakespeare | 1 shilling 6 pence |
| Book | Inventory of Doctor Gustavus Brown (1762) | Abernathis Sermons, valued in Charles County, Maryland, 1762 | 6 shillings |
| Book | Inventory of Doctor Gustavus Brown (1762) | Nelsons Festiables, valued in Charles County, Maryland, 1762 | 8 shillings |
| Book | Account Invoice of E. Man (1764) | Cost for a complete Hebrew Bible with a Greek Supplement at the end at Harvard College, 1764 | 1 pound, 4 shillings |
| Book | Account Invoice of E. Man (1764) | Cost for a Latin Bible, 8 vo at Harvard College, 1764 | 8 shillings, 2 pence |
| Book | Account Invoice of E. Man (1764) | A five volume edition of Homer's Odyssey by Pope - sold in Boston for students atteding Harvard, 1764 | 1 pound 8 shillings |
| Book | Account Invoice of E. Man (1764) | A eight volume edition of Aristole's Ethic - sold in Boston for students atteding Harvard, 1764 | 12 shillings |
| Book | Account Invoice of E. Man (1764) | Introduction to the Latin Tongue by Clerk - sold in Boston for students atteding Harvard | 10 shillings |
| Book | Account Invoice of E. Man (1764) | Boyle's Voyages - A eight volume text sold to students attending Harvard, 1764 | 12 shillings |

| Item | Data Source | Description | Price |
|------|-------------|-------------|-------|
| Book | Account Invoice of E. Man (1764) | Book of Job - In Greek heroic verse - text sold to students attending Harvard, 1764 | 4 shillings |
| Book | Account Invoice of E. Man (1764) | Travels of a Englishman to Jerusalem - text sold to students attending Harvard | 6 shillings |
| Book | Account Invoice of E. Man (1764) | Drake's Voyages - text sold to students attending Harvard, 1764 | 12 shillings |
| Book | Account Invoice of E. Man (1764) | Smith's Theory of Moral Sentiments - text sold to students atteding Harvard, 1764 | 12 shillings |
| Book | Account Invoice of S. Ames (1764) | An English Dictionary- purchased by a Harvard student, 1764 | 10 shillings |
| Book | Account Invoice of S. Ames (1764) | A Greek Catechism - purchased by a Harvard student, 1764 | 8 pence |
| Magazine | Inventory of Samuel Kennastons (1754) | Lilliputians Magazine in Charles Town, South Carolina, 1754 | 10 pence |
| Magazine | Inventory of Charles Pury (1756) | London Magazines 1738, Present State of Great Britian - value in the Town of Beaufort, South Carolina, 1756 | 1 pound |
| Magazine | Joseph Willard Account (appox 1760) | 1 Vol of Spectator | 6 shillings |
| Magazine | Joseph Willard Account (appox 1760) | 1 Vol of the Rambler | 6 shillings |

## Real Estate

| Item | Data Source | Description | Price |
|------|-------------|-------------|-------|
| Boarding | Vestry Book of Camden Parish 1771 | Payment for boarding minister in Halifax County | 340 lbs of Tobacco |
| Construction | Account Book of John Smith in Pittsylvania Virginia (1762) | For the construction of a "Dwelling House" | 45 pounds |
| Construction | Account Book of John Smith in Halifax, Virginia (1762) | For the construction of two chimneys to a house | 6 pounds 10 shillings |
| House | The Pennsylvania Gazette (1762) | Three story brick house in Philadelphia, Pennsylvania on Race Street, 1762 | 250 pounds plus 3 years' interest |
| Property | Halifax Deed Book (1764) | Property purchase of 794 acres in Virginia on Sandy Creek, 1764 | 350 pounds |
| Property | Deed in Henry County (1772) | Lands on the Pigg River which include an iron mine Henry County, Virginia, 1772 | 4,000 pounds |
| Rent | The Pennsylvania Gazette (1754) | Rent offered for a 60 by 40 foot Mill with servants both black and white in East New Jersey, 1754 | 500 pounds |

## Based Upon the British Currency System

| Year | Pound in 2002 US Dollars | Shilling in 2002 US Dollars | Pence in 2002 US Dollars |
|------|--------------------------|------------------------------|---------------------------|
| 1750 | $216.00 | $10.80 | $0.90 |
| 1755 | $216.00 | $10.80 | $0.90 |
| 1760 | $192.00 | $ 9.60 | $0.80 |
| 1765 | $168.00 | $ 8.40 | $0.70 |
| 1770 | $168.00 | $ 8.40 | $0.70 |
| 1774 | $144.00 | $ 7.20 | $0.60 |

*Calculations are approximate values based upon economic historical data*

| Item | Data Source | Description | Price |
|------|-------------|-------------|-------|
| Rent | The Journal of the Commons House of Assembly (1759) | Rent to William Henderson for hire of a House for a Free School in South Carolina, 1759 | 193 pounds 3 shillings |

**Servants**

| Item | Data Source | Description | Price |
|------|-------------|-------------|-------|
| Indentured servant | Inventory of Maj. Wm. Palmers (1754) | 3 years time of an Indeted Servant Boy in Charlestown, South Carolina, 1754 | 40 pounds |
| Indentured servant | Inventory of James Summers (1754) | A Servant man having about 2½ years to serve in Charlestown, South Carolina, 1754 | 60 pounds |
| Indentured servant | Inventory of John Fendall (1763) | William Brown 6 Years to serve in Charles County, Maryland, 1763 | 12 pounds |
| Indentured servant | Inventory of John Fendall (1763) | Grace Brown 3 Years and 10 Months to serve in Charles County, Maryland, 1763 | 7 pounds |
| Indentured servant | Inventory of Solom Isaac (1757) | 2 years and 8 months time of a Dutch Servant man a Cooper in Charlestown, South Carolina, 1757 | 50 pounds |
| Indentured servant | Inventory of Daniel Dulany (1754) | John Reaves a Taylor, 1 year to serve in Annapolis, Maryland, 1754 | 5 pounds |
| Indentured servant | Inventory of John Brice (1767) | Convict Man John Matthews Carpenter 3¼ yrs to serve in Ann Arundel, Maryland, 1767 | 10 pounds |
| Indentured servant | Inventory of Doctor Adam Thomson (1768) | White servant Man named James Lash about 16 Months to serve in Prince George, Maryland, 1768 | 7 pounds 10 shillings |
| Indentured servant | Inventory of Daniel Dulany (1754) | John Chaney, Gardiner, 3 years to Serve in Annapolis, Maryland, 1754 | 15 pounds |
| Indentured servant | Inventory of Daniel Dulany (1754) | Maria Fisher a dutch Woman 1½ years to serve in Annapolis, Maryland, 1754 | 5 pounds |
| Indentured servant | Inventory of Thomas Lewis (1750) | Griffeth Merrick a servant 14 months to serve in Fairfax County, Virginia, 1750 | 3 pounds |
| Indentured servant | Inventory of Thomas Lewis (1750) | Mary Haden a servant woman 14 months to serve in Fairfax County, Virginia, 1750 | 2 pounds |
| Indentured servant | Inventory of Thomas Lewis (1750) | Margt Winford 6 months to serve in Fairfax County, Virginia, 1750 | 1 pound 5 shillings |
| Indentured servant | Inventory of John Dart (1755) | An Indented Dutch boy to serve 6 years in Charlestown, South Caorlina, 1755 | 50 pounds |
| Slave | Inventory of Thomas Lewis (1750) | Negro Sam a man in Fairfax County, Virginia, 1750 | 30 pounds |
| Slave | Inventory of Thomas Lewis (1750) | Negro Sue a young wench in Fairfax County, Virginia, 1750 | 30 pounds |
| Slave | Inventory of Jedathan Ball (1750) | James (a boy) in King George County, Virginia, 1750 | 40 pounds |
| Slave | Inventory of Jedathan Ball (1750) | Dick a young negro man troubled with fitts in King George County, Virginia, 1750 | 20 pounds |
| Slave | Inventory of William Air (1754) | One Negro woman Leah sent off the Province in Capt Hutchinson for Sale being very Vecious in Beaufort, South Carolina, 1754 | 150 pounds |
| Slave | Inventory of Hugh Cartwright (1754) | Cyrus, a Bricklayer in Charles Town, South Carolina, 1754 | 350 pounds |
| Slave | Inventory of Hugh Cartwright (1754) | Smart, a Bricklayer in Charles Town, South Carolina, 1754 | 400 pounds |
| Slave | Inventory of Hugh Cartwright (1754) | Simon, A Tanner and Currier in Charles Town, South Carolina, 1754 | 300 pounds |
| Slave | Inventory of Hugh Cartwright (1754) | Jack, a Blacksmith in Charles Town, South Carolina, 1754 | 300 pounds |
| Slave | Inventory of Hugh Cartwright (1754) | York, a Carpenter in Charles Town, South Carolina, 1754 | 500 pounds |
| Slave | Inventory of Hugh Cartwright (1754) | Greenwich, a Brickmaker in Charles Town, South Carolina, 1754 | 200 pounds |

| Item | Data Source | Description | Price |
|------|-------------|-------------|-------|
| Slave | Inventory of Hugh Cartwright (1754) | George, a Boatman in Charles Town, South Carolina, 1754 | 323 pounds |
| Slave | Inventory of Hugh Cartwright (1754) | Carolina, a Shoemaker in Charles Town, South Carolina, 1754 | 456 pounds |
| Slave | Inventory of William Screven (1755) | Friday in Beaufort, South Carolina, 1755 | 300 pounds |
| Slave | Inventory of William Screven (1755) | Grace, Frydays Wife, in Beaufort, South Carolina, 1755 | 200 pounds |
| Slave | Inventory of William Screven (1755) | Little Case in Beaufort, South Carolina, 1755 | 60 pounds |
| Slave | Inventory of William Screven (1755) | Old Mingo in Beaufort, South Carolina, 1755 | 50 pounds |
| Slave | Inventory of William Screven (1755) | Penelepey in Beaufort, South Carolina, 1755 | 230 pounds |
| Slave | Inventory of Josheph Fox (1756) | Negro fellow nam'd Abraham in Charles Town, South Carolina, 1756 | 270 pounds |
| Slave | Inventory of Josheph Fox (1756) | Negro fellow named London in Charles Town, South Carolina, 1756 | 270 pounds |
| Slave | Inventory of Josheph Fox (1756) | Negro Woman Named Sarah in Charles Town, South Carolina, 1756 | 230 pounds |
| Slave | Inventory of James Boisseau (1756) | Negro Man Call'd Brass in Charles Town, South Carolina, 1756 | 300 pounds |
| Slave | Inventory of James Boisseau (1756) | Negro Man Call'd Josey in Charles Town, South Carolina, 1756 | 300 pounds |
| Slave | Inventory of James Boisseau (1756) | Boy called Simpa in Charles Town, South Carolina, 1756 | 200 pounds |
| Slave | Inventory of James Boisseau (1756) | One Wench called Tenah in Charles Town, South Carolina, 1756 | 250 pounds |
| Slave | Inventory of James Boisseau (1756) | One Girl called Phebe in Charles Town, South Carolina, 1756 | 100 pounds |
| Slave | Inventory of Thomas Holman (1756) | One Negro Man Peter in Charles Town, South Carolina, 1756 | 300 pounds |
| Slave | Inventory of Thomas Holman (1756) | One Negro Man Justice in Charles Town, South Carolina, 1756 | 200 pounds |
| Slave | Inventory of Thomas Holman (1756) | One Mulatto Man Dick in Charles Town, South Carolina, 1756 | 280 pounds |
| Slave | Inventory of Thomas Holman (1756) | One Negro Woman Sue and Child Prosper in Charles Town, South Carolina, 1756 | 320 pounds |

### Based Upon the British Currency System

| Year | Pound in 2002 US Dollars | Shilling in 2002 US Dollars | Pence in 2002 US Dollars |
|------|--------------------------|------------------------------|---------------------------|
| 1750 | $216.00 | $10.80 | $0.90 |
| 1755 | $216.00 | $10.80 | $0.90 |
| 1760 | $192.00 | $ 9.60 | $0.80 |
| 1765 | $168.00 | $ 8.40 | $0.70 |
| 1770 | $168.00 | $ 8.40 | $0.70 |
| 1774 | $144.00 | $ 7.20 | $0.60 |

*Calculations are approximate values based upon economic historical data*

| Item | Data Source | Description | Price |
|------|-------------|-------------|-------|
| Slave | Inventory of John Pinney (1756) | One Negro Man named Prince in Charles Town, South Carolina, 1756 | 350 pounds |
| Slave | Inventory of William Brunston (1756) | One Wench Lezett in Charles Town, South Carolina, 1756 | 160 pounds |
| Slave | Inventory of William Edings (1756) | One Negro Woman Called Moll in Charles Town, South Carolina, 1756 | 225 pounds |
| Slave | Inventory of William Edings (1756) | One Negro Man Called Tamerlain in Charles Town, South Carolina, 1756 | 265 pounds |
| Slave | Inventory of William Edings (1756) | One Negro Woman Called Dye in Charles Town, South Carolina, 1756 | 120 pounds |
| Slave | Inventory of Charles Pury (1756) | Old Negro Man named Guy in Beaufort, South Carolina, 1756 | 50 pounds |
| Slave | Inventory of Charles Pury (1756) | A Woman named Jenny in Beaufort, South Carolina, 1756 | 250 pounds |
| Slave | Inventory of Charles Pury (1756) | A Woman Guys Wife named Clarinda in Beaufort, South Carolina, 1756 | 100 pounds |
| Slave | Inventory of Charles Pury (1756) | A Girl named Silvia in Beaufort, South Carolina, 1756 | 100 pounds |
| Slave | Inventory of Jedathan Ball (1750) | Jack a Negro Man/Carpenter in King George County, Virginia, 1750 | 50 pounds |

## Tobacco Products

| Item | Data Source | Description | Price |
|------|-------------|-------------|-------|
| Pipe | Inventory of William Air (1754) | Gross of Long pipes in Beaufort County, South Carolina, 1754 | 7 shillings 6 pence |
| Pipe | Inventory of William Air (1754) | Gross of Short pipes in Beaufort County, South Carolina, 1754 | 7 shillings 6 pence |
| Snuff | Inventory of Samuel Kennastons (1754) | Pound of Rappee Snuff in Charles Town, South Carolina, 1754 | 2 shillings |
| Snuff | Inventory of Samuel Kennastons (1754) | Bottle of snuff in Charles Town, South Carolina, 1754 | 1 shilling 8 pence |
| Snuff | Inventory of Samuel Kennastons (1754) | Ounce of head ack Snuff in Charles Town, South Carolina,1754 | 10 pence |
| Snuff box | Inventory of Samuel Kennastons (1754) | Snuff Box in Charles Town, South Carolina, 1754 | 2 pence |
| Tobacco | Inventory of Samuel Kennastons (1754) | Pound of cut tobacco in Charles Town, South Carolina, 1754 | 7 pence |
| Tobacco | Inventory of Samuel Kennastons (1754) | Pound of Pig Tail Tobacco in Charles Town, South Carolina, 1754 | 10 pence |
| Tobacco | Inventory of John Brice (1767) | Per pound of Leaf Tobacco in Ann Arundel, Maryland, 1767 | 1½ pence |

## Trade Equipment & Tools

| Item | Data Source | Description | Price |
|------|-------------|-------------|-------|
| Adze | Inventory of Charles Pury (1756) | Carpenters & Coopers Adzes in the Town of Beaufort, South Carolina, 1756 | 15 shillings |
| Adze | Inventory of John Brice (1767) | Coopers adze in Ann Arundel, Maryland, 1767 | 5 pence |
| Apron | Inventory of Samuel Kennastons (1754) | Free Masons Apron in Charles Town, South Carolina, 1754 | 15 shillings |
| Axe | Inventory of Daniel Dulany (1754) | Coopers Ax in Annapolis, Maryland, 1754 | 2 shillings 6 pence |
| Bit | Inventory of Daniel Dulany (1754) | Coopers dowling Bit in Annapolis, Maryland, 1754 | 1 pence |
| Book | Inventory of Daniel Dulany (1754) | Blank Leidger - about 4 quire - in Annapolis, Maryland, 1754 | 6 shillings |
| Brick | Inventory of William Edings (1756) | Approximate value of 3 unburnt brick in Tooboodoe, South Carolina, 1756 | 1 pence |

| Item | Data Source | Description | Price |
|------|-------------|-------------|-------|
| Brick molds | Inventory of Daniel Huger (1755) | Brick Moulds in Beaufort, South Carolina, 1755 | 5 shillings |
| Carpenter's tools | Inventory of Daniel Huger (1755) | Set of Carpenters Tools in Beaufort, South Carolina, 1755 | 2 pounds |
| Chisel | Inventory of William Eilbeck (1765) | Joiners Chissel in Charles County, Maryland, 1765 | 1 shilling |
| Clamp | Inventory of Charles Pury (1756) | Clamp in the Town of Beaufort, South Carolina, 1756 | 2 shillings 6 pence |
| Cooper's tools | Inventory of Daniel Huger (1755) | Set of Coopers tools in Beaufort, South Carolina, 1755 | 2 pounds |
| Cooper's tools | Inventory of Charles Pury (1756) | Coopers Howel & round Sheafe in the Town of Beaufort, South Carolina, 1756 | 15 shillings |
| Gouge | Inventory of Charles Pury (1756) | Gouge in the Town of Beaufort, South Carolina, 1756 | 4 shillings |
| Hinge | Inventory of John Brice (1767) | Pair of table hinges in Ann Arundel, Maryland, 1767 | 4 pence |
| Knife | Inventory of Daniel Dulany (1754) | Coopers drawing knife in Annapolis, Maryland, 1754 | 2 shillings 6 pence |
| Latch | Inventory of John Brice (1767) | Table latch in Ann Arundel, Maryland, 1767 | 6 pence |
| Leather | Inventory of Daniel Dulany (1754) | Sole Leather in Annapolis, Maryland, 1754 | 1 shilling |
| Maps | Inventory of John Fendall (1763) | Map of Nova Scotia & Evans Map much soiled in Charles County, Maryland, 1763 | 5 shillings |
| Nails | Inventory of Doctor Gustavus Brown (1762) | One thousand twenty peny nailes in Charles County, Maryland, 1762 | 12 shillings 6 pence |
| Net | Inventory of William Edings (1756) | Casting net in Tooboodoe, South Carolina, 1756 | 3 pounds |
| Net | Inventory of John Fendall (1763) | Twine Nett in Charles County, Maryland, 1763 | 1 shilling |
| Quilting frame | Inventory of William Edings (1756) | Quiliting frame in Tooboodoe, South Carolina, 1756 | 1 pound 5 shillings |
| Rubbers | Inventory of Charles Pury (1756) | Smiths Rubbers in the Town of Beaufort, South Carolina, 1756 | 10 shillings |
| Rule | Inventory of William Eilbeck (1765) | Carpenters Rule in Charles County, Maryland, 1765 | 6 pence |
| Sail | Inventory of Nathenial Chapman (1761) | One new sail for the Boat in Charles County, Maryland, 1761 | 1 pound 15 shillings |
| Sail fabric | Inventory of John Brice (1767) | Yard of Sail Fabic in Ann Arundel, Maryland, 1767 | 1 shilling 3 pence |

### Based Upon the British Currency System

| Year | Pound in 2002 US Dollars | Shilling in 2002 US Dollars | Pence in 2002 US Dollars |
|------|--------------------------|------------------------------|---------------------------|
| 1750 | $216.00 | $10.80 | $0.90 |
| 1755 | $216.00 | $10.80 | $0.90 |
| 1760 | $192.00 | $ 9.60 | $0.80 |
| 1765 | $168.00 | $ 8.40 | $0.70 |
| 1770 | $168.00 | $ 8.40 | $0.70 |
| 1774 | $144.00 | $ 7.20 | $0.60 |

*Calculations are approximate values based upon economic historical data*

| Item | Data Source | Description | Price |
|---|---|---|---|
| Sail twine | Inventory of John Brice (1767) | One pound of sail twine in Ann Arundel, Maryland, 1767 | 1 shilling 4 pence |
| Saw | Inventory of Daniel Dulany (1754) | Cross Cut saw of 6 feet length in Annapolis, Maryland, 1754 | 15 shillings |
| Scales | Inventory of Daniel Dulany (1754) | Brass Money Weights and Scales in Annapolis, Maryland, 1754 | 2 shillings 6 pence |
| Screws | Inventory of Daniel Dulany (1754) | Thirteen wood screws in Annapolis, Maryland, 1754 | 4 pence |
| Screws | Inventory of John Fendall (1763) | Dozen Window Screws in Charles County, Maryland, 1763 | 1 shilling |
| Shear | Inventory of Daniel Dulany (1754) | Pair of Taylors Small Shears in Annapolis, Maryland, 1754 | 1 shilling |
| Skin | Inventory of Charles Pury (1756) | Pound of skins in the Town of Beaufort, South Carolina, 1756 | 10 shillings |
| Spyglass | Inventory of John Fendall (1763) | Old Spy Glass in Charles County, Maryland, 1763 | 10 shillings |
| Surgeon's instruments | Inventory of Doctor Adam Thomson (1768) | Medicines, Surgeons Instruments & utensils in Prince George, Maryland, 1768 | 19 pounds |
| Surveying equipment | Inventory of William Edings (1756) | Curveyers Compass and Chain in Tooboodoe, South Carolina, 1756 | 2 pounds 10 shillings |
| Tacks | Inventory of Daniel Dulany (1754) | Thousand 3-penny Tacks in Annapolis, Maryland, 1754 | 1 shilling 4 pence |
| Tacks | Inventory of John Fendall (1763) | 72 Brass Tacks in Charles County, Maryland, 1763 | 1 shilling |
| Tallow | Inventory of William Edings (1756) | Pound of tallow in Tooboodoe, South Carolina, 1756 | 2 shillings 6 pence |
| Tar | Inventory of Daniel Huger (1755) | Barrel of tar in Beaufort, South Carolina, 1755 | 1 pound |
| Tools | Inventory of William Brunston (1756) | Parcell of Shoe makers tools in Charles Town, South Carolina, 1756 | 15 shillings |
| Tools | Inventory of William Edings (1756) | Lott of Coopers Tools in Tooboodoe, South Carolina, 1756 | 3 pounds |
| Tools | Inventory of William Edings (1756) | Lott of Carpenters tools in Tooboodoe, South Carolina, 1756 | 8 pounds 10 shillings |
| Tools | Inventory of John Brice (1767) | Joiners Tools in Ann Arundel, Maryland, 1767 | 8 pounds 10 shillings 2 pence |
| Tread | Inventory of William Eilbeck (1765) | One pound shoe tread in Charles County, Maryland, 1765 | 2 shillings |

### Travel & Transportation

| Item | Data Source | Description | Price |
|---|---|---|---|
| Boat | Inventory of William Edings (1756) | Old boat in Tooboodoe, South Carolina, 1756 | 10 pounds |
| Boat | Inventory of William Edings (1756) | Value of one boat in order with Sails in Tooboodoe, South Carolina, 1756 | 17 shillings 6 pence |
| Boat | Inventory of Nathenial Chapman (1761) | Old Boat & grapling in Charles County, Maryland, 1761 | 10 shillings |
| Boat | Inventory of John Brice (1767) | Boat in Stocks unfinished in Ann Arundel, Maryland, 1767 | 50 pounds |
| Canoe | Inventory of Jedathan Ball (1750) | Canoe in King George County, Virginia, 1750 | 25 pounds |
| Canoe | Inventory of Daniel Huger (1755) | Canoe with Oars in Beaufort, South Carolina, 1755 | 5 pounds |
| Canoe | Inventory of Thomas Holman (1756) | Old cannoe in St Andrews, South Carolina, 1756 | 25 pounds |

| | | | |
|---|---|---|---|
| Cart | Inventory of Thomas Holman (1756) | Old cart in St Andrews, South Carolina, 1756 | 20 pounds |
| Freight | The Journal of the Commons House of Assembly (1759) | Freight of Great Guns & ca for the Look-Out at Winyaw Inlett, South Carolina, 1759 | 50 pounds |
| Freight | The Journal of the Commons House of Assembly (1759) | Carriage of Rum to Fort Prince George, South Carolina, 1759 | 300 pounds |
| Freight expense | Letter from John Smith of Halifax, Virginia (1771) | Payment for the carriage of 27 hogsheads of tobacco from Lynch's Ferry to Westham Virginia via batteaux | 750 pounds |
| Lodging | Alan D. Watson, Society In Early North Carolina (2000) | Lodging per night good bed and Clean Sheets in Rowan County, North Carolina, 1774 | 4 pence |
| Meal | Alan D. Watson, Society In Early North Carolina (2000) | Breakfast or Supper with hott meal and Small beer drink in Rowan County, North Carolina, 1774 | 8 pence |
| Meal | Alan D. Watson, Society In Early North Carolina (2000) | Breakfast or Supper with hott meal with coffee in Rowan County, North Carolina, 1774 | 4 pence |
| Ox Cart | Inventory of William Edings (1756) | Ox Cart in Tooboodoe, South Carolina, 1756 | 8 pence |
| Passage servant | Foundations for Teaching Economics (1999) | Cost of passage for an indendtured servent, including recruitment costs | 10 pounds |
| Prisoner transport | Statutes at Large of South Carolina, Vol. Fourth (1838) | Pay for passage of several prisoners of war to Great Britain from South Carolina, 1758 | 1 shilling |
| Schooner | Inventory of Daniel Huger (1755) | Schooner in Beaufort, South Carolina, 1755 | 600 pounds |
| Scout Boat | Statutes at Large of South Carolina, Vol. Fourth (1838) | Cost for a Scout Boat for service of the colony's soldiers, South Carolina, 1758 | 12 pounds |

## Based Upon the British Currency System

| Year | Pound in 2002 US Dollars | Shilling in 2002 US Dollars | Pence in 2002 US Dollars |
|---|---|---|---|
| 1750 | $216.00 | $10.80 | $0.90 |
| 1755 | $216.00 | $10.80 | $0.90 |
| 1760 | $192.00 | $ 9.60 | $0.80 |
| 1765 | $168.00 | $ 8.40 | $0.70 |
| 1770 | $168.00 | $ 8.40 | $0.70 |
| 1774 | $144.00 | $ 7.20 | $0.60 |

*Calculations are approximate values based upon economic historical data*

# MISCELLANY 1750-1774

### Patriotic Poesy

Copied by Milcah Martha Moore of Philadelphia, 1768

*Since the Men from a Party, on fear of a Frown,*
*Are kept by a Sugar-Plumb, quietly down,*
*Supinely asleep, and depriv'd of their Sight*
*Are strip'd of their Freedom, and rob'd of their*
*Right.*
*If the Sons (so degenerate) the Blessing despise,*
*Let the Daughters of Liberty, nobly arise,*
*And tho' we've no Voice, but a negative here,*
*The use of the Taxables, let us forbear,*
*(Then Merchants import till yr. Stores are all full*
*May the Buyers be few and yr. Traffick be dull.)*
*Stand firmly resolved and bid Grenville to see*
*That rather than Freedom, we'll part with our Tea*
*And well as we love the dear Draught when adry,*
*As American Patriots, - our Taste we deny.*

. . . . . . . . . . . . . . . . .

*And Paper sufficient (at home) still we have,*
*To assure the Wise-acre, we will not sign Slave.*

Source: Linda K. Kerber, Women of the Republic

### Search for Indentured Servant: 1763

Henry Laurens of South Carolina sent a letter to Captain Thomas Courtin in 1763 searching for a servant. Conditions described were as follows:

I shall be much obliged to you to procure for me on terms of three years a sober steady Man, a Cooper that is a good hand at his business, provided he will come out for £25 Stg. Per Annum & his board & diet; his passage to be paid by me but deducted out of his Wages, which I may abate if he behaves well.

Source: White Servitude in Colonial South Carolina,
Warren B. Smith (1961)

### Shipping Conditions of the Irish – 1767

Nathaniel Russell in 1767 described the conditions on which Irish immigrants were brought into Charles Town, South Carolina.

*About six weeks past a ship arriv'd hear from Belfast with a number of passengers the woners or merchants there being very anxious to procure as many passengers as possible. Instead of two hundred (Which was the most they could bring with comfort) they brot out 450 & their agreement was for 19 inches room in width for each person but they scarcely had seven, their being so much crowed and the bad usage they met with from the master of the ship who cut them off in their allowances of Provis*

*almost three Quarters brot on a distemper which carried off upwards of a hundred on the passage. The survivors were in a most pitifull condition when they arrivd here There were parents who buried all their children & many children without Parent Friend or Relation. As soon as they Landed they were ordered into the Barracks The Church Wardens immediately carried about subscriptions to raise a sum of money for their relief & in two days had upwards of two hundred pound sterling subscribed exclusive of Blankets, Linen, Cloaths, & every necessary that the sick & naked stood in need of.*

Source: Letter from Nathaniel Russell to Rev. Ezra Stiles,
Charles Town, July 19, 1767 (Gratz Collection –
Pennsylvania Historical Society)

### Real Estate Advertisement

To be sold by public Vendue, on Wednesday, the 15th Instant, on the Premises, a large thre- Story Brick House, and Lot of Ground, with a good Kitchen, two Stories high, situate in Saflafras or Race-street, next Door but one to the fix square Church in said Street, with the

Privilege of a four Feet Alley at the back End of said Lot, late the Estate of Mary Bartholomew, deceased, by EDWARD BARTHOLOMEW, AUSTIN BARTHOLOMEW, and BENJAMIN DAVIS, Executors.

N.B. THE Purchaser may have £250 of the Purchase Money on Interest three Years, giving good Security for the fame.

Source: The Pennsylvania Gazette, December, 1762

### Reward for Lost Purse

Dropt, the 28th of October last, near Mr. Nieman's, living near the Swedes Church, Philadelphia, A brown Cloth Pocket-Book, with Forty Shillings of Money in it, two Bonds, one of Forty Pounds, the other of Twenty-five Pounds, Eleven Shillings, and a Note of Forty Pounds. Whoever finds the Pocket-Book, with the Writings, and brings them to Alexander Woodrow, in

Lower-Providence, Chester County, or to Samuel Minshall, living in Pewter-Platter-Alley, Philadelphia, shall have Fifteen Shillings Reward, besides the Money that is in it.

*Source:* The Pennsylvania Gazette, *December 1762*

## Separation from Wife

Whereas Catherine Haselton, wife of Isaac Haselton, hath behaved herself very unbecoming, and left his house and abode; this is to forewarn all people from trusting her on his account, for he will not pay debts of her contracting after the date hereof.

*Source:* The Pennsylvania Gazette, *April, 1768*

## Diary Entry on North Carolina Inhabitants

The inhabitants of North Carolina are of two kinds. Some have been born in the country, and they bear the climate well, but are lazy and do not compare to our northern colonists. Others have moved here from the northern colonies or from England, Scotland, or Ireland, etc. Many of the first comers were brought by poverty, for they were too poor to buy land in Pennsylvania or Jersey, and yet wished to have land of their own; from these the Colonies receives no harm. Others, however, were refuges from debt, and had deserted wives and children, or had fled to escape punishment for evil deeds, and thought that here no one would find them, and they could go on in impunity. Whole bands of horse thieves have moved here, and constantly show their skill in this neighborhood; this has given North Carolina a very bad name in the adjoining Provinces.

*Source: Alan D. Watson,* Society In Early North Carolina, *Division of Archives and History, North Carolina Department of Cultural Resources, Raleigh, NC, 2000*

## Account on a Kitchen and Food in North Carolina

I shall & must build a good Kitchen, which I can do for forty Pounds Sterling of 30 f X 40 f. The garden has nothing to Boast of except Fruit Trees. Peaches, Nectrs Figgs annd Plumbs are in perfection of good Sorts. I cut a Musk Melon this week that weighed 17½ Pounds. Apples grow extremely well here, I have tasted excellent Cyder and Produce of this Province. Most if not all kinds of garden greens and Pot herbs grow luxuriant with us. We are in want of nothing but Industry & skill, to bring every Vegetable to a greater peerfection in this Province. Indian corn, Rice, and American

Beans are the grain that is Cultivated within a hundred and fifty yards of the Sea Board.

*Source: Correspondence of William Tryon, Western North Carolina, 1765 Alan D. Watson,* Society In Early North Carolina, *Division of Archives and History, North Carolina Department of Cultural Resources, Raleigh, N.C. 2000*

## Runaway Slave – Advertisement

RUN away, last Night, from the Subscribers, two Negroe Men, one named Cain, about 30 Years of Age, about 5 Feet 6 Inches high, has two Coats, one light coloured, with Mohair Buttons, the other Blue, with white Linings, a black Cotton Velvet Jacket, with Jet Buttons, a new Pair of Buckskin Breeches, several Pair of Thread, Worsted and Yarn Stockings, two Pair of new Shoes, two Pair of Silver carved Shoe Buckles, a Pair of Silver carved Knee Buckles, several good Linen Shirts, some of them ruffled, a Beaver Hat, with Silver Loop and Button, plays on the Fiddle, and it is thought has one with him, as it is missing, a mannerly Fellow, speaks good English, but stammers a little, and may pass himself for a Gentleman waiting Man; the other named Phill, of much the same Stature, about 24 Years of age, took with him a Blanket Coat, but perhaps may wear one of the other Negroe, a red Flannel Jacket, a Pair of brown Yarn Stockings, new Shoes, with Steel Buckles, his Hands and Fingers have a natural Cast outwards very remarkable, a new Wool Hat, a red and white Calfskin Knapsack. Whoever takes up and secures said Negroes, so as their Masters may have them again, shall receive for each Twenty Shillings, if taken in Cumberland County, or Forty Shillings, if taken out of the County, with reasonable charges, from JOHN STEEL, V.D.M. and ROBERT GIBSON.

*Source:* The Pennsylvania Gazette, *July 11, 1765*

## Eyewitness Account of the Boston Tea Party

The tea destroyed was contained in three ships, lying near each other at what was called at that time Griffin's wharf, and were surrounded by armed ships of war, the commanders of which had publicly declared that if the rebels, as they were pleased to style the Bostonians, should not withdraw their opposition to the landing of the tea before a certain day, the 17th day of December, 1773, they should on that day force it on shore, under the cover of their cannon's mouth.

On the day preceding the seventeenth, there was a meeting of the citizens of the county of Suffolk, convened at one of the churches in Boston, for the purpose of consulting on what measures might be considered expedient to prevent the landing of the tea, or secure the people from the collection of the duty. At that meeting a committee was appointed to wait on Governor Hutchinson, and request him to inform them whether he would take any measures to satisfy the people on the object of the meeting.

To the first application of this committee, the Governor told them he would give them a definite answer by five o'clock in the afternoon. At the hour appointed, the committee again repaired to the Governor's house, and on inquiry found he had gone to his country seat at Milton, a distance of about six miles. When the committee returned and informed the meeting of the absence of the Governor, there was a confused murmur among the members, and the meeting was immediately dissolved, many of them crying out, "Let every man do his duty, and be true to his country"; and there was a general huzza for Griffin's wharf.

It was now evening, and I immediately dressed myself in the costume of an Indian, equipped with a small hatchet, which I and my associates denominated the tomahawk, with which, and a club, after having painted my face and hands with coal dust in the shop of a blacksmith, I repaired to Griffin's wharf, where the ships lay that contained the tea. When I first appeared in the street after being thus disguised, I fell in with many who were dressed, equipped and painted as I was, and who fell in with me and marched in order to the place of our destination.

When we arrived at the wharf, there were three of our number who assumed an authority to direct our operations, to which we readily submitted. They divided us into three parties, for the purpose of boarding the three ships which contained the tea at the same time. The name of him who commanded the division to which I was assigned was Leonard Pitt. The names of the other commanders I never knew.

We were immediately ordered by the respective commanders to board all the ships at the same time, which we promptly obeyed. The commander of the division to which I belonged, as soon as we were on board the ship appointed me boatswain, and ordered me to go to the captain and demand of him the keys to the hatches and a dozen candles. I made the demand accordingly, and the captain promptly replied, and delivered the articles; but requested me at the same time to do no damage to the ship or rigging.

We then were ordered by our commander to open the hatches and take out all the chests of tea and throw them overboard, and we immediately proceeded to execute his orders, first cutting and splitting the chests with our tomahawks, so as thoroughly to expose them to the effects of the water.

In about three hours from the time we went on board, we had thus broken and thrown overboard every tea chest to be found in the ship, while those in the other ships were disposing of the tea in the same way, at the same time. We were surrounded by British armed ships, but no attempt was made to resist us.

We then quietly retired to our several places of residence, without having any conversation with each other, or taking any measures to discover who were our associates; nor do I recollect of our having had the knowledge of the name of a single individual concerned in that affair, except that of Leonard Pitt, the commander of my division, whom I have mentioned. There appeared to be an understanding that each individual should volunteer his services, keep his own secret, and risk the consequence for himself. No disorder took place during that transaction, and it was observed at that time that the stillest night ensued that Boston had enjoyed for many months.

George Hewes

*Source: The History Place Website*
*(http://www.historyplace.com/unitedstates/revolution/teaparty.htm)*

## Patriotic Quote: Samuel Adams

*The natural liberty of man is to be free from any superior power on earth, and not to be under the will or legislative authority of man, but only to have the law of nature for his rule.*

*Source:* The Rights of the Colonist, *by Samuel Adams, November 20, 1772*

# 1775-1799

# The Revolution Births a Debt-Plagued Nation

## PRESIDENTS

| George Washington | 1789-1797 |
| John Adams | 1797-1801 |

When the Continental Congress boldly signed the Declaration of Independence, the colonial militias were outnumbered five to one by the wealthiest and most powerful nation in the world. The British navy commanded the sea and was fully capable of a complete blockade of the American coastline. The British army was seasoned and feared. And America was far from unified. Within America's citizenry lived thousands of loyalists eager to do the bidding of the king. Of the 700,000 potential soldiers within the colonies, approximately a third opposed the war or sided with England.

The American advantages were few: an aroused leadership, a hatred of taxation, and a difficult location for England to reach and supply an army. America possessed few major cities to attack. Britain's large, highly organized army disliked the idea of attacking small, scattered communities reachable only on poorly maintained roads that hampered the procurement of supplies and the distribution of troops. As a result, The British never settled on a single war strategy, shifting their objectives and thus their resources during the course of war. This confusion gave hope to the colonials and robbed the British regulars of a sense of easy victory. To make full use of its meager assets, the Americans adopted a defensive strategy that forced the British to spread their resources over wide areas, resulting in an eight-year, very tiresome and expensive war.

The revolution started in April 1775 when British troops quartered in Boston attempted to seize munitions stored by colonial militias at Concord, Massachusetts. Conflict spread and the outnumbered British garrisons were quickly defeated. Fort Ticonderoga fell in May, Boston was evacuated by British troops in October. By the end of 1775, Britain's holdings in North America had been reduced to a few garrisons in Canada.

The following year, the British sent 75,000 troops to North America to squash the rebellion. The colonial army proved hardly a match for the well-armed British and suffered an embarrassing series of defeats. By the end of 1776, Quebec, New York City and much of New Jersey were in British hands. However, during Christmas week, General George Washington crossed the Delaware River back into New Jersey and rolled up victories at the outlying British garrisons of Trenton and Princeton. This established a pattern that held for the rest of the war. The British controlled the territory they occupied-primarily New York City and Philadelphia-with major forces. The colonists controlled-intermittently-everything else.

At the outbreak of the revolution, Congress did not have a standing army or the necessary wealth to wage war. The entire money supply in the colonies was under $10 million. Nor did Congress have the power to tax a disparate, disunited people, so it turned to the printing press to finance its revolution against the mother country. In all, the revolutionary government printed and floated $450 million in paper money to purchase goods needed to support the military-driving down the value of colonial money and inspiring the phrase, "Not worth a continental." As a result, during these disruptive years, wages for labor doubled to a dollar a day in specie, or coin, compared with the $6.60 a month in continental dollars paid to revolutionary soldiers.

In addition to battling the British, the American revolutionaries were attacked by both rampant inflation and blockade-imposed shortages. To fight back, a wide swath of the citizenry decided that public good should come before private gain. This belief liberated crowds of people, frequently women, to physically set upon traders in tea or salt and demand that they charge no more than the "just price," which the buyers set themselves.

The war economy also spoke with a distinctly French accent. Eighty thousand muskets and 60 percent of the gunpowder the colonials used came from France. In all, during the war for American independence, the French contributed $8 million in loans plus thousands of military men. Their involvement arrived early, in 1777, when the British were still in an excellent position to quell the rebellion. But when the British army's attempts to cut off New England ended in a series of defeats, including the Battle of Saratoga, New York, direct French military support began to flow, a critical turning point in the war. At the decisive battle of Yorktown, all the navy and half the army was French. In addition, Britain's other European enemies jumped in for their own purposes. Spain entered the war hoping to regain Gibraltar, lost to the British in 1713, as did Holland, a major commercial rival of England and a prominent financier of the American war effort. The Navigation Act had locked the Netherlands out of the burgeoning American market, and the revolution offered the perfect opportunity to reset the rules.

The signing of the Treaty of Paris in 1783 created its own problems. British merchants flooded the newly opened American market with luxuries, creating a boom that evolved into a postwar depression. American merchants lost their favored position with Britain as a trade partner and were excluded from the British West Indies. In addition, as wartime demand declined, agricultural prices fell and cities faced high unemployment rates. American merchants maintained trade with Mediterranean countries, and opened limited trade with China in the 1780s. Mediterranean trade, however, was hampered by pirate attacks where American ships no longer had the protection of the British navy.

The losers also included many of the leading lights of America-wealthy merchants, professionals, prominent priests and politicians who had stayed loyal to the crown during the war. In retaliation, the property of many was confiscated, and nearly 100,000 loyalists, or Tories, were expelled to Canada, the Caribbean or South America. Large estates belonging to loyalist families were broken up into smaller plots, some of which were set aside for educational purposes. The ancient British practice of passing on a family's entire estate to the eldest son known as primogeniture largely ended. Both these policies provided increased opportunities for small, independent farmers.

At the same time, the newly independent, but hardly unified, young nation began to wrestle a wide variety of policy issues including slavery and the proper role of the individual states. From its founding, America struggled to balance the repugnant immorality of slavery with its wealth-generating opportunities, often with little success.

Peace also ignited a western wanderlust. By 1790, the United States had embarked on an era of expansion. After decades of abiding by the king's prohibition against western expansion, the new Americans rushed to lay claim to the land beyond the Appalachian Mountains. The Land Ordinance of 1784 provided for the formation of 10 states northwest of the Ohio River. This was followed the next year by an ordinance that prescribed in advance that the land should be systematically surveyed into townships of six miles square, each subdivided into 36 sections of 640 parcels each, costing one dollar per acre. These decisions often placed the new government and its legions of settlers in direct conflict with the culture and traditions of the native American peoples.

Even though a centralized government ran counter to the fundamental beliefs of many who had fought to be free of British control, the creation of the Constitution was a major landmark in political and monetary development. The original Articles of Confederation simply provided for the establishment of a perpetual "league of friendship " for common defense and general welfare between the 13 states. Under it each state retained its sovereignty, its independence and all rights not given to the central government. But it quickly became clear that that the country also needed a chief executive, the power to tax and the power to control commerce to be successful. Heavily in debt, the country was torn between differing states interests and vulnerable to another foreign invasion. The new Constitution was an economic and political document that gave the federal government a framework for balancing competing interests through an executive department distinct from the legislative and judicial departments, the right to issue money and gained the power to regulate interstate and foreign commerce. "The Federal Constitution was the work of the commercial people of the seaboard towns, of the slave holding states, of the officers of the Revolutionary army, and the property holders everywhere," according to John Adams.

This new country, with its abundance of rich land and a long heritage in shipping, was aided by two events in 1793: the invention of the cotton gin and the outbreak of yet another war between England and France that lasted until 1815. Most of Europe was drawn into the conflict, but America remained neutral and traded with both sides.

# HISTORICAL SNAPSHOTS 1775-1799

## 1775–1784

### 1775

- As tensions with Great Britain increased, Massachusetts colonists bought military equipment for 15,000 men
- American revolutionary Patrick Henry made a plea for independence from Britain, saying, "Give me liberty, or give me death!"
- An act forbidding trade with any country other than Britain and Ireland was extended to include South Carolina, Virginia, Pennsylvania, New Jersey and Maryland
- Paul Revere, William Dawes and Samuel Prescott warned American colonists that "the British are coming!"
- The Second Continental Congress convened in Pennsylvania and named George Washington as its supreme commander
- Ethan Allen and his 83 Green Mountain Boys captured the British-held fortress at Ticonderoga, New York, on the western shore of Lake Champlain
- The United Colonies changed its name to the United States
- Congregationalists, Anglicans and Presbyterians comprised the three largest religious denominations in the American colonies
- The Continental Congress established a postal system for the colonies with Benjamin Franklin as the first postmaster general
- Thomas Paine advocated women's rights in an article for *Pennsylvania Magazine*
- Lord Dunmore promised freedom to male slaves who would join the British army
- The U.S. Marines were organized under the authority of the Continental Congress

### 1776

- The Continental Congress wrote and signed the Declaration of Independence
- Virginia adopted a Bill of Rights that protected an individual's enjoyment of life and liberty and the acquisition and possession of property
- George Washington established an American arsenal to manufacture guns and ammunition for his army
- The $2 bill was issued by the Continental Congress to pay for the "defense of America"
- Rhode Island declared its freedom from England two months before the Declaration of Independence was adopted
- The Assembly of New Hampshire adopted its first state constitution
- Thomas Paine anonymously published *Common Sense*, a scathing attack on King George III's reign over the colonies; it sold more than 500,000 copies in just a few months
- American revolutionaries forced British troops to abandon Boston
- The British army took New York and Rhode Island

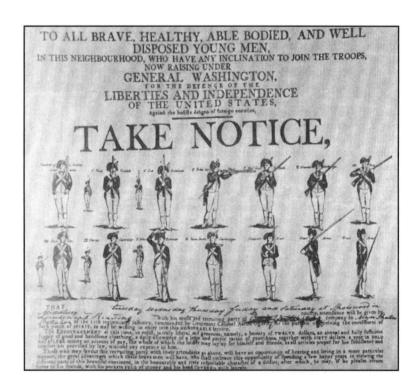

- Both France and Spain donated arms to the American rebels
- Colonists repulsed a British sea attack on Charleston, South Carolina
- The statue of King George III was pulled down in New York City
- American Captain Nathan Hale was hanged as a spy by the British in New York City
- Congress borrowed five million dollars to halt the depreciation of the value of paper money in the colonies
- Benedict Arnold and his Patriot army were defeated at Lake Champlain by the British
- George Washington's retreating revolutionary army crossed the Delaware River from New Jersey to Pennsylvania
- Captain Juan Bautista de Anza, Lieutenant Jose Moraga, and Franciscan priest Pedro Font reached San Francisco
- Phi Beta Kappa was organized at William and Mary College in Williamsburg, Virginia

## 1777

- The Continental Congress adopted the Articles of Confederation
- General George Washington's army defeated the British in the Battle of Princeton, New Jersey
- Two thousand American soldiers died at the Valley Forge, Pennsylvania, encampment during a harsh winter

- The Marquis de Lafayette arrived in the United States to assist the American cause
- Abigail Adams encouraged her husband John to give women voting privileges in the new American government
- New England's Minutemen routed British regulars at the Battle of Bennington
- The Stars and Stripes was adopted as the national flag
- The Continental frigate *Hancock* was captured by the British
- English General William Howe conquered Philadelphia, driving the U.S. Congress out of the city
- Five thousand British troops were captured at the battle of Saratoga, encouraging more overt French support of the Americans
- Scientists proved that air consists mainly of oxygen and nitrogen
- Captain James Cook reported seeing surfers using long-boards in Tahiti and Oahu
- American engineer David Bushnell invented the torpedo

## 1778

- American troops stationed at West Point nicknamed the place "Point Purgatory"
- The United States won official recognition from France and Holland
- Congress prohibited the importation of slaves
- American patriot Mary Ludwig Hays McCauley earned the name

"Molly Pitcher" when she carried water to the victorious soldiers during the Battle of Monmouth, New Jersey
- George Washington appointed Benedict Arnold as military governor of Philadelphia
- Four hundred American settlers were killed by the British in the Wyoming Massacre in Pennsylvania
- British troops recaptured Fort Sackville near Vincennes, Indiana
- British troops captured Savannah, the capital of Georgia at the time
- In England the Catholic Relief Act ignited unrest in London
- Oliver Pollock, a New Orleans businessman, created the "$" symbol
- Britain's Joseph Bramah improved the water closet

## 1779

- The British army numbered between 6,500 and 8,000 soldiers, compared to the 3,468 commanded by George Washington
- American forces gained effective control of the Old Northwest with the recapture of Fort Sackville near Vincennes, Indiana
- General Anthony Wayne captured Stony Point, New York, from the British
- Americans under Major Henry Lee took the British garrison at Paulus Hook, New Jersey

- Frederick II of Prussia condemned the increased use of coffee and called for the increased consumption of beer
- John Adams was named to negotiate the Revolutionary War's peace terms with Britain
- The Luddite riots in Manchester, England, began in reaction to the introduction of machinery for spinning cotton
- Louis XVI of France freed the last remaining serfs on royal land
- Polish nobleman General Casimir Pulaski was killed while fighting for American independence during the Battle of Savannah, Georgia

## 1780

- To consolidate the debts from the Revolutionary War, Alexander Hamilton proposed the creation of a central bank
- John Paul Jones's war ship was captured by the British at the fall of Charleston, South Carolina
- Pennsylvania began freeing the newborn children of slaves
- British Lieutenant Colonel Banastre Tarleton massacred a group of surrendering Virginia soldiers
- London exploded in riots in opposition to the Catholic Relief Act of 1778
- American General Benedict Arnold secretly promised to surrender the fort at West Point to the British army

- American troops were badly defeated by the British at the Battle of Camden, South Carolina
- Colonial militia defeated the British at the Battle of King's Mountain in South Carolina
- King Louis XVI abolished torture as a means of forcing suspects to confess
- The giant Mosasaurus dinosaur head was discovered in the Netherlands
- Sheep were introduced into Ireland from Scotland
- The American Academy of Sciences was founded in Boston, Massachusetts
- The English and the Dutch began a four-year battle
- The circular saw was invented

## 1781

- A British naval expedition led by traitor Benedict Arnold burned Richmond, Virginia
- Continental regiments routed British forces at Cowpens, South Carolina
- The Continental Congress ratified the Articles of Confederation
- General Nathanael Greene engaged British forces under General Cornwallis at Guilford Court-House, North Carolina
- The Peace Commission, composed of John Adams, John Jay, Benjamin Franklin, Henry Laurens and Thomas Jefferson, was instructed to seek independence and sovereignty

- A fleet of 24 French ships arrived in Chesapeake Bay to aid the American Revolution
- American forces defeated the British at the Battle of Yorktown in Virginia, the last battle of the Revolutionary War
- Mexican Provincial Governor Felipe de Neve founded Los Angeles
- Immanuel Kant published his *Critique of Pure Reason*
- Astronomer William Herschel discovered the planet Uranus, which he named Georgium Sidus in honor of King George III

## 1782

- The first English Bible in America was published
- The Continental Congress elected John Hanson of Maryland as its chairman, giving him the title of "President of the United States in Congress Assembled"
- The bald eagle was declared the national symbol of the United States
- The first United States commercial bank, the Bank of North America, opened in Philadelphia
- Ninety Gnadenhutten Indians were slain by militiamen in Ohio in retaliation for raids carried out by other Indians
- General George Washington created the Order of the Purple Heart for soldiers wounded in combat

- Charleston, South Carolina, was evacuated by the British army
- The first American nautical almanac was published in Boston by Samuel Stearns
- James Watt invented the double-acting rotary steam engine

## 1783

- The Treaty of Paris between the United States and Great Britain officially ended the Revolutionary War
- The city of Annapolis, Maryland, became the first peacetime state capital
- The homes of families loyal to the defeated British in Maine were dismantled, moved to New Brunswick, Canada, and reassembled there
- Noah Webster's Spelling Book was first published as "A Grammatical Institute of the English Language"
- In Britain, William Pitt became prime minister at age 24
- Spain and Sweden formally recognized United States
- The *Pennsylvania Evening Post*, a daily newspaper, began publishing in Philadelphia
- Joseph and Jacques Montgolfier publicly flew a hot-air balloon over Versailles, France with a sheep, a rooster and a duck as passengers
- Benjamin Hanks patented a self-winding clock
- Virginia emancipated slaves who had fought for independence during the war
- George Washington ordered the Continental Army disbanded, resigned as commander-in-chief of the army and retired to his home at Mount Vernon, Virginia

## 1784

- Thomas Jefferson excavated an Indian burial mound on his property in Virginia
- New York State awarded Thomas Paine 227 acres for his war service
- U.S. merchant ship *Empress of China* left New York City for the Far East
- The Peace of Versailles ended the war among France, England, and Holland

- Russian trappers established a colony on Kodiak Island, Alaska
- Maryland granted citizenship to the Marquis de Lafayette and his descendents
- Thomas Rowlandson drew the first political cartoon
- Joseph Bramah constructed the first patent lock

# 1785–1794

## 1785

- The Continental Congress convened in New York City
- Congress created the country's monetary system based on a silver coin called a dollar
- The University of Georgia was chartered
- A commercial treaty was signed between the United States and Russia
- Loyalist graduates of Harvard and King's College founded the University of New Brunswick, Canada
- *Memorial and Remonstrance* by James Madison opposed the use of public funds for Christian education
- Land for schools was set aside by the Land Grant Act of 1785
- Barbary pirates seized American ships and imprisoned their crew in Algiers
- The first balloon flight across the English Channel was made by Frenchman Jean-Pierre Blanchard and American Dr. John Jeffries
- Thomas Jefferson was appointed minister to France, succeeding Benjamin Franklin
- Benjamin Franklin invented bifocals
- France placed restrictions on the importation of goods from Britain
- Chippewa, Delaware, Ottawa and Wyandot Indians signed a treaty at Fort McIntosh, ceding present-day Ohio to the United States
- Chlorine bleach was invented

## 1786

- George Washington called for the abolition of slavery
- Defeated British General Lord Cornwallis was appointed governor general of India

- Revolutionary war veteran Daniel Shay led a rebellion to protest the seizure of property for the non-payment of debts in cash in Massachusetts
- George Morland painted *The Wreck of the Haswell*
- Robert Burns published his first book of poetry in Scotland
- Mission Santa Barbara in California was founded as a place for the Franciscan friars to assemble and convert the native Chumash Indians
- The Council of Virginia guaranteed religious freedom
- The opera *The Marriage of Figaro* by Wolfgang Amadeus Mozart premiered in Vienna
- Morocco agreed to stop attacking American ships in the Mediterranean for a payment of $10,000

## 1787

- A majority of delegates completed and signed the Constitution of the United States at the Constitutional Convention in Philadelphia, then submitted it to the states for ratification
- The College of Electors or electoral college was established at the Constitutional Convention
- The first of the 77 essays called the Federalist Papers, calling for ratification of the U.S. Constitution, was published
- Britain continued exporting its convicted criminals to the United States despite the Treaty of Paris
- Alexander Hamilton became the first United States Treasury secretary
- A private mint struck the first penny made of copper and called the Fugio cent
- The Northwest Ordinance established the rules for governing the Northwest Territory
- Inventor John Fitch demonstrated his steamboat on the Delaware River
- Mozart's opera *Don Giovanni* opened in Prague with Mozart as conductor
- The first Unitarian minister in the United States was ordained in Boston

- Quatremiere de Quincy coined the term "Baroque" and defined it as "absurdity carried to excess"
- Shoes were first made to fit right and left feet
- The moons of Uranus were discovered by William Herschel
- In France, Louis XVI called for tolerance, granting civil status to Protestants

### 1788

- The Congress of the Confederation authorized the first national election and declared New York City the temporary national capital
- Maryland voted to cede a 100-square-mile area for the seat of the national government; about two-thirds of which became the District of Columbia
- John Adams published *A Defense of the Constitutions*
- The *Times* of London was first published
- Quakers in Pennsylvania emancipated their slaves
- English settlers arrived in Australia's Botany Bay to establish a penal colony
- Almost the entire city of New Orleans, Louisiana, was destroyed by fire
- Food shortages sparked riots in the poorer districts of Paris

- French artist Pierre-Paul Prud'hon painted *Love Seduces Innocence, Pleasure Entraps, and Remorse Follows*

### 1789

- The Constitution of the United States went into effect; the first Federal Congress met in New York City
- Democratically selected electors chose George Washington to be the nation's first president
- Georgetown University was established by Jesuits in present-day Washington, DC
- The U.S. Post Office was established
- Tammany Hall in New York City was founded by Revolutionary war soldiers as a fraternal benevolent society
- The first tobacco advertisement appeared in the United States depicting an Indian smoking a long clay pipe
- The first tariff protection passed in America included a 15 percent duty on imported nails
- Antoine-Laurent Lavoisier theorized that Earth's sea level fluctuated over time
- The French Revolution. brought down the government; the Third Estate declared itself a national assembly and undertook to frame a constitution

- The bankruptcy of the French government created a banking crisis across Europe
- William Blake published *Songs of Innocence*
- The Church of England Episcopal Church became the Protestant Episcopal Church of the United States

### 1790

- The first U.S. census counted 3,929,625 persons; the most populous state was Virginia, while the most populous city was Philadelphia
- President Washington delivered the first "State of the Union" address
- Philadelphia was established as the federal capital
- The Coast Guard was born as the Revenue Cutter Service
- The Society of Friends petitioned Congress for the emancipation of slaves
- The *Philadelphia Spelling Book* became the first American work to be copyrighted.
- The American government issued $80 million in bonds to cover Revolutionary War debts
- The Trade and Intercourse Act prohibited states from acquiring Indian lands without federal approval
- The Patent and Trademark Office was established

*Tobacco & Snuff of the best quality & flavor,*
At the Manufactory, No. 4, Chatham street, near the Gaol
**By Peter and George Lorillard,**
Where may be had as follows :

| | |
|---|---|
| Cut tobacco, | Prig or carrot do. |
| Common kitefoot do. | Maccuba fnuff, |
| Common fmoaking do. | Rappee do. |
| Segars do. | Strafburgh do. |
| Ladies twift do. | Common rappee do. |
| Pigtail do. in fmall rolls, | Scented rappee do. of dif- |
| Plug do. | ferent kinds, |
| Hogtail do. | Scotch do. |

The above Tobacco and Snuff will be fold reafonable, and warranted as good as any on the continent. If not found to prove good, any part of it may be returned, if not damaged.
N. B. Proper allowance will be made to those that purchafe a quantity. May 27—1m.

- In Paris, the celerifere two-wheeler bicycle appeared, propelled by striking the ground with one's feet
- Pineapples were introduced to the Sandwich Islands
- Denmark abolished slavery
- Rhode Island became the last of the 13 original colonies to ratify the United States Constitution
- An Aztec calendar stone was discovered in Mexico City
- Samuel Slater began production of the first American spinning mill in Pawtucket, Rhode Island

## 1791

- The Bill of Rights, composed of the first 10 amendments to the U.S. Constitution, took effect
- The First Bank of the United States was created
- Vermont was admitted as the fourteenth state
- Virginia plantation owner Robert Carter III freed all 500 of his slaves in a private emancipation
- Indians killed 637 soldiers in the Battle of Wabash
- Austrian composer Wolfgang Amadeus Mozart died in Vienna, Austria, at age 35
- New York City traffic regulation created the first one-way street
- National Guard troops in Paris opened fire on a crowd of demonstrators calling for the deposition of the king
- Maximilien Robespierre expelled all Jacobins-members of an extremist republican club— opposed to the principles of the French Revolution
- Toussaint L'Ouverture led a slave rebellion against plantation owners in Haiti, and later a colonial revolt against France
- James Boswell authored *The Life of Samuel Johnson*
- France's King Louis XVI accepted a constitution
- Mozart's opera *The Magic Flute* premiered in Vienna, Austria

## 1792

- George Washington was re-elected president; John Adams was re-elected vice president
- The cornerstone of the White House was laid

150

- The Coinage Act authorized establishment of the United States Mint
- Treasury bonds displayed the dollar sign for the first time
- The Columbia River was discovered and named by Captain Robert Gray
- The New York Stock Exchange was informally created
- Kentucky became the fifteenth state of the union
- Gas lighting was developed in Scotland
- Captain Bligh published *A Voyage to the South Sea* after his return from the mutiny on the *Bounty*
- Mary Wollstonecraft wrote *Vindication of the Rights of Women*
- Treasury Secretary Alexander Hamilton was accused of illegal speculation in government securities
- Columbus Day was first celebrated
- The *Old Farmer's Almanac* was first published.
- The French Republic was proclaimed
- France declared war on Austria, Prussia and Sardinia to begin the French Revolutionary Wars
- President Washington declared American neutrality in the war in Europe
- Franz Joseph Haydn's *Surprise Symphony* was performed publicly for the first time

## 1793

- The German Reformed Church was established in the United States by Calvinist Puritans
- China's Emperor Qianlong turned away the British fleet and declared China possessed all things in abundance and had no need of British goods
- Ralph Hodgson of Lansingburg, New York, patented oiled silk
- The fugitive slave law required the return of all escaped slaves
- The "Reign of Terror," a purge of those suspected of treason against the French Republic, began
- Louis XVI was executed by guillotine
- Eli Whitney applied for a patent on the cotton gin to clean seeds from short-staple cotton

- The Louvre opened in Paris as a museum

## 1794

- Congress passed the Neutrality Act, which prohibited Americans from enlisting in the service of a foreign power
- The St. Louis Cathedral in New Orleans was rebuilt
- George Washington established a national armory at Springfield, Massachusetts
- The first American silver dollar was minted
- Farmers in western Pennsylvania staged a violent protest against a new federal tax on whiskey makers
- French inventor Nicolas Conte fired ground graphite mixed with clay and water to make pencil leads
- The Russian Orthodox mission was founded in Alaska
- Two stars were added to the American flag, following the admission of Vermont and Kentucky to the union
- Congress prohibited future slave trade with foreign countries
- President Washington and Congress authorized the creation of the U.S. Navy
- Maximilien Robespierre, a leading figure of the French Revolution, was sent to the guillotine as crowds cheered
- American General "Mad Anthony" Wayne defeated the Ohio Indians at the Battle of Fallen Timbers in the Northwest territory to end Indian resistance in the area
- The United States and Britain signed the Jay Treaty, which resolved some issues left over from the Revolutionary War
- William Blake painted his *Elohim Creating Adam*

## 1795–1799

### 1795

- Thomas Paine defended the principle of universal suffrage at the Constitutional Convention in Paris
- General Napoleon Bonaparte routed the counterrevolutionaries in the streets of Paris to begin his rise to power

- The Treaty of San Lorenzo between the United States and Spain provided for free navigation of the Mississippi River
- America paid $800,000 and a frigate as tribute to Algiers and Tunis
- The National Convention of Revolutionary France adopted a new calendar that began with the autumn equinox
- Bourbon whiskey producer Jim Beam was founded
- Lime juice was issued to all British sailors to prevent scurvy
- The South African Cape was occupied by the British

## 1796

- Electors chose John Adams to be the second president of the United States
- Campaign supporters of John Adams accused Thomas Jefferson of being "an atheist, anarchist, demagogue, coward, mountebank, trickster and Francomaniac"
- Cuba exported Havana cigars to Britain
- Napoleon conquered northern Italy and defeated the Austrians at Lodi and Arcol
- English physician Edward Jenner administered the first smallpox vaccination to an 8-year-old boy
- Congress acted to restrict white encroachment on Indian hunting grounds
- Tennessee became the sixteenth state of the union
- The first United States Independence Day celebration was held
- Cleveland, Ohio, was founded by General Moses Cleaveland
- President George Washington counseled young America to avoid "entangling alliances" in his "Farewell Address" to Congress
- The *Baltimore Monitor* published the first American Sunday newspaper
- Immanuel Kant wrote his *Perpetual Peace*, advocating a world government

## 1797

- John Frere published his paper *The Beginnings of Paleolithic Archaeology*
- Charges concerning the alleged financial misdeeds of Alexander Hamilton were published
- French forces attacked Britain at the port of Fishguard
- Albany became the capital of New York State, replacing New York City
- The British destroyed the Spanish fleet at the battle of Cape St. Vincent, off Portugal
- The Directory of Great Britain authorized vessels of war to board and seize neutral vessels, particularly if the ships were American
- Nathaniel Briggs of New Hampshire patented a washing machine
- Mission San Juan Bautista, in California, was founded in the lands of the Mutsun Indians
- Hatchards bookstore was founded in Piccadilly, London
- The U.S. frigate *Constitution*, also known as Old Ironsides, was launched in Boston
- French balloonist Andre-Jacques Garnerin made the first parachute descent
- Henry Maudslay invented the carriage lathe

## 1798

- Congress agreed to pay a yearly tribute to Tripoli to protect U.S. shipping
- The Sedition Act made it unlawful to write, publish or utter false or malicious statements about the U.S. president and the U.S. Government
- Congressman Matthew Lyon was convicted of sedition for printing his unvarnished opinion of President John Adams
- The United States Supreme Court ruled that Congress and the states could not pass any "ex post facto law," a law that makes illegal an act that was legal when committed

- The 11th Amendment regarding judicial powers was ratified
- The British boarded the U.S. frigate *Baltimore* and impressed into service a number of crewmen as alleged deserters
- David Wilkinson of Rhode Island patented a nut and bolt machine
- Napoleon Bonaparte's army annexed Egypt, seized Malta and conquered Naples
- Judith Sargent Murray wrote *The Gleaner*, essays on women's education and alternatives to marriage
- Samuel Taylor Coleridge and William Wordsworth published *Lyrical Ballads*
- Twenty-two sea captains founded the Peabody Essex Museum in Marblehead, Massachusetts, to preserve the exotic treasures they brought back from their voyages

## 1799

- Pennsylvania pioneered the printed ballot
- The Rosetta Stone was discovered in Egypt by an officer in Napoleon's army
- The last known blaauwboch or blue antelope was shot in Africa
- The Dutch East India Company was liquidated and the Dutch government took control over the islands of Indonesia
- The Russian government granted the Russian-American Company a trade monopoly in Alaska
- Eli Whitney received a government contract for 10,000 muskets
- The *USS Constellation* captured the French frigate *Insurgente* off the coast of Wisconsin
- Jacques Louis David painted *The Rape of the Sabine Women*
- Napoleon Bonaparte participated in a coup and declared himself first consul, or dictator, of France
- The metric system was established in France
- George Washington died at age 67 at his Mount Vernon, Virginia home

# Financing Revolution & Government

Independence, and the attempts to attain it from Britain, created financial hardship on the American colonies' efforts for liberty. The Continental Congress and its supporters struggled to raise monies for the developing nation, and to develop a volunteer army, a new government, and the support of the international community. All of this required available financial capital that the Continental Congress lacked.

Many of the colonists at the time were comfortable to follow their Congress against their common enemy, England, but showed little acceptance of a government with no authority to tax the population. This severely limited the delegates' ability to raise funds and required them to undertake financing methods that were as revolutionary as the war itself. By issuing bills of credit, borrowing from abroad and within the states, the government financed the cause with great difficulty. Within time, the systems of financing rapidly crumbled based upon the deficits in the financial schemes.

Initially, reliance was placed upon the bills of credit, but as additional bills were issued, valuations fluctuated greatly. Financial backing of the Continental paper money arrived from the credit of the states' ability to service the debt. By 1779, 40 separate issues of paper money were authorized by the states totaling over $240 million. This rapid rate of issues, in conjunction with the failed public support to back the currency, led to an accelerated monetary depreciation. In March of 1778, 1.75 Continental dollars equaled one Spanish milled dollar. By March of 1780, the exchange was 40 Continental dollars for one Spanish milled dollar. By 1781, Pelatiah Webster stated that the Continental dollar "..ceased to pass as currency, but was afterwards bought and sold as an article of speculation, at very uncertain and desultory prices, from five hundred to one thousand to one."

Loans, both foreign and domestic, compounded the financial issues following the war. The states' taxing ability was the primary instrument of servicing the debt obligations. If the Continental Congress asked for a fixed sum to pay a foreign nation, it had no power to acquire the monies from the states. At the war's end and the establishment of the Articles of Confederation, the new nation still lacked sufficient power to tax and raise funds.

When the new nation was governed by the Articles of Confederation, many lawmakers believed in leaving commerce as free as possible. The principle was to keep commercial enterprises free from government influence to encourage growth of the business community. Despite the intended efforts of this doctrine, the states' necessity to meet fiscal obligations required them to reintroduce tariffs.

Many of the industries developing in America supported the tariffs as protective support from European imports. It also permitted businesses time to attract new customers because their former customers were within the British Empire. Americans were viewed as aliens to their former mother country, and Britain only traded with loyal parts of its empire. Hindered by limited access to British customers, the tariffs were supported by the population as a protective measure to the young nation. They also enabled the new nation to generate revenues on imports, but the funds generated were not enough.

The weakening financial situation revealed the power struggle between the states and Congress, and the limitations of the new nation. Under the Articles, commerce suffered because Congress could not regulate the laws of trade among the states or enforce a taxation system. This rapidly led to a deterioration of the nation's fiscal situation. Creditors were alarmed. If the republic was to continue, then it must be restructured to resolve its financial and commercial issues. Leadership expressed the need to meet and overcome the nation's problems at the National Convention in Philadelphia in 1887. After the convention ended, the body formed the Constitution of the United States.

Once the Constitution was ratified, Congress was granted additional fiscal powers not found in the Articles of Confederation. This included the governing of taxation, loans and coinage of money. The founding leaders began establishing rules for interstate commerce, collection of import tariffs, establishing a national currency and collecting taxes. All rules applied evenly throughout the states and created a developing commercial environment within the nation.

With the new powers, the United States' initial efforts were to restore the nation's credit. The states held significant amounts of debt accrued during the war with Britain and under the Articles of Confederation. Many individuals who held devalued notes sold them under face value. Alexander Hamilton, the nation's treasurer, recommended the United States pay the notes at face value and acquire the financial burden from the states. This proposed scheme created a whirlwind of debate within the new nation.

This federal assumption of the states' debt would move the new debt to the nation, but the controversy revolved around the debate on whom to pay. Those in line to receive this payment were wealthy speculators who bought the certificates on pennies to the dollar from the original owners. Speculators were to receive a huge financial gain. States like Massachusetts were to gain because they had more debt and it pleased state leaders to give up their heavy debt burden. States with fewer debt obligations fought this measure out of concern of being taxed more by a federal government because of poor fiscal management of other states. The controversy resulted in a struggle between the Northern and Southern states. In the end, a compromise was developed for the nation to assume the states' debt in return for moving the nation's capital from Philadelphia to a site on the Potomac River.

With the increased national debt, the nation had to create the necessary financial infrastructure and collections to operate the government. One method was the creation of the First United States Bank. This national bank, modeled after the Bank of England, was constructed and chartered for 20 years. This institution's purpose was to increase the circulation of currency, to simplify the ability to acquire loans for the government, and to provide a source of individuals to pay the government. Constitutional controversy and debate evolved upon its creation, but in the end, Congress supported its creation.

Revenues were needed to pay the nation's debt obligations. One method was the issuance of low import tariffs. These tariffs generated needed revenues while providing protection to the nation's growing industries. Another method was internal taxes upon the population. One was a tax on whiskey and other distilled spirits. Taxes ranged from 9 to 25 cents a gallon and typically hurt farmers in rural regions of the United States. Many farmers could not transport corn and other grains to market due to long distances. By converting the grain into alcohol, they possessed a commodity easily transported and traded. These farmers viewed the tax as oppression of their liberty. In western Pennsylvania, many protested the tax and actively tarred and feathered revenue officers. President Washington called upon the militia to halt this "Whiskey Rebellion" and sent a force far stronger than his army in the Revolutionary War to quell the revolt. The result of this fiscal revolt showed the strength of the new United States Government and its ability to maintain order within its population.

As a new nation, the United States accomplished a significant feat in creating a strong fiscal foundation. It established a national revenue system that was varied in scope, implemented an administrative system for the treasury, and restored the credit of the United States, thereby instituting the beginnings of a financial system that could support the new republic.

Bank of the United States, July 6. — 1793.

PAY to Adam May — or Bearer, twenty seven dollars & thirty seven cents of Dollars.

27 DOLLARS 37 cents

# SELECTED INCOMES 1775-1799

| Occupation | Data Source | Description | Price |
|---|---|---|---|
| Artisan | US Census (1976) | Daily wage rate for an artisan in Philadelphia, 1785 | $1.33 |
| Artisan | US Census (1976) | Daily wage rate for an artisan in Philadelphia, 1792 | $1.00 |
| Artisan | US Census (1976) | Daily wage rate for an artisan in Philadelphia, 1799 | $1.62 |
| Agricultural Worker | US Census (1976) | Daily wage rate an agricultural worker in Philadelphia area, 1798 | $0.40 |
| Bricklayer | US Census (1976) | Daily wages of a bricklayer paid in local currency without board furnished in Rhode Island, 1776 | 6 shillings 6 pence |
| Bricklayer | US Census (1976) | Daily wages of a bricklayer paid in local currency without board furnished in Providence, Rhode Island, 1779 | 3 pounds 2 shillings |
| Bricklayer | US Census (1976) | Daily wages of a bricklayer paid in local currency without board furnished in Virginia, 1781 | 5 shillings |
| Cabinetmaker | Brock Jobe, New England Furniture: The Colonial Era (1984) | Approximate annual income earned by Lemuel Tobey for furniture making in Dartmouth, Massachusetts, 1777 | 87 pounds 17 shillings |
| Cabinetmaker | Brock Jobe, New England Furniture: The Colonial Era (1984) | Approximate annual income earned by Lemuel Tobey for furniture making in Dartmouth, Massachusetts, 1781 | 23 pounds 12 shillings 6 pence |
| Captain | Kitman, George Washington's Expense Account (1970) | Monthly pay for a Captain in the Continental Army during the American Revolution | $20.00 |
| Carpenter | US Census (1976) | Daily wages of a carpenter paid in local currency without board furnished in Rhode Island, 1776 | 5 shillings |
| Carpenter | US Census (1976) | Daily wages of a carpenter paid in local currency without board furnished in Providence, Rhode Island, 1779 | 3 pounds 1 shilling |
| Carpenter | US Census (1976) | Daily wages of a carpenter paid in local currency without board furnished in Virginia, 1781 | 5 shillings |
| Clock Repair | Winthrop Gardiner Jr. Collection | For repairing one clock - New York, 1799 | 3 pounds 5 shillings |
| Commander in Chief | Kitman, George Washington's Expense Account (1970) | Monthly pay the Continental Congress offered George Washington during the American Revolution Washington accepted the position without pay | $500.00 |
| Cooper | US Census (1976) | Daily wages of a cooper paid in local currency without board furnished in Rhode Island, 1776 | 5 shillings |
| Cooper | US Census (1976) | Daily wages of a cooper paid in local currency without board furnished in Virginia, 1781 | 5 shillings |
| Corporal | Kitman, George Washington's Expense Account (1970) | Monthly pay for a Corporal in the Continental Army during the American Revolution | $7.33 |
| Doctor's Visit | Joseph I. Waring, A History of Medicine in South Carolina, 1670-1825 (1967) | Cost for a doctors visit during the daylight hours, 1792 | 5 shillings |
| Doctor's Visit | Joseph I. Waring, A History of Medicine in South Carolina, 1670-1825 (1967) | Cost for a doctor to visit at night in poor weather, 1792 | 2 pounds |

| Occupation | Data Source | Description | Price |
|---|---|---|---|
| Drum Major | Lt. Col. Drury's Pay Roll (1781) | Monthly income for a Drum Major in the Continental Army, 1781 | $10.00 |
| Drummer | Kitman, George Washington's Expense Account (1970) | Monthly pay for a Drummer in the Continental Army during the American Revolution | $6.33 |
| Enlistment Bounty | Continental Army Recruitment Poster (1776) | Enlistment bounty for men in General Washington in the Continental Army, 1776 | $12.00 |
| Furniture Maker | Winthrop Gardiner Jr. Collection | Value of daily New York laborer crafting furniture for Nathaniel Dominy in 1791 | 7 shillings 6 pence |
| General | Kitman, George Washington's Expense Account (1970) | Monthly pay for a Brigadier General in the Continental Army during the American Revolution | $125.00 |
| General | Kitman, George Washington's Expense Account (1970) | Monthly pay for a Major General in the Continental Army during the American Revolution | $166.00 |
| Joiner | US Census (1976) | Daily wages of a joiner paid in local currency without board furnished in Rhode Island, 1776 | 5 shillings |
| Joiner | US Census (1976) | Daily wages of a joiner paid in local currency without board furnished in Providence, Rhode Island, 1779 | 3 pounds 1 shilling |
| Laborer | US Census (1976) | Daily wages of a laborer paid in local currency without board furnished in Rhode Island, 1776 | 3 shillings |
| Laborer | US Census (1976) | Daily wages of a laborer paid in local currency without board furnished in Providence, Rhode Island, 1779 | 2 pounds 1 shilling 6 pence |
| Laborer | US Census (1976) | Daily wage rate for laborer in Philadelphia, 1785 | $0.72 |
| Laborer | US Census (1976) | Daily wage rate for laborer in Philadelphia, 1792 | $0.66 |
| Laborer | US Census (1976) | Daily wage rate for laborer in Philadelphia, 1799 | $1.00 |
| Lieutenant | Kitman, George Washington's Expense Account (1970) | Monthly pay for a Lieutenant in the Continental Army during the American Revolution | $13.33 |
| Mason | US Census (1976) | Daily wages of a mason paid in local currency without board furnished in Rhode Island, 1776 | 6 shillings 6 pence |
| Mason | US Census (1976) | Daily wages of a mason paid in local currency without board furnished in Providence, Rhode Island, 1779 | 3 pounds 2 shillings |

## Based Upon the British Currency System

| Year | Pound in 2002 US Dollars | Shilling in 2002 US Dollars | Pence in 2002 US Dollars |
|---|---|---|---|
| 1775 | $144.00 | $7.20 | $0.60 |
| 1780 | $168.00 | $8.40 | $0.70 |
| 1785 | $144.00 | $7.20 | $0.60 |
| 1790 | $144.00 | $7.20 | $0.60 |
| 1795 | $120.00 | $6.00 | $0.50 |
| 1799 | $120.00 | $6.00 | $0.50 |

*Calculations are approximate values based upon economic historical data*

| Occupation | Data Source | Description | Price |
|---|---|---|---|
| Mason | US Census (1976) | Daily wages of a mason paid in local currency without board furnished in Virginia, 1781 | 5 shillings |
| Military Service | Claim Records of Pittsylvania County, Virginia (1785) | Col Peter Perkins for 90 days service as commissary to the General Hospital at his house | 45 pounds |
| Paymaster General | Kitman, George Washington's Expense Account (1970) | Monthly income of the paymaster general of the Continental Army, 1775 | $100.00 |
| Pension | Kitman, George Washington's Expense Account (1970) | Annual pension offered to each of Benedict Arnold's children for his services to the British Crown, 1782 | 100 pounds |
| Pension | Kitman, George Washington's Expense Account (1970) | Annual pension offered to Benedict Arnold's wife for his services to the British Crown, 1782 | 500 pounds |
| Privates | Kitman, George Washington's Expense Account (1970) | Monthly pay for a Private in the Continental Army during the American Revolution | $6.33 |
| Rigger | US Census (1976) | Daily wages of a rigger paid in local currency without board furnished in Rhode Island, 1776 | 5 shillings |
| Rigger | US Census (1976) | Daily wages of a rigger paid in local currency without board furnished in Providence, Rhode Island, 1779 | 3 pounds 1 shilling |
| Sergeant | Kitman, George Washington's Expense Account (1970) | Monthly pay for a Sergeant in the Continental Army during the American Revolution | $8.00 |
| Secretary of State | Kitman, George Washington's Expense Account (1970) | Annual salary of Thomas Jefferson as Secretary of State, 1794 | $3,500.00 |
| Soldier | Lt. Col. Drury's Pay Roll (1781) | Monthly income for a Lieutenant Colonel in the Continental Army, 1781 | $75.00 |
| Soldier | Lt. Col. Drury's Pay Roll (1781) | Monthly income for a Major in the Continental Army, 1781 | $50.00 |
| Soldier | Lt. Col. Drury's Pay Roll (1781) | Monthly income for a Sergeant Major in the Continental Army, 1781 | $10.00 |
| Steward | Kitman, George Washington's Expense Account (1970) | Monthly pay for Ebenezer Austin, Steward of General George Washington at his headquarters, 1775 | 7 pounds 10 shillings |
| Surgeon | Lt. Col. Drury's Pay Roll (1781) | Monthly income for a Surgeon in the Continental Army, 1781 | $65.00 |
| Tailor | US Census (1976) | Per suit charges of a tailor paid in local currency without board furnished in Providence, Rhode Island, 1779 | 17 pounds |
| Tailor | US Census (1976) | Daily wages of a tailor paid in local currency without board furnished in Virginia, 1781 | 5 shillings |
| United States President | Kitman, George Washington's Expense Account (1970) | Annual salary of George Washington as President of the United States | $25,000.00 |

# SERVICES & FEES 1775-1799

| Service/Fee | Data Source | Description | Price |
|---|---|---|---|
| Architect Fee | American Heritage (1959) | Fee offered to the architect designing a suitable plan for the President's house in Washington DC, 1792 | $500.00 |
| Bridge Construction | Pace & McGee, The life and Times of Ridgeway, Virginia. | Payment to Edward Daniel for building a bridge across Marrowbone Creek in Henry County, Virginia, 1793 | 80 pounds 9 shillings 6 pence |
| Door | Peterson, The Carpenters' Company 1786 Rule Book (1992) | Crafting DOORS framed squared, two or four pannels, raised on one side, per yard cost in Philadelphia, Pennsylvania, 1786 | 5 shillings |
| Entertainment | Kitman, George Washington's Expense Account (1970) | Entertainment expense from May 18 to June 30, 1776 charged to the New York Provincial Congress by Fraunces Tavern, | 45 pounds |
| Expense Account | Kitman, George Washington's Expense Account (1970) | General George Washington's expenses for his eight years of personal expenses as Commander, 1783 | $449,261.51 |
| Fence | Peterson, The Carpenters' Company 1786 Rule Book (1992) | Crafting PALISADE fence, with pointed or round heads, in a plain manner, not exceeding four feet high, per foot cost in Philadelphia, Pennsylvania, 1786 | 1 shilling 8 pence |
| Framing | Peterson, The Carpenters' Company 1786 Rule Book (1992) | Framing floors of joists, of 9 inches deep, per square in Philadelphia, Pennsylvania, 1786 | 8 shillings |
| Government Expense | Kitman, George Washington's Expense Account (1970) | Expenditures report by the colony of Pennsylvania for peacetime operations 1775 | 3,000 pounds |
| Gutters | Peterson, The Carpenters' Company 1786 Rule Book (1992) | Crafting GUTTERS of plank shingled in roofs, per foot lineal cost in Philadelphia, Pennsylvania, 1786 | 1 shilling 3 pence |
| Ladder | Peterson, The Carpenters' Company 1786 Rule Book (1992) | Crafting a step ladder, made of boards, per foot lineal cost in Philadelphia, Pennsylvania, 1786 | 10 pence |
| Printing | Peterson, The Carpenters' Company 1786 Rule Book (1992) | Fee charged by Hall & Sellers for printing the Carpenters' Company 1786 Rule Book, Philadelphia, Pennsylvania, 1786 | 15 pounds |

## Based Upon the British Currency System

| Year | Pound in 2002 US Dollars | Shilling in 2002 US Dollars | Pence in 2002 US Dollars |
|---|---|---|---|
| 1775 | $144.00 | $7.20 | $0.60 |
| 1780 | $168.00 | $8.40 | $0.70 |
| 1785 | $144.00 | $7.20 | $0.60 |
| 1790 | $144.00 | $7.20 | $0.60 |
| 1795 | $120.00 | $6.00 | $0.50 |
| 1799 | $120.00 | $6.00 | $0.50 |

*Calculations are approximate values based upon economic historical data*

| Service/Fee | Data Source | Description | Price |
|---|---|---|---|
| Reward | The Pennsylvania Gazette (1776) | Reward for deserters from Captain John Miller's company in the Fifth Battalion, Philadelphia, Pennsylvania, 1776 | 1 pound |
| Reward | The Pennsylvania Gazette (1777) | Reward for deserters from Captain James Silson's Company of the First Pennsylvania regiment, Philadelphia, 1777 | $8.00 |
| Sashes | Peterson, The Carpenters' Company 1786 Rule Book (1992) | Crafting SASHES, as common for glass 10 by 8 inches, per light cost in Philadelphia, Pennsylvania, 1786 | 7 pence |
| Stairs | Peterson, The Carpenters' Company 1786 Rule Book (1992) | Crafting WINDING stairs, not fap'd, from two feet six inches to three feet going, per step cost in Philadelphia, Pennsylvania, 1786 | 1 shilling 9 pence |
| Stud Fee | The Pennsylvania Gazette (1776) | Stud fee for the horse Liberty for the entire season in Philadelphia, Pennsylvania, 1776 | 1 pound 10 shillings |
| Stud Fee | The Pennsylvania Gazette (1776) | Stud fee for the horse Liberty for a single leap in Philadelphia, Pennsylvania, 1776 | 12 shillings |
| Stud Fee | The Pennsylvania Gazette (1776) | Stud fee for the horse Young Bellsize for the entire season in Philadelphia, Pennsylvania, 1776 | $4.00 |
| Swearing | Pace & McGee, The life and Times of Ridgeway, Virginia. | Fine charged to Walter King Cole for swearing an oath in the presence of the court in Henry County, Virginia, 1784 | 5 shillings |
| Tariff | Dewey, Early Financial History of the United States (1934) | Per pound tariff on brown sugar imported into the United States, 1789 | $0.01 |
| Tariff | Dewey, Early Financial History of the United States (1934) | Per pair tariff on men's leather boots imported into the United States, 1789 | $0.50 |
| Tariff | Dewey, Early Financial History of the United States (1934) | Per pound tariff on candle tallows imported into the United States, 1789 | $0.02 |
| Tariff | Dewey, Early Financial History of the United States (1934) | Per pound tariff on nails imported into the United States, 1789 | $0.01 |
| Tariff | Dewey, Early Financial History of the United States (1934) | Per bushell tariff on salt imported into the United States, 1789 | $0.10 |
| Treason | Kitman, George Washington's Expense Account (1970) | Amount offered by the British to General Benedict Arnold for delivering West Pont to the British Army, 1780 | 10,000 pounds |
| Washing | Kitman, George Washington's Expense Account (1970) | Monthly fees paid to Peggy Lee to wash General George Washington's clothing at Valley Forge, 1778 | 2 pounds |
| Washing | Kitman, George Washington's Expense Account (1970) | Washing one dozen pieces of clothing for Continental soliders at Valley Forge, 1778 | 4 shillings |
| Window Framing | Peterson, The Carpenters' Company 1786 Rule Book (1992) | Crafting window frames full trimmed, of the best kind, per foot in Philadelphia, Pennsylvania, 1786 | 7 pence |

# FINANCIAL RATES & EXCHANGES
## 1775-1799

| Year | British Official Price of Gold (per Ounce) | United States Official Price of Gold (per Ounce) | Inflation Rate in Colonial America & United States | Yield of Long-Term British Government Securities | US Federal Government High Grade Bond Yields - New Issue | US Federal Government High Grade Bond Yields - Select Market | New England Municipal Bond Yields |
|------|------|------|------|------|------|------|------|
| 1775 | £4.25 | — | −5.15% | 3.39% | — | — | — |
| 1776 | £4.25 | — | 14.13% | 3.57% | — | — | — |
| 1777 | £4.25 | — | 21.90% | 3.85% | — | — | — |
| 1778 | £4.25 | — | 29.69% | 4.51% | — | — | — |
| 1779 | £4.25 | — | −11.45% | 4.88% | — | — | — |
| 1780 | £4.25 | — | 12.24% | 4.88% | — | — | — |
| 1781 | £4.25 | — | −19.39% | 5.22% | — | — | — |
| 1782 | £4.25 | — | 9.77% | 5.26% | — | — | — |
| 1783 | £4.25 | — | −12.33% | 4.76% | — | — | — |
| 1784 | £4.25 | — | −3.91% | 5.41% | — | — | — |
| 1785 | £4.25 | — | −4.88% | 4.76% | — | — | — |
| 1786 | £4.25 | $19.49 | −2.56% | 4.06% | — | — | — |
| 1787 | £4.25 | $19.49 | −1.75% | 4.08% | — | — | — |
| 1788 | £4.25 | $19.49 | −4.46% | 4.06% | — | — | — |
| 1789 | £4.25 | $19.49 | −0.93% | 3.92% | — | — | — |
| 1790 | £4.25 | $19.49 | 3.77% | 3.90% | — | — | — |
| 1791 | £4.25 | $19.49 | 2.73% | 3.58% | — | — | — |
| 1792 | £4.25 | $19.39 | 1.77% | 3.33% | — | — | — |
| 1793 | £4.25 | .$19.39 | 3.48% | 3.96% | — | — | — |
| 1794 | £4.25 | $19.39 | 10.98% | 4.40% | — | — | — |
| 1795 | £4.25 | $19.39 | 14.39% | 4.52% | — | — | — |
| 1796 | £4.25 | $19.39 | 5.30% | 4.80% | — | — | — |
| 1797 | £4.25 | $19.39 | −3.77% | 5.90% | — | — | — |
| 1798 | £4.25 | $19.39 | −3.27% | 5.94% | — | 7.56% | 6.30% |
| 1799 | £4.25 | $19.39 | 0.00% | 5.07% | 8.00% | 7.42% | 6.16% |

### Based Upon the British Currency System

| Year | Pound in 2002 US Dollars | Shilling in 2002 US Dollars | Pence in 2002 US Dollars |
|------|------|------|------|
| 1775 | $144.00 | $7.20 | $0.60 |
| 1780 | $168.00 | $8.40 | $0.70 |
| 1785 | $144.00 | $7.20 | $0.60 |
| 1790 | $144.00 | $7.20 | $0.60 |
| 1795 | $120.00 | $6.00 | $0.50 |
| 1799 | $120.00 | $6.00 | $0.50 |

*Calculations are approximate values based upon economic historical data*

# SLAVE TRADES 1775-1799

### Average Price of British American and West African Slaves
*Price in Pounds Sterling*

| Year | Price | Year | Price | Year | Price |
|------|-------|------|-------|------|-------|
| 1775 | 33 | 1780 | 33 | 1790 | 50 |
| 1776 | 33 | 1781 | 33 | 1791 | 50 |
| 1777 | 33 | 1782 | 33 | 1792 | 50 |
| 1778 | 33 | 1783 | 33 | 1793 | 50 |
| 1779 | 33 | 1784 | 33 | 1794 | 50 |
|      |    | 1785 | 37 | 1795 | 50 |
|      |    | 1786 | 37 | 1796 | 50 |
|      |    | 1787 | 37 | 1797 | 50 |
|      |    | 1788 | 37 | 1798 | 50 |
|      |    | 1789 | 37 | 1799 | 50 |

# COMMODITIES 1775-1799

| Commodity | Year | Philadelphia Currency | New York Currency | Boston Currency | Charleston Currency |
|-----------|------|----------------------|-------------------|-----------------|---------------------|
| Bacon, per pound | 1784 | 0.13 | N/R | N/R | N/R |
| | 1785 | 0.12 | N/R | N/R | N/R |
| | 1786 | 0.10 | N/R | N/R | N/R |
| | 1787 | 0.09 | N/R | N/R | N/R |
| | 1788 | 0.09 | N/R | N/R | N/R |
| | 1789 | 0.06 | N/R | N/R | N/R |
| | 1790 | 0.06 | N/R | N/R | N/R |
| | 1792 | $0.09 | N/R | N/R | N/R |
| | 1793 | $0.10 | N/R | N/R | N/R |
| | 1794 | $0.11 | N/R | N/R | N/R |
| | 1795 | $0.11 | N/R | N/R | 0.09 |
| | 1796 | $0.13 | N/R | N/R | 0.12 |
| | 1797 | $0.13 | $0.09 | N/R | 0.23 |
| | 1798 | $0.13 | $0.13 | N/R | 0.12 |
| | 1799 | N/R | $0.12 | N/R | 0.7 |
| Beef, per barrel | 1775 | 7.33 | 6.00 | N/R | N/R |
| | 1781 | N/R | N/R | N/R | 17.14 |
| | 1782 | N/R | N/R | N/R | 23.57 |
| | 1783 | N/R | N/R | N/R | 6.21 |
| | 1784 | 11.12 | N/R | N/R | 6.75 |
| | 1785 | 10.67 | 8.13 | N/R | 8.83 |
| | 1786 | 10.67 | 8.13 | N/R | N/R |
| | 1787 | 10.67 | 8.81 | N/R | 9.49 |
| | 1788 | 10.67 | 5.63 | N/R | 7.99 |
| | 1789 | 7.33 | 5.63 | N/R | 7.99 |
| | 1790 | 7.33 | 5.94 | N/R | 5.99 |
| | 1792 | $7.50 | N/R | N/R | N/R |
| | 1793 | $12.00 | 5.63 | N/R | N/R |
| | 1794 | $10.50 | 8.00 | N/R | N/R |
| | 1795 | $5.25 | 10.00 | N/R | N/R |
| | 1796 | $17.50 | $13.00 | N/R | N/R |
| | 1797 | $15.50 | $10.75 | N/R | N/R |
| | 1798 | $14.50 | $9.00 | N/R | N/R |
| | 1799 | $11.00 | $8.50 | N/R | N/R |
| Bread, per hundredweight | 1775 | 4.26 | 1.88 | N/R | N/R |
| (Charleston per barrel 1795-1799) | 1780 | N/R | N/R | N/R | 4.67 |
| | 1781 | N/R | N/R | N/R | 5.33 |
| | 1782 | N/R | N/R | N/R | 4.00 |

Values are expressed in Silver Dollars, the most common currency in the Colonies, unless noted with a Dollar Sign ($), indicating US Dollars.

| Commodity | Year | Philadelphia Currency | New York Currency | Boston Currency | Charleston Currency |
|-----------|------|----------------------|-------------------|-----------------|---------------------|
| | 1784 | 2.47 | N/R | N/R | 1.86 |
| | 1785 | 3.2 | N/R | N/R | 2.44 |
| | 1786 | 2.56 | 2.38 | N/R | 1.60 |
| | 1787 | 2.56 | 2.63 | N/R | 2.40 |
| | 1788 | 1.93 | 2.00 | N/R | 1.60 |
| | 1789 | 1.73 | 2.25 | N/R | 1.60 |
| | 1790 | 3.33 | 2.81 | N/R | 2.66 |
| | 1791 | 2.16 | 2.13 | N/R | 1.86 |
| | 1792 | 1.93 | N/R | N/R | N/R |
| | 1793 | 2.26 | 2.00 | N/R | N/R |
| | 1794 | $3.33 | 2.38 | N/R | $3.00 |
| | 1795 | 4.00 | 3.13 | N/R | $3.25 |
| | 1796 | $6.25 | N/R | N/R | 3.66 |
| | 1797 | $6.03 | $4.50 | N/R | $4.50 |
| | 1798 | $4.00 | $2.75 | N/R | N/R |
| | 1799 | $4.00 | $4.13 | N/R | N/R |
| Butter, per pound | 1784 | 0.14 | N/R | N/R | 0.19 |
| | 1785 | 0.12 | N/R | N/R | 0.13 |
| | 1786 | 0.12 | N/R | N/R | 0.18 |
| | 1787 | 0.10 | N/R | N/R | 0.14 |
| | 1788 | 0.08 | N/R | N/R | 0.11 |
| | 1789 | 0.07 | N/R | N/R | 0.11 |
| | 1790 | 0.11 | N/R | N/R | 0.11 |
| | 1792 | $0.11 | N/R | N/R | 0.13 |
| | 1793 | $0.13 | N/R | N/R | N/R |
| | 1794 | $0.17 | N/R | N/R | 0.19 |
| | 1795 | $0.17 | N/R | N/R | 0.18 |
| | 1796 | $0.15 | N/R | N/R | 0.17 |
| | 1797 | $0.15 | $0.16 | N/R | 0.17 |
| | 1798 | $0.16 | $0.18 | N/R | 0.17 |
| | 1799 | $0.16 | $0.19 | N/R | 0.17 |
| Candles, per pound | 1775 | N/R | N/R | 0.43 | N/R |
| | 1784 | 0.14 | N/R | N/R | 0.12 |
| | 1785 | 0.13 | N/R | N/R | 0.13 |
| | 1786 | 0.13 | 0.54 | N/R | 0.13 |
| | 1787 | 0.16 | 0.44 | N/R | 0.20 |
| | 1788 | 0.13 | 0.44 | N/R | 0.18 |
| | 1789 | 0.11 | 0.38 | N/R | 0.18 |
| | 1790 | 0.10 | 0.38 | N/R | 0.14 |
| | 1791 | 0.13 | 0.38 | N/R | 0.14 |
| | 1792 | $0.11 | N/R | N/R | 0.12 |
| | 1793 | $0.12 | 0.38 | N/R | 0.16 |

Values are expressed in Silver Dollars, the most common currency in the Colonies, unless noted with a Dollar Sign ($), indicating US Dollars.

| Commodity | Year | Philadelphia Currency | New York Currency | Boston Currency | Charleston Currency |
|---|---|---|---|---|---|
| | 1794 | $0.18 | 0.44 | N/R | 0.32 |
| | 1795 | $0.22 | 0.47 | N/R | 0.32 |
| | 1796 | $0.18 | $0.50 | N/R | 0.21 |
| | 1797 | $0.17 | $0.52 | N/R | 0.21 |
| | 1798 | $0.15 | $0.52 | N/R | N/R |
| | 1799 | $0.20 | $0.50 | N/R | N/R |
| Coal, per ton | 1784 | 0.29 | N/R | N/R | N/R |
| *(Philadelphia per bushel 1784-1799)* | 1785 | 0.20 | N/R | N/R | 4.29 |
| *(New York per chaldron 1797-1799)* | 1786 | 0.21 | N/R | N/R | 4.14 |
| *(Charleston per bushel 1796-1797)* | 1787 | 0.19 | N/R | N/R | 3.00 |
| | 1788 | 0.14 | N/R | N/R | 7.72 |
| | 1789 | 0.17 | N/R | N/R | N/R |
| | 1790 | 0.15 | N/R | N/R | N/R |
| | 1791 | 0.20 | N/R | N/R | 5.36 |
| | 1792 | $0.21 | N/R | N/R | N/R |
| | 1793 | $0.21 | N/R | N/R | N/R |
| | 1794 | $0.29 | N/R | N/R | 7.72 |
| | 1795 | $0.29 | N/R | N/R | 7.50 |
| | 1796 | $0.40 | N/R | N/R | 0.60 |
| | 1797 | $0.29 | $10.50 | N/R | 0.60 |
| | 1798 | $0.33 | $10.00 | N/R | N/R |
| | 1799 | $0.33 | $10.50 | N/R | N/R |
| Codfish, per hundredweight | 1775 | N/R | N/R | 2.00 | N/R |
| | 1784 | 4.06 | N/R | 3.33 | N/R |
| | 1785 | 3.53 | N/R | 3.67 | N/R |
| | 1786 | 3.53 | N/R | 2.50 | N/R |
| | 1787 | 3.53 | N/R | 2.33 | N/R |
| | 1788 | 3.52 | N/R | 2.25 | N/R |
| | 1789 | 2.78 | N/R | 1.83 | N/R |
| Coffee, per pound | 1775 | N/R | N/R | 0.13 | N/R |
| | 1776 | N/R | N/R | 0.14 | N/R |
| | 1781 | N/R | N/R | 0.12 | N/R |
| | 1782 | N/R | N/R | 0.17 | N/R |
| | 1783 | N/R | N/R | 0.15 | N/R |
| | 1784 | 0.13 | N/R | 0.13 | 0.125 |
| | 1785 | 0.16 | N/R | 0.13 | 0.157 |
| | 1786 | 0.17 | N/R | 0.15 | 0.133 |
| | 1787 | 0.17 | N/R | 0.19 | 0.196 |
| | 1788 | 0.16 | N/R | 0.18 | 0.178 |
| | 1789 | 0.21 | N/R | 0.20 | 0.179 |
| | 1790 | 0.18 | N/R | 0.17 | 0.214 |

Values are expressed in Silver Dollars, the most common currency in the Colonies, unless noted with a Dollar Sign ($), indicating US Dollars.

| Commodity | Year | Philadelphia Currency | New York Currency | Boston Currency | Charleston Currency |
|---|---|---|---|---|---|
| | 1792 | $0.18 | N/R | 0.18 | 0.205 |
| | 1793 | $0.15 | N/R | 0.16 | 0.179 |
| | 1794 | $0.16 | N/R | 0.16 | 0.196 |
| | 1795 | $0.22 | N/R | 0.19 | 0.200 |
| | 1796 | $0.24 | N/R | N/R | 0.259 |
| | 1797 | $0.25 | $0.23 | N/R | 0.259 |
| | 1798 | $0.24 | $0.23 | N/R | N/R |
| | 1799 | $0.30 | $0.30 | N/R | N/R |
| Copper, per pound | 1784 | 0.24 | N/R | N/R | N/R |
| | 1785 | 0.27 | N/R | N/R | N/R |
| | 1786 | 0.25 | N/R | N/R | N/R |
| | 1787 | 0.26 | N/R | N/R | N/R |
| | 1788 | 0.25 | N/R | N/R | N/R |
| | 1789 | 0.25 | N/R | N/R | N/R |
| | 1790 | 0.25 | N/R | N/R | N/R |
| | 1791 | 0.25 | N/R | N/R | N/R |
| | 1795 | $0.37 | N/R | N/R | N/R |
| | 1796 | $0.37 | N/R | N/R | N/R |
| | 1797 | $0.40 | $0.29 | N/R | N/R |
| | 1798 | $0.46 | $0.46 | N/R | N/R |
| | 1799 | $0.48 | $0.48 | N/R | N/R |
| Corn meal, per barrel | 1784 | 4.66 | N/R | N/R | N/R |
| | 1785 | 1.66 | N/R | N/R | N/R |
| | 1786 | 3.33 | N/R | N/R | N/R |
| | 1787 | 2.60 | N/R | N/R | N/R |
| | 1788 | 2.20 | N/R | N/R | N/R |
| | 1789 | 2.00 | N/R | Boston | N/R |
| | 1790 | 3.33 | N/R | N/R | N/R |
| | 1792 | $2.67 | N/R | N/R | N/R |
| | 1793 | $3.00 | N/R | N/R | N/R |
| | 1794 | $2.25 | N/R | N/R | N/R |
| | 1795 | 3.66 | N/R | N/R | N/R |
| | 1796 | $5.00 | N/R | N/R | N/R |
| | 1797 | $3.93 | N/R | N/R | N/R |
| | 1798 | $3.25 | N/R | N/R | N/R |
| | 1799 | $2.67 | N/R | N/R | N/R |
| Corn, per bushel | 1775 | 0.37 | 0.42 | N/R | N/R |
| (Charleston per hundredweight 1784-1787) | 1784 | 0.77 | N/R | N/R | 0.46 |
| | 1785 | 0.50 | 0.56 | N/R | 0.75 |
| | 1786 | 0.53 | 0.53 | N/R | 0.75 |
| | 1787 | 0.46 | 0.80 | N/R | 0.63 |

Values are expressed in Silver Dollars, the most common currency in the Colonies, unless noted with a Dollar Sign ($), indicating US Dollars.

| Commodity | Year | Philadelphia Currency | New York Currency | Boston Currency | Charleston Currency |
|---|---|---|---|---|---|
| | 1788 | 0.36 | 0.43 | N/R | 0.47 |
| | 1789 | 0.40 | 0.50 | N/R | 0.47 |
| | 1790 | 0.66 | N/R | N/R | 0.52 |
| | 1792 | $0.42 | N/R | N/R | N/R |
| | 1793 | $0.57 | 0.69 | N/R | N/R |
| | 1794 | 0.50 | 0.58 | N/R | 0.98 |
| | 1795 | 0.65 | 0.75 | N/R | 0.86 |
| | 1796 | $0.98 | N/R | N/R | 1.13 |
| | 1797 | $0.70 | $0.84 | N/R | 0.51 |
| | 1798 | $0.45 | $0.53 | N/R | 0.50 |
| | 1799 | $0.47 | $0.54 | N/R | 0.59 |
| Cotton, per pound | 1775 | 0.27 | N/R | 0.34 | N/R |
| | 1776 | N/R | N/R | 0.57 | N/R |
| | 1781 | N/R | N/R | 0.33 | N/R |
| | 1782 | N/R | N/R | 0.39 | N/R |
| | 1783 | N/R | N/R | 0.30 | N/R |
| | 1784 | 0.28 | N/R | 0.26 | N/R |
| | 1785 | 0.32 | N/R | 0.36 | N/R |
| | 1786 | 0.42 | 0.42 | 0.34 | N/R |
| | 1787 | 0.4 | 0.44 | 0.45 | N/R |
| | 1788 | 0.37 | 0.38 | 0.36 | N/R |
| | 1789 | 0.27 | 0.31 | 0.25 | N/R |
| | 1790 | 0.25 | 0.22 | 0.25 | N/R |
| | 1791 | 0.22 | 0.31 | 0.22 | N/R |
| | 1792 | $0.36 | N/R | 0.32 | N/R |
| | 1793 | $0.32 | N/R | 0.35 | N/R |
| | 1794 | $0.30 | 0.25 | 0.31 | N/R |
| | 1795 | 0.37 | 0.29 | 0.32 | N/R |
| | 1796 | $0.31 | $0.37 | N/R | 0.32 |
| | 1797 | $0.25 | $0.29 | N/R | 0.23 |
| | 1798 | $0.27 | $0.29 | N/R | 0.30 |
| | 1799 | $0.27 | $0.32 | N/R | 0.31 |
| Duck Cloth, per piece | 1782 | N/R | N/R | 25.55 | N/R |
| *(Philadelphia per bolt 1788-1799)* | 1783 | N/R | N/R | 0.15 | N/R |
| | 1784 | 9.33 | N/R | 9.58 | N/R |
| | 1785 | 7.43 | N/R | 11.16 | N/R |
| | 1786 | 8.66 | N/R | 13.00 | N/R |
| | 1787 | 9.66 | N/R | 10.83 | N/R |
| | 1788 | 9.33 | N/R | 10.50 | N/R |
| | 1789 | 9.33 | N/R | 11.00 | N/R |
| | 1790 | 9.00 | N/R | 10.00 | N/R |
| | 1791 | 9.30 | N/R | N/R | N/R |

Values are expressed in Silver Dollars, the most common currency in the Colonies, unless noted with a Dollar Sign ($), indicating US Dollars.

| Commodity | Year | Philadelphia Currency | New York Currency | Boston Currency | Charleston Currency |
|---|---|---|---|---|---|
| | 1792 | $9.30 | N/R | 12.26 | N/R |
| | 1793 | $10.67 | N/R | 12.00 | N/R |
| | 1794 | $11.00 | N/R | N/R | N/R |
| | 1795 | $11.50 | N/R | 15.50 | N/R |
| | 1796 | $10.50 | N/R | N/R | N/R |
| | 1797 | $12.00 | $17.75 | N/R | N/R |
| | 1798 | $12.13 | $19.50 | N/R | N/R |
| | 1799 | $10.75 | $16.75 | N/R | N/R |
| | | | | | |
| Fish, per hundredweight | 1790 | 3.17 | N/R | 2.12 | N/R |
| | 1792 | $3.19 | 1.75 | 2.33 | N/R |
| | 1793 | $3.53 | N/R | 3.66 | N/R |
| | 1794 | $3.53 | N/R | 2.25 | 3.64 |
| | 1795 | $6.46 | N/R | 3.33 | 3.64 |
| | 1796 | $6.50 | N/R | N/R | $5.50 |
| | 1797 | $7.50 | $4.75 | N/R | $5.50 |
| | 1798 | $8.01 | $4.10 | N/R | N/R |
| | 1799 | $4.08 | $3.25 | N/R | N/R |
| | | | | | |
| Flour, per hundredweight | 1781 | N/R | N/R | 5.83 | N/R |
| (New York per barrel 1784-1799) | 1782 | N/R | N/R | 4.66 | N/R |
| (Philadelphia per barrel 1784-1799) | 1783 | N/R | N/R | 5.50 | N/R |
| | 1784 | 6.23 | N/R | 3.08 | 8.00 |
| | 1785 | 6.00 | 7.00 | 3.25 | 7.87 |
| | 1786 | 5.33 | 5.13 | 3.33 | 5.57 |
| | 1787 | 5.33 | 5.44 | 2.86 | 7.51 |
| | 1788 | 4.93 | 5.00 | 2.91 | 5.19 |
| | 1789 | 5.33 | 5.38 | 2.80 | 5.19 |
| | 1790 | 8.33 | 8.00 | 3.96 | 9.40 |
| | 1791 | 5.33 | 4.88 | 5.33 | 3.43 |
| | 1792 | 5.00 | N/R | 2.45 | N/R |
| | 1793 | 6.00 | 6.19 | 3.30 | N/R |
| | 1794 | 6.66 | 6.25 | 3.00 | N/R |
| | 1795 | 11.00 | 10.75 | 4.18 | N/R |
| | 1796 | $14.00 | $13.50 | N/R | N/R |
| | 1797 | $9.00 | 7.75 | N/R | N/R |
| | 1798 | $7.00 | $6.50 | N/R | N/R |
| | 1799 | $9.50 | $8.38 | N/R | N/R |
| | | | | | |
| Gin, per gallon | 1784 | 0.50 | N/R | N/R | N/R |
| (New York per 1786-1795) | 1785 | 0.50 | N/R | N/R | 4.44 |
| (Charleston per case 1785-1790) | 1786 | 0.51 | 3.63 | N/R | 3.88 |
| | 1787 | 0.60 | 3.50 | N/R | 3.86 |
| | 1788 | 0.60 | 3.75 | N/R | 3.86 |

Values are expressed in Silver Dollars, the most common currency in the Colonies, unless noted with a Dollar Sign ($), indicating US Dollars.

| Commodity | Year | Philadelphia Currency | New York Currency | Boston Currency | Charleston Currency |
|---|---|---|---|---|---|
| | 1789 | 0.60 | 3.63 | N/R | 3.86 |
| | 1790 | 0.63 | N/R | N/R | 4.29 |
| | 1792 | $1.00 | N/R | N/R | N/R |
| | 1793 | $0.85 | 4.13 | N/R | N/R |
| | 1794 | $0.85 | 4.38 | N/R | N/R |
| | 1795 | 1.10 | 4.50 | N/R | N/R |
| | 1796 | $2.00 | N/R | N/R | N/R |
| | 1797 | $1.26 | $0.78 | N/R | N/R |
| | 1798 | $0.88 | $0.99 | N/R | N/R |
| | 1799 | $0.85 | $0.94 | N/R | N/R |
| Hops, per pound | 1790 | 0.33 | N/R | N/R | N/R |
| *(Per hundredweight 1795-96)* | 1791 | 0.27 | N/R | N/R | N/R |
| | 1792 | $0.27 | N/R | N/R | N/R |
| | 1793 | $0.27 | N/R | N/R | N/R |
| | 1794 | $0.13 | N/R | N/R | N/R |
| | 1795 | $7.00 | N/R | N/R | N/R |
| | 1796 | $7.00 | N/R | N/R | N/R |
| | 1797 | $0.13 | N/R | N/R | N/R |
| Indigo, per pound | 1783 | N/R | N/R | N/R | 1.07 |
| | 1784 | 1.64 | N/R | N/R | 0.96 |
| | 1785 | 1.28 | N/R | N/R | 1.00 |
| | 1786 | 1.40 | N/R | N/R | 1.07 |
| | 1787 | 1.13 | N/R | N/R | 1.11 |
| | 1788 | 1.40 | N/R | N/R | 1.07 |
| | 1789 | 1.40 | N/R | N/R | 1.07 |
| | 1790 | 1.40 | N/R | N/R | 0.96 |
| | 1791 | 1.27 | N/R | N/R | 0.96 |
| | 1792 | 1.30 | N/R | N/R | 1.11 |
| | 1793 | $1.36 | N/R | N/R | 0.66 |
| | 1794 | $1.67 | N/R | N/R | 0.56 |
| | 1795 | 1.49 | N/R | N/R | 0.86 |
| | 1796 | $1.50 | N/R | N/R | 0.54 |
| | 1797 | $1.30 | $1.69 | N/R | 0.60 |
| | 1798 | $1.20 | $1.88 | N/R | 0.75 |
| | 1799 | $1.20 | $2.13 | N/R | 0.54 |
| Iron - Bar, per ton | 1775 | 63.73 | N/R | N/R | N/R |
| | 1784 | 98.67 | N/R | N/R | 139.13 |
| | 1785 | 88.00 | N/R | N/R | 77.39 |
| | 1786 | 70.67 | 72.50 | N/R | 82.61 |
| | 1787 | 68.00 | 70.00 | N/R | 82.61 |
| | 1788 | 69.33 | 75.00 | N/R | 86.96 |

Values are expressed in Silver Dollars, the most common currency in the Colonies, unless noted with a Dollar Sign ($), indicating US Dollars.

| Commodity | Year | Philadelphia Currency | New York Currency | Boston Currency | Charleston Currency |
|---|---|---|---|---|---|
| | 1789 | 69.33 | 75.00 | N/R | N/R |
| | 1790 | 74.67 | 72.50 | N/R | 86.95 |
| | 1791 | 80.00 | 72.50 | N/R | 86.95 |
| | 1792 | 82.67 | N/R | N/R | N/R |
| | 1793 | $84.00 | 90.00 | N/R | N/R |
| | 1794 | 82.66 | 90.00 | N/R | N/R |
| | 1795 | 90.66 | 90.00 | N/R | N/R |
| | 1796 | $116.00 | N/R | N/R | N/R |
| | 1797 | $114.00 | $107.50 | N/R | N/R |
| | 1798 | $103.70 | $102.50 | N/R | N/R |
| | 1799 | $100.00 | $97.50 | N/R | N/R |
| Iron-Pig, per ton | 1784 | 26.66 | N/R | N/R | N/R |
| | 1785 | 26.66 | N/R | N/R | N/R |
| | 1786 | 24.00 | 27.50 | N/R | N/R |
| | 1787 | 22.67 | 27.50 | N/R | N/R |
| | 1788 | 22.67 | 22.50 | N/R | N/R |
| | 1789 | 22.67 | 22.50 | N/R | N/R |
| | 1790 | 22.67 | 21.88 | N/R | N/R |
| | 1791 | 25.68 | 22.88 | N/R | N/R |
| | 1792 | $25.30 | N/R | N/R | N/R |
| | 1793 | $24.00 | 21.88 | N/R | N/R |
| | 1794 | $25.00 | 21.88 | N/R | N/R |
| | 1795 | 29.33 | 21.88 | N/R | N/R |
| | 1796 | $32.00 | N/R | N/R | N/R |
| | 1797 | $34.00 | $31.20 | N/R | N/R |
| | 1798 | $33.30 | $31.20 | N/R | N/R |
| | 1799 | $39.00 | $36.20 | N/R | N/R |
| Lard, per pound | 1784 | 0.10 | N/R | N/R | N/R |
| | 1785 | 0.10 | N/R | N/R | N/R |
| | 1786 | 0.10 | N/R | N/R | N/R |
| | 1787 | 0.10 | N/R | N/R | N/R |
| | 1788 | 0.09 | N/R | N/R | N/R |
| | 1789 | 0.06 | N/R | N/R | N/R |
| | 1790 | 0.08 | N/R | N/R | N/R |
| | 1792 | $0.10 | N/R | N/R | N/R |
| | 1793 | $0.11 | N/R | N/R | N/R |
| | 1794 | $0.14 | N/R | N/R | 0.15 |
| | 1795 | 0.16 | N/R | N/R | 0.13 |
| | 1796 | $0.16 | N/R | N/R | 0.15 |
| | 1797 | $0.15 | $0.13 | N/R | 0.18 |
| | 1798 | $0.16 | $0.14 | N/R | 0.16 |
| | 1799 | $0.11 | $0.12 | N/R | 0.16 |

Values are expressed in Silver Dollars, the most common currency in the Colonies, unless noted with a Dollar Sign ($), indicating US Dollars.

| Commodity | Year | Philadelphia Currency | New York Currency | Boston Currency | Charleston Currency |
|---|---|---|---|---|---|
| Leather - Sole, per pound | 1784 | 0.22 | N/R | N/R | N/R |
| | 1785 | 0.21 | N/R | N/R | 0.13 |
| | 1786 | 0.20 | N/R | N/R | 0.13 |
| | 1787 | 0.18 | N/R | N/R | 0.17 |
| | 1788 | 0.20 | N/R | N/R | 0.16 |
| | 1789 | 0.16 | N/R | N/R | 0.16 |
| | 1790 | 0.18 | N/R | N/R | 0.16 |
| | 1791 | 0.17 | N/R | N/R | 0.18 |
| | 1792 | $0.18 | N/R | N/R | N/R |
| | 1793 | $0.18 | N/R | N/R | N/R |
| | 1794 | $0.19 | N/R | N/R | 0.18 |
| | 1795 | 0.22 | N/R | N/R | 0.19 |
| | 1796 | $0.22 | N/R | N/R | 0.17 |
| | 1797 | $0.17 | $0.18 | N/R | 0.17 |
| | 1798 | $0.18 | $0.16 | N/R | 0.16 |
| | 1799 | $0.18 | $0.14 | N/R | 0.16 |
| Linseed Oil, per gallon | 1784 | 0.62 | N/R | N/R | N/R |
| | 1785 | 0.77 | N/R | N/R | N/R |
| | 1786 | 1.00 | 1.13 | N/R | N/R |
| | 1787 | 0.83 | 1.13 | N/R | N/R |
| | 1788 | 0.59 | 0.50 | N/R | N/R |
| | 1789 | 0.38 | 0.56 | N/R | N/R |
| | 1790 | 0.41 | 0.50 | N/R | N/R |
| | 1791 | 0.48 | 0.56 | N/R | 0.62 |
| | 1792 | $0.54 | N/R | N/R | N/R |
| | 1793 | $0.63 | 0.81 | N/R | N/R |
| | 1794 | $0.54 | 0.75 | N/R | 0.91 |
| | 1795 | $0.67 | 0.75 | N/R | 0.75 |
| | 1796 | $1.06 | N/R | N/R | 1.34 |
| | 1797 | $1.20 | $0.81 | N/R | 1.39 |
| | 1798 | $0.70 | $0.78 | N/R | N/R |
| | 1799 | $0.65 | $1.00 | N/R | N/R |
| Lumber Boards, per one thousand | 1784 | 18.00 | N/R | N/R | 20.26 |
| | 1785 | 19.33 | N/R | N/R | 19.04 |
| | 1786 | 16.00 | N/R | N/R | 15.22 |
| | 1787 | 16.00 | N/R | N/R | 15.74 |
| | 1788 | 16.00 | N/R | N/R | 13.04 |
| | 1789 | 16.00 | N/R | N/R | 13.04 |
| | 1790 | 16.00 | N/R | N/R | 11.96 |
| | 1791 | 14.66 | N/R | N/R | 13.04 |
| | 1792 | $23.30 | N/R | N/R | N/R |
| | 1793 | 20.66 | N/R | N/R | N/R |

Values are expressed in Silver Dollars, the most common currency in the Colonies, unless noted with a Dollar Sign ($), indicating US Dollars.

| Commodity | Year | Philadelphia Currency | New York Currency | Boston Currency | Charleston Currency |
|---|---|---|---|---|---|
| | 1794 | $22.00 | N/R | N/R | N/R |
| | 1795 | 25.33 | N/R | N/R | N/R |
| | 1796 | $28.70 | N/R | N/R | N/R |
| | 1797 | $28.30 | $17.50 | N/R | N/R |
| | 1798 | $46.00 | $17.00 | N/R | N/R |
| | 1799 | $36.00 | $17.00 | N/R | N/R |
| Molasses, per gallon | 1775 | 0.22 | 0.25 | 0.26 | N/R |
| | 1776 | N/R | 0.34 | N/R | N/R |
| | 1782 | N/R | N/R | 0.47 | N/R |
| | 1783 | N/R | N/R | 0.29 | N/R |
| | 1784 | 0.25 | N/R | 0.26 | 0.18 |
| | 1785 | 0.23 | N/R | 0.22 | 0.23 |
| | 1786 | 0.23 | 0.23 | 0.20 | 0.21 |
| | 1787 | 0.23 | 0.21 | 0.24 | 0.27 |
| | 1788 | 0.25 | N/R | 0.20 | 0.25 |
| | 1789 | 0.28 | N/R | 0.22 | 0.25 |
| | 1790 | 0.29 | N/R | 0.28 | 0.28 |
| | 1791 | 0.44 | N/R | 0.35 | 0.28 |
| | 1792 | $0.46 | N/R | 0.42 | 0.47 |
| | 1793 | $0.46 | 0.43 | 0.38 | N/R |
| | 1794 | $0.53 | N/R | 0.63 | 0.55 |
| | 1795 | 0.55 | N/R | 0.52 | 0.61 |
| | 1796 | $0.57 | N/R | N/R | 0.52 |
| | 1797 | $0.64 | $0.55 | N/R | 0.59 |
| | 1798 | $0.57 | $0.53 | N/R | 0.57 |
| | 1799 | $0.64 | $0.53 | N/R | 0.64 |
| Nails, per pound | 1784 | 0.10 | N/R | N/R | N/R |
| | 1785 | 0.10 | N/R | N/R | N/R |
| | 1786 | 0.10 | N/R | N/R | N/R |
| | 1787 | 0.10 | N/R | N/R | N/R |
| | 1788 | 0.10 | N/R | N/R | N/R |
| | 1789 | 0.10 | N/R | N/R | N/R |
| | 1790 | 0.09 | N/R | N/R | N/R |
| | 1791 | 0.10 | N/R | N/R | N/R |
| | 1792 | $0.10 | N/R | N/R | N/R |
| | 1793 | $0.10 | N/R | N/R | N/R |
| | 1794 | $0.10 | N/R | N/R | N/R |
| | 1795 | 0.12 | N/R | N/R | N/R |
| | 1796 | $0.12 | N/R | N/R | N/R |
| | 1797 | $0.12 | $0.12 | N/R | N/R |
| | 1798 | $0.12 | $0.12 | N/R | N/R |
| | 1799 | $0.12 | $0.12 | N/R | N/R |

Values are expressed in Silver Dollars, the most common currency in the Colonies, unless noted with a Dollar Sign ($), indicating US Dollars.

| Commodity | Year | Philadelphia Currency | New York Currency | Boston Currency | Charleston Currency |
|---|---|---|---|---|---|
| Pork, per barrel | 1775 | 8.00 | 8.13 | 9.00 | N/R |
| | 1784 | 11.18 | N/R | N/R | 6.75 |
| | 1785 | 13.13 | 13.75 | N/R | 10.71 |
| | 1786 | 12.50 | 13.75 | N/R | N/R |
| | 1787 | 11.25 | 11.95 | N/R | 13.39 |
| | 1788 | 9.20 | N/R | N/R | 12.00 |
| | 1789 | 8.13 | N/R | N/R | 12.00 |
| | 1790 | 8.13 | N/R | N/R | 12.00 |
| | 1792 | $11.17 | N/R | N/R | $13.00 |
| | 1793 | $13.33 | 12.50 | N/R | 16.43 |
| | 1794 | $15.00 | 15.31 | N/R | $18.00 |
| | 1795 | 15.00 | 12.00 | N/R | $17.00 |
| | 1796 | $18.00 | $21.00 | N/R | $18.00 |
| | 1797 | $18.50 | $24.50 | N/R | $19.00 |
| | 1798 | $18.50 | $20.00 | N/R | 19.29 |
| | 1799 | $14.75 | $16.50 | N/R | 19.29 |
| Pot Ashes, per ton | 1784 | 80.00 | N/R | N/R | N/R |
| | 1785 | 160.00 | N/R | N/R | N/R |
| | 1786 | 106.00 | N/R | N/R | N/R |
| | 1787 | 100.00 | N/R | N/R | N/R |
| | 1788 | 100.00 | N/R | N/R | N/R |
| | 1789 | 100.00 | N/R | N/R | N/R |
| | 1790 | 103.46 | N/R | N/R | N/R |
| | 1791 | 109.33 | N/R | N/R | N/R |
| | 1792 | $95.00 | N/R | N/R | N/R |
| | 1793 | $122.50 | N/R | N/R | N/R |
| | 1794 | $120.00 | N/R | N/R | N/R |
| | 1795 | 120.00 | N/R | N/R | N/R |
| | 1796 | $175.50 | N/R | N/R | N/R |
| | 1797 | $156.20 | $120.00 | N/R | N/R |
| | 1798 | $142.50 | $142.50 | N/R | N/R |
| | 1799 | $183.80 | $177.50 | N/R | N/R |
| Rice, per hundredweight | 1775 | 1.89 | N/R | N/R | N/R |
| | 1784 | 3.86 | N/R | N/R | 1.86 |
| | 1785 | 3.46 | N/R | N/R | 1.60 |
| | 1786 | 2.86 | 3.00 | N/R | 1.37 |
| | 1787 | 3.40 | 3.88 | N/R | 2.20 |
| | 1788 | 2.82 | N/R | N/R | 1.60 |
| | 1789 | 2.66 | N/R | N/R | 1.36 |
| | 1790 | 3.00 | N/R | N/R | 1.60 |
| | 1792 | $2.67 | N/R | N/R | 1.09 |
| | 1793 | $3.00 | 2.50 | N/R | 1.80 |

Values are expressed in Silver Dollars, the most common currency in the Colonies, unless noted with a Dollar Sign ($), indicating US Dollars.

| Commodity | Year | Philadelphia Currency | New York Currency | Boston Currency | Charleston Currency |
|---|---|---|---|---|---|
| | 1794 | 3.00 | N/R | N/R | 1.33 |
| | 1795 | 5.00 | N/R | N/R | 2.24 |
| | 1796 | $7.25 | N/R | N/R | 3.22 |
| | 1797 | $3.33 | $2.69 | N/R | 1.26 |
| | 1798 | $3.00 | $2.31 | N/R | 1.13 |
| | 1799 | $2.33 | $2.44 | N/R | 0.93 |

Values are expressed in Silver Dollars, the most common currency in the Colonies, unless noted with a Dollar Sign ($), indicating US Dollars.

| Commodity | Year | Philadelphia Currency | New York Currency | Boston Currency | Charleston Currency |
|---|---|---|---|---|---|
| Rum, per gallon | 1775 | 0.30 | 0.31 | 0.29 | N/R |
| | 1782 | N/R | N/R | 0.57 | N/R |
| | 1783 | N/R | N/R | 0.54 | N/R |
| | 1784 | 0.37 | N/R | 0.31 | 0.37 |
| | 1785 | 0.32 | 0.56 | 0.25 | 0.32 |
| | 1786 | 0.32 | 0.47 | 0.24 | 0.3 |
| | 1787 | 0.34 | 0.59 | 0.28 | 0.41 |
| | 1788 | 0.32 | 0.56 | 0.26 | 0.36 |
| | 1789 | 0.33 | 0.58 | 0.28 | 0.36 |
| | 1790 | 0.37 | 0.64 | 0.32 | 0.46 |
| | 1792 | $0.67 | N/R | 0.63 | N/R |
| | 1793 | $0.63 | 0.79 | 0.57 | 0.64 |
| | 1794 | $0.87 | 1.13 | 0.75 | 0.86 |
| | 1795 | 0.75 | 1.06 | 0.75 | N/R |
| | 1796 | $1.00 | $1.81 | N/R | 0.89 |
| | 1797 | $0.88 | $1.22 | N/R | 0.86 |
| | 1798 | $0.85 | $1.33 | N/R | 0.86 |
| | 1799 | $0.80 | $1.11 | N/R | 0.86 |
| Salt petre, per pound | 1784 | 0.21 | N/R | N/R | N/R |
| (Per hundredweight 1789-1794) | 1785 | 0.22 | N/R | N/R | N/R |
| | 1786 | 0.22 | N/R | N/R | N/R |
| | 1787 | 0.23 | N/R | N/R | N/R |
| | 1788 | 0.20 | N/R | N/R | N/R |
| | 1789 | 17.33 | N/R | N/R | N/R |
| | 1790 | 16.00 | N/R | N/R | N/R |
| | 1791 | 12.00 | N/R | N/R | N/R |
| | 1792 | $13.70 | N/R | N/R | N/R |
| | 1793 | $14.30 | N/R | N/R | N/R |
| | 1794 | $14.30 | N/R | N/R | N/R |
| | 1795 | $0.87 | N/R | N/R | N/R |
| | 1796 | $0.80 | N/R | N/R | N/R |
| | 1797 | $0.55 | $0.44 | N/R | N/R |
| | 1798 | $0.37 | $0.45 | N/R | N/R |
| | 1799 | $0.50 | $0.37 | N/R | N/R |
| Salt, per bushel | 1775 | 0.40 | 0.41 | N/R | N/R |
| | 1776 | N/R | 0.41 | N/R | N/R |
| | 1784 | 0.38 | N/R | N/R | 0.30 |
| | 1785 | 0.27 | 0.50 | N/R | 0.47 |
| | 1786 | 0.24 | 0.44 | N/R | 0.23 |
| | 1787 | 0.24 | 0.25 | N/R | 0.32 |
| | 1788 | 0.24 | 0.25 | N/R | 0.19 |
| | 1789 | 0.25 | 0.25 | N/R | 0.24 |

Values are expressed in Silver Dollars, the most common currency in the Colonies, unless noted with a Dollar Sign ($), indicating US Dollars.

| Commodity | Year | Philadelphia Currency | New York Currency | Boston Currency | Charleston Currency |
|---|---|---|---|---|---|
| | 1790 | 0.25 | 0.25 | N/R | 0.28 |
| | 1792 | $0.29 | N/R | N/R | N/R |
| | 1793 | $0.33 | 0.31 | N/R | N/R |
| | 1794 | $1.00 | 0.88 | N/R | 0.75 |
| | 1795 | 0.733 | 0.50 | N/R | 0.59 |
| | 1796 | $0.67 | N/R | N/R | 0.59 |
| | 1797 | $0.61 | $0.55 | N/R | 0.54 |
| | 1798 | $0.55 | $0.56 | N/R | 0.80 |
| | 1799 | $0.76 | $0.55 | N/R | 1.39 |
| Sheeting, per piece | 1784 | 13.00 | N/R | N/R | N/R |
| | 1785 | 13.75 | N/R | N/R | N/R |
| | 1786 | 13.76 | N/R | N/R | 17.62 |
| | 1787 | 14.17 | N/R | N/R | 20.36 |
| | 1788 | 12.00 | N/R | N/R | 19.29 |
| | 1789 | 12.00 | N/R | N/R | 19.29 |
| | 1790 | 12.00 | N/R | N/R | 14.47 |
| | 1791 | 12.00 | N/R | N/R | 14.47 |
| | 1792 | $12.00 | N/R | N/R | N/R |
| | 1793 | $15.00 | N/R | N/R | N/R |
| | 1794 | $18.33 | N/R | N/R | 19.29 |
| | 1795 | $16.33 | N/R | N/R | 16.61 |
| | 1796 | $16.75 | N/R | N/R | 16.01 |
| | 1797 | $16.75 | $18.38 | N/R | 16.01 |
| | 1798 | $18.50 | $18.50 | N/R | N/R |
| | 1799 | $17.50 | N/R | N/R | N/R |
| Staves, per 1200 units | 1775 | 18.66 | N/R | N/R | N/R |
| | 1784 | 26.66 | N/R | N/R | 14.13 |
| | 1785 | 22.66 | N/R | N/R | 22.82 |
| | 1786 | 20.00 | 15.95 | N/R | 16.87 |
| | 1787 | 18.66 | 18.75 | N/R | 17.39 |
| | 1788 | 16.00 | 20.00 | N/R | 17.39 |
| | 1789 | 18.66 | 15.00 | N/R | 15.22 |
| | 1790 | 18.66 | 16.25 | N/R | 12.61 |
| | 1791 | 19.33 | 16.25 | N/R | 13.04 |
| | 1792 | 20.00 | N/R | N/R | N/R |
| | 1793 | 22.66 | 23.75 | N/R | N/R |
| | 1794 | $20.30 | 27.50 | N/R | N/R |
| | 1795 | 36.00 | 45.00 | N/R | 20.65 |
| | 1796 | $46.00 | N/R | N/R | 21.74 |
| | 1797 | $45.00 | $32.50 | N/R | 26.09 |
| | 1798 | $35.00 | $27.50 | N/R | 21.73 |
| | 1799 | $37.00 | $30.00 | N/R | 21.74 |

Values are expressed in Silver Dollars, the most common currency in the Colonies, unless noted with a Dollar Sign ($), indicating US Dollars.

| Commodity | Year | Philadelphia Currency | New York Currency | Boston Currency | Charleston Currency |
|---|---|---|---|---|---|
| Steel, per pound | 1784 | 13.08 | N/R | N/R | N/R |
| *(Philadelphi per hundredweight 1784-1794)* | 1785 | 12.02 | N/R | N/R | 0.20 |
| *(Charleston per hundredweight 1796-1797)* | 1786 | 12.00 | 0.09 | N/R | 0.20 |
| | 1787 | 11.00 | 0.09 | N/R | 0.17 |
| | 1788 | 11.00 | 0.09 | N/R | N/R |
| | 1789 | 11.00 | 0.09 | N/R | N/R |
| | 1790 | 10.66 | N/R | N/R | N/R |
| | 1791 | 10.00 | 0.09 | N/R | N/R |
| | 1792 | 10.66 | N/R | N/R | N/R |
| | 1793 | 10.66 | 0.09 | N/R | N/R |
| | 1794 | $10.00 | 0.10 | N/R | N/R |
| | 1795 | 0.12 | 0.10 | N/R | N/R |
| | 1796 | $0.13 | N/R | N/R | 10.66 |
| | 1797 | $0.13 | $0.14 | N/R | 10.66 |
| | 1798 | $0.14 | $0.14 | N/R | N/R |
| | 1799 | $0.12 | $0.14 | N/R | N/R |
| Sugar, per hundredweight | 1775 | 6.84 | 8.00 | 8.00 | N/R |
| | 1776 | N/R | 8.00 | 10.50 | N/R |
| | 1781 | N/R | N/R | 8.75 | N/R |
| | 1782 | N/R | N/R | 9.16 | N/R |
| | 1783 | N/R | N/R | 9.25 | N/R |
| | 1784 | 8.66 | N/R | 6.00 | 5.14 |
| | 1785 | 6.13 | 6.25 | 7.50 | 7.50 |
| | 1786 | 7.33 | 7.50 | 6.75 | 7.25 |
| | 1787 | 7.33 | 7.50 | N/R | 9.10 |
| | 1788 | 7.33 | 8.75 | 7.75 | 8.57 |
| | 1789 | 8.51 | 7.50 | 6.33 | 8.57 |
| | 1790 | 8.16 | 9.50 | 7.66 | 10.97 |
| | 1792 | $15.00 | N/R | N/R | 14.46 |
| | 1793 | $14.00 | 11.88 | N/R | 11.57 |
| | 1794 | 11.00 | 13.75 | 13.50 | 10.61 |
| | 1795 | 12.13 | 11.25 | 13.00 | 12.86 |
| | 1796 | $14.00 | N/R | N/R | 13.39 |
| | 1797 | $16.00 | N/R | N/R | 13.39 |
| | 1798 | $14.00 | N/R | N/R | 13.50 |
| | 1799 | $14.00 | N/R | N/R | 13.93 |
| Tallow, per pound | 1785 | 0.10 | N/R | N/R | 0.11 |
| | 1786 | 0.12 | N/R | N/R | N/R |
| | 1787 | 0.12 | N/R | N/R | 0.14 |
| | 1788 | 0.09 | N/R | N/R | 0.11 |
| | 1789 | 0.08 | N/R | N/R | 0.11 |
| | 1790 | 0.10 | N/R | N/R | 0.09 |

Values are expressed in Silver Dollars, the most common currency in the Colonies, unless noted with a Dollar Sign ($), indicating US Dollars.

| Commodity | Year | Philadelphia Currency | New York Currency | Boston Currency | Charleston Currency |
|---|---|---|---|---|---|
| | 1791 | 0.09 | N/R | N/R | 0.09 |
| | 1792 | $0.09 | N/R | N/R | N/R |
| | 1793 | $0.09 | N/R | N/R | N/R |
| | 1794 | $0.11 | N/R | N/R | 0.17 |
| | 1795 | 0.18 | N/R | N/R | 0.18 |
| | 1796 | $0.13 | N/R | N/R | 0.15 |
| | 1797 | $0.11 | $0.13 | N/R | 0.15 |
| | 1798 | $0.14 | $0.13 | N/R | 0.16 |
| | 1799 | $0.14 | $0.16 | N/R | 0.16 |
| Tea, per pound | 1775 | 0.51 | 0.56 | N/R | N/R |
| | 1781 | N/R | N/R | 1.75 | N/R |
| | 1782 | N/R | N/R | 1.23 | N/R |
| | 1783 | N/R | N/R | 0.60 | N/R |
| | 1784 | 0.44 | N/R | 0.45 | N/R |
| | 1785 | 0.39 | N/R | 0.38 | 0.50 |
| | 1786 | 0.37 | 1.06 | 0.27 | 0.40 |
| | 1787 | 0.35 | 1.22 | 0.31 | 0.43 |
| | 1788 | 0.35 | 2.50 | 0.34 | 0.43 |
| | 1789 | 0.27 | 2.19 | 0.26 | 0.43 |
| | 1790 | 0.31 | 1.43 | 0.25 | 0.35 |
| | 1791 | N/R | N/R | N/R | N/R |
| | 1792 | $0.32 | N/R | 0.39 | 0.38 |
| | 1793 | $0.34 | 0.97 | 0.33 | 0.38 |
| | 1794 | $0.35 | 1.25 | 0.37 | 0.36 |
| | 1795 | 0.37 | 1.28 | 0.32 | 0.35 |
| | 1796 | $0.33 | $1.50 | N/R | 0.38 |
| | 1797 | $0.35 | $1.31 | N/R | 0.38 |
| | 1798 | $0.54 | $1.41 | N/R | N/R |
| | 1799 | $0.74 | $1.38 | N/R | N/R |
| Tobacco, per hundredweight | 1784 | 7.84 | N/R | N/R | 4.44 |
| (New York per pound) | 1785 | 7.33 | N/R | N/R | 5.38 |
| | 1786 | 5.33 | 0.05 | N/R | 3.88 |
| | 1787 | 6.00 | 0.05 | N/R | 4.86 |
| | 1788 | 6.33 | 0.06 | N/R | 4.24 |
| | 1789 | 6.33 | 0.06 | N/R | 4.24 |
| | 1790 | 6.33 | 0.04 | N/R | 3.69 |
| | 1791 | 4.82 | 0.04 | N/R | 3.11 |
| | 1792 | $4.67 | N/R | N/R | 2.68 |
| | 1793 | $4.67 | 0.04 | N/R | 3.75 |
| | 1794 | $4.75 | 0.04 | N/R | 3.87 |
| | 1795 | 6.66 | 0.07 | N/R | 4.75 |
| | 1796 | $7.50 | $0.06 | N/R | 6.00 |

Values are expressed in Silver Dollars, the most common currency in the Colonies, unless noted with a Dollar Sign ($), indicating US Dollars.

| Commodity | Year | Philadelphia Currency | New York Currency | Boston Currency | Charleston Currency |
|---|---|---|---|---|---|
| | 1797 | $10.00 | $0.10 | N/R | 6.00 |
| | 1798 | $12.50 | $0.10 | N/R | 7.99 |
| | 1799 | $13.00 | $0.10 | N/R | 7.75 |
| Turpentine, per barrel | 1784 | 4.33 | N/R | N/R | 4.01 |
| | 1785 | 3.33 | N/R | N/R | 3.26 |
| | 1786 | 1.60 | 2.81 | N/R | 1.54 |
| | 1787 | 1.60 | 3.13 | N/R | 1.99 |
| | 1788 | 1.60 | 1.75 | N/R | 1.50 |
| | 1789 | 1.66 | 1.38 | N/R | 1.50 |
| | 1790 | 2.33 | 2.38 | N/R | 3.00 |
| | 1791 | 1.84 | 2.00 | N/R | 1.82 |
| | 1792 | $1.84 | N/R | N/R | N/R |
| | 1793 | $2.33 | 2.00 | N/R | N/R |
| | 1794 | $2.00 | 1.50 | N/R | $2.00 |
| | 1795 | 3.20 | 2.50 | N/R | 2.14 |
| | 1796 | $3.33 | $3.00 | N/R | 2.51 |
| | 1797 | $3.75 | $2.69 | N/R | 3.49 |
| | 1798 | $3.50 | $2.50 | N/R | 2.79 |
| | 1799 | $2.50 | $1.87 | N/R | 1.50 |
| Whale Oil, per gallon | 1784 | 0.40 | N/R | N/R | N/R |
| *(New York per barrel in 1786-1795)* | 1785 | 0.35 | N/R | N/R | N/R |
| | 1786 | 0.30 | 7.75 | N/R | N/R |
| | 1787 | 0.37 | 8.75 | N/R | N/R |
| | 1788 | 0.37 | 9.06 | N/R | N/R |
| | 1789 | 0.27 | 9.06 | N/R | N/R |
| | 1790 | 0.28 | 6.63 | N/R | N/R |
| | 1791 | 0.27 | 6.63 | N/R | N/R |
| | 1792 | 0.27 | N/R | N/R | N/R |
| | 1793 | 0.27 | 6.63 | N/R | N/R |
| | 1794 | $0.29 | 6.63 | N/R | N/R |
| | 1795 | 0.35 | 10.00 | N/R | N/R |
| | 1796 | $0.47 | N/R | N/R | N/R |
| | 1797 | $0.40 | $0.33 | N/R | N/R |
| | 1798 | $0.47 | $0.34 | N/R | N/R |
| | 1799 | $0.27 | $0.30 | N/R | N/R |
| Wheat, per bushel | 1775 | 0.77 | 0.79 | 1.00 | N/R |
| | 1776 | N/R | 0.69 | 1.25 | N/R |
| | 1781 | N/R | N/R | 1.25 | N/R |
| | 1782 | N/R | N/R | 1.50 | N/R |
| | 1783 | N/R | N/R | 1.75 | N/R |
| | 1784 | 0.97 | N/R | 1.25 | N/R |

Values are expressed in Silver Dollars, the most common currency in the Colonies, unless noted with a Dollar Sign ($), indicating US Dollars.

| Commodity | Year | Philadelphia Currency | New York Currency | Boston Currency | Charleston Currency |
|---|---|---|---|---|---|
| | 1785 | 1.07 | 1.09 | 1.16 | N/R |
| | 1786 | 0.92 | 0.81 | 0.91 | N/R |
| | 1787 | 0.90 | 0.96 | 1.00 | N/R |
| | 1788 | 0.90 | 0.83 | 0.92 | N/R |
| | 1789 | 0.95 | 1.00 | 0.92 | N/R |
| | 1790 | 1.77 | 1.34 | 1.41 | N/R |
| | 1791 | 1.03 | 0.91 | 0.92 | N/R |
| | 1792 | $0.98 | N/R | 1.00 | N/R |
| | 1793 | $1.18 | 1.14 | 1.25 | N/R |
| | 1794 | $1.05 | 1.06 | 1.25 | N/R |
| | 1795 | 1.80 | 2.13 | 1.75 | N/R |
| | 1796 | $2.25 | $2.50 | 1.75 | N/R |
| | 1797 | $1.00 | $1.41 | 1.58 | N/R |
| | 1798 | $1.10 | $1.21 | 1.41 | N/R |
| | 1799 | $1.58 | $1.56 | N/R | N/R |
| Whisky, per gallon | 1797 | $0.67 | N/R | N/R | N/R |
| | 1798 | $0.58 | N/R | N/R | N/R |
| | 1799 | $0.51 | N/R | N/R | N/R |

Values are expressed in Silver Dollars, the most common currency in the Colonies, unless noted with a Dollar Sign ($), indicating US Dollars.

| Commodity | Year | Philadelphia Currency | New York Currency | Boston Currency | Charleston Currency |
|---|---|---|---|---|---|
| Wine, per pipe | 1775 | 220.67 | N/R | N/R | N/R |
| *(New York per gallon 1797-1799)* | 1784 | 250.00 | N/R | N/R | 163.04 |
| | 1785 | 233.33 | 175.00 | N/R | 163.04 |
| | 1786 | 200.00 | 200.00 | N/R | 173.91 |
| | 1787 | 200.00 | 200.00 | N/R | 239.13 |
| | 1788 | 200.00 | 187.50 | N/R | 239.13 |
| | 1789 | 200.00 | 187.50 | N/R | 239.13 |
| | 1790 | 200.00 | 187.50 | N/R | 173.91 |
| | 1792 | $153.30 | N/R | N/R | N/R |
| | 1793 | $201.00 | 187.50 | N/R | N/R |
| | 1794 | $201.00 | 187.50 | N/R | 239.13 |
| | 1795 | N/R | 200.00 | N/R | 250.00 |
| | 1796 | $263.00 | N/R | N/R | 228.26 |
| | 1797 | $283.50 | $1.59 | N/R | 315.22 |
| | 1798 | $246.70 | $1.59 | N/R | N/R |
| | 1799 | $293.30 | $1.59 | N/R | N/R |

Values are expressed in Silver Dollars, the most common currency in the Colonies, unless noted with a Dollar Sign ($), indicating US Dollars.

# SELECTED PRICES 1775-1799

| Item | Data Source | Description | Price |
|------|-------------|-------------|-------|
| **Alcohol** | | | |
| Ale | Inventory of John Baynes (1790) | Cask of ale in Prince George County, Maryland, 1790 | 7 shillings 6 pence |
| Brandy | Inventory of Richard Mitchell (1781) | Gallon of brandy in Lancaster County, Virginia, 1781 | 4 shillings |
| Brandy | Inventory of Richard Mitchell (1781) | Gallon of brandy in Lancaster County, Virginia, 1781 | 4 shillings |
| Cag | Inventory of Margaret Ball (1783) | Brandy Cag in Lancaster County, Virginia, 1783 | 3 shillings |
| Case | Inventory of John Baynes (1790) | Rum Case in Prince George County, Maryland, 1790 | 10 shillings |
| Cask | Inventory of Margaret Anderson (1783) | Rum Cask in Kershaw, South Carolina, 1783 | 2 pounds 10 shillings |
| Cider | Economic and Social History of New England, 1620-1789 by William Weeden | Barrel of Cider in New England, 1775 | 1 pound, 12 shillings, 2 pence |
| Cider | Inventory of Richard Mitchell (1781) | 100 gallon cask of Cyder in Lancaster County, Virginia, 1781 | 10 shillings |
| Cordial | Inventory of Doctor Nicholas Flood (1776) | One small cask, 20 gallons, orange peel cordial in Richmond County, Virginia, 1776 | 3 pounds |
| Flask | Inventory of Doctor Nicholas Flood (1776) | Flask in Richmond County, Virginia, 1776 | 1 pence |
| Port | Kitman, George Washington's Expense Account (1970) | Bottle of Port in Fraunces Tavern in New York City, 1776 | 6 shillings |
| Rum | Inventory of Doctor Nicholas Flood (1776) | One cask, 23 gallons, common rum in Richmond County, Virginia, 1776 | 3 pounds |
| Rum | Economic and Social History of New England, 1620-1789 by William Weeden | Gallon of rum in New England, 1779 | 1 pound |
| Sherry | Inventory of Doctor Nicholas Flood (1776) | Bottle of sherry in Richmond County, Virginia, 1776 | 1 shilling 3½ pence |
| Sherry | Inventory of Isaac Walker (1797) | Gallon of sherry in Prince George County, Maryland, 1797 | 7 shillings 6 pence |
| Spirit | Inventory of Doctor Nicholas Flood (1776) | Large bottle of Chain Spirit in Richmond County, Virginia, 1776 | 8 shillings |
| Spirit | Inventory of Doctor Nicholas Flood (1776) | Gallon of Barbadoes Spirits in Richmond County, Virginia, 1776 | 10 shillings |
| Spirit | Inventory of Doctor Nicholas Flood (1776) | One hogshead, 45 gallons, Demirara spirits in Richmond County, Virginia, 1776 | 18 pounds 15 shillings |
| Still | Inventory of Doctor Nicholas Flood (1776) | Small Still & Worm in Richmond County, Virginia, 1776 | 3 pounds |
| Still | Inventory of John Baynes (1790) | Copper Still in Prince George County, Maryland, 1790 | 12 pounds 13 shillings 4 pence |
| Still | Inventory of John Riley (1795) | Still in Newberry, South Carolina, 1795 | 2 pounds 11 shillings 9 pence |
| Wine | Inventory of Doctor Nicholas Flood (1776) | Bottle of Madira Wine (Wharton's) in Richmond County, Virginia, 1776 | 2 shillings 6 pence |
| Wine | Inventory of Doctor Nicholas Flood (1776) | Bottle of old white wine in Richmond County, Virginia, 1776 | 2 shillings |

| Item | Data Source | Description | Price |
|------|-------------|-------------|-------|
| Wine | Inventory of John Baynes (1790) | Cask of port wine in Prince George County, Maryland, 1790 | 15 shillings |
| Worm | Inventory of John Baynes (1790) | Worm for Still in Prince George County, Maryland, 1790 | 4 pounds 9 shillings |

### Apparel - Children

| Item | Data Source | Description | Price |
|------|-------------|-------------|-------|
| Hat | Inventory of John Baynes (1790) | Boys Caster Hatt in Prince George County, Maryland, 1790 | 3 shillings |
| Hat | Inventory of John Baynes (1790) | Boys felt Hatt in Prince George County, Maryland, 1790 | 9 pence |
| Hose | Inventory of Isaac Walker (1797) | Pair of Boys Hose in Prince George County, Maryland, 1797 | 8 pence |
| Shoes | Inventory of John Baynes (1790) | Pair Girls Leather Shoes in Prince George County, Maryland, 1790 | 2 shillings 6 pence |
| Shoes | Inventory of John Baynes (1790) | Pair of Girls Callamo Shoes in Prince George County, Maryland, 1790 | 3 shillings 6 pence |

### Apparel - Men

| Item | Data Source | Description | Price |
|------|-------------|-------------|-------|
| Boots | Inventory of John Baynes (1790) | Pair of boots in Prince George County, Maryland, 1790 | 2 pounds |
| Breeches | Inventory of John Riley (1795) | Pair of old Sea Breaches in Newberry, South Carolina, 1795 | 2 shillings |
| Buckles | Inventory of Doctor Nicholas Flood (1776) | Pair Silver Shoe and knee buckles in Richmond County, Virginia, 1776 | 1 pound 5 shillings |
| Buckles | Inventory of Doctor Nicholas Flood (1776) | Pair carved silver shoe and knee buckles in Richmond County, Virginia, 1776 | 1 pound |
| Buckles | Inventory of Daniel Diman (1798) | Silver shoe buckles in Plymouth, Massachusetts, 1798 | $1.50 |
| Buckles | Inventory of Daniel Diman (1798) | Silver knee buckles in Plymouth, Massachusetts, 1798 | $0.62 |
| Buttons | Inventory of Daniel Diman (1798) | Silver sleeve buttons in Plymouth, Massachusetts, 1798 | $0.25 |
| Cap | Inventory of Doctor Nicholas Flood (1776) | Leather cap in Richmond County, Virginia, 1776 | 3 shillings 9 pence |
| Cap | Inventory of Isaac Walker (1797) | Milled Cap in Prince George County, Maryland, 1797 | 4½ pence |
| Cloak | Inventory of John Baynes (1790) | Black Silk Cloak in Prince George County, Maryland, 1790 | 2 pounds |

## Based Upon the British Currency System

| Year | Pound in 2002 US Dollars | Shilling in 2002 US Dollars | Pence in 2002 US Dollars |
|------|--------------------------|------------------------------|---------------------------|
| 1775 | $144.00 | $7.20 | $0.60 |
| 1780 | $168.00 | $8.40 | $0.70 |
| 1785 | $144.00 | $7.20 | $0.60 |
| 1790 | $144.00 | $7.20 | $0.60 |
| 1795 | $120.00 | $6.00 | $0.50 |
| 1799 | $120.00 | $6.00 | $0.50 |

*Calculations are approximate values based upon economic historical data*

| Item | Data Source | Description | Price |
|---|---|---|---|
| Cloak | Inventory of Isaac Walker (1797) | Scarlet Cloak in Prince George County, Maryland, 1797 | 1 pound 2 shillings 6 pence |
| Coat | Inventory of John Baynes (1790) | Horsemans Coat in Prince George County, Maryland, 1790 | 1 pound 9 shillings |
| Garters | Inventory of Doctor Nicholas Flood (1776) | Pair of Silk knee Garters in Richmond County, Virginia, 1776 | 6 shillings |
| Gloves | Inventory of Doctor Nicholas Flood (1776) | Pair of Mens Gloves in Richmond County, Virginia, 1776 | 2 shillings |
| Gloves | Inventory of John Baynes (1790) | Pair of men's silk gloves in Prince George County, Maryland, 1790 | 3 shillings |
| Gloves | Inventory of Isaac Walker (1797) | Pair of Mens Beaver Gloves in Prince George County, Maryland, 1797 | 2 shillings 9 pence |
| Gloves | Inventory of Isaac Walker (1797) | Pair Rabbit Gloves in Prince George County, Maryland, 1797 | 2 shillings 10 pence |
| Handkerchief | Inventory of Doctor Nicholas Flood (1776) | Coarse Pocket Handkerchief in Richmond County, Virginia, 1776 | 1 shilling 3 pence |
| Handkerchief | Inventory of Isaac Walker (1797) | Mens Neck Handkfs in Prince George County, Maryland, 1797 | 6 shillings |
| Hat | Inventory of Doctor Nicholas Flood (1776) | Mens felt Hatt in Richmond County, Virginia, 1776 | 5 shillings |
| Hat | Inventory of Doctor Nicholas Flood (1776) | Tincel'd laced hat in Richmond County, Virginia, 1776 | 5 shillings |
| Hat | Inventory of John Baynes (1790) | Mens Castor Hatt in Prince George County, Maryland, 1790 | 5 shillings |
| Hose | Calland's Account Book - Captain James Robert's Account(1784) | Cost for one pair of plaid hose | 2 shillings |
| Hose | Inventory of John Baynes (1790) | Pair of men's threaded hose in Prince George County, Maryland, 1790 | 2 shillings 3 pence |
| Hose | Inventory of John Baynes (1790) | Pair of White worsted Hose in Prince George County, Maryland, 1790 | 4 shillings |
| Shoes | Calland's Account Book - Captain James Robert's Account(1784) | Cost for Best Men's Shoes | 7 shillings 5 pence |
| Shoes | Inventory of John Baynes (1790) | Pair of Mens Shoes in Prince George County, Maryland, 1790 | 4 shillings 6 pence |
| Slippers | Inventory of Doctor Nicholas Flood (1776) | Pair of slippers in Richmond County, Virginia, 1776 | 3 shillings |
| Stockings | Inventory of Doctor Nicholas Flood (1776) | Pair of men's brown threaded stockings in Richmond County, Virginia, 1776 | 5 shillings |
| Trousers | Inventory of Ebenezer Wells (1784) | Two 2 pair of striped trousers in Deerfield, Massachusetts, 1784 | 8 pounds |
| Waist Coat | Inventory of John Riley (1795) | Blue Waist Coat in Newberry, South Carolina, 1795 | 3 shillings |
| Waist Coat | Inventory of John Riley (1795) | Mixed Coulored Waistcoat in Newberry, South Carolina, 1795 | 3 shillings |

## Apparel - Women

| Item | Data Source | Description | Price |
|---|---|---|---|
| Apron | Inventory of Margaret Anderson (1783) | Linen Apron in Kershaw, South Carolina, 1783 | 6 pounds |
| Apron | Inventory of Isaac Walker (1797) | Muslin Apron in Prince George County, Maryland, 1797 | 5 shillings 6 pence |
| Bonnet | Inventory of John Baynes (1790) | Satten Bonnet in Prince George County, Maryland, 1790 | 7 shillings 6 pence |
| Bonnet | Inventory of John Baynes (1790) | Full Trimed Bonnet in Prince George County, Maryland, 1790 | 7 shillings 6 pence |

| Item | Data Source | Description | Price |
|------|-------------|-------------|-------|
| Buckles | Calland's Account Book - Captain James Robert's Account(1784) | One pair of women's shoe buckles | 3 shillings |
| Cloak | Inventory of Doctor Nicholas Flood (1776) | Woman's scarlet broadcloth cloak in Richmond County, Virginia, 1776 | 15 shillings |
| Cloak | Inventory of Margaret Anderson (1783) | Black Cloak Sattin lined in Kershaw, South Carolina, 1783 | 8 pounds 10 shillings 5 pence |
| Cloak | Inventory of Margaret Anderson (1783) | White Silk Cloak in Kershaw, South Carolina, 1783 | 10 pounds |
| Fan | Inventory of John Baynes (1790) | Fan in Prince George County, Maryland, 1790 | 10 pence |
| Gloves | Inventory of John Baynes (1790) | Pair of women's silk gloves in Prince George County, Maryland, 1790 | 3 shillings |
| Gloves | Inventory of John Baynes (1790) | Pair of Woms Wash Gloves in Prince George County, Maryland, 1790 | 1 shilling 1 pence |
| Gown | Inventory of Margaret Anderson (1783) | Linen Gown in Kershaw, South Carolina, 1783 | 12 pounds 10 shillings |
| Gown | Inventory of Margaret Anderson (1783) | Flowered silk Gown in Kershaw, South Carolina, 1783 | 30 pounds |
| Gown | Inventory of Margaret Anderson (1783) | Paplin Gown plane in Kershaw, South Carolina, 1783 | 12 pounds 10 shillings |
| Handkerchief | Inventory of Doctor Nicholas Flood (1776) | Coarse Pocket Handkerchief in Richmond County, Virginia, 1776 | 1 shilling 3 pence |
| Handkerchief | Calland's Account Book - Captain James Robert's Account(1784) | Cost for a fine women's hankercheif | 5 shillings |
| Hat | Inventory of Isaac Walker (1797) | Ladies Hatt in Prince George County, Maryland, 1797 | 9 shillings |
| Hat | Inventory of Isaac Walker (1797) | Ladies Black Hat in Prince George County, Maryland, 1797 | 9 shillings |
| Hose | Inventory of John Baynes (1790) | Pair of women's threaded hose in Prince George County, Maryland, 1790 | 1 shilling 10 pence |
| Hose | Inventory of John Baynes (1790) | Pair of womens worsted hose in Prince George County, Maryland, 1790 | 2 shillings 6 pence |
| Mitts | Inventory of John Baynes (1790) | Pair of women's Mitts in Prince George County, Maryland, 1790 | 2 shillings 3 pence |

## Based Upon the British Currency System

| Year | Pound in 2002 US Dollars | Shilling in 2002 US Dollars | Pence in 2002 US Dollars |
|------|--------------------------|-----------------------------|--------------------------|
| 1775 | $144.00 | $7.20 | $0.60 |
| 1780 | $168.00 | $8.40 | $0.70 |
| 1785 | $144.00 | $7.20 | $0.60 |
| 1790 | $144.00 | $7.20 | $0.60 |
| 1795 | $120.00 | $6.00 | $0.50 |
| 1799 | $120.00 | $6.00 | $0.50 |

*Calculations are approximate values based upon economic historical data*

| Item | Data Source | Description | Price |
|------|-------------|-------------|-------|
| Petticoat | Inventory of Margaret Anderson (1783) | Callimanco petti/coat in Kershaw, South Carolina, 1783 | 10 pounds |
| Petticoat | Inventory of Margaret Anderson (1783) | Red petticoat Quilted in Kershaw, South Carolina, 1783 | 12 pounds 10 shillings |
| Pin | Inventory of Isaac Walker (1797) | Hat pin in Prince George County, Maryland, 1797 | 2 pence |
| Pumps | Inventory of John Baynes (1790) | Pair of Woms Pumps in Prince George County, Maryland, 1790 | 3 Shoes 4 pence |
| Sandals | Inventory of Isaac Walker (1797) | Pair of Morocco Sandals in Prince George County, Maryland, 1797 | 9 shillings 4½ pence |
| Shawl | Inventory of Isaac Walker (1797) | Cotton long Shawl in Prince George County, Maryland, 1797 | 4 shillings 5 pence |
| Shift | Inventory of Margaret Anderson (1783) | Linen Shift ruffled in Kershaw, South Carolina, 1783 | 8 pounds 10 shillings |
| Shoes | Inventory of John Baynes (1790) | Pair of Woms Leather Shoes in Prince George County, Maryland, 1790 | 3 shillings |

## Commodities

| Item | Data Source | Description | Price |
|------|-------------|-------------|-------|
| Beans | Inventory of Isaac Walker (1797) | Bushel of beans in Prince George County, Maryland, 1797 | 4 shillings |
| Boards | Inventory of Rev. Thomas Ainger (1797) | 100 ft sap pine in New Castle County, Delaware, 1797 | $8.00 |
| Coal | Letter from James Walsh (1776) | Bushel of coal in Philadelphia, 1776 | 4 pence |
| Corn | Inventory of Elizabeth Chappell (1782) | Bushel of corn in Kershaw, South Carolina, 1782 | 15 shillings |
| Feathers | Inventory of Doctor Nicholas Flood (1776) | Bag of Feathers in Richmond County, Virginia, 1776 | 12 shillings 6 pence |
| Flax | Inventory of Isaac Walker (1797) | Bushel of flax seed in Prince George County, Maryland, 1797 | 3 shillings 9 pence |
| Flour | Inventory of Elizabeth Chappell (1782) | Barrel of flour in Kershaw, South Carolina, 1782 | 15 pounds |
| Hay | Inventory of John Riley (1795) | Stack of hay in Newberry, South Carolina, 1795 | 1 pound |
| Indigo | Inventory of Doctor Nicholas Flood (1776) | Pound of indigo in Richmond County, Virginia, 1776 | 8 shillings |
| Indigo Seed | Inventory of William Howell (1784) | Bushel of indigo seed in Kershaw, South Carolina, 1784 | 1 pound 10 shillings |
| Lead | Inventory of Doctor Nicholas Flood (1776) | Pound of Barr lead in Richmond County, Virginia, 1776 | 4 pence |
| Oats | Inventory of William Oneall (1789) | Bushel of oats in Newberry, South Carolina, 1789 | 1 shilling 6 pence |
| Oats | Inventory of John Riley (1795) | One stack of oats in Newberry, South Carolina, 1795 | 1 pound 4 shillings 8 pence |
| Oil | Inventory of Richard Mitchell (1781) | Jug of Lintseed Oyl in Lancaster County, Virginia, 1781 | 1 shilling |
| Rye | Inventory of Richard Mitchell (1781) | Bushel of rye in Lancaster County, Virginia, 1781 | 2 shillings 6 pence |
| Rye | Inventory of Isaac Walker (1797) | Bushel of rye in Prince George County, Maryland, 1797 | 15 shillings |
| Salt | Inventory of Doctor Nicholas Flood (1776) | Bushel of fine salt in Richmond County, Virginia, 1776 | 3 pence |
| Steel | Inventory of Elizabeth Chappell (1782) | Pound of steel in Kershaw, South Carolina, 1782 | 1 shilling 3 pence |

| Item | Data Source | Description | Price |
|------|-------------|-------------|-------|
| Tar | Inventory of Doctor Nicholas Flood (1776) | Barrel of Tarr in Richmond County, Virginia, 1776 | 12 shillings 6 pence |
| Tea | Inventory of John Baynes (1790) | Pound of Bohea Tea in Prince George County, Maryland, 1790 | 2 shillings 6 pence |
| Tea | Inventory of John Baynes (1790) | Pound of Singloe Tea in Prince George County, Maryland, 1790 | 4 shillings |
| Tobacco | Inventory of Doctor Nicholas Flood (1776) | Hogshead of Tobacco in Richmond County, Virginia, 1776 | 5 pounds |
| Tobacco | Inventory of Elizabeth Chappell (1782) | Hogshead of Prized Tobacco in Kershaw, South Carolina, 1782 | 73 pounds 10 shillings |
| Turpentine | Inventory of Doctor Nicholas Flood (1776) | Barrel of turpentine in Richmond County, Virginia, 1776 | 15 shillings |
| Wheat | Inventory of Richard Mitchell (1781) | Bushel of new wheat in Lancaster County, Virginia, 1781 | 4 shillings |
| Wheat | Inventory of Richard Mitchell (1781) | Bushel of old wheat in Lancaster County, Virginia, 1781 | 1 shilling 6 pence |

## Entertainment

| Item | Data Source | Description | Price |
|------|-------------|-------------|-------|
| Backgammon | Inventory of Doctor Nicholas Flood (1776) | Backgamon Table in Richmond County, Virginia, 1776 | 3 pounds 5 shillings |
| Checkers | Inventory of Doctor Nicholas Flood (1776) | Checker board & men in Richmond County, Virginia, 1776 | 2 shillings 6 pence |

## Fabrics & Sewing Materials

| Item | Data Source | Description | Price |
|------|-------------|-------------|-------|
| Buttons | Inventory of Doctor Nicholas Flood (1776) | One card of black sleeve buttons in Richmond County, Virginia, 1776 | 2 shillings 4 pence |
| Buttons | Inventory of Doctor Nicholas Flood (1776) | One card of Children's sleeve buttons in Richmond County, Virginia, 1776 | 1 shilling |
| Buttons | Inventory of Doctor Nicholas Flood (1776) | Dozen Coat Gilt Buttons in Richmond County, Virginia, 1776 | 1 shilling |
| Cloth | American Heritage (1958) | Cost per yard of good cotton cloth produced by Samuel Slater, 1790 | $0.09 |
| Cloth | Inventory of John Baynes (1790) | Yard of Printed Linen in Prince George County, Maryland, 1790 | 1 shilling 10 pence |
| Coating | Inventory of Isaac Walker (1797) | Yard of bro Twil'd Coating in Prince George County, Maryland, 1797 | 4 shillings |

### Based Upon the British Currency System

| Year | Pound in 2002 US Dollars | Shilling in 2002 US Dollars | Pence in 2002 US Dollars |
|------|--------------------------|-----------------------------|--------------------------|
| 1775 | $144.00 | $7.20 | $0.60 |
| 1780 | $168.00 | $8.40 | $0.70 |
| 1785 | $144.00 | $7.20 | $0.60 |
| 1790 | $144.00 | $7.20 | $0.60 |
| 1795 | $120.00 | $6.00 | $0.50 |
| 1799 | $120.00 | $6.00 | $0.50 |

*Calculations are approximate values based upon economic historical data*

| Item | Data Source | Description | Price |
|---|---|---|---|
| Cord | Inventory of John Baynes (1790) | Yard of Ells Velvet Cord in Prince George County, Maryland, 1790 | 4 shillings 6 pence |
| Cord | Inventory of John Baynes (1790) | Yard of Satten Cord in Prince George County, Maryland, 1790 | 3 shillings 4 pence |
| Crape | Inventory of John Baynes (1790) | Yard of Mourning Crape in Prince George County, Maryland, 1790 | 1 shilling 1½ pence |
| Crape | Inventory of Isaac Walker (1797) | Yard of crape in Prince George County, Maryland, 1797 | 3 shillings 10 pence |
| Fabric | Inventory of Doctor Nicholas Flood (1776) | Yard of Blue half Thicks in Richmond County, Virginia, 1776 | 3 shillings |
| Fabric | Inventory of Doctor Nicholas Flood (1776) | Yard of black velvet in Richmond County, Virginia, 1776 | 16 shillings |
| Fabric | Inventory of Doctor Nicholas Flood (1776) | Yard of White flowered Silk in Richmond County, Virginia, 1776 | 10 shillings |
| Fabric | Inventory of Doctor Nicholas Flood (1776) | Yard of Virginia Cotton in Richmond County, Virginia, 1776 | 4 shillings |
| Fabric | Calland's Account Book - Captain James Robert's Account(1784) | Cost for one yard of finest chintz fabric | 17 shillings |
| Lace | Inventory of John Baynes (1790) | Yard of black lace in Prince George County, Maryland, 1790 | 7½ pence |
| Lace | Inventory of Isaac Walker (1797) | Dozen thread laces in Prince George County, Maryland, 1797 | 1 shilling 6 pence |
| Linen | Calland's Account Book - Captain James Robert's Account(1784) | Cost for 26 yards of Linen in Virginia | 3 pounds 15 shillings 6 pence |
| Needles | Calland's Account Book - Captain James Robert's Account(1784) | Cost to purchase 25 needles | 1 shilling |
| Pattern | Inventory of Isaac Walker (1797) | Pair of Cotton Breeches pattern in Prince George County, Maryland, 1797 | 13 shillings |
| Pattern | Inventory of Isaac Walker (1797) | Vest Patterns in Prince George County, Maryland, 1797 | 4 shillings 10 pence |
| Pins | Inventory of John Baynes (1790) | Dozen Common pins in Prince George County, Maryland, 1790 | 6 shillings |
| Plaiding | Calland's Account Book - Captain James Robert's Account(1784) | Cost of 1 yard of plaiding | 2 shillings |
| Ribbon | Inventory of Isaac Walker (1797) | Yard of Wire Ribbon in Prince George County, Maryland, 1797 | 2 pence |
| Ribbon | Inventory of Isaac Walker (1797) | Yard of Velvet Ribbon in Prince George County, Maryland, 1797 | 11 pence |
| Scissors | Inventory of Isaac Walker (1797) | Pair large Scissars in Prince George County, Maryland, 1797 | 1 shilling |
| Silk | Inventory of John Baynes (1790) | Pound of Black Sewing Silk in Prince George County, Maryland, 1790 | 1 pound 4 shillings |
| Tape | Inventory of John Baynes (1790) | Stay tape in Prince George County, Maryland, 1790 | 5 shillings |
| Thimble | Inventory of Doctor Nicholas Flood (1776) | Brass thimble in Richmond County, Virginia, 1776 | 2 pence |
| Thread | Inventory of Doctor Nicholas Flood (1776) | Pound of black thread in Richmond County, Virginia, 1776 | 5 shillings |

## Farm Equipment & Tools

| Item | Data Source | Description | Price |
|---|---|---|---|
| Auger | Inventory of John Riley (1795) | Screw augur in Newberry, South Carolina, 1795 | 9 pence |

| Item | Data Source | Description | Price |
|---|---|---|---|
| Axe | Inventory of Margaret Anderson (1783) | Club ax in Kershaw, South Carolina, 1783 | 2 pounds 10 shillings |
| Axe | Inventory of Doctor Nicholas Flood (1776) | Brod Axe in Richmond County, Virginia, 1776 | 5 shillings |
| Barrel | Inventory of John Riley (1795) | Old barrel in Newberry, South Carolina, 1795 | 9 pence |
| Barrel | Inventory of Rev. Thomas Ainger (1797) | Pork barrel in New Castle County, Delaware, 1797 | $1.00 |
| Bee Hive | Inventory of Rev. Thomas Ainger (1797) | Bee hive in New Castle County, Delaware, 1797 | $1.00 |
| Branding Iron | Inventory of Doctor Nicholas Flood (1776) | Brand Iron in Richmond County, Virginia, 1776 | 4 pence |
| Brush | Inventory of Doctor Nicholas Flood (1776) | Paint brush in Richmond County, Virginia, 1776 | 6 pence |
| Bucket | Inventory of Doctor Nicholas Flood (1776) | Leather Buckett in Richmond County, Virginia, 1776 | 2 shillings 6 pence |
| Chain | Inventory of John Young (1790) | Log chain in Plymouth, Massachusetts, 1790 | $4.00 |
| Chicken Coop | Inventory of Isaac Walker (1797) | Chicken coop in Prince George County, Maryland, 1797 | 15 shillings |
| Chisel | Inventory of John Baynes (1790) | Chizel in Prince George County, Maryland, 1790 | 6½ pence |
| Dung | Inventory of James Adam, Sr. (1793) | Heap dung in New Castle County, Delaware, 1793 | 1 pound 5 shillings |
| Fork | Inventory of Doctor Nicholas Flood (1776) | Dung fork in Richmond County, Virginia, 1776 | 1 shilling |
| Froe | Inventory of Margaret Ball (1783) | Froe in Lancaster County, Virginia, 1783 | 2 shillings 6 pence |
| Gimlet | Inventory of John Baynes (1790) | Gimblet in Prince George County, Maryland, 1790 | 10 pence |
| Gin | Inventory of Richard Mitchell (1781) | Ginn in Lancaster County, Virginia, 1781 | 1 shilling |
| Grindstone | Inventory of John Young (1790) | Grindstone in Plymouth, Massachusetts, 1790 | $4.00 |
| Hammer | Inventory of John Riley (1795) | Claw hammer in Newberry, South Carolina, 1795 | 7 pence |
| Hayfork | Inventory of Doctor Nicholas Flood (1776) | Hay Fork in Richmond County, Virginia, 1776 | 1 shilling |

## Based Upon the British Currency System

| Year | Pound in 2002 US Dollars | Shilling in 2002 US Dollars | Pence in 2002 US Dollars |
|---|---|---|---|
| 1775 | $144.00 | $7.20 | $0.60 |
| 1780 | $168.00 | $8.40 | $0.70 |
| 1785 | $144.00 | $7.20 | $0.60 |
| 1790 | $144.00 | $7.20 | $0.60 |
| 1795 | $120.00 | $6.00 | $0.50 |
| 1799 | $120.00 | $6.00 | $0.50 |

*Calculations are approximate values based upon economic historical data*

| Item | Data Source | Description | Price |
|---|---|---|---|
| Hive | Inventory of John Riley (1795) | Bee hive in Newberry, South Carolina, 1795 | 1 shilling 8 pence |
| Hoe | Inventory of Margaret Anderson (1783) | Grubbing hoe in Kershaw, South Carolina, 1783 | 1 pound 5 shillings |
| Hoe | Inventory of John Baynes (1790) | Broad hoe in Prince George County, Maryland, 1790 | 1 shilling 6 pence |
| Hogshead | Inventory of Doctor Nicholas Flood (1776) | Empty hogshead in Richmond County, Virginia, 1776 | 3 shillings |
| Hook | Inventory of Richard Mitchell (1781) | Reap hook in Lancaster County, Virginia, 1781 | 1 shilling |
| Hooks | Inventory of Doctor Nicholas Flood (1776) | Reep hooks in Richmond County, Virginia, 1776 | 9 pence |
| Horse | Inventory of John Young (1790) | Wooden Horse in Plymouth, Massachusetts, 1790 | $0.33 |
| Milk Pan | Inventory of Doctor Nicholas Flood (1776) | Earthen Milk Pan in Richmond County, Virginia, 1776 | 6 pence |
| Mill Stone | Inventory of Doctor Nicholas Flood (1776) | Pair of small mill stones in Richmond County, Virginia, 1776 | 1 pound 10 shillings |
| Pail | Inventory of John Riley (1795) | Water pail in Newberry, South Carolina, 1795 | 1 shilling 9 pence |
| Paint | Inventory of Doctor Nicholas Flood (1776) | Cask of paint in Richmond County, Virginia, 1776 | 3 shillings |
| Pitchfork | Inventory of John Riley (1795) | Pitch fork in Newberry, South Carolina, 1795 | 1 shilling 4 pence |
| Pitchfork | Inventory of Doctor Nicholas Flood (1776) | Pitch Fork in Richmond County, Virginia, 1776 | 1 shilling |
| Plane | Inventory of John Riley (1795) | Plane in Newberry, South Carolina, 1795 | 1 shilling 2 pence |
| Plow | Inventory of Richard Mitchell (1781) | Weeding Plough in Lancaster County, Virginia, 1781 | 7 shillings |
| Plow | Inventory of Margaret Anderson (1783) | Barshare plow in Kershaw, South Carolina, 1783 | 1 pound 10 shillings |
| Plow and Irons | Inventory of Ebenezer Wells (1784) | Plow and Iron in Deerfield, Massachusetts, 1784 | 1 pound |
| Pulley | Inventory of Doctor Nicholas Flood (1776) | Screw pulley in Richmond County, Virginia, 1776 | 1 shilling |
| Pulley | Inventory of Doctor Nicholas Flood (1776) | Lash pulley in Richmond County, Virginia, 1776 | 3¼ pence |
| Saw | Inventory of Richard Mitchell (1781) | Whip saw in Lancaster County, Virginia, 1781 | 1 pound 5 shillings |
| Saw | Inventory of Ebenezer Wells (1784) | One saw in Deerfield, Massachusetts, 1784 | 2 shillings |
| Saw | Inventory of John Young (1790) | Hand saw in Plymouth, Massachusetts, 1790 | $0.50 |
| Saw | Inventory of John Baynes (1790) | Seven feet whip saw, 2 shillings 3 pence per foot, in Prince George County, Maryland, 1790 | 15 shillings 9 pence |
| Saw | Inventory of John Baynes (1790) | Seven feet cross saw in Prince George County, Maryland, 1790 | 15 shillings 9 pence |
| Scythe | Inventory of John Flowers (1790) | Scythe in Darlington, South Carolina, 1790 | 6 shillings 6 pence |
| Sieve | Inventory of Richard Mitchell (1781) | Wheat Seive in Lancaster County, Virginia, 1781 | 1 shilling 3 pence |
| Shears | Inventory of Doctor Nicholas Flood (1776) | Pair of Sheep Sheares in Richmond County, Virginia, 1776 | 1 shilling 3 pence |
| Sled | Inventory of John Young (1790) | Horse sled in Plymouth, Massachusetts, 1790 | $1.33 |

| Item | Data Source | Description | Price |
|------|-------------|-------------|-------|
| Spade | Inventory of John Baynes (1790) | Garden Spade in Prince George County, Maryland, 1790 | 2 shillings 6 pence |
| Steelyard | Inventory of John Young (1790) | Pair Steel yards in Plymouth, Massachusetts, 1790 | $1.25 |
| Tools | Inventory of Doctor Nicholas Flood (1776) | Chest of tools in Richmond County, Virginia, 1776 | 7 shillings 6 pence |
| Tub | Inventory of Isaac Walker (1797) | Pickle tub in Prince George County, Maryland, 1797 | 7 shillings 6 pence |
| Wedge | Inventory of John Riley (1795) | Iron wedge in Newberry, South Carolina, 1795 | 1 shilling 2 pence |

## Firearms & Supplies

| Item | Data Source | Description | Price |
|------|-------------|-------------|-------|
| Flask | Inventory of Isaac Walker (1797) | Powder Flask in Prince George County, Maryland, 1797 | 5 shillings |
| Gun | Inventory of Doctor Nicholas Flood (1776) | Gun double Breach'd in Richmond County, Virginia, 1776 | 3 pounds |
| Gun | Claim Records of Arbemarle Barracks (1781) | One smooth bored gun impressed from Robert Williams for Continental Troop | 5 pounds |
| Gun | Inventory of John Riley (1795) | Rifle Gunn in Newberry, South Carolina, 1795 | 3 shillings |
| Gun Flints | Inventory of Doctor Nicholas Flood (1776) | 250 gun flints in Richmond County, Virginia, 1776 | 1 pound |
| Gun Lock | Inventory of John Baynes (1790) | Gun lock in Prince George County, Maryland, 1790 | 1 shilling 11 pence |
| Gunpowder | Inventory of Doctor Nicholas Flood (1776) | Quart of Gun Powder in Richmond County, Virginia, 1776 | 6 shillings |
| Gunpowder | Inventory of Isaac Walker (1797) | Pound of Gun Powder in Prince George County, Maryland, 1797 | 7 shillings 6 pence |
| Knife | Inventory of Isaac Walker (1797) | Hunting Knife in Prince George County, Maryland, 1797 | 7 shillings 6 pence |
| Musket | Arcadi Gluckman, Identifying Old U.S. Muskets, Rifles & Carbines (1965) | Price fo a French musket purchased by the Continental troops, 1778 | 24 livres |
| Musket | Arcadi Gluckman, Identifying Old U.S. Muskets, Rifles & Carbines (1965) | Average contract price for American made muskets for the Continental troops, 1778 | $12.30 |
| Rifle | Inventory of Hermon Kinseler (1783) | Rifle gun in Kershaw, South Carolina, 1783 | 4 pounds 6 pence |

### Based Upon the British Currency System

| Year | Pound in 2002 US Dollars | Shilling in 2002 US Dollars | Pence in 2002 US Dollars |
|------|--------------------------|------------------------------|---------------------------|
| 1775 | $144.00 | $7.20 | $0.60 |
| 1780 | $168.00 | $8.40 | $0.70 |
| 1785 | $144.00 | $7.20 | $0.60 |
| 1790 | $144.00 | $7.20 | $0.60 |
| 1795 | $120.00 | $6.00 | $0.50 |
| 1799 | $120.00 | $6.00 | $0.50 |

*Calculations are approximate values based upon economic historical data*

| Item | Data Source | Description | Price |
|---|---|---|---|
| Saltpeter | Inventory of Doctor Nicholas Flood (1776) | Pound of sal petr in Richmond County, Virginia, 1776 | 2½ pence |
| Shot | Inventory of Doctor Nicholas Flood (1776) | Fifty pounds of buck Shott in Richmond County, Virginia, 1776 | 1 pound 17 shillings |
| Shot Bag | Inventory of Isaac Walker (1797) | Shot bag in Prince George County, Maryland, 1797 | 7 shillings 6 pence |
| Sword | Inventory of Richard Mitchell (1781) | Sword Bayonet & Belt in Lancaster County, Virginia, 1781 | 15 shillings |
| Food Alum | Inventory of Isaac Walker (1797) | Pound of Allum in Prince George County, Maryland, 1797 | 6 pence |
| Bacon | Inventory of Richard Mitchell (1781) | Pound of bacon in Lancaster County, Virginia, 1781 | 6 pence |
| Barley | Inventory of John Riley (1795) | Bushel of barley in Newberry, South Carolina, 1795 | 1 shilling 9 pence |
| Beans | Inventory of Isaac Walker (1797) | Bushel of beans in Prince George County, Maryland, 1797 | 4 shillings |
| Beef | Economic and Social History of New England, 1620-1789 by William Weeden | Pound of beef in New England, 1775 | 3 pence |
| Bread | The Pennsylvania Gazette (1776) | Price for a 4 lb, 3 oz loaf of white bread in Philadelphia, Pennsylvania, 1776 | 8 pence |
| Bread | Kitman, George Washington's Expense Account (1970) | Bread supplied by Zaccheus Morton to the Continental Army from February 26 to April 2, in Cambridge, Massachusetts 1776 | 6 pounds 8 shillings |
| Butter | Economic and Social History of New England, 1620-1789 by William Weeden | Pound of Butter in New England, 1776 | 9 pence |
| Cabbage | Inventory of Isaac Walker (1797) | Lot of cabbage in Prince George County, Maryland, 1797 | 7 shillings 6 pence |
| Cheese | Economic and Social History of New England, 1620-1789 by William Weeden | Pound of cheese in New England, 1775 | 4 pence |
| Chocolate | Inventory of Doctor Nicholas Flood (1776) | Pound of chocolate in Richmond County, Virginia, 1776 | 2 shillings 6 pence |
| Coffee | Inventory of Doctor Nicholas Flood (1776) | Pound of coffee in Richmond County, Virginia, 1776 | 1 pound |
| Corn | Inventory of John Riley (1795) | Bushel of corn in Newberry, South Carolina, 1795 | 1 shilling 8 pence |
| Eggs | Economic and Social History of New England, 1620-1789 by William Weeden | Dozen eggs in New England, 1775 | 7 pence |
| Honey | Inventory of John Riley (1795) | Gallon of honey in Newberry, South Carolina, 1795 | 4 shillings 8 pence |
| Lemons | Economic and Social History of New England, 1620-1789 by William Weeden | Dozen lemons in New England, 1775 | 2 shillings |
| Milk | Kitman, George Washington's Expense Account (1970) | Quart of milk in Cambridge, Massachusetts, 1776 | 2¾ pence |
| Molasses | Economic and Social History of New England, 1620-1789 by William Weeden | Gallon of molasses in New England, 1775 | 18 shillings |
| Mustard | Inventory of Isaac Walker (1797) | Bottle of Mustard in Prince George County, Maryland, 1797 | 1 shilling 10½ pence |

| Item | Data Source | Description | Price |
|---|---|---|---|
| Mutton | Economic and Social History of New England, 1620-1789 by William Weeden | Pound of mutton in New England, 1775 | 3$^{1}$/$_{2}$ pence |
| Peas | Inventory of Richard Mitchell (1781) | Bushel of Indian Pease in Lancaster County, Virginia, 1781 | 3 shillings |
| Pig | Kitman, George Washington's Expense Account (1970) | Amount George Washington paid for a pig to feed the Continental Army, 1775 | $3.50 |
| Pork | Economic and Social History of New England, 1620-1789 by William Weeden | Pound of pork in New England, 1776 | 6 pence |
| Pork | Economic and Social History of New England, 1620-1789 by William Weeden | Pound of pork in New England, 1780 | 9 pence |
| Pork | Inventory of William Howell (1784) | Pound of pork in Kershaw, South Carolina, 1784 | 2½ pence |
| Potatoes | Inventory of John Riley (1795) | Bushel of Sweet Potatoes in Newberry, South Carolina, 1795 | 1 shilling |
| Potatoes | Economic and Social History of New England, 1620-1789 by William Weeden | Bushel of potatoes in New England, 1775 | 11 shillings, 1 pence |
| Potatoes | Inventory of John Young (1790) | Bushel of potatoes in Plymouth, Massachusetts, 1790 | $0.33 |
| Rice | Inventory of John Riley (1795) | Bushel of Ruff Rice in Newberry, South Carolina, 1795 | 2 shillings |
| Rye meal | Economic and Social History of New England, 1620-1789 by William Weeden | Bushel of rye meal in New England, 1775 | 3 shillings, 9 pence |
| Spice | Inventory of Doctor Nicholas Flood (1776) | Pound of White Ginger in Richmond County, Virginia, 1776 | 1 shilling |
| Spice | Inventory of Doctor Nicholas Flood (1776) | Pound of brown ginger in Richmond County, Virginia, 1776 | 1 shilling |
| Spice | Inventory of Doctor Nicholas Flood (1776) | Pound of nutmeg in Richmond County, Virginia, 1776 | 2 shillings |
| Spice | Inventory of Doctor Nicholas Flood (1776) | Ounce of Mace in Richmond County, Virginia, 1776 | 2 shillings |
| Spice | Inventory of Doctor Nicholas Flood (1776) | Pound of cinnamon in Richmond County, Virginia, 1776 | 1 pound |

### Based Upon the British Currency System

| Year | Pound in 2002 US Dollars | Shilling in 2002 US Dollars | Pence in 2002 US Dollars |
|---|---|---|---|
| 1775 | $144.00 | $7.20 | $0.60 |
| 1780 | $168.00 | $8.40 | $0.70 |
| 1785 | $144.00 | $7.20 | $0.60 |
| 1790 | $144.00 | $7.20 | $0.60 |
| 1795 | $120.00 | $6.00 | $0.50 |
| 1799 | $120.00 | $6.00 | $0.50 |

*Calculations are approximate values based upon economic historical data*

| Item | Data Source | Description | Price |
|------|-------------|-------------|-------|
| Spice | Inventory of Doctor Nicholas Flood (1776) | Pound of pepper in Richmond County, Virginia, 1776 | 3 shillings |
| Spice | Inventory of Doctor Nicholas Flood (1776) | Pound of allspice in Richmond County, Virginia, 1776 | 2 shillings |
| Sugar | Economic and Social History of New England, 1620-1789 by William Weeden | Pound of sugar in New England, 1775 | 6$\frac{1}{2}$ pence |
| Sugar | Economic and Social History of New England, 1620-1789 by William Weeden | Pound of sugar in New England, 1780 | 7 pence |
| Sugar | Inventory of Doctor Nicholas Flood (1776) | Per pound price of a loaf of sugar in Richmond County, Virginia, 1776 | 1 shilling 3 pence |
| Tea | Inventory of Doctor Nicholas Flood (1776) | Pound of Bohea Tea in Richmond County, Virginia, 1776 | 2 shillings |
| Tea | Inventory of Isaac Walker (1797) | Pound of Imperial Tea in Prince George County, Maryland, 1797 | 15 shillings |
| Vanilla Pod | Kimball, Thomas Jefferson's Cook Book (1976) | Price of one baton (pod) of vanilla, 1794 | 1 pound 4 shilling |
| Wheat | Economic and Social History of New England, 1620-1789 by William Weeden | Bushel of wheat in New England, 1775 | 1 pound, 17 shillings |
| Wheat | Inventory of Ebenezer Wells (1784) | 25 bushels of wheat (unthreshed) in Deerfield, Massachusetts, 1784 | 4 pounds, 11 shillings, 8 pence |
| Wheat | Inventory of John Riley (1795) | Bushel of wheat in Newberry, South Carolina, 1795 | 2 shillings |

### Household Furniture

| Item | Data Source | Description | Price |
|------|-------------|-------------|-------|
| Bed | Inventory of Richard Mitchell (1781) | High bed with pair of sheets, pair double blankets, 2 pillows with cases and coverlet in Lancaster County, Virginia, 1781 | 8 pounds |
| Bed | Inventory of Isaac Walker (1797) | Feather Bed, with 1 pr Sheets, 1 pr Blankets, 1 Bolster, 2 pillows, 1 white Cotton Counterpain and Curtians in Prince George County, Maryland, 1797 | 15 pounds |
| Bed | Inventory of Daniel Adams (1797) | Trunk bed, bedding, bedstead for children in New Castle County, Delaware, 1797 | $15.00 |
| Bed | Inventory of Rev. Thomas Ainger (1797) | Bed bolser & pillows, woolen & callico cover in New Castle County, Delaware, 1797 | $20.00 |
| Bed | Inventory of Rev. Thomas Ainger (1797) | Feather bed in New Castle County, Delaware, 1797 | $12.00 |
| Bedstead | Inventory of Rev. Thomas Ainger (1797) | Chaff feather bed & bedstead & bedding in New Castle County, Delaware, 1797 | $5.00 |
| Blankets | Inventory of Ebenezer Wells (1784) | 2 blankets in Deerfield, Massachusetts, 1784 | 1 pound |
| Bureau | Inventory of Daniel Adams (1797) | Bureau set in New Castle County, Delaware, 1797 | $8.00 |
| Bureau | Inventory of Rev. Thomas Ainger (1797) | Beaureau in New Castle County, Delaware, 1797 | $6.00 |
| Carpet | Inventory of Doctor Nicholas Flood (1776) | Large carpet in Richmond County, Virginia, 1776 | 5 shillings |
| Case Drawer | Inventory of Daniel Adams (1797) | Case drawer in New Castle County, Delaware, 1797 | $40.00 |
| Chair | Inventory of Doctor Nicholas Flood (1776) | Easy Chaire in Richmond County, Virginia, 1776 | 3 pounds |
| Chair | Inventory of Doctor Nicholas Flood (1776) | Chair with blue Damsk Bottom in Richmond County, Virginia, 1776 | 12 shillings 6 pence |

| Item | Data Source | Description | Price |
|------|-------------|-------------|-------|
| Chair | Inventory of John Baynes (1790) | Childrens Chair in Prince George County, Maryland, 1790 | 1 shilling |
| Chair | Inventory of James Adam, Sr. (1793) | Mahagony chair in New Castle County, Delaware, 1793 | 15 shillings |
| Chair | Inventory of James Adam, Sr. (1793) | Winsor chair in New Castle County, Delaware, 1793 | 4 shillings |
| Chair | Inventory of Daniel Diman (1798) | Leather button great chair in Plymouth, Massachusetts, 1798 | $1.25 |
| Chairs | Inventory of Ebenezer Wells (1784) | Six black chairs in Deerfield, Massachusetts, 1784 | 30 shillings |
| Chest | Winthrop Gardiner Jr. Collection | Chest made in New York, 1792 | 1 pound 16 shillings |
| Chest | Inventory of Rev. Thomas Ainger (1797) | Old chest of stamped paper in New Castle County, Delaware, 1797 | $2.00 |
| Chest of Drawers | Inventory of Rev. Thomas Ainger (1797) | Pine chest in New Castle County, Delaware, 1797 | $2.00 |
| Chest of Drawers | Inventory of Daniel Diman (1798) | Mahogany chest drawers in Plymouth, Massachusetts, 1798 | $20.00 |
| Chest on Chests | Winthrop Gardiner Jr. Collection | Cherry Chest on chests -11 drawers; white pine and tulip secondary woods H 72⅜", W 40⅞", D 20¼ crafted in New York, 1796 | 10 pounds |
| Clock | Winthrop Gardiner Jr. Collection | Pine Timepiece with pewter dial and brass works H 79½", W 12⅛", D 7½" made in New York, 1789 | 6 pounds |
| Clock | Inventory of James Adam, Sr. (1793) | Eight day clock in New Castle County, Delaware, 1793 | 12 pounds |
| Clock | Winthrop Gardiner Jr. Collection | Repeating-Alarm telltale clock made in New York, 1797 | 38 pounds |
| Clock | Winthrop Gardiner Jr. Collection | Horologiographical, Repeating Alarm Monition Clock made in New York, 1799 | 36 pounds |
| Couch | Inventory of Doctor Nicholas Flood (1776) | Couch with Leather Bottom in Richmond County, Virginia, 1776 | 3 pounds 10 shillings |
| Cradle | Inventory of John Young (1790) | Cradle in Plymouth, Massachusetts, 1790 | $1.00 |
| Cupboard | Inventory of John Baynes (1790) | Cupboard in Prince George County, Maryland, 1790 | 1 pound |
| Cupboard | Inventory of Doctor Nicholas Flood (1776) | Corner cupbords with Glass doors in Richmond County, Virginia, 1776 | 2 pounds 10 shillings |
| Desk | Inventory of Doctor Nicholas Flood (1776) | Desk & Book Case in Richmond County, Virginia, 1776 | 7 pounds 10 shillings |

## Based Upon the British Currency System

| Year | Pound in 2002 US Dollars | Shilling in 2002 US Dollars | Pence in 2002 US Dollars |
|------|--------------------------|------------------------------|---------------------------|
| 1775 | $144.00 | $7.20 | $0.60 |
| 1780 | $168.00 | $8.40 | $0.70 |
| 1785 | $144.00 | $7.20 | $0.60 |
| 1790 | $144.00 | $7.20 | $0.60 |
| 1795 | $120.00 | $6.00 | $0.50 |
| 1799 | $120.00 | $6.00 | $0.50 |

*Calculations are approximate values based upon economic historical data*

| Item | Data Source | Description | Price |
|------|-------------|-------------|-------|
| Desk | Winthrop Gardiner Jr. Collection | Writing Desk made in New York, 1794 | 1 pound |
| Drawers | Inventory of Daniel Adams (1797) | High case walnut drawers in New Castle County, Delaware, 1797 | $10.00 |
| Dressing Table | Inventory of Doctor Nicholas Flood (1776) | Dressing table and glass in Richmond County, Virginia, 1776 | 15 shillings |
| Looking Glass | Inventory of Doctor Nicholas Flood (1776) | Small Old looking Glass in Richmond County, Virginia, 1776 | 7 shillings |
| Looking Glass | Inventory of James Adam, Sr. (1793) | Oval looking glass in New Castle County, Delaware, 1793 | 2 pounds 5 shillings |
| Picture | Inventory of Daniel Adams (1797) | Framed picture in New Castle County, Delaware, 1797 | $0.25 |
| Rug | Inventory of Ebenezer Wells (1784) | Red and white rug in Deerfield, Massachusetts, 1784 | 24 shillings |
| Rug | Inventory of Ebenezer Wells (1784) | Black and blue rug in Deerfield, Massachusetts, 1784 | 25 shillings |
| Stand | Winthrop Gardiner Jr. Collection | Mahogany stand made in New York, 1799 | 1 pound |
| Table | Inventory of Doctor Nicholas Flood (1776) | Angle Table in Richmond County, Virginia, 1776 | 1 pound 5 shillings |
| Table | Inventory of Doctor Nicholas Flood (1776) | Round Tea Table in Richmond County, Virginia, 1776 | 1 pound 10 shillings |
| Table | Inventory of Richard Mitchell (1781) | Square Poplar Table in Lancaster County, Virginia, 1781 | 1 shilling |
| Table | Inventory of Daniel Diman (1798) | Black walnut square table in Plymouth, Massachusetts, 1798 | $1.75 |
| Table | Inventory of Daniel Diman (1798) | Round maple table in Plymouth, Massachusetts, 1798 | $1.25 |
| Timepiece | Winthrop Gardiner Jr. Collection | Timepiece made in New York, 1783 | 6 pounds 10 shillings |
| Trunk | Inventory of Isaac Walker (1797) | Large flat top'd leather Trunk in Prince George County, Maryland, 1797 | 15 shillings |
| Waiter | Inventory of Doctor Nicholas Flood (1776) | Gilt Japan'd Waiter in Richmond County, Virginia, 1776 | 5 shillings |
| Wardrobe | Winthrop Gardiner Jr. Collection | Wardrobe from New York during 1798 | 13 pounds |

### Household Products

| Item | Data Source | Description | Price |
|------|-------------|-------------|-------|
| Andirons | Inventory of Daniel Adams (1797) | Small pair of andirons in New Castle County, Delaware, 1797 | $1.00 |
| Basin | Inventory of Daniel Adams (1797) | Pewter basin in New Castle County, Delaware, 1797 | $0.50 |
| Basket | Inventory of Doctor Nicholas Flood (1776) | Wicker'd Bread Basket in Richmond County, Virginia, 1776 | 2 shillings 6 pence |
| Basin | Inventory of Doctor Nicholas Flood (1776) | Large pewter bason in Richmond County, Virginia, 1776 | 3 shillings 3 pence |
| Basin | Inventory of Margaret Ball (1783) | White Stone Wash Bason in Lancaster County, Virginia, 1783 | 1 shilling |
| Bathing Cap | Inventory of Isaac Walker (1797) | Oil Cloth bathing Cap in Prince George County, Maryland, 1797 | 2 shillings 6 pence |
| Bedstead | Inventory of John Riley (1795) | Bedstead and cord in Newberry, South Carolina, 1795 | 7 shillings |
| Bed | Inventory of Elizabeth Chappell (1782) | Feather Bed, Blanket & bolster in Kershaw, South Carolina, 1782 | 30 pounds |
| Bedspread | Inventory of Rev. Thomas Ainger (1797) | Callico bedspread in New Castle County, Delaware, 1797 | $2.00 |

| Item | Data Source | Description | Price |
|------|-------------|-------------|-------|
| Bird Cage | Inventory of Doctor Nicholas Flood (1776) | Bird cage in Richmond County, Virginia, 1776 | 1 pound 3 shillings |
| Bird Fountain | Inventory of John Baynes (1790) | Bird fountain in Prince George County, Maryland, 1790 | 5 pence |
| Blanket | Inventory of Daniel Diman (1798) | Blanket in Plymouth, Massachusetts, 1798 | $1.25 |
| Bottles | Inventory of Richard Mitchell (1781) | Dozen quart bottles in Lancaster County, Virginia, 1781 | 4 shillings |
| Bowl | Inventory of Doctor Nicholas Flood (1776) | Queens China Wate Bowl in Richmond County, Virginia, 1776 | 1 shilling 3 pence |
| Bowl | Inventory of Doctor Nicholas Flood (1776) | Large gold burnt China Bowl in Richmond County, Virginia, 1776 | 1 pound |
| Bowl | Calland's Account Book - Captain James Robert's Account(1784) | One large punch bowl | 2 shillings |
| Box | Inventory of Richard Mitchell (1781) | Tin Candle box in Lancaster County, Virginia, 1781 | 2 shillings |
| Box | Inventory of Isaac Walker (1797) | Shaving box in Prince George County, Maryland, 1797 | 1 shilling 6 pence |
| Box | Inventory of Isaac Walker (1797) | Oval Egyptian Sugar Box in Prince George County, Maryland, 1797 | 1 shillings 6 pence |
| Box | Inventory of Isaac Walker (1797) | Walnut Knife Box in Prince George County, Maryland, 1797 | 7 shillings 6 pence |
| Brass Knob | Inventory of Doctor Nicholas Flood (1776) | Long bolt with brass knob in Richmond County, Virginia, 1776 | 2 shillings 6 pence |
| Broom | Inventory of Isaac Walker (1797) | Hair Broom in Prince George County, Maryland, 1797 | 1 shilling 1¾ pence |
| Brush | Inventory of John Baynes (1790) | Shoe brush in Prince George County, Maryland, 1790 | 3 pence |
| Brush | Inventory of John Baynes (1790) | Buckle brush in Prince George County, Maryland, 1790 | 2 pence |
| Brush | Inventory of Isaac Walker (1797) | Hearth brush in Prince George County, Maryland, 1797 | 9 pence |
| Butter Boat | Inventory of Doctor Nicholas Flood (1776) | Blue and white China Butter Boat in Richmond County, Virginia, 1776 | 2 shillings 6 pence |
| Candle | Inventory of Doctor Nicholas Flood (1776) | White wax Candle in Richmond County, Virginia, 1776 | 5 shillings |

## Based Upon the British Currency System

| Year | Pound in 2002 US Dollars | Shilling in 2002 US Dollars | Pence in 2002 US Dollars |
|------|--------------------------|------------------------------|---------------------------|
| 1775 | $144.00 | $7.20 | $0.60 |
| 1780 | $168.00 | $8.40 | $0.70 |
| 1785 | $144.00 | $7.20 | $0.60 |
| 1790 | $144.00 | $7.20 | $0.60 |
| 1795 | $120.00 | $6.00 | $0.50 |
| 1799 | $120.00 | $6.00 | $0.50 |

*Calculations are approximate values based upon economic historical data*

| Item | Data Source | Description | Price |
|------|-------------|-------------|-------|
| Candle | Inventory of Doctor Nicholas Flood (1776) | Pound of Perminto Candles in Richmond County, Virginia, 1776 | 2 shillings 6 pence |
| Candle box | Winthrop Gardiner Jr. Collection | Candlebox made in New York, 1790 | 1 shilling 9 pence |
| Candlestick | Inventory of John Baynes (1790) | Pair of brass candlesticks in Prince George County, Maryland, 1790 | 10 shillings |
| Candlestick | Inventory of Isaac Walker (1797) | Plated Candlestick in Prince George County, Maryland, 1797 | 10 shillings |
| Card | Inventory of Margaret Ball (1783) | Pair of cotton cards in Lancaster County, Virginia, 1783 | 3 shillings |
| Carpet | Inventory of Isaac Walker (1797) | Carpet 2½ × 3-7½ yards in Prince George County, Maryland, 1797 | 1 pound 6 shillings 3 pence |
| Carpet | Inventory of Isaac Walker (1797) | Carpet 4 × 4½ - 18 yards in Prince George County, Maryland, 1797 | 3 pounds 3 shillings |
| Carpet | Inventory of Rev. Thomas Ainger (1797) | Rag carpet in New Castle County, Delaware, 1797 | $3.00 |
| Case & Silver | Inventory of Doctor Nicholas Flood (1776) | Shagreen Case with a dozen forks silverhandl in Richmond County, Virginia, 1776 | 3 pounds |
| Chamber Pot | Inventory of Doctor Nicholas Flood (1776) | Chamber pot in Richmond County, Virginia, 1776 | 2 shillings 6 pence |
| Chimney Screen | Inventory of Doctor Nicholas Flood (1776) | Chimny Skreen and Cricket in Richmond County, Virginia, 1776 | 15 shillings |
| China | C. Nicholes, Historical Sketches of Sumter County (1975) | 550 pieces of china bought in England and delivered to Sumter, South Carolina, 1797 | $1,100.00 |
| Churn | Inventory of John Riley (1795) | Churn in Newberry, South Carolina, 1795 | 2 shillings 4 pence |
| Coffee Pot | Inventory of Richard Mitchell (1781) | Copper Coffee Pot in Lancaster County, Virginia, 1781 | 2 shillings |
| Comb | Calland's Account Book - Captain James Robert's Account(1784) | Cost for one ivory comb | 2 shillings 6 pence |
| Corkscrew | Inventory of John Baynes (1790) | Cork Screw in Prince George County, Maryland, 1790 | 6½ pence |
| Cup | Inventory of Doctor Nicholas Flood (1776) | Coffee cup in Richmond County, Virginia, 1776 | 1 shilling 1½ pence |

| Item | Data Source | Description | Price |
|------|-------------|-------------|-------|
| Cup | Inventory of John Baynes (1790) | Blue & white Coffee Cup in Prince George County, Maryland, 1790 | 6 pence |
| Cups | Inventory of Isaac Walker (1797) | Dozen Choclate Cups & Saucers in Prince George County, Maryland, 1797 | 1 shilling 6 pence |
| Curtains | Inventory of Richard Mitchell (1781) | Sett strip'd Callo Curtians in Lancaster County, Virginia, 1781 | 2 pounds 10 shillings |
| Curtains | Inventory of James Adam, Sr. (1793) | Window curtain in New Castle County, Delaware, 1793 | 3 shillings |
| Decanter | Inventory of John Baynes (1790) | Decanter in Prince George County, Maryland, 1790 | 2 shillings |
| Dial | Inventory of Doctor Nicholas Flood (1776) | Horizontal Dial in Richmond County, Virginia, 1776 | 5 shillings |
| Dish | Inventory of Doctor Nicholas Flood (1776) | Blue and white China dish in Richmond County, Virginia, 1776 | 5 shillings |
| Dishes | Inventory of Doctor Nicholas Flood (1776) | Dozen Queen Ovel Dishes in Richmond County, Virginia, 1776 | 1 pound |
| Dishes | Inventory of Daniel Adams (1797) | Three pewter dishes in New Castle County, Delaware, 1797 | $1.25 |
| Egg Cup | Inventory of Doctor Nicholas Flood (1776) | Egg cup in Richmond County, Virginia, 1776 | 3 pence |
| Fire screen | Inventory of Doctor Nicholas Flood (1776) | Fire Skreen in Richmond County, Virginia, 1776 | 1 pound |
| Flatware | Inventory of John Baynes (1790) | Dozen knives and forks in Prince George County, Maryland, 1790 | 2 shillings |
| Flower Pot | Inventory of Doctor Nicholas Flood (1776) | Flower Pot in Richmond County, Virginia, 1776 | 6 pence |
| Fork | Inventory of John Baynes (1790) | Dessert fork in Prince George County, Maryland, 1790 | 10 pence |
| Fork | Inventory of John Riley (1795) | Flesh Fork in Newberry, South Carolina, 1795 | 1 shilling 8 pence |
| Frame | Inventory of Doctor Nicholas Flood (1776) | A new picture frame in Richmond County, Virginia, 1776 | 6 pence |
| Glass | Inventory of John Baynes (1790) | Wine glass in Prince George County, Maryland, 1790 | 5 pence |
| Glass | Inventory of John Baynes (1790) | Beer glass in Prince George County, Maryland, 1790 | 5 pence |

## Based Upon the British Currency System

| Year | Pound in 2002 US Dollars | Shilling in 2002 US Dollars | Pence in 2002 US Dollars |
|------|--------------------------|------------------------------|---------------------------|
| 1775 | $144.00 | $7.20 | $0.60 |
| 1780 | $168.00 | $8.40 | $0.70 |
| 1785 | $144.00 | $7.20 | $0.60 |
| 1790 | $144.00 | $7.20 | $0.60 |
| 1795 | $120.00 | $6.00 | $0.50 |
| 1799 | $120.00 | $6.00 | $0.50 |

*Calculations are approximate values based upon economic historical data*

| Item | Data Source | Description | Price |
|---|---|---|---|
| Glasses | Inventory of Isaac Walker (1797) | Dozen Wine Glasses in Prince George County, Maryland, 1797 | 4 shillings |
| Goblet | Inventory of John Baynes (1790) | Goblet in Prince George County, Maryland, 1790 | 1 shilling 3 pence |
| Goblet | Inventory of Isaac Walker (1797) | Water Goblet in Prince George County, Maryland, 1797 | 1 shilling 4 pence |
| Hand Irons | Inventory of Richard Mitchell (1781) | Pair of hand irons in Lancaster County, Virginia, 1781 | 15 shillings |
| Hat Box | Inventory of Isaac Walker (1797) | Box for a Ladies Hat in Prince George County, Maryland, 1797 | 2 shillings 3 pence |
| Ironing table | Inventory of Doctor Nicholas Flood (1776) | Ironing table in Richmond County, Virginia, 1776 | 2 shillings |
| Jelly Glasses | Inventory of Doctor Nicholas Flood (1776) | Dozen jelly glasses in Richmond County, Virginia, 1776 | 9 shillings |
| Jug | Inventory of Doctor Nicholas Flood (1776) | Water jug in Richmond County, Virginia, 1776 | 2 shillings |
| Jug | Inventory of Daniel Diman (1798) | Stone jug in Plymouth, Massachusetts, 1798 | $0.50 |
| Kettle | Inventory of Margaret Anderson (1783) | Copper Tea Kettle in Kershaw, South Carolina, 1783 | 1 pound 5 shillings |
| Knife | Calland's Account Book - Captain James Robert's Account(1784) | Cost for one pen knife | 1 shilling |
| Knife | Inventory of John Baynes (1790) | Oyster knife in Prince George County, Maryland, 1790 | 4 pence |
| Lantern | Inventory of Doctor Nicholas Flood (1776) | Magic Lanthorn in Richmond County, Virginia, 1776 | 10 shillings |
| Lantern | Inventory of Richard Mitchell (1781) | Old Tin Lanthorn in Lancaster County, Virginia, 1781 | 6 pence |
| Lock | Inventory of Doctor Nicholas Flood (1776) | Cupbord Lock in Richmond County, Virginia, 1776 | 1 shilling 3 pence |
| Lock | Inventory of John Baynes (1790) | Chest Lock in Prince George County, Maryland, 1790 | 1 shilling 2 pence |
| Lock | Inventory of Isaac Walker (1797) | Desk Lock in Prince George County, Maryland, 1797 | 5 pence |
| Looking Glass | Inventory of Doctor Nicholas Flood (1776) | Looking glass in Richmond County, Virginia, 1776 | 10 shillings |
| Looking Glass | Inventory of Daniel Adams (1797) | Small looking glass in New Castle County, Delaware, 1797 | $1.50 |
| Map | Inventory of Daniel Adams (1797) | Framed map in New Castle County, Delaware, 1797 | $0.50 |
| Mat | Inventory of Richard Mitchell (1781) | Table Matt in Lancaster County, Virginia, 1781 | 1 shilling |
| Milk Pot | Calland's Account Book - Captain James Robert's Account(1784) | One blue milk pott | 1 shilling |
| Mug | Inventory of Richard Mitchell (1781) | Queens China Chocolate Mug in Lancaster County, Virginia, 1781 | 1 shilling |
| Napkin | Inventory of Rev. Thomas Ainger (1797) | Napkin in New Castle County, Delaware, 1797 | 12½ cents |
| Pan | Inventory of James Adams, Sr. (1793) | Warming pan in New Castle County, Delaware, 1793 | 5 shillings |
| Pictures | Inventory of James Adams, Sr. (1793) | Two pictures - King & Queen of France in New Castle County, Delaware, 1793 | 7 shillings 6 pence |
| Pictures | Inventory of Daniel Adams (1797) | 14 framed pictures in New Castle County, Delaware, 1797 | $4.00 |

| Item | Data Source | Description | Price |
|------|-------------|-------------|-------|
| Pillowcase | Inventory of Doctor Nicholas Flood (1776) | Pair of Cotton pillow Cases in Richmond County, Virginia, 1776 | 2 shillings |
| Pinchers | Inventory of Isaac Walker (1797) | Pair of Shoe Pinchers in Prince George County, Maryland, 1797 | 2 shillings 7 pence |
| Pitcher | Inventory of Isaac Walker (1797) | Blue & White Bitcher in Prince George County, Maryland, 1797 | 1 shilling 6 pence |
| Plate | Inventory of Doctor Nicholas Flood (1776) | Blue and white China plate in Richmond County, Virginia, 1776 | 1 shilling 6 pence |
| Plate | Inventory of Doctor Nicholas Flood (1776) | Shallow white stone plate in Richmond County, Virginia, 1776 | 3 pence |
| Plate | Inventory of Elizabeth Chappell (1782) | Deep pewter plate in Kershaw, South Carolina, 1782 | 1 pound 13 shillings 4 pence |
| Plates | Inventory of Daniel Adams (1797) | Ten small pewter plates in New Castle County, Delaware, 1797 | $1.67 |
| Porringer | Calland's Account Book - Captain James Robert's Account(1784) | Cost for one pewter porriinger | 2 shillings |
| Pot | Inventory of Doctor Nicholas Flood (1776) | Garden pott in Richmond County, Virginia, 1776 | 1 shilling |
| Pot | Inventory of Margaret Ball (1783) | Stone Butter pot in Lancaster County, Virginia, 1783 | 2 shillings |
| Pot | Inventory of Margaret Ball (1783) | Coffee Pot in Lancaster County, Virginia, 1783 | 6 shillings |
| Pot | Inventory of John Baynes (1790) | Oval Tea Pott in Prince George County, Maryland, 1790 | 2 shillings |
| Press | Inventory of Daniel Adams (1797) | Clothes press in New Castle County, Delaware, 1797 | $2.00 |
| Print | Inventory of Doctor Nicholas Flood (1776) | Varnished print in Richmond County, Virginia, 1776 | 2 shillings |
| Print | Inventory of Doctor Nicholas Flood (1776) | Print in frames without Glass in Richmond County, Virginia, 1776 | 2½ pence |
| Quilt | Inventory of Daniel Diman (1798) | Callico bed quilt in Plymouth, Massachusetts, 1798 | $2.50 |
| Razor | Inventory of Isaac Walker (1797) | Razor in Prince George County, Maryland, 1797 | 1 shilling ½ pence |
| Razor Case | Inventory of John Baynes (1790) | Case for Razors in Prince George County, Maryland, 1790 | 5 pence |

### Based Upon the British Currency System

| Year | Pound in 2002 US Dollars | Shilling in 2002 US Dollars | Pence in 2002 US Dollars |
|------|--------------------------|------------------------------|---------------------------|
| 1775 | $144.00 | $7.20 | $0.60 |
| 1780 | $168.00 | $8.40 | $0.70 |
| 1785 | $144.00 | $7.20 | $0.60 |
| 1790 | $144.00 | $7.20 | $0.60 |
| 1795 | $120.00 | $6.00 | $0.50 |
| 1799 | $120.00 | $6.00 | $0.50 |

*Calculations are approximate values based upon economic historical data*

| Item | Data Source | Description | Price |
|---|---|---|---|
| Rug | Inventory of Richard Mitchell (1781) | Silk Rugg in Lancaster County, Virginia, 1781 | 1 pound |
| Rug | Inventory of Richard Mitchell (1781) | Purple Worsted Rug in Lancaster County, Virginia, 1781 | 7 shillings 6 pence |
| Scales | Inventory of Richard Mitchell (1781) | Pair money Weights & Scales in Lancaster County, Virginia, 1781 | 7 shillings 6 pence |
| Server | Inventory of Daniel Adams (1797) | Walnut server in New Castle County, Delaware, 1797 | $3.00 |
| Shears | Inventory of Richard Mitchell (1781) | Pair of Garden Sheers in Lancaster County, Virginia, 1781 | 1 shilling 3 pence |
| Sheets | Inventory of Richard Mitchell (1781) | Pair of cotton sheets in Lancaster County, Virginia, 1781 | 1 pound 10 shillings |
| Sheets | Inventory of Daniel Diman (1798) | Pair of cotton sheets in Plymouth, Massachusetts, 1798 | $1.50 |
| Shovel & Tongs | Inventory of Rev. Thomas Ainger (1797) | Shovel & tongs in New Castle County, Delaware, 1797 | $1.50 |
| Soap | Inventory of John Baynes (1790) | Pound of soap in Prince George County, Maryland, 1790 | 5½ pence |
| Soap | Inventory of Isaac Walker (1797) | Piece of shaving soap in Prince George County, Maryland, 1797 | 1 shilling 3 pence |
| Spice Mill | Inventory of John Baynes (1790) | Spice mill in Prince George County, Maryland, 1790 | 5 shillings |
| Spinning Wheel | Inventory of Doctor Nicholas Flood (1776) | Spinning Wheel and 1 pr Cards in Richmond County, Virginia, 1776 | 15 shillings |
| Spinning Wheel | Inventory of Richard Mitchell (1781) | Spinning wheel in Lancaster County, Virginia, 1781 | 6 shillings |
| Spoon | Inventory of Margaret Ball (1783) | Silver tablespoon in Lancaster County, Virginia, 1783 | 10 shillings |
| Spoons | Inventory of Isaac Walker (1797) | Dozen Silver Tea Spoons new Marked I W in Prince George County, Maryland, 1797 | 3 pounds |
| Stool | Inventory of James Adam, Sr. (1793) | Close stool in New Castle County, Delaware, 1793 | 1 pound 10 shillings |
| Stool Box | Inventory of John Baynes (1790) | Close Stool Box in Prince George County, Maryland, 1790 | 7 shillings 6 pence |
| Strop | Inventory of Isaac Walker (1797) | Elastic Razor Strop in Prince George County, Maryland, 1797 | 3 shillings 6 pence |
| Sugar Dish | Inventory of Richard Mitchell (1781) | Glass Sugar Dish in Lancaster County, Virginia, 1781 | 2 shillings |
| Sugar Tongs | Inventory of Richard Mitchell (1781) | Pair of sugar tongs in Lancaster County, Virginia, 1781 | 3 shillings |
| Table | Inventory of James Adam, Sr. (1793) | Tea table in New Castle County, Delaware, 1793 | 8 shillings |
| Tablecloth | Inventory of James Adam, Sr. (1793) | Table cloth in New Castle County, Delaware, 1793 | 11 shillings 3 pence |
| Tablecloth | Inventory of Richard Mitchell (1781) | Damask Table Cloth in Lancaster County, Virginia, 1781 | 1 pound 10 shillings |
| Tablecloth | Inventory of Margaret Anderson (1783) | Diaper Table Cloth in Kershaw, South Carolina, 1783 | 8 pounds |
| Tea Canister | Inventory of Doctor Nicholas Flood (1776) | Large Tea Cannister in Richmond County, Virginia, 1776 | 1 shilling 3 pence |
| Tea Cup | Inventory of Ebenezer Wells (1784) | One soft white tea cup in Deerfield, Massachusetts, 1784 | 1 shilling, 8 pence |
| Tea Cups | Inventory of Doctor Nicholas Flood (1776) | Dozen Gold burnt Tea Cups and Saucers in Richmond County, Virginia, 1776 | 1 pound |
| Tea Pot | Inventory of Isaac Walker (1797) | Tea pot in Prince George County, Maryland, 1797 | 7 pence |

| Item | Data Source | Description | Price |
|---|---|---|---|
| Tea Set | Inventory of Rev. Thomas Ainger (1797) | 1 tea pot, sugar bowl & cream jug in New Castle County, Delaware, 1797 | $0.50 |
| Teaspoons | Inventory of Ebenezer Wells (1784) | Six silver teaspoons in Deerfield, Massachusetts, 1784 | 18 shillings |
| Tongs & Poker | Inventory of Rev. Thomas Ainger (1797) | Tongs in New Castle County, Delaware, 1797 | $0.40 |
| Towel | Inventory of Isaac Walker (1797) | Huckaback towel in Prince George County, Maryland, 1797 | 1 shilling |
| Tray | Inventory of Doctor Nicholas Flood (1776) | Square Tea Tray in Richmond County, Virginia, 1776 | 1 pound |
| Tray | Inventory of Isaac Walker (1797) | Large handsome Tea Tray in Prince George County, Maryland, 1797 | 2 pounds 5 shillings |
| Tub | Inventory of John Young (1790) | Wash tub in Plymouth, Massachusetts, 1790 | $1.00 |
| Tub | Inventory of John Young (1790) | Dye tub in Plymouth, Massachusetts, 1790 | $0.33 |
| Tumbler | Inventory of Isaac Walker (1797) | Dozen pint Tumbers in Prince George County, Maryland, 1797 | 8 shillings |
| Twine | Inventory of Doctor Nicholas Flood (1776) | Pound of twine in Richmond County, Virginia, 1776 | 2 shillings |
| Watch Holder | Inventory of Doctor Nicholas Flood (1776) | Watch holder in Richmond County, Virginia, 1776 | 5 shillings |
| Wax | Inventory of Doctor Nicholas Flood (1776) | Pound of Myrtle wax in Richmond County, Virginia, 1776 | 1 pound |
| Wax | Inventory of Doctor Nicholas Flood (1776) | Pound of bees wax in Richmond County, Virginia, 1776 | 1 pound |
| Wheel | Inventory of James Adam, Sr. (1793) | Big wheel & reel in New Castle County, Delaware, 1793 | 12 shillings 6 pence |
| Wine glasses | Inventory of Ebenezer Wells (1784) | Two wine glasses in Deerfield, Massachusetts, 1784 | 1 shilling, 11 pence |

## Investments

| | | | |
|---|---|---|---|
| Stock Interest | Kitman, George Washington's Expense Account (1970) | Intrest earned by Martha Washington on her Bank of England stocks, 1786 | 4,168 pounds |

## Jewelry

| | | | |
|---|---|---|---|
| Locket | Inventory of Isaac Walker (1797) | Gold Locket Set and ciphered IEW in Prince George County, Maryland, 1797 | 1 pound 17 shillings 6 pence |

## Based Upon the British Currency System

| Year | Pound in 2002 US Dollars | Shilling in 2002 US Dollars | Pence in 2002 US Dollars |
|---|---|---|---|
| 1775 | $144.00 | $7.20 | $0.60 |
| 1780 | $168.00 | $8.40 | $0.70 |
| 1785 | $144.00 | $7.20 | $0.60 |
| 1790 | $144.00 | $7.20 | $0.60 |
| 1795 | $120.00 | $6.00 | $0.50 |
| 1799 | $120.00 | $6.00 | $0.50 |

*Calculations are approximate values based upon economic historical data*

| Item | Data Source | Description | Price |
|---|---|---|---|
| Necklace | Inventory of Isaac Walker (1797) | Neck Lace in Prince George County, Maryland, 1797 | 3 shillings |
| Ring | Inventory of Doctor Nicholas Flood (1776) | Gold stone ring in Richmond County, Virginia, 1776 | 1 pound |
| Watch | Inventory of Doctor Nicholas Flood (1776) | Gold watch in Richmond County, Virginia, 1776 | 15 pounds |
| Watch | Inventory of Richard Mitchell (1781) | Silver watch in Lancaster County, Virginia, 1781 | 2 pounds |

### Kitchen Items

| Item | Data Source | Description | Price |
|---|---|---|---|
| Basket | Inventory of Margaret Ball (1783) | Bread basket in Lancaster County, Virginia, 1783 | 1 shilling 3 pence |
| Box | Inventory of John Young (1790) | Sugar box in Plymouth, Massachusetts, 1790 | $0.17 |
| Box | Inventory of Isaac Walker (1797) | Small Tin peper box in Prince George County, Maryland, 1797 | 4 pence |
| Cake Molds | Inventory of Doctor Nicholas Flood (1776) | Mould for Cake in Richmond County, Virginia, 1776 | 2 pence |
| Chaffing Dish | Inventory of Doctor Nicholas Flood (1776) | Chaffing dish in Richmond County, Virginia, 1776 | 1 shilling |
| Coffee Mill | Inventory of William Howell (1784) | Coffee mill in Kershaw, South Carolina, 1784 | 9 shillings 4 pence |
| Coffee Mill | Inventory of Daniel Diman (1798) | Coffee mill in Plymouth, Massachusetts, 1798 | $0.75 |
| Coffee Pot | Inventory of Rev. Thomas Ainger (1797) | Coffee pot in New Castle County, Delaware, 1797 | $0.50 |
| Colander | Inventory of John Baynes (1790) | Cullender in Prince George County, Maryland, 1790 | 10 pence |
| Cruet | Inventory of Isaac Walker (1797) | Vinegar Cruit in Prince George County, Maryland, 1797 | 6 pence |
| Cutlery | Calland's Account Book - Captain James Robert's Account(1784) | Cost for one dozen knives and forks | 7 shillings 6 pence |
| Frying Pan | Inventory of Isaac Walker (1797) | Frying pan in Prince George County, Maryland, 1797 | 4 shillings |
| Funnel | Inventory of John Baynes (1790) | Large Funnel in Prince George County, Maryland, 1790 | 1 shilling |
| Grater | Inventory of Doctor Nicholas Flood (1776) | Nutmeg Grater in Richmond County, Virginia, 1776 | 1 shilling 3 pence |
| Griddle | Inventory of Isaac Walker (1797) | Griddle in Prince George County, Maryland, 1797 | 3 shillings 6 pence |
| Gridiron | Inventory of Daniel Diman (1798) | Grid Iron in Plymouth, Massachusetts, 1798 | $0.50 |
| Grindstone | Inventory of James Adam, Sr. (1793) | Grindstone in New Castle County, Delaware, 1793 | 1 shilling 6 pence |
| Hogshead | Inventory of James Adam, Sr. (1793) | Hogshead in New Castle County, Delaware, 1793 | 5 shillings |
| Ice Cream Freezer | Kimball, Thomas Jefferson's Cook Book (1976) | Cream machine for Ice - General George Washington, 1784 | 1 pound 13 shillings 4 pence |
| Iron | Inventory of Rev. Thomas Ainger (1797) | Baking iron in New Castle County, Delaware, 1797 | $1.50 |
| Jar | Inventory of Rev. Thomas Ainger (1797) | Stone jarr in New Castle County, Delaware, 1797 | $0.75 |
| Kettle | Inventory of John Young (1790) | Large Iron kettle in Plymouth, Massachusetts, 1790 | $2.50 |
| Kettle | Inventory of John Baynes (1790) | Tin Tea Kettle in Prince George County, Maryland, 1790 | 2 shillings 9 pence |

| Item | Data Source | Description | Price |
|---|---|---|---|
| Kettle | Inventory of John Baynes (1790) | Copper Tea Kittle in Prince George County, Maryland, 1790 | 7 shillings 6 pence |
| Kitchen Iron | Inventory of James Adam, Sr. (1793) | One griddle, iron toaster, two bake irons & little pot in New Castle County, Delaware, 1793 | 2 pounds |
| Knife | Inventory of John Baynes (1790) | Butcher knife in Prince George County, Maryland, 1790 | 3 shillings |
| Measure | Inventory of Rev. Thomas Ainger (1797) | Peck measure in New Castle County, Delaware, 1797 | $0.50 |
| Mortar & Pestle | Inventory of Doctor Nicholas Flood (1776) | Bell mettle Mortar and Pestle in Richmond County, Virginia, 1776 | 2 shillings 6 pence |
| Mug | Inventory of Doctor Nicholas Flood (1776) | Quart mug in Richmond County, Virginia, 1776 | 1 shilling 3 pence |
| Mug | Inventory of Doctor Nicholas Flood (1776) | Pint mug in Richmond County, Virginia, 1776 | 7½ pence |
| Nipper | Inventory of Isaac Walker (1797) | Sugar Nipper in Prince George County, Maryland, 1797 | 2 shillings |
| Oven | Inventory of Doctor Nicholas Flood (1776) | Dutch Oven in Richmond County, Virginia, 1776 | 6 shillings 3 pence |
| Pan | Inventory of Doctor Nicholas Flood (1776) | Frying pan in Richmond County, Virginia, 1776 | 2 shillings 6 pence |
| Pan | Inventory of Doctor Nicholas Flood (1776) | Pudden Pan in Richmond County, Virginia, 1776 | 1 shilling |
| Pan | Inventory of John Baynes (1790) | Quart pan in Prince George County, Maryland, 1790 | 5 pence |
| Pan | Inventory of Isaac Walker (1797) | Old Tin baking pan in Prince George County, Maryland, 1797 | 7 shillings 6 pence |
| Pan | Inventory of Daniel Adams (1797) | Dripping pan & skillet in New Castle County, Delaware, 1797 | $0.50 |
| Pepper Box | Inventory of John Baynes (1790) | Pepper Box in Prince George County, Maryland, 1790 | 1¾ pence |
| Pestle | Inventory of Doctor Nicholas Flood (1776) | Large iron pestle in Richmond County, Virginia, 1776 | 3 shillings 6 pence |
| Pitcher | Inventory of Rev. Thomas Ainger (1797) | Pitcher in New Castle County, Delaware, 1797 | $0.50 |
| Pot | Inventory of Doctor Nicholas Flood (1776) | Brown China Chocolate pot in Richmond County, Virginia, 1776 | 5 shillings |
| Pot | Inventory of Richard Mitchell (1781) | Large Fat Pot in Lancaster County, Virginia, 1781 | 5 shillings |

## Based Upon the British Currency System

| Year | Pound in 2002 US Dollars | Shilling in 2002 US Dollars | Pence in 2002 US Dollars |
|---|---|---|---|
| 1775 | $144.00 | $7.20 | $0.60 |
| 1780 | $168.00 | $8.40 | $0.70 |
| 1785 | $144.00 | $7.20 | $0.60 |
| 1790 | $144.00 | $7.20 | $0.60 |
| 1795 | $120.00 | $6.00 | $0.50 |
| 1799 | $120.00 | $6.00 | $0.50 |

*Calculations are approximate values based upon economic historical data*

| Item | Data Source | Description | Price |
|---|---|---|---|
| Pot | Inventory of Rev. Thomas Ainger (1797) | Iron pot in New Castle County, Delaware, 1797 | $1.50 |
| Pot Hooks | Inventory of John Baynes (1790) | Pott Hook in Prince George County, Maryland, 1790 | 1 shilling 6 pence |
| Pot Rack | Inventory of John Baynes (1790) | Iron pott Rack in Prince George County, Maryland, 1790 | 10 shillings |
| Press | Inventory of Doctor Nicholas Flood (1776) | Linseed Oyl Press in Richmond County, Virginia, 1776 | 5 shillings |
| Rack | Inventory of Margaret Ball (1783) | Iron Pot Rack in Lancaster County, Virginia, 1783 | 7 shillings 6 pence |
| Racks | Inventory of Richard Mitchell (1781) | Iron Pot Rack in Lancaster County, Virginia, 1781 | 10 shillings |
| Salt Cellar | Inventory of Rev. Thomas Ainger (1797) | Salt cellar in New Castle County, Delaware, 1797 | $0.25 |
| Sieve | Inventory of William Howell (1784) | Sieve in Kershaw, South Carolina, 1784 | 6 shillings |
| Skillet | Inventory of Doctor Nicholas Flood (1776) | Small Bell Mettle Skillet in Richmond County, Virginia, 1776 | 7 shillings |
| Spit | Inventory of John Baynes (1790) | Iron Spit in Prince George County, Maryland, 1790 | 5 shillings |
| Steel Mill | Inventory of Doctor Nicholas Flood (1776) | Old Steel Mill in Richmond County, Virginia, 1776 | 1 pound |
| Stove | Inventory of James Adam, Sr. (1793) | Open stove in New Castle County, Delaware, 1793 | 3 shillings |
| Stove | Inventory of James Adam, Sr. (1793) | Stove (6 plate) & pipe in New Castle County, Delaware, 1793 | 2 pounds 5 shillings |
| Tins | Inventory of Rev. Thomas Ainger (1797) | Four tins in New Castle County, Delaware, 1797 | $0.25 |
| Toaster | Inventory of Daniel Diman (1798) | Toaster in Plymouth, Massachusetts, 1798 | $0.25 |
| Tongs | Inventory of Richard Mitchell (1781) | Pair of tongs in Lancaster County, Virginia, 1781 | 2 shillings |
| Tub | Inventory of Richard Mitchell (1781) | Powdering Tub in Lancaster County, Virginia, 1781 | 2 shillings 6 pence |
| Waffle Iron | Kimball, Thomas Jefferson's Cook Book (1976) | Purchase of waffle iron by Thomas Jefferson in 1788 | 1.3 Florins |
| Wood | Inventory of Rev. Thomas Ainger (1797) | Cord H wood in New Castle County, Delaware, 1797 | $7.00 |

### Livery Animals & Tools

| Item | Data Source | Description | Price |
|---|---|---|---|
| Bag | Inventory of John Young (1790) | Meal bag in Plymouth, Massachusetts, 1790 | $1.00 |
| Bit | Inventory of Doctor Nicholas Flood (1776) | New Kirb Bridle Bit in Richmond County, Virginia, 1776 | 3 shillings |
| Bridle | Inventory of Doctor Nicholas Flood (1776) | Snaffl Bridle in Richmond County, Virginia, 1776 | 3 shillings |
| Brush | Inventory of John Baynes (1790) | Horse Brush in Prince George County, Maryland, 1790 | 11½ pence |
| Cart | Inventory of Margaret Ball (1783) | Ox Cart and Wheels two yokes &c & Chain in Lancaster County, Virginia, 1783 | 2 pounds 10 shillings |
| Cart | Inventory of Ebenezer Wells (1784) | One cart, cart wheels, and irons in Deerfield, Massachusetts, 1784 | 3 pounds 13 shillings |
| Chain | Inventory of Margaret Ball (1783) | Ox Chain in Lancaster County, Virginia, 1783 | 4 shillings 6 pence |
| Cloth | Inventory of John Baynes (1790) | Saddle Cloth in Prince George County, Maryland, 1790 | 2 shillings 8 pence |

| Item | Data Source | Description | Price |
|------|-------------|-------------|-------|
| Colt | Inventory of William Oneall (1789) | One year old mare colt in Newberry, South Carolina, 1789 | 7 pounds |
| Girth | Inventory of John Baynes (1790) | Single Girth in Prince George County, Maryland, 1790 | 10 pence |
| Harness | Kitman, George Washington's Expense Account (1970) | Double harness purchased by General George Washington for chariot, 1775 | $201.50 |
| Horse | Inventory of Richard Mitchell (1781) | Bay Horse in Lancaster County, Virginia, 1781 | 25 pounds |
| Horse | Inventory of Isaac Walker (1797) | Sorrel Horse said to be 7 years old last Spring in Prince George County, Maryland, 1797 | 65 pounds |
| Horse | Inventory of Isaac Walker (1797) | Dark bay Horse Said to be about 10 years old last Spring in Prince George County, Maryland, 1797 | 20 pounds |
| Horse saddle and bridle | Botetourt County, VA Tax Record (1788) | Saddle and bridle given to shoemaker's apprentice Michael Miller, 1788 | 20 pounds |
| Ladder | Inventory of John Young (1790) | Cart ladder in Plymouth, Massachusetts, 1790 | $0.50 |
| Locks | Inventory of Isaac Walker (1797) | Steel Saddle bag Locks in Prince George County, Maryland, 1797 | 1 shilling 1¼ pence |
| Mare | Inventory of John Baynes (1790) | Mare 14 years old in Prince George County, Maryland, 1790 | 10 pounds |
| Oxen | Inventory of John Baynes (1790) | Ox in Prince George County, Maryland, 1790 | 5 pounds |
| Portmanteau | Inventory of Isaac Walker (1797) | Portmantua with Pad in Prince George County, Maryland, 1797 | 3 pounds |
| Reins | Inventory of John Baynes (1790) | Dble Reined Bridle in Prince George County, Maryland, 1790 | 5 shillings |
| Saddle | Inventory of John Young (1790) | Saddle in Plymouth, Massachusetts, 1790 | $2.00 |
| Saddle | Inventory of John Baynes (1790) | Mens Saddle in Prince George County, Maryland, 1790 | 16 shillings |
| Saddle | Inventory of John Baynes (1790) | Boys Saddle in Prince George County, Maryland, 1790 | 15 shillings 6 pence |
| Saddle | Inventory of John Riley (1795) | Womans Saddle in Newberry, South Carolina, 1795 | 2 pounds |
| Saddle Bags | Inventory of Isaac Walker (1797) | Pair of saddle bags in Prince George County, Maryland, 1797 | 2 pounds 2 shillings 6 pence |

## Based Upon the British Currency System

| Year | Pound in 2002 US Dollars | Shilling in 2002 US Dollars | Pence in 2002 US Dollars |
|------|--------------------------|------------------------------|---------------------------|
| 1775 | $144.00 | $7.20 | $0.60 |
| 1780 | $168.00 | $8.40 | $0.70 |
| 1785 | $144.00 | $7.20 | $0.60 |
| 1790 | $144.00 | $7.20 | $0.60 |
| 1795 | $120.00 | $6.00 | $0.50 |
| 1799 | $120.00 | $6.00 | $0.50 |

*Calculations are approximate values based upon economic historical data*

| Item | Data Source | Description | Price |
|------|-------------|-------------|-------|
| Saddle Tree | Inventory of John Riley (1795) | Saddle tree in Newberry, South Carolina, 1795 | 5 shillings |
| Spurs | Inventory of John Baynes (1790) | Pair of steel spurs in Prince George County, Maryland, 1790 | 9 pence |
| Stirrup | Inventory of Doctor Nicholas Flood (1776) | Stirrup leathers in Richmond County, Virginia, 1776 | 1 shilling 6 pence |
| Travel Bags | Inventory of James Adam, Sr. (1793) | Two old portmanteaus & two pair saddle bags in New Castle County, Delaware, 1793 | 0-7-6 |
| Wagon | Inventory of John Baynes (1790) | Wagon & Harness for 2 Horses in Prince George County, Maryland, 1790 | 15 pounds |
| Whip | Inventory of Doctor Nicholas Flood (1776) | Horse whip in Richmond County, Virginia, 1776 | 12 shillings 6 pence |

## Livestock

| Item | Data Source | Description | Price |
|------|-------------|-------------|-------|
| Boar | Inventory of Margaret Ball (1783) | Large Boar in Lancaster County, Virginia, 1783 | 1 pound 10 shillings |
| Bull | Inventory of Richard Mitchell (1781) | Bull in Lancaster County, Virginia, 1781 | 2 pounds |
| Cattle | Inventory of John Riley (1795) | One head of cattle in Newberry, South Carolina, 1795 | 18 shillings 4 pence |
| Cow | Inventory of Richard Mitchell (1781) | Best Cow in Lancaster County, Virginia, 1781 | 2 pounds 5 shillings |
| Cow | Inventory of Richard Mitchell (1781) | Old Black Cow in Lancaster County, Virginia, 1781 | 1 pound 5 shillings |
| Cow | Inventory of Ebenezer Wells (1784) | 1 blach and white cow (with horns) in Deerfield, Massachusetts, 1784 | 3 pounds, 5 shillings |
| Goose | Inventory of William Oneall (1789) | Goose in Newberry, South Carolina, 1789 | 2 shillings |
| Heifer | Inventory of Ebenezer Wells (1784) | 15-year-old heifer in Deerfield, Massachusetts, 1784 | 24 shillings |
| Heifer | Inventory of John Baynes (1790) | Heifer in Prince George County, Maryland, 1790 | 1 pound 10 shillings |
| Hog | Inventory of Isaac Walker (1797) | Hog in Prince George County, Maryland, 1797 | 1 pound |
| Lamb | Inventory of Richard Mitchell (1781) | Best lamb in Lancaster County, Virginia, 1781 | 6 shillings |
| Pig | Inventory of John Young (1790) | Pig in Plymouth, Massachusetts, 1790 | $7.00 |
| Poultry | Inventory of John Riley (1795) | Poultry in Newberry, South Carolina, 1795 | 2 shillings |
| Ram | Inventory of Richard Mitchell (1781) | Old Ram in Lancaster County, Virginia, 1781 | 8 shillings |
| Sheep | Inventory of John Riley (1795) | One sheep in Newberry, South Carolina, 1795 | 4 shillings 8 pence |
| Shoat | Inventory of John Riley (1795) | One shoat in Newberry, South Carolina, 1795 | 3 shillings 2½ pence |
| Sow | Inventory of Richard Mitchell (1781) | Breeding Sow in Lancaster County, Virginia, 1781 | 15 shillings |
| Sow | Inventory of John Riley (1795) | One sow in Newberry, South Carolina, 1795 | 13 shillings 3 pence |
| Steer | Inventory of Ebenezer Wells (1784) | 1 yoke of steer in Deerfield, Massachusetts, 1784 | 8 pounds |
| Yearling | Inventory of John Young (1790) | Yearling in Plymouth, Massachusetts, 1790 | $5.00 |

## Medical Care & Medicine

| Item | Data Source | Description | Price |
|------|-------------|-------------|-------|
| Bark | Inventory of John Baynes (1790) | One pound Best Peruvian Bark in Prince George County, Maryland, 1790 | 8 shillings |

| Item | Data Source | Description | Price |
|------|-------------|-------------|-------|
| Bleeding | Joseph I. Waring, A History of Medicine in South Carolina, 1670-1825 (1980) | Cost for a doctor to bleed a white patient (around 1792) | 9 shillings 4 pence |
| Bleeding | Joseph I. Waring, A History of Medicine in South Carolina, 1670-1825 (1980) | Cost for a doctor to bleed a black patient (around 1792) | 4 shillings 8 pence |
| Cordial | Inventory of Isaac Walker (1797) | Bottle of Godfreys Cordial in Prince George County, Maryland, 1797 | 1 shilling |
| Drug | Inventory of Doctor Nicholas Flood (1776) | One pound of Gum Ammone in Richmond County, Virginia, 1776 | 16 shillings |
| Drug | Inventory of Doctor Nicholas Flood (1776) | One ounce of Assafetid in Richmond County, Virginia, 1776 | 1 shilling |
| Drug | Inventory of Doctor Nicholas Flood (1776) | One of Drs Aniss in Richmond County, Virginia, 1776 | 3 pence |
| Drug | Inventory of Doctor Nicholas Flood (1776) | One of Drs Coriander in Richmond County, Virginia, 1776 | 3 pence |
| Drug | Inventory of Doctor Nicholas Flood (1776) | One pound Alloes H&S in Richmond County, Virginia, 1776 | 16 shillings |
| Drug | Inventory of Doctor Nicholas Flood (1776) | One dram of Gum Galbancem in Richmond County, Virginia, 1776 | 3 pence |
| Drug | Inventory of Doctor Nicholas Flood (1776) | One ounce of Ether Virtiol in Richmond County, Virginia, 1776 | 1 shilling |
| Drug | Inventory of Doctor Nicholas Flood (1776) | One ounce of Emetic Tart in Richmond County, Virginia, 1776 | 1 shilling |
| Drug | Inventory of Doctor Nicholas Flood (1776) | One pound of quick Silver in Richmond County, Virginia, 1776 | 16 shillings |
| Grater | Inventory of Doctor Nicholas Flood (1776) | Rhubarb Grater in a doctor's shop in Richmond County, Virginia, 1776 | 6 pence |
| Hair Formula | The Pennsylvania Gazette (1776) | Pot of Pomade de Venus that prevents hair loss and can also be used as a lip salve, Philadelphia, Pennsylvania, 1776 | 3 shillings |
| Marble | Inventory of Doctor Nicholas Flood (1776) | Marble Slab in doctor's shop in Richmond County, Virginia, 1776 | 2 shillings 6 pence |
| Measures | Inventory of Doctor Nicholas Flood (1776) | Five pewter measures for medicine in Richmond County, Virginia, 1776 | 2 shillings 6 pence |
| Medicine | Joseph I. Waring, A History of Medicine in South Carolina, 1670-1825 (1980) | Cost of one dose of pills given to a patient (around 1792) | 1 shilling |

### Based Upon the British Currency System

| Year | Pound in 2002 US Dollars | Shilling in 2002 US Dollars | Pence in 2002 US Dollars |
|------|--------------------------|-----------------------------|--------------------------|
| 1775 | $144.00 | $7.20 | $0.60 |
| 1780 | $168.00 | $8.40 | $0.70 |
| 1785 | $144.00 | $7.20 | $0.60 |
| 1790 | $144.00 | $7.20 | $0.60 |
| 1795 | $120.00 | $6.00 | $0.50 |
| 1799 | $120.00 | $6.00 | $0.50 |

*Calculations are approximate values based upon economic historical data*

| Item | Data Source | Description | Price |
|------|-------------|-------------|-------|
| Medicine | Smith, Early American Home Remedies (1968) | Bottle of Henkle's Vermifuge - Compound Oil of Worm-seed  The medicine is a powerful anthelmintic and a mild cathartic, expelling every species of worms infesting the intestinal canal | $0.25 |
| Operation | Joseph I. Waring, A History of Medicine in South Carolina, 1670-1825 (1980) | Operation of "the trepan" - a procedure that requires perforating the skull (around 1792) | 10 pounds |
| Pills | Inventory of Isaac Walker (1797) | Box of Andersons pills in Prince George County, Maryland, 1797 | 1 shilling 4¾ pence |
| Pipe | Inventory of Doctor Nicholas Flood (1776) | Clyster Pipe in Richmond County, Virginia, 1776 | 6 pence |
| Salts | Inventory of John Baynes (1790) | Pound of Best Glauber Salts in Prince George County, Maryland, 1790 | 6 pence |
| Scales | Inventory of Doctor Nicholas Flood (1776) | Pair of scales for drug measurements in Richmond County, Virginia, 1776 | 3 shillings 3 pence |
| Snuff | The Pennsylvania Gazette (1776) | Bottle of Golden Medical Cephalic Snuff Used for headaches and curing recent deafness Philadelphia, Pennsylvania, 1776 | 2 shillings 6 pence |
| Spatula | Inventory of Doctor Nicholas Flood (1776) | Spatula in a doctor's shop in Richmond County, Virginia, 1776 | 3 pence |
| Syringe | Inventory of Doctor Nicholas Flood (1776) | Glister Syringe in Richmond County, Virginia, 1776 | 2 shillings 6 pence |
| Tooth Powder | The Pennsylvania Gazette (1776) | Bottle of British Tooth-powder and Tincture Said to take foulness of teeth and gums  Philadelphia, Pennsylvania, 1776 | 2 shillings 6 pence |
| Toothache Powder | The Pennsylvania Gazette (1776) | Bottle of Toothache powder sold in Philadelphia, Pennsylvania, 1776 | 5 shillings |
| Treatment | Joseph I. Waring, A History of Medicine in South Carolina, 1670-1825 (1980) | Cost for a doctor to provide blistering plasters (cost around 1792) | 2 shillings 4 pence |

## Music

| Item | Data Source | Description | Price |
|------|-------------|-------------|-------|
| Fiddle | Inventory of Isaac Walker (1797) | Fiddle in Prince George County, Maryland, 1797 | 1 pound 2 shillings 6 pence |
| String | Inventory of Isaac Walker (1797) | Knots Fiddle String in Prince George County, Maryland, 1797 | 7½ pence |

## Other

| Item | Data Source | Description | Price |
|------|-------------|-------------|-------|
| Bell | Inventory of Isaac Walker (1797) | House Bell with appendages in Prince George County, Maryland, 1797 | 11 shillings 3 pence |
| Book | Inventory of Doctor Nicholas Flood (1776) | Memo Book in Richmond County, Virginia, 1776 | 1 shillings 6 pence |
| Bottle | Inventory of John Young (1790) | Wood bottle in Plymouth, Massachusetts, 1790 | $0.33 |
| Cask | Inventory of John Young (1790) | Beer cask in Plymouth, Massachusetts, 1790 | $0.25 |
| Child Support | Minutes of Marlboro General Court Sessions (1786) | Annual child support payment charged to prevent a bastard child charged to Marlboro Parish | 9 pounds 4 shillings |
| Coffin | Winthrop Gardiner Jr. Collection | Coffin made in New York, 1792 | 12 shillings |
| Corks | Inventory of Doctor Nicholas Flood (1776) | Small barrel of corks in Richmond County, Virginia, 1776 | 15 shillings |
| Feather | Inventory of John Baynes (1790) | One Ostrich Feather in Prince George County, Maryland, 1790 | 10 shillings |
| Fountain Pen | Inventory of Doctor Nicholas Flood (1776) | Fountain pin & Case in Richmond County, Virginia, 1776 | 6 pence |

| Item | Data Source | Description | Price |
|------|-------------|-------------|-------|
| Funnel | Inventory of Richard Mitchell (1781) | Large Tin Funnel in Lancaster County, Virginia, 1781 | 6 pence |
| Glass | Inventory of Doctor Nicholas Flood (1776) | A perspective Glass in Richmond County, Virginia, 1776 | 10 shillings |
| Glass | Inventory of Doctor Nicholas Flood (1776) | One Box Containing 38 pains of Glass 11 by 9 in Richmond County, Virginia, 1776 | 2 pounds 8 shillings |
| Ink Case | Inventory of Doctor Nicholas Flood (1776) | Pocket Ink Case in Richmond County, Virginia, 1776 | 2 shillings 6 pence |
| Ink Pot | Inventory of Isaac Walker (1797) | Brass Ink pot in Prince George County, Maryland, 1797 | 1 shilling |
| Ink Powder | Inventory of John Baynes (1790) | Package of ink powder in Prince George County, Maryland, 1790 | 5 pence |
| Journal | Inventory of Isaac Walker (1797) | Blank Journal in Prince George County, Maryland, 1797 | 19 shillings |
| Key | Inventory of Isaac Walker (1797) | Steel key in Prince George County, Maryland, 1797 | 11 pence |
| Knife | Inventory of Isaac Walker (1797) | Clasp knife in Prince George County, Maryland, 1797 | 11½ pence |
| Letter Case | Kitman, George Washington's Expense Account (1970) | Leather letter-case purchased by Washington from Robert Aitken Philadelphia, 1775 | 3 pounds |
| Lottery Ticket | United States Lottery Ticket (1776) | Lottery tickey issued by Contential Congress - United States Lottery - Call the Fourth - Ther Bearer of this ticket will be entitled to such Prize as shall belong thereto in the Fourth Class of the Lottery of the United States, agreeable to a Resolution of Congress, 1776 | $40.00 |
| Microscope | Inventory of Doctor Nicholas Flood (1776) | Solar Microscope & Book in Richmond County, Virginia, 1776 | 5 pounds |
| Money Book | Inventory of Doctor Nicholas Flood (1776) | Small money book in Richmond County, Virginia, 1776 | 1 pound |
| Money Purse | Inventory of Isaac Walker (1797) | Money Purse in Prince George County, Maryland, 1797 | 4 shillings 6 pence |
| Oyster Tongs | Inventory of Richard Mitchell (1781) | Pair of oyster tongs in Lancaster County, Virginia, 1781 | 3 shillings |
| Paint | Inventory of William Howell (1784) | One Cag of Paint in Kershaw, South Carolina, 1784 | 16 shillings 8 pence |
| Paper | Inventory of Doctor Nicholas Flood (1776) | Quire bro Paper in Richmond County, Virginia, 1776 | 6 pence |

## Based Upon the British Currency System

| Year | Pound in 2002 US Dollars | Shilling in 2002 US Dollars | Pence in 2002 US Dollars |
|------|--------------------------|------------------------------|---------------------------|
| 1775 | $144.00 | $7.20 | $0.60 |
| 1780 | $168.00 | $8.40 | $0.70 |
| 1785 | $144.00 | $7.20 | $0.60 |
| 1790 | $144.00 | $7.20 | $0.60 |
| 1795 | $120.00 | $6.00 | $0.50 |
| 1799 | $120.00 | $6.00 | $0.50 |

*Calculations are approximate values based upon economic historical data*

| Item | Data Source | Description | Price |
|---|---|---|---|
| Pen | Inventory of Doctor Nicholas Flood (1776) | Fountain pen in Richmond County, Virginia, 1776 | 6 pence |
| Pen Knife | Inventory of Isaac Walker (1797) | Pen knife in Prince George County, Maryland, 1797 | 1 shilling 3 pence |
| Pencil | Inventory of Doctor Nicholas Flood (1776) | Black lead pencil in Richmond County, Virginia, 1776 | 6 pence |
| Reading Glass | Inventory of Doctor Nicholas Flood (1776) | Reading glass in Richmond County, Virginia, 1776 | 3 shillings |
| School | Horance F. Rudisill, Saint David's Society | Contribution provided by St David's Society to establish a school | 9000 pounds |
| Shells | Inventory of Doctor Nicholas Flood (1776) | Three coconut shells in Richmond County, Virginia, 1776 | 5 shillings |
| Speaking Trumpet | Inventory of Richard Mitchell (1781) | Speaking Trumpet in Lancaster County, Virginia, 1781 | 6 pounds |
| Spectacles | Inventory of Doctor Nicholas Flood (1776) | Pair of Temple Spectacles in Richmond County, Virginia, 1776 | 3 shillings |
| Spectacles | Inventory of Richard Mitchell (1781) | Pair of Temple Spectacles in Lancaster County, Virginia, 1781 | 15 shillings |
| Spy Glass | Inventory of Doctor Nicholas Flood (1776) | Spy Glass in Richmond County, Virginia, 1776 | 15 shillings |
| Treaty | American Heritage (1958) | Annual annuities agreed in the Treaty of Greenville between the US Government and the Indian population, 1795 | $9,500.00 |
| Umbrella | Inventory of Isaac Walker (1797) | Umbrella in Prince George County, Maryland, 1797 | 1 pound 2 shillings 6 pence |
| Walking Stick | Inventory of Doctor Nicholas Flood (1776) | Walking stick in Richmond County, Virginia, 1776 | 12 shillings 6 pence |

## Publications

| Item | Data Source | Description | Price |
|---|---|---|---|
| Bible | Inventory of Doctor Nicholas Flood (1776) | Large family Bible in Richmond County, Virginia, 1776 | 1 pound 10 shillings |
| Bible | Inventory of James Adams, Sr. (1793) | School Bible in New Castle County, Delaware, 1793 | 4 shillings |
| Bible | Inventory of James Adams, Sr. (1793) | Pocket Bible in New Castle County, Delaware, 1793 | 6 shillings |
| Book | Inventory of Doctor Nicholas Flood (1776) | The History of China - Two Volumes, in Richmond County, Virginia, 1776 | 1 pound 10 shillings |
| Book | Inventory of Doctor Nicholas Flood (1776) | Berklays Naval History of Britian - One Volume, in Richmond County, Virginia, 1776 | 1 pound |
| Book | Inventory of Doctor Nicholas Flood (1776) | Puffendore's Laws of Natures & Nations - One Volume, in Richmond County, Virginia, 1776 | 10 shillings |
| Book | Inventory of Rev. Thomas Ainger (1797) | Dictionary in New Castle County, Delaware, 1797 | $0.50 |
| Book | Inventory of Rev. Thomas Ainger (1797) | Hymn book in New Castle County, Delaware, 1797 | $0.50 |
| Book | Inventory of Daniel Diman (1798) | Barnards Life & Journal | $1.00 |
| Magazine | Inventory of Daniel Diman (1798) | Evangelical Magazine found in Plymouth, Massachusetts, 1798 | $0.75 |
| Pamphlet | Inventory of Doctor Nicholas Flood (1776) | Octavair, a medical & chirergical pamphlet, in Richmond County, Virginia, 1776 | 1 shilling |
| Pamphlet | Inventory of James Adams, Sr. (1793) | Aporisms pamphlets in New Castle County, Delaware, 1793 | 1¾ pence |
| Pamphlet | Inventory of James Adams, Sr. (1793) | Plain Planter in pamphlet in New Castle County, Delaware, 1793 | 2 pence |

| Item | Data Source | Description | Price |
|---|---|---|---|
| Pamphlet | Inventory of James Adams, Sr. (1793) | Geography in New Castle County, Delaware, 1793 | 1 pence |
| Pamphlet | Inventory of James Adams, Sr. (1793) | Descriptions of Virtuous Women in New Castle County, Delaware, 1793 | ½ Penny |
| Pamphlet | Inventory of James Adams, Sr. (1793) | Baptism of Believers in New Castle County, Delaware, 1793 | 3 pence |
| Sheet | Inventory of James Adams, Sr. (1793) | Family Prayers in sheets in New Castle County, Delaware, 1793 | 2 shillings 3¼ pence |
| Testament | Calland's Account Book - Captain James Robert's Account (1784) | One Testament | 2 shillings 4 pence |

## Real Estate

| Item | Data Source | Description | Price |
|---|---|---|---|
| Construction | Maud Carter Clement, History of Pittsylvania County Virginia (1929) | Cost to constructed a court house of brick with tall white collumns in front in 1782 | 4,000 lbs of tobacco |
| Land | Milner, Oxford History of the American West | Price per acre sold to the Ohio Company of Associates who purchased 35 million acres in 1787 | $0.09 |
| Land | Milner, Oxford History of the American West | Price per acre sold in western New York when state sold 5 million acres in 1792 | $0.20 |
| Land | Milner, Oxford History of the American West | Price of one acre in the Northwest Terriority in 1796 | $2.00 |
| Ledford Estate | Will of William Ledford, (1796) | Total worth of entire Ledford estate in Botetourt County, Virginia, 1796 | 888 pounds, 12 shillings, 8 pence |
| Property | Estate of John Twitty (1786) | Price of 440 acres in Marlboro, South Carolina on the Pee Dee River near the falls of Hicks Creek | 2000 pounds |
| Rent | Claim Records of Pittsylvania County, Virginia (1785) | Three months rent of Harrison house, beds and etc. for the use of the General Hospital for Contential Army | 35 pounds |
| Rent | Claim Records of Pittsylvania County, Virginia (1785) | Three months rent of C Perkins house, beds and etc. for the use of the General Hospital for Contential Army | 40 pounds |
| Rent | Claim Records of Pittsylvania County, Virginia (1785) | Three months rent of P Perkins house, beds and ect, for the use of the General Hospital for Contential Army | 50 pounds |

## Based Upon the British Currency System

| Year | Pound in 2002 US Dollars | Shilling in 2002 US Dollars | Pence in 2002 US Dollars |
|---|---|---|---|
| 1775 | $144.00 | $7.20 | $0.60 |
| 1780 | $168.00 | $8.40 | $0.70 |
| 1785 | $144.00 | $7.20 | $0.60 |
| 1790 | $144.00 | $7.20 | $0.60 |
| 1795 | $120.00 | $6.00 | $0.50 |
| 1799 | $120.00 | $6.00 | $0.50 |

*Calculations are approximate values based upon economic historical data*

| Item | Data Source | Description | Price |
|---|---|---|---|
| **Servant** | | | |
| Indentured Servant | Inventory of James Adams, Sr. (1793) | Alexander Kilpatrick - an apprentice in New Castle County, Delaware, 1793 | 5 pounds |
| Indentured Servant | Inventory of James Adams, Sr. (1793) | Mary Kilpatrick - apprentice girl in New Castle County, Delaware, 1793 | 1 pound |
| Slave | Inventory of Doctor Nicholas Flood (1776) | Fanny & Child in Richmond County, Virginia, 1776 | 60 pounds |
| Slave | Inventory of Elizabeth Chappell (1782) | Negro Wench Jane in Kershaw, South Carolina, 1782 | 77 pounds |
| Slave | Inventory of Hermon Kinseler (1783) | One Negro Wench in Kershaw, South Carolina, 1783 | 138 pounds |
| Slave | Inventory of Margaret Ball (1783) | Negro Man Harry in Lancaster County, Virginia, 1783 | 70 pounds |
| Slave | Inventory of Margaret Ball (1783) | Cate an old Wench in Lancaster County, Virginia, 1783 | 10 pounds |
| Slave | Inventory of John Baynes (1790) | Jenny 70 years in Prince George County, Maryland, 1790 | 5 pounds |
| Slave | Inventory of John Baynes (1790) | Milly 25 years in Prince George County, Maryland, 1790 | 45 pounds |
| Slave | Inventory of John Baynes (1790) | Rachel 2 years in Prince George County, Maryland, 1790 | 12 pounds 10 shillings |
| Slave | Inventory of John Baynes (1790) | W Haven 40 years in Prince George County, Maryland, 1790 | 100 pounds |
| Slave | Inventory of John Baynes (1790) | Ben 25 years in Prince George County, Maryland, 1790 | 45 pounds |
| Slave | Inventory of Isaac Walker (1797) | Negro Jack to be free by Will in 5 years from Mr Walkers death, Prince George County, Maryland, 1797 | 40 pounds |
| Slave | Inventory of Isaac Walker (1797) | Mulatto George about 2 years of age - Slave for Life - son of Henny, Prince George County, Maryland, 1797 | 15 pounds |
| **Tobacco Products** | | | |
| Box | Inventory of Isaac Walker (1797) | Tortoise Shell Tobacco Box in Prince George County, Maryland, 1797 | 3 shillings 9 pence |
| Snuff | Inventory of Isaac Walker (1797) | Large bottle of Snuff in Prince George County, Maryland, 1797 | 3 shillings 6 pence |
| Snuff Bottle | Inventory of Doctor Nicholas Flood (1776) | Snuff bottle in Richmond County, Virginia, 1776 | 15 shillings |
| Snuff Box | Inventory of Isaac Walker (1797) | Snuff Box in Prince George County, Maryland, 1797 | 10 pence |
| Tobacco | Economic and Social History of New England, 1620-1789 by William Weeden | Pound of Tobacco in New England, 1775 | 4 shillings |
| **Trade Equipment & Tools** | | | |
| Anvil | Inventory of John Young (1790) | Anvil in Plymouth, Massachusetts, 1790 | $3.00 |
| Auger | Inventory of John Riley (1795) | Screw augur in Newberry, South Carolina, 1795 | 9 pence |
| Ballots | Inventory of James Adams, Sr. (1793) | Six reams of ballots in New Castle County, Delaware, 1793 | 3 pounds |
| Bank | Inventory of James Adams, Sr. (1793) | Bank in New Castle County, Delaware, 1793 | 7 shillings 6 pence |
| Bellows | Inventory of John Young (1790) | Pair Smith's bellows in Plymouth, Massachusetts, 1790 | $15.00 |
| Bench | Inventory of James Adams, Sr. (1793) | Old work bench in New Castle County, Delaware, 1793 | 6 pence |

| Item | Data Source | Description | Price |
|------|-------------|-------------|-------|
| Blacksmith's Shop | Inventory of Richard Mitchell (1781) | An anvil, bellows, 2 sledge hammers, 2 hand hammers, a large vice, a hand vice, 3 screw plates, 3 pair of tongs, a shovel & poker, pair of nippers, a small hammer, 2 rasps and parcel of old files in Lancaster County, Virginia, 1781 | 15 pounds |
| Blade | Inventory of Isaac Walker (1797) | Awl Blade in Prince George County, Maryland, 1797 | 2½ pence |
| Can | Inventory of James Adam, Sr. (1793) | Pair of print shop cans in New Castle County, Delaware, 1793 | 11 shillings 3 pence |
| Chisel | Inventory of Doctor Nicholas Flood (1776) | Sockett Chizzel in Richmond County, Virginia, 1776 | 1 shilling |
| Chisel | Inventory of Doctor Nicholas Flood (1776) | Stone Chizzell in Richmond County, Virginia, 1776 | 9 pence |
| Compass & Chains | Inventory of Doctor Nicholas Flood (1776) | Surveying Compasses & 2 Chains in Richmond County, Virginia, 1776 | 1 pound 10 shillings |
| Copy Plate | Inventory of James Adam, Sr. (1793) | Copy plate in New Castle County, Delaware, 1793 | 10 pence |
| Cutting Plow | Inventory of James Adam, Sr. (1793) | Bookbinders cutting plow in New Castle County, Delaware, 1793 | 4 shillings 6 pence |
| Cutting Press | Inventory of James Adam, Sr. (1793) | Bookbinders cutting press in New Castle County, Delaware, 1793 | 10 shillings |
| Fishing Line | Inventory of Doctor Nicholas Flood (1776) | Small fishing line in Richmond County, Virginia, 1776 | 6 pence |
| Fishing Line | Inventory of Doctor Nicholas Flood (1776) | Large fishing line in Richmond County, Virginia, 1776 | 1 shilling |
| Flax Wheel | Inventory of Richard Mitchell (1781) | Flax wheel in Lancaster County, Virginia, 1781 | 10 shillings |
| Fonts | Inventory of James Adam, Sr. (1793) | 2 fonts of type pica & long in New Castle County, Delaware, 1793 | 15 pounds |
| Fonts | Inventory of James Adam, Sr. (1793) | 1 font brevior &c in New Castle County, Delaware, 1793 | 70 pounds |
| Frame | Inventory of James Adam, Sr. (1793) | Double frame in print shop in New Castle County, Delaware, 1793 | 11 shillings 3 pence |
| Galleys | Inventory of James Adam, Sr. (1793) | Three galleys located in a print shop in New Castle County, Delaware, 1793 | 3 shillings |
| Hammer | Inventory of John Young (1790) | Hammer in Plymouth, Massachusetts, 1790 | $0.25 |
| Indenter | Inventory of Rev. Thomas Ainger (1797) | Indenter in New Castle County, Delaware, 1797 | $2.00 |

### Based Upon the British Currency System

| Year | Pound in 2002 US Dollars | Shilling in 2002 US Dollars | Pence in 2002 US Dollars |
|------|------|------|------|
| 1775 | $144.00 | $7.20 | $0.60 |
| 1780 | $168.00 | $8.40 | $0.70 |
| 1785 | $144.00 | $7.20 | $0.60 |
| 1790 | $144.00 | $7.20 | $0.60 |
| 1795 | $120.00 | $6.00 | $0.50 |
| 1799 | $120.00 | $6.00 | $0.50 |

*Calculations are approximate values based upon economic historical data*

| Item | Data Source | Description | Price |
|------|-------------|-------------|-------|
| Ink | Inventory of James Adams, Sr. (1793) | Seven pounds of ink in New Castle County, Delaware, 1793 | 1 pound 17 shillings 6 pence |
| Instruments | Inventory of Doctor Nicholas Flood (1776) | Sett of plotting instruments in Richmond County, Virginia, 1776 | 10 shillings |
| Iron | Inventory of Richard Mitchell (1781) | Pound of bar iron in Lancaster County, Virginia, 1781 | 4 pence |
| Knife | Inventory of Isaac Walker (1797) | Shoe knife in Prince George County, Maryland, 1797 | 4½ pence |
| Leather | Inventory of John Riley (1795) | Piece of tanned leather in Newberry, South Carolina, 1795 | 3 shillings |
| Line | Inventory of Doctor Nicholas Flood (1776) | 4½ Knotts Drum Line in Richmond County, Virginia, 1776 | 13 shillings 6 pence |
| Loom | Inventory of Margaret Ball (1783) | Weavers Loom & Geer in Lancaster County, Virginia, 1783 | 1 pound |
| Magnet | Inventory of Doctor Nicholas Flood (1776) | Artificial Magnet in Richmond County, Virginia, 1776 | 6 pence |
| Nails | Inventory of Doctor Nicholas Flood (1776) | 100 flatt headed four-penny nails in Richmond County, Virginia, 1776 | 4½ pence |
| Nails | Inventory of Doctor Nicholas Flood (1776) | 1,000 slender two-penny nails in Richmond County, Virginia, 1776 | 2 shillings |
| Nails | Inventory of Doctor Nicholas Flood (1776) | 1,000 brass nails in Richmond County, Virginia, 1776 | 2 shillings |
| Paper | Inventory of James Adams, Sr. (1793) | Ream demi printing paper in New Castle County, Delaware, 1793 | 12 shillings 6 pence |
| Paper | Inventory of James Adams, Sr. (1793) | Ream wrapping paper in New Castle County, Delaware, 1793 | 4 shillings |
| Plane | Inventory of John Riley (1795) | Plane in Newberry, South Carolina, 1795 | 1 shilling 2 pence |
| Press | Inventory of James Adams, Sr. (1793) | Printers press in New Castle County, Delaware, 1793 | 18 pounds |
| Rivets | Inventory of Rev. Thomas Ainger (1797) | Dozen rivets in New Castle County, Delaware, 1797 | $0.36 |
| Shaving Horse | Inventory of Rev. Thomas Ainger (1797) | Shaving horse & bench in New Castle County, Delaware, 1797 | $0.75 |
| Shears | Inventory of James Adams, Sr. (1793) | Large shears in print shop in New Castle County, Delaware, 1793 | 2 shillings 6 pence |
| Shears | Inventory of James Adams, Sr. (1793) | Pair of printer's bookbinder shears in New Castle County, Delaware, 1793 | 7 shillings 6 pence |
| Skin | Inventory of Doctor Nicholas Flood (1776) | Lambs Skin in Richmond County, Virginia, 1776 | 1 pound |
| Skin | Inventory of John Riley (1795) | Fox skin in Newberry, South Carolina, 1795 | 1 shilling 6 pence |
| Skin | Inventory of John Riley (1795) | Mink skin in Newberry, South Carolina, 1795 | 13 shillings |
| Skin | Inventory of John Riley (1795) | Rackoon skin in Newberry, South Carolina, 1795 | 7 shillings |
| Skins | Inventory of James Adams, Sr. (1793) | 16½ dozen sheep skins in a printing shop in New Castle County, Delaware, 1793 | 10 pounds 11 shillings 3 pence |
| Slay | Inventory of Richard Mitchell (1781) | Weavers slay in Lancaster County, Virginia, 1781 | 5 shillings |
| Staves | Inventory of Rev. Thomas Ainger (1797) | 1000 cast hoop staves in New Castle County, Delaware, 1797 | $36.68 |
| Staves | Inventory of Rev. Thomas Ainger (1797) | 100 cast head staves in New Castle County, Delaware, 1797 | $5.37 |
| Steel | Inventory of Elizabeth Chappell (1782) | Pound of steel in Kershaw, South Carolina, 1782 | 1 shilling 3 pence |

| Item | Data Source | Description | Price |
|---|---|---|---|
| Sticks | Inventory of James Adam, Sr. (1793) | Two print shop composing sticks in New Castle County, Delaware, 1793 | 15 shillings |
| Tacks | Inventory of John Baynes (1790) | Gross of shoe tacks in Prince George County, Maryland, 1790 | 5½ pence |
| Thimbles | Inventory of John Baynes (1790) | Dozen Taylors Thimbles in Prince George County, Maryland, 1790 | 3 shillings 6 pence |
| Thread | Inventory of John Baynes (1790) | Pound of shoe thread in Prince George County, Maryland, 1790 | 1 shilling 2½ pence |
| Tools | Inventory of Doctor Nicholas Flood (1776) | Parcel of Carpenters tools in Richmond County, Virginia, 1776 | 15 shillings |
| Tools | Inventory of John Flowers (1790) | Shoemakers tools in Darlington, South Carolina, 1790 | 6 shillings |
| Trowel | Inventory of Doctor Nicholas Flood (1776) | Masons Trowel for laying Bricks in Richmond County, Virginia, 1776 | 1 shilling |
| Trowel | Inventory of Doctor Nicholas Flood (1776) | Masons Trowel for Plasterring in Richmond County, Virginia, 1776 | 1 shilling 3 pence |
| Trusshoops | Inventory of Rev. Thomas Ainger (1797) | 2 sets round ash trusshoops in New Castle County, Delaware, 1797 | $3.50 |
| Types | Inventory of James Adam, Sr. (1793) | 43 types of pica & long in New Castle County, Delaware, 1793 | 160 pounds |
| Vise | Inventory of Doctor Nicholas Flood (1776) | Smiths Vice in Richmond County, Virginia, 1776 | 1 pound 10 shillings |
| Vise | Inventory of John Riley (1795) | Hand Vice in Newberry, South Carolina, 1795 | 12 shillings 9 pence |
| Wheel | Inventory of Richard Mitchell (1781) | Weaver's quill wheel in Lancaster County, Virginia, 1781 | 2 shillings 4 pence |

### Travel & Transportation

| Item | Data Source | Description | Price |
|---|---|---|---|
| Canoe | Claim Records of Arbemarle Barracks (1781) | Cost of a canoe impressed for Continental use | 5 pounds |
| Carriage | Inventory of Daniel Adams (1797) | Carriage in New Castle County, Delaware, 1797 | $6.00 |
| Freight Expense | Calland's Account Book (1784) | Cost paid to Captian Francis Graves for 2400 pounds of freight | 4 pounds 16 shillings |
| Freight Expense | Maud Carter Clement, History of Pittsylvania County Virginia (1929) | Charge for carrying one hogshead of tobacco from Staunton River to Manchester Virginia in 1784 | 3 pounds 3 shillings 7 pence |

## Based Upon the British Currency System

| Year | Pound in 2002 US Dollars | Shilling in 2002 US Dollars | Pence in 2002 US Dollars |
|---|---|---|---|
| 1775 | $144.00 | $7.20 | $0.60 |
| 1780 | $168.00 | $8.40 | $0.70 |
| 1785 | $144.00 | $7.20 | $0.60 |
| 1790 | $144.00 | $7.20 | $0.60 |
| 1795 | $120.00 | $6.00 | $0.50 |
| 1799 | $120.00 | $6.00 | $0.50 |

*Calculations are approximate values based upon economic historical data*

| Item | Data Source | Description | Price |
|---|---|---|---|
| Passage | Kitman, George Washington's Expense Account (1970) | Cost to send a recruiting officer to England from the American colonies, 1775 | 2 pounds 10 shillings |
| Sleigh | Inventory of Daniel Adams (1797) | Sleigh in New Castle County, Delaware, 1797 | $8.00 |
| Freight Expense | Receipt of Thomas Silk (1798) | Transportation of a parcel of stones from Pittsburg to the Senaca Nation as a gift from the Society of Friends at Philadelphia | $133.97 |
| Wagon | Inventory of William Oneall (1789) | Wagon & Geers in Newberry, South Carolina, 1789 | 18 pounds |
| Wagon | Inventory of John Riley (1795) | Truck Waggon in Newberry, South Carolina, 1795 | 4 pounds |
| Wheels | Inventory of Doctor Nicholas Flood (1776) | Pair new Cart Wheels in Richmond County, Virginia, 1776 | 1 pound 5 shillings |
| Wheels | Inventory of Doctor Nicholas Flood (1776) | Pair large Charot wheels in Richmond County, Virginia, 1776 | 2 pounds |
| Wheels | Inventory of Doctor Nicholas Flood (1776) | Pair Small Charot Wheels in Richmond County, Virginia, 1776 | 1 pound |
| Cart | Inventory of John Young (1790) | Cart in Plymouth, Massachusetts, 1790 | $20.00 |

# MISCELLANY 1775-1799

## Reward for General George Washington's Lost Pistol, 1776

From the General Orders of March 9, 1776

His Excellency the General lost one of his pistols yesterday upon Dorchester Neck. Whoever will bring it to him or leave it with General Thomas shall receive two dollars reward and no questions asked; it is a screwed barreled pistol mounted with silver and a head resembling that of a pug dog at the butt.

*Source: Marvin Kitman,* George Washington's Account Book *(1970)*

Reason and free inquiry are the only effectual agents against error . . . . They are the natural enemies of error, and of error only . . . . If [free enquiry] be restrained now, the present corruptions will be protected, and new ones encouraged.

*Thomas Jefferson:* Notes on Virginia, *1782*

*The preservation of the sacred fire of liberty and the destiny of the republican model of government are justly considered . . . deeply, . . . finally, staked on the experiment entrusted to the hands of the American people.*

*President George Washington, First Inaugural Address, Apr. 30, 1789*

*I know not what course others may take, but as for me, give me liberty, or give me death.*

*Patrick Henry, Virginia Convention, March 23, 1775*

*It has been observed that a pure democracy if it were practicable would be the most perfect government. Experience has proved that no position is more false than this. The ancient democracies in which the people themselves deliberated never possessed one good feature of government. Their very character was tyranny; their figure deformity.*

*Alexander Hamilton, Speech on 21 June 1788 urging ratification of the Constitution in New York*

## Confession of a Continental Private, 1776

The soldiers at New York had an idea that the enemy, when they took possession of the town, would make a general seizure of all property that could be of use to them as military or commissary stores. Hence they imagined that it was no injury to supply themselves when they thought they could do so with impunity . . . .

I was stationed in Stone Street . . . . Directly opposite to my quarters was a wine cellar; there were in the cellar at this time several pipes of Madeira wine. By some means the soldiers had "melt it out." Some of the men had, at mid-day taken the iron grating from a window in the backyard, and one hand entered the cellar and, by means of a powder-horn divested of its bottom, had supplied himself with wine, and was helping his comrades through the window with a "delicious draught" when the owner of the wine having discovered what they were about, very wisely, as it seemed, came into the street and opened an outer door to the cellar in open view of every passenger. The soldiers quickly filled the cellar, when he, to save his property, proposed to sell it at what he called a cheap rate—I think a dollar a gallon . . . . While the owner was drawing for his purchasers on one side of the cellar, behind him on the other side another set of purchasers were drawing for themselves (with empty flasks found in the corner of the cellar). As it appeared to have a brisk sale, especially in the latter case, I concluded I would take a flask amongst the rest, which I accordingly did, and conveyed it in safety to my room, and went back in the street to see the end.

The owner of the wine soon found out what was going forward on is premises, and began remonstrating, but he preached to the wind. Finding that he could effect nothing with them, he went to Gen. Putnam's quarters, which was not more than three or four rods off. The General immediately repaired in person to the field of action. The soldiers getting word of his approach hurried out into the street when he, mounting himself upon the doorsteps of my quarters, began "haranguing the multitude," threatening to hang every mother's son of them. Whether he was to be the hangman or not, he did not say, but I took every word he said for gospel, and expecting nothing else but to be hanged before the morrow night. I sincerely wished him hanged and out of the way, for fixing himself upon the step of our door; but he soon ended his discourse and come down from his rostrum, and the soldiers dispersed, no doubt much edified.

I got home as soon as the General had left the coast clear, took a draught of the wine, and then flung the flask and the remainder of the wine out the window, from the third story, into the water cistern in the back yard, where it remains to this day for aught I know. However I might have kept it if I had not been in too much haste to free myself from being hanged by General Putnam, or by his order. I never heard any thing further about the wine or being hanged about it; he doubtless forgot it.

*Source: Marvin Kitman,* George Washington's Account Book *(1970)*

## Beware the Ides of March
### (excerpt), Hannah Griffitts

. . . for the sake of Freedom's name,
   (Since British Wisdom scorns repealing,)
Come, sacrifice to Patriot fame,
   And give up Tea, by way of Healing,
This done, within ourselves retreat,
   The Industrious arts of life to follow,
Let the Proud Nabobs storm & fret,
   They Cannot force our lips to swallow.

*Source: Linda K. Kerber,* Women of the Republic *(1980)*

## Account of a Country Doctor (1783)

We lived in the same house with a doctor who, like many country-doctors in America, had all his medicines exposed in the window; his store was very restricted, little besides tartar-emetik, flowers of antimony, tartar, saltpeter, Peruvian bark, and a few other mixtures of sorts. He complained of slow and small pay. As yet there are no medical regulations in America, and if any one thinks his doctor's charge too high it is the custom to submit the matter to some neighboring practitioner, or to several of them, who allow or reduce the amount according to the circumstances or the degree or friendship or spite they have for their colleague. But if injustice is done, the charge can be very easily made good by an affidavit.

*Source: Johann David Schoepf,* Travels in the Confederation, *Edenton, North Carolina, December, 1783*

## Funeral Ceremony, 1789

Funerals take place in the following manner: if the church is too far removed the dead are buried at their home, occasionally also at the home of a good neighbor where then generally a sort of churchyard is formed. If, however, as is usually the case, they are brought to the church, (the regular cemetery) the coffin is first placed before the front door of the house. At the foot of the corpse stands the preacher, and around the coffin, on all sides, the congregation. No invitations to a funeral are sent out. Everybody considers it his duty to come, and indeed on horseback. Then the pastor has a song, or at least a few verses, sung, after which he gives a short address of about eight to ten minutes. Meanwhile the lid of the coffin is removed and the women crowd around uttering a pitiful wail. Then the pastor orders the coffin to be closed and placed in a wagon while the people mount their horses. This after refreshments of bread and rum at the house of the deceased the procession moves to the church. Upon arriving at the church the pastor commands a halt, the corpse is let down from the wagon, a few verses are sung, the coffin is again opened, and while singing the crowd marches by twos to the grave. After the body is lowered a silent prayer is offered and the grave is filled during the singing of a song. Then still continuing their chant they betake themselves to the church where the funeral sermon is given from the pulpit.

*Source: Rev. Mr. Roschen,* German Tracts, 1789

## Runaway Slave Advertisement

Carlisle, Mar 3, 1778. EIGHT DOLLARS REWARD. RUN away from the subscriber living at Carlisle Iron Works, a Mulattoe slave, named Anthony, about 26 years of age, 5 feet 6 or 7 inches high; had on an old blanket coat with brown stripes; buckskin breeches, white woollen stockings and old shoes. Whoever takes up the said slave, so as his master may have him again, shall have the above reward, and reasonable charges, paid by THOMAS MAYBURY

*Source: The Pennsylvania Gazette, May 30, 1778*

## Slave for Sale

TO BE SOLD, A HEALTHY stout Mulatto WENCH, 16 years old; she has had the small-pox and measles, can cook, wash, and do most sorts of house-work. Inquire of Mr. ROBERT WHITE, Tavern-keeper, in Carlisle

*Source: The Pennsylvania Gazette, February 14, 1778*

## Punishment for Desertion, 1780

September 13, 1780

This day the army was paraded & reviewed by his Excellency Genl. Washington and [a] Number of Indian Chifes after which sat on a Genl. Court Martial / Tried a Serjeant for Desertion who was found Guilty & sentenced to be reduced & received 100 Lashes on his naked back.

*Source: Edited by Robert Bray & Paul Bushnell, Diary of a Common Soldier in the American Revolution, 1775-1783 (1978)*

## Punishment for Stealing, 1780

October 1, 1780

This day on Genl. Court Martial tried one Soldier for being drunk on his post & suffering bread to be stole from the Commiserys Stores / found Guilty & sentinced to receive 100 Lashes on his naked back.

*Source: Edited by Robert Bray & Paul Bushnell, Diary of a Common Soldier in the American Revolution, 1775-1783 (1978)*

---

### In Council of Safety.

Philadelphia, December 2, 1776.

*RESOLVED,*

THAT it is the Opinion of this Board, that all the Shops in this City be shut up, that the Schools be broke up, and the Inhabitants engaged solely in providing for the Defence of this City, at this Time of extreme Danger.

*By Order of Council,*

DAVID RITTENHOUSE, Vice-Prefident.

[Philadelphia, Printed by Henry Miller, in Race-ftreet.]

---

## Housing the Family in Connecticut, 1778

I could not help remarking that the houses are all after the same plan [in Connecticut], and what was rather singular, most of them having only the rough timbers that support the building; upon enquiry I found, that when a man builds a house, he leaves it in this state till his son marries, when he fits it up for his family, and the father and son live under one roof, as though there were two distinct houses; but as the houses are entirely compleat on the outside, the windows all glazed, they have the appearance of being finished, but on entering a house, you cannot help lamenting that the owner was unable to complete it.

*Source: Thomas Anburey, Travels Through the Interior Parts of America, ed. William Harding Carter (1923)*

## Treaty with the Shawnee, 1786

*Articles of a Treaty concluded at the Mouth of the Great Miami, on the North-western Bank of the Ohio, the thirty-first day of January, one thousand seven hundred arid eighty-six, between the Commissioners Plenipotentiary of the United States of America, of the one Part, and the Chiefs and Warriors of the Shawnoe Nation, of the other Part.*

ARTICLE 1.

THREE hostages shall be immediately delivered to the Commissioners, to remain in the possession of the United States until all the prisoners, white and black, taken in the late war from among the citizens of the United States, by the Shawanoe nation, or by any other Indian or Indians residing in their towns, shall be restored.

ARTICLE II.

The Shawanoe nation do acknowledge the United States to be the sole and absolute sovereigns of all the territory ceded to them by treaty of peace, made between them and the King of Great Britain the fourteenth day of January, one thousand seven hundred and eighty-four.

ARTICLE III.

If any Indian or Indians of the Shawanoe nation, or any other Indian or Indians residing in their towns, shall commit murder or robbery on, or do any injury to the citizens of the United States, or any of them, that nation shall deliver such offender or offenders to the officer commending the nearest post of the United States, to be punished according to the ordinances of Congress; and in like manner, any citizen of the United States, who shall do an injury to any Indian of the Shawanoe nation, or to any other Indian or Indians residing in their towns, and under their protection, shall be punished according to the laws of the United States.

ARTICLE IV.

The Shawanoe nation having knowledge of the intention of any nation or body of Indians to make war on the citizens of the United States, or of their counselling together for that purpose, and neglecting to give information thereof to the commanding officer of the nearest post of the United States, shall be considered as parties in such war and be punished accordingly: and the United States shall in like manner inform the Shawanoes of any injury designed against them.

ARTICLE V.

The United States do grant peace to the Shawanoe nation, and do receive them into their friendship and protection.

ARTICLE VI.

The United Sates do allot to the Shawanoe nation, lands within their territory to live and hunt upon, beginning at the south line of the lands allotted to the Wiandots and Delaware nations, at the place where the main branch of the Great Miami, which falls into the Ohio, intersects said line; then down the river Miami, to the fork of that river, next below the old fort which was taken by the French in one thousand seven hundred and fifty-two; thence due west to the river de la Panse; then down that river to the river Wabash, beyond which lines none of the citizens of the United States shall settle, nor disturb the Shawanoes in their settlement and possessions; and the Shawanoes do relinquish to the United States, all title, or presence of title, they ever had to the lands east, west and south, of the east, west and south lines before described.

ARTICLE VII.

If any citizen or citizens of the United States, shall presume to settle upon the lands allotted to the Shawanoes by this treaty, he or they shall be put out of the protection of the United States.

*Source: Avalon Project at Yale Law School*

## Diary of 16-year-old Elizabeth Fuller, Princeton, Massachusetts, October 1792

**Oct. 2**  I wove to-day.

**Oct. 3**  Cold. I wove.

**Oct. 4**  I wove to-day. Pleasant.

**Oct. 5**  I wove to-day.

**Oct. 6**  Muster at Lancaster. John Allen here.

**Oct. 7**  I wove.

**Oct. 8**  I wove.

**Oct. 9**  Sabbath. I went to church.

**Oct. 10**  I wove to-day.

**Oct. 11**  I wove A.M. Miss Polly Mirick & Miss Polly Baxter here P.M.

**Oct. 12**  I wove got out the Piece before night 27 yards of it.

**Oct. 13**  My birth day. I am sixteen Years old. How many years have been past by me in thoughtlesness & vanity.

**Oct. 14**  Mr. & Mrs Warren here. Ma is making Pa a Surtout.

**Oct. 15**  I made Pyes to-day.

**Oct. 16**  Mr. Goodridge Preached. Miss Eliza Harris came here, she is to keep us company whilst Ma is gone.

**Oct. 17**  Pa & Ma set out for Sandwich broke the Chaise *(a two-wheeled carriage)* before they got to Lieut. Miricks but got it mended again & pursued their journey.

**Oct. 18**  I spun to-day.

**Oct. 19**  Elisha Brooks & Lucretia & Parmelia Mirick here this eve. Ordination to-day at Gardner.

**Oct. 20**  Cloudy. Nathan Perry here part of the afternoon & evening.

**Oct. 21**  Elisha Brooks here.

**Oct. 22**  Mr. Cutting here.

**Oct. 23**  Sabbath. There came a considerable snow last night, so much that I shall not go to church but Sally is a going. (after Meeting) Sally has got home from Meeting. She went ankle deep in snow & mud all the way. I am glad I had not so much Zeal.

**Oct. 24**  Anna Davis & Ichabod Perry here this eve. Anna took offense at something & went away about eight o'clock, went to Mr. Hasting's till eleven. David stayed and sung with us an hour after she was gone. Nathan Perry here.

**Oct. 25**  Elisha Brooks & John spent the evening here.

**Oct. 26**  Nathan Perry here this morning.

**Oct. 27**  Elisha Brooks & Nathan Cutting here this P.M.–David Perry here this eve to sing with us we had a fine concert.

**Oct. 28**  Sally Gleason, Nancy Hastings, Lucretia Mirick & John Brooks here this eve we Danced, Played, and sung all the evening, had an exceedingly agreeable evening.

**Oct. 29**  Olive Parmenter here a few moments.

**Oct. 30**  Sabbath. Rainy weather we all stayed at home but Timmy.

**Oct. 31**  Timmy went to Mr. Hastings to help Wareham Husk Corn.

*Source: "Diary Kept by Elizabeth Fuller, Daughter of Rev. Timothy Fuller of Princeton," in Francis Everett Blake, History of the Town of Princeton, Vol. I, Narrative (Princeton, Mass.: Published by the Town, 1915)*

# 1800-1824

# Another War, Manufacturing, Self-Sufficiency and Prosperity

## PRESIDENTS

| | |
|---|---|
| John Adams | 1797-1801 |
| Thomas Jefferson | 1801-1809 |
| James Madison | 1809-1817 |
| James Monroe | 1817-1825 |

Thanks to the cost of fighting the revolutionary war, the United States began the new century as a debtor nation. Few in Europe had really expected the young, restless country to survive for this long. Most were waiting for a chance to gain an advantage over it through trade domination or conquest. Even the French, whose money, sailors and arms had played a critical role in the fight against England, assumed a decidedly condescending attitude toward its protégé.

Yet by the turn of the new century, nearly everyone had to acknowledge that the American political "revolution" was working. When the Republicans under the leadership of Thomas Jefferson swept the Federalists, the party of George Washington, from office, the peaceful power shift was hailed as a political first and a model for the world. Just as significant, the event that stripped the aristocratic Federalists of the presidency and their majorities in both Houses of Congress was initiated by America's common folk-farmers and small-town merchants-who banded together for a popular government opposed to the creation of a large standing army, heavy taxes and a federal government that subverted individual liberties.

Still, the upstart nation showed considerable signs of being vulnerable to a world still watching for a misstep. Not only was there a danger of being drawn into the Napoleonic wars raging in Europe, but also, as the century began, America was hardly a financially sound nation. The money supply was no more than $30 million, or less than $6.00 per person. The nation's transportation network was so poorly developed that shipping a ton of goods 3.000 miles from Europe to America's seacoast towns cost $9.00, but to move the same goods 30 miles to the interior of the nation also cost $9.00. Yet, America retained the same brash,

ambitious nature that had ignited the revolt against England. Long-term growth is traditionally dependent on a nation expanding its land area, the exploitation of its natural resources, an increase in the size and quality of its workforce, or the availability of capital. America enthusiastically selected all of the above. Even Jefferson's avowed goal of reducing the size and power of the central government was shelved when Napoleon Bonaparte offered to sell 1.2 million acres in the Louisiana Purchase, doubling the land area of the United States. Jefferson justified the purchase using the same constitutional arguments he had rejected in his disagreements with Alexander Hamilton. America took another leap in 1819 with the purchase of Florida. By 1824, not only land area had increased, but also the population had doubled to more than 10 million.

However, the most tenuous phase of this political experiment known as the United States of America arrived in 1812 with another divisive war with England. For years America had avoided another costly war through a self-imposed trade embargo that forbade land- and sea-borne commerce with foreign nations, virtually eliminating American exports, largely shutting down East Coast seaports, and resulting in falling farm prices, failed industries and widespread unemployment. At the same time, traders and settlers in the West were convinced that England was both arming and inciting the native-Americans against them. War hawks, largely elected from the Western and Southern states, declared that America's rights must be asserted, despite the risks. President James Madison's war message cited British interference with American trade, a blockade of the Eastern seaboard, impressments of American sailors and British-inspired Indian attacks. The two-year struggle resulted in several major battles over ownership of parts of Canada, the British invasion and burning of Washington, DC, and little territorial change. But the intensity of the war of 1812 had a psychological impact on the economy and the nation. Political conversations that insisted that secession was the right of every state virtually vanished and unity took precedence. Even the Federalists' attempts in 1814 to brand the conflict as "Mr. Madison's War" backfired. The Federalists were labeled traitors, and the party never recovered.

One lasting impact of the War of 1812 was the name Uncle Sam, a nickname for the United States. Workers at Samuel Wilson's meat-packing plant in Troy, New York, which supplied provisions to the U.S. Army, joked that the U.S. stamped on the barrels bound for the troops actually stood for their boss Uncle Sam Wilson. The story spread and as time went on government property in general became referred to as "Uncle Sam's."

After the war, American industry grew, driven by new concepts in industrialization and the efficient energy supplied by steam engines, which measured their efficiency in horsepower, or how many horses the machine replaced. Expenditures for new and improved roads, bridges and canals also increased, including the publicly financed Erie Canal in New York State, which dramatically reduced freight charges on internal commerce. Yet economically, the United States was still tethered to Europe. With the shipping lanes liberated, the South could once again send most of its annual 125 million-pound cotton crop to England, whose industries continued to dominate manufacturing. Many American factories failed because they were unable to produce the same quality textiles at a competitive price in this global atmosphere. America then suffered another economic blow in the Panic of 1819 with the collapse of European markets for American export products. This three-year depression revealed deep political and sectional divisions in the United States, marked by bank failure, the halving of farm prices, widespread joblessness and the collapse of Western land prices.

The early 1820s also placed the issue of slavery back on the political table via the Missouri Compromise. The much-debated decision to admit Missouri as a slave state and Maine as a free state calmed the day but was a flimsy band-aid over a festering wound that would not be treated for 40 years. The quarter-century would conclude with the contested election of 1824. Andrew Jackson won the popular vote in a four-way race, but not an electoral majority. In the House of Representatives, Henry Clay threw his support behind John Quincy Adams in a deal widely branded as "a corrupt bargain" that relegated Adams to one term and propelled the election of populist Jackson four years later.

# HISTORICAL SNAPSHOTS 1800-1824

## 1800–1809

### 1800

♦ In the presidential voting, Thomas Jefferson and Aaron Burr tied, forcing the decision into the House of Representatives, which selected Jefferson on the thirty-sixth ballot

♦ The Library of Congress in Washington, DC, was created with a $5,000 allocation

♦ Congress convened for the first time in Washington, DC

♦ The French regained the territory of Louisiana from Spain by secret treaty

♦ The world's population was believed to be 800 million people, double the population in 1500

♦ The population of New York topped 60,000

♦ John Chapman, known as Johnny Appleseed, began planting orchards across western Pennsylvania, Ohio and Indiana

♦ Rev. Mason Locke Weems authored the biography *A History of the Life and Death, Virtues and Exploits of General George Washington*

♦ Alessandro Volta demonstrated an early battery known as an electricity pile

♦ Robert Fulton tested a 20-foot model of his torpedo-armed submarine

♦ The textile industry dramatically expanded in Belgium after Lieven Bauwens smuggled from Britain a working spinning "mule jenny" machine that could be copied

♦ Martha Washington set all her slaves free

### 1801

♦ Thomas Jefferson became the first president to be inaugurated in Washington, DC

♦ The North African state of Tripoli declared war on the United States in a dispute over safe passage of merchant vessels through the Mediterranean

♦ The District of Columbia was placed under the jurisdiction of Congress

♦ Thomas Jefferson proposed rules for proper conduct in the Senate, including, "No one is to disturb another in his speech by hissing, coughing, spitting, speaking, or whispering to another."

♦ A nine-day revival at the Cane Ridge Presbyterian Church in Bourbon County, Kentucky, drew 20,000 people

♦ Kentucky banned dueling

♦ *The New York Evening Post* was first published, with Alexander Hamilton as its editor

♦ Haitian slaves under Toussaint L'Ouverture seized power in Haiti and overthrew French control

♦ The Union Jack became the official flag of the United Kingdom of Great Britain

♦ Rembrandt Peale painted his brother's portrait *Rubens Peale with Geranium*

♦ Thomas Bruce, British ambassador to the Ottoman Empire, shipped the Parthenon's 2,500-year-old bas-reliefs to England

♦ Napoleon Bonaparte opened the Louvre to the public

## 1802

- Congress repealed all taxes except for those on salt, leaving the government dependent on import tariffs
- The *Richmond Virginia Recorder* published a story accusing President Thomas Jefferson of having a relationship with the slave Sally Hemmings
- Eleuthere Irenee du Pont de Nemours set up a saltpeter mill in Wilmington, Delaware that would become America's largest black-powder plant
- The United States Military Academy opened its doors at West Point, New York
- The U.S. Army Corps of Engineers was re-established
- The first non-Indian settlement in Oklahoma was created
- John Dalton introduced atomic theory into chemistry
- England began to regulate child labor
- Great Britain declared war on Napoleon's France; an English income tax was established to finance the war
- Napoleon Bonaparte was proclaimed "Consul for Life" by the French Senate

## 1803

- President Thomas Jefferson purchased the Louisiana Territory from France for about $15 million to double the size of the United States territory
- The government sponsored a transcontinental expedition under the leadership of Captain Merewether Lewis and Lieutenant William Clark
- John Dalton, British chemist and physicist, described the grouping together of atoms to form units called molecules
- The French Academy of Sciences insisted that meteorites could not exist because no specimens had been found
- Haiti became the first independent black republic
- The Supreme Court ruled itself the final interpreter of constitutional issues in *Marbury v. Madison*
- Ohio became the seventeenth state

224

## 1804

- Thomas Jefferson was re-elected president; George Clinton, the governor of New York, was elected vice president
- Congress ordered the removal of Indians east of the Mississippi to Louisiana
- The 12th Amendment was ratified, requiring electors to vote separately for the president and vice president.
- John Quincy Adams published his travel book, *Letters on Silesia*
- Fort Dearborn was erected on the Chicago River on the site of present-day downtown Chicago
- Ohio legislature passed laws restricting the movement of free blacks
- The French civil code, the "Code Napoleon," was adopted
- Vice President Aaron Burr mortally wounded Alexander Hamilton in a pistol duel
- England mobilized to protect against an expected French invasion by Napoleon
- Both The British Royal Horticultural Society and the Royal Watercolour Society were formed.
- Empress Josephine, wife of Napoleon I, began a rose collection that sparked wide interest in rose culture
- Alice Meynell became the first English woman jockey

## 1805

- U.S. Marines attacked and captured the town of Derna in Tripoli from the Barbary pirates; Tripoli concluded peace with United States
- Bostonian Frederic Tudor began exporting ice from New England to the tropics
- The Michigan Territory was created
- Chief Justice Samuel Chase was acquitted by the Senate impeachment trial, ending the Republican campaign against the Federalist bench
- Virginia required all freed slaves to leave the state or risk imprisonment or deportation
- The Lewis and Clark expedition reached the Pacific Ocean
- Lieutenant Zebulon Montgomery Pike paid the Sioux $2,000 for a

nine-square-mile tract of land at the mouth of the Minnesota River to establish Fort Snelling, a military post
- Napoleon Bonaparte was crowned king of Italy
- Austria joined Britain, Russia and Sweden in the Third Coalition against Napoleonic France and Spain
- A British fleet commanded by Vice Admiral Horatio Nelson defeated a French-Spanish fleet in the Battle of Trafalgar fought off Cape Trafalgar, Spain
- French Revolutionary calendar law was abolished

## 1806

- A catalog of the plants at Elgin Botanical Garden in New York City was published
- A printed reference to a mixed-drink cocktail first appeared
- Shoemakers in Philadelphia formed a union
- The British took control of South Africa from the Dutch
- Napoleon attempted to restrict European trade with Britain
- Andrew Jackson killed Charles Dickinson in a duel over a horse racing debt
- Lewis and Clark began their trip home after an 8,000-mile trek of the Mississippi basin and the Pacific Coast
- During an expedition to locate the source of the Mississippi River, Zebulon Pike discovered the structure that would become known as Pike's Peak
- The Holy Roman Empire was dissolved when Emperor Francis I abdicated the throne
- Carbon paper was patented in London by inventor Ralph Wedgwood.
- Emperor Napoleon entered Berlin
- Napoleon's army was checked by the Russians at the Battle of Pultusk
- The Spanish army repelled Britain's attempt to retake Buenos Aires, Argentina

## 1807

- President Jefferson imposed a trade embargo with Europe to keep American ships neutral in the Napoleonic wars

♦ The British blockaded continental Europe

♦ British seamen boarded the *USS Chesapeake*, a provocation that led to the War of 1812

♦ President Jefferson exposed a plot by former Vice President Aaron Burr to form a new republic in the Southwest

♦ British Parliament abolished the slave trade

♦ Czar Alexander of Russia met with Napoleon Bonaparte to divide Europe between themselves and isolate Britain

♦ Averaging five miles per hour, Robert Fulton's steamboat the *Clermont* successfully made the round-trip journey up New York's Hudson River to Albany

♦ The Geological Society of London, devoted to the earth sciences, was established

♦ Englishmen William and John Cockerill promoted the Industrial Revolution to continental Europe by developing machine shops in Liège, Belgium

### 1808

♦ James Madison was elected president

♦ The first newspaper west of the Mississippi was founded in St. Louis by Joseph Charles and funded by Merewether Lewis, the local territorial governor, who needed to print the local laws

♦ The United States Supreme Court affirmed the constitutional rights of the federal government, and not individual states, to determine the legality of captures on the high seas

♦ The first American land-grant university was founded in Athens, Ohio

♦ America abolished the importing of slaves

♦ Elizabeth Seton established a school for girls in Baltimore, Maryland

♦ Artist Charles Willson Peale painted the only known portrait of naturalist William Bartram

♦ Pellegrino Turri built a crude typewriter for the blind Countess Carolina Fantoni da Fivizono in Italy

♦ Sir Humphrey Davy showed that electricity could produce heat or light between two electrodes separated in space

♦ Excavations began at Pompeii, the site of the eruption of Mount Vesuvius in 79 AD

♦ The Bayonne Decree by Napoleon ordered the seizure of United States ships

♦ The citizens of Madrid unsuccessfully rose up against Napoleon; hundreds were slaughtered in reprisal

♦ France's General Junot was defeated by Wellington at the first Battle of the Peninsular War at Vimiero, Spain

♦ Johann Wolfgang von Goethe completed the first part of *Faust*

♦ The political rights of Jews were suspended in Duchy of Warsaw

### 1809

♦ The first railroad track in the United States was laid at Crum Creek, Pennsylvania, by Thomas Leiper

♦ Explorer Merewether Lewis died of self-inflicted gunshot wounds in Tennessee

♦ The Territory of Illinois was created

♦ President James Madison ordered the annexation of West Florida from Spain

♦ Peregrine Williamson of Baltimore patented a steel pen

♦ Wearing masks at balls was forbidden in Boston

♦ Great Britain signed a treaty with Persia, forcing the French out of the country

♦ Austrian forces entered Bavaria as Austria declared war on France

♦ Napoleon was divorced from the Empress Josephine by an act of the French Senate

## 1810–1819
### 1810

♦ The U.S. Census recorded the United States population at 7,239,881, 19 percent of whom were recorded as black

♦ The Maryland legislature authorized a lottery to build a memorial to George Washington

♦ First United States fire insurance joint-stock company was organized in Philadelphia

♦ The British Bullion Committee condemned the practice of governments printing too much money and causing inflation

♦ The British acquired Mauritius from France

♦ John Jacob Astor organized the Pacific Fur Company

♦ Wilhelm von Humboldt founded Humboldt University in Berlin to give students a broad humanist education

♦ King Kamehameha conquered and unified all the Hawaiian islands

♦ Argentina and Chile declared their independence and began their revolt against Napoleonic Spain

♦ The first billiard rooms were established in London, England

### 1811

♦ The Bank of the United States, established as a central bank and a mechanism for government borrowing, was abolished

♦ Robert Fulton's steamboat, *New Orleans*, became the first steamboat in western waters when it sailed down the Ohio and Mississippi Rivers; passage cost $30

♦ Jane Austen published *Sense and Sensibility*

♦ Francis Cabot Lowell started the modern textile industry in New England

♦ An uprising of over 400 slaves was put down in New Orleans, resulting in the deaths of 66 blacks

♦ Congress made secret plans to annex Spanish eastern Florida

♦ Mary Anning of England excavated a 17-foot-long skeleton fossil later named icthyosaurus and sold it for £23

♦ Ned Ludd organized a group of craftsmen, known as Luddites, who violently protested industrialization in England

♦ General William Henry Harrison routed the Shawnee Indians at the Battle of Tippecanoe in the Indiana Territory

### 1812

♦ The War of 1812 began as the United States declared war against Great Britain

♦ John Jacob Astor and Stephen Girard were called upon to personally finance the war

- United States forces led by General William Hull invaded Canada
- The Cherokee Indians sided with the United States
- Maine separated from the state of Massachusetts
- George Clinton, the fourth vice president of the United States, became the first vice president to die while in office
- Massachusetts Governor Elbridge Gerry signed a redistricting law that favored his party, giving rise to the term "gerrymandering"
- Louisiana became the eighteenth state; the Louisiana Territory was renamed the Missouri Territory
- Jacob and Wilhelm Grimm published their first collection of *Folk Tales for Children and the Home*
- Napoleon and his army invaded Russia
- Great Britain signed the Treaty of Orebro, making peace with Russia and Sweden

## 1813

- Nearly broke from the cost of war, Congress chartered the Second Bank of the United States
- Americans forces under General Zebulon Pike captured York, now Toronto
- Americans captured Fort George, Canada
- The U.S. Navy gained its motto as the mortally wounded commander of the U.S. frigate *Chesapeake*, Captain James Lawrence, was heard to say, "Don't give up the ship!" during a losing battle with a British frigate *Shannon*
- The U.S. invasion of Canada was halted at Stoney Creek, Ontario
- The Creek Indians massacred over 500 whites at Fort Mims, Alabama
- The *Demologos*, the first steam-powered warship, was launched in New York City
- American militiamen burned down the town of Niagara-on-the-Lake in Canada
- The British announced a blockade of Long Island Sound, leaving only the New England coast open to shipping
- The British burned Buffalo, New York

- The first raw cotton-to-cloth mill was founded in Waltham, Massachusetts
- The first mass production factory began making pistols
- Rubber was patented
- A Swiss traveler discovered the Great and Small Temples of Ramses II at Abu Simbel in Egypt
- Jane Austin published *Pride and Prejudice*
- The Russians fighting against Napoleon reached Berlin

## 1814

- British forces landed on the Patuxent River and routed the Americans in the Battle of Bladensburg, and then marched to Washington
- The U.S. Capitol and White House were burned and sacked by the British
- British forces destroyed the Library of Congress, which contained 3,000 books
- An American fleet scored a decisive victory over the British in the Battle of Lake Champlain
- Lawyer Francis Scott Key witnessed the bombardment of Fort McHenry, the last American defense before Baltimore, and wrote "The Star-Spangled Banner"
- Five Indian tribes in Ohio made peace with the United States and declared war on Britain
- The British attacked Ft. Ontario, Oswego, New York
- British and American forces fought each other to a stand-off at Lundy's Lane, Canada
- Andrew Jackson and the Creek Indians signed the Treaty of Fort Jackson, giving the whites 23 million acres of Mississippi Creek territory
- The Treaty of Fontainebleau exiled Napoleon to Elba, a small island in the Mediterranean, where he retained the title of emperor and 400 volunteers to act as his guard
- Lord Byron completed *The Corsair*
- U.S. soldiers killed 700 Creek Indians at Horseshoe Bend, Louisiana
- The Duke of Wellington led 60,000 troops against 325,000 French troops at Toulouse and defeated them, just days after Napoleon abdicated the throne

- Sir Walter Scott published his novel *Waverly* anonymously to avoid damaging his reputation as a poet
- Andrew Jackson attacked and captured Pensacola, Florida, defeating the Spanish and driving out a British force

## 1815

- The burned Library of Congress was re-established with Thomas Jefferson's collection of 6,500 volumes
- Congress appropriated funds for the restoration of the White House and hired James Hoban, the original designer and builder, to do the work
- The United States declared war on Algiers to put an end to robberies by the Barbary pirates
- John Roulstone of Sterling, Massachusetts, penned the first three stanzas of the poem "Mary Had a Little Lamb" after his classmate Mary Sawyer came to school followed by her pet lamb
- Milan forbade gambling in the back rooms of the opera houses
- The first New England missionaries arrived in Hawaii
- Switzerland became officially neutral
- U.S. forces led by General Andrew Jackson and French pirate Jean Lafitte defeated 8,000 British veterans in the Battle of New Orleans, the closing engagement of the War of 1812

- Napoleon escaped from the island of Elba, and with 1,200 of his men, started the 100-day reconquest of France
- British and Prussian troops under the Duke of Wellington defeated the French in Waterloo, Belgium

## 1816

- James Monroe of Virginia was elected president of the United States after defeating Federalist Rufus King
- The United States passed the first tariff laws to protect its industries
- The U.S. Supreme Court, in *Martin v. Hunter's Lessee*, affirmed its right to review state court decisions
- Pittsburgh was incorporated on the site of old Fort Pitt
- Lord Elgin sold his Parthenon sculptures to the British government for £35,000
- Dr. Rene Theophile Hyacinthe Laennec of France invented the stethoscope
- Joseph Nicephore Niepce developed the first photographic negative
- France decreed the Bonaparte family to be exiled from the country forever
- Argentina declared independence from Spain
- Louis XVIII of France dissolved the chamber of deputies, which had been challenging his authority
- The first savings bank in the United States, the Philadelphia Savings Fund Society, opened for business
- Indiana became the nineteenth state
- A patent for a dry dock was issued to John Adamson in Boston
- Giocchino Rossini composed his opera *The Barber of Seville*, and introduced it to the public of Rome
- The American Bible Society was established

## 1817

- Work began on the Erie Canal, designed to connect Lake Erie with the Hudson; workers were paid a $1 a day plus a quart of whiskey

- The University of Michigan was founded
- The New York Stock and Exchange Board was formalized and established its first quarters in a rented room at 40 Wall Street
- Frederick Eberle was tried for trying to prevent the use of the English language in German Lutheran church services in Philadelphia
- A street in Baltimore was lighted with gas from America's first gas company
- The first American school for the deaf opened in Hartford, Connecticut
- Scottish naturalist John Bradbury authored *Travels in the Interior of America in the Years 1809, 1810 and 1811*
- David Ricardo published *Principles of Political Economy and Taxation*
- President and Mrs. James Monroe moved back into the restored White House
- U.S. soldiers attacked a Florida Indian village and began the Seminole War
- Mississippi was admitted as the twentieth state of the union
- The first Hawaiian coffee was planted in Kona

## 1818

- Congress decided the flag of the United States would consist of seven red and six white stripes, and 20 stars, with a new star to be added for every new state of the union
- The United States and Britain established the 49th Parallel as the boundary between Canada and the United States
- President Monroe proclaimed naval disarmament on the Great Lakes and Lake Champlain
- The American Bible Society published the Epistles of John in the language of the Delaware Indians
- Brooks Brothers haberdashery was founded
- Illinois became the twenty-first state
- The Libbey Glass Company of Toledo, Ohio, was founded as the New England Glass Company

- The Smirnoff family went into the vodka business in Russia
- The first successful educational magazine, *Academician*, began publication in New York City
- A regiment of Indians and blacks was defeated at the Battle of Suwanna in Florida, ending the first Seminole War
- Mary Wollstonecraft Shelley wrote *Frankenstein*
- John Keats published his poem "Endymion"
- David Young began publishing the *Farmers' Almanac*

## 1819

- The paddle-wheel steamship *Savannah* became the first steamship to successfully cross the Atlantic when it arrived in Liverpool, England, after a voyage lasting 27 days
- The Territory of Arkansas was created
- Thomas Blanchard patented the lathe
- The first ship passed through the Erie Canal
- Alabama was admitted as the twenty-second state, making 11 slave states and 11 free states
- Washington Irving published *The Sketch Book of Geoffrey Crayon*, which included "The Legend of Sleepy Hollow" and "Rip Van Winkle"
- The opera *La Donna del Lago* by Gioacchino Antonio Rossini premiered in Naples
- Chief Justice John Marshall, in *Dartmouth College v. Woodward*, described the corporation as "an artificial being, invisible, intangible"
- King Kamehameha II abolished the brutal kapu system of laws in Hawaii
- Spain signed a treaty with the United States ceding eastern Florida

## 1820–1824

### 1820

- James Monroe was elected president for a second term
- The Missouri Compromise was enacted, providing for the admission of Missouri into the

227

union as a slave state but prohibiting slavery in the rest of the northern Louisiana Purchase territory

- Congress passed the Land Act, paving the way for westward expansion
- Maine became the twenty-third state
- Thomas Jefferson wrote of slavery: "We have a wolf by the ears and can neither hold him, nor safely let him go"
- More than a thousand ships were engaged in transporting timber from North America to the British Isles
- Danish physicist Hans Christian Oersted discovered that an electric current created a magnetic field around a conductor
- The Greek Venus de Milo marble statue was found on Melos
- Grain prices collapsed in Britain
- Czar Alexander declared that Russian influence in North America extended as far south as Oregon, and attempted to close the Alaskan waters to foreigners
- The Royal Astronomical Society was founded in England
- George III of England died insane and was succeeded by his son George IV, who had been regent for nine years
- U.S. Navy Captain Nathaniel B. Palmer discovered the frozen continent of Antarctica
- Missouri imposed a $1 bachelor tax on unmarried men between the ages of 21 and 50

## 1821

- John Quincy Adams, Secretary of State, wrote: "America does not go abroad in search of monsters to destroy. She is the well-wisher to the freedom and independence of all. She is the champion only of her own"
- Denmark Vessey mounted a major slave rebellion in South Carolina
- The Boston English High School, the first public high school, held its opening classes
- Spain sold eastern Florida to the U.S. for $5 million
- Napoleon died in exile on the island of St. Helena

- Peru declared its independence from Spain
- Missouri became the twenty-fourth state
- After 11 years of war, Spain granted Mexico independence
- The first pharmacy college held its first classes in Philadelphia
- Kentucky abolished debtor's prisons
- Thomas Jefferson wrote his autobiography
- Owen Chase ghost-wrote the *Narrative of the Most Extraordinary and Distressing Shipwreck of the White-Whale Ship Essex*

## 1822

- The Superintendent of Mails in Washington, DC, complained that the growing popularity of sending Christmas cards had become a burden for the United States Postal System
- California became part of Mexico
- Christian Buschmann constructed the first primitive accordion
- American colonists landed in Liberia and founded Monrovia, the colony's capital city, named in honor of President James Monroe
- Boston was granted a charter to incorporate as a city
- The first patent for false teeth was requested
- Brazil declared its independence from Portugal
- The first edition of the London *Sunday Times* was published
- Eleven-year-old Franz Liszt made his debut as a pianist
- J.F. Champollion published a paper on deciphering the Rosetta Stone
- Thomas DeQuincey wrote *Confessions of an English Opium Eater*

## 1823

- President Monroe proclaimed the Monroe Doctrine, stating "that the American continents. . . are henceforth not to be considered as subjects for future colonization by European powers"
- Mission San Francisco de Solano de Sonoma was established by Father Jose Altimira, set up to

convert the native Indians and develop the local resources

- Franz Schubert composed his song cycle *Die Schöne Müllerin*
- The Reverend Hiram Bingham, leader of a group of New England Calvinist missionaries, began translating the Bible into Hawaiian
- Louis Joseph Dufilho, Jr. established a pharmacy in New Orleans
- Charles Macintosh of Scotland began selling raincoats
- Georgia passed the first state birth registration law
- The poem "A Visit from St. Nicholas" by Clement C. Moore, often called "T'was the Night before Christmas," was published in the Troy, New York *Sentinel*

## 1824

- The presidential election was decided by the U.S. House of Representatives when a deadlock developed among John Quincy Adams, Andrew Jackson, William H. Crawford and Henry Clay; John Quincy Adams was declared the winner
- Hens called Rhode Island Reds were first bred in Little Compton, Rhode Island
- The first animal welfare group was founded in England
- The Mexican governor of California offered all missions for sale under a program of secularization
- The Camp Street Theatre opened as the first English-language playhouse in New Orleans
- The United States War Department created the Bureau of Indian Affairs
- Newfoundland became a British colony
- The Saud family of Arabia established a new capital at Riyadh
- Russia abandoned all claims to North America south of 54' 40'
- The Ninth Symphony by Beethoven had its premiere
- Dean William Buckland of Oxford University discovered the bones of the meat-eating Megalosaurus, "huge reptile"

# Banking and the Economy

A growing nation requires a stable economy, a sound monetary system and a strong government. The United States had all of these characteristics at some point during this period, but not necessary all at the same time. Fluctuations in the currency, the economy and governmental stability played a role in the new nation and created financial gain and hardship for many individuals.

By the turn of the nineteenth century, the nation's banking system was developed upon the Bank of the United States. This privately owned entity was the primary depository of revenue collected by the United States government, but was also the primary facilitator for developing the nation's money supply. The Bank of America provided 20% of the nation's money supply, while private banks accounted for the rest of the currency in the United States. This system enabled the country to have a stable currency and engage actively in commerce.

Trade greatly improved in the United States when France deliberately redeveloped its war with Great Britain in 1803. Under a neutral stance, the nation actively exported with both countries to support their war efforts. The neutral commerce expanded at an unprecedented rate with exports rapidly growing along with prices of raw materials in demand.

Foreign trade came to a sudden halt as the British began the impressments of American sailors and mandating that all ships traveling to France must first visit British ports for inspection. With the United States possessing a weak navy and unable to react militarily and European countries in need of American products, the United States, under the encouragement of President Jefferson, hastily passed the Embargo Act of 1807. This law forbade export of all goods from the United States as an act of defiance to European powers in need of American goods. Instead, it created fiscal hardship on many American citizens as commerce slowed considerably. After much protest, an alarmed Congress repealed the embargo 15 months later in 1809.

Protest over foreign influences continued and the nation was alarmed by the number of international investors in the Bank of the United States. Over 70% of the ownership was in foreign holdings with the bank's dividends being passed into foreign hands. Though the international members held no voting rights, it was viewed that this ownership could exercise malicious influence. Supporters of the Bank of the United States who saw the benefits the institution provided to the nation typically were scorned as enemies of the Republic. By 1811, Congress decided that the bank was a threat to the nation and undemocratic, and declined to renew the charter. Without a federal institution into which to deposit federal revenue, it became necessary for the federal government to turn to local banks.

Many of the local banks were organized with little to no restrictions, and state legislatures lacked the experience to develop appropriate guidelines for these private institutions. With no system to inform the public of the fiscal conditions of the banks, many operations across the country acted poorly and weakened the nation's currency system. When war was declared in 1812 against Britain, a demand for funds required a stimulus for federal debt under these banks. This increased the federal debt, compounded by a lax credit system in selling public lands in the west, led the United States into inflation. The impact of the war rapidly revealed that the nation lacked the financial resources to adequately support the nation during times of war and in peace. Steps were required to restore a solid financial infrastructure and a national currency.

Within five years after Congress failed to renew the First Bank of the United States, Congress chartered its successor, the Second Bank of the United States. Patterned on the first bank, it attempted to resolve the nation's currency and financial troubles after the war. Though it was modeled after the first bank, it encountered a number of difficulties within the first years.

The Second Bank's appointed head provided poor judgment for the nation's fiscal well-being. It was not uncommon for the bank to provide loans to Congress without demanding payment and permit political objectives to guide loan decisions. Oversight of the bank's regional branches was also weak and created problems of corruption.

Fortunately, the United States was experiencing a postwar boom driven by the effects of the Napoleonic Wars. American products, particularly agricultural, were in high demand due to the devastation that occurred throughout Europe at this time. Supporting the boom efforts were the careless lending practices accepted by the Second Bank of the United States. Many Americans were speculating on land in the west, and loans provided by the bank accelerated the land values. By 1818 the bank management began to control its lending practices, which in turned slowed down land sales. Europe's recovery was noticeable in that it was capable of supplying its own manufactured and agricultural products. The tightening lending polices, coupled with the improved economic conditions in Europe, led to the Panic of 1819.

Bank directors questioned the quality of the loans offered to state banks in 1818-1819. Many of the local banks that had provided risky loans received payment demands from the Bank of the United States, resulting in the local banks calling loans it had made to land speculators. Because many speculators lacked sufficient funds to repay the banks, many of the banks were unable to repay the Bank of the United States and collapsed. This crashing banking system was compounded by the strong competition of manufactured goods coming from Europe, thus weakening the country's exports.

Many businesses and farms failed, resulting in numerous bankruptcies and high unemployment. It was the worst fiscal crisis the country encountered as a new nation. Over the next six years, Congress proposed numerous remedies from increasing tariffs to restricting bank credit. By 1824, the effects of the economic downturn faded and the country's economy recovered.

# SELECTED INCOMES 1800-1824

| Occupation | Data Source | Description | Price |
|---|---|---|---|
| Agricultural Worker | U.S. Census (1976) | Average daily wage of a farm worker in the Philadelphia area, 1806 | $0.40 |
| Agricultural Worker | U.S. Census (1976) | Average daily wage of a farm worker in the Philadelphia area, 1822 | $0.40 |
| Artisan | U.S. Census (1976) | Average daily wage of an artisan in the Philadelphia area, 1805 | $1.57 |
| Artisan | U.S. Census (1976) | Average daily wage of an artisan in the Philadelphia area, 1822 | $1.65 |
| Artist | American Heritiage (1958) | Commission fee by the US Congress to John Trumbull to paint four historical paintings for the Capitol's rotunda, 1816 | $32,000.00 |
| Artist | American Heritage (1959) | Price per chalk portrait by James Audubon, 1819 | $5.00 |
| Assistant Keeper | Statutes at Large of Virginia (1803) | Annual salary for assistant keeper of the penitentiary house in Virginia, 1803 | $250.00 |
| Captain | American Heritage (1956) | Monthly Income, ship's captain from New England, 1805 | $40.00 |
| Caretaker | Pace & McGee, The Life and Times of Ridgeway, Virginia (1990) | Annual income of George Hairston to keep the Martinsville, Virginia Courthouse clean and furnished with wood | $15.00 |
| Clearing Timber | Thomas Johnson Contract (1805) | Cost per acre to clear heavy timber and fit it for plow in Wayne County New York in 1805 | $14.00 |
| Contractor's Fee | Pace & McGee, The Life and Times of Ridgeway, Virginia (1990) | One of three installments paid to Richard Stockton to construct a courthouse in Martinsville, Virginia, 1800 | 77 pounds 13 shillings 4 pence |
| Director | William Dutton, Du Pont (1949) | Annual Salary of EI du Pont for Gunpowder Operations in Wilmington, Delaware, 1801 | $1,800.00 |
| Door Keeper | Statutes at Large of Virginia (1803) | Annual salary for the door keeper of the capitol to keep the capitol clean in Virginia, 1803 | $300.00 |

## Based Upon US Dollars

| Year | Value of 19th Century Dollar in 2002 US Dollars |
|---|---|
| 1800 | $14.00 |
| 1805 | $15.00 |
| 1810 | $14.00 |
| 1815 | $11.00 |
| 1820 | $15.00 |
| 1824 | $18.00 |

*Calculations are approximate values based upon economic historical data*

| Occupation | Data Source | Description | Price |
|---|---|---|---|
| Farm Laborer | U.S. Census (1976) | Average monthly earnings for a farm laborer in New England, 1818 | $11.90 |
| Farm Laborer | U.S. Census (1976) | Average monthly earnings for a farm laborer in the Middle Atlantic states, 1818 | $9.82 |
| Farm Laborer | U.S. Census (1976) | Average monthly earnings for a farm laborer in South Atlantic states, 1818 | $8.10 |
| Glassworker | McKearin, American Bottles & Flasks (1978) | Daily income for a glassworker at Pitkin, Woodbridge & Company in East Hartford, Connecticut, 1817 | $0.58 |
| Governor | Statutes at Large of South Carolina (1808) | Annual Salary of the South Carolina's governor, 1806 | $2,572.00 |
| Horseshoeing | Business Accounts of Hampshire Furnance (1815) | Blacksmith's earnings for a providing a new pair of horseshoes and shoeing in Hampshire, Virginia in 1815 | $1.16 |
| Hunter/Interpreter | Milner, Oxford History of the American West (1996) | Monthly salary of George Drouillard when working with Corps of Discovery, led by Lewis and Clarke in 1804 | $25.00 |
| Inspector | Statutes at Large of Virginia (1803) | Annual salary of tobacco inspector in Virginia, 1803 | $250.00 |
| Judge | Statutes at Large of South Carolina (1808) | Annual salary of a Judge of the Court of Equity in South Carolina, 1806 | $2,142.00 |
| Labor - Construction | Business Accounts of Hampshire Furnance (1815) | Earnings to build on new Saw Mill in Hampshire, Virginia in 1815 | $323.00 |
| Labor -Chopping | Business Accounts of Hampshire Furnance (1816) | Charge for cutting one cord of wood in Hampshire, Virginia in 1815 | $0.42 |
| Laborer | U.S. Census (1976) | Average daily wage of a laborer in the Philadelphia area, 1805 | $1.00 |
| Laborer | U.S. Census (1976) | Average daily wage of a laborer in the Philadelphia area, 1822 | $0.75 |
| Minister | Wells, The Origins of the South Middle Class (2004) | Annual Income of a Baptist Minister in 1820 | $1,500.00 |
| Painter | American Heritage (1958) | Cost to paint portrait of Thomas Jefferson by Gilbert Stuart, 1805 | $100.00 |
| Painter | American Heritage (1961) | Income from Samuel Morse for painting an portrait, 1809 | $5.00 |
| Painter | American Heritage (1961) | Income from Samuel Morse for painting an ivory miniature, 1820 | $300.00 |
| Penitentiary Keeper | Statutes at Large of Virginia (1803) | Annual salary for keeper of the penitentiary house in Virginia, 1803 | $1,200.00 |
| Physician | Statutes at Large of Virginia (1803) | Annual salary paid to the physician to visit the Virginia's jail or penitentiary, 1803 | $500.00 |
| Physician | Statutes at Large of South Carolina (1808) | Annual salary of the Port Physician of Charleston, 1806 | $600.00 |
| Portrait Painting | American Heritage (1960) | Charge by a portrait painter for a young person's portrait, 1814 | $2.92 |
| Seamstress | A. Kessler-Harris, Out to Work (1982) | Seamstress, woman working at home, Philadelphia, 1821 | $58.00 |
| Steam boat pilot | The Vanderbilts by Jerry E. Patterson (1989) | Cornelius Vanderbilt's annual wages as a steam boat pilot in Staten Island, New York in 1818 | $1,000.00 |

| Occupation | Data Source | Description | Price |
|---|---|---|---|
| Steeling | Business Accounts of Hampshire Furnance (1815) | Blacksmith's earnings for steeling one axe in Hampshire, Virginia in 1815 | $0.75 |
| Textile worker | A. Kessler-Harris, Out to Work (1982) | To card one pound of wool in New England, 1801 | $0.12½ |
| Tool Sharping | Business Accounts of Hampshire Furnance (1815) | Blacksmith's earnings for sharping tow shovel plows in Hampshire, Virginia in 1815 | $0.08 |

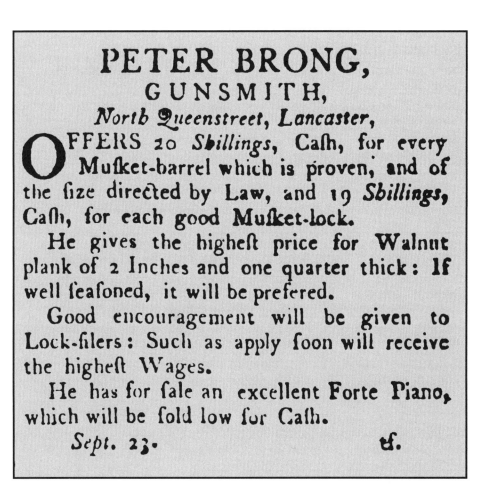

# SERVICES & FEES 1800-1824

| Service/Fee | Data Source | Description | Price |
|---|---|---|---|
| Appraiser | Inventory of James Moore (1820) | Appraiser's fee for a probate inventory in Franklin County, Indiana, 1820 | $1.00 |
| Chaplain | Statutes at Large of Virginia (1803) | Weekly income to chaplain for services during the legislative session in Virginia, 1803 | $20.00 |
| Clerk | Inventory of James Moore (1820) | Clerk's fees for a probate inventory in Franklin County, Indiana, 1820 | $1.00 |
| Coffin | Brock Jobe, New England Furniture: The Colonial Era (1984) | Cost to make a coffin by a joiner in Massachusetts, 1812 | $2.50 |
| Fine | Wells, The Origins of the South Middle Class (2004) | South Carolina fine for dueling plus 12 months in prison for anyone remotely involved in 1813 | $2,000.00 |
| Hospital Care | Cheraw Intlligencer and Southern Register (1823) | Daily cost to provide nursing care and proper diet for sick Negros in South Carolina | $1.00 |
| Inspection Fee | Statutes at Large of Virginia (1803) | Fee paid for by tobacco warehouses for inspection, 1803 | $1.00 |
| Inspection Fee | Statutes at Large of Virginia (1803) | Fee paid by tobacco manufacturer for inspection, 1803 | $0.25 |
| Library Admission Fee | Wells, The Origins of the South Middle Class (2004) | Charleston Library Society - Entry Fee to join the society in 1813 | $50.00 |
| Library Annual Dues | Wells, The Origins of the South Middle Class (2004) | Charleston Library Society - Annual dues in 1811 | $8.00 |
| Minister | Statutes at Large of South Carolina (1808) | Fee for performing divine service during the South Carolina legislative session, 1806 | $100.00 |
| Physician | Statutes at Large of South Carolina (1808) | Fee for attending prisoners in Edgefield, South Carolina, 1806 | $25.75 |
| Printing | Statutes at Large of Virginia (1803) | Fee paid to Samuel Pleasants for print the journals of the Virginia senate, 1803 | $275.00 |
| Reward | Giles County Records (1813) | Fee for capturing a dangerous horse thief in Giles County, Virginia | $17.62 |
| Servant | Statutes at Large of Virginia (1806) | Payment to Philip Woodson of Goochland, Virginia for lost negro named Lewis for services to the commonwealth, 1806 | $400.00 |
| Tariff | McKearin, American Bottles & Flasks (1978) | Government tariff charged on a gross of black-glass bottles needed by brewers, 1816 | $1.44 |
| Toll | Statutes at Large of Virginia (1804) | Toll for the Roanoke Canal in Virginia for every pipe or hogshead of wine containing more than 65 gallons, 1804 | $0.75 |
| Toll | Statutes at Large of Virginia (1804) | Toll for the Roanoke Canal in Virginia for every bushel of wheat, peas, beans, rice or flax seed, 1804 | 1½ cents |
| Toll | Statutes at Large of Virginia (1804) | Toll for the Roanoke Canal in Virginia for every hogshead of tobacco, 1804 | $0.42 |
| Toll | Statutes at Large of Virginia (1804) | Toll for the Roanoke Canal in Virginia for every barrel of pork or flour, 1804 | 12½ cents |
| Toll | Statutes at Large of Virginia (1804) | Toll for the Roanoke Canal in Virginia for every canoe, boat or vessel under ton, 1804 | $0.33 |

# FINANCIAL RATES & EXCHANGES
## 1800-1824

| Year | United States Official Price of Gold (per ounce) | Inflation Rate in the United States | United States Exchange Rate for One British Pound | US Federal Government High Grade Bond Yields, New Issue | US Federal Government High Grade Bond Yields, Select Market | Government High Grade Bond Yields, New Issue Yields | New England Municipal Bond Yields |
|---|---|---|---|---|---|---|---|
| 1800 | $19.39 | 2.03% | $4.55 | 7.34% | 6.94% | 7.34% | 6.13% |
| 1801 | $19.39 | 1.32% | $4.38 | — | 6.44% | — | 5.63% |
| 1802 | $19.39 | −15.69% | $4.49 | — | 6.02% | — | 5.25% |
| 1803 | $19.39 | 5.43% | $4.54 | — | 6.16% | — | 5.06% |
| 1804 | $19.39 | 4.41% | $4.55 | — | 6.29% | — | 5.14% |
| 1805 | $19.39 | −0.70% | $4.35 | — | 6.38% | — | 5.36% |
| 1806 | $19.39 | 4.26% | $4.43 | — | 6.14% | — | 5.32% |
| 1807 | $19.39 | −5.44% | $4.42 | 6.00% | 6.08% | 6.00% | 5.29% |
| 1808 | $19.39 | 8.63% | $4.63 | — | 5.96% | — | 5.19% |
| 1809 | $19.39 | −1.99% | $4.57 | — | 5.85% | — | 5.02% |
| 1810 | $19.39 | 0.00% | $4.30 | — | 5.82% | — | 5.02% |
| 1811 | $19.39 | 6.76% | $3.82 | — | 5.95% | — | 5.09% |
| 1812 | $19.39 | 1.27% | $3.62 | 6.00% | 6.12% | 6.00% | 5.13% |
| 1813 | $19.39 | 20.00% | $3.75 | 6.83% | 6.30% | 6.83% | 5.03% |
| 1814 | $19.39 | 9.90% | $4.24 | 7.50% | 7.64% | 7.50% | 5.26% |
| 1815 | $19.39 | −12.32% | $4.90 | 7.75% | 7.30% | 7.75% | 5.29% |
| 1816 | $19.39 | −8.65% | $5.22 | — | 7.25% | — | 5.72% |
| 1817 | $19.39 | −5.33% | $4.60 | — | 5.86% | — | 5.27% |
| 1818 | $19.39 | −4.38% | $4.50 | — | 5.78% | — | 5.08% |
| 1819 | $19.39 | 0.00% | $4.51 | — | 5.90% | — | 5.17% |
| 1820 | $19.39 | −7.84% | $4.52 | 5.88% | 5.16% | 5.75% | 5.00% |
| 1821 | $19.39 | −3.55% | $4.82 | 4.50% | 4.57% | 4.50% | 4.93% |
| 1822 | $19.39 | 3.68% | $4.98 | — | 4.65% | — | — |
| 1823 | $19.39 | −10.64% | $4.80 | — | 4.72% | — | 5.00% |
| 1824 | $19.39 | −7.94% | $4.87 | 4.50% | 4..25% | 4.50% | 4.52% |

# SLAVE TRADES 1800-1824

### Average Price of British American and West African Slaves
*Price in Pounds Sterling*

| Year | Price |
|------|-------|
| 1800 | 50 |
| 1801 | 60 |
| 1802 | 60 |
| 1803 | 60 |
| 1804 | 60 |
| 1805 | 60 |
| 1806 | 60 |
| 1807 | 60 |

# COMMODITIES 1800-1824

Currency expressed in US dollars.

| Commodity | Year | Philadelphia Currency | New York Currency | Charleston Currency | New Orleans Currency | Cincinnati Currency |
|---|---|---|---|---|---|---|
| Bacon, per pound | 1800 | $0.100 | $0.100 | $0.075 | $0.12 | N/R |
| | 1801 | $0.125 | $0.150 | $0.060 | $0.12 | N/R |
| | 1802 | $0.110 | $0.100 | $0.070 | $0.15 | N/R |
| | 1803 | $0.095 | $0.110 | $0.060 | $0.12 | N/R |
| | 1804 | $0.095 | $0.105 | $0.070 | $0.08 | N/R |
| | 1805 | $0.125 | $0.120 | $0.090 | $0.08 | N/R |
| | 1806 | $0.145 | $0.145 | $0.070 | $0.09 | N/R |
| | 1807 | $0.125 | $0.135 | $0.070 | $0.12 | N/R |
| | 1808 | $0.095 | $0.085 | $0.110 | $0.09 | N/R |
| | 1809 | $0.130 | $0.115 | $0.112 | $0.10 | N/R |
| | 1810 | $0.140 | $0.120 | $0.120 | $0.04 | N/R |
| | 1811 | $0.145 | $0.115 | $0.112 | $0.13 | N/R |
| | 1812 | $0.130 | $0.105 | $0.100 | $0.10 | N/R |
| | 1813 | $0.130 | $0.110 | $0.095 | N/R | N/R |
| | 1814 | $0.170 | $0.155 | $0.125 | N/R | N/R |
| | 1815 | $0.168 | $0.145 | $0.150 | N/R | N/R |
| | 1816 | $0.155 | $0.160 | $0.160 | N/R | $0.090 |
| | 1817 | $0.170 | $0.155 | $0.170 | N/R | $0.095 |
| | 1818 | $0.175 | $0.145 | $0.165 | N/R | $0.090 |
| | 1819 | $0.142 | $0.128 | $0.145 | N/R | $0.090 |
| | 1820 | $0.120 | $0.090 | $0.100 | $0.11 | $0.070 |
| | 1821 | $0.100 | $0.085 | $0.065 | $0.05 | $0.052 |
| | 1822 | $0.110 | $0.095 | $0.090 | $0.10 | $0.040 |
| | 1823 | $0.100 | $0.080 | $0.082 | $0.06 | $0.035 |
| | 1824 | $0.100 | $0.083 | $0.065 | $0.08 | $0.045 |
| Beef, per barrel | 1800 | $15.00 | $9.88 | N/R | N/R | N/R |
| | 1801 | $15.50 | $20.50 | N/R | N/R | N/R |

## Based Upon US Dollars

| Year | Value of 19th Century Dollar in 2002 US Dollars |
|---|---|
| 1800 | $14.00 |
| 1805 | $15.00 |
| 1810 | $14.00 |
| 1815 | $11.00 |
| 1820 | $15.00 |
| 1824 | $18.00 |

*Calculations are approximate values based upon economic historical data*

| Commodity | Year | Philadelphia Currency | New York Currency | Charleston Currency | New Orleans Currency | Cincinnati Currency |
|---|---|---|---|---|---|---|
| | 1802 | $14.00 | $12.00 | N/R | N/R | N/R |
| | 1803 | $15.00 | $14.00 | $60.70 | N/R | N/R |
| | 1804 | $15.50 | $11.75 | $56.00 | N/R | N/R |
| | 1805 | $13.75 | $11.75 | $10.50 | N/R | N/R |
| | 1806 | $13.75 | $11.50 | $12.00 | N/R | N/R |
| | 1807 | $15.50 | $11.75 | $12.50 | N/R | N/R |
| | 1808 | $13.00 | $11.00 | $12.50 | N/R | N/R |
| | 1809 | $13.50 | $12.00 | $15.00 | N/R | N/R |
| | 1810 | $14.50 | $11.00 | $12.50 | N/R | N/R |
| | 1811 | $15.50 | $9.25 | $13.25 | N/R | N/R |
| | 1812 | $15.50 | $10.75 | $12.25 | N/R | N/R |
| | 1813 | $15.50 | $10.00 | N/R | N/R | N/R |
| | 1814 | $17.00 | $9.88 | N/R | N/R | N/R |
| | 1815 | $20.00 | $17.25 | N/R | N/R | N/R |
| | 1816 | $19.00 | $13.50 | $14.50 | N/R | N/R |
| | 1817 | $16.50 | $14.75 | $14.50 | N/R | N/R |
| | 1818 | $17.00 | $13.25 | $16.00 | $12.48 | N/R |
| | 1819 | $18.00 | $15.38 | $16.00 | $9.36 | N/R |
| | 1820 | $13.50 | $9.38 | $13.00 | $10.72 | N/R |
| | 1821 | $12.00 | $10.88 | $11.75 | $5.75 | N/R |
| | 1822 | $11.00 | $8.63 | $10.00 | $8.75 | N/R |
| | 1823 | $11.00 | $8.00 | $10.50 | $7.50 | N/R |
| | 1824 | $12.00 | $8.88 | $9.25 | $6.50 | N/R |
| Bread, per hundredweight | 1800 | $4.00 | $5.63 | N/R | N/R | N/R |
| *(Charleston & Cinncinati per barrel)* | 1801 | $4.75 | $6.00 | N/R | N/R | N/R |
| | 1802 | $4.05 | $3.50 | N/R | N/R | N/R |
| | 1803 | $3.12 | $3.25 | $3.00 | N/R | N/R |
| | 1804 | $3.12 | $3.25 | $3.00 | $11.00 | N/R |
| | 1805 | $4.25 | $5.50 | $5.00 | $11.00 | N/R |
| | 1806 | $4.25 | $4.50 | N/R | $10.50 | N/R |
| | 1807 | $4.50 | $4.50 | N/R | $10.50 | N/R |
| | 1808 | $4.00 | $4.00 | N/R | $10.50 | N/R |
| | 1809 | $4.50 | $4.25 | N/R | $7.50 | N/R |
| | 1810 | $4.50 | $4.25 | N/R | $7.50 | N/R |
| | 1811 | $5.75 | $5.63 | N/R | $7.50 | N/R |
| | 1812 | $5.00 | $5.00 | N/R | $9.00 | N/R |
| | 1813 | $5.50 | $5.00 | N/R | N/R | N/R |
| | 1814 | $5.36 | $4.50 | N/R | N/R | N/R |
| | 1815 | $6.00 | $4.50 | N/R | N/R | N/R |
| | 1816 | $5.00 | $4.25 | N/R | N/R | $5.00 |
| | 1817 | $8.50 | $9.00 | N/R | N/R | $6.00 |
| | 1818 | $6.25 | $5.38 | N/R | N/R | N/R |
| | 1819 | $4.62 | $3.88 | N/R | N/R | $4.88 |
| | 1820 | $4.00 | $3.63 | N/R | N/R | $4.88 |
| | 1821 | $3.00 | $2.88 | N/R | N/R | N/R |
| | 1822 | $3.25 | $3.75 | N/R | N/R | N/R |
| | 1823 | $3.25 | $3.88 | N/R | $5.62 | N/R |
| | 1824 | $3.25 | $3.38 | N/R | $5.50 | $3.00 |

| Commodity | Year | Philadelphia Currency | New York Currency | Charleston Currency | New Orleans Currency | Cincinnati Currency |
|---|---|---|---|---|---|---|
| Butter, per pound | 1800 | $0.124 | $0.170 | $0.120 | $0.25 | N/R |
| | 1801 | $0.165 | $0.180 | $0.120 | N/R | N/R |
| | 1802 | $0.125 | $0.100 | $0.100 | N/R | N/R |
| | 1803 | $0.085 | $0.090 | $0.095 | N/R | N/R |
| | 1804 | $0.190 | $0.190 | $0.245 | $0.28 | N/R |
| | 1805 | $0.190 | $0.150 | $0.225 | $0.25 | N/R |
| | 1806 | $0.175 | $0.180 | $0.200 | $0.28 | N/R |
| | 1807 | $0.150 | $0.160 | $0.200 | $0.16 | N/R |
| | 1808 | $0.120 | $0.075 | $0.200 | $0.21 | N/R |
| | 1809 | $0.135 | $0.130 | $0.225 | $0.18 | N/R |
| | 1810 | $0.155 | $0.140 | $0.162 | $0.18 | N/R |
| | 1811 | $0.150 | $0.170 | N/R | $0.19 | N/R |
| | 1812 | $0.125 | $0.125 | $0.190 | $0.21 | N/R |
| | 1813 | $0.122 | $0.155 | $0.190 | N/R | N/R |
| | 1814 | $0.170 | $0.200 | $0.375 | $0.23 | N/R |
| | 1815 | $0.205 | $0.225 | $0.275 | N/R | N/R |
| | 1816 | $0.210 | $0.165 | $0.273 | $0.22 | $0.140 |
| | 1817 | $0.175 | $0.180 | N/R | $0.24 | $0.140 |
| | 1818 | $0.135 | $0.170 | $0.260 | $0.22 | $0.175 |
| | 1819 | $0.125 | $0.130 | $0.238 | $0.23 | $0.170 |
| | 1820 | $0.100 | $0.110 | $0.235 | $0.12 | $0.125 |
| | 1821 | $0.095 | $0.110 | $0.275 | $0.15 | $0.150 |
| | 1822 | $0.130 | $0.105 | $0.210 | $0.20 | N/R |
| | 1823 | $0.090 | $0.085 | $0.230 | $0.15 | N/R |
| | 1824 | $0.080 | $0.080 | $0.225 | $0.10 | $0.066 |
| Candles, per pound | 1800 | $0.200 | $0.480 | N/R | $0.750 | N/R |
| | 1801 | $0.190 | $0.480 | N/R | N/R | N/R |
| | 1802 | $0.170 | $0.480 | N/R | N/R | N/R |
| | 1803 | $0.150 | $0.480 | N/R | N/R | N/R |
| | 1804 | $0.180 | $0.540 | N/R | $0.700 | N/R |
| | 1805 | $0.200 | $0.580 | N/R | $0.700 | N/R |
| | 1806 | $0.200 | $0.515 | N/R | $0.625 | N/R |
| | 1807 | $0.195 | $0.490 | N/R | $0.525 | N/R |

## Based Upon US Dollars

| Year | Value of 19th Century Dollar in 2002 US Dollars |
|---|---|
| 1800 | $14.00 |
| 1805 | $15.00 |
| 1810 | $14.00 |
| 1815 | $11.00 |
| 1820 | $15.00 |
| 1824 | $18.00 |

*Calculations are approximate values based upon economic historical data*

| Commodity | Year | Philadelphia Currency | New York Currency | Charleston Currency | New Orleans Currency | Cincinnati Currency |
|---|---|---|---|---|---|---|
| | 1808 | $0.160 | $0.470 | N/R | $0.560 | N/R |
| | 1809 | $0.190 | $0.470 | N/R | $0.500 | N/R |
| | 1810 | $0.200 | $0.470 | N/R | $0.450 | N/R |
| | 1811 | $0.195 | $0.440 | N/R | $0.470 | N/R |
| | 1812 | $0.190 | $0.390 | N/R | $0.470 | N/R |
| | 1813 | $0.190 | $0.390 | N/R | N/R | N/R |
| | 1814 | $0.180 | $0.435 | N/R | N/R | N/R |
| | 1815 | $0.210 | $0.410 | N/R | N/R | N/R |
| | 1816 | $0.235 | $0.495 | N/R | $0.475 | $0.250 |
| | 1817 | $0.190 | $0.450 | N/R | N/R | $0.250 |
| | 1818 | $0.185 | $0.440 | $0.475 | $0.560 | $0.250 |
| | 1819 | $0.200 | $0.430 | $0.475 | $0.490 | $0.250 |
| | 1820 | $0.180 | $0.410 | $0.450 | $0.510 | $0.250 |
| | 1821 | $0.155 | $0.390 | $0.435 | $0.465 | N/R |
| | 1822 | $0.145 | $0.358 | $0.400 | $0.410 | $0.100 |
| | 1823 | $0.115 | $0.265 | $0.250 | $0.400 | $0.125 |
| | 1824 | $0.115 | $0.270 | N/R | $0.335 | $0.095 |
| Coal, per bushel | 1800 | $0.300 | $0.100 | N/R | N/R | N/R |
| | 1801 | $0.003 | $0.080 | N/R | N/R | N/R |
| | 1802 | $0.290 | $0.112 | N/R | N/R | N/R |
| | 1803 | $0.290 | $0.112 | N/R | N/R | N/R |
| | 1804 | $0.290 | $0.120 | N/R | N/R | N/R |
| | 1805 | $0.405 | $0.115 | N/R | N/R | N/R |
| | 1806 | $0.360 | $0.105 | N/R | N/R | N/R |
| | 1807 | $0.295 | $0.115 | N/R | N/R | N/R |
| | 1808 | $0.280 | $0.120 | N/R | N/R | N/R |
| | 1809 | $0.290 | $0.110 | N/R | N/R | N/R |
| | 1810 | $0.357 | $0.140 | N/R | N/R | N/R |
| | 1811 | $0.320 | $0.145 | N/R | N/R | N/R |
| | 1812 | $0.425 | $0.280 | N/R | N/R | N/R |
| | 1813 | $1.000 | $0.300 | N/R | N/R | N/R |
| | 1814 | $1.050 | N/R | N/R | N/R | N/R |
| | 1815 | $0.460 | $0.150 | N/R | N/R | N/R |
| | 1816 | $0.350 | $0.115 | N/R | N/R | N/R |
| | 1817 | $0.300 | $0.085 | N/R | N/R | N/R |
| | 1818 | $0.330 | $0.130 | N/R | N/R | N/R |
| | 1819 | $0.360 | $0.100 | N/R | N/R | $0.190 |
| | 1820 | $0.325 | $0.100 | N/R | N/R | N/R |
| | 1821 | $0.325 | $0.120 | N/R | N/R | N/R |
| | 1822 | $0.325 | $0.115 | N/R | N/R | N/R |
| | 1823 | $0.325 | $0.100 | N/R | N/R | $0.102 |
| | 1824 | $0.325 | $0.110 | N/R | N/R | $0.055 |
| Coffee, per pound | 1800 | $0.250 | $0.255 | N/R | N/R | N/R |
| | 1801 | $0.245 | $0.240 | N/R | $0.310 | N/R |
| | 1802 | $0.230 | $0.220 | N/R | N/R | N/R |
| | 1803 | $0.285 | $0.265 | $0.285 | $0.320 | N/R |
| | 1804 | $0.265 | $0.265 | $0.270 | $0.250 | N/R |
| | 1805 | $0.320 | $0.310 | $0.340 | $0.345 | N/R |

| Commodity | Year | Philadelphia Currency | New York Currency | Charleston Currency | New Orleans Currency | Cincinnati Currency |
|---|---|---|---|---|---|---|
| | 1806 | $0.285 | $0.295 | $0.310 | $0.345 | N/R |
| | 1807 | $0.295 | $0.295 | $0.295 | $0.360 | N/R |
| | 1808 | $0.230 | $0.235 | $0.275 | $0.255 | N/R |
| | 1809 | $0.230 | $0.240 | $0.200 | $0.250 | N/R |
| | 1810 | $0.205 | $0.220 | $0.215 | $0.255 | N/R |
| | 1811 | $0.155 | $0.180 | $0.185 | $0.215 | N/R |
| | 1812 | $0.135 | $0.135 | $0.140 | $0.150 | N/R |
| | 1813 | $0.200 | $0.205 | $0.215 | $0.190 | N/R |
| | 1814 | $0.270 | $0.210 | N/R | $0.300 | N/R |
| | 1815 | $0.252 | $0.255 | $0.255 | $0.260 | N/R |
| | 1816 | $0.225 | $0.220 | $0.260 | $0.290 | $0.400 |
| | 1817 | $0.175 | $0.195 | $0.190 | $0.190 | $0.320 |
| | 1818 | $0.240 | $0.265 | $0.278 | $0.272 | $0.340 |
| | 1819 | $0.265 | $0.290 | $0.310 | $0.345 | $0.525 |
| | 1820 | $0.230 | $0.265 | $0.280 | $0.290 | $0.475 |
| | 1821 | $0.255 | $0.290 | $0.280 | $0.265 | $0.400 |
| | 1822 | $0.260 | $0.268 | $0.295 | $0.320 | $0.420 |
| | 1823 | $0.228 | $0.255 | $0.252 | $0.250 | $0.290 |
| | 1824 | $0.178 | $0.220 | $0.208 | $0.225 | $0.250 |
| Copper, per pound | 1800 | $0.55 | $0.55 | N/R | N/R | N/R |
| | 1801 | $0.42 | $0.59 | N/R | N/R | N/R |
| | 1802 | $0.41 | $0.40 | N/R | N/R | N/R |
| | 1803 | $0.39 | $0.40 | N/R | N/R | N/R |
| | 1804 | $0.48 | $0.43 | N/R | N/R | N/R |
| | 1805 | $0.48 | $0.42 | N/R | N/R | N/R |
| | 1806 | $0.52 | N/R | N/R | N/R | N/R |
| | 1807 | $0.51 | N/R | N/R | N/R | N/R |
| | 1808 | $0.46 | N/R | N/R | N/R | N/R |
| | 1809 | $0.45 | N/R | N/R | N/R | N/R |
| | 1810 | $0.42 | $0.40 | N/R | N/R | N/R |
| | 1811 | $0.35 | $0.32 | N/R | N/R | N/R |
| | 1812 | $0.36 | $0.40 | N/R | N/R | N/R |
| | 1813 | $0.48 | $0.58 | N/R | N/R | N/R |

### Based Upon US Dollars

| Year | Value of 19th Century Dollar in 2002 US Dollars |
|---|---|
| 1800 | $14.00 |
| 1805 | $15.00 |
| 1810 | $14.00 |
| 1815 | $11.00 |
| 1820 | $15.00 |
| 1824 | $18.00 |

*Calculations are approximate values based upon economic historical data*

| Commodity | Year | Philadelphia Currency | New York Currency | Charleston Currency | New Orleans Currency | Cincinnati Currency |
|---|---|---|---|---|---|---|
| | 1814 | $0.52 | $0.68 | N/R | N/R | N/R |
| | 1815 | $0.50 | $0.40 | N/R | $0.17 | N/R |
| | 1816 | $0.40 | $0.34 | N/R | $0.19 | N/R |
| | 1817 | $0.27 | $0.27 | N/R | N/R | N/R |
| | 1818 | $0.28 | $0.28 | N/R | N/R | N/R |
| | 1819 | $0.30 | $0.30 | N/R | $0.18 | N/R |
| | 1820 | $0.28 | $0.30 | N/R | N/R | N/R |
| | 1821 | $0.30 | $0.26 | N/R | N/R | N/R |
| | 1822 | $0.28 | $0.26 | N/R | N/R | N/R |
| | 1823 | $0.26 | $0.25 | N/R | N/R | N/R |
| | 1824 | $0.24 | $0.24 | N/R | N/R | N/R |
| Corn meal, per barrel | 1800 | $4.00 | N/R | N/R | N/R | N/R |
| *(Cinncinati per bushel)* | 1801 | $5.25 | N/R | N/R | N/R | N/R |
| | 1802 | $2.54 | $2.88 | N/R | N/R | N/R |
| | 1803 | $3.00 | $3.62 | N/R | N/R | N/R |
| | 1804 | $3.50 | $4.25 | N/R | N/R | N/R |
| | 1805 | $5.50 | $5.00 | N/R | N/R | N/R |
| | 1806 | $3.38 | $4.00 | N/R | N/R | N/R |
| | 1807 | $3.25 | N/R | N/R | N/R | N/R |
| | 1808 | $3.38 | N/R | N/R | N/R | N/R |
| | 1809 | $4.00 | N/R | N/R | N/R | N/R |
| | 1810 | $4.25 | N/R | N/R | N/R | N/R |
| | 1811 | $4.50 | N/R | N/R | N/R | N/R |
| | 1812 | $4.50 | N/R | N/R | N/R | N/R |
| | 1813 | $4.88 | N/R | N/R | N/R | N/R |
| | 1814 | $4.50 | N/R | N/R | N/R | N/R |
| | 1815 | $4.00 | N/R | N/R | N/R | N/R |
| | 1816 | $4.88 | N/R | N/R | $3.25 | $0.44 |
| | 1817 | $9.00 | $9.38 | N/R | $6.50 | $0.75 |
| | 1818 | $4.00 | $5.00 | N/R | $2.50 | $0.75 |
| | 1819 | $2.94 | $3.63 | N/R | $3.00 | $0.68 |
| | 1820 | $3.00 | $3.09 | N/R | $2.12 | $0.28 |
| | 1821 | $2.00 | $2.56 | N/R | N/R | $0.25 |
| | 1822 | $3.62 | $4.13 | N/R | $2.25 | $0.18 |
| | 1823 | $3.25 | $3.44 | N/R | N/R | $0.40 |
| | 1824 | $2.12 | $2.44 | N/R | N/R | $0.21 |
| Corn, per bushel | 1800 | $0.605 | $0.840 | $0.043 | N/R | N/R |
| *(New Orleans, per barrel)* | 1801 | $0.815 | $0.905 | $0.054 | N/R | N/R |
| | 1802 | $0.485 | $0.560 | $0.033 | N/R | N/R |
| | 1803 | $0.500 | $0.600 | $0.725 | N/R | N/R |
| | 1804 | $0.775 | $0.750 | $0.047 | $1.00 | N/R |
| | 1805 | $1.020 | $1.030 | $1.125 | $1.00 | N/R |
| | 1806 | $0.520 | $0.650 | $0.680 | $0.88 | N/R |
| | 1807 | $0.615 | $0.750 | $1.140 | $1.00 | N/R |
| | 1808 | $0.475 | $0.530 | $0.600 | $0.75 | N/R |
| | 1809 | $0.600 | $0.750 | $0.550 | $0.88 | N/R |
| | 1810 | $0.700 | $0.790 | $0.710 | $0.88 | N/R |
| | 1811 | $0.700 | $0.780 | $0.800 | $0.88 | N/R |

| Commodity | Year | Philadelphia Currency | New York Currency | Charleston Currency | New Orleans Currency | Cincinnati Currency |
|---|---|---|---|---|---|---|
| | 1812 | $0.775 | $0.610 | $0.836 | $0.73 | N/R |
| | 1813 | $0.625 | $1.120 | $0.800 | N/R | N/R |
| | 1814 | $0.680 | $1.000 | $0.725 | N/R | N/R |
| | 1815 | $0.710 | $0.870 | $0.900 | N/R | N/R |
| | 1816 | $0.910 | $0.970 | $0.950 | N/R | $0.438 |
| | 1817 | $1.725 | $1.750 | $1.550 | N/R | $0.625 |
| | 1818 | $0.750 | $0.935 | $0.925 | N/R | $0.500 |
| | 1819 | $0.510 | $0.740 | $0.625 | N/R | $0.500 |
| | 1820 | $0.475 | $0.555 | $0.550 | N/R | $0.275 |
| | 1821 | $0.315 | $0.500 | $0.410 | N/R | $0.208 |
| | 1822 | $0.790 | $0.855 | $0.950 | $0.75 | $0.150 |
| | 1823 | $0.560 | $0.580 | $0.680 | $0.56 | $0.250 |
| | 1824 | $0.360 | $0.425 | $0.380 | $0.44 | $0.190 |
| Cotton, per pound | 1800 | $0.29 | $0.26 | N/R | $0.19 | N/R |
| | 1801 | $0.26 | $0.28 | N/R | $0.22 | N/R |
| | 1802 | $0.22 | $0.20 | $0.18 | $0.27 | N/R |
| | 1803 | $0.18 | $0.18 | $0.15 | $0.15 | N/R |
| | 1804 | $0.18 | $0.18 | $0.17 | $0.14 | N/R |
| | 1805 | $0.24 | $0.25 | $0.22 | $0.26 | N/R |
| | 1806 | $0.20 | $0.22 | $0.18 | $0.22 | N/R |
| | 1807 | $0.22 | $0.21 | $0.20 | $0.22 | N/R |
| | 1808 | $0.14 | $0.13 | $0.14 | $0.15 | N/R |
| | 1809 | $0.16 | $0.16 | $0.14 | $0.14 | N/R |
| | 1810 | $0.18 | $0.16 | $0.12 | $0.14 | N/R |
| | 1811 | $0.14 | $0.12 | $0.12 | $0.14 | N/R |
| | 1812 | $0.10 | $0.10 | $0.09 | $0.08 | N/R |
| | 1813 | $0.16 | $0.18 | $0.10 | N/R | N/R |
| | 1814 | $0.24 | $0.24 | $0.15 | N/R | N/R |
| | 1815 | $0.19 | $0.17 | $0.17 | $0.18 | N/R |
| | 1816 | $0.30 | $0.32 | $0.30 | $0.32 | $0.30 |
| | 1817 | $0.27 | $0.29 | $0.30 | $0.30 | $0.35 |
| | 1818 | $0.34 | $0.33 | $0.30 | $0.27 | $0.36 |
| | 1819 | $0.18 | $0.15 | $0.14 | $0.20 | $0.28 |

### Based Upon US Dollars

| Year | Value of 19th Century Dollar in 2002 US Dollars |
|---|---|
| 1800 | $14.00 |
| 1805 | $15.00 |
| 1810 | $14.00 |
| 1815 | $11.00 |
| 1820 | $15.00 |
| 1824 | $18.00 |

*Calculations are approximate values based upon economic historical data*

| Commodity | Year | Philadelphia Currency | New York Currency | Charleston Currency | New Orleans Currency | Cincinnati Currency |
|---|---|---|---|---|---|---|
| | 1820 | $0.18 | $0.16 | $0.16 | $0.18 | $0.34 |
| | 1821 | $0.16 | $0.13 | $0.12 | $0.16 | $0.18 |
| | 1822 | $0.16 | $0.15 | $0.14 | $0.22 | $0.18 |
| | 1823 | $0.11 | $0.10 | $0.10 | $0.14 | $0.10 |
| | 1824 | $0.14 | $0.16 | $0.15 | $0.17 | $0.14 |
| Duck Cloth, per bolt | 1800 | $11.00 | $15.75 | N/R | N/R | N/R |
| *(New Orleans per piece from 1822-24)* | 1801 | $13.00 | $19.00 | N/R | N/R | N/R |
| | 1802 | $9.50 | $15.00 | N/R | N/R | N/R |
| | 1803 | $11.50 | $20.00 | N/R | N/R | N/R |
| | 1804 | $11.50 | $19.75 | N/R | $20.00 | N/R |
| | 1805 | $14.88 | $20.00 | N/R | $20.00 | N/R |
| | 1806 | $15.00 | $20.50 | N/R | N/R | N/R |
| | 1807 | $14.00 | $21.50 | N/R | $22.50 | N/R |
| | 1808 | $14.75 | $24.50 | N/R | $28.50 | N/R |
| | 1809 | $22.00 | $40.00 | N/R | $45.00 | N/R |
| | 1810 | $16.00 | $29.00 | N/R | $45.00 | N/R |
| | 1811 | $11.00 | $24.00 | N/R | $27.50 | N/R |
| | 1812 | $11.00 | $23.50 | N/R | $13.00 | N/R |
| | 1813 | $18.25 | $35.00 | N/R | N/R | N/R |
| | 1814 | $16.00 | $40.00 | N/R | N/R | N/R |
| | 1815 | $17.00 | $30.00 | N/R | $26.00 | N/R |
| | 1816 | $13.50 | $27.50 | N/R | $26.00 | N/R |
| | 1817 | $10.75 | $22.50 | N/R | N/R | N/R |
| | 1818 | $11.50 | $21.75 | N/R | $18.00 | N/R |
| | 1819 | $11.25 | $21.75 | N/R | $19.00 | N/R |
| | 1820 | $10.75 | $21.25 | N/R | N/R | N/R |
| | 1821 | $9.62 | $20.75 | N/R | N/R | N/R |
| | 1822 | $10.50 | $19.75 | N/R | $16.00 | N/R |
| | 1823 | $10.50 | $19.50 | N/R | $18.50 | N/R |
| | 1824 | $9.00 | $18.75 | N/R | $18.00 | N/R |
| Fish, per hundredweight | 1800 | $2.50 | $2.88 | N/R | N/R | N/R |
| *(Charleston & Cinncinati per barrel 1819-24)* | 1801 | $4.75 | $4.75 | N/R | N/R | N/R |
| | 1802 | $5.00 | $4.38 | N/R | N/R | N/R |
| | 1803 | $4.25 | $1.75 | $9.00 | N/R | N/R |
| | 1804 | $4.25 | $4.25 | $6.00 | $4.50 | N/R |
| | 1805 | $4.25 | $4.50 | $7.75 | $7.00 | N/R |
| | 1806 | $4.25 | $4.63 | $8.00 | $6.50 | N/R |
| | 1807 | $4.75 | $4.63 | N/R | $5.50 | N/R |
| | 1808 | $2.25 | $4.80 | N/R | $4.00 | N/R |
| | 1809 | $3.75 | $4.25 | N/R | $5.00 | N/R |
| | 1810 | $3.62 | $3.25 | N/R | $5.00 | N/R |
| | 1811 | $5.00 | $3.75 | N/R | $3.25 | N/R |
| | 1812 | $4.50 | $3.50 | N/R | $5.50 | N/R |
| | 1813 | $4.25 | $3.75 | N/R | N/R | N/R |
| | 1814 | $5.75 | $5.00 | N/R | N/R | N/R |
| | 1815 | $5.00 | $5.00 | N/R | $4.25 | N/R |
| | 1816 | $4.75 | $4.50 | N/R | $6.00 | N/R |
| | 1817 | $3.25 | $3.75 | N/R | N/R | N/R |

| Commodity | Year | Philadelphia Currency | New York Currency | Charleston Currency | New Orleans Currency | Cincinnati Currency |
|---|---|---|---|---|---|---|
| | 1818 | $3.88 | $3.38 | $10.50 | $3.25 | N/R |
| | 1819 | $3.25 | $3.44 | $8.50 | $3.25 | $38.00 |
| | 1820 | $2.88 | $2.69 | $6.50 | N/R | $34.00 |
| | 1821 | $2.50 | $2.63 | $3.20 | N/R | N/R |
| | 1822 | $3.00 | $2.88 | $4.10 | N/R | N/R |
| | 1823 | $2.88 | $2.63 | $4.00 | N/R | N/R |
| | 1824 | $2.88 | $2.75 | $4.10 | N/R | $13.50 |
| Flour, per hundredweight | 1801 | $11.50 | $10.75 | N/R | $9.00 | N/R |
| *(Philadelphia & New York per barrel* | 1802 | $7.00 | $6.50 | N/R | $7.50 | N/R |
| *1801-1808)* | 1803 | $6.00 | $6.38 | $7.12 | $7.00 | N/R |
| | 1804 | $6.50 | $5.38 | $7.62 | $7.50 | N/R |
| | 1805 | $11.75 | $11.50 | $12.00 | $9.50 | N/R |
| | 1806 | $7.80 | $8.88 | $7.25 | $5.50 | N/R |
| | 1807 | $7.25 | $7.13 | $9.00 | $5.50 | N/R |
| | 1808 | $5.00 | $5.25 | $7.00 | $5.50 | N/R |
| | 1809 | $7.00 | $8.00 | $8.00 | $7.00 | N/R |
| | 1810 | $9.00 | $7.88 | $7.50 | $7.50 | N/R |
| | 1811 | $10.25 | $10.25 | $12.25 | $5.50 | N/R |
| | 1812 | $7.88 | $7.75 | $12.56 | $7.25 | N/R |
| | 1813 | $7.88 | $11.63 | $16.90 | N/R | N/R |
| | 1814 | $7.25 | $8.75 | $9.70 | N/R | N/R |
| | 1815 | $8.50 | $7.13 | $8.10 | $5.75 | N/R |
| | 1816 | $7.87 | $7.25 | $8.00 | $6.50 | $4.50 |
| | 1817 | $14.25 | $13.00 | $15.50 | $11.50 | $8.25 |
| | 1818 | $10.00 | $9.44 | $10.80 | $7.00 | $5.50 |
| | 1819 | $6.37 | $6.81 | $9.80 | $5.00 | $5.75 |
| | 1820 | $4.62 | $5.00 | $5.50 | $4.00 | $3.44 |
| | 1821 | $4.00 | $4.44 | $5.00 | $2.62 | $2.00 |
| | 1822 | $7.12 | $6.38 | $7.40 | $5.25 | $2.62 |
| | 1823 | $7.37 | $6.94 | $8.10 | $4.12 | $3.75 |
| | 1824 | $6.00 | $5.94 | $6.00 | $5.25 | $4.14 |

### Based Upon US Dollars

| Year | Value of 19th Century Dollar in 2002 US Dollars |
|---|---|
| 1800 | $14.00 |
| 1805 | $15.00 |
| 1810 | $14.00 |
| 1815 | $11.00 |
| 1820 | $15.00 |
| 1824 | $18.00 |

*Calculations are approximate values based upon economic historical data*

| Commodity | Year | Philadelphia Currency | New York Currency | Charleston Currency | New Orleans Currency | Cincinnati Currency |
|---|---|---|---|---|---|---|
| Gin, per gallon | 1800 | $1.11 | $1.09 | N/R | $1.62 | N/R |
| *(New York per case 1800-1803)* | 1801 | $1.34 | $1.18 | N/R | N/R | N/R |
| | 1802 | $1.20 | $1.09 | N/R | N/R | N/R |
| | 1803 | $1.18 | $1.14 | N/R | N/R | N/R |
| | 1804 | $1.00 | $0.96 | N/R | $1.06 | N/R |
| | 1805 | $0.98 | $0.94 | N/R | $0.75 | N/R |
| | 1806 | $1.18 | $1.16 | N/R | $0.88 | N/R |
| | 1807 | $0.98 | $0.97 | N/R | $0.75 | N/R |
| | 1808 | $1.18 | $1.18 | N/R | $0.62 | N/R |
| | 1809 | $1.50 | $1.25 | N/R | $0.88 | N/R |
| | 1810 | $1.88 | N/R | N/R | $0.94 | N/R |
| | 1811 | $1.95 | N/R | N/R | $0.94 | N/R |
| | 1812 | $2.75 | N/R | N/R | $0.72 | N/R |
| | 1813 | $2.50 | N/R | $1.22 | N/R | N/R |
| | 1814 | $1.88 | N/R | N/R | N/R | N/R |
| | 1815 | $2.12 | N/R | $1.55 | N/R | N/R |
| | 1816 | $1.42 | N/R | $1.25 | N/R | N/R |
| | 1817 | $1.55 | $1.31 | $1.45 | N/R | N/R |
| | 1818 | $1.55 | $1.47 | $1.62 | N/R | N/R |
| | 1819 | $1.01 | $0.92 | $1.05 | N/R | N/R |
| | 1820 | $1.03 | $0.89 | $0.92 | N/R | N/R |
| | 1821 | $1.00 | $0.85 | $0.90 | $0.42 | N/R |
| | 1822 | $1.00 | $0.86 | $0.98 | $0.43 | N/R |
| | 1823 | $1.10 | $0.88 | $0.95 | $0.40 | N/R |
| | 1824 | $1.20 | $0.90 | N/R | $0.41 | N/R |
| Hops, per pound | 1801 | $0.20 | N/R | N/R | N/R | N/R |
| | 1802 | $0.20 | N/R | N/R | N/R | N/R |
| | 1803 | $0.11 | N/R | N/R | N/R | N/R |
| | 1804 | $0.11 | N/R | N/R | N/R | N/R |
| | 1805 | $0.07 | N/R | N/R | N/R | N/R |
| | 1806 | $0.15 | N/R | N/R | N/R | N/R |
| | 1807 | $0.16 | N/R | N/R | N/R | N/R |
| | 1808 | $0.15 | N/R | N/R | N/R | N/R |
| | 1809 | $0.15 | N/R | N/R | N/R | N/R |
| | 1810 | $0.18 | N/R | N/R | N/R | N/R |
| | 1811 | $0.27 | N/R | N/R | N/R | N/R |
| | 1812 | $0.10 | N/R | N/R | N/R | N/R |
| | 1813 | $0.19 | N/R | N/R | N/R | N/R |
| | 1814 | $0.30 | $0.20 | N/R | N/R | N/R |
| | 1815 | $0.35 | $0.20 | N/R | N/R | N/R |
| | 1816 | $0.50 | $0.30 | N/R | N/R | $0.25 |
| | 1817 | $0.29 | $0.34 | N/R | N/R | $0.31 |
| | 1818 | $0.42 | $0.38 | N/R | N/R | $0.31 |
| | 1819 | $0.09 | $0.07 | N/R | N/R | $0.37 |
| | 1820 | $0.06 | $0.07 | N/R | N/R | N/R |
| | 1821 | $0.08 | $0.08 | N/R | N/R | N/R |
| | 1822 | $0.12 | $0.11 | N/R | N/R | $0.18 |
| | 1823 | $0.12 | $0.12 | N/R | N/R | N/R |
| | 1824 | $0.32 | $0.35 | N/R | N/R | $0.12 |

| Commodity | Year | Philadelphia Currency | New York Currency | Charleston Currency | New Orleans Currency | Cincinnati Currency |
|---|---|---|---|---|---|---|
| Indigo, per pound | 1800 | $1.29 | $1.47 | N/R | $0.62 | N/R |
| | 1801 | $1.25 | $2.13 | N/R | N/R | N/R |
| | 1802 | $1.55 | $1.50 | N/R | N/R | N/R |
| | 1803 | $2.00 | $2.53 | N/R | N/R | N/R |
| | 1804 | $1.75 | $2.00 | N/R | $1.62 | N/R |
| | 1805 | $1.75 | $2.22 | N/R | $1.62 | N/R |
| | 1806 | $1.71 | $2.63 | N/R | $1.63 | N/R |
| | 1807 | $1.71 | $2.22 | N/R | $1.63 | N/R |
| | 1808 | $1.50 | $2.06 | $0.88 | $1.25 | N/R |
| | 1809 | $1.50 | $2.25 | $0.88 | $1.12 | N/R |
| | 1810 | $1.50 | $2.90 | $1.01 | $1.06 | N/R |
| | 1811 | $1.50 | $2.31 | $0.85 | $1.03 | N/R |
| | 1812 | $1.25 | $1.88 | $0.70 | $0.88 | N/R |
| | 1813 | $1.62 | $2.50 | $0.78 | N/R | N/R |
| | 1814 | $1.48 | $2.50 | $0.95 | N/R | N/R |
| | 1815 | $1.84 | $2.28 | $0.78 | $1.25 | N/R |
| | 1816 | $1.21 | $2.19 | $0.78 | N/R | N/R |
| | 1817 | $1.24 | $2.22 | N/R | N/R | N/R |
| | 1818 | $1.32 | $1.79 | $0.78 | $1.50 | N/R |
| | 1819 | $1.32 | $1.90 | N/R | $1.25 | $3.00 |
| | 1820 | $1.32 | $1.82 | N/R | $1.00 | $3.00 |
| | 1821 | $1.32 | $1.82 | N/R | N/R | N/R |
| | 1822 | $1.62 | $3.00 | N/R | N/R | N/R |
| | 1823 | $2.08 | $2.38 | N/R | N/R | $2.75 |
| | 1824 | $1.95 | $2.06 | N/R | N/R | $2.56 |
| Iron - Bar, per ton | 1800 | $110.00 | $102.50 | N/R | N/R | N/R |
| *(Charleston Per hundredweight)* | 1801 | $113.30 | $142.50 | N/R | N/R | N/R |
| | 1802 | $110.00 | $107.50 | N/R | N/R | N/R |
| | 1803 | $100.00 | $102.50 | N/R | N/R | N/R |
| | 1804 | $100.00 | $102.50 | N/R | N/R | N/R |
| | 1805 | $107.00 | $107.50 | N/R | N/R | N/R |
| | 1806 | $113.00 | $112.50 | $6.50 | N/R | N/R |
| | 1807 | $117.50 | $112.50 | $6.25 | N/R | N/R |

## Based Upon US Dollars

| Year | Value of 19th Century Dollar in 2002 US Dollars |
|---|---|
| 1800 | $14.00 |
| 1805 | $15.00 |
| 1810 | $14.00 |
| 1815 | $11.00 |
| 1820 | $15.00 |
| 1824 | $18.00 |

*Calculations are approximate values based upon economic historical data*

| Commodity | Year | Philadelphia Currency | New York Currency | Charleston Currency | New Orleans Currency | Cincinnati Currency |
|---|---|---|---|---|---|---|
| | 1808 | $117.50 | $112.50 | N/R | N/R | N/R |
| | 1809 | $112.50 | $110.00 | N/R | N/R | N/R |
| | 1810 | $112.50 | $110.00 | N/R | N/R | N/R |
| | 1811 | $109.00 | $102.50 | N/R | N/R | N/R |
| | 1812 | $97.50 | $102.50 | N/R | N/R | N/R |
| | 1813 | $97.50 | $102.50 | N/R | N/R | N/R |
| | 1814 | $117.50 | $107.50 | N/R | N/R | N/R |
| | 1815 | $107.50 | $130.00 | N/R | N/R | N/R |
| | 1816 | $137.50 | $112.50 | N/R | $122.50 | $235.00 |
| | 1817 | $115.00 | $95.00 | N/R | N/R | $215.00 |
| | 1818 | $115.00 | $87.50 | $4.25 | $100.00 | $204.00 |
| | 1819 | $107.50 | $92.50 | $4.50 | $115.00 | $225.00 |
| | 1820 | $110.00 | $95.00 | $4.50 | $120.00 | $165.00 |
| | 1821 | $110.00 | $77.50 | $4.38 | $92.00 | $130.00 |
| | 1822 | $97.50 | $81.50 | $4.50 | $100.00 | $112.50 |
| | 1823 | $97.50 | $77.50 | $4.12 | $97.50 | $125.00 |
| | 1824 | $89.50 | $76.50 | $4.12 | $90.00 | $127.50 |
| Iron-Pig, per ton | 1800 | $36.00 | $36.20 | N/R | N/R | N/R |
| | 1801 | $34.00 | $39.00 | N/R | N/R | N/R |
| | 1802 | $30.00 | $32.50 | N/R | N/R | N/R |
| | 1803 | $30.00 | $29.00 | N/R | N/R | N/R |
| | 1804 | $30.00 | $30.00 | N/R | N/R | N/R |
| | 1805 | $31.00 | $29.00 | N/R | N/R | N/R |
| | 1806 | $35.50 | $32.50 | N/R | N/R | N/R |
| | 1807 | $40.00 | $38.00 | N/R | N/R | N/R |
| | 1808 | $40.00 | $38.00 | N/R | N/R | N/R |
| | 1809 | $40.00 | $38.00 | N/R | N/R | N/R |
| | 1810 | $40.00 | $38.00 | N/R | N/R | N/R |
| | 1811 | $47.50 | $45.00 | N/R | N/R | N/R |
| | 1812 | $47.50 | $45.00 | N/R | N/R | N/R |
| | 1813 | $47.50 | $45.00 | N/R | N/R | N/R |
| | 1814 | $45.00 | $45.00 | N/R | N/R | N/R |
| | 1815 | $55.00 | $55.00 | N/R | N/R | N/R |
| | 1816 | $50.00 | $50.00 | N/R | N/R | N/R |
| | 1817 | $50.00 | $45.00 | N/R | N/R | N/R |
| | 1818 | $42.50 | $37.50 | N/R | N/R | N/R |
| | 1819 | $35.50 | $37.50 | N/R | N/R | N/R |
| | 1820 | $35.00 | $35.00 | N/R | N/R | N/R |
| | 1821 | $35.00 | $35.00 | N/R | N/R | N/R |
| | 1822 | $35.00 | $35.00 | N/R | N/R | N/R |
| | 1823 | $37.50 | $35.00 | N/R | N/R | N/R |
| | 1824 | $40.00 | $40.00 | N/R | N/R | N/R |
| Lard, per pound | 1800 | $0.100 | $0.110 | N/R | N/R | N/R |
| | 1801 | $0.165 | $0.145 | N/R | N/R | N/R |
| | 1802 | $0.130 | $0.105 | N/R | $0.070 | N/R |
| | 1803 | $0.095 | $0.095 | N/R | N/R | N/R |
| | 1804 | $0.105 | $0.105 | N/R | $0.120 | N/R |
| | 1805 | $0.125 | $0.160 | N/R | $0.125 | N/R |

| Commodity | Year | Philadelphia Currency | New York Currency | Charleston Currency | New Orleans Currency | Cincinnati Currency |
|---|---|---|---|---|---|---|
| | 1806 | $0.200 | $0.165 | N/R | $0.150 | N/R |
| | 1807 | $0.135 | $0.140 | N/R | $0.120 | N/R |
| | 1808 | $0.110 | $0.085 | N/R | $0.110 | N/R |
| | 1809 | $0.125 | $0.115 | N/R | $0.140 | N/R |
| | 1810 | $0.150 | $0.125 | N/R | $0.105 | N/R |
| | 1811 | $0.130 | $0.120 | N/R | $0.090 | N/R |
| | 1812 | $0.125 | $0.115 | N/R | $0.100 | N/R |
| | 1813 | $0.128 | $0.120 | $0.100 | N/R | N/R |
| | 1814 | $0.155 | $0.165 | $0.130 | N/R | N/R |
| | 1815 | $0.145 | $0.160 | $0.150 | $0.290 | N/R |
| | 1816 | $0.185 | $0.150 | $0.180 | $0.162 | $0.100 |
| | 1817 | $0.210 | $0.190 | $0.200 | $0.140 | $0.120 |
| | 1818 | $0.195 | $0.150 | $0.165 | $0.160 | $0.100 |
| | 1819 | $0.128 | $0.135 | $0.145 | $0.115 | $0.138 |
| | 1820 | $0.112 | $0.098 | $0.105 | $0.105 | $0.095 |
| | 1821 | $0.095 | $0.100 | $0.085 | $0.055 | $0.040 |
| | 1822 | $0.095 | $0.083 | $0.100 | $0.070 | $0.040 |
| | 1823 | $0.085 | $0.061 | $0.100 | $0.065 | $0.060 |
| | 1824 | $0.095 | $0.083 | $0.092 | $0.075 | $0.058 |
| Leather, Tanned, per pound | 1800 | $0.19 | $0.16 | $0.75 | N/R | N/R |
| | 1801 | $0.19 | $0.18 | $1.08 | N/R | N/R |
| | 1802 | $0.19 | $0.22 | $1.12 | N/R | N/R |
| | 1803 | $0.23 | $0.22 | $1.08 | N/R | N/R |
| | 1804 | $0.23 | $0.22 | $1.12 | $2.00 | N/R |
| | 1805 | $0.23 | $0.22 | $1.12 | $2.00 | N/R |
| | 1806 | $0.23 | $0.25 | $1.12 | $2.00 | N/R |
| | 1807 | $0.23 | $0.22 | $1.12 | $0.29 | N/R |
| | 1808 | $0.24 | $0.22 | N/R | $0.29 | N/R |
| | 1809 | $0.22 | $0.18 | N/R | $0.29 | N/R |
| | 1810 | $0.25 | $0.21 | N/R | $0.29 | N/R |
| | 1811 | $0.22 | $0.21 | N/R | $0.29 | N/R |
| | 1812 | $0.20 | $0.20 | N/R | $0.20 | N/R |
| | 1813 | $0.21 | $0.20 | N/R | N/R | N/R |

## Based Upon US Dollars

| Year | Value of 19th Century Dollar in 2002 US Dollars |
|---|---|
| 1800 | $14.00 |
| 1805 | $15.00 |
| 1810 | $14.00 |
| 1815 | $11.00 |
| 1820 | $15.00 |
| 1824 | $18.00 |

*Calculations are approximate values based upon economic historical data*

| Commodity | Year | Philadelphia Currency | New York Currency | Charleston Currency | New Orleans Currency | Cincinnati Currency |
|---|---|---|---|---|---|---|
| | 1814 | $0.26 | $0.31 | N/R | N/R | N/R |
| | 1815 | $0.21 | $0.24 | N/R | N/R | N/R |
| | 1816 | $0.28 | $0.24 | N/R | N/R | N/R |
| | 1817 | $0.28 | $0.22 | N/R | N/R | N/R |
| | 1818 | $0.27 | $0.32 | N/R | $0.25 | N/R |
| | 1819 | $0.28 | $0.32 | N/R | $0.25 | $0.48 |
| | 1820 | $0.27 | $0.26 | N/R | N/R | $0.39 |
| | 1821 | $0.27 | $0.21 | N/R | N/R | N/R |
| | 1822 | $0.27 | $0.24 | N/R | $0.20 | $0.28 |
| | 1823 | $0.27 | $0.26 | N/R | $0.28 | $0.26 |
| | 1824 | $0.27 | $0.26 | N/R | $0.21 | $0.28 |
| Linseed Oil, per gallon | 1800 | $0.77 | $0.81 | N/R | $1.50 | N/R |
| | 1801 | $0.66 | $1.15 | N/R | N/R | N/R |
| | 1802 | $1.05 | $1.25 | N/R | N/R | N/R |
| | 1803 | $1.33 | $1.44 | $1.28 | $2.00 | N/R |
| | 1804 | $1.04 | $1.37 | $1.50 | $1.62 | N/R |
| | 1805 | $1.20 | $1.22 | $1.25 | $1.75 | N/R |
| | 1806 | $0.88 | $1.00 | N/R | $1.75 | N/R |
| | 1807 | $0.76 | $0.97 | N/R | $1.12 | N/R |
| | 1808 | $0.68 | $0.81 | N/R | $1.12 | N/R |
| | 1809 | $0.85 | $1.06 | N/R | $1.38 | N/R |
| | 1810 | $0.98 | N/R | N/R | $1.38 | N/R |
| | 1811 | $0.89 | $0.90 | N/R | $1.38 | N/R |
| | 1812 | $0.82 | $1.03 | N/R | $1.25 | N/R |
| | 1813 | $0.75 | $0.80 | N/R | N/R | N/R |
| | 1814 | $0.72 | $0.81 | N/R | N/R | N/R |
| | 1815 | $0.72 | $0.81 | N/R | N/R | N/R |
| | 1816 | $1.04 | $1.08 | N/R | $1.12 | $1.38 |
| | 1817 | $0.90 | $0.97 | N/R | N/R | $1.25 |
| | 1818 | $1.36 | $1.39 | N/R | N/R | $1.12 |
| | 1819 | $1.45 | $1.25 | N/R | $1.31 | $1.25 |
| | 1820 | $0.88 | $0.95 | N/R | N/R | $1.25 |
| | 1821 | $0.78 | $0.83 | N/R | N/R | $0.69 |
| | 1822 | $0.68 | $0.76 | N/R | $0.75 | $0.69 |
| | 1823 | $0.50 | $0.58 | N/R | $0.68 | $0.64 |
| | 1824 | $0.64 | $0.66 | N/R | $0.88 | $0.64 |
| Lumber Boards, per one thousand feet | 1800 | $28.00 | $15.00 | N/R | N/R | N/R |
| | 1801 | $28.00 | $17.50 | N/R | N/R | N/R |
| | 1802 | $28.00 | $17.50 | N/R | N/R | N/R |
| | 1803 | $26.50 | $15.00 | $6.50 | N/R | N/R |
| | 1804 | $29.00 | $15.60 | $4.75 | N/R | N/R |
| | 1805 | $28.00 | $17.50 | $4.66 | N/R | N/R |
| | 1806 | $30.00 | $16.20 | $20.00 | N/R | N/R |
| | 1807 | $30.00 | $17.50 | $20.00 | N/R | N/R |
| | 1808 | $30.00 | $18.80 | N/R | N/R | N/R |
| | 1809 | $30.00 | $17.50 | N/R | N/R | N/R |
| | 1810 | $35.00 | $17.50 | N/R | N/R | N/R |
| | 1811 | $35.50 | $15.00 | N/R | N/R | N/R |

| Commodity | Year | Philadelphia Currency | New York Currency | Charleston Currency | New Orleans Currency | Cincinnati Currency |
|---|---|---|---|---|---|---|
| | 1812 | $35.50 | $15.00 | N/R | N/R | N/R |
| | 1813 | $40.00 | $15.00 | N/R | N/R | N/R |
| | 1814 | $40.00 | $15.00 | N/R | N/R | N/R |
| | 1815 | $40.00 | $18.00 | N/R | N/R | N/R |
| | 1816 | $40.00 | $22.00 | N/R | $40.00 | N/R |
| | 1817 | $0.31 | $0.20 | N/R | N/R | N/R |
| | 1818 | $37.50 | $16.50 | $26.00 | $19.00 | N/R |
| | 1819 | $35.00 | $16.50 | $26.00 | $22.50 | N/R |
| | 1820 | $35.00 | $16.50 | $23.50 | N/R | N/R |
| | 1821 | $27.50 | $16.50 | $24.50 | N/R | $4.00 |
| | 1822 | $27.50 | $16.50 | $27.00 | $19.00 | $4.00 |
| | 1823 | $27.50 | $16.50 | $27.00 | $18.50 | N/R |
| | 1824 | $27.50 | $14.00 | $25.50 | $17.50 | $15.00 |
| Molasses, per gallon | 1800 | $4.25 | $0.43 | N/R | N/R | N/R |
| | 1801 | $0.54 | $0.42 | N/R | N/R | N/R |
| | 1802 | $0.38 | $0.40 | N/R | N/R | N/R |
| | 1803 | $0.45 | $0.42 | $0.42 | N/R | N/R |
| | 1804 | $0.52 | $0.48 | $0.50 | $0.38 | N/R |
| | 1805 | $0.45 | $0.39 | $0.39 | $0.32 | N/R |
| | 1806 | $0.39 | $0.36 | $0.34 | $0.33 | N/R |
| | 1807 | $0.30 | $0.36 | $0.36 | $0.32 | N/R |
| | 1808 | $0.46 | $0.44 | $0.47 | $0.36 | N/R |
| | 1809 | $0.35 | $0.40 | $0.39 | $0.40 | N/R |
| | 1810 | $0.48 | $0.47 | $0.39 | $0.41 | N/R |
| | 1811 | $0.52 | $0.48 | $0.55 | $0.42 | N/R |
| | 1812 | $0.57 | $0.52 | $0.47 | $0.42 | N/R |
| | 1813 | $0.85 | $0.76 | $0.60 | N/R | N/R |
| | 1814 | $1.12 | $0.70 | N/R | N/R | N/R |
| | 1815 | $0.74 | $0.72 | $0.76 | $0.31 | N/R |
| | 1816 | $0.48 | $0.46 | $0.52 | $0.40 | N/R |
| | 1817 | $0.49 | $0.46 | $0.52 | N/R | N/R |
| | 1818 | $0.55 | $0.52 | $0.53 | $0.41 | N/R |
| | 1819 | $0.42 | $0.44 | $0.45 | $0.38 | $1.20 |

| **Based Upon US Dollars** | |
|---|---|
| Year | Value of 19th Century Dollar in 2002 US Dollars |
| 1800 | $14.00 |
| 1805 | $15.00 |
| 1810 | $14.00 |
| 1815 | $11.00 |
| 1820 | $15.00 |
| 1824 | $18.00 |

*Calculations are approximate values based upon economic historical data*

| Commodity | Year | Philadelphia Currency | New York Currency | Charleston Currency | New Orleans Currency | Cincinnati Currency |
|---|---|---|---|---|---|---|
| | 1820 | $0.34 | $0.28 | $0.34 | $0.18 | $0.65 |
| | 1821 | $0.26 | $0.26 | $0.29 | $0.18 | $0.50 |
| | 1822 | $0.32 | $0.28 | $0.38 | $0.28 | $0.50 |
| | 1823 | $0.30 | $0.24 | $0.30 | $0.18 | $0.36 |
| | 1824 | $0.26 | $0.24 | $0.28 | $0.20 | $0.36 |
| Nails, per pound | 1800 | $0.108 | $0.115 | N/R | $0.37 | N/R |
| | 1801 | $0.104 | $0.115 | N/R | $0.27 | N/R |
| | 1802 | $0.120 | $0.115 | N/R | N/R | N/R |
| | 1803 | $0.105 | $0.115 | N/R | N/R | N/R |
| | 1804 | $0.105 | $0.115 | N/R | $0.13 | N/R |
| | 1805 | $0.105 | $0.115 | N/R | $0.15 | N/R |
| | 1806 | $0.095 | $0.115 | N/R | $0.15 | N/R |
| | 1807 | $0.095 | $0.115 | N/R | $0.16 | N/R |
| | 1808 | $0.095 | $0.115 | N/R | $0.16 | N/R |
| | 1809 | $0.095 | $0.125 | N/R | $0.17 | N/R |
| | 1810 | $0.095 | $0.125 | N/R | $0.16 | N/R |
| | 1811 | $0.095 | $0.125 | N/R | $0.15 | N/R |
| | 1812 | $0.085 | $0.125 | N/R | $0.14 | N/R |
| | 1813 | $0.085 | $0.125 | N/R | N/R | N/R |
| | 1814 | $0.110 | $0.125 | N/R | N/R | N/R |
| | 1815 | $0.125 | $0.145 | N/R | N/R | N/R |
| | 1816 | $0.125 | $0.135 | N/R | $0.13 | N/R |
| | 1817 | $0.098 | $0.100 | N/R | N/R | N/R |
| | 1818 | $0.098 | $0.100 | N/R | $0.09 | N/R |
| | 1819 | $0.098 | $0.095 | N/R | $0.09 | $0.160 |
| | 1820 | $0.098 | $0.095 | N/R | $0.09 | $0.170 |
| | 1821 | $0.098 | $0.090 | N/R | $0.09 | $0.113 |
| | 1822 | $0.098 | $0.090 | N/R | $0.08 | $0.093 |
| | 1823 | $0.098 | $0.080 | N/R | $0.08 | $0.085 |
| | 1824 | $0.098 | $0.070 | N/R | $0.07 | $0.095 |
| Pork, per barrel | 1800 | $13.38 | $14.50 | N/R | $11.00 | N/R |
| | 1801 | $19.50 | $28.00 | N/R | $13.50 | N/R |
| | 1802 | $15.50 | $16.75 | N/R | $8.00 | N/R |
| | 1803 | $15.50 | $18.00 | N/R | $10.00 | N/R |
| | 1804 | $18.00 | $15.50 | N/R | $8.00 | N/R |
| | 1805 | $14.50 | $22.50 | $18.00 | $9.50 | N/R |
| | 1806 | $22.00 | $22.50 | $20.00 | $11.50 | N/R |
| | 1807 | $18.50 | $20.75 | $19.50 | $13.00 | N/R |
| | 1808 | $13.00 | $14.75 | $12.17 | $15.00 | N/R |
| | 1809 | $16.50 | $16.50 | $15.50 | $13.00 | N/R |
| | 1810 | $20.50 | $21.50 | $16.00 | $13.00 | N/R |
| | 1811 | $21.00 | $19.50 | $16.50 | $9.00 | N/R |
| | 1812 | $16.00 | $16.00 | $16.50 | $9.70 | N/R |
| | 1813 | $16.50 | $21.50 | N/R | N/R | N/R |
| | 1814 | $28.00 | $29.00 | N/R | N/R | N/R |
| | 1815 | $26.50 | $27.75 | N/R | $21.80 | N/R |
| | 1816 | $23.50 | $22.75 | N/R | $24.60 | $13.00 |
| | 1817 | $29.50 | $30.00 | N/R | $21.00 | $8.00 |

| Commodity | Year | Philadelphia Currency | New York Currency | Charleston Currency | New Orleans Currency | Cincinnati Currency |
|---|---|---|---|---|---|---|
| | 1818 | $27.00 | $24.25 | $24.50 | $22.30 | $14.00 |
| | 1819 | $18.00 | $19.00 | $22.50 | $20.30 | $18.00 |
| | 1820 | $15.75 | $13.75 | $14.00 | $12.50 | $13.50 |
| | 1821 | $12.50 | $11.63 | $12.00 | $8.50 | $9.00 |
| | 1822 | $13.75 | $13.75 | $15.00 | $11.20 | $9.00 |
| | 1823 | $14.75 | $12.75 | $14.00 | $11.50 | $10.00 |
| | 1824 | $14.50 | $13.63 | $14.20 | $11.80 | $9.25 |
| Pot Ashes, per ton | 1800 | $172.50 | $172.50 | N/R | N/R | N/R |
| *(Cinncinati per pound)* | 1801 | $145.00 | $120.00 | N/R | N/R | N/R |
| | 1802 | $97.50 | $95.00 | N/R | N/R | N/R |
| | 1803 | $155.00 | $150.00 | N/R | N/R | N/R |
| | 1804 | $132.50 | $145.00 | N/R | N/R | N/R |
| | 1805 | $140.00 | $180.00 | N/R | N/R | N/R |
| | 1806 | $140.00 | $185.00 | N/R | N/R | N/R |
| | 1807 | $140.00 | $215.00 | N/R | N/R | N/R |
| | 1808 | $140.00 | $160.00 | N/R | N/R | N/R |
| | 1809 | $137.50 | $172.50 | N/R | N/R | N/R |
| | 1810 | $145.00 | $163.80 | N/R | N/R | N/R |
| | 1811 | $180.40 | $120.00 | N/R | N/R | N/R |
| | 1812 | $127.40 | $80.00 | N/R | N/R | N/R |
| | 1813 | $141.90 | $100.00 | N/R | N/R | N/R |
| | 1814 | $9.50 | $140.00 | N/R | N/R | N/R |
| | 1815 | $172.50 | $157.50 | N/R | N/R | N/R |
| | 1816 | $220.00 | $262.50 | N/R | N/R | $0.10 |
| | 1817 | $220.00 | $175.00 | N/R | N/R | $0.10 |
| | 1818 | $200.00 | $163.80 | N/R | N/R | $0.10 |
| | 1819 | $172.50 | $113.80 | N/R | N/R | $0.08 |
| | 1820 | $110.00 | $107.50 | N/R | N/R | $0.08 |
| | 1821 | $110.00 | $111.20 | N/R | N/R | N/R |
| | 1822 | $110.00 | $127.50 | N/R | N/R | N/R |
| | 1823 | $110.00 | $161.20 | N/R | N/R | N/R |
| | 1824 | $130.00 | $120.00 | N/R | N/R | N/R |

### Based Upon US Dollars

| Year | Value of 19th Century Dollar in 2002 US Dollars |
|---|---|
| 1800 | $14.00 |
| 1805 | $15.00 |
| 1810 | $14.00 |
| 1815 | $11.00 |
| 1820 | $15.00 |
| 1824 | $18.00 |

*Calculations are approximate values based upon economic historical data*

| Commodity | Year | Philadelphia Currency | New York Currency | Charleston Currency | New Orleans Currency | Cincinnati Currency |
|---|---|---|---|---|---|---|
| Rice, per hundredweight | 1800 | $6.12 | $5.38 | N/R | N/R | N/R |
| (New Orleans per barrel 1804-1812) | 1801 | $6.50 | $5.50 | N/R | N/R | N/R |
| | 1802 | $4.00 | $4.75 | N/R | N/R | N/R |
| | 1803 | $6.25 | $6.25 | $5.00 | N/R | N/R |
| | 1804 | $4.75 | $4.75 | $3.62 | $8.50 | N/R |
| | 1805 | $6.25 | $5.94 | $5.00 | $9.00 | N/R |
| | 1806 | $4.88 | $4.00 | $3.25 | $8.50 | N/R |
| | 1807 | $4.50 | $4.75 | $3.50 | $8.50 | N/R |
| | 1808 | $2.75 | $3.00 | $2.00 | $6.25 | N/R |
| | 1809 | $3.75 | $3.75 | $2.50 | $6.25 | N/R |
| | 1810 | $3.50 | $3.75 | $2.17 | $6.25 | N/R |
| | 1811 | $3.25 | $3.63 | $2.88 | $4.00 | N/R |
| | 1812 | $4.25 | $4.00 | $3.75 | $4.00 | N/R |
| | 1813 | $6.50 | $7.50 | $3.50 | N/R | N/R |
| | 1814 | $7.25 | $11.13 | $2.75 | N/R | N/R |
| | 1815 | $3.30 | $2.88 | $2.38 | N/R | N/R |
| | 1816 | $4.88 | $4.25 | $3.50 | N/R | N/R |
| | 1817 | $7.62 | $7.25 | $6.31 | N/R | N/R |
| | 1818 | $6.88 | $6.63 | $6.38 | N/R | N/R |
| | 1819 | $4.00 | $3.75 | $3.50 | N/R | $20.00 |
| | 1820 | $3.80 | $3.44 | $2.88 | N/R | $10.00 |
| | 1821 | $3.12 | $3.38 | $2.88 | $2.75 | N/R |
| | 1822 | $3.38 | $3.38 | $3.06 | $4.00 | N/R |
| | 1823 | $3.75 | $3.63 | $3.50 | $3.00 | $5.00 |
| | 1824 | $3.44 | $3.38 | $3.00 | $3.12 | $5.25 |
| Rum, per gallon | 1800 | $0.72 | $1.06 | $3.50 | N/R | N/R |
| | 1801 | $0.78 | $1.17 | $3.75 | N/R | N/R |
| | 1802 | $0.68 | $0.98 | $3.00 | N/R | N/R |
| | 1803 | $0.57 | $1.04 | $2.50 | N/R | N/R |
| | 1804 | $0.64 | $0.96 | $3.25 | $0.75 | N/R |
| | 1805 | $0.56 | $0.91 | $0.62 | $0.75 | N/R |
| | 1806 | $0.53 | $0.89 | $0.55 | $0.62 | N/R |
| | 1807 | $0.48 | $0.89 | $0.56 | $0.60 | N/R |
| | 1808 | $0.56 | $1.06 | $0.51 | $0.60 | N/R |
| | 1809 | $0.58 | $1.22 | $0.55 | $0.97 | N/R |
| | 1810 | $0.70 | $1.25 | $0.58 | $0.72 | N/R |
| | 1811 | $0.69 | $1.22 | $0.65 | $0.72 | N/R |
| | 1812 | $0.68 | $1.50 | $0.70 | $0.60 | N/R |
| | 1813 | $0.92 | $1.62 | N/R | $0.94 | N/R |
| | 1814 | $1.13 | $2.50 | N/R | N/R | N/R |
| | 1815 | $1.16 | $1.94 | N/R | N/R | N/R |
| | 1816 | $0.75 | $1.35 | $0.78 | N/R | N/R |
| | 1817 | $0.68 | $1.17 | $0.71 | N/R | N/R |
| | 1818 | $0.66 | $1.27 | $0.64 | N/R | N/R |
| | 1819 | $0.54 | $1.13 | $0.54 | N/R | N/R |
| | 1820 | $0.40 | $1.09 | $0.35 | $0.52 | N/R |
| | 1821 | $0.34 | $1.12 | $0.36 | N/R | N/R |
| | 1822 | $0.40 | $1.06 | $0.38 | $0.46 | N/R |
| | 1823 | $0.36 | $0.88 | $0.38 | $0.40 | $0.38 |
| | 1824 | $0.34 | $0.87 | $0.34 | $0.32 | N/R |

| Commodity | Year | Philadelphia Currency | New York Currency | Charleston Currency | New Orleans Currency | Cincinnati Currency |
|---|---|---|---|---|---|---|
| Salt petre, per pound | 1800 | $0.43 | $0.30 | N/R | $0.50 | N/R |
| | 1801 | $0.30 | $0.35 | N/R | N/R | N/R |
| | 1802 | $0.24 | $0.24 | N/R | N/R | N/R |
| | 1803 | $0.25 | $0.20 | N/R | N/R | N/R |
| | 1804 | $0.28 | $0.29 | N/R | $0.75 | N/R |
| | 1805 | $0.24 | $0.25 | N/R | $0.22 | N/R |
| | 1806 | $0.25 | $0.23 | N/R | $0.22 | N/R |
| | 1807 | $0.21 | $0.26 | N/R | $0.27 | N/R |
| | 1808 | $0.33 | $0.30 | N/R | $0.27 | N/R |
| | 1809 | $0.40 | $0.62 | N/R | $0.27 | N/R |
| | 1810 | $0.62 | $0.52 | N/R | N/R | N/R |
| | 1811 | $0.60 | $0.58 | N/R | N/R | N/R |
| | 1812 | $0.50 | $0.50 | N/R | N/R | N/R |
| | 1813 | $0.50 | $0.52 | N/R | N/R | N/R |
| | 1814 | $0.48 | $0.45 | N/R | N/R | N/R |
| | 1815 | $0.28 | $0.24 | N/R | $0.40 | N/R |
| | 1816 | $0.33 | $0.34 | N/R | $0.38 | N/R |
| | 1817 | $0.18 | $0.16 | N/R | N/R | N/R |
| | 1818 | $0.14 | $0.14 | N/R | $0.20 | N/R |
| | 1819 | $0.12 | $0.12 | N/R | $0.20 | $0.30 |
| | 1820 | $0.12 | $0.10 | N/R | N/R | N/R |
| | 1821 | $0.10 | $0.11 | N/R | N/R | N/R |
| | 1822 | $0.19 | $1.00 | N/R | N/R | N/R |
| | 1823 | $0.10 | $0.11 | N/R | $0.12 | N/R |
| | 1824 | $0.08 | $0.08 | N/R | $0.11 | $0.09 |
| Salt, per bushel (N.O. - per barrel) | 1800 | $0.667 | $0.60 | N/R | $1.17 | N/R |
| *(New Orleans per barrel 1800-1819;* | 1801 | $0.550 | $0.60 | N/R | N/R | N/R |
| *per sack 1820-1824)* | 1802 | $0.525 | $0.45 | N/R | N/R | N/R |
| *(Charleston per four bushels 1818-1824l)* | 1803 | $0.470 | $0.51 | N/R | N/R | N/R |
| | 1804 | $0.685 | $0.65 | N/R | $2.50 | N/R |
| | 1805 | $0.875 | $0.62 | $0.58 | $4.00 | N/R |
| | 1806 | $0.775 | $0.58 | $0.95 | $4.00 | N/R |
| | 1807 | $0.450 | $0.35 | $0.45 | $3.25 | N/R |

### Based Upon US Dollars

| Year | Value of 19th Century Dollar in 2002 US Dollars |
|---|---|
| 1800 | $14.00 |
| 1805 | $15.00 |
| 1810 | $14.00 |
| 1815 | $11.00 |
| 1820 | $15.00 |
| 1824 | $18.00 |

*Calculations are approximate values based upon economic historical data*

| Commodity | Year | Philadelphia Currency | New York Currency | Charleston Currency | New Orleans Currency | Cincinnati Currency |
|---|---|---|---|---|---|---|
| | 1808 | $0.500 | $0.48 | $0.76 | $1.25 | N/R |
| | 1809 | $0.900 | $0.70 | $0.68 | $3.00 | N/R |
| | 1810 | $0.450 | $0.60 | $0.65 | $3.50 | N/R |
| | 1811 | $0.500 | $0.50 | $0.45 | $1.13 | N/R |
| | 1812 | $0.675 | $1.00 | $0.70 | $2.50 | N/R |
| | 1813 | $1.075 | $0.90 | N/R | N/R | N/R |
| | 1814 | $1.693 | $1.88 | N/R | N/R | N/R |
| | 1815 | $0.900 | $1.06 | N/R | N/R | N/R |
| | 1816 | $0.625 | $0.40 | N/R | $1.38 | $1.25 |
| | 1817 | $0.550 | $0.42 | N/R | N/R | $1.25 |
| | 1818 | $0.575 | $0.44 | $2.20 | N/R | $1.50 |
| | 1819 | $0.650 | $0.46 | $2.40 | $2.13 | $1.50 |
| | 1820 | $0.675 | $0.46 | $2.30 | $2.00 | $1.25 |
| | 1821 | $0.535 | $0.44 | $1.80 | $1.75 | $0.78 |
| | 1822 | $0.550 | $0.43 | $1.76 | $2.50 | $0.75 |
| | 1823 | $0.600 | $0.44 | $1.90 | $2.50 | $0.43 |
| | 1824 | $0.500 | $0.46 | $2.00 | $2.31 | $0.34 |
| Sheeting, per piece | 1800 | $17.50 | N/R | N/R | N/R | N/R |
| *(New Orlean per yard 1823-24)* | 1801 | $17.75 | N/R | N/R | N/R | N/R |
| | 1802 | $16.00 | N/R | N/R | N/R | N/R |
| | 1803 | $16.00 | N/R | N/R | N/R | N/R |
| | 1804 | $19.50 | $19.00 | N/R | $23.50 | N/R |
| | 1805 | $21.75 | $19.75 | N/R | $25.50 | N/R |
| | 1806 | $22.50 | $21.50 | N/R | $25.00 | N/R |
| | 1807 | $21.00 | $20.25 | N/R | $23.50 | N/R |
| | 1808 | $22.75 | $20.25 | N/R | $23.50 | N/R |
| | 1809 | $26.00 | $25.00 | N/R | $23.50 | N/R |
| | 1810 | $22.00 | $23.50 | N/R | $27.00 | N/R |
| | 1811 | $19.00 | $18.00 | N/R | $19.00 | N/R |
| | 1812 | $16.50 | $17.00 | N/R | $19.00 | N/R |
| | 1813 | $21.50 | $21.00 | N/R | N/R | N/R |
| | 1814 | $22.57 | $22.50 | N/R | N/R | N/R |
| | 1815 | $19.00 | $22.50 | N/R | N/R | N/R |
| | 1816 | $19.10 | $18.00 | N/R | N/R | N/R |
| | 1817 | $18.50 | $18.75 | N/R | N/R | N/R |
| | 1818 | $17.75 | $17.50 | N/R | N/R | N/R |
| | 1819 | $16.50 | $15.50 | N/R | N/R | N/R |
| | 1820 | $16.00 | $15.75 | N/R | N/R | N/R |
| | 1821 | $16.00 | $15.75 | N/R | N/R | N/R |
| | 1822 | $14.50 | $15.75 | N/R | N/R | N/R |
| | 1823 | $14.50 | $15.25 | N/R | $0.19 | N/R |
| | 1824 | $11.25 | $11.25 | N/R | $0.17 | N/R |
| Staves, per 1200 units | 1800 | $40.00 | $30.00 | $5.00 | N/R | N/R |
| | 1801 | $40.00 | $40.00 | $5.00 | N/R | N/R |
| | 1802 | $33.00 | $41.20 | $4.20 | N/R | N/R |
| | 1803 | $47.00 | $38.80 | $4.20 | N/R | N/R |
| | 1804 | $47.00 | $45.00 | $4.20 | $27.50 | N/R |
| | 1805 | $47.00 | $45.00 | $4.20 | $27.50 | N/R |

| Commodity | Year | Philadelphia Currency | New York Currency | Charleston Currency | New Orleans Currency | Cincinnati Currency |
|---|---|---|---|---|---|---|
| | 1806 | $44.00 | $42.50 | $20.00 | $27.50 | N/R |
| | 1807 | $45.00 | $40.00 | $20.00 | $22.00 | N/R |
| | 1808 | $45.00 | $42.50 | $28.00 | $22.00 | N/R |
| | 1809 | $44.00 | $47.50 | $30.00 | N/R | N/R |
| | 1810 | $42.50 | $42.50 | $30.00 | N/R | N/R |
| | 1811 | $44.00 | $46.20 | N/R | N/R | N/R |
| | 1812 | $44.00 | $41.20 | N/R | N/R | N/R |
| | 1813 | $44.00 | $41.20 | N/R | N/R | N/R |
| | 1814 | $44.00 | $50.00 | N/R | N/R | N/R |
| | 1815 | $56.00 | $65.00 | N/R | N/R | N/R |
| | 1816 | $48.00 | $55.00 | $35.00 | $40.00 | N/R |
| | 1817 | $54.00 | $42.50 | $22.50 | N/R | N/R |
| | 1818 | $48.00 | $45.00 | $23.50 | $50.00 | N/R |
| | 1819 | $47.00 | $50.00 | N/R | $35.00 | N/R |
| | 1820 | $40.00 | $43.00 | N/R | N/R | N/R |
| | 1821 | $31.50 | $35.00 | N/R | N/R | N/R |
| | 1822 | $38.00 | $38.00 | N/R | $26.50 | N/R |
| | 1823 | $38.00 | $28.00 | N/R | $24.00 | N/R |
| | 1824 | $35.00 | $31.50 | N/R | $15.50 | N/R |
| Steel, per pound | 1800 | $0.14 | $0.16 | N/R | N/R | N/R |
| | 1801 | $0.14 | $0.16 | N/R | N/R | N/R |
| | 1802 | $0.18 | $0.11 | N/R | N/R | N/R |
| | 1803 | $0.16 | $0.11 | $0.12 | N/R | N/R |
| | 1804 | $0.16 | $0.12 | $0.12 | $0.18 | N/R |
| | 1805 | $0.16 | $0.12 | $0.12 | $0.19 | N/R |
| | 1806 | $19.00 | $0.12 | $0.07 | N/R | N/R |
| | 1807 | $19.00 | $0.12 | N/R | $0.10 | N/R |
| | 1808 | $19.00 | $0.14 | N/R | $0.10 | N/R |
| | 1809 | $27.00 | $0.16 | N/R | $0.28 | N/R |
| | 1810 | $21.00 | $0.25 | N/R | $0.28 | N/R |
| | 1811 | $17.00 | $0.25 | N/R | $0.28 | N/R |
| | 1812 | $22.00 | $0.29 | N/R | $0.22 | N/R |
| | 1813 | $25.00 | $0.40 | N/R | N/R | N/R |

## Based Upon US Dollars

| Year | Value of 19th Century Dollar in 2002 US Dollars |
|---|---|
| 1800 | $14.00 |
| 1805 | $15.00 |
| 1810 | $14.00 |
| 1815 | $11.00 |
| 1820 | $15.00 |
| 1824 | $18.00 |

*Calculations are approximate values based upon economic historical data*

| Commodity | Year | Philadelphia Currency | New York Currency | Charleston Currency | New Orleans Currency | Cincinnati Currency |
|---|---|---|---|---|---|---|
| | 1814 | $38.70 | $0.32 | N/R | N/R | N/R |
| | 1815 | $22.50 | $0.18 | N/R | $25.00 | N/R |
| | 1816 | $20.00 | $0.16 | N/R | $16.50 | N/R |
| | 1817 | $20.00 | $0.14 | N/R | N/R | N/R |
| | 1818 | $0.14 | $0.12 | N/R | $16.50 | N/R |
| | 1819 | $0.15 | $0.13 | N/R | N/R | $0.18 |
| | 1820 | $0.15 | $0.13 | N/R | $0.14 | $0.18 |
| | 1821 | $0.15 | $0.13 | N/R | $0.14 | N/R |
| | 1822 | $0.15 | $0.13 | N/R | $0.15 | N/R |
| | 1823 | $0.15 | $0.12 | N/R | $0.15 | $0.11 |
| | 1824 | $0.15 | $0.13 | N/R | $0.14 | $0.12 |
| Sugar, per hundredweight | 1800 | $12.84 | N/R | N/R | $9.00 | N/R |
| | 1801 | $11.00 | N/R | N/R | $8.50 | N/R |
| | 1802 | $11.50 | N/R | N/R | $7.50 | N/R |
| | 1803 | $12.00 | N/R | N/R | $6.25 | N/R |
| | 1804 | $14.00 | N/R | $7.50 | N/R | N/R |
| | 1805 | $13.75 | N/R | $11.00 | $9.75 | N/R |
| | 1806 | $12.00 | N/R | $10.50 | $11.00 | N/R |
| | 1807 | $12.50 | N/R | $8.50 | $10.00 | N/R |
| | 1808 | $11.00 | N/R | $9.00 | $7.75 | N/R |
| | 1809 | $11.50 | N/R | $7.75 | $8.75 | N/R |
| | 1810 | $11.50 | N/R | $9.50 | $7.50 | N/R |
| | 1811 | $12.80 | $9.75 | N/R | $7.50 | N/R |
| | 1812 | $12.75 | N/R | $11.00 | $10.17 | N/R |
| | 1813 | $18.75 | N/R | N/R | $9.00 | N/R |
| | 1814 | $17.75 | N/R | N/R | $12.00 | N/R |
| | 1815 | $19.25 | N/R | N/R | $11.50 | N/R |
| | 1816 | $19.25 | $16.50 | N/R | $16.50 | $25.00 |
| | 1817 | $17.25 | $13.75 | N/R | $12.00 | $20.00 |
| | 1818 | $14.28 | $13.00 | $13.10 | $9.75 | $15.50 |
| | 1819 | $16.18 | $13.00 | $13.00 | $10.50 | $16.67 |
| | 1820 | $10.25 | $10.88 | $9.20 | $6.25 | $15.50 |
| | 1821 | $10.75 | $10.50 | $9.20 | $7.25 | $9.50 |
| | 1822 | $12.25 | $10.75 | $9.00 | $9.00 | $14.50 |
| | 1823 | $11.75 | $9.50 | $8.20 | $6.50 | $10.00 |
| | 1824 | $12.25 | $9.00 | $8.80 | $7.25 | $9.00 |
| Tallow, per pound | 1800 | $0.13 | $0.16 | $10.00 | N/R | N/R |
| | 1801 | $0.14 | $0.16 | $9.50 | N/R | N/R |
| | 1802 | $0.12 | $0.13 | $7.50 | N/R | N/R |
| | 1803 | $0.10 | $0.11 | $7.00 | $0.13 | N/R |
| | 1804 | $0.10 | $0.13 | $9.00 | $0.19 | N/R |
| | 1805 | $0.14 | $0.17 | $0.17 | $0.14 | N/R |
| | 1806 | $0.15 | $0.17 | $0.17 | $0.12 | N/R |
| | 1807 | $0.12 | $0.14 | $0.16 | $0.13 | N/R |
| | 1808 | $0.12 | $0.10 | N/R | $0.13 | N/R |
| | 1809 | $0.13 | $0.16 | N/R | $0.12 | N/R |
| | 1810 | $0.14 | $0.16 | N/R | $0.12 | N/R |
| | 1811 | $0.14 | $0.14 | N/R | $0.12 | N/R |

| Commodity | Year | Philadelphia Currency | New York Currency | Charleston Currency | New Orleans Currency | Cincinnati Currency |
|---|---|---|---|---|---|---|
| | 1812 | $0.14 | $0.13 | N/R | $0.12 | N/R |
| | 1813 | $0.14 | $0.13 | $0.14 | N/R | N/R |
| | 1814 | $0.13 | $0.18 | $0.14 | N/R | N/R |
| | 1815 | $0.15 | N/R | $0.17 | N/R | N/R |
| | 1816 | $0.22 | $0.21 | $0.19 | $0.22 | $0.11 |
| | 1817 | $0.15 | $0.13 | $0.18 | N/R | $0.12 |
| | 1818 | $0.16 | $0.12 | $0.16 | $0.11 | $0.11 |
| | 1819 | $0.14 | $0.14 | $0.18 | $0.10 | $0.12 |
| | 1820 | $0.14 | $0.15 | $0.18 | N/R | $0.12 |
| | 1821 | $0.12 | $0.12 | $0.18 | N/R | $0.12 |
| | 1822 | $0.10 | $0.10 | $0.14 | $0.11 | $0.08 |
| | 1823 | $0.08 | $0.08 | $0.08 | $0.08 | $0.07 |
| | 1824 | $0.08 | $0.08 | $0.08 | $0.06 | $0.05 |
| Tea, per pound | 1800 | $0.36 | $1.31 | N/R | $2.00 | N/R |
| | 1801 | $0.36 | $1.03 | N/R | N/R | N/R |
| | 1802 | $0.37 | $0.97 | N/R | N/R | N/R |
| | 1803 | $0.33 | $1.47 | $0.40 | N/R | N/R |
| | 1804 | $0.32 | $1.17 | $0.34 | $1.65 | N/R |
| | 1805 | $0.30 | $1.17 | $0.30 | $1.37 | N/R |
| | 1806 | $0.38 | $1.18 | N/R | $1.37 | N/R |
| | 1807 | $0.31 | $1.09 | N/R | $1.37 | N/R |
| | 1808 | $0.35 | $1.03 | N/R | $1.12 | N/R |
| | 1809 | $0.40 | $1.03 | N/R | $1.50 | N/R |
| | 1810 | $0.35 | $0.98 | N/R | $1.19 | N/R |
| | 1811 | $0.32 | $0.95 | N/R | $0.95 | N/R |
| | 1812 | $0.28 | $0.83 | N/R | $0.95 | N/R |
| | 1813 | $0.70 | $1.53 | N/R | N/R | N/R |
| | 1814 | $0.65 | $1.63 | N/R | N/R | N/R |
| | 1815 | $0.59 | $1.56 | N/R | $1.75 | N/R |
| | 1816 | $0.42 | $2.00 | N/R | $1.45 | N/R |
| | 1817 | $0.31 | $1.25 | N/R | N/R | N/R |
| | 1818 | $0.32 | $1.13 | $1.22 | $1.25 | N/R |

### Based Upon US Dollars

| Year | Value of 19th Century Dollar in 2002 US Dollars |
|---|---|
| 1800 | $14.00 |
| 1805 | $15.00 |
| 1810 | $14.00 |
| 1815 | $11.00 |
| 1820 | $15.00 |
| 1824 | $18.00 |

*Calculations are approximate values based upon economic historical data*

| Commodity | Year | Philadelphia Currency | New York Currency | Charleston Currency | New Orleans Currency | Cincinnati Currency |
|---|---|---|---|---|---|---|
| | 1819 | $0.32 | $1.03 | $1.22 | $1.25 | $1.48 |
| | 1820 | $0.34 | $0.99 | $1.02 | $1.25 | $1.35 |
| | 1821 | $0.34 | $0.97 | $0.98 | $1.00 | N/R |
| | 1822 | $0.34 | $1.03 | $0.90 | $0.95 | N/R |
| | 1823 | $0.34 | $1.00 | $1.02 | $1.20 | $1.12 |
| | 1824 | $0.29 | $0.98 | $1.00 | $1.05 | $1.11 |
| Tobacco, per hundredweight | 1800 | $6.00 | $0.06 | $22.20 | $4.50 | N/R |
| (New York 1800-1824 and Philadelphia | 1801 | $6.25 | $0.06 | $22.20 | $4.00 | N/R |
| 1814-24, per pound) | 1802 | $7.50 | $0.06 | $19.80 | $4.00 | N/R |
| | 1803 | $6.75 | $0.06 | $26.80 | $5.25 | N/R |
| | 1804 | $7.75 | $0.07 | $28.60 | $5.50 | N/R |
| | 1805 | $7.75 | $0.08 | $5.50 | $5.50 | N/R |
| | 1806 | $7.25 | $0.07 | $5.25 | $6.25 | N/R |
| | 1807 | $7.50 | $0.08 | $6.25 | $5.75 | N/R |
| | 1808 | $6.75 | $0.07 | $3.25 | $4.25 | N/R |
| | 1809 | $6.50 | $0.06 | $7.00 | $4.00 | N/R |
| | 1810 | $7.00 | $0.06 | $5.50 | $4.25 | N/R |
| | 1811 | $6.50 | $0.06 | $4.88 | $3.38 | N/R |
| | 1812 | $5.75 | $0.06 | $4.50 | $4.00 | N/R |
| | 1813 | $8.00 | $0.08 | $4.00 | $5.25 | N/R |
| | 1814 | $0.07 | $0.08 | $5.00 | N/R | N/R |
| | 1815 | $0.09 | $0.10 | $10.50 | $8.50 | N/R |
| | 1816 | $0.22 | $0.18 | $15.00 | $17.00 | $18.00 |
| | 1817 | $0.14 | $0.10 | $8.25 | $7.75 | $13.50 |
| | 1818 | $0.12 | $0.12 | $8.50 | $7.75 | $12.00 |
| | 1819 | $0.12 | $0.08 | $8.25 | $5.50 | $18.50 |
| | 1820 | $0.08 | $0.06 | $5.25 | $4.00 | $18.75 |
| | 1821 | $0.08 | $0.06 | $4.38 | $4.25 | N/R |
| | 1822 | $0.08 | $0.06 | $4.75 | $4.38 | $8.00 |
| | 1823 | $0.08 | $0.06 | $3.75 | $2.12 | N/R |
| | 1824 | $0.08 | $0.06 | $3.75 | $4.38 | $5.25 |
| Turpentine, per barrel | 1800 | $2.50 | $2.75 | $9.30 | N/R | N/R |
| (New Orleans per gallon 1807-1824) | 1801 | $2.50 | $3.24 | $13.00 | N/R | N/R |
| | 1802 | $3.25 | $3.12 | $23.30 | N/R | N/R |
| | 1803 | $3.50 | $2.69 | $2.00 | N/R | N/R |
| | 1804 | $3.50 | $3.75 | $5.00 | $18.00 | N/R |
| | 1805 | $3.62 | $3.50 | $3.00 | $18.00 | N/R |
| | 1806 | $3.00 | $2.63 | $2.00 | $0.62 | N/R |
| | 1807 | $2.06 | $2.25 | $2.00 | $0.45 | N/R |
| | 1808 | $3.12 | $3.00 | $2.00 | $0.45 | N/R |
| | 1809 | $4.50 | $5.00 | $3.75 | $0.55 | N/R |
| | 1810 | $4.50 | $4.00 | $4.25 | $0.55 | N/R |
| | 1811 | $3.75 | $2.63 | $2.50 | $0.76 | N/R |
| | 1812 | $2.38 | $2.13 | $2.25 | $0.76 | N/R |
| | 1813 | $2.50 | $4.00 | N/R | N/R | N/R |
| | 1814 | $8.00 | $12.00 | N/R | N/R | N/R |
| | 1815 | $3.00 | $3.25 | N/R | $0.75 | N/R |
| | 1816 | $3.75 | $3.25 | $3.00 | $1.00 | N/R |

| Commodity | Year | Philadelphia Currency | New York Currency | Charleston Currency | New Orleans Currency | Cincinnati Currency |
|---|---|---|---|---|---|---|
| | 1817 | $2.88 | $2.75 | $3.00 | N/R | N/R |
| | 1818 | $3.62 | $3.25 | $4.50 | N/R | N/R |
| | 1819 | $3.12 | $2.44 | $3.25 | $1.00 | N/R |
| | 1820 | $2.38 | $2.00 | $2.25 | $1.00 | N/R |
| | 1821 | $1.94 | $2.00 | $1.75 | N/R | N/R |
| | 1822 | $3.75 | $2.63 | $3.25 | $0.50 | N/R |
| | 1823 | $2.62 | $2.88 | $2.62 | $0.60 | N/R |
| | 1824 | $2.81 | $3.00 | $3.12 | $0.66 | N/R |
| Whale Oil, per gallon | 1800 | $0.42 | $0.39 | N/R | N/R | N/R |
| | 1801 | $0.50 | $0.62 | N/R | N/R | N/R |
| | 1802 | $0.42 | $0.53 | N/R | N/R | N/R |
| | 1803 | $0.42 | $0.45 | N/R | N/R | N/R |
| | 1804 | $0.48 | $0.50 | N/R | $1.00 | N/R |
| | 1805 | $0.52 | $0.50 | N/R | $0.78 | N/R |
| | 1806 | $0.40 | $0.57 | N/R | $0.78 | N/R |
| | 1807 | $0.42 | $0.44 | N/R | $0.78 | N/R |
| | 1808 | $0.38 | $0.43 | N/R | $0.78 | N/R |
| | 1809 | $0.36 | $0.38 | N/R | $0.78 | N/R |
| | 1810 | $0.38 | $0.35 | N/R | $0.78 | N/R |
| | 1811 | $0.45 | $0.44 | N/R | $0.78 | N/R |
| | 1812 | $0.50 | $0.45 | N/R | $0.78 | N/R |
| | 1813 | $0.85 | $0.98 | N/R | N/R | N/R |
| | 1814 | $1.16 | $1.16 | N/R | N/R | N/R |
| | 1815 | $0.88 | $0.88 | N/R | $1.44 | N/R |
| | 1816 | $0.72 | $0.78 | N/R | $1.38 | N/R |
| | 1817 | $0.52 | $0.53 | N/R | N/R | N/R |
| | 1818 | $0.60 | $0.60 | N/R | N/R | N/R |
| | 1819 | $0.45 | $0.45 | N/R | $1.25 | N/R |
| | 1820 | $0.36 | $0.36 | N/R | N/R | N/R |
| | 1821 | $0.34 | $0.30 | N/R | N/R | N/R |
| | 1822 | $0.38 | $0.30 | N/R | $0.42 | N/R |
| | 1823 | $0.30 | $0.26 | N/R | $0.30 | N/R |
| | 1824 | $0.26 | $0.23 | N/R | $0.29 | N/R |

### Based Upon US Dollars

| Year | Value of 19th Century Dollar in 2002 US Dollars |
|---|---|
| 1800 | $14.00 |
| 1805 | $15.00 |
| 1810 | $14.00 |
| 1815 | $11.00 |
| 1820 | $15.00 |
| 1824 | $18.00 |

*Calculations are approximate values based upon economic historical data*

| Commodity | Year | Philadelphia Currency | New York Currency | Charleston Currency | New Orleans Currency | Cincinnati Currency |
|---|---|---|---|---|---|---|
| Wheat, per bushel | 1801 | $2.25 | $1.78 | N/R | N/R | N/R |
| | 1802 | $1.22 | $1.22 | N/R | N/R | N/R |
| | 1803 | $1.10 | $1.27 | N/R | N/R | N/R |
| | 1804 | $1.18 | $1.12 | N/R | N/R | N/R |
| | 1805 | $2.40 | $2.31 | N/R | N/R | N/R |
| | 1806 | $1.45 | $1.50 | N/R | N/R | N/R |
| | 1807 | $1.45 | $1.50 | N/R | N/R | N/R |
| | 1808 | $1.00 | $1.03 | N/R | N/R | N/R |
| | 1809 | $1.42 | $1.75 | N/R | N/R | N/R |
| | 1810 | $1.72 | $1.75 | N/R | N/R | N/R |
| | 1811 | $2.00 | $2.12 | N/R | N/R | N/R |
| | 1812 | $1.75 | $1.48 | N/R | N/R | N/R |
| | 1813 | $1.50 | $2.56 | N/R | N/R | N/R |
| | 1814 | $1.58 | $1.78 | N/R | N/R | N/R |
| | 1815 | $1.40 | $1.62 | N/R | N/R | N/R |
| | 1816 | $1.60 | $1.41 | N/R | N/R | $0.62 |
| | 1817 | $3.11 | $2.43 | N/R | N/R | $1.00 |
| | 1818 | $2.10 | $2.00 | N/R | $1.50 | $0.80 |
| | 1819 | $14.45 | $1.39 | N/R | $1.12 | $0.94 |
| | 1820 | $1.02 | $0.96 | N/R | $1.00 | $0.56 |
| | 1821 | $0.82 | $0.89 | N/R | N/R | $0.36 |
| | 1822 | $1.35 | $1.35 | N/R | N/R | $0.36 |
| | 1823 | $1.52 | $1.34 | N/R | N/R | $0.50 |
| | 1824 | $1.22 | $1.21 | N/R | N/R | $0.55 |
| Whisky, per gallon | 1800 | $0.55 | N/R | N/R | $0.75 | N/R |
| | 1801 | $0.54 | N/R | N/R | $0.75 | N/R |
| | 1802 | $0.51 | N/R | N/R | $0.50 | N/R |
| | 1803 | $0.46 | N/R | N/R | $0.62 | N/R |
| | 1804 | $0.48 | N/R | N/R | $0.62 | N/R |
| | 1805 | $0.53 | N/R | N/R | $0.62 | N/R |
| | 1806 | $0.48 | N/R | N/R | $0.75 | N/R |
| | 1807 | $0.46 | N/R | N/R | $0.56 | N/R |
| | 1808 | $0.40 | N/R | N/R | $0.38 | N/R |
| | 1809 | $0.46 | N/R | N/R | $0.62 | N/R |
| | 1810 | $0.62 | N/R | N/R | $0.50 | N/R |
| | 1811 | $0.50 | N/R | N/R | $0.48 | N/R |
| | 1812 | $0.42 | N/R | N/R | $0.60 | N/R |
| | 1813 | $0.54 | N/R | $0.88 | N/R | N/R |
| | 1814 | $0.48 | $0.72 | N/R | $0.62 | N/R |
| | 1815 | $0.78 | N/R | $0.80 | $0.88 | N/R |
| | 1816 | $0.62 | $0.50 | $0.61 | $0.67 | $0.62 |
| | 1817 | $0.71 | $0.71 | $0.76 | $0.75 | $0.62 |
| | 1818 | $0.52 | $0.53 | $0.57 | $0.48 | $0.40 |
| | 1819 | $0.38 | $0.36 | $0.44 | $0.50 | $0.45 |
| | 1820 | $0.30 | $0.28 | $0.34 | $0.40 | $0.29 |
| | 1821 | $0.26 | $0.24 | $0.28 | $0.22 | $0.17 |
| | 1822 | $0.32 | $0.30 | $0.33 | $0.24 | $0.14 |
| | 1823 | $0.33 | $0.26 | $0.34 | $0.26 | $0.25 |
| | 1824 | $0.26 | $0.25 | $0.26 | $0.26 | $0.20 |

| Commodity | Year | Philadelphia Currency | New York Currency | Charleston Currency | New Orleans Currency | Cincinnati Currency |
|---|---|---|---|---|---|---|
| Wine, per gallon | 1800 | $240.00 | $1.59 | N/R | $2.75 | N/R |
| *(Charleston & Philadelphia per pipe* | 1801 | $240.00 | $1.59 | N/R | N/R | N/R |
| *1800-1804)* | 1802 | $258.00 | $1.59 | N/R | N/R | N/R |
| | 1803 | $283.30 | $1.59 | $190.00 | $2.50 | N/R |
| | 1804 | $275.00 | $1.59 | $295.00 | $2.88 | N/R |
| | 1805 | $2.58 | $2.18 | N/R | $2.50 | N/R |
| | 1806 | $2.33 | $2.18 | N/R | $2.75 | N/R |
| | 1807 | $2.50 | $2.18 | N/R | $2.75 | N/R |
| | 1808 | $2.67 | $2.18 | N/R | $2.75 | N/R |
| | 1809 | $2.75 | $2.18 | N/R | $3.50 | N/R |
| | 1810 | $2.84 | $2.18 | N/R | $4.00 | N/R |
| | 1811 | $3.38 | $2.18 | N/R | $3.00 | N/R |
| | 1812 | $3.00 | $2.18 | N/R | $3.00 | N/R |
| | 1813 | $3.50 | $2.18 | N/R | N/R | N/R |
| | 1814 | $3.75 | $3.17 | N/R | N/R | N/R |
| | 1815 | $3.50 | $3.17 | N/R | $3.75 | N/R |
| | 1816 | $3.88 | $5.25 | N/R | $4.25 | N/R |
| | 1817 | $3.75 | $3.38 | N/R | N/R | N/R |
| | 1818 | $3.50 | $2.63 | $3.75 | $4.00 | N/R |
| | 1819 | $3.75 | $2.63 | $3.00 | $4.00 | $4.75 |
| | 1820 | $3.75 | $2.38 | $3.00 | $1.00 | $4.75 |
| | 1821 | $3.75 | $2.38 | $3.00 | $0.89 | N/R |
| | 1822 | $3.75 | $2.38 | N/R | $0.75 | N/R |
| | 1823 | $3.00 | $2.75 | N/R | $0.56 | $4.50 |
| | 1824 | $3.00 | $2.75 | N/R | $0.62 | $3.75 |

# SELECTED PRICES 1800-1824

| Item | Data Source | Description | Price |
|------|-------------|-------------|-------|
| **Alcohol** | | | |
| Brandy | Roland Clapp's Store Day Book (1816) | Cost for one gallon of brandy in Roland Clapp Store in Turin, New York | $3.00 |
| Cider | Inventory of William Alexander (1811) | Barrel of cider in New Castle County, Delaware, 1811 | $1.50 |
| Gin | Inventory of Samuel Ash (1822) | Gallon of corn gin in New Castle County, Delaware, 1822 | $0.34 |
| Keg | Inventory of John Hanna (1814) | Whiskey keg in Franklin County, Indiana, 1814 | $0.50 |
| Rum | Inventory of Samuel Ash (1822) | Gallon of New England rum in New Castle County, Delaware, 1822 | $0.40 |
| Still | Inventory of Dr. Gustavus Richard Brown (1804) | Copper still containing 52 gallons with lead worm in Charles County, Maryland, 1804 | $60.00 |
| Whiskey | Inventory of Samuel Ash (1822) | Gallon of whiskey in New Castle County, Delaware, 1822 | $0.39 |
| Wine | Inventory of Samuel Ash (1822) | Gallon of Malorga wine in New Castle County, Delaware, 1822 | $0.73 |
| **Apparel - Children** | | | |
| Shoes | Aurora General Advertiser (1810) | Boy's fine shoes, best quality in Philadelphia, 1810 | $1.00 |
| **Apparel - Men** | | | |
| Bandanna | Inventory of James Winchill (1817) | Red bandanna in Franklin County, Indiana, 1817 | $1.00 |
| Boots | Aurora General Advertiser (1810) | Gentlemen's best Philadelphia made and warranted boots, 1810 | $4.00 |
| Breeches | Inventory of Asahel Churchill (1812) | Pare breeches in Franklin County, Indiana, 1812 | $0.75 |
| Buckles | Inventory of Richard Cramplin (1807) | Pair of knee buckles set with brister stones in Prince George County, Maryland, 1807 | $2.00 |
| Buckles | Inventory of Richard Cramplin (1807) | Pair of silver boot buckles in Prince George County, Maryland, 1807 | $1.00 |
| Coat | Inventory of Charles Tillier (1812) | Big coat in Franklin County, Indiana, 1812 | $12.00 |
| Coat | Inventory of Asahel Churchill (1812) | Servant coat in Franklin County, Indiana, 1812 | $9.00 |
| Handkerchief | Inventory of James Winchill (1817) | Black handkercheif in Franklin County, Indiana, 1817 | 12½ cents |
| Hat | Inventory of John Stogdale (1815) | Fur hat in Franklin County, Indiana, 1815 | $3.50 |
| Hat | Inventory of James Winchill (1817) | Wool hat in Franklin County, Indiana, 1817 | $1.50 |
| Hose | Inventory of James Winchill (1817) | Pair white cotton hose in Franklin County, Indiana, 1817 | $1.00 |
| Mittens | Inventory of Asahel Churchill (1812) | Pair of striped mittens in Franklin County, Indiana, 1812 | $0.90 |
| Outfit | Inventory of Peter Dellue (1812) | Buckskin hunting shirt, overhall & leggins in Franklin County, Indiana, 1812 | $0.25 |
| Pantaloons | Inventory of Nathaniel French (1819) | Pair of cloth pantaloons in Franklin County, Indiana, 1819 | $1.00 |

| Item | Data Source | Description | Price |
|------|-------------|-------------|-------|
| Pantaloons | Inventory of Reuben Brackney (1820) | Pair of linnen pantaloons in Franklin County, Indiana, 1820 | $0.25 |
| Shirt | Inventory of Richard Cramplin (1807) | Flannel shirt in Prince George County, Maryland, 1807 | $1.50 |
| Shoes | Inventory of James Winchill (1817) | Pair of shoes in Franklin County, Indiana, 1817 | 12½ cents |
| Slippers | Inventory of James Knight (1816) | Pair of slippers in Franklin County, Indiana, 1816 | $0.25 |
| Stockings | Inventory of John Trammel (1818) | Pair white cotton stockings in Greenville, South Carolina, 1820 | $1.21½ |
| Suspenders | Inventory of James Winchill (1817) | Pair of suspenders in Franklin County, Indiana, 1817 | $0.25 |
| Trousers | Inventory of Asahel Churchill (1812) | Pare stiped trowsers in Franklin County, Indiana, 1812 | $0.25 |
| Vest | Inventory of Asahel Churchill (1812) | Striped vest in Franklin County, Indiana, 1812 | $0.50 |
| Waistcoat | Inventory of Richard Cramplin (1807) | Winter waistcoat in Prince George County, Maryland, 1807 | $2.00 |

### Apparel - Women

| Item | Data Source | Description | Price |
|------|-------------|-------------|-------|
| Bodice | Inventory of John Hadley (1818) | Stait bodice blue coat in Franklin County, Indiana, 1818 | $4.00 |
| Bonnet | Inventory of James Winchill (1817) | Silk bonnet in Franklin County, Indiana, 1817 | $1.00 |
| Gloves | Inventory of James Winchill (1817) | Pair cotton gloves in Franklin County, Indiana, 1817 | 12½ cents |
| Hose | Inventory of James Winchill (1817) | Pair of woman's cotton hose in Franklin County, Indiana, 1817 | $1.00 |
| Shawl | Inventory of James Winchill (1817) | Yellow cotton shawl in Franklin County, Indiana, 1817 | $1.00 |
| Shoes | Aurora General Advertiser (1810) | Ladies' Valencia shoes, full trimmed in Philadelphia, 1810 | $1.00 |
| Stockings | Inventory of James Winchill (1817) | Pair of silk stockings in Franklin County, Indiana, 1817 | $1.00 |
| Umbrella | Estate of Alfred Yeomans (1817) | Silk umbrella in a South Carolina, 1817 | $5.00 |

## Based Upon US Dollars

| Year | Value of 19th Century Dollar in 2002 US Dollars |
|------|--------------------------------------------------|
| 1800 | $14.00 |
| 1805 | $15.00 |
| 1810 | $14.00 |
| 1815 | $11.00 |
| 1820 | $15.00 |
| 1824 | $18.00 |

*Calculations are approximate values based upon economic historical data*

| Item | Data Source | Description | Price |
|------|-------------|-------------|-------|
| **Commodity** | | | |
| Ashes | Roland Clapp's Store Day Book (1816) | One bushel of field ashes accepted as payment in Roland Clapp Store in Turin, New York | $0.09 |
| Board | Inventory of Asahel Churchill (1812) | 45 feet poplar plank in Franklin County, Indiana, 1812 | $0.50 |
| Coffee | Inventory of John Anderson (1822) | Pound of coffee in Sumter, South Carolina, 1822 | $0.30 |
| Corn | Inventory of Richard Cramplin (1807) | Barrel of corn in Prince George County, Maryland, 1807 | $3.33 |
| Cotton | Inventory of George Frute (1811) | Pound of cotton in Franklin County, Indiana, 1811 | $0.25 |
| Flax | Inventory of George Frute (1811) | Stack of flax in Franklin County, Indiana, 1811 | $3.00 |
| Flax seed | Inventory of Richard Cramplin (1807) | Bushel of flax seed in Prince George County, Maryland, 1807 | $1.00 |
| Flour | Inventory of John G. Flagler (1815) | Barrel of flour in Sumter, South Carolina, 1815 | $6.00 |
| Fodder | Inventory of John Taylor (1822) | Hunder pounds of fodder in Sumter, South Carolina, 1822 | $1.00 |
| Hay | Inventory of Richard Cramplin (1807) | Thousand pounds of hay in Prince George County, Maryland, 1807 | $5.00 |
| Hemp | Inventory of John Hanna (1814) | Pound of hemp in Franklin County, Indiana, 1814 | $0.05 |
| Indigo | Inventory of Samuel Ash (1822) | Pound of spanish indigo in New Castle County, Delaware, 1822 | $2.00 |
| Indigo Seed | Inventory of John Anderson (1822) | Bushel of indigo seed in Sumter, South Carolina, 1822 | $3.00 |
| Oats | Inventory of Isaac Kimmy (1817) | Bushel of oats in Franklin County, Indiana, 1817 | $0.25 |
| Peas | Inventory of Margaret Gordon (1815) | Bushel of peas in Sumter, South Carolina, 1815 | 37½ cents |
| Plank | Inventory of Richard Cramplin (1807) | Hundred feet of old plank in Prince George County, Maryland, 1807 | $1.00 |
| Potatoes | Inventory of Legrand Guerry (1811) | Bushel of potatoes in Sumter, South Carolina, 1811 | $0.25 |
| Rice | Inventory of James Gamble (1812) | Bushel of Rough rice in Sumter, South Carolina, 1812 | $0.50 |
| Rye | Inventory of Richard Cramplin (1807) | Bushel of rye in Prince George County, Maryland, 1807 | $0.66 |
| Salt | Business Accounts of Hampshire Furnance (1816) | One barrel of salt in Hampshire, Virginia in 1815 | $22.00 |
| Saltpeter | William Dutton, Du Pont (1949) | Pound of saltpeter from Mammoth Cave, Kentucy, 1813 | $0.32 |
| Sugar | Inventory of John Anderson (1822) | Pound of sugar in Sumter, South Carolina, 1822 | 12½ cents |
| Sugar | Inventory of Samuel Ash (1822) | Barrel of sugar in New Castle County, Delaware, 1822 | $20.08 |
| Tea | Inventory of Samuel Ash (1822) | Pound of Hyson tea in New Castle County, Delaware, 1822 | $0.60 |
| Tobacco | Inventory of Richard Cramplin (1807) | Hundred pounds of tobacco in Prince George County, Maryland, 1807 | $5.00 |
| Turnips | Inventory of Richard Cramplin (1807) | Stak of turnips, containing on average 18 bushells to the stack in Prince George County, Maryland, 1807 | $2.00 |
| Wheat | Inventory of George Frute (1811) | Stack of wheat in Franklin County, Indiana, 1811 | $8.00 |

| Item | Data Source | Description | Price |
|------|-------------|-------------|-------|
| Wood Ashes | Roland Clapp's Store Day Book (1816) | Cost for one bushel of in Turin, New York in 1816 | 1 shilling |
| Wool | Inventory of Richard Cramplin (1807) | Pound of wool in Prince George County, Maryland, 1807 | 37½ cents |

### Education

| | | | |
|------|-------------|-------------|-------|
| Tuition | Virginia Gazette (1803) | Cost for a "gentlemen to have his son" taught Latin language. Does not include board | $16.00 |
| Tuition | Virginia Gazette (1803) | Cost for a "gentlemen to have his son" taught English. Does not include board | $8.00 |

### Entertainment

| | | | |
|------|-------------|-------------|-------|
| Backgammon | Inventory of Thomas Lee (1806) | Back gammon box in Prince William County, Virginia, 1806 | $2.50 |
| Menagerie | Aurora General Advertiser (1810) | Admission to a menagerie of 21 living animals, including a lion, a polar bear and an elephant, Philadelphia, 1810 | $0.25 |
| Theater | Aurora General Advertiser (1810) | Box seat ticket for the play John Bull at New Theater in Philadelphia, 1810 | $1.00 |
| Theater | Aurora General Advertiser (1810) | Pit seat ticket for the play John Bull at New Theater in Philadelphia, 1810 | $0.75 |
| Theater | Aurora General Advertiser (1810) | Gallery seat ticket for the play The Poor Soldier at the New Theater in Philadelphia, 1810 | $0.50 |

| Item | Data Source | Description | Price |
|------|-------------|-------------|-------|
| **Fabrics & Sewing Materials** | | | |
| Buttons | Inventory of James Winchill (1817) | Paper box of shirt buttons in Franklin County, Indiana, 1817 | $2.00 |
| Clock Reel | Laurence A. Johnson, Over The Counter and On The Shelf 1620-1920 (1961) | Wooden clock reel to measure spun thread | $1.50 |
| Cord | Inventory of James Winchill (1817) | Yard of Bedford cord in Franklin County, Indiana, 1817 | $2.00 |
| Cotton Cards | Inventory of John Hanna (1814) | Pair of cotton cards in Franklin County, Indiana, 1814 | $0.50 |
| Fabric | Inventory of James Winchill (1817) | Yard of blue cassimere in Franklin County, Indiana, 1817 | $1.75 |
| Fabric | Inventory of James Winchill (1817) | Yard of nicest cloth in Franklin County, Indiana, 1817 | $2.50 |
| Fabric | Inventory of James Winchill (1817) | Yard of olive velvet in Franklin County, Indiana, 1817 | $0.50 |
| Molds | Inventory of James Winchill (1817) | Box of button molds in Franklin County, Indiana, 1817 | $4.00 |
| Moleskin | Inventory of James Winchill (1817) | Yard of black Kersey moleskin in Franklin County, Indiana, 1817 | $2.00 |
| Needles | Inventory of Caleb Odle (1812) | Two pair of nitting needles in Franklin County, Indiana, 1812 | 12½ cents |
| Needles | Inventory of James Winchill (1817) | Box of needles in Franklin County, Indiana, 1817 | $0.50 |
| Pattern | Inventory of John Hadley (1818) | Vest pattern in Franklin County, Indiana, 1818 | $1.50 |
| Ribbon | Inventory of John Trammel (1818) | ¼ yard of pink ribon in Greenville, South Carolina, 1820 | $0.36 |
| Silk | Inventory of James Winchill (1817) | Ounce of sewing silk in Franklin County, Indiana, 1817 | $9.00 |
| Tape | Inventory of James Winchill (1817) | Tape in Franklin County, Indiana, 1817 | $0.06 |
| Thimbles | Inventory of James Winchill (1817) | Box of thimbles in Franklin County, Indiana, 1817 | $1.50 |
| Thread | Inventory of George Frute (1811) | Pound of thread in Franklin County, Indiana, 1811 | $0.21 |
| Thread | Inventory of James Winchill (1817) | Bundle of quilting thread in Franklin County, Indiana, 1817 | $1.06½ |
| **Farm Equipment & Tools** | | | |
| Auger | Inventory of Adam Carsn (1816) | Large auger in Franklin County, Indiana, 1816 | $0.75 |
| Axe | Business Accounts of Hampshire Furnance (1815) | Price for one new axe in Hampshire, Virginia in 1815 | $2.00 |
| Barrel | Inventory of Samuel Ash (1822) | Empty barrel in New Castle County, Delaware, 1822 | $0.50 |
| Bee Gum | Inventory of James Gamble (1812) | Bee gum in Sumter, South Carolina, 1812 | $1.00 |
| Beehive | Inventory of George Frute (1811) | Beehive in Franklin County, Indiana, 1811 | $1.50 |
| Bin | Inventory of Major Cyrus Ball (1820) | Bin in Lancaster County, Virginia, 1820 | $0.25 |
| Bit | Inventory of Dr. Gustavus Richard Brown (1804) | Bryer bitt in Charles County, Maryland, 1804 | $0.50 |
| Box | Inventory of William Alexander (1811) | Cutting box in New Castle County, Delaware, 1811 | $4.00 |

| Item | Data Source | Description | Price |
|------|-------------|-------------|-------|
| Bucket | Inventory of John Kennedy (1811) | Old well bucket in Franklin County, Indiana, 1811 | $0.25 |
| Cabbage cutter | Inventory of George Frute (1811) | Cabbage cutter in Franklin County, Indiana, 1811 | $1.50 |
| Chain | Business Accounts of Hampshire Furnance (1816) | One iron log chain in Hampshire, Virginia in 1815 | $5.78 |
| Chisel | Inventory of Adam Carsn (1816) | Chissel in Franklin County, Indiana, 1816 | $0.50 |
| Churn | Inventory of James Moore (1820) | Churn in Franklin County, Indiana, 1820 | $0.50 |
| Comb | Inventory of Julius Nickrols (1816) | Curry comb in Greenville, South Carolina, 1816 | $0.25 |
| Corn Mill | Inventory of James Gamble (1812) | Corn mill grind stone in Sumter, South Carolina, 1812 | $8.00 |
| Cotton Cards | Inventory of James Gamble (1812) | Pair of Cotton Cards in Sumter, South Carolina, 1812 | $1.50 |
| Cotton Gin | Inventory of Legrand Guerry (1811) | Cotton gin in Sumter, South Carolina, 1811 | $85.00 |
| Cotton Machine | Inventory of James Gamble (1812) | Cotton machine in Sumter, South Carolina, 1812 | $25.00 |
| Cultivator | Inventory of Richard Cramplin (1807) | Cultivator in Prince George County, Maryland, 1807 | $2.50 |
| Cutting Box | Inventory of John Ridgill (1820) | Cutting box in Sumter, South Carolina, 1820 | $10.00 |
| Fan | Inventory of Dr. Gustavus Richard Brown (1804) | Wheat fan in Charles County, Maryland, 1804 | $16.00 |
| File | Inventory of James Winchill (1817) | File in Franklin County, Indiana, 1817 | $0.50 |
| Gears | Inventory of John Milholland (1814) | Set of geers in Franklin County, Indiana, 1814 | $3.50 |
| Gin | Inventory of Benjm. Hodge (1815) | Gin in Sumter, South Carolina, 1815 | $75.00 |
| Grindstone | Inventory of John Ridgill (1820) | Grindstone in Sumter, South Carolina, 1820 | $2.50 |
| Hammer | Business Accounts of Hampshire Furnance (1816) | One hammer made at a blacksmith shop in Hampshire, Virginia in 1815 | $0.37 |
| Hand Mill | Inventory of John Ridgill (1820) | Hand mill in Sumter, South Carolina, 1820 | $12.00 |
| Harrow | Inventory of Dr. Gustavus Richard Brown (1804) | Iron tooth harrow in Charles County, Maryland, 1804 | $3.00 |

## Based Upon US Dollars

| Year | Value of 19th Century Dollar in 2002 US Dollars |
|------|--------------------------------------------------|
| 1800 | $14.00 |
| 1805 | $15.00 |
| 1810 | $14.00 |
| 1815 | $11.00 |
| 1820 | $15.00 |
| 1824 | $18.00 |

*Calculations are approximate values based upon economic historical data*

| Item | Data Source | Description | Price |
|------|-------------|-------------|-------|
| Hoe | Inventory of Richard Cramplin (1807) | New weeding hoe in Prince George County, Maryland, 1807 | $0.80 |
| Hoe | Inventory of James Gamble (1812) | Broad hoe in Sumter, South Carolina, 1812 | $0.50 |
| Knife | Inventory of George Frute (1811) | Drawing knife in Franklin County, Indiana, 1811 | $0.50 |
| Log chain | Inventory of Malchi Richardson (1815) | Log chain in Franklin County, Indiana, 1815 | $2.00 |
| Loom | Inventory of Margaret Gordon (1815) | Loom and harness in Sumter, South Carolina, 1815 | $4.50 |
| Machine | Inventory of Major Cyrus Ball (1820) | Crashing machine in Lancaster County, Virginia, 1820 | $5.00 |
| Molds | Inventory of John Milholland (1814) | Candle moles in Franklin County, Indiana, 1814 | 12½ cents |
| Nails | Inventory of John Hanna (1814) | Pound of nails in Franklin County, Indiana, 1814 | $0.25 |
| Pail | Inventory of James Winchill (1817) | Milk bucket in Franklin County, Indiana, 1817 | 12½ cents |
| Pitchfork | Inventory of John Milholland (1814) | Pitchfork in Franklin County, Indiana, 1814 | $0.50 |
| Plane | Inventory of John Hanna (1814) | Plain in Franklin County, Indiana, 1814 | $0.42 |
| Plough | Inventory of Adam Carsn (1816) | Small plough in Franklin County, Indiana, 1816 | $4.00 |
| Plough | Inventory of John Anderson (1822) | Plough and gears in Sumter, South Carolina, 1822 | $15.00 |
| Pot | Inventory of James Gamble (1812) | Watering pot in Sumter, South Carolina, 1812 | $0.25 |
| Riddle | Inventory of John Stogdale (1815) | Riddle in Franklin County, Indiana, 1815 | $0.25 |
| Rope | Roland Clapp's Store Day Book (1816) | Cost for 3½ pounds of rope sold in Roland Clapp Store in Turin, New York | $0.15 |
| Salt | Business Accounts of Hampshire Furnance (1816) | One quart of salt for livestock in Hampshire, Virginia in 1815 | $0.08 |
| Saw | Inventory of Dr. Gustavus Richard Brown (1804) | Hand saw in Charles County, Maryland, 1804 | $1.00 |
| Saw | Inventory of Thomas Lee (1806) | Tennon saw in Prince William County, Virginia, 1806 | $0.50 |
| Saw | Inventory of Richard Cramplin (1807) | Good whip saw in Prince George County, Maryland, 1807 | $5.00 |
| Saw | Inventory of John Ridgill (1820) | Cross cut saw in Sumter, South Carolina, 1820 | $3.00 |
| Scale | Inventory of James Gamble (1812) | Scales & weights in Sumter, South Carolina, 1812 | $6.00 |
| Screws | Inventory of James Winchill (1817) | Gross of screws in Franklin County, Indiana, 1817 | $1.00 |
| Scythe | Inventory of Richard Cramplin (1807) | Grass scythe in Prince George County, Maryland, 1807 | $0.66 |
| Scythe | Inventory of Richard Cramplin (1807) | Bramble scythe in Prince George County, Maryland, 1807 | $0.40 |
| Shears | Inventory of John Ridgill (1820) | Sheep shears in Sumter, South Carolina, 1820 | 87½ cents |
| Shovel | Inventory of John Kennedy (1811) | Old shovel in Franklin County, Indiana, 1811 | $0.25 |
| Sickle | Inventory of James Moore (1820) | Sickle in Franklin County, Indiana, 1820 | $0.25 |
| Sieve | Inventory of John Stogdale (1815) | Wire sieve in Franklin County, Indiana, 1815 | $1.75 |

| Item | Data Source | Description | Price |
| --- | --- | --- | --- |
| Sifter | Inventory of George Frute (1811) | Meal sifter in Franklin County, Indiana, 1811 | 12½ cents |
| Spade | Inventory of Samuel Ash (1822) | Old spade in New Castle County, Delaware, 1822 | $1.10 |
| Steelyard | Inventory of James Gamble (1812) | Steelyard in Sumter, South Carolina, 1812 | $1.00 |
| Steelyards | Inventory of Malchi Richardson (1815) | Pair of steelyards in Franklin County, Indiana, 1815 | $3.00 |
| Task Basket | Inventory of John Anderson (1822) | Task basket in Sumter, South Carolina, 1822 | 18¾ cents |
| Trough | Inventory of Charles Tillier (1812) | Trough in Franklin County, Indiana, 1812 | $0.50 |
| Twine | Roland Clapp's Store Day Book (1816) | Cost for 3¼ pounds of twine sold in Roland Clapp Store in Turin, New York | $0.47 |
| Wedge | Inventory of Dr. Gustavus Richard Brown (1804) | Iron wedge in Charles County, Maryland, 1804 | $0.50 |
| Wire Sieve | Inventory of Dr. Daniel Jenifer (1809) | Wire seive & riddle in Charles County, Maryland, 1809 | $1.00 |
| Wool Cards | Inventory of James Gamble (1812) | Pair of Wool Cards in Sumter, South Carolina, 1812 | $1.50 |

## Firearms & Supplies

| Item | Data Source | Description | Price |
| --- | --- | --- | --- |
| Brace | Inventory of Major Cyrus Ball (1820) | Brace of horsemans pistols & houlsters in Lancaster County, Virginia, 1820 | $15.00 |
| Flints | Inventory of Samuel Ash (1822) | 100 gun flints in New Castle County, Delaware, 1822 | $0.10 |
| Gun | Inventory of John Hanna (1814) | Gun in Franklin County, Indiana, 1814 | $12.00 |
| Gunpowder | William Dutton, Du Pont (1949) | Pound of gunpowder imported into the United States, 1811 | $0.40 |
| Lock | Inventory of James Winchill (1817) | Gunn lock in Franklin County, Indiana, 1817 | $1.50 |
| Musket | Arcadi Gluckman, Identifying Old U.S. Muskets, Rifles & Carbines (1965) | Contract price per stand of for 1812 Musket Model for the US Government, manufactured by Elias Earle, Centerville South Carolina, 1815 | $15.00 |
| Pistols | Inventory of Dr. Daniel Jenifer (1809) | Pair of holster pistols in Charles County, Maryland, 1809 | $25.00 |
| Rifle | Arcadi Gluckman, Identifying Old U.S. Muskets, Rifles & Carbines (1965) | Price per rifle, US Flintlock-Model 1814, manufactured by Henry Deringer, 1821 | $17.00 |

## Based Upon US Dollars

| Year | Value of 19th Century Dollar in 2002 US Dollars |
| --- | --- |
| 1800 | $14.00 |
| 1805 | $15.00 |
| 1810 | $14.00 |
| 1815 | $11.00 |
| 1820 | $15.00 |
| 1824 | $18.00 |

*Calculations are approximate values based upon economic historical data*

| Item | Data Source | Description | Price |
|---|---|---|---|
| Rifle | Arcadi Gluckman, Identifying Old U.S. Muskets, Rifles & Carbines (1965) | Price per rifle, US Flintlock Breach-Loading Rifle - Model 1819, manufactured by John H Hall 1817 | $25.00 |
| Rifle Barrel Lock | Inventory of John G. Flagler (1815) | Rifle barrel lock & mounting in Sumter, South Carolina, 1815 | $10.00 |
| Rifle Moulds | Inventory of James Gamble (1812) | Rifle Moulds in Sumter, South Carolina, 1812 | $15.00 |
| Screw | Inventory of James Winchill (1817) | Musket screw in Franklin County, Indiana, 1817 | $0.10 |
| Shot | Inventory of James Winchill (1817) | Pound of shot in Franklin County, Indiana, 1817 | $0.16 |
| Shotgun | Inventory of John Ridgill (1820) | Double barrel shot gun in Sumter, South Carolina, 1820 | $80.00 |
| Shotgun | Inventory of John Ridgill (1820) | Single barrel shot gun in Sumter, South Carolina, 1820 | $18.25 |
| Sword | Inventory of Major Cyrus Ball (1820) | Sword and belt in Lancaster County, Virginia, 1820 | $15.00 |
| Sword Belt | Inventory of John P. Felder (1815) | Sword belt in Sumter, South Carolina, 1815 | $9.00 |
| Tomahawk | Inventory of Peter Dellue (1812) | Tomahawk in Franklin County, Indiana, 1812 | $0.25 |

## Food Products

| Item | Data Source | Description | Price |
|---|---|---|---|
| Alum | Roland Clapp's Store Day Book (1816) | Cost for one pound of alum sold in Roland Clapp Store in Turin, New York | $0.21 |
| Bacon | Inventory of John Hanna (1814) | Pound of bacon in Franklin County, Indiana, 1814 | $0.10 |
| Beans | Business Accounts of Hampshire Furnance (1816) | Cost for one bushel of beans in Hampshire, Virginia in 1815 | $1.00 |
| Biscuits | Aurora General Advertiser (1810) | Pound of biscuits sold by a confectionary in Philadelphia, 1810 | $0.50 |
| Cabbage | Inventory of Richard Cramplin (1807) | Head of cabbage in Prince George County, Maryland, 1807 | $0.01 |
| Cake | Aurora General Advertiser (1810) | Almond cake sold by a confectionary in Philadelphia, 1810 | $0.75 |
| Candied Fruit | Aurora General Advertiser (1810) | Candied peaches sold by a confectionary in Philadelphia, 1810 | $1.00 |
| Candy | Aurora General Advertiser (1810) | Caramel sold by a confectionary in Philadelphia, 1810 | $1.00 |
| Chocolate | Inventory of James Winchill (1817) | Pound of chocolate in Franklin County, Indiana, 1817 | $0.30 |
| Coffee | Roland Clapp's Store Day Book (1816) | Cost for one pound of coffee sold in Roland Clapp Store in Turin, New York | $0.10 |
| Dried Fruit | Aurora General Advertiser (1810) | Dried peaches sold by a confectionary in Philadelphia, 1810 | $0.75 |
| Dried Fruit | Aurora General Advertiser (1810) | Dried black walnuts sold by a confectionary in Philadelphia, 1810 | $1.50 |
| Drops | Aurora General Advertiser (1810) | Peppermint drops sold by a confectionary in Philadelphia, 1810 | $0.75 |
| Flour | Inventory of John Hanna (1814) | Barrel of flour in Franklin County, Indiana, 1814 | $4.50 |
| Ham | Inventory of Dr. Daniel Jenifer (1809) | Ham in Charles County, Maryland, 1809 | $1.50 |
| Herring | Inventory of Samuel Ash (1822) | 1 box ornery smoked herring in New Castle County, Delaware, 1822 | $0.25 |
| Jelly | Aurora General Advertiser (1810) | Pot of strawberry jelly sold by a confectionary in Philadelphia, 1810 | $0.50 |
| Jelly | Aurora General Advertiser (1810) | Pot of guave jelly sold by a confectionary in Philadelphia, 1810 | $1.50 |

| Item | Data Source | Description | Price |
| --- | --- | --- | --- |
| Molasses | Roland Clapp's Store Day Book (1816) | Cost for one gallon of molasses sold in Roland Clap Store in Turin, New York | $0.35 |
| Oats | Inventory of William Alexander (1811) | Three acres of oats in New Castle County, Delaware, 1811 | $18.00 |
| Pork | Inventory of Richard Cramplin (1807) | Pound of salted pork in Prince George County, Maryland, 1807 | $0.06 |
| Raisins | Roland Clapp's Store Day Book (1816) | Cost for one pound of raisins sold in Roland Clapp Store in Turin, New York | $0.10 |
| Rice | Inventory of Samuel Ash (1822) | Pound of rice in New Castle County, Delaware, 1822 | 4½ cents |
| Rye | Inventory of Julius Nickrols (1816) | Bushel of rye in Greenville, South Carolina, 1816 | $0.75 |
| Salartus | Roland Clapp's Store Day Book (1816) | Cost for one pound of salartus sold in Roland Clapp Store in Turin, New York | $0.09 |
| Spice | Inventory of James Winchill (1817) | Ounce of nutmeg in Franklin County, Indiana, 1817 | $0.36 |
| Spice | Inventory of James Winchill (1817) | Pound of pepper in Franklin County, Indiana, 1817 | $0.33 |
| Spice | Inventory of James Winchill (1817) | Pound of allspice in Franklin County, Indiana, 1817 | $0.40 |
| Spice | Inventory of James Winchill (1817) | Pound of ginger in Franklin County, Indiana, 1817 | $0.30 |
| Starch | Roland Clapp's Store Day Book (1816) | Cost for 7½ pounds of starch sold in Roland Clapp Store in Turin, New York | $0.55 |
| Sugar | Inventory of John Hanna (1814) | Pound of sugar in Franklin County, Indiana, 1814 | $0.10 |
| Sugar | Inventory of Samuel Ash (1822) | Ten pounds of common sugar in New Castle County, Delaware, 1822 | $0.20 |
| Tarts | Aurora General Advertiser (1810) | Cream tarts sold by a confectionary in Philadelphia, 1810 | $0.50 |
| Tea | Roland Clapp's Store Day Book (1816) | Cost for one pound of tea sold in Roland Clapp Store in Turin, New York | $1.50 |
| Tea | Roland Clapp's Store Day Book (1816) | Cost for one chest of green tea sold in Roland Clapp Store in Turin, New York | $0.50 |
| Turnips | Inventory of Richard Cramplin (1807) | Bushel of turnips in Prince George County, Maryland, 1807 | $0.11 |
| Vinegar | Inventory of Samuel Ash (1822) | Gallon of vinegar in New Castle County, Delaware, 1822 | $0.12 |
| Wheat | Inventory of Caleb Odle (1812) | Bushel of Wheat in Franklin County, Indiana, 1812 | $0.50 |

## Based Upon US Dollars

| Year | Value of 19th Century Dollar in 2002 US Dollars |
| --- | --- |
| 1800 | $14.00 |
| 1805 | $15.00 |
| 1810 | $14.00 |
| 1815 | $11.00 |
| 1820 | $15.00 |
| 1824 | $18.00 |

*Calculations are approximate values based upon economic historical data*

| Item | Data Source | Description | Price |
|---|---|---|---|
| **Household Furniture** | | | |
| Armchair | Inventory of Margaret J. Bail (1817) | Large armchair in New Castle County, Delaware, 1817 | $0.75 |
| Bed | Inventory of William Black (1804) | Bed, bedstead & blue bedding in New Castle County, Delaware, 1804 | $25.00 |
| Bench | Inventory of James Gamble (1812) | Cyprus bench in Sumter, South Carolina, 1812 | $0.25 |
| Bookcase | Inventory of Dr. Daniel Jenifer (1809) | Small mahogany book case in Charles County, Maryland, 1809 | $8.00 |
| Bottle case | Winthrop Gardiner Jr. Collection | Bottle case made in New York, 1802 | 12 Shllings |
| Bureau | Inventory of Margaret J. Bail (1817) | Bureau in New Castle County, Delaware, 1817 | $6.00 |
| Carpet | Inventory of James Gamble (1812) | Hearth carpert in Sumter, South Carolina, 1812 | $5.00 |
| Case of drawers | Inventory of William Black (1804) | High case of drawers in New Castle County, Delaware, 1804 | $6.00 |
| Cellarette | Inventory of James Gamble (1812) | Cellarette in Sumter, South Carolina, 1812 | $15.00 |
| Chair | Inventory of James Brice (1802) | Mahogany chair with damask bottom and old brass nails in Anne Arundel County, Maryland, 1802 | $4.58 |
| Chair | Inventory of William Black (1804) | Winsor chair in New Castle County, Delaware, 1804 | $0.50 |
| Chair | Inventory of William Black (1804) | Children's chair in New Castle County, Delaware, 1804 | $0.75 |
| Chest | Inventory of John Hadley (1818) | Large pine chest in Franklin County, Indiana, 1818 | $1.50 |
| Chest of Drawers | Winthrop Gardiner Jr. Collection | Mahogany Chest of Drawers made in New York during 1800 | 18 pounds |
| Chest of Drawers | Inventory of James Brice (1802) | Very old walnut chest of drawers in Anne Arundel County, Maryland, 1802 | $2.00 |
| Clock | Winthrop Gardiner Jr. Collection | Silent clock; pine case with enameled sheet-iron dial, brass works H 83", W 13", D 8" crafted in New York, 1804 | 10 pounds |
| Clock | Winthrop Gardiner Jr. Collection | Timepiece with minute hand made in New York, 1814 | 10 pounds |
| Clock | Winthrop Gardiner Jr. Collection | Eight day repeating clock made in New York, 1818 | 10 pounds 8 shillings |
| Clotheshorse | Winthrop Gardiner Jr. Collection | Clotheshorse made in New York, 1803 | 10 shillings |
| Couch | Inventory of Margaret J. Bail (1817) | Couch in New Castle County, Delaware, 1817 | $1.00 |
| Cradle | Inventory of Margaret J. Bail (1817) | Cradle in New Castle County, Delaware, 1817 | $2.00 |
| Crib | Inventory of Major Cyrus Ball (1820) | Childs crib in Lancaster County, Virginia, 1820 | $2.00 |
| Cupboard | Inventory of Dr. Daniel Jenifer (1809) | Cupboard with glass door in Charles County, Maryland, 1809 | $12.00 |
| Desk | Winthrop Gardiner Jr. Collection | Desk with bookcase: Maple; cherry and pine secondary woods H 87¼"; W 37¾"; D 20 ⅝" in New York during 1800 | 20 pounds 8 shillings |
| Desk | Winthrop Gardiner Jr. Collection | Mahogany desk with white pine and cherry secondary woods H 42"; W 37¼", D 19⅞" crafted in New York, 1802 | 11 pounds |
| Dish | Inventory of Major Cyrus Ball (1820) | White dish in Lancaster County, Virginia, 1820 | $0.05 |

| Item | Data Source | Description | Price |
|------|-------------|-------------|-------|
| Drawers | Inventory of James Gamble (1812) | Chest drawers in Sumter, South Carolina, 1812 | $20.00 |
| Dressing Glass | Inventory of Richard Cramplin (1807) | Oval dressing glass in Prince George County, Maryland, 1807 | $2.00 |
| Lamp | Inventory of James Brice (1802) | Old fashioned passage lamp in Anne Arundel County, Maryland, 1802 | $3.00 |
| Liquor Case | Inventory of James Brice (1802) | Liquor case in Anne Arundel County, Maryland, 1802 | $1.00 |
| Mattress | Inventory of James Brice (1802) | New mattrass and bed wth a blanket, a coverlet and pair of sheets boulster in Anne Arundel County, Maryland, 1802 | $20.00 |
| Mattress | Inventory of Peter Doty (1811) | Cost for a pigeon featherbed mattress in Shaticoke, New York | $5.00 |
| Screen | Inventory of James Gamble (1812) | Chamber screen in Sumter, South Carolina, 1812 | $10.00 |
| Stand | Inventory of Thomas Lee (1806) | Wash stand in Prince William County, Virginia, 1806 | $4.00 |
| Stand | Inventory of James Knight (1816) | Candle stand in Franklin County, Indiana, 1816 | $0.30 |
| Stool | Inventory of James Gamble (1812) | Office stool in Sumter, South Carolina, 1812 | $0.25 |
| Stool | Winthrop Gardiner Jr. Collection | Footstool made in New York, 1820 | 7 shillings |
| Table | Inventory of James Brice (1802) | Old round walnut table in Anne Arundel County, Maryland, 1802 | $1.50 |
| Table | Inventory of James Brice (1802) | Mahogany card table in Anne Arundel County, Maryland, 1802 | $8.00 |
| Table | Inventory of James Brice (1802) | Oval breakfast table in Anne Arundel County, Maryland, 1802 | $8.00 |
| Trunk | Inventory of Margaret J. Bail (1817) | Large leather trunk in New Castle County, Delaware, 1817 | $0.50 |
| Waiter | Inventory of Margaret J. Bail (1817) | Waiter in New Castle County, Delaware, 1817 | $0.17 |
| Wardrobe | Inventory of James Brice (1802) | Mahogany wardrobe in Anne Arundel County, Maryland, 1802 | $6.00 |

## Household Products

| Item | Data Source | Description | Price |
|------|-------------|-------------|-------|
| Acquafortier | Inventory of John Ridgill (1820) | Acquafortier in Sumter, South Carolina, 1820 | $1.50 |
| Andirons | Inventory of William Black (1804) | Pair brass andirons in New Castle County, Delaware, 1804 | $4.50 |
| Basket | Inventory of John Kennedy (1811) | Bread basket in Franklin County, Indiana, 1811 | $1.00 |
| Basket | Inventory of Malchi Richardson (1815) | Willow basket in Franklin County, Indiana, 1815 | 37½ cents |
| Basket | Inventory of John Hadley (1818) | Clothes basket in Franklin County, Indiana, 1818 | 12½ cents |
| Basin | Inventory of George Frute (1811) | Pewter bason in Franklin County, Indiana, 1811 | $0.66 |
| Basin | Inventory of James Gamble (1812) | Blue bason and goblet in Sumter, South Carolina, 1812 | $3.00 |
| Bed | Inventory of James Gamble (1812) | Feather bed in Sumter, South Carolina, 1812 | $35.00 |
| Bed Cords | Roland Clapp's Store Day Book (1816) | Cost for one dozen bed cords sold in Roland Clapp Store in Turin, New York | $3.38 |
| Bedcover | Inventory of James Gamble (1812) | Bed cover in Sumter, South Carolina, 1812 | $5.00 |
| Bedspread | Inventory of Margaret J. Bail (1817) | Callico bedspread in New Castle County, Delaware, 1817 | $1.50 |
| Bell | Inventory of Dr. Gustavus Richard Brown (1804) | Chamber bell in Charles County, Maryland, 1804 | $0.25 |
| Blanket | Inventory of William Black (1804) | Pair of blankets in New Castle County, Delaware, 1804 | $2.50 |
| Bolster | Inventory of James Gamble (1812) | Bolster in Sumter, South Carolina, 1812 | $1.00 |
| Bolt | Inventory of James Winchill (1817) | Window bolt in Franklin County, Indiana, 1817 | 6¼ cents |
| Bottles | McKearin, American Bottles & Flasks (1978) | Dozen Hollow Ware gallon bottles from Pittsburgh, Pennslyvania, 1809 | $4.00 |
| Bottles | McKearin, American Bottles & Flasks (1978) | Gross of Inferior twisted glass bottles in Philadelphia, Pennsylvania, 1818 | $7.50 |
| Bowl | Inventory of Dr. Gustavus Richard Brown (1804) | Large china bowl in Charles County, Maryland, 1804 | $1.50 |
| Box | Inventory of John Stogdale (1815) | Old writing box in Franklin County, Indiana, 1815 | $0.25 |
| Broom | Inventory of Dr. Gustavus Richard Brown (1804) | Hearth broom in Charles County, Maryland, 1804 | $0.25 |
| Brush | Inventory of John Kennedy (1811) | Clothes brush in Franklin County, Indiana, 1811 | $0.50 |
| Brush | Inventory of John Hanna (1814) | Hat brush in Franklin County, Indiana, 1814 | 12½ cents |
| Brush | Inventory of Samuel Ash (1822) | Sweeping brush #2 in New Castle County, Delaware, 1822 | $0.25 |
| Brush | Inventory of James Winchill (1817) | Hair brush in Franklin County, Indiana, 1817 | $0.25 |
| Bucket | Inventory of Charles Tillier (1812) | Tin bucket in Franklin County, Indiana, 1812 | $1.25 |
| Candlestick | Roland Clapp's Store Day Book (1816) | Cost for one brass candlestick sold at Roland Clapp Store in Turin, New York | 31½ cents |
| Candlesticks | Inventory of Margaret J. Bail (1817) | Pair plated candlesticks in New Castle County, Delaware, 1817 | $1.00 |

| Item | Data Source | Description | Price |
|------|-------------|-------------|-------|
| Carpet | Inventory of James Brice (1802) | Passage carpet in Anne Arundel County, Maryland, 1802 | $1.50 |
| Case | Inventory of Margaret J. Bail (1817) | Bolster case in New Castle County, Delaware, 1817 | $0.04 |
| Castors | Inventory of James Gamble (1812) | Set of Mahogony Castors in Sumter, South Carolina, 1812 | $2.00 |
| Chair | Inventory of John Anderson (1822) | Sitting chair in Sumter, South Carolina, 1822 | $0.25 |
| Chamber Pot | Roland Clapp's Store Day Book (1816) | Cost for one chamber pot sold in Roland Clapp Store in Turin, New York | $0.37 |
| Chimney Board | Inventory of Margaret J. Bail (1817) | Chimney board in New Castle County, Delaware, 1817 | $0.25 |
| China Set | Inventory of Dr. Gustavus Richard Brown (1804) | Set of china containing 32 pieces in Charles County, Maryland, 1804 | $4.00 |
| Churn | Inventory of Julius Nickrols (1816) | Churn in Greenville, South Carolina, 1816 | $0.50 |
| Clock | Inventory of John Anderson (1822) | Yankee Clock in Sumter, South Carolina, 1822 | 12½ cents |
| Coffee & Tea Set | Inventory of James Gamble (1812) | Set of plated coffee and tea pots with sugar dish & milk pot, 1812 | $12.00 |
| Coffee Roaster | Inventory of Dr. Gustavus Richard Brown (1804) | Coffee roaster in Charles County, Maryland, 1804 | $0.50 |
| Comforter | Inventory of Margaret J. Bail (1817) | Comforters in New Castle County, Delaware, 1817 | $5.00 |
| Cot | Inventory of William Black (1804) | Cot bedstead in New Castle County, Delaware, 1804 | $1.00 |
| Coverlet | Inventory of John Bulkley (1819) | Coverlit in Franklin County, Indiana, 1819 | $7.00 |
| Cruet | Inventory of Thomas Lee (1806) | Cruett in Prince William County, Virginia, 1806 | 12½ cents |
| Cup | Inventory of George Frute (1811) | Tin cup in Franklin County, Indiana, 1811 | $0.10 |
| Cup | Inventory of James Gamble (1812) | Fruit cup in Sumter, South Carolina, 1812 | $0.10 |
| Curtains | Inventory of Thomas Lee (1806) | Suit chintz bed curtains in Prince William County, Virginia, 1806 | $25.00 |
| Curtains | Inventory of Thomas Lee (1806) | Suit callico bed curtains in Prince William County, Virginia, 1806 | $20.00 |

## Based Upon US Dollars

| Year | Value of 19th Century Dollar in 2002 US Dollars |
|------|-------------------------------------------------|
| 1800 | $14.00 |
| 1805 | $15.00 |
| 1810 | $14.00 |
| 1815 | $11.00 |
| 1820 | $15.00 |
| 1824 | $18.00 |

*Calculations are approximate values based upon economic historical data*

| Item | Data Source | Description | Price |
|---|---|---|---|
| Decanter | Inventory of Thomas Lee (1806) | Fluted decanter in Prince William County, Virginia, 1806 | $2.00 |
| Dish | Inventory of Thomas Lee (1806) | Deep blue edge scallop dish in Prince William County, Virginia, 1806 | $0.25 |
| Dish | Inventory of Thomas Lee (1806) | Glass dish in Prince William County, Virginia, 1806 | $1.00 |
| Dish | Inventory of George Frute (1811) | Earthen dish in Franklin County, Indiana, 1811 | $0.25 |
| Fire dogs | Inventory of James Gamble (1812) | Fire dogs shovel & tongs in Sumter, South Carolina, 1812 | $10.00 |
| Firescreen | Inventory of Thomas Lee (1806) | Fire screen in Prince William County, Virginia, 1806 | $1.00 |
| Flask | McKearin, American Bottles & Flasks (1978) | Dozen pint green flasks in Philadelphia, Pennsylvania, 1818 | $1.00 |
| Flatware | Inventory of James Winchill (1817) | Sett of knives and forks in Franklin County, Indiana, 1817 | $1.50 |
| Frame | Inventory of Malchi Richardson (1815) | Picture frame in Franklin County, Indiana, 1815 | $0.25 |
| Frame | Winthrop Gardiner Jr. Collection | Frame for looking glass made in New York, 1820 | 4 shillings |
| Glasses | Inventory of Thomas Lee (1806) | Dozen fluted sweet meat glasses in Prince William County, Virginia, 1806 | $6.00 |
| Glasses | Inventory of Thomas Lee (1806) | 23 jelly glasses in Prince William County, Virginia, 1806 | $4.00 |
| Goblet | Inventory of Thomas Lee (1806) | Goblett in Prince William County, Virginia, 1806 | $20.00 |
| Inkstand | Inventory of James Gamble (1812) | Mahogy Inkstd in Sumter, South Carolina, 1812 | $0.50 |
| Irons | Inventory of James Brice (1802) | Pair of flat irons in Anne Arundel County, Maryland, 1802 | $0.25 |
| Jar | McKearin, American Bottles & Flasks (1978) | Dozen Hollow Ware quart jars from Pittsburgh, Pennslyvania, 1808 | $1.60 |
| Jug | Inventory of Thomas Lee (1806) | Water jug in Prince William County, Virginia, 1806 | $0.25 |
| Knife | Inventory of John Trammel (1818) | Pen knife in Greenville, South Carolina, 1820 | 37½ cents |
| Knife box | Inventory of Margaret J. Bail (1817) | 1 knife box with knives in New Castle County, Delaware, 1817 | $10.00 |
| Ladle | Inventory of Dr. Daniel Jenifer (1809) | Silver soop laddle in Charles County, Maryland, 1809 | $8.00 |
| Lamp | Roland Clapp's Store Day Book (1816) | Cost for one glass lamp sold at Roland Clapp Store in Turin, New York | $0.72 |
| Lantern | Inventory of Dr. Gustavus Richard Brown (1804) | Tin lanthorn in Charles County, Maryland, 1804 | $0.50 |
| Lantern | Inventory of Thomas Lee (1806) | Glass lanthorn in Prince William County, Virginia, 1806 | $4.00 |
| Lining | Inventory of Samuel Ash (1822) | Bed lining in New Castle County, Delaware, 1822 | $0.06 |
| Lock | Inventory of John Hanna (1814) | Brass lock in Franklin County, Indiana, 1814 | $0.50 |
| Loom | Inventory of John Taylor (1822) | Loom and gears in Sumter, South Carolina, 1822 | $5.00 |
| Mattress | Inventory of James Gamble (1812) | Mattress in Sumter, South Carolina, 1812 | $18.00 |
| Medicine Chest | Inventory of James Gamble (1812) | Medicine chest and trunk in Sumter, South Carolina, 1812 | $12.50 |

| Item | Data Source | Description | Price |
|------|-------------|-------------|-------|
| Mirror | Inventory of John Stogdale (1815) | Mirror in Franklin County, Indiana, 1815 | $2.00 |
| Mop Stick | Roland Clapp's Store Day Book (1816) | Cost for one mop stick sold at Roland Clapp Store in Turin, New York | $0.10 |
| Mug | Inventory of James Gamble (1812) | Mug in Sumter, South Carolina, 1812 | $0.25 |
| Napkins | Inventory of James Brice (1802) | Eight old Damask napkins in Anne Arundel County, Maryland, 1802 | $1.50 |
| Pan | Inventory of Dr. Daniel Jenifer (1809) | Earthen pan in Charles County, Maryland, 1809 | $0.20 |
| Pepper Mill | Inventory of James Brice (1802) | Pepper mill in Anne Arundel County, Maryland, 1802 | $0.25 |
| Picture | Inventory of James Brice (1802) | Family picture in Anne Arundel County, Maryland, 1802 | $0.50 |
| Pillow | Inventory of James Gamble (1812) | Pair of bed pillows in Sumter, South Carolina, 1812 | $1.00 |
| Pillow case | Inventory of James Gamble (1812) | Pillow case in Sumter, South Carolina, 1812 | $0.50 |
| Pitcher | Inventory of George Frute (1811) | Earthen pitcher in Franklin County, Indiana, 1811 | $0.25 |
| Plate | Inventory of Dr. Gustavus Richard Brown (1804) | Glass plate in Charles County, Maryland, 1804 | $0.33 |
| Plate | Inventory of John Kennedy (1811) | Butter plate in Franklin County, Indiana, 1811 | 37½ cents |
| Plates | Inventory of James Brice (1802) | Dozen green edged queens ware breakfast plates in Anne Arundel County, Maryland, 1802 | $0.50 |
| Pot | Inventory of Dr. Gustavus Richard Brown (1804) | Stone butter pot in Charles County, Maryland, 1804 | $0.25 |
| Pot | Inventory of Thomas Lee (1806) | Cream pot in Prince William County, Virginia, 1806 | $1.25 |
| Pot | Inventory of Dr. Daniel Jenifer (1809) | Silver coffee pot in Charles County, Maryland, 1809 | $60.00 |
| Pot | Inventory of James Gamble (1812) | Large iron pot in Sumter, South Carolina, 1812 | $4.00 |
| Press | Inventory of Dr. Gustavus Richard Brown (1804) | Black walnut press in Charles County, Maryland, 1804 | $8.00 |
| Print | Inventory of Richard Cramplin (1807) | Print, representative of Genl Washington - larger gilt frame | $12.00 |

### Based Upon US Dollars

| Year | Value of 19th Century Dollar in 2002 US Dollars |
|------|-------------------------------------------------|
| 1800 | $14.00 |
| 1805 | $15.00 |
| 1810 | $14.00 |
| 1815 | $11.00 |
| 1820 | $15.00 |
| 1824 | $18.00 |

*Calculations are approximate values based upon economic historical data*

| Item | Data Source | Description | Price |
|------|-------------|-------------|-------|
| Print | Inventory of Richard Cramplin (1807) | Print, Surender of Tippo's sons to Genl Harrison | $2.50 |
| Quilt | Inventory of Margaret J. Bail (1817) | Callico quilt in New Castle County, Delaware, 1817 | $0.90 |
| Razor | Roland Clapp's Store Day Book (1816) | Cost for one razor sold in Roland Clapp Store in Turin, New York | $0.05 |
| Razor Case | Inventory of Asahel Churchill (1812) | Rasure case in Franklin County, Indiana, 1812 | $0.75 |
| Razor strap | Roland Clapp's Store Day Book (1816) | Cost for one razor strop sold in Roland Clapp Store in Turin, New York | $0.17 |
| Rug | Inventory of Margaret J. Bail (1817) | Rugg in New Castle County, Delaware, 1817 | $2.00 |
| Salt Cellar | Inventory of John Kennedy (1811) | Salt seller in Franklin County, Indiana, 1811 | $1.00 |
| Scales | Inventory of Samuel Ash (1822) | 1 pair scales in New Castle County, Delaware, 1822 | $1.50 |
| Scrub | Inventory of Samuel Ash (1822) | Hand Scrub in New Castle County, Delaware, 1822 | 12½ cents |
| Secretary | Inventory of John Anderson (1822) | Mahogany secretary in Sumter, South Carolina, 1822 | $20.00 |
| Shade | Inventory of James Brice (1802) | Glass candle shade in Anne Arundel County, Maryland, 1802 | $1.50 |
| Shaving Apparatus | Inventory of Richard Cramplin (1807) | Shaving apparatus, rasors, straps, &c in Prince George County, Maryland, 1807 | $2.50 |
| Sheets | Inventory of James Gamble (1812) | Pair of sheets in Sumter, South Carolina, 1812 | $13.00 |
| Shovel | Inventory of John Milholland (1814) | Fire shovel in Franklin County, Indiana, 1814 | $1.00 |
| Shovel & Tongs | Inventory of William Black (1804) | Shovel and tongs in New Castle County, Delaware, 1804 | $2.00 |
| Snuffer | Inventory of James Gamble (1812) | Plated candlestick snuffers and stand in Sumter, South Carolina, 1812 | $3.00 |
| Soap | Inventory of John Hanna (1814) | Shaving soap in Franklin County, Indiana, 1814 | $0.25 |
| Soap | Inventory of Samuel Ash (1822) | Box lye soap in New Castle County, Delaware, 1822 | $5.22 |
| Spinning Wheel | Inventory of William Alexander (1811) | Spinning wheel & reel in New Castle County, Delaware, 1811 | $2.00 |
| Spoons | Inventory of Dr. Gustavus Richard Brown (1804) | Dozen silver tea spoons in Charles County, Maryland, 1804 | $5.00 |
| Spoons | Inventory of James Winchill (1817) | Dozen pewter tea spoons in Franklin County, Indiana, 1817 | $0.33 |
| Stand | Inventory of John Hanna (1814) | Water stand in Franklin County, Indiana, 1814 | 12½ cents |
| Stand & Bowl | Inventory of Dr. Gustavus Richard Brown (1804) | Glass stand & bowl in Charles County, Maryland, 1804 | $4.00 |
| Stool | Inventory of Richard Cramplin (1807) | Fineared close stool in Prince George County, Maryland, 1807 | $4.00 |
| Stove | Inventory of George Frute (1811) | Iron stove in Franklin County, Indiana, 1811 | $12.00 |
| Stove | Inventory of Margaret J. Bail (1817) | Open stove in New Castle County, Delaware, 1817 | $3.00 |
| Strainer | Inventory of Dr. Daniel Jenifer (1809) | Silver punch strainer in Charles County, Maryland, 1809 | $4.00 |
| Sugar Dish | Inventory of Richard Cramplin (1807) | Blue glass sugar dish in Prince George County, Maryland, 1807 | $0.25 |

| Item | Data Source | Description | Price |
|---|---|---|---|
| Sun Glass | Inventory of John Ridgill (1820) | Sun glass in Sumter, South Carolina, 1820 | $1.00 |
| Tablecloth | Inventory of James Brice (1802) | Dining table cloth in Anne Arundel County, Maryland, 1802 | $2.00 |
| Tea cup | Inventory of James Gamble (1812) | Dozen tea cups and saucers in Sumter, South Carolina, 1812 | $3.00 |
| Teapot | Inventory of James Brice (1802) | Brown tea pot in Anne Arundel County, Maryland, 1802 | $0.25 |
| Teapot | Inventory of Dr. Gustavus Richard Brown (1804) | Silver tea pot in Charles County, Maryland, 1804 | $10.00 |
| Teaware | Inventory of George Frute (1811) | Set of teaware in Franklin County, Indiana, 1811 | $1.00 |
| Toilet | Inventory of Jno. R. Beaty (1815) | Toilet in Franklin County, Indiana, 1815 | $1.00 |
| Toothbrush | Roland Clapp's Store Day Book (1816) | Cost for one toothbrush sold in Roland Clapp Store in Turin, New York | $0.07 |
| Towel | Inventory of Margaret J. Bail (1817) | Dinner towel in New Castle County, Delaware, 1817 | $0.18 |
| Towel | Inventory of Dr. Daniel Jenifer (1809) | Diaper towel in Charles County, Maryland, 1809 | $0.50 |
| Trunk | Inventory of Richard Cramplin (1807) | Seal skin trunk in Prince George County, Maryland, 1807 | $1.00 |

| Item | Data Source | Description | Price |
|------|-------------|-------------|-------|
| Tub | Inventory of Margaret J. Bail (1817) | Large tub in New Castle County, Delaware, 1817 | $0.50 |
| Tumbler | Inventory of Dr. Gustavus Richard Brown (1804) | Small glass tumbler in Charles County, Maryland, 1804 | $0.05 |
| Umbrella | Inventory of James Winchill (1817) | Umbrella in Franklin County, Indiana, 1817 | $0.50 |
| Warming Pan | Inventory of James Brice (1802) | Very old warming pan in Anne Arundel County, Maryland, 1802 | $0.75 |
| Water Jug | Inventory of Margaret Gordon (1815) | Water jug in Sumter, South Carolina, 1815 | $1.50 |
| Watering Can | Inventory of George Frute (1811) | Watering can in Franklin County, Indiana, 1811 | $0.50 |
| Wax | Inventory of James Winchill (1817) | Ball of bees wax in Franklin County, Indiana, 1817 | $0.25 |

## Investment

| Item | Data Source | Description | Price |
|------|-------------|-------------|-------|
| Stock | Statutes at Large of South Carolina (1808) | Share of stock in the Broad River Company, 1806 | $230.78 |
| Stock | Inventory of Eli Allen (1817) | Per share price of Wilmington & Brandywine held in New Castle County, Delaware, 1817 | $2.77 |

## Jewelry

| Item | Data Source | Description | Price |
|------|-------------|-------------|-------|
| Locket | Inventory of Richard Cramplin (1807) | Gold lockett with the letters ALG in Prince George County, Maryland, 1807 | $5.00 |
| Watch | Inventory of Richard Cramplin (1807) | Gold watch in Prince George County, Maryland, 1807 | $50.00 |
| Watch | Inventory of John Stogdale (1815) | Silver watch in Franklin County, Indiana, 1815 | $15.00 |

## Kitchen Items

| Item | Data Source | Description | Price |
|------|-------------|-------------|-------|
| Andirons | Inventory of Dr. Gustavus Richard Brown (1804) | Pair of kitchen andirons in Charles County, Maryland, 1804 | $1.00 |
| Basin | Inventory of Margaret J. Bail (1817) | Pewter basin in New Castle County, Delaware, 1817 | $0.25 |
| Boiler | Inventory of Margaret J. Bail (1817) | Tin boiler in New Castle County, Delaware, 1817 | $0.25 |
| Bottle | Inventory of John Kennedy (1811) | 1½ Gallon bottle in Franklin County, Indiana, 1811 | $0.50 |
| Bucket | Inventory of Margaret J. Bail (1817) | Water bucket in New Castle County, Delaware, 1817 | $0.37 |
| Canister | Inventory of Margaret J. Bail (1817) | Tin cannister in New Castle County, Delaware, 1817 | $0.25 |
| Cleaver | Inventory of Dr. Daniel Jenifer (1809) | Butchers cleaver in Charles County, Maryland, 1809 | $1.00 |
| Coffee Mill | Inventory of Samuel Ash (1822) | Box coffee mill in New Castle County, Delaware, 1822 | $1.00 |
| Coffee pot | Inventory of Margaret J. Bail (1817) | Black tin coffee pot in New Castle County, Delaware, 1817 | $2.00 |
| Cooler | Inventory of Dr. Daniel Jenifer (1809) | Cooler with brass hoops in Charles County, Maryland, 1809 | $10.00 |
| Crock | Inventory of Richard Cramplin (1807) | Crock for lard in Prince George County, Maryland, 1807 | $0.50 |
| Colander | Inventory of Margaret J. Bail (1817) | Cullander in New Castle County, Delaware, 1817 | $0.12 |
| Dish | Inventory of Margaret J. Bail (1817) | Pewter dish in New Castle County, Delaware, 1817 | 12½ cents |

| Item | Data Source | Description | Price |
|------|-------------|-------------|-------|
| Doughtrough | Inventory of William Alexander (1811) | Doughtrough in New Castle County, Delaware, 1811 | $1.00 |
| Dutch Oven | Inventory of Legrand Guerry (1811) | Dutch oven in Sumter, South Carolina, 1811 | $2.00 |
| Egg Slicer | Inventory of Margaret J. Bail (1817) | Egg slicer in New Castle County, Delaware, 1817 | $0.06 |
| Fire Brick | Inventory of Margaret J. Bail (1817) | Pair fire bricks in New Castle County, Delaware, 1817 | $5.00 |
| Funnel | Inventory of Margaret J. Bail (1817) | Funnel in New Castle County, Delaware, 1817 | $0.06 |
| Griddle | Inventory of Malchi Richardson (1815) | Griddle in Franklin County, Indiana, 1815 | $1.25 |
| Gridiron | Inventory of John Kennedy (1811) | Grid iron in Franklin County, Indiana, 1811 | $1.25 |
| Hooks | Inventory of Margaret J. Bail (1817) | Half dozen pot hooks in New Castle County, Delaware, 1817 | $1.00 |
| Jar | Inventory of Margaret J. Bail (1817) | Earthen jar in New Castle County, Delaware, 1817 | $0.10 |
| Kettle | Inventory of Dr. Gustavus Richard Brown (1804) | Small copper fish kettle with cover in Charles County, Maryland, 1804 | $4.00 |
| Kettle | Inventory of Richard Cramplin (1807) | Iron tea kettle with brass handles in Prince George County, Maryland, 1807 | $2.00 |
| Knife | Inventory of James Winchill (1817) | Carving knife in Franklin County, Indiana, 1817 | $0.50 |
| Measure | Inventory of James Winchill (1817) | Half-gallon measure in Franklin County, Indiana, 1817 | $0.25 |
| Measures | Roland Clapp's Store Day Book (1816) | Cost for 1½ sets of measureing tins sold in Roland Clapp Store in Turin, New York | $1.75 |
| Milk Strainer | Inventory of James Gamble (1812) | Milk strainer and skimer in Sumter, South Carolina, 1812 | $0.50 |
| Mill | Inventory of James Gamble (1812) | Coffee mill in Sumter, South Carolina, 1812 | $1.50 |
| Mortar | Business Accounts of Hampshire Furnance (1816) | One spice mortar in Hampshire, Virginia in 1815 | $1.04 |
| Mortar & Pestle | Inventory of Margaret J. Bail (1817) | Mortar & pestle in New Castle County, Delaware, 1817 | $0.50 |
| Mortar | Inventory of Thomas Lee (1806) | Spice mortar & pestle in Prince William County, Virginia, 1806 | $1.00 |
| Muffin Rings | Inventory of Margaret J. Bail (1817) | Dozen muffin rings in New Castle County, Delaware, 1817 | $0.25 |
| Oven | Inventory of William Black (1804) | Dutch oven in New Castle County, Delaware, 1804 | $0.50 |
| Pan | Business Accounts of Hampshire Furnance (1816) | A frying pan casted by blacksmith in Hampshire, Virginia in 1815 | $1.08 |
| Pan | Inventory of Margaret J. Bail (1817) | Warming pan in New Castle County, Delaware, 1817 | $1.50 |
| Pickling cask | Inventory of Margaret J. Bail (1817) | Pickling cask in New Castle County, Delaware, 1817 | $1.50 |
| Plates | Inventory of Margaret J. Bail (1817) | Box of pewter plates in New Castle County, Delaware, 1817 | $2.00 |
| Pot | Inventory of Margaret J. Bail (1817) | Iron pot in New Castle County, Delaware, 1817 | $0.50 |
| Pot racks | Inventory of Dr. Daniel Jenifer (1809) | Three iron pot racks in Charles County, Maryland, 1809 | $7.00 |
| Potato chest | Inventory of Margaret J. Bail (1817) | Potato chest in New Castle County, Delaware, 1817 | $1.50 |

| Item | Data Source | Description | Price |
|------|-------------|-------------|-------|
| Rack | Inventory of Julius Nickrols (1816) | Pot rack in Greenville, South Carolina, 1816 | $2.00 |
| Sausage Stuffer | Inventory of Margaret J. Bail (1817) | Sausage stuffer in New Castle County, Delaware, 1817 | $6.00 |
| Skillet | Business Accounts of Hampshire Furnance (1816) | One frying skillet with lid in Hampshire, Virginia in 1815 | $1.13 |
| Soap barrel | Inventory of Margaret J. Bail (1817) | Soap barrel in New Castle County, Delaware, 1817 | $0.50 |
| Spice Box | Inventory of James Gamble (1812) | Spice box in Sumter, South Carolina, 1812 | $1.50 |
| Spider | Inventory of Dr. Daniel Jenifer (1809) | Dutch spider in Charles County, Maryland, 1809 | $0.50 |
| Spit | Inventory of Dr. Gustavus Richard Brown (1804) | Spit in Charles County, Maryland, 1804 | $1.00 |
| Sugar Box | Inventory of Legrand Guerry (1811) | Sugar box in Sumter, South Carolina, 1811 | $0.25 |
| Tea kettle | Inventory of Adam Carsn (1816) | Tea kittle in Franklin County, Indiana, 1816 | $1.75 |
| Toaster | Inventory of Richard Cramplin (1807) | Iron bread toaster in Prince George County, Maryland, 1807 | $0.50 |
| Tongs | Inventory of Jno. R. Beaty (1815) | Pair of tongs in Franklin County, Indiana, 1815 | $1.00 |
| Tongs & spoons | Inventory of Margaret J. Bail (1817) | Pair sugar tongs & tea spoons in New Castle County, Delaware, 1817 | $2.00 |
| Tub | Inventory of Margaret J. Bail (1817) | Washing tubs in New Castle County, Delaware, 1817 | $0.50 |
| Utensils | Business Accounts of Hampshire Furnance (1816) | One set of knives and forks in Hampshire, Virginia in 1815 | $3.13 |
| Waffle Iron | Inventory of James Gamble (1812) | Waffle Iron and wafer Iron in Sumter, South Carolina, 1812 | $7.00 |

## Livery Animals & Tools

| Item | Data Source | Description | Price |
|------|-------------|-------------|-------|
| Bell | Roland Clapp's Store Day Book (1816) | Cost for one sleigh bell sold in Roland Clapp Store in Turin, New York | $0.25 |
| Bit | Inventory of Thomas Lee (1806) | Bridle bit in Prince William County, Virginia, 1806 | 12½ cents |
| Carriage | Inventory of James Gamble (1812) | Carriage and harness in Sumter, South Carolina, 1812 | $250.00 |
| Cart | Inventory of Thomas Lee (1806) | Ox cart in Prince William County, Virginia, 1806 | $2.00 |
| Cart | Inventory of William Alexander (1811) | Cart & harness in New Castle County, Delaware, 1811 | $20.00 |
| Chariot | Inventory of James Brice (1802) | Old chariot without harness in Anne Arundel County, Maryland, 1802 | $106.00 |
| Chariot | Inventory of Dr. Gustavus Richard Brown (1804) | Old chariot, very much damaged with harness in Charles County, Maryland, 1804 | $20.00 |
| Colt | Inventory of John Hanna (1814) | Colt in Franklin County, Indiana, 1814 | $10.00 |
| Harness | Estate of Alfred Yeomans (1817) | Gilt harness in Marlboro County, South Carolina in 1817 | $40.00 |
| Horse | Inventory of Dr. Gustavus Richard Brown (1804) | Sorrel mare 8 years of age in Charles County, Maryland, 1804 | $50.00 |
| Horse | Inventory of Dr. Gustavus Richard Brown (1804) | Small gray horse 5 years of age in Charles County, Maryland, 1804 | $20.00 |
| Horses | Inventory of Dr. Gustavus Richard Brown (1804) | Pair carriage horses 7 & 8 years of age in Charles County, Maryland, 1804 | $120.00 |

| Item | Data Source | Description | Price |
|------|-------------|-------------|-------|
| Horseshoes | Inventory of John Hanna (1814) | Pair of horse shoes in Franklin County, Indiana, 1814 | $0.50 |
| Jack | Inventory of James Gamble (1812) | Old jack in Sumter, South Carolina, 1812 | $20.00 |
| Martingale | Inventory of James Knight (1816) | Martingale in Franklin County, Indiana, 1816 | $3.00 |
| Mule | Inventory of Thomas Lee (1806) | Large black mule in Prince William County, Virginia, 1806 | $80.00 |
| Ox | Inventory of Julius Nickrols (1816) | Stear ox in Greenville, South Carolina, 1816 | $20.00 |
| Portmanteau | Inventory of Asahel Churchill (1812) | Portmanteau in Franklin County, Indiana, 1812 | $1.00 |
| Riding Chair | Inventory of John G. Flagler (1815) | Riding chair in Sumter, South Carolina, 1815 | $30.00 |
| Saddle | Inventory of John Milholland (1814) | Man's saddle in Franklin County, Indiana, 1814 | $4.00 |
| Saddle | Inventory of John Milholland (1814) | Women's saddle in Franklin County, Indiana, 1814 | $5.00 |
| Saddle | Inventory of John Hanna (1814) | Side saddle in Franklin County, Indiana, 1814 | $4.00 |
| Saddle & Bag | Inventory of William Alexander (1811) | Saddle & bags in New Castle County, Delaware, 1811 | $7.00 |
| Spurs | Inventory of Jacob Giger (1818) | Pair of spurs in Franklin County, Indiana, 1818 | $0.75 |
| Stirrup irons | Inventory of James Winchill (1817) | Pair of sturrup irons in Franklin County, Indiana, 1817 | $0.50 |
| Sulkey | Inventory of James Gamble (1812) | Sulkey and harness in Sumter, South Carolina, 1812 | $15.00 |
| Wagon | Inventory of Thomas Lee (1806) | New waggon gear & tent in Prince William County, Virginia, 1806 | $130.00 |
| Wagon | Inventory of Richard Cramplin (1807) | Waggon and gear for 4 horses in Prince George County, Maryland, 1807 | $40.00 |
| Wheels | Inventory of Dr. Daniel Jenifer (1809) | Par new cart wheels in Charles County, Maryland, 1809 | $28.00 |
| Whip | Business Accounts of Hampshire Furnance (1816) | One wagon whip and collar in Hampshire, Virginia in 1815 | $2.50 |

## Based Upon US Dollars

| Year | Value of 19th Century Dollar in 2002 US Dollars |
|------|--------------------------------------------------|
| 1800 | $14.00 |
| 1805 | $15.00 |
| 1810 | $14.00 |
| 1815 | $11.00 |
| 1820 | $15.00 |
| 1824 | $18.00 |

*Calculations are approximate values based upon economic historical data*

| Item | Data Source | Description | Price |
|------|-------------|-------------|-------|
| **Livestock** | | | |
| Bull | Inventory of Dr. Gustavus Richard Brown (1804) | Bull in Charles County, Maryland, 1804 | $20.00 |
| Bull | Inventory of Charles Tillier (1812) | Small bull in Franklin County, Indiana, 1812 | $3.00 |
| Calf | Inventory of Adam Carsn (1816) | Yearlen calf in Franklin County, Indiana, 1816 | $3.00 |
| Cattle | Inventory of Legrand Guerry (1811) | Head of cattle in Sumter, South Carolina, 1811 | $5.50 |
| Cow | Inventory of Dr. Gustavus Richard Brown (1804) | Cow in Charles County, Maryland, 1804 | $10.00 |
| Deer | Inventory of Benjm. Hodge (1815) | Deer in Sumter, South Carolina, 1815 | $1.00 |
| Duck | Inventory of John Fruit (1815) | Duck in Franklin County, Indiana, 1815 | $0.12 |
| Goat | Inventory of Benjm. Hodge (1815) | Goat in Sumter, South Carolina, 1815 | $1.00 |
| Goose | Inventory of John Taylor (1822) | Goose in Sumter, South Carolina, 1822 | $0.50 |
| Heifer | Inventory of John Kennedy (1811) | White heffer in Franklin County, Indiana, 1811 | $5.00 |
| Hog | Inventory of Richard Cramplin (1807) | Young hog in Prince George County, Maryland, 1807 | $5.00 |
| Hog | Inventory of Dr. Daniel Jenifer (1809) | Grown hog in Charles County, Maryland, 1809 | $2.25 |
| Ox | Inventory of Dr. Daniel Jenifer (1809) | Working ox in Charles County, Maryland, 1809 | $14.00 |
| Pig | Inventory of Richard Cramplin (1807) | Pigs abut 18 days old in Prince George County, Maryland, 1807 | 33½ cents |
| Sheep | Inventory of Dr. Gustavus Richard Brown (1804) | Sheep in Charles County, Maryland, 1804 | $2.00 |
| Shoat | Inventory of Dr. Daniel Jenifer (1809) | Shoat in Charles County, Maryland, 1809 | $1.00 |
| Shoat | Inventory of John Milholland (1814) | Shoat in Franklin County, Indiana, 1814 | $1.66 |
| Sow | Inventory of Richard Cramplin (1807) | Breeding sow in Prince George County, Maryland, 1807 | $6.00 |
| Steer | Inventory of Adam Carsn (1816) | Three year old steer in Franklin County, Indiana, 1816 | $11.00 |
| Yearling | Inventory of Major Cyrus Ball (1820) | Buffaloe bull yearling in Lancaster County, Virginia, 1820 | $3.00 |
| **Manufactured Products** | | | |
| Bottle | McKearin, American Bottles & Flasks (1978) | Gross of Lavender or Honey Water Perfumery bottles in Boston, Massachusetts, 1819 | $6.00 |
| Bottle | McKearin, American Bottles & Flasks (1978) | Per Dozen - Bottles, Long Neck, Small Quarts from Philadelphia and Kensington Vial and Bottle Factory, 1824 | $1.00 |
| Demijohns | McKearin, American Bottles & Flasks (1978) | Per Dozen - Demijohns, 2 Gallons from Philadelphia and Kensington Vial and Bottle Factory, 1824 | $9.00 |
| Flasks | McKearin, American Bottles & Flasks (1978) | Per Dozen Flasks, Eagle and Washington, Pint from Philadelphia and Kensington Vial and Bottle Factory, 1824 | 62½ cents |
| Jar | McKearin, American Bottles & Flasks (1978) | Per Dozen - Jars, Stratight or turned over Tops, Quart from Philadelphia and Kensington Vial and Bottle Factory, 1824 | $1.00 |

| Item | Data Source | Description | Price |
|------|-------------|-------------|-------|
| Loom | Inventory of James Gamble (1812) | Loom and gears in Sumter, South Carolina, 1812 | $8.50 |
| Tinctures | McKearin, American Bottles & Flasks (1978) | Per Dozen - Tinctures, Gro Stoppers 1 Quart from Philadelphia and Kensington Vial and Bottle Factory, 1824 | $2.00 |
| Vial | McKearin, American Bottles & Flasks (1978) | Per Gross - Vials, assorted from 1/2 to 8 ounces in 5 and 10 Gross Packages from Philadelphia Vial and Bottle Factory, 1824 | $2.50 |

### Medical Equipment

| Item | Data Source | Description | Price |
|------|-------------|-------------|-------|
| Desk | Inventory of Dr. Daniel Jenifer (1809) | Medical desk with furniture in Charles County, Maryland, 1809 | $10.00 |
| Electric Machine | Estate of Alfred Yeomans (1817) | Medical device doctors used to treat paralysis in patients | $10.00 |
| Medical Supplies | Inventory of Julius Nickrols (1816) | Paper box vials & Medicine Apothecary sacles & weights in Greenville, South Carolina, 1816 | $5.00 |
| Surgical Instruments | Inventory of Dr. Daniel Jenifer (1809) | Surgical instruments in Charles County, Maryland, 1809 | $8.00 |

### Music

| Item | Data Source | Description | Price |
|------|-------------|-------------|-------|
| Book | Inventory of John Milholland (1814) | Music book in Franklin County, Indiana, 1814 | $0.45 |
| Fiddle | Inventory of Dr. Daniel Jenifer (1809) | Fiddle with mahogany case in Charles County, Maryland, 1809 | $10.00 |
| Flute | Inventory of Samuel Ash (1822) | German flute in New Castle County, Delaware, 1822 | $1.00 |
| Guitar | Inventory of Thomas Lee (1806) | Guitar in Prince William County, Virginia, 1806 | $25.00 |
| Hand Organ | Inventory of Thomas Lee (1806) | Hand organ in Prince William County, Virginia, 1806 | $0.25 |
| Piano | Inventory of Thomas Lee (1806) | Peannoe forte music in Prince William County, Virginia, 1806 | $133.33 |

### Other

| Item | Data Source | Description | Price |
|------|-------------|-------------|-------|
| Bricks | Inventory of Jacob Giger (1818) | Thousand bricks in Franklin County, Indiana, 1818 | $4.00 |
| Coffin | Winthrop Gardiner Jr. Collection | Mahogany and Pine coffin made in New York, 1816 | 10 pounds |

### Based Upon US Dollars

| Year | Value of 19th Century Dollar in 2002 US Dollars |
|------|------------------------------------------------|
| 1800 | $14.00 |
| 1805 | $15.00 |
| 1810 | $14.00 |
| 1815 | $11.00 |
| 1820 | $15.00 |
| 1824 | $18.00 |

*Calculations are approximate values based upon economic historical data*

| Item | Data Source | Description | Price |
|------|-------------|-------------|-------|
| Comb | Inventory of John Trammel (1818) | Fine comb in Greenville, South Carolina, 1820 | $0.28 |
| Compass | Inventory of James Moore (1820) | Pocket compass in Franklin County, Indiana, 1820 | $0.25 |
| Cork | Inventory of John Trammel (1818) | Brass cork in Greenville, South Carolina, 1820 | $0.50 |
| Corps of Discovery | Milner, Oxford History of the American West (1996) | Project cost recommended by the US President's plan, and approved by Congress, for the Lewis and Clarke expedition in 1803 | $2,500.00 |
| Feathers | Inventory of William Black (1804) | One bag of feathers in New Castle County, Delaware, 1804 | $6.00 |
| Gate | Roland Clapp's Store Day Book (1816) | Cost for one molasses gate sold in Roland Clapp Store in Turin, New York | $1.00 |
| Handcuffs | Inventory of Richard Cramplin (1807) | Pair of iron hand cuffs in Prince George County, Maryland, 1807 | $0.25 |
| Hinges | Inventory of John Kennedy (1811) | Pair of hinges in Franklin County, Indiana, 1811 | $0.25 |
| Hooks | Inventory of James Winchill (1817) | Bundle of fish hooks in Franklin County, Indiana, 1817 | $0.75 |
| Indigo | Inventory of James Winchill (1817) | Pound of Spanish indigo in Franklin County, Indiana, 1817 | $2.54 |
| Indispensables | Inventory of James Winchill (1817) | Ladys indispensible in Franklin County, Indiana, 1817 | $0.25 |
| Ink Powder | Inventory of James Winchill (1817) | Paper of ink powder in Franklin County, Indiana, 1817 | $0.08 |
| Inkstand | Inventory of Dr. Gustavus Richard Brown (1804) | Lead inkstand in Charles County, Maryland, 1804 | $0.50 |
| Knife | Inventory of James Winchill (1817) | Pen knife in Franklin County, Indiana, 1817 | $0.25 |
| Lock | Inventory of Adam Carsn (1816) | Lock in Franklin County, Indiana, 1816 | $0.50 |
| Map | Inventory of Richard Cramplin (1807) | Bradleys map of the United States in Prince George County, Maryland, 1807 | $4.00 |
| Measure | Inventory of James Winchill (1817) | English two foot rule in Franklin County, Indiana, 1817 | $0.37 |
| Net | Inventory of Peter Doty (1811) | Cost of a pigeon net and rope in Shaticoke, New York | $1.25 |
| Paper | Inventory of Samuel Ash (1822) | Ream wrapping paper in New Castle County, Delaware, 1822 | $0.75 |
| Pencil | Inventory of James Winchill (1817) | Pencil in Franklin County, Indiana, 1817 | $0.02 |
| Quills | Inventory of Jno. R. Beaty (1815) | Quills in Franklin County, Indiana, 1815 | $0.50 |
| Seeds | Roland Clapp's Store Day Book (1816) | Cost for one paper of garden seed | 6¼ cents |
| Seeds | Roland Clapp's Store Day Book (1816) | Cost for one paper of onion seed | 12½ cents |
| Shell | Inventory of Caleb Odle (1812) | Konk shell in Franklin County, Indiana, 1812 | $0.25 |
| Shingles | Inverntory of John Dickerson (1817) | Thousand shingles in Franklin County, Indiana, 1817 | $2.60 |
| Slate | Roland Clapp's Store Day Book (1816) | Slate and pencil sold in Roland Clapp Store in Turin, New York | $0.40 |
| Spectacles | Inventory of John Hanna (1814) | Spectacles & case in Franklin County, Indiana, 1814 | $1.75 |

| Item | Data Source | Description | Price |
|------|-------------|-------------|-------|
| Spectacles | Roland Clapp's Store Day Book (1816) | Cost for one pair of spectacles sold in Roland Clapp Store in Turin, New York | $0.61 |
| Spyglass | Inventory of Major Cyrus Ball (1820) | Spy glass in Lancaster County, Virginia, 1820 | $3.50 |
| Toothbrushes | Inventory of James Winchill (1817) | Lot of toothbrushes in Franklin County, Indiana, 1817 | $0.50 |
| Trap | Inventory of John Stogdale (1815) | Steel trap in Franklin County, Indiana, 1815 | $0.50 |
| Umbrella | Inventory of John Hanna (1814) | Umberella in Franklin County, Indiana, 1814 | $1.00 |
| Wagon | Inventory of William Black (1804) | Child's waggon in New Castle County, Delaware, 1804 | $0.25 |

## Publications

| Item | Data Source | Description | Price |
|------|-------------|-------------|-------|
| Bible | Inventory of George Frute (1811) | Large jarman Bible in Franklin County, Indiana, 1811 | $10.00 |
| Bible | Inventory of Julius Nickrols (1816) | Large Bible with maps | $2.00 |
| Book | Inventory of James Brice (1802) | Book of Architecture in Anne Arundel County, Maryland, 1802 | $3.50 |
| Book | Inventory of William Black (1804) | Quire of blank books, half bound in New Castle County, Delaware, 1804 | $23.80 |
| Book | Inventory of Nathaniel French (1819) | Life of Napoleon Boneparte in Franklin County, Indiana, 1819 | $0.50 |
| Dictionary | Inventory of John Kennedy (1811) | Dictionary in Franklin County, Indiana, 1811 | $0.25 |
| Digest | Inventory of Nathaniel French (1819) | American Digest in Franklin County, Indiana, 1819 | $4.00 |
| Encyclopedia | Inventory of Major Cyrus Ball (1820) | 12 vols Nicholsons Encycleopedia & box | $12.00 |
| Magazine | Inventory of Jno. R. Beaty (1815) | Clerks Magazine in Franklin County, Indiana, 1815 | $1.00 |
| Play | Inventory of Jno. R. Beaty (1815) | Play by George Coleman in Franklin County, Indiana, 1815 | $0.25 |
| Testament | Inventory of John Kennedy (1811) | Illustrated testament | $7.00 |

## Based Upon US Dollars

| Year | Value of 19th Century Dollar in 2002 US Dollars |
|------|------------------------------------------------|
| 1800 | $14.00 |
| 1805 | $15.00 |
| 1810 | $14.00 |
| 1815 | $11.00 |
| 1820 | $15.00 |
| 1824 | $18.00 |

*Calculations are approximate values based upon economic historical data*

| Item | Data Source | Description | Price |
|---|---|---|---|

**Real Estate**

| Building | Statutes at Large of South Carolina (1808) | Amount to rebuild a court house in the Darlington District, South Carolina, 1806 | $3,000.00 |
| Farm Land | William Dutton, Du Pont (1949) | Value of ninety-five acres in Delaware, 1802 | $6,740.00 |
| House | Statutes at Large of South Carolina (1808) | Cost to build the president's house for the South Carolina College, 1806 | $8,000.00 |
| House | Aurora General Advertiser (1810) | Building on Water Street in Philadelphia that is 5 stories tall has right to a wharf landing, 1810 | $6,000.00 |
| House | American Heritage (1957) | Value of a residence at the corner of Broadway and Park Place in New York City, 1821 | $25,000.00 |
| Land | Inventory of William H. McIntosh (1822) | One acre in a tract of land of over 400 acres in Sumter, South Carolina, 1823 | $2.00 |
| Rent | Statutes at Large of Virginia (1803) | Legal rent for one hogshead of tobacco in a brick warehouse in Virginia, 1803 | $0.50 |
| Rent | Statutes at Large of Virginia (1803) | Legal rent for one hogshead of tobacco in a wood built warehouse in Virginia, 1803 | 37½ cents |
| Rent | Statutes at Large of South Carolina (1808) | Annual rent of the Governor's house in Columbia, 1806 | $250.00 |

**Servants**

| Slave | Inventory of James Brice (1802) | Nan aged about 36 years in Anne Arundel County, Maryland, 1802 | $140.00 |
| Slave | Inventory of James Brice (1802) | Tom aged about 58 years in Anne Arundel County, Maryland, 1802 | $30.00 |
| Slave | Inventory of Dr. Gustavus Richard Brown (1804) | Joe aged 14 years in Charles County, Maryland, 1804 | $250.00 |
| Slave | Inventory of Dr. Gustavus Richard Brown (1804) | Edward aged 26 years (Gardiner) in Charles County, Maryland, 1804 | $300.00 |
| Slave | Inventory of Richard Cramplin (1807) | Sarah aged 65 years in Prince George County, Maryland, 1807 | $20.00 |
| Slave | Inventory of Richard Cramplin (1807) | George an infant 2 weeks old in Prince George County, Maryland, 1807 | $20.00 |
| Slave | Inventory of Dr. Daniel Jenifer (1809) | Caesar (Blk Smith) 65 years old in Charles County, Maryland, 1809 | $40.00 |
| Slave | Inventory of Dr. Daniel Jenifer (1809) | Mary 57 years old, sickly, in Charles County, Maryland, 1809 | $0.00 |
| Slave | Inventory of Dr. Daniel Jenifer (1809) | Ann 8 years old in Charles County, Maryland, 1809 | $150.00 |

**Tobacco Products**

| Chewing Tobacco | Joel Hull Account (1801) | Cost for one yard of pig tail tobacco | $0.03 |
| Cigars | Inventory of Samuel Ash (1822) | Ten spanish segar in New Castle County, Delaware, 1822 | $0.08 |
| Papers | Inventory of James Winchill (1817) | Two papers of smoking tobacco in Franklin County, Indiana, 1817 | $0.25 |
| Pipes | Roland Clapp's Store Day Book (1816) | Cost for one box of pipes sold in Roland Clapp Store in Turin, New York | $1.19 |
| Snuff | Peter Lorillard Invoice (1805) | Pound cost of British snuff shipped to New York, 1805 | 2 shillings |
| Tobacco | Joel Hull Account (1801) | Cost per pound of Cavendish tobacoo in Dryden, New York in 1801 | 3 shillings |

**Trade Equipment & Tools**

| Adze | Inventory of Thomas Lee (1806) | Carpenters addz in Prince William County, Virginia, 1806 | $0.75 |

| Item | Data Source | Description | Price |
|------|-------------|-------------|-------|
| Ax | Inventory of Thomas Lee (1806) | Coopers ax in Prince William County, Virginia, 1806 | $0.75 |
| Blacksmith Tools | Inventory of Benjm. Hodge (1815) | Black smiths Tools Bellows, Anvil &c in Sumter, South Carolina, 1815 | $45.00 |
| Brush | Inventory of James Winchill (1817) | Weavers brush in Franklin County, Indiana, 1817 | $0.38 |
| Carpenter's Tools | Inventory of Dr. Daniel Jenifer (1809) | Chest of carpenters tools in Charles County, Maryland, 1809 | $20.00 |
| Case | Inventory of William Black (1804) | Pair of cases in New Castle County, Delaware, 1804 | $2.50 |
| Composing Sticks | Inventory of William Black (1804) | Six printer's composing sticks in New Castle County, Delaware, 1804 | $5.00 |
| Driver | Business Accounts of Hampshire Furnance (1816) | Cost of a driver for textile manufacturing in Hampshire, Virginia in 1815 | $0.26 |
| Font | Inventory of William Black (1804) | 1 small font - 8 line Pica in New Castle County, Delaware, 1804 | $10.00 |
| Font | Inventory of William Black (1804) | 24 lb French common font in New Castle County, Delaware, 1804 | $4.80 |
| Frame | Inventory of William Black (1804) | Printer's frame in New Castle County, Delaware, 1804 | $4.00 |
| Gallies | Inventory of William Black (1804) | Two printer gallies in New Castle County, Delaware, 1804 | $1.00 |
| Gunsmith Tools | Inventory of John Ridgill (1820) | Gunsmith Tools in Sumter, South Carolina, 1820 | $16.00 |
| Hammer | Inventory of John Hanna (1814) | Hammer in Franklin County, Indiana, 1814 | $0.25 |
| Hammer & Trowel | Inventory of George Frute (1811) | Mason hammer and trowel in Franklin County, Indiana, 1811 | $1.45 |
| Hide | Inventory of Julius Nickrols (1816) | Cowhide in Greenville, South Carolina, 1816 | $2.00 |
| Ink | Inventory of William Black (1804) | Two pounds of printing ink in New Castle County, Delaware, 1804 | $0.80 |
| Iron | Inventory of George Frute (1811) | Pound of iron in Franklin County, Indiana, 1811 | $0.09 |
| Leather | Inventory of Legrand Guerry (1811) | Side leather in Sumter, South Carolina, 1811 | $1.50 |
| Loom | Inventory of William H. McIntosh (1822) | Loom Wheel and Swifts | $8.00 |

## Based Upon US Dollars

| Year | Value of 19th Century Dollar in 2002 US Dollars |
|------|-------------------------------------------------|
| 1800 | $14.00 |
| 1805 | $15.00 |
| 1810 | $14.00 |
| 1815 | $11.00 |
| 1820 | $15.00 |
| 1824 | $18.00 |

*Calculations are approximate values based upon economic historical data*

| Item | Data Source | Description | Price |
|------|-------------|-------------|-------|
| Molds | Inventory of Thomas Lee (1806) | 8 brick molds in Prince William County, Virginia, 1806 | $3.00 |
| Paper | Inventory of William Black (1804) | 12 quires strong wrapping paper in New Castle County, Delaware, 1804 | $1.00 |
| Paper | Inventory of William Black (1804) | Ream medium printing paper in New Castle County, Delaware, 1804 | $2.00 |
| Paper | Inventory of William Black (1804) | Ream of cap writing paper in New Castle County, Delaware, 1804 | $0.81 |
| Pewter | Inventory of Caleb Odle (1812) | Pound of pewter in Franklin County, Indiana, 1812 | $0.55 |
| Printing Press | Inventory of William Black (1804) | Printers press in New Castle County, Delaware, 1804 | $60.00 |
| Rack | Inventory of William Black (1804) | Rack in a printer's shop in New Castle County, Delaware, 1804 | $3.50 |
| Reed | Inventory of James Winchill (1817) | Weavers reed in Franklin County, Indiana, 1817 | $1.00 |
| Rules | Inventory of William Black (1804) | Brass rules in New Castle County, Delaware, 1804 | $6.00 |
| Scissors | Inventory of John Hanna (1814) | Pair of scissors in Franklin County, Indiana, 1814 | 12½ cents |
| Shoemaker's Tools | Inventory of William Alexander (1811) | Shoemakers tools in New Castle County, Delaware, 1811 | $2.00 |
| Skin | Inventory of Benjm. Hodge (1815) | Goat skin in Sumter, South Carolina, 1815 | $1.80 |
| Skin | Inventory of Jael Belk (1819) | Otter skin in Franklin County, Indiana, 1819 | $1.00 |
| Smith Tools | Inventory of John Stogdale (1815) | Sett of smith tools in Franklin County, Indiana, 1815 | $90.00 |
| Spindle | Business Accounts of Hampshire Furnance (1816) | Cost for one spindle for textile manufacturing in Hampshire, Virginia in 1815 | $1.80 |
| Spools | Inventory of John Stogdale (1815) | Set of weavers spools in Franklin County, Indiana, 1815 | $1.25 |
| Steel | Business Accounts of Hampshire Furnance (1816) | Cost of one ounce of steel for Blacksmith Shop in Hampshire, Virginia in 1815 | $0.18 |
| Surveyor's Instruments | Inventory of Major Cyrus Ball (1820) | Broken set of surveyors instruments in Lancaster County, Virginia, 1820 | $5.00 |
| Tacks | Inventory of James Winchill (1817) | Gross of shoe tacks in Franklin County, Indiana, 1817 | $2.50 |
| Tools | Inventory of John Hanna (1814) | Shoe makers tools in Franklin County, Indiana, 1814 | $1.12½ |
| Tub | Inventory of Julius Nickrols (1816) | Dye tub in Greenville, South Carolina, 1816 | $0.50 |
| Vat | Inventory of Asahel Churchill (1812) | Tan vat in Franklin County, Indiana, 1812 | $1.00 |
| Wheelwright Tools | Inverntory of John Dickerson (1817) | Lot of wheelwrite tools in Franklin County, Indiana, 1817 | $13.00 |

### Travel & Transportation

| Item | Data Source | Description | Price |
|------|-------------|-------------|-------|
| Boat | Inventory of Jno. R. Beaty (1815) | Great boat in Franklin County, Indiana, 1815 | $10.00 |
| Boat fare | "The Vanderbilts", by Jerry E. Patterson (1989) | Fare for passage form Staten Island, NY to Philadelphia, PA, ca 1818 | $5.00 |
| Bribe | American Heritiage (1957) | Bribe, per head, to Spanish officials in Havanna for each slave being transported to the United States, 1821 | $15.00 |
| Canoe | Inventory of John Stogdale (1815) | Canoe & chain in Franklin County, Indiana, 1815 | $4.00 |

| Item | Data Source | Description | Price |
|------|-------------|-------------|-------|
| Carriage Ride | Blackstone Canal Company Records (1825) | Fare for a 12-14 hour ride between Providence, Rhode Island and Worcester, Massachusetts in 1823 | $3.00 |
| Cart | Inventory of Benjm. Hodge (1815) | Cart in Sumter, South Carolina, 1815 | $8.00 |
| Freight Expense | Blackstone Canal Company Records (1825) | One ton of freight of goods between Providence, Rhode Island and Worcester, Massachusetts in 1823 | $25.00 |
| Paddleboat | American Heritage (1957) | Cost to build the New Orleans, a 148 long steampowerd paddleboat, 1811 | $38,000.00 |
| Piragua | "The Vanderbilts", by Jerry E. Patterson (1989) | Small Indian boat, said to have been bought by Cornelius Vanderblit in 1811 | $100.00 |
| Toll | Maud Carter Clement, History of Pittsylvania County Virginia | Cost for horse to cross bridge of the Dan River outside Danville, Virginia in 1818 | $0.04 |
| Toll | Maud Carter Clement, History of Pittsylvania County Virginia | Cost for man to cross bridge of the Dan River outside Danville, Virginia in 1818 | $0.04 |
| Toll | Maud Carter Clement, History of Pittsylvania County Virginia (1929) | Cost for a 4 wheel carriage to cross bridge of the Dan River outside Danville, Virginia in 1818 | $0.24 |
| Toll | Maud Carter Clement, History of Pittsylvania County Virginia (1929) | Cost for a 2 wheel carriage to cross bridge of the Dan River outside Danville, Virginia in 1818 | $0.08 |
| Wagon | Inventory of John Anderson (1822) | Waggon & Gears in Sumter, South Carolina, 1822 | $60.00 |

## Based Upon US Dollars

| Year | Value of 19th Century Dollar in 2002 US Dollars |
|------|-------------------------------------------------|
| 1800 | $14.00 |
| 1805 | $15.00 |
| 1810 | $14.00 |
| 1815 | $11.00 |
| 1820 | $15.00 |
| 1824 | $18.00 |

*Calculations are approximate values based upon economic historical data*

# MISCELLANY 1800-1824

### Advertising to Prevent Counterfeiting of Medicine

#### Swaim's Panacea
Price Two Dollars Per Bottle
*To the Public*

In consequence of the numerous frauds and impositions practiced in reference to my medicine, I am again induced to change the form of my BOTTLES. In future, the PANACEA will be put in round bottles, fluted longitudinally, with the following words blown in the glass, "*Swaim's Panacea, Philada,*" as represented above.

These bottles are much stronger than those heretofore used, and will have but one label, which covers the cork with my own signature on it, so that the cork cannot be drawn without destroying the signature, without which none is genuine. The medicine may consequently be known to be genuine when my signature is visible; *to counterfeit which will be punishable with forgery.*

*Source:* New York, Commercial Advertiser, Oct. 7, 1828.

### House made of shells, 1821

Exhibition of Shell Work. At no. 73, Market-street. One and hundred and fifty thousand SHELLS of the most elegant Polish and Brilliant colours, collected from all parts of the World, and arranged so as to show the different Orders of *Architecture,* and facilitate the study of *Conchology*—in the form of the BOSTON STATE HOUSE, A Modern Dwelling House, and a Temple surrounded with a variety of Flowers, and specimens of about 100 different kinds of SHELLS. To be opened every day, from 9 A.M. till sunset. Admittance 25 cents.

*Source:* Columbian Centinel, *Boston, September 26, 1821.*

### Menagerie in Philadelphia, 1810

#### Menagerie
Grand Exhibition

Of Twenty-one Living Animals.

MUCH the Largest and most valuable collection ever exhibited in America.

No. 272, Market street, Third door above Eight-street.

African Lion, full grown. This Lion was taken by the Arabs from the interior and brought to Senegal....

The large and learned elephant, which for sagacity and docility much exceeds any one ever imported into this country. The animal will go through its astonishing performances which have excited the admiration of every beholder.

Two Arabian Camels, Male and Female, full grown. The male is between 7 and 8 feet high. The Female is about 5 years old and 6 feet high....

Wild two legged Hog, from Canton. A very singular and savage animal. Another hog, from the Mountains of Peru, coated with fur. This is savage as the Tyger of India.

Ourang Outang, or Wild Man of Africa.

Troglouyte, or Wild Man of Sierra Leone...

Learned Polar Bear

Three large living Rattle Snakes

Two Calves from South America and other Animals.

Admission 25 cents, Children half price.

*Source: Aurora General Advertiser (1810)*

### Furs for Sale, 1810

A Large parcel of valuable FURS collected at the United States Factories on the Missouri and Upper Mississippi, will be offered at public auction in lots, at the stores of the *superintendent of Indian trade* in Georgetown (Columbia) on Monday, the 16th of April at 11 o'clock, among these are about 2800 pounds of *Beaver,* a considerable quantity of *Racoon, Muskrats,* and other *small furs* – at same time will be sold a parcel of Indian dressed *deer skins.*

Approved notes at ninety days will be received in payment for all sums exceeding one hundred dollars.

John Mason, Sup. Ind. Trade.

*Source: Aurora General Advertiser (1810)*

## Account of Travel in East Hampton, New York

There was so little traveling that the road consisted of two ruts worn through the green turf for the wheels, and two narrow paths for the horses. The wide green street was generally covered with flocks of white geese. On Sunday, all the families from the villages came riding to meeting in great two-horse, uncovered wagons, with three seats, carrying nine persons. It is probable that more than half of the inhabitants of these two retired villages made no other journey during their whole lives. There was not a store in town and all our purchases were made in New York by a small schooner that ran once a week.

*Source: Presbyterian pastor Lyman Beecher on East Hampton, New York, around 1807*

## Reward Advertisement

"Ten Dollars Reward. Ran away from the subscriber, living in Susquehanna township, Dauphin county, on the morning of Wednesday the 29th March, a black girl, named CHARLOTTE.

She is about 22 Years of age, small in stature; she took with her a black silk bonnet, one white muslin dress, a large blue shawl, and a number of other articles of wearing apparel, principally of linsey.

The above reward will be given for the apprehension of the runaway, and securing her in any jail so that I can get her again; and all reasonable expenses if brought home. John Foster May 5, 1820"

*Source: Harrisburg Republican; May 05, 1820*

## Excerpt from the diary of George Cutler, 1820

Aug. 31st [1820]

I carry my gallantry so far as to say that though a woman ought never to engage herself to a man for any great length of time before consummation of the nuptials, if she can retain her lover without so doing,—yet, if this is necessary, of which she is to be the Judge, & she does so bind herself by her promise to marry, still I go to the length of allowing her to take a better husband, or one more agree-

able to her, if she has the opportunity— I give her the liberty of violating her engagement in lieu of her power of choice. Shall women be compelled to take the first creature that offers himself lest they should not find another? Shall they be compelled to love him (on the one hand) by denying, when they do not know that they shall ever see another man in their lives, who comes near them, nor have the power of making a selection— this I think is but a fair balance for the great advantage which our sex possess in their opportunities to suit themselves in this important concern—& more, if there is to be an advantage on either side, it certainly ought not to be on ours,—because the contract is so much more important in its consequences to females than to males—for besides leaving everything else to unite themselves to one man they subject themselves to his authority— they depend more upon their husband than he does upon the wife for society & for the happiness & enjoyment of their lives,—he is their all—their only relative—their only hope—but as for him— business leads him out of doors, far from the company of his wife, & it engages his mind & occupies his thoughts so as frequently to engross them almost entirely & then it is upon his employment that he depends almost entirely for the happiness of his life—certainly then, unfortunate, helpless, interesting woman ought to have all the advantage in the matrimonial contract & instead of her present oppression ought to be allowed to make the most of every advantage & opportunity which fortune throws in her way—I will go further & apply the case. I would justify any woman in treating me in that way—provided she did it in a delicate manner—than which nothing is more easy—& which no woman of sense & judgment would fail to do.

*Source "Journal of George Younglove Cutler," New Haven, Conn., 1820. Published in Chronicles of a Pioneer School, Emily Noyes Vanderpoel, compiler (Cambridge, Mass.: University Press, 1903)*

## Excerpts from the diary of Moses Porter, 1824

*Moses Porter, 30 years old, lived in Danvers, Massachusetts. He kept a diary about his work on his father's farm and his courtship with a certain young lady, named Fanny Giddings. Because the family farm was close to Salem, Massachusetts, Porter made frequent trips to the nearby market to sell produce.*

## January

**5** Mr. Wyatt came between 9 & 10 and we got thro' with the butchering very comfortable. He ate dinner. I paid him, he brot in the large hog for us & then went home.

**6** While I was milking this morning, Uncle David came up here and said that old Mrs. Baker was dead & to be buried this afternoon, funeral set at 10. Sir and I made some mortar & laid a new hearth in the front East room today.

**7** Sir cut up the pork today. I cut & split wood at the door & went over to Eben. Wilkins' to see if he had done my thin boots which I carried over there some days since, found he had not got back yet from Middleton or somewhere else. Zadock said he would mend them for me on the morrow if Eben did not return soon enough...Whole weight of pork this year, 597 lbs.

**8** Went to market, carried 1 bushel of long red potatoes, 1 pk. apples & the harsletts, sold the milk at 5 cents per q. as usual, potatoes at 2/* to 40 cts. pr. b., apples 20 cts., harsletts /9 to 1/, met with a tolerable good market. Got back about sunset, went over to Eben's again; he has not returned yet, neither has Zadock done my boots.

**11** Sunday, Wrote some & read some of the N. England Farmers*, found them interesting.

**16** I tended the cattle, hauled the remainder of the logs out of the pasture & cut them all up. Sir went over to Eben Wilkins' shop to mend his boots & brought home mine that Zadock had mended. Sophia T. staid here thro' the day & at night I carried her home, spent a few minutes there, then went into Mr. Putnam's, had a short interview with Fanny after the folks went to bed, but was too much interupted by Charles (who was not well) to stay long.

**17** Went to market, sold eggs for 25 cts. pr. doz. Carried a good lot of Salt Beef to Mrs. Farrington, which Aunt Sally sent her. Went to Mrs. Millett's & didn't get home till after dark...Heard Mr. John Proctor dyed yesterday, was not sick more than a week with a fever

**26** Snowed most of the day, and in the evening made some ax handles.

## November

**8** I went to picking over the Cider apples & putting them into the cart. Sir thought it best to go to digging potatoes and because I wouldn't, he got so affronted that he went to bed before breakfast & did nothing more all day. William went to Salem to work for Mr. Batchelder where he worked some last week, but he returned tonight not liking the business.

**9** I carried the remainder of the apples over to the mill with some of the barrels. Joel ground them all today.

**11** I set off early with the Cider, got down as far as Uncle Porter's before sunrise, found them up and stirring. Took an old trunk there of Mary Millett's & carried it home from her. Brought up a plank for Sir from Putnam & Cheever's. This day was the Annual Thanksgiving in N. Hampshire.

*Source: Old Sturbridge Village*

## Quote

*Though the will of the majority is in all cases to prevail, that will, to be rightful, must be reasonable; the minority possesses their equal right, which equal laws must protect, and to violate would be oppression.*

*Source: Thomas Jefferson, Inaugural Address, 1801*

# 1825-1849

# Western Expansion, Canal Transportation and American Confidence

## PRESIDENTS

| | |
|---|---|
| John Quincy Adams | 1825-1829 |
| Andrew Jackson | 1829-1837 |
| Martin Van Buren | 1837-1841 |
| William Henry Harrison | 1841-1841 *(Died in Office)* |
| John Tyler | 1841-1845 |
| James K. Polk | 1845-1849 |
| Zachary Taylor | 1849-1850 *(Died in Office)* |

This quarter-century was marked by peace, innovation, and western expansion, entwined with the role of slavery in the new territories. America was growing in size and character, showing no reluctance to test new ideas or images of self. From 1815 until the Mexican War in 1846, America enjoyed a period of uninterrupted peace-the longest in the young nation's history-which contributed to the economic prosperity. During this crucial time, both agriculture and industry underwent fundamental changes that resulted in improved productivity and more self-sufficiency. As a result, less labor was needed on the farms, freeing up workers for the burgeoning industries of New England, eager to supply the national market. Lowell, Massachusetts, in particular, pioneered the industrial system, characterized by innovative technology, professional management and female labor, envisioned by Francis Cabot Lowell. Western migration accelerated in the 1830s; settlers from the northern free states followed the shores of the Great Lakes, bringing commerce to Michigan and Wisconsin. Land seekers from the coastal slave states found Mississippi, Alabama and points west to their liking. The population of some old-line eastern towns actually decreased-causing enormous distress among established politicians-while breathing life into Ohio, Kentucky, Tennessee and locations beyond. Of the 6.3 million inhabitants of the Western states in 1840, more than 4.1 million had moved to the region after 1820.

This economic expansion was driven by the era of canals that dramatically opened the interior of the county to eastern manufactured goods. This grand innovation in travel efficiency quickly melted into the railroad age-a technological revolution that opened up huge swaths of the country to development, settlement and exploitation. Both canals and railroads suffered through periods of overbuilding and bankruptcy, but improved transportation changed the way Americans thought about their boundaries. Railroads in particular allowed people to reorient the west, opening up vast new territory to farming. At the same time, improved transportation and reduced freight costs played a critical role in ending the ideal and necessity of near self-sufficiency many rural farmers held so dear. In 1817, a shipment of goods from New York to Cincinnati took two months; by 1847, the trip took two weeks. For the first time, mass-produced household goods from the manufacturing centers were available-and affordable-to farm families. A coffee mill selling for $5 in 1813 could be acquired for $2 in 1836, and $1.50 by 1846. Between 1809 and 1836, the price of candles fell by a third.

The new economy that was developing in America was less tied to agriculture and European manufactured imports and more to home-grown factories and internal expansion. Factories with 10, 50 or 100 wage earners were common, producing gunpowder, wool blankets or cast-iron plates. These facilities provided real wages to farmers frustrated by intermittent crop failures and isolation. In exchange, workers of this new industrial age were expected to work 12-hour days, six days a week. Holidays were few: Independence Day, Thanksgiving and the first day of spring. And as competition grew, so did the work load. Between 1840 and 1854, the work load of the average textile weaver doubled. He or she was required to tend more machines that were made to perform faster. At the same time, more work was sent to private homes for completion, where it was often women who earned a weekly wage. By 1831, in just the four largest cities, approximately 13,000 women worked at home making items such as paper boxes, hoopskirts, shirts and collars, artificial flowers and ladies' cloaks. When outworkers are calculated into the working rolls, women in 1840 made up almost half of all manufacturing workers in America and about two-thirds of workers in New England. But wages were low and profits high. By the late 1830s, the cost of ready-made clothing was five times what it cost to produce. Women, on average, made $1.50 to 2.00 a week for sewing and many, based on high, employer-set production levels, made less than one dollar per week.

Americans worshipped independence and commerce simultaneously. The New England Farmer of 1835 said, "Our Sons from the very cradle breathe the air of independence-and we teach them to owe no man. It is to gratify this love of independence that they rake the ocean and the earth for money." At the same time, Britain began repealed laws restricting the emigration of its skilled artisans in a display of its commitment to an international economy. And emigrate they did. Thousands of skilled English, representing a broad segment of British society, flooded into America bringing specialized craft skills to a market both ripe and eager for innovation. More than 100,000 Europeans a year flowed to the land of the free remaking the map of America: more than half the German immigrants found last west of the mountains, the Scandinavians found homes in Illinois, Wisconsin and Minnesota, while approximately five sixths of the Irish, retreating from failed crops and starvation, stayed in the east. America's reputation as the land of opportunity was already well established and documented in the lives of millions of immigrant families.

But despite all the economic change and innovation, the South continued to be mired in an economic model of slavery that was not only repugnant to millions, but also, its efficiency was declining, especially in the coastal states. Few political issues escaped the debate. The slavery issue was also entwined with America's ideal of expansion when in 1836, an army of Texans led by Sam Houston defeated Mexican General Santa Anna, declared themselves an independent republic, and called for annexation to the United States as a slave state. But even slavery was not immune to American innovation. Just as the New England factory system was increasing the demand for raw cotton fiber, Eli Whitney 's mechanized cotton gin was transforming the southern plantation, strengthening the slave system.

The populist movement, whose roots went back decades, got its champion in 1828 with the election of President Andrew Jackson, who invigorated the hopes of the common man and struck fear in the nation's most prosperous. When the president, for example, vetoed the re-chartering of the Second Bank of the United States in 1832, he pitted the common man against the Eastern moneyed interests. That same year, Jackson tangled with Vice President John C. Calhoun over high tariffs. South Carolina opposed the cost of the taxes on imported goods, fearing that economic instability would damage its hold on slavery, already weakened by falling cotton prices and soil exhaustion. Calhoun and others began to reassert a belief that the United States was actually a compact of states, each of which retained the right to declare certain federal laws null and void. This argument set the stage for Southern secession and resulting civil war three decades later.

James Polk's election in 1844 brought another important turn to American politics. The national government committed itself totally to a policy of national expansion known as Manifest Destiny. The annexation of Texas in 1845 gave rise to the U.S. - Mexican war of 1846 - 1848, a controversial war that heightened the conflict between North and South. In addition to Texas, growth was ever present with the acquisition of the Oregon Territory in 1846, California in 1848 and the Gadsden Purchase in 1854. These rich resources focused America on its own internal expansion opportunities and away from its preoccupation with the economies of Western Europe.

# HISTORICAL SNAPSHOTS 1825-1849

## 1825–1834

### 1825

- Sing Sing Prison opened on the banks of the Hudson River, New York
- Franciscan missionaries planted vineyards north of San Francisco to make sacramental wine
- Philadelphia druggist Elie Magliore Durand promoted effervescent soda water as a health drink
- Congress created The Bureau of Indian Affairs
- Englishman William Sturgeon discovered that an electric current flowing through a coil of wire could be used to create a magnet
- The Rensselaer School, the first private engineering college in the U.S., opened in Troy, New York
- Scottish factory owner Robert Owen bought 30,000 acres in Indiana to create New Harmony utopian community
- Russia and Britain established the Alaska and Canada boundary
- The first locomotive to haul a passenger train was operated by George Stephenson in England
- The first college social fraternity, the Kappa Alpha Society, was formed at Union College in Schenectady, New York

### 1826

- John Adams, the nation's second president, and Thomas Jefferson, the nation's third president, both died within hours of each other, 50 years to the day after the Declaration of Independence was adopted
- The 387-mile-long Erie Canal was completed, connecting Lake Erie at Buffalo to the Hudson River at Albany, New York; passenger travel was reduced from 10 days by stage service to three and a half days
- The first exhibition of Clydesdale horses, bred for hauling coal, occurred at the Glasgow Exhibition in Scotland
- Samuel Mory patented the internal combustion engine
- Construction of the Pennsylvania Grand Canal began
- The *USS Vincennes* became the first warship to circumnavigate the globe
- Jebediah Smith's expedition reached San Diego to be the first Americans to cross the southwestern part of the continent
- John J. Audubon read a technical paper before the Natural History Society of Edinburgh entitled: "Account of the habits of the turkey buzzard, particularly with the view of exploding the opinion generally entertained of its extraordinary power of smelling"

### 1827

- The first Mardi Gras celebration was held in New Orleans
- The first U.S. railroad chartered to carry passengers and freight, the Baltimore and Ohio Railroad Company, was incorporated
- *Freedom's Journal*, an African-American newspaper, was published in New York City by John Russworm and Samuel Cornish
- Ludwig van Beethoven was buried in Vienna amidst a crowd of over 10,000 mourners
- New York state law emancipated adult slaves
- The Creek Indians lost all their property in America
- John Herschel proposed the idea of contact lenses
- Friction matches were first produced
- Jean-Baptist-Joseph Fourier compared the interaction of Earth and its atmosphere to the setting in a hothouse
- Moravian missionary David Zeisberger published *Grammar of the Language of the Lenni-Lenape*, a Delaware Indian tribe
- Franz Schubert composed his song cycle *Winterreise*

### 1828

- Andrew Jackson was elected the seventh president of the United States, propelled by resentment over the restrictive credit policies of the Bank of the United States
- John Rubens Smith painted the watercolor *West Front of the United States Capital*
- The first issue of the *Cherokee Phoenix* was printed, both in English and in the newly invented Cherokee alphabet
- The first edition of Noah Webster's *American Dictionary of the English Language* was published after nearly 20 years of work
- The Tariff of Abominations, which raised duties on manufactured goods from abroad, caused South Carolina to declare the tariff null and void within its borders
- Groundbreaking ceremonies were held for construction of the Baltimore and Ohio Railroad
- Sister Mary Elizabeth Lange of Haiti co-founded the first black Catholic school in the United States
- Uruguay, created as a buffer state between Argentina and Brazil, declared its independence

### 1829

- The American Bible Society published scripture in the Seneca Indian language
- In England, the ban on Catholic voting was lifted
- An unruly crowd mobbed the White House during the inaugural reception for Andrew Jackson
- The cornerstone was laid for the United States Mint
- William Austin Burt of Michigan received a patent for the typographer, the forerunner of the typewriter
- The original Siamese twins, Chang and Eng Bunker, arrived in Boston to be exhibited to the Western world

- Giachinno Rossini's final opera *William Tell* was produced in Paris
- Frederic Chopin at 19 published his *Waltz #10, Op. 69/2*, and *Waltz #13, Op. 70/3*

**1830**

- President Andrew Jackson signed the Indian Removal Act, which banished the Cherokee Indians and other eastern tribes to land beyond the Mississippi River
- "Mary Had a Little Lamb" was published by Sarah Josepha Hale of Newport, New Hampshire, in a collection of children's poems
- The length of a yard was standardized at 36 inches
- The Bowie knife was created
- Annual alcohol consumption reached 7.1 gallons per capita
- Forty million buffalo inhabited the American West
- William Lloyd Garrison began *The Liberator*, which called for the complete and immediate emancipation of all slaves in the United States
- The Church of Jesus Christ of Latter-day Saints was organized by Joseph Smith and five others in Fayette, Seneca County, New York
- Railroad passenger service began between Baltimore and Elliott's Mills, Maryland
- Plans for the city of Chicago were laid out
- The "Tom Thumb" steam locomotive raced a horse-drawn car and lost when the engine failed
- The National Negro Convention convened in Philadelphia with the purpose of abolishing slavery

**1831**

- American copyright protections were expanded to cover musical compositions
- Cincinnati picked up the nickname "Porkopolis" after it became America's largest meat packing center
- The lawn mower was invented in England

- Slaves in Jamaica were emancipated
- The first recorded bank robbery, which occurred at the City Bank in New York, netted $245,000
- Quebec City and Montreal were incorporated
- Preacher and former slave Nat Turner led a violent insurrection that killed 57 people in Southampton, Virginia
- Englishman Michael Faraday demonstrated an electric transformer
- Naturalist Charles Darwin set out on a voyage to the Pacific aboard the *HMS Beagle*
- *The Hunchback of Notre Dame* by Victor Hugo was published
- Stendhal wrote his novel *The Red and the Black*
- The Order of Skull and Bones was founded at Yale

**1832**

- President Jackson vetoed legislation to re-charter the Second Bank of the United States
- Alfred Mosher Butts, an architect in Poughkeepsie, New York, invented the game Scrabble
- The Black Hawk War with the Sauk Indians began in Wisconsin
- The song "America" was sung publicly for the first time at a Fourth of July celebration in Boston
- Henry Schoolcraft discovered the source of the Mississippi River in Minnesota
- South Carolina passed an Ordinance of Nullification and threatened to secede from the union to protest the passage of higher tariff laws
- John C. Calhoun became the first vice president of the United States to resign, stepping down over differences with President Jackson
- Public streetcar service began in New York City; the fare was 12½ cents
- Johann Wolfgang von Goethe completed *Faust* just before his death

**1833**

- The first penny newspaper, the *New York Sun*, was founded by Benjamin Day
- An improved version of the typewriter was made in France
- Susan Hayhurst became the first woman to graduate from a pharmacy college
- A lock stitching sewing machine was invented in New York, but was never patented
- England passed stronger measures regulating child labor
- The British Emancipation Act began the abolition of slavery in the West Indies
- The United States and Siam concluded a commercial treaty in Bangkok
- The first tax-supported public library was founded in Peterborough, New Hampshire
- The New York Anti-Slavery Society was organized
- Oberlin College in Ohio, allowing coeducation, opened its doors
- The American Anti-Slavery Society was formed by Arthur Tappan in Philadelphia

**1834**

- "Turkey in the Straw" became a popular tune in the United States
- Federal troops were used to control a labor dispute near Williamsport, Maryland, among Irish laborers constructing the Chesapeake and Ohio Canal
- New York and New Jersey made a compact over ownership of Ellis Island
- Sardines were canned in Europe for the first time
- Horace Greeley published *New Yorker*, a weekly literary and news magazine
- The U.S. Senate voted to censure President Jackson for the removal of federal deposits from the Bank of the United States
- Cyrus Hall McCormick received a patent for his reaping machine
- One of New York City's finest restaurants, Delmonico's, sold a meal of soup, steak, coffee and half a pie for 12 cents

♦ The first dental society was organized in New York

## 1835–1844

### 1835

♦ Alexis de Tocqueville published *Democracy in America, Volume I*

♦ President Jackson retired the national debt

♦ Natural gas was used for cooking

♦ Madame Tussaud opened her London Wax Museum

♦ A foreign embassy in Hawaii was established

♦ The Liberty Bell in Philadelphia cracked while being tolled for Chief Justice John Marshall

♦ A mob in Charleston, South Carolina, seized mail containing abolitionist literature and burned it in public

♦ Charles Darwin on the *HMS Beagle* reached the Galapagos Islands, a scattering of 19 small islands

♦ Texans officially proclaimed independence from Mexico, and called itself the Lone Star Republic

♦ Texas settlers defeated the Mexican cavalry near the Guadalupe River

♦ Henry Burden invented the first machine for manufacturing horseshoes in Troy, New York

♦ Cherokee Indians were forced to move across the Mississippi River after gold was discovered in Georgia

♦ Frederic Chopin composed his *Waltz #2 in C# Minor*

### 1836

♦ George Yount built the first structure in Sonoma, California, and planted the first grapes

♦ Sam Houston was named president of the Republic of Texas

♦ Some 3,000 Mexicans under General Santa Ana launched a 13-day assault on the Alamo, with its 182 Texan defenders

♦ Samuel Colt patented the first revolving barrel multishot firearm

♦ The first monthly installment of *The Pickwick Papers* by Charles Dickens was published in London

♦ The Territory of Wisconsin was established

♦ At the Battle of San Jacinto, Texas won independence from Mexico

♦ Arkansas became the twenty-fifth state

♦ Congress approved the Deposit Act, which contained a provision for turning over surplus federal revenue to the states

♦ Charles Darwin returned to England after five years of travel in Brazil, the Galapagos Islands, and New Zealand

♦ Spain recognized the independence of Mexico

### 1837

♦ Samuel F.B. Morse demonstrated the first practical telegraph machine

♦ Sir Thomas Crapper came out with a flush model, valve-controlled water closet

♦ Queen Victoria ascended the British throne following the death of her uncle, King William IV

♦ Pharmacists John Lea and William Perrins began to manufacture Worcestershire sauce

♦ Charles Tiffany founded his jewelry and china stores

♦ Nathaniel Hawthorne wrote *Twice-Told Tales*

♦ Washington Irving wrote *The Adventures of Captain Bonneville*

♦ The Presbyterian Church split into two denominations

♦ By treaty, the Chippewa Indians in Minnesota were guaranteed their right to hunt and fish, and gather wild rice on certain lands

♦ Under a flag of truce during peace talks, U.S. troops captured the Indian Seminole Chief Osceola in Florida

♦ Mount Holyoke Seminary, exclusively for women, opened in South Hadley, Massachusetts

♦ A steam-powered threshing machine was patented in Winthrop, Maine

### 1838

♦ New York passed the Free Banking Act popularizing the idea of state-chartered banks

♦ The Proctor & Gamble Company was formed

♦ The National Gallery opened on Trafalgar Square, London

♦ Greece made an attempt to restart the Olympics

♦ Soprano Jenny Lind made her debut in Weber's opera *Der Freischultz*

♦ The Iowa Territory was organized

♦ Two thousand Cherokee Indians were forced to follow the Trail of Tears to eastern Oklahoma

♦ Charles Babbage published his paper on "Time Reckoning by Tree Ring Counts"

♦ The first Braille Bible was published by the American Bible Society

♦ Mammoth Cave in Kentucky was purchased by Franklin Gorin as a tourist attraction

♦ Frederick Douglass, American Negro abolitionist, escaped slavery disguised as a sailor

♦ Mexico declared war on France

### 1839

♦ Louis Jacques Mande Daguerre announced his process for fixing a photographic image

♦ The Virginia Military Institute for young men was founded in Lexington, Virginia

♦ The basic idea for electrocombustion, which combines oxygen and hydrogen to generate electricity, was conceived

♦ France began to mass-produce women's corsets

♦ Jews in Mashad, Iran, were forcibly converted to Shiite Islam following a pogrom.

♦ John Herschel took the first glass plate photograph

♦ The first Opium War between China and Britain erupted

### 1840

♦ President Martin Van Buren issued an executive order limiting work to 10 hours for all laborers and mechanics employed on federal public works projects

♦ South Carolina confiscated 140,000 acres from the Catawba Indians

- Whig candidate William Henry Harrison was elected president, defeating incumbent Martin Van Buren
- The emergence of railroads made milk available to inland communities
- More than 2,000 ships were engaged full-time carrying timber from North America to the British Isles
- The word "tuberculosis" appeared in print for the first time
- Louis Agassiz theorized that Earth had experienced an ice age
- The British seized Hong Kong following the first Opium War
- The World Anti-Slavery Convention in London excluded Lucretia Mott and Elizabeth Cady Stanton because of their gender
- Britain issued the world's first postage stamp, featuring a picture of Queen Victoria
- Stereographs were emerging as popular parlor entertainment
- Stephen Perry patented the rubber band
- The first grapefruit trees were planted in Florida
- New York merchants brought red bananas from Cuba
- An Atlantic crossing aboard the Cunard Line took just over 14 days
- The Boston rocker appeared in New England

## 1841

- Vice President John Tyler became the tenth president upon William Henry Harrison's unexpected death of pneumonia; Harrison was the first chief executive to die in office
- Volney B. Palmer of Philadelphia began the first advertising agency to sell newspaper space to out-of-town advertisers
- Horace Greeley , abolitionist newspaper editor, founded *The New York Tribune*
- Former President John Quincy Adams won the acquittal of a group of Africans who rebelled and killed the crew aboard the Spanish slave ship *Amistad*
- John Sutter built a fort on the Sacramento River
- The first steam fire engine was tested in New York City
- Edgar Allen Poe's first detective story, "Murders in Rue Morgue," was published.
- The ballet *Giselle* premiered in Paris, the brain-child of Theophile Gautier, a leading voice of the Romantic Age
- The British humor magazine *Punch* was first published
- Life preservers made of cork were patented by Napoleon Guerin in New York

## 1842

- The United States and Canada signed the Webster-Ashburton Treaty, resolving a border dispute between Maine and Canada's New Brunswick
- *Around the World in 80 Days* was written by Jules Verne, featuring science-fiction adventurer Phileas Fogg
- Prague mathematician Christian Johann Doppler proposed the Doppler effect describing the change in pitch in a sound passing by a stationary observer
- Mount St. Helens began 15 years of intermittent eruptions and then became relatively quiet for 123 years
- Naturalist artist John James Audubon made sketches and collected specimens for his book *The Viviparous Quadrupeds of North America*
- Adhesive postage stamps were issued by a private delivery company in New York City
- Ether was first used as an anesthetic during a minor operation
- Micah Rugg patented a nuts and bolts machine
- The New York Philharmonic gave its first concert.
- Walt Whitman published his poem "A Sketch" in *The New York New World*

## 1843

- Former slave Isabella Van Wagenen renamed herself Sojourner Truth and began her career as antislavery activist
- James Wilson, a Scottish writer, founded *The Economist* magazine
- The population in New York City was estimated to be 350,000
- A comet sighting led William Miller and his 50,000 New York religious cult, the Millerites, to proclaim the end of the world
- The Jewish organization B'nai B'rith was founded in New York City
- *A Christmas Carol* by Charles Dickens was published

## 1844

- James K. Polk was elected president
- Samuel F.B. Morse tapped out the message, "What hath God wrought?" to his partner 37 miles away in Baltimore to demonstrate the range of the telegraph machine
- Charles Goodyear received a patent for the vulcanization of rubber
- Brigham Young was chosen to lead the Mormons following the death of Joseph Smith.
- Edward Hicks began his painting *The Peaceable Kingdom*
- John Middleton published a paper describing how a fluorine test could be used to determine the geologic age of fossil bones
- The great auk, known as the "penguin of the north," was hunted to extinction
- The University of Notre Dame received its charter from the state of Indiana
- Richard Theodore Greener became the first African-American to graduate from Harvard University
- Iron ore was discovered in Minnesota's Mesabi Range
- Nitrous oxide was used for a dental procedure in Hartford, Connecticut
- The Young Men's Christian Association (YMCA) was founded in London

# 1845–1849

## 1845

- Congress declared that future national elections would be held on the first Tuesday after the first Monday in November

- The Eastern Hotel in Boston became one of the first buildings heated by steam
- Richard Fox founded the *National Police Gazette*
- New York newspaperman John L. O'Sullivan coined the term "Manifest Destiny" to describe American intentions to annex Texas
- Button-fly pants were introduced to the United States despite protests from the religious community, who saw the flap as a license to sin
- Beriah Swift of Millbrook, New York patented a coffee mill
- Ireland's potato crop was destroyed by blight, triggering famine, the loss of one million lives and a mass migration to America
- Edgar Allan Poe's poem "The Raven" was first published in the *New York Evening Mirror*
- Frederick Douglass, African-American abolitionist, published his autobiography
- Florida and Texas became the twenty-seventh and twenty-eighth states
- American writer Henry David Thoreau began his 26-month experiment in simple living at Walden Pond in Concord, Massachusetts
- The U.S. Naval Academy opened in Annapolis, Maryland, with 50 midshipmen students and seven professors

## 1846

- The United States declared war against Mexico
- Americans in Northern California rebelled against Mexican authorities in the Bear Flag Revolt and proclaimed the Republic of California
- Sarah Josepha Hale, editor of *Godey's Lady's Book*, promoted Thanksgiving as a national holiday each November
- A major immigration of Swedes began to the United States
- American troops invaded and captured Mexico City
- The first Pacific Coast newspaper, *Oregon Spectator*, was published

- United States and Britain settled a boundary dispute in the Pacific Northwest at the 49th parallel
- The first baseball game was played at the Elysian Field in Hoboken, New Jersey
- Congress chartered the Smithsonian Institution, named after English scientist James Smithson, whose bequest of $500,000 made it possible

## 1847

- Rescuers reached the ill-fated Donner Party in the Sierras to discover they had resorted to cannibalism to survive
- American troops under General Zachary Taylor defeated Mexican General Santa Anna at the Battle of Buena Vista in Mexico
- Some 12,000 U.S. forces led by General Winfield Scott occupied the city of Vera Cruz
- The American Medical Association was established
- Doctors began the practice of washing their hands between examinations
- Marx and Engels founded the Communist League in Brussels
- The California town of Yerba Buena was renamed San Francisco
- The cookbook *The Carolina Housewife* by Sarah Rutledge was published
- *Jane Eyre* by Charlotte Bronte was published
- The American Medical Association was founded in Philadelphia
- The faces of Benjamin Franklin and George Washington were pictured on the first U.S. Government-sponsored postage stamps
- Mormon leader Brigham Young and his followers arrived in the valley of the Great Salt Lake in present-day Utah
- Stephen Foster's "Oh! Susanna" was first performed in a Pittsburgh saloon

## 1848

- Gold was discovered at Johann August Sutter's sawmill on the American River, near Coloma, California, igniting gold mania across the nation

303

- In the Treaty of Guadalupe Hidalgo, Mexico ceded one-third of its territory to the United States including California, ending the 17-month-old conflict
- Karl Marx and Frederich Engels published "The Communist Manifesto"
- Wisconsin became the thirtieth state
- William Young patented the ice cream freezer
- Women's rights convention convened in Seneca Falls, New York, to discuss voting, property rights and divorce laws
- The Oregon Territory was established.
- General Zachary Taylor was elected president
- Gas lights were installed at the White House

- Elizabeth Ellet authored her two-volume work: *Women of the American Revolution*
- The Associated Press was founded
- Antoine Zegera established a macaroni factory in Brooklyn, New York
- Golf balls were introduced, molded from white gum of the Malayan gutta-percha tree
- The Pacific Mail Steamship Company was incorporated to carry people, goods and mail from San Francisco to Asia and South America

## 1849

- Americans raced to California for the gold rush; 23,000 people arrived in San Francisco by land and 62,000 by sea
- The Pfizer drug company was founded by Charles Pfizer and cousin Charles Erhart in Brooklyn

- The safety pin was invented by Walter Hunt
- The Anglican Church of Christ was built in Jerusalem by the British
- French officer Claude-Etienne Minie invented a bullet, the Minie ball
- Elizabeth Blackwell became the first woman in America to receive a medical degree, from the Medical Institution of Geneva, New York
- Congress created the Minnesota Territory
- Louisa May Alcott wrote her first novel *The Inheritance*
- The gas mask was patented by L. P. Haslett
- California asked to be admitted into the Union as a free state
- Harriet Tubman escaped from slavery in Maryland

# The Politics of Banking

The Second Bank of the United States and the nation's economy were on a solid footing in the late 1820s. The Bank proved important to the government and the nation on multiple levels. It provided safeguards against improper bank note issues and protected the financial stability of commerce and industry. Secretary of the Treasury Rush indicated in 1828 that "the Treasury to apply public funds at the proper moment in every part of the country . . . has been essentially augmented by the Bank of the United States." Numerous banking experts wrote that United States paper currency was as sound as any under this monetary system. With the positive impact the Bank provided to the nation, it was a surprise that President Andrew Jackson was so openly opposed to the renewal of the Bank's charter.

As early as 1829, Jackson made it clear to the nation that he opposed the Second Bank of the United States. When Congress passed legislation in 1832 to renew the Bank's charter, Jackson vetoed the measure and Congress was unable to override the veto. Jackson's objections were based on the idea that rechartering would continue a perceived monopoly, benefit shareholders with an investment return and risk the influence from foreign shareholders in the event of war. The primary issue for Jackson was simple: He perceived the Bank as unconstitutional.

Even though the constitutional issue was resolved by the Supreme Court in 1819 (*McCulloch v. Maryland*), the Bank was used as a political weapon by Jackson's enemies. Jackson hastened to limit the Bank's strength by authorizing the Secretary of the Treasury to place government monies into state banks by 1833. From 1833 to 1836, the Bank of the United States gradually diminished its loans and was dissolved. The growth and development of state banks grew to the great financial risk of the nation.

During the period of 1830 to 1836, the number of banks increased over 200%, with the circulation of currency rising over 100%. This increase in currency created an inordinate amount of inflation that was equal to that during the American Revolution and its discredited continental currency. The Secretary of the Treasury in 1836 reported that many of the state banks were used not only for land speculation, but risky loans on canals, roads and railroads. To protect the limited funds within the Treasury, Jackson issued the Specie Circular in 1836 which required gold or silver, instead of paper bank notes, as a means of protecting the financial stability of the United States.

Besides the demands of the U.S. Treasury, the European financial markets weakened and many banks overseas began calling in their loans. Because many state banks lacked the required gold and silver to repay account obligations, many lenders called in outstanding loans. Instead of a rush of repayment with available gold or silver currency, many of the loans defaulted, resulting in the failure of hundreds of banks. Many banks that held the U.S. Treasury's funds also failed and greatly weakened the fiscal strength of the country. The collapse of the banking system led to the Panic of 1837. A diary account of a

| | **Based Upon US Dollars** |
|---|---|
| **Year** | **Value of 19th Century Dollar in 2002 US Dollars** |
| 1825 | $18.00 |
| 1830 | $19.00 |
| 1835 | $20.00 |
| 1840 | $20.00 |
| 1845 | $23.00 |
| 1849 | $23.00 |

*Calculations are approximate values based upon economic historical data*

New York businessman recounts the events:

*The savings-bank also sustained a most grievous run yesterday. They paid 375 depositors $81,000. The press was awful; the hour for closing the bank is six o'clock, but they did not get through the paying of those who were in at the time till nine o'clock. I was there with the other trustees and witnessed the madness of the people—women nearly pressed to death, and the stoutest men could scarcely sustain themselves...*

*Phillip Hone (May 10, 1837)*

The Panic of 1837 lasted seven years and resulted in many congressmen being elected in 1838 who supported an independent treasury system to manage the nation's revenue. Debate revolved around the constitutionality of the proposed legislation and the requirement for banks to pay with hard currency. After much debate and numerous attempts, legislation was passed in 1840. Under the new treasury system, the government established treasuries in Boston, New York, Charleston and St. Louis. To protect the federal institution and the government's finances, gold and silver were the only currency it would receive.

The new treasury system was short-lived and repealed in 1841 by President John Tyler. A supporter of states' rights, he viewed the independent treasury authorizing branches within the states without their consent as unconstitutional. With the treasury system dissolved, the nation's financial systems returned to the system prior to the First Bank of the United States.

It was not until 1846 under the presidency of James Polk that legislation was reintroduced and passed which supported an independent treasury system. With this federal treasury system in place, coupled with the growth in commerce and trade, the United States' fiscal conditions improved through the remaining 1840s.

# SELECTED INCOMES 1825-1849

| Occupation | Data Source | Description | Price |
|---|---|---|---|
| Apprentice Clerk | Wells, The Origins of the South Middle Class (2004) | Annual salary for accounting clerk in North Carolina for a mercantile business in 1827 | $500.00 |
| Arsenal keeper | Statutes at Large of South Carolina (1828) | Annual income of the arsenal kepper in Charleston, South Carolina, 1828 | $450.00 |
| Artist | American Heritiage (1958) | Annual annuities to John Trumbull from Yale in exchange of paintings provided, 1832 | $1,000.00 |
| Author | American Heritiage (1957) | Annual royalties to William McGruffey for the various McGuffey, Texts, 1834 | $1,000.00 |
| Baritone | McKearin, American Bottles & Flasks (1978) | Annual income for Jenny Lind's baritone to perform with her on stage Paid for by PT Barnum 1848 | $12,000.00 |
| Bookkeeper | American Heritage (1961) | Weekly income for a bookkeeper at a textile operation in New England, 1840 | $9.50 |
| Bottle Maker | McKearin, American Bottles & Flasks (1978) | *Daily earning for making 100 Common Pugeants bottles at the Boston and Sandwich Glass Works, 1825* | $5.00 |
| College President | Statutes at Large of South Carolina (1836) | Annual salary of the President of South Carolina College, 1836 | $3,000.00 |
| Domestic | A. Kessler-Harris, Out to Work (1982) | Domestic, weekly income plus board, New York, 1841 | $1.25 |
| Domestic | A. Kessler-Harris, Out to Work (1982) | Domestic, monthly income, for Irish servant in New York City, 1846 | $6.00 |
| Female Worker | A. Kessler-Harris, Out to Work (1982) | Estimated average daily wage, woman, by *National Labor* in "*every branch of business*", 1836 | $0.37½ |
| Female Worker | A. Kessler-Harris, Out to Work (1982) | Estimated average weekly wage, woman-nondomestic, by New York *Tribune*, 1845 | $2.00 |
| Gold Prospectors | Milner, Oxford History of the American West | Daily amount of gold discovered by early prospectors in 1848 | $8,000.00 |
| Governor | Statutes at Large of South Carolina (1827) | Annual income of the Governor of South Carolina, 1827 | $3,500.00 |
| Judge | Statutes at Large of South Carolina (1828) | Annual salary of Judge of the Court of Appeals in South Carolina, 1828 | $3,000.00 |

## Based Upon US Dollars

| Year | Value of 19th Century Dollar in 2002 US Dollars |
|---|---|
| 1825 | $18.00 |
| 1830 | $19.00 |
| 1835 | $20.00 |
| 1840 | $20.00 |
| 1845 | $23.00 |
| 1849 | $23.00 |

*Calculations are approximate values based upon economic historical data*

| Occupation | Data Source | Description | Price |
|---|---|---|---|
| Librarian | Statutes at Large of South Carolina (1828) | Annual income of the Librarian of the Legislative Library of South Carolina, 1828 | $100.00 |
| Librarian | Statutes at Large of South Carolina (1836) | Annual salary of the Librarian of the College of South Carolina, 1836 | $600.00 |
| Military Service | Encyclopedia of Collectibles (1978) | Award by the US Congress to Marquis de Lafayette for his services to the Revolution, 1825 | $18,000.00 |
| Musical Director | McKearin, American Bottles & Flasks (1978) | Annual income for Jenny Lind's musical director paid for by PT Barnum, 1848 | $25,000.00 |
| Overseer | American Heritage (1961) | Weekly income for an overseer at a textile operation in New England, 1840 | $12.00 |
| Physician | Statutes at Large of South Carolina (1836) | Annual salary of the port physician in Charleston, South Carolina - includes boat hire and incidental expenses, 1836 | $800.00 |
| Professor | Statutes at Large of South Carolina (1836) | Annual salary of professor at South Carolina College, 1836 | $2,500.00 |
| Professor | American Heritage (1961) | Annual salary to Abbott Lawrence to chair zoology and geology at Harvard's Lawrence Scientific School, 1848 | $15,000.00 |
| Rector | C. Nicholes, Historical Sketches of Sumter County (1975) | Annual salary of a rector in Sumter, South Carolina, 1841 | $300.00 |
| Spinner | American Heritage (1961) | Weekly income for a woman spinner at a textile operation in New England, 1840 | $3.00 |
| Superintendents | American Heritage (1961) | Weekly income for a superintendent at a textile operation in New England, 1840 | $25.00 |
| Teacher | A. Kessler-Harris, Out to Work (1982) | Teacher, weekly income, New York, 1841 | $1.25 |
| Textile worker | A. Kessler-Harris, Out to Work (1982) | Woman textile worker, weekly wages plus board, in Massachusetts, 1842 | $1.90 |
| Textile worker | A. Kessler-Harris, Out to Work (1982) | Harness knitter, weekly wage, in Massachusetts, 1848 | $2.00 |
| Treasurer | Statutes at Large of South Carolina (1828) | Annual income of the Treasurer of South Carolina, 1828 | $2,000.00 |
| Weaver | American Heritage (1961) | Per "piece" earning of a weaver at a textile operation in New England, 1840 | $0.25 |
| Worker | A. Kessler-Harris, Out to Work (1982) | Daily wage, female paper mill worker, Hadley, Massachusetts, 1832 | $0.33 |
| Worker | A. Kessler-Harris, Out to Work (1982) | Daily wage, male paper mill worker, Hadley, Massachusetts, 1832 | $0.85 |
| Farm Laborer | U.S. Census (1976) | Average monthly earnings for a farm laborer in New England, 1826 | $8.83 |
| Farm Laborer | U.S. Census (1976) | Average monthly earnings for a farm laborer in New England, 1830 | $8.85 |
| Farm Laborer | U.S. Census (1976) | Average monthly earnings for a farm laborer in the Middle Atlantic states, 1826 | $8.38 |
| Farm Laborer | U.S. Census (1976) | Average monthly earnings for a farm laborer in the Middle Atlantic states, 1830 | $8.52 |
| Farm Laborer | U.S. Census (1976) | Average monthly earnings for a farm laborer in South Atlantic states, 1826 | $7.18 |
| Farm Laborer | U.S. Census (1976) | Average monthly earnings for a farm laborer in South Atlantic states, 1830 | $7.16 |

| Occupation | Data Source | Description | Price |
|---|---|---|---|
| Agricultural Worker | US Census (1976) | Average daily wage of a farm worker in the Philadelphia area, 1827 | $0.40 |
| Agricultural Worker | US Census (1976) | Average daily wage of a farm worker in the Philadelphia area, 1829 | $0.50 |
| Artisan | US Census (1976) | Average daily wage of an artisan in the Philadelphia area, 1826 | $1.70 |
| Artisan | US Census (1976) | Average daily wage of an artisan in the Philadelphia area, 1830 | $1.73 |
| Carpenter | US Census (1976) | Daily rate for carpenters on the Erie Canal in 1830 | $1.25 |
| Carpenter | US Census (1976) | Daily rate for carpenters on the Erie Canal in 1840 | $1.50 |
| Carpenter | US Census (1976) | Daily rate for carpenters on the Erie Canal in 1849 | $1.00 |
| Carpenter | US Census (1976) | Daily rate for carpenters on the Erie Canal in 1845 | $1.63 |
| Common Labor | US Census (1976) | Daily rate for a common laborer on the Erie Canal in 1830 | $0.75 |
| Common Labor | US Census (1976) | Daily rate for a common laborer on the Erie Canal in 1840 | $0.88 |
| Common Labor | US Census (1976) | Daily rate for a common laborer on the Erie Canal in 1845 | $0.75 |
| Common Labor | US Census (1976) | Daily rate for a common laborer on the Erie Canal in 1849 | $0.88 |
| Laborer | US Census (1976) | Average daily wage of a laborer in the Philadelphia area, 1826 | $1.00 |
| Laborer | US Census (1976) | Average daily wage of a laborer in the Philadelphia area, 1830 | $1.00 |
| Mason | US Census (1976) | Daily rate for masons on the Erie Canal in 1830 | $1.31 |
| Mason | US Census (1976) | Daily rate for masons on the Erie Canal in 1840 | $1.75 |
| Mason | US Census (1976) | Daily rate for masons on the Erie Canal in 1845 | $1.25 |
| Mason | US Census (1976) | Daily rate for masons on the Erie Canal in 1849 | $1.75 |
| Teamwork | US Census (1976) | Daily rate for a driver of horses on the Erie Canal in 1830 | $1.75 |
| Teamwork | US Census (1976) | Daily rate for a driver of horses on the Erie Canal in 1840 | $2.40 |
| Teamwork | US Census (1976) | Daily rate for a driver of horses on the Erie Canal in 1845 | $1.75 |
| Teamwork | US Census (1976) | Daily rate for a driver of horses on the Erie Canal in 1849 | $2.00 |

# SERVICES & FEES 1825-1849

| Service/Fee | Data Source | Description | Price |
|---|---|---|---|
| Bail | Statutes at Large of South Carolina (1827) | Fee charged by attorney for issuing bail in South Carolina, 1827 | $1.00 |
| Cabin Boy | American Heritage (1960) | Cabinboy's share of earning for transporting goods on a single voyage netting over $51,000, 1833 | $255.00 |
| Cadaver | Edward McGill Narrative of Reminiscences in Williamsburg County (1952) | Cost to obtain one cadaver from a potter's field (around 1841) | $5.00 |
| Captain | American Heritage (1960) | Captain's share of earnings for transporting goods on a single voyage netting over $51,000 1833 | $5,100.00 |
| Doctor's Visit | Wells, The Origins of the South Middle Class (2004) | Visit for a routine call in Florida in 1842 | $2.00 |
| Domestic | A. Kessler-Harris, Out to Work (1982) | Bonus, for maintaining one year's service to employer in New York, 1826 | 1 Bible |
| Emancipation | Maud Carter Clement, History of Pittsylvania County Virginia (1990) | Major John Ward of Pittsylvania, Virginia bequeathed $20 to his former slaves over fifteen years of age along with their freedom | $20 and freedom |
| Fine | Statutes at Large of South Carolina (1828) | Fine for destroying or cutting trees along public roads in South Carolina, 1828 | $12.00 |
| Initiation Fee | The Nature of Jacksonian America, edited by Douglas T. Miller (1972) | Initiation fee for entrance into the Society for the Promotion of Internal Improvements, ca 1825 | $100.00 |
| Lecture Fee | Wells, The Origins of the South Middle Class (2004) | Fee to attend the lecture series of the Young Men's Library Society in Augusta in 1848 | $1.00 |
| Lecture Fee | Wells, The Origins of the South Middle Class (2004) | Fee to attend an individual lecture provided by the Young Men's Library Society in 1848 | $0.25 |
| Library Admission Fee | Wells, The Origins of the South Middle Class (2004) | Washington Library Society in Charleston - Fee is to join Society in 1834 | $1.00 |
| Library Annual Dues | Wells, The Origins of the South Middle Class (2004) | Washington Library Society's Annual dues in Charleston, South Carolina in 1834 | $6.00 |
| Library Annual Dues | Wells, The Origins of the South Middle Class (2004) | Fee to have borrowing privileges at the Augusta Georgia Library Society in 1848 | $4.00 |
| Pasturage | Pace & McGee, The life and Times of Ridgeway, Virginia. | Pasturage per head for horse and cattle for 12 hours at a tavern in Ridgeway, Virginia, 1849 | $0.05 |
| Performer | McKearin, American Bottles & Flasks (1978) | Performance fee paid to opera singer Jenny Lind for 150 performances within a year throughout North America, 1848 | $1,000.00 |
| Plea | Statutes at Large of South Carolina (1827) | Fee charged by attorney for filing plea to the court in South Carolina, 1827 | $4.00 |
| Public School Cost | Pace & McGee, The life Times of Ridgeway, and Virginia (1990) | Average daily cost per pupil in a public school in a Henry County, Virginia, 1838 | $0.04 |
| Rent | Statutes at Large of South Carolina (1828) | Payment for state's governor to find housing in Columbia, South Carolina, 1828 | $400.00 |
| Stableage | Pace & McGee, The life and Times of Ridgeway, Virginia (1990) | Stableage for 24 hours for a hourse without food at a tavern in Ridgeway, Virginia, 1849 | $1.00 |

| Service/Fee | Data Source | Description | Price |
|---|---|---|---|
| Tariff | Dewey, Early Financial History of the United States (1934) | Per square yard tariff on carpets imported into the United States, 1846 | $0.30 |
| Toll | Statutes at Large of South Carolina (1828) | Toll for every head of cattle at establish toll gates in South Carolina, 1828 | $0.02 |
| Wagon Construction | Statutes at Large of South Carolina (1836) | Fee charged by William Lloyd for making carriage and mounting cannon for the Marion Flying Artillery, South Carolina, 1836 | $60.00 |
| Writ | Statutes at Large of South Carolina (1827) | Fee charged for issuing a writ for contempt of court in South Carolina, 1827 | $3.00 |

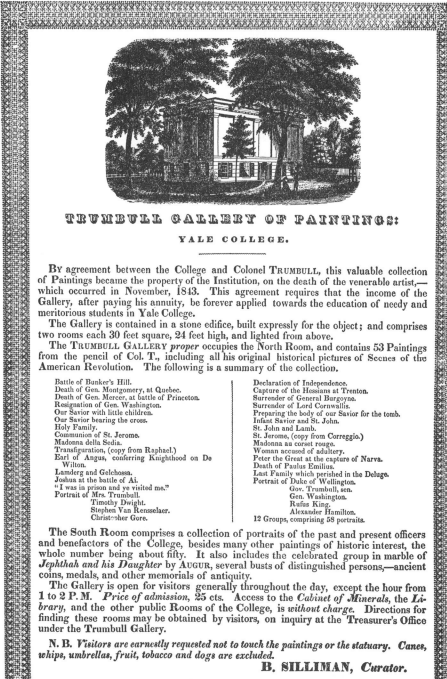

**TRUMBULL GALLERY OF PAINTINGS:**

**YALE COLLEGE.**

BY agreement between the College and Colonel TRUMBULL, this valuable collection of Paintings became the property of the Institution, on the death of the venerable artist,—which occurred in November, 1843. This agreement requires that the income of the Gallery, after paying his annuity, be forever applied towards the education of needy and meritorious students in Yale College.

The Gallery is contained in a stone edifice, built expressly for the object; and comprises two rooms each 30 feet square, 24 feet high, and lighted from above.

The TRUMBULL GALLERY *proper* occupies the North Room, and contains 53 Paintings from the pencil of Col. T., including all his original historical pictures of Scenes of the American Revolution. The following is a summary of the collection.

Battle of Bunker's Hill.
Death of Gen. Montgomery, at Quebec.
Death of Gen. Mercer, at battle of Princeton.
Resignation of Gen. Washington.
Our Savior with little children.
Our Savior bearing the cross.
Holy Family.
Communion of St. Jerome.
Madonna della Sedia.
Transfiguration, (copy from Raphael.)
Earl of Angus, conferring Knighthood on De Wilton.
Lamderg and Gelchossa.
Joshua at the battle of Ai.
"I was in prison and ye visited me."
Portrait of Mrs. Trumbull.
    Timothy Dwight.
    Stephen Van Rensselaer.
    Christopher Gore.

Declaration of Independence.
Capture of the Hessians at Trenton.
Surrender of General Burgoyne.
Surrender of Lord Cornwallis.
Preparing the body of our Savior for the tomb.
Infant Savior and St. John.
St. John and Lamb.
St. Jerome, (copy from Correggio.)
Madonna au corset rouge.
Woman accused of adultery.
Peter the Great at the capture of Narva.
Death of Paulus Emilius.
Last Family which perished in the Deluge.
Portrait of Duke of Wellington.
    Gov. Trumbull, sen.
    Gen. Washington.
    Rufus King.
    Alexander Hamilton.
12 Groups, comprising 58 portraits.

The South Room comprises a collection of portraits of the past and present officers and benefactors of the College, besides many other paintings of historic interest, the whole number being about fifty. It also includes the celebrated group in marble of *Jephthah and his Daughter* by AUGUR, several busts of distinguished persons,—ancient coins, medals, and other memorials of antiquity.

The Gallery is open for visitors generally throughout the day, except the hour from **1 to 2 P.M.** *Price of admission,* **25 cts.** Access to the *Cabinet of Minerals,* the *Library,* and the other public Rooms of the College, is *without charge.* Directions for finding these rooms may be obtained by visitors, on inquiry at the **Treasurer's Office** under the Trumbull Gallery.

**N. B.** *Visitors are earnestly requested not to touch the paintings or the statuary. Canes, whips, umbrellas, fruit, tobacco and dogs are excluded.*

**B. SILLIMAN,** *Curator.*

PRINTED BY B. L. HAMLEN.

# FINANCIAL RATES & EXCHANGES
## 1825-1849

| Year | United States Official Price of Gold (per Ounce) | Inflation Rate in the United States | United States Exchange Rate for One British Pound | US Federal Government High Grade Bond Yields - New Issue | US Federal Government High Grade Bond Yields - Select Market | New England Municipal Bond Yields |
|---|---|---|---|---|---|---|
| 1825 | $19.39 | 2.59% | $4.83 | 4.50% | 4.32% | 4.52% |
| 1826 | $19.39 | 0.00% | $4.92 | — | 4.50% | — |
| 1827 | $19.39 | 0.84% | $4.94 | — | 4.37% | 4.61% |
| 1828 | $19.39 | −5.00% | $4.93 | — | 4.48% | — |
| 1829 | $19.39 | −1.75% | $4.86 | — | 4.50% | 4.77% |
| 1830 | $19.39 | −0.89% | $4.76 | — | 4.37% | 4.90% |
| 1831 | $19.39 | −6.31% | $4.86 | — | 4.41% | — |
| 1832 | $19.39 | −0.96% | $4.86 | — | 4.45% | 5.00% |
| 1833 | $19.39 | −1.94% | $4.79 | — | — | 4.87% |
| 1834 | $19.94 | 1.98% | $4.64 | — | — | 4.87% |
| 1835 | $20.69 | 2.91% | $4.85 | — | — | 4.83% |
| 1836 | $20.69 | 5.66% | $4.82 | — | — | 4.96% |
| 1837 | $21.64 | 2.68% | $5.10 | — | — | 4.95% |
| 1838 | $20.86 | −2.61% | $4.89 | — | — | 5.01% |
| 1839 | $20.67 | 0.00% | $4.99 | — | — | 5.21% |
| 1840 | $20.67 | −7.14% | $5.00 | — | — | 5.07% |
| 1841 | $20.67 | 0.96% | $4.99 | 5.50% | — | 4.99% |
| 1842 | $20.67 | −6.67% | $4.80 | 6.00% | 6.07% | 4.95% |
| 1843 | $20.67 | −9.18% | $4.79 | 4.95% | 5.03% | 4.88% |
| 1844 | $20.67 | 1.12% | $4.86 | — | 4.85% | 4.84% |
| 1845 | $20.67 | 1.11% | $4.87 | — | 5.16% | 4.86% |
| 1846 | $20.67 | 1.00% | $4.82 | 6.00% | 5.50% | 4.92% |
| 1847 | $20.67 | 7.61% | $4.79 | 5.88% | 5.77% | 5.14% |
| 1848 | $20.67 | −4.04% | $4.87 | 5.76% | 5.71% | 5.31% |
| 1849 | $20.67 | −3.16% | $4.81 | — | 5.16% | 5.31% |

# COMMODITIES 1825-1849

Currency expressed in US dollars.

| Commodity | Year | Philadelphia Currency | New York Currency | Charleston Currency | New Orleans Currency | Cincinnati Currency |
|---|---|---|---|---|---|---|
| Bacon, per pound | 1825 | $0.105 | $0.085 | $0.070 | $0.095 | $0.045 |
| | 1826 | $0.090 | $0.085 | $0.065 | $0.065 | $0.035 |
| | 1827 | $0.090 | $0.105 | $0.060 | $0.065 | $0.028 |
| | 1828 | $0.095 | $0.090 | $0.062 | $0.075 | $0.035 |
| | 1829 | $0.100 | $0.095 | $0.060 | $0.072 | $0.048 |
| | 1830 | $0.095 | $0.095 | $0.080 | $0.072 | $0.052 |
| | 1831 | $0.100 | $0.105 | $0.072 | $0.065 | $0.055 |
| | 1832 | $0.095 | $0.105 | $0.062 | $0.072 | $0.065 |
| | 1833 | $0.095 | $0.090 | $0.065 | $0.078 | $0.060 |
| | 1834 | $0.095 | $0.095 | $0.080 | $0.075 | $0.048 |
| | 1835 | $0.106 | $0.105 | $0.095 | $0.100 | $0.075 |
| | 1836 | $0.150 | $0.135 | $0.115 | $0.135 | $0.092 |
| | 1837 | $0.120 | $0.095 | $0.090 | $0.082 | $0.062 |
| | 1838 | $0.118 | $0.115 | $0.092 | $0.095 | $0.068 |
| | 1839 | $0.124 | $0.115 | $0.112 | $0.110 | $0.088 |
| | 1840 | $0.100 | N/R | $0.095 | $0.085 | $0.069 |
| | 1841 | $0.080 | N/R | $0.072 | $0.068 | $0.050 |
| | 1842 | $0.058 | N/R | $0.038 | $0.038 | $0.025 |
| | 1843 | $0.069 | $0.045 | $0.052 | $0.029 | $0.031 |
| | 1844 | $0.055 | $0.040 | $0.049 | $0.028 | $0.036 |
| | 1845 | $0.093 | $0.061 | $0.074 | $0.050 | $0.064 |
| | 1846 | $0.062 | $0.051 | $0.069 | $0.030 | $0.049 |
| | 1847 | $0.109 | $0.068 | $0.098 | $0.055 | $0.081 |
| | 1848 | $0.068 | $0.044 | $0.051 | $0.025 | $0.032 |
| | 1849 | $0.081 | $0.051 | $0.061 | $0.039 | $0.048 |

### Based Upon US Dollars

| Year | Value of 19th Century Dollar in 2002 US Dollars |
|---|---|
| 1825 | $18.00 |
| 1830 | $19.00 |
| 1835 | $20.00 |
| 1840 | $20.00 |
| 1845 | $23.00 |
| 1849 | $23.00 |

*Calculations are approximate values based upon economic historical data*

| Commodity | Year | Philadelphia Currency | New York Currency | Charleston Currency | New Orleans Currency | Cincinnati Currency |
|---|---|---|---|---|---|---|
| Beef, per barrel | 1825 | $10.50 | $9.25 | $10.25 | $7.50 | N/R |
| | 1826 | $10.50 | $9.60 | $10.50 | $7.50 | N/R |
| | 1827 | $10.50 | $9.41 | $10.00 | $8.25 | N/R |
| | 1828 | $10.50 | $9.50 | $10.50 | $7.00 | N/R |
| | 1829 | $10.50 | $10.40 | $11.50 | $5.75 | N/R |
| | 1830 | $10.25 | $9.72 | $9.75 | $7.40 | N/R |
| | 1831 | $10.15 | $9.25 | $10.00 | $7.25 | N/R |
| | 1832 | $10.25 | $9.67 | $1.25 | $7.50 | N/R |
| | 1833 | $10.75 | $9.60 | $11.50 | $8.00 | N/R |
| | 1834 | $11.00 | $9.50 | $10.50 | $9.25 | N/R |
| | 1835 | $11.75 | $12.66 | $11.75 | $9.25 | N/R |
| | 1836 | $12.00 | $11.87 | $14.25 | $11.75 | N/R |
| | 1837 | $14.50 | $14.50 | $13.75 | $9.50 | N/R |
| | 1838 | $14.50 | $14.50 | $16.50 | $12.75 | N/R |
| | 1839 | $15.75 | $15.50 | $16.50 | $13.00 | N/R |
| | 1840 | $14.50 | $14.25 | $15.50 | $12.50 | $16.00 |
| | 1841 | $11.50 | $9.25 | $15.50 | $12.20 | N/R |
| | 1842 | $7.75 | $8.00 | $10.00 | $9.50 | N/R |
| | 1843 | $8.00 | $8.00 | N/R | $7.60 | N/R |
| | 1844 | $7.12 | $7.90 | N/R | $8.80 | N/R |
| | 1845 | $8.62 | $7.65 | N/R | $10.20 | N/R |
| | 1846 | $8.25 | $7.75 | N/R | $8.60 | N/R |
| | 1847 | $14.00 | $8.00 | N/R | $15.20 | N/R |
| | 1848 | $10.50 | $8.26 | N/R | $11.60 | N/R |
| | 1849 | $12.75 | $11.30 | N/R | $14.50 | N/R |
| Bread, per hundredweight *(Charleston & Cincinnati per barrel)* | 1825 | $3.25 | $2.62 | $2.50 | $4.50 | $2.38 |
| | 1826 | $2.75 | $2.63 | N/R | $4.00 | $2.38 |
| | 1827 | $3.25 | $3.25 | N/R | $4.38 | $2.38 |
| | 1828 | $2.75 | $3.00 | N/R | $5.00 | $2.38 |
| | 1829 | $4.00 | $3.50 | N/R | $6.00 | $3.50 |
| | 1830 | $3.12 | $3.00 | N/R | $4.42 | $2.75 |
| | 1831 | $4.75 | $3.25 | N/R | $4.62 | $2.75 |
| | 1832 | $3.50 | $3.25 | N/R | $4.62 | N/R |
| | 1833 | $3.50 | $3.25 | N/R | $4.38 | N/R |
| | 1834 | $3.50 | $3.00 | N/R | $4.50 | $2.75 |
| | 1835 | $4.00 | $3.13 | N/R | $4.50 | $2.75 |
| | 1836 | $4.12 | $3.75 | N/R | $6.38 | $2.00 |
| | 1837 | $5.75 | $4.25 | N/R | $6.00 | $2.75 |
| | 1838 | $4.75 | $4.25 | N/R | $6.00 | $2.75 |
| | 1839 | $4.75 | $4.00 | N/R | $5.50 | N/R |
| | 1840 | $3.88 | $3.25 | N/R | $5.00 | $2.25 |
| | 1841 | $3.00 | $3.00 | N/R | $4.00 | $2.00 |
| | 1842 | $3.12 | $3.00 | N/R | $4.50 | $5.00 |
| | 1843 | $2.75 | $2.50 | N/R | $3.25 | $2.00 |
| | 1844 | $3.12 | $2.25 | N/R | $3.38 | $2.50 |
| | 1845 | $2.75 | $2.50 | N/R | $3.38 | $2.44 |
| | 1846 | $3.38 | $2.75 | N/R | $3.38 | $2.50 |
| | 1847 | $5.12 | $4.25 | N/R | $4.12 | $3.12 |
| | 1848 | $3.75 | $3.50 | N/R | $4.25 | $2.62 |
| | 1849 | $3.50 | $3.00 | N/R | $4.00 | $2.62 |

| Commodity | Year | Philadelphia Currency | New York Currency | Charleston Currency | New Orleans Currency | Cincinnati Currency |
|---|---|---|---|---|---|---|
| Butter, per pound | 1825 | $0.090 | $0.160 | $0.250 | $0.200 | $0.065 |
| | 1826 | $0.095 | $0.145 | $0.180 | $0.175 | $0.070 |
| | 1827 | $0.090 | $0.200 | $0.250 | $0.240 | $0.065 |
| | 1828 | $0.075 | $0.160 | $0.215 | $0.180 | $0.060 |
| | 1829 | $0.082 | $0.140 | $0.175 | $0.205 | $0.095 |
| | 1830 | $0.065 | $0.135 | $0.210 | $0.122 | $0.080 |
| | 1831 | $0.105 | $0.150 | $0.210 | $0.195 | $0.050 |
| | 1832 | $0.120 | $0.145 | $0.281 | $0.197 | $0.090 |
| | 1833 | $0.118 | $0.180 | $0.200 | $0.200 | $0.110 |
| | 1834 | $0.085 | $0.140 | $0.200 | $0.205 | $0.090 |
| | 1835 | $0.105 | $0.195 | $0.250 | $0.260 | $0.110 |
| | 1836 | $0.160 | $0.210 | $0.312 | $0.235 | $0.150 |
| | 1837 | $0.138 | $0.140 | $0.300 | $0.215 | $0.155 |
| | 1838 | $0.135 | $0.260 | $0.335 | $0.265 | $0.115 |
| | 1839 | $0.150 | $0.210 | $0.290 | $0.260 | $0.165 |
| | 1840 | $0.088 | $0.190 | $0.228 | $0.215 | $0.080 |
| | 1841 | $0.082 | $0.100 | $0.200 | $0.190 | $0.051 |
| | 1842 | $0.072 | $0.130 | $0.305 | $0.285 | $0.065 |
| | 1843 | $0.065 | $0.080 | $0.145 | $0.150 | $0.058 |
| | 1844 | $0.085 | $0.100 | $0.190 | $0.170 | $0.090 |
| | 1845 | $0.105 | $0.130 | $0.190 | $0.195 | $0.092 |
| | 1846 | $0.085 | $0.100 | $0.205 | $0.170 | $0.120 |
| | 1847 | $0.132 | $0.210 | $0.305 | $0.270 | $0.150 |
| | 1848 | $0.135 | $0.190 | $0.235 | $0.290 | $0.140 |
| | 1849 | $0.075 | $0.130 | $0.195 | $0.250 | $0.130 |
| Candles, per pound | 1825 | $0.110 | $0.340 | N/R | $0.400 | $0.098 |
| | 1826 | $0.118 | $0.325 | N/R | $0.365 | $0.125 |
| | 1827 | $0.125 | $0.310 | N/R | $0.340 | $0.125 |
| | 1828 | $0.110 | $0.270 | N/R | $0.295 | $0.125 |
| | 1829 | $0.100 | $0.230 | N/R | $0.255 | $0.115 |
| | 1830 | $0.090 | $0.220 | N/R | $0.218 | $0.115 |
| | 1831 | $0.108 | $0.285 | N/R | $0.302 | $0.115 |
| | 1832 | $0.120 | $0.310 | N/R | $0.315 | $0.135 |

## Based Upon US Dollars

| Year | Value of 19th Century Dollar in 2002 US Dollars |
|---|---|
| 1825 | $18.00 |
| 1830 | $19.00 |
| 1835 | $20.00 |
| 1840 | $20.00 |
| 1845 | $23.00 |
| 1849 | $23.00 |

*Calculations are approximate values based upon economic historical data*

| Commodity | Year | Philadelphia Currency | New York Currency | Charleston Currency | New Orleans Currency | Cincinnati Currency |
|---|---|---|---|---|---|---|
| | 1833 | $0.120 | $0.335 | $0.345 | $0.335 | $0.115 |
| | 1834 | $0.120 | $0.290 | $0.345 | $0.330 | $0.115 |
| | 1835 | $0.110 | $0.310 | $0.335 | $0.350 | $0.115 |
| | 1836 | $0.120 | $0.335 | N/R | $0.368 | $0.122 |
| | 1837 | $0.145 | $0.335 | N/R | $0.335 | $0.132 |
| | 1838 | $0.145 | $0.315 | N/R | $0.385 | $0.125 |
| | 1839 | $0.152 | $0.415 | N/R | $0.450 | $0.128 |
| | 1840 | $0.125 | $0.395 | N/R | $0.455 | $0.110 |
| | 1841 | $0.120 | $0.385 | N/R | $0.440 | $0.100 |
| | 1842 | $0.102 | $0.285 | N/R | $0.285 | $0.085 |
| | 1843 | $0.100 | $0.210 | N/R | $0.260 | $0.070 |
| | 1844 | $0.095 | $0.305 | N/R | $0.295 | $0.078 |
| | 1845 | $0.090 | $0.280 | N/R | $0.295 | $0.082 |
| | 1846 | $0.095 | $0.270 | N/R | $0.260 | $0.080 |
| | 1847 | $0.115 | $0.310 | N/R | $0.330 | $0.105 |
| | 1848 | $0.120 | $0.315 | N/R | $0.315 | $0.100 |
| | 1849 | $0.110 | $0.345 | N/R | $0.355 | $0.082 |
| Coal, per bushel | 1825 | $0.250 | $0.108 | N/R | N/R | $0.080 |
| *(New York per ton)* | 1826 | $0.236 | $0.110 | N/R | N/R | $0.080 |
| *(New Orleans per barrel)* | 1827 | $0.208 | $0.110 | N/R | N/R | $0.100 |
| | 1828 | $0.194 | $0.110 | N/R | N/R | $0.080 |
| | 1829 | $0.194 | $0.110 | N/R | N/R | $0.105 |
| | 1830 | $0.194 | $0.089 | N/R | $0.625 | $0.088 |
| | 1831 | $0.167 | $0.065 | N/R | $0.625 | $0.110 |
| | 1832 | $0.235 | $0.105 | N/R | $1.000 | $0.130 |
| | 1833 | $0.245 | $0.065 | N/R | $1.000 | $0.115 |
| | 1834 | $0.245 | $0.060 | N/R | $0.500 | $0.125 |
| | 1835 | $0.225 | $0.065 | $0.065 | $0.530 | $0.118 |
| | 1836 | $0.250 | $0.090 | N/R | $0.625 | $0.112 |
| | 1837 | $0.280 | $0.105 | N/R | $2.000 | $0.162 |
| | 1838 | $0.235 | $0.078 | N/R | $0.500 | $0.140 |
| | 1839 | $0.230 | $0.082 | N/R | $0.562 | $0.140 |
| | 1840 | $0.270 | $0.082 | $0.072 | $0.562 | $0.125 |
| | 1841 | $0.245 | $0.072 | N/R | $0.438 | $0.088 |
| | 1842 | $0.240 | $0.061 | N/R | $0.500 | $0.062 |
| | 1843 | $0.215 | $0.071 | $0.052 | $0.362 | $0.124 |
| | 1844 | $0.165 | $0.050 | N/R | $0.500 | $0.105 |
| | 1845 | $0.160 | $0.098 | $0.055 | $0.385 | $0.090 |
| | 1846 | $0.210 | $0.055 | N/R | $1.125 | $0.140 |
| | 1847 | $0.162 | $0.072 | $0.055 | $0.950 | $0.140 |
| | 1848 | $0.168 | $0.088 | $0.058 | $0.500 | $0.122 |
| | 1849 | $0.145 | $0.076 | $0.055 | $0.500 | $0.125 |
| Coffee, per pound | 1825 | $0.170 | $0.215 | $0.205 | $0.205 | $0.023 |
| | 1826 | $0.158 | $0.160 | $0.170 | $0.160 | $0.195 |
| | 1827 | $0.135 | $0.145 | $0.162 | $0.145 | $0.170 |
| | 1828 | $0.122 | $0.125 | $0.155 | $0.152 | $0.162 |
| | 1829 | $0.118 | $0.125 | $0.145 | $0.145 | $0.158 |
| | 1830 | $0.112 | $0.115 | $0.132 | $0.122 | $0.148 |

| Commodity | Year | Philadelphia Currency | New York Currency | Charleston Currency | New Orleans Currency | Cincinnati Currency |
|---|---|---|---|---|---|---|
| | 1831 | $0.108 | $0.110 | $0.119 | $0.110 | $0.135 |
| | 1832 | $0.122 | $0.120 | $0.145 | $132.000 | $0.152 |
| | 1833 | $0.112 | $0.115 | $0.132 | $0.120 | $0.138 |
| | 1834 | $0.108 | $0.115 | $0.140 | $0.132 | $0.142 |
| | 1835 | $0.118 | $0.125 | $0.148 | $0.145 | $0.152 |
| | 1836 | $0.118 | $0.120 | $0.148 | $0.148 | $0.142 |
| | 1837 | $0.100 | $0.110 | $0.115 | $0.108 | $0.138 |
| | 1838 | $0.090 | $0.095 | $0.126 | $0.118 | $0.132 |
| | 1839 | $0.102 | $0.110 | $0.121 | $0.111 | $0.130 |
| | 1840 | $0.100 | $0.095 | $0.114 | $0.111 | $0.122 |
| | 1841 | $0.096 | $0.095 | $0.120 | $0.111 | $0.122 |
| | 1842 | $0.070 | $0.090 | $0.101 | $0.088 | $0.110 |
| | 1843 | $0.061 | $0.075 | $0.082 | $0.077 | $0.089 |
| | 1844 | $0.056 | $0.065 | $0.075 | $0.069 | $0.076 |
| | 1845 | $0.061 | $0.070 | $0.078 | $0.072 | $0.085 |
| | 1846 | $0.070 | $0.075 | $0.085 | $0.075 | $0.088 |
| | 1847 | $0.068 | $0.070 | $0.086 | $0.073 | $0.088 |
| | 1848 | $0.061 | $0.065 | $0.074 | $0.068 | $0.080 |
| | 1849 | $0.060 | $0.065 | $0.064 | $0.064 | $0.076 |
| Copper, per pound | 1825 | $0.32 | $0.32 | N/R | N/R | N/R |
| | 1826 | $0.30 | $0.30 | N/R | N/R | N/R |
| | 1827 | $0.27 | $0.26 | N/R | N/R | N/R |
| | 1828 | $0.26 | $0.24 | N/R | N/R | N/R |
| | 1829 | $0.25 | $0.24 | N/R | N/R | N/R |
| | 1830 | $0.23 | $0.22 | N/R | $0.27 | N/R |
| | 1831 | $0.22 | $0.22 | N/R | $0.26 | N/R |
| | 1832 | $0.23 | $0.22 | N/R | $0.24 | N/R |
| | 1833 | $0.24 | $0.24 | N/R | $0.24 | N/R |
| | 1834 | $0.24 | $0.24 | N/R | $0.24 | N/R |
| | 1835 | $0.23 | $0.22 | N/R | $0.25 | N/R |
| | 1836 | $0.28 | $0.28 | N/R | $0.29 | N/R |
| | 1837 | $0.29 | $0.26 | N/R | $0.30 | N/R |
| | 1838 | $0.27 | $0.26 | N/R | $0.30 | N/R |

## Based Upon US Dollars

| Year | Value of 19th Century Dollar in 2002 US Dollars |
|---|---|
| 1825 | $18.00 |
| 1830 | $19.00 |
| 1835 | $20.00 |
| 1840 | $20.00 |
| 1845 | $23.00 |
| 1849 | $23.00 |

*Calculations are approximate values based upon economic historical data*

| Commodity | Year | Philadelphia Currency | New York Currency | Charleston Currency | New Orleans Currency | Cincinnati Currency |
|---|---|---|---|---|---|---|
| | 1839 | $0.26 | $0.26 | N/R | N/R | N/R |
| | 1840 | $0.27 | $0.26 | N/R | N/R | N/R |
| | 1841 | $0.26 | $0.26 | N/R | N/R | N/R |
| | 1842 | $0.25 | $0.23 | N/R | N/R | N/R |
| | 1843 | $0.22 | $0.22 | N/R | N/R | $0.30 |
| | 1844 | $0.22 | $0.22 | N/R | N/R | $0.28 |
| | 1845 | $0.22 | $0.22 | N/R | N/R | $0.28 |
| | 1846 | $0.23 | $0.24 | N/R | N/R | N/R |
| | 1847 | $0.23 | $0.24 | N/R | N/R | N/R |
| | 1848 | $0.22 | $0.22 | N/R | N/R | $0.28 |
| | 1849 | $0.22 | $0.22 | N/R | N/R | $0.28 |
| Corn meal, per barrel | 1825 | $2.38 | $2.69 | N/R | N/R | $0.17 |
| *(Cincinnati per bushel)* | 1826 | $3.50 | $4.00 | N/R | N/R | $0.38 |
| | 1827 | $2.62 | $3.31 | N/R | N/R | $0.22 |
| | 1828 | $2.38 | $2.62 | N/R | N/R | $0.28 |
| | 1829 | $2.12 | $2.50 | N/R | N/R | $0.44 |
| | 1830 | $2.25 | $2.50 | N/R | $2.50 | $0.30 |
| | 1831 | $3.22 | $3.63 | N/R | $2.50 | $0.30 |
| | 1832 | $2.62 | $2.94 | N/R | $2.00 | N/R |
| | 1833 | $3.50 | $3.94 | N/R | $3.00 | N/R |
| | 1834 | $2.88 | $3.19 | N/R | $2.75 | $0.38 |
| | 1835 | $3.94 | $3.81 | N/R | $2.25 | $0.42 |
| | 1836 | $4.18 | $4.62 | N/R | $2.00 | $0.64 |
| | 1837 | $4.00 | $4.38 | N/R | $2.88 | N/R |
| | 1838 | $3.50 | $3.75 | N/R | $2.38 | N/R |
| | 1839 | $4.00 | $4.25 | N/R | N/R | $0.88 |
| | 1840 | $2.91 | $2.81 | N/R | N/R | $0.34 |
| | 1841 | $2.62 | $2.84 | N/R | N/R | $0.28 |
| | 1842 | $2.84 | $3.06 | N/R | N/R | $0.26 |
| | 1843 | $2.69 | $2.75 | N/R | N/R | $0.26 |
| | 1844 | $2.44 | $2.69 | N/R | N/R | $0.38 |
| | 1845 | $2.25 | $2.47 | N/R | N/R | N/R |
| | 1846 | $3.12 | $3.31 | N/R | N/R | $0.30 |
| | 1847 | $5.00 | $4.66 | N/R | N/R | N/R |
| | 1848 | $2.38 | $2.37 | N/R | N/R | N/R |
| | 1849 | $2.75 | $2.75 | N/R | N/R | N/R |
| Corn, per bushel | 1825 | $0.385 | $0.500 | $0.500 | $0.660 | $0.150 |
| *(New Orleans, per barrel 1825-39)* | 1826 | $0.690 | $0.740 | $0.760 | $0.750 | $0.350 |
| | 1827 | $0.490 | $0.545 | $0.580 | $0.410 | $0.160 |
| | 1828 | $0.400 | $0.490 | $0.400 | $0.500 | $0.200 |
| | 1829 | $0.475 | $0.550 | $0.440 | $1.250 | $0.250 |
| | 1830 | $0.392 | $0.485 | $0.470 | $0.620 | $0.250 |
| | 1831 | $0.660 | $0.735 | $0.810 | $0.500 | $0.465 |
| | 1832 | $0.515 | $0.570 | $0.570 | $1.120 | $0.200 |
| | 1833 | $0.675 | $0.740 | $0.720 | $1.250 | $0.310 |
| | 1834 | $0.600 | $0.645 | $0.700 | $1.190 | $0.290 |
| | 1835 | $0.805 | $0.850 | $0.840 | $1.120 | $0.475 |
| | 1836 | $0.805 | $0.890 | $0.760 | $0.750 | $0.315 |

| Commodity | Year | Philadelphia Currency | New York Currency | Charleston Currency | New Orleans Currency | Cincinnati Currency |
|---|---|---|---|---|---|---|
| | 1837 | $0.855 | $1.000 | $1.000 | $1.060 | $0.425 |
| | 1838 | $0.740 | $0.840 | $0.800 | $0.750 | $0.560 |
| | 1839 | $0.905 | $0.910 | $0.820 | $0.880 | $0.610 |
| | 1840 | $0.495 | $0.555 | $0.510 | $0.435 | $0.250 |
| | 1841 | $0.500 | $0.545 | $0.650 | $0.410 | $0.190 |
| | 1842 | $0.570 | $0.635 | $0.620 | $0.345 | $0.225 |
| | 1843 | $0.515 | $0.540 | $0.680 | $0.355 | $0.190 |
| | 1844 | $0.470 | $0.525 | $0.580 | $0.385 | $0.310 |
| | 1845 | $0.405 | $0.470 | $0.500 | $0.355 | $0.350 |
| | 1846 | $0.630 | $0.690 | $0.690 | $0.330 | $0.335 |
| | 1847 | $1.030 | $0.940 | $0.925 | $0.725 | $0.420 |
| | 1848 | $0.510 | $0.525 | $0.555 | $0.320 | $0.250 |
| | 1849 | $0.610 | $0.625 | $0.570 | $0.455 | $0.285 |
| Cotton yarn, per pound | 1825 | N/R | N/R | N/R | N/R | $0.465 |
| | 1826 | N/R | N/R | N/R | N/R | $0.320 |
| | 1827 | N/R | N/R | N/R | N/R | $0.300 |
| | 1828 | N/R | N/R | N/R | N/R | $0.270 |
| | 1829 | N/R | N/R | N/R | N/R | $0.285 |
| | 1830 | N/R | N/R | N/R | N/R | $0.230 |
| | 1831 | N/R | N/R | N/R | N/R | $0.225 |
| | 1832 | N/R | N/R | N/R | N/R | $0.290 |
| | 1833 | N/R | N/R | N/R | N/R | $0.265 |
| | 1834 | N/R | N/R | N/R | N/R | $0.275 |
| | 1835 | N/R | N/R | N/R | N/R | $0.280 |
| | 1836 | N/R | N/R | N/R | N/R | $0.340 |
| | 1837 | N/R | N/R | N/R | N/R | $0.340 |
| | 1838 | N/R | N/R | N/R | N/R | $0.290 |
| | 1839 | N/R | N/R | N/R | N/R | $0.290 |
| | 1840 | N/R | N/R | N/R | N/R | $0.275 |
| | 1841 | N/R | N/R | N/R | N/R | $0.275 |
| | 1842 | N/R | N/R | N/R | N/R | $0.278 |
| | 1843 | N/R | N/R | N/R | N/R | $0.175 |
| | 1844 | N/R | N/R | N/R | N/R | $0.180 |

## Based Upon US Dollars

| Year | Value of 19th Century Dollar in 2002 US Dollars |
|---|---|
| 1825 | $18.00 |
| 1830 | $19.00 |
| 1835 | $20.00 |
| 1840 | $20.00 |
| 1845 | $23.00 |
| 1849 | $23.00 |

*Calculations are approximate values based upon economic historical data*

| Commodity | Year | Philadelphia Currency | New York Currency | Charleston Currency | New Orleans Currency | Cincinnati Currency |
|---|---|---|---|---|---|---|
| | 1845 | N/R | N/R | N/R | N/R | $0.160 |
| | 1846 | N/R | N/R | N/R | N/R | $0.155 |
| | 1847 | N/R | N/R | N/R | N/R | $0.190 |
| | 1848 | N/R | N/R | N/R | N/R | $0.145 |
| | 1849 | N/R | N/R | N/R | N/R | $0.150 |
| Cotton, per pound | 1825 | $0.21 | $0.25 | $0.27 | $0.32 | $0.24 |
| | 1826 | $0.11 | $0.10 | $0.10 | $0.12 | $0.12 |
| | 1827 | $0.10 | $0.10 | $0.09 | $0.10 | $0.08 |
| | 1828 | $0.11 | $0.11 | $0.10 | $0.12 | $0.08 |
| | 1829 | $0.10 | $0.10 | $0.08 | $0.10 | $0.12 |
| | 1830 | $0.10 | $0.10 | $0.10 | $0.10 | $0.09 |
| | 1831 | $0.10 | $0.09 | $0.08 | $0.10 | $0.10 |
| | 1832 | $0.10 | $0.10 | $0.10 | $0.11 | $0.10 |
| | 1833 | $0.12 | $0.12 | $0.11 | $0.13 | $0.10 |
| | 1834 | $0.14 | $0.12 | $0.12 | $0.13 | $0.12 |
| | 1835 | $0.18 | $0.18 | $0.16 | $0.20 | $0.18 |
| | 1836 | $0.19 | $0.18 | $0.16 | $0.18 | $0.18 |
| | 1837 | $0.12 | $0.10 | $0.07 | $0.13 | $0.10 |
| | 1838 | $0.11 | $0.09 | $0.09 | $0.12 | $0.10 |
| | 1839 | $0.16 | $0.15 | $0.15 | $0.17 | $0.14 |
| | 1840 | $0.09 | $0.08 | $0.08 | $0.10 | $0.09 |
| | 1841 | $0.11 | $0.10 | $0.10 | $0.12 | $0.11 |
| | 1842 | $0.08 | $0.07 | $0.08 | $0.11 | $0.10 |
| | 1843 | $0.07 | $0.07 | $0.06 | $0.06 | $0.06 |
| | 1844 | $0.08 | $0.07 | $0.07 | $0.07 | $0.08 |
| | 1845 | $0.06 | $0.06 | $0.06 | $0.06 | $0.05 |
| | 1846 | $0.08 | $0.08 | $0.07 | $0.06 | $0.08 |
| | 1847 | $0.13 | $0.12 | $0.12 | $0.11 | $0.12 |
| | 1848 | $0.07 | $0.06 | $0.06 | $0.05 | $0.06 |
| | 1849 | $0.08 | $0.08 | $0.07 | $0.07 | $0.06 |
| Duck Cloth, per bolt | 1825 | $7.75 | $21.50 | N/R | $18.50 | N/R |
| *(New Orleans per piece from 1822-24)* | 1826 | $6.50 | $21.25 | N/R | $19.00 | N/R |
| | 1827 | $5.88 | $21.25 | N/R | $18.00 | N/R |
| | 1828 | $6.12 | $20.13 | N/R | $18.00 | N/R |
| | 1829 | $7.00 | $19.00 | N/R | $18.00 | N/R |
| | 1830 | $8.75 | $17.50 | N/R | $18.00 | N/R |
| | 1831 | $9.00 | $19.50 | N/R | $19.00 | N/R |
| | 1832 | $8.75 | $18.75 | N/R | $21.00 | N/R |
| | 1833 | $6.75 | $17.50 | N/R | $17.50 | N/R |
| | 1834 | $6.25 | $16.88 | N/R | $17.00 | N/R |
| | 1835 | $6.25 | $16.50 | N/R | $16.50 | N/R |
| | 1836 | $7.12 | $16.13 | N/R | $16.50 | N/R |
| | 1837 | $8.00 | $16.75 | N/R | $17.00 | N/R |
| | 1838 | $8.25 | $19.00 | N/R | $21.50 | N/R |
| | 1839 | $8.25 | $20.00 | N/R | $20.25 | N/R |
| | 1840 | $7.50 | N/R | N/R | $20.25 | N/R |
| | 1841 | $7.50 | N/R | N/R | $20.50 | N/R |
| | 1842 | $7.25 | N/R | N/R | $20.50 | N/R |

| Commodity | Year | Philadelphia Currency | New York Currency | Charleston Currency | New Orleans Currency | Cincinnati Currency |
|---|---|---|---|---|---|---|
| | 1843 | $7.25 | N/R | N/R | $20.50 | N/R |
| | 1844 | $6.38 | N/R | N/R | $19.50 | N/R |
| | 1845 | $6.38 | N/R | N/R | $17.00 | N/R |
| | 1846 | $6.38 | $17.00 | N/R | N/R | N/R |
| | 1847 | $6.38 | N/R | N/R | $17.00 | N/R |
| | 1848 | $6.38 | N/R | N/R | $17.00 | N/R |
| | 1849 | $6.38 | $15.75 | N/R | N/R | N/R |
| Fish, per hundredweight | 1825 | $2.62 | $2.75 | $3.60 | $2.25 | $11.50 |
| (Charleston & Cincinnati per barrel) | 1826 | $2.38 | $2.25 | $2.80 | $1.88 | $11.00 |
| (New Orleans per box) | 1827 | $4.00 | $3.38 | $4.50 | $1.88 | $9.25 |
| | 1828 | $3.00 | $3.00 | $3.80 | $1.50 | $9.50 |
| | 1829 | $2.25 | $2.63 | $4.20 | $1.75 | $10.00 |
| | 1830 | $2.25 | $2.25 | $3.60 | $1.42 | $10.00 |
| | 1831 | $3.12 | $3.00 | $3.50 | $1.50 | $9.25 |
| | 1832 | $2.62 | $2.88 | $2.90 | $1.75 | $9.18 |
| | 1833 | $3.00 | $2.69 | $3.60 | $0.88 | $9.50 |
| | 1834 | $2.38 | $2.50 | $5.00 | $1.20 | $9.75 |
| | 1835 | $2.81 | $3.13 | $6.00 | $1.38 | $11.75 |
| | 1836 | $3.62 | $3.69 | $7.00 | $1.25 | $14.00 |
| | 1837 | $3.75 | $3.63 | $6.60 | $1.30 | $14.75 |
| | 1838 | $3.50 | $3.37 | $6.20 | $1.38 | $14.50 |
| | 1839 | $4.25 | $4.30 | $7.20 | $1.54 | $18.75 |
| | 1840 | $2.12 | $2.44 | $8.20 | $1.12 | $19.25 |
| | 1841 | $3.00 | $2.75 | $7.50 | $0.82 | $18.00 |
| | 1842 | $2.53 | $2.09 | $8.00 | $0.81 | $16.50 |
| | 1843 | $2.44 | $2.50 | N/R | $1.50 | $11.50 |
| | 1844 | $2.88 | $3.00 | N/R | $0.75 | $13.75 |
| | 1845 | $2.75 | $2.94 | N/R | $0.88 | $14.75 |
| | 1846 | $2.88 | $3.03 | N/R | $0.92 | $13.75 |
| | 1847 | $3.38 | $3.89 | N/R | $1.05 | $13.75 |
| | 1848 | $3.12 | $3.69 | N/R | $1.06 | $10.00 |
| | 1849 | $2.56 | $2.63 | N/R | $0.75 | $12.00 |

## Based Upon US Dollars

| Year | Value of 19th Century Dollar in 2002 US Dollars |
|---|---|
| 1825 | $18.00 |
| 1830 | $19.00 |
| 1835 | $20.00 |
| 1840 | $20.00 |
| 1845 | $23.00 |
| 1849 | $23.00 |

*Calculations are approximate values based upon economic historical data*

| Commodity | Year | Philadelphia Currency | New York Currency | Charleston Currency | New Orleans Currency | Cincinnati Currency |
|---|---|---|---|---|---|---|
| Flour, per barrel | 1825 | $6.00 | $5.31 | $5.80 | $5.00 | $3.22 |
| | 1826 | $4.25 | $4.13 | $4.20 | $3.25 | $2.68 |
| | 1827 | $5.00 | $5.19 | $5.60 | $4.19 | $3.12 |
| | 1828 | $4.75 | $4.56 | $5.00 | $4.00 | $3.28 |
| | 1829 | $6.62 | $6.44 | $7.00 | $6.25 | $5.88 |
| | 1830 | $4.75 | $4.87 | $5.30 | $4.35 | $2.75 |
| | 1831 | $6.00 | $5.88 | $6.40 | $5.00 | $4.12 |
| | 1832 | $5.50 | $5.44 | $5.90 | $5.12 | $4.24 |
| | 1833 | $5.50 | $5.56 | $6.00 | $5.38 | $3.62 |
| | 1834 | $5.38 | $4.75 | $6.00 | $4.62 | $2.88 |
| | 1835 | $6.00 | $5.31 | $6.50 | $6.06 | $4.90 |
| | 1836 | $6.50 | $6.75 | $7.60 | $6.00 | $5.00 |
| | 1837 | $9.00 | $7.50 | $10.60 | $6.00 | $6.00 |
| | 1838 | $7.80 | $7.13 | $8.80 | $8.75 | $6.06 |
| | 1839 | $7.25 | $7.63 | $7.70 | $6.69 | $5.65 |
| | 1840 | $4.62 | $5.19 | $6.00 | $3.92 | $3.20 |
| | 1841 | $4.82 | $5.00 | $6.00 | $4.28 | $3.88 |
| | 1842 | $5.75 | $5.87 | $7.20 | $4.62 | $4.00 |
| | 1843 | $4.32 | $5.06 | $5.12 | $3.69 | $3.44 |
| | 1844 | $4.47 | $4.93 | $5.44 | $4.06 | $3.61 |
| | 1845 | $4.45 | $4.62 | $5.38 | $3.95 | $3.64 |
| | 1846 | $4.31 | $4.75 | $5.25 | $3.12 | $3.42 |
| | 1847 | $7.90 | $7.69 | $6.75 | $6.19 | $5.19 |
| | 1848 | $5.87 | $6.28 | $6.38 | $4.88 | $4.45 |
| | 1849 | $4.68 | $5.69 | $5.31 | $4.28 | $3.68 |
| Gin, per gallon | 1825 | $0.82 | $0.83 | N/R | $0.36 | N/R |
| | 1826 | $0.76 | $0.78 | N/R | $0.24 | N/R |
| | 1827 | $1.00 | $1.06 | N/R | $0.40 | N/R |
| | 1828 | $1.00 | $0.96 | N/R | $0.32 | N/R |
| | 1829 | $1.02 | $0.98 | N/R | $0.34 | N/R |
| | 1830 | $1.02 | $1.02 | N/R | $0.28 | N/R |
| | 1831 | $1.02 | $1.22 | N/R | $0.40 | N/R |
| | 1832 | $1.02 | $1.15 | $1.12 | $0.42 | N/R |
| | 1833 | $1.25 | $1.20 | $1.12 | $0.44 | N/R |
| | 1834 | $1.25 | $1.09 | $1.10 | $0.36 | N/R |
| | 1835 | $1.18 | $1.13 | $1.10 | $0.40 | N/R |
| | 1836 | $1.11 | $1.09 | N/R | $0.49 | N/R |
| | 1837 | $1.11 | $1.20 | $1.10 | $0.52 | N/R |
| | 1838 | $1.11 | $1.20 | N/R | $0.51 | N/R |
| | 1839 | $1.11 | $1.18 | N/R | $0.58 | N/R |
| | 1840 | $1.11 | $1.14 | N/R | $0.48 | N/R |
| | 1841 | $1.06 | $1.14 | N/R | $0.38 | N/R |
| | 1842 | $1.00 | $1.05 | N/R | $0.28 | N/R |
| | 1843 | $1.25 | $1.23 | N/R | $0.30 | N/R |
| | 1844 | $1.21 | $1.23 | N/R | $0.30 | N/R |
| | 1845 | $1.29 | $1.23 | N/R | $0.30 | N/R |
| | 1846 | $1.35 | $1.30 | N/R | $0.31 | N/R |
| | 1847 | $1.32 | $1.37 | N/R | $0.31 | N/R |
| | 1848 | $1.22 | $1.37 | N/R | $0.44 | N/R |
| | 1849 | $1.22 | $1.23 | N/R | $0.44 | N/R |

| Commodity | Year | Philadelphia Currency | New York Currency | Charleston Currency | New Orleans Currency | Cincinnati Currency |
|---|---|---|---|---|---|---|
| Hides, per pound | 1825 | N/R | N/R | N/R | N/R | N/R |
| | 1826 | N/R | N/R | N/R | N/R | N/R |
| | 1827 | N/R | N/R | N/R | N/R | N/R |
| | 1828 | N/R | N/R | N/R | N/R | N/R |
| | 1829 | N/R | N/R | N/R | N/R | N/R |
| | 1830 | N/R | N/R | N/R | N/R | N/R |
| | 1831 | N/R | N/R | N/R | N/R | N/R |
| | 1832 | N/R | N/R | N/R | N/R | N/R |
| | 1833 | N/R | N/R | N/R | N/R | N/R |
| | 1834 | N/R | N/R | N/R | N/R | N/R |
| | 1835 | N/R | N/R | N/R | N/R | N/R |
| | 1836 | N/R | N/R | N/R | N/R | N/R |
| | 1837 | N/R | N/R | N/R | N/R | N/R |
| | 1838 | N/R | N/R | N/R | N/R | N/R |
| | 1839 | N/R | N/R | N/R | N/R | N/R |
| | 1840 | N/R | N/R | N/R | $0.07 | N/R |
| | 1841 | N/R | N/R | N/R | $0.09 | N/R |
| | 1842 | N/R | N/R | N/R | $0.08 | N/R |
| | 1843 | N/R | N/R | N/R | $0.06 | N/R |
| | 1844 | N/R | N/R | N/R | $0.08 | N/R |
| | 1845 | N/R | N/R | N/R | $0.08 | N/R |
| | 1846 | N/R | N/R | N/R | $0.08 | N/R |
| | 1847 | N/R | N/R | N/R | $0.06 | N/R |
| | 1848 | N/R | N/R | N/R | $0.05 | N/R |
| | 1849 | N/R | N/R | N/R | $0.06 | N/R |
| Hops, per pound | 1825 | $0.28 | $0.16 | N/R | N/R | $0.11 |
| | 1826 | $0.16 | $0.12 | N/R | N/R | $0.29 |
| | 1827 | $0.18 | $0.14 | N/R | N/R | $0.20 |
| | 1828 | $0.07 | $0.05 | N/R | N/R | $0.14 |
| | 1829 | $0.08 | $0.06 | N/R | N/R | $0.12 |
| | 1830 | $0.15 | $0.13 | N/R | N/R | $0.12 |
| | 1831 | $0.11 | $0.09 | N/R | N/R | $0.12 |
| | 1832 | $0.24 | $0.16 | N/R | N/R | $0.14 |

### Based Upon US Dollars

| Year | Value of 19th Century Dollar in 2002 US Dollars |
|---|---|
| 1825 | $18.00 |
| 1830 | $19.00 |
| 1835 | $20.00 |
| 1840 | $20.00 |
| 1845 | $23.00 |
| 1849 | $23.00 |

*Calculations are approximate values based upon economic historical data*

| Commodity | Year | Philadelphia Currency | New York Currency | Charleston Currency | New Orleans Currency | Cincinnati Currency |
|---|---|---|---|---|---|---|
| | 1833 | $0.36 | $0.29 | N/R | N/R | $0.11 |
| | 1834 | $0.16 | $0.10 | N/R | N/R | $0.18 |
| | 1835 | $0.16 | $0.18 | N/R | N/R | $0.24 |
| | 1836 | $0.16 | $0.16 | N/R | N/R | $0.19 |
| | 1837 | $0.10 | $0.08 | N/R | N/R | $0.15 |
| | 1838 | $0.07 | $0.04 | N/R | N/R | $0.11 |
| | 1839 | $0.17 | $0.16 | N/R | N/R | $0.26 |
| | 1840 | $0.45 | $0.45 | N/R | N/R | $1.00 |
| | 1841 | $0.26 | $0.22 | N/R | N/R | $0.38 |
| | 1842 | $0.14 | $0.14 | N/R | N/R | $0.20 |
| | 1843 | $0.11 | $0.10 | N/R | N/R | $0.08 |
| | 1844 | $0.08 | $0.08 | N/R | N/R | $0.11 |
| | 1845 | $0.13 | $0.14 | N/R | N/R | $0.11 |
| | 1846 | $0.23 | $0.23 | N/R | N/R | $0.30 |
| | 1847 | $0.09 | $0.08 | N/R | N/R | $0.13 |
| | 1848 | $0.07 | $0.06 | N/R | N/R | $0.10 |
| | 1849 | $0.08 | $0.08 | N/R | N/R | $0.07 |
| Indigo, per pound | 1825 | $2.35 | $2.38 | N/R | N/R | $3.12 |
| | 1826 | $2.05 | $2.00 | N/R | N/R | $2.75 |
| | 1827 | $1.88 | $1.91 | N/R | N/R | $2.38 |
| | 1828 | $1.88 | $1.31 | N/R | N/R | $2.40 |
| | 1829 | $1.15 | $1.09 | N/R | N/R | $1.94 |
| | 1830 | $0.90 | $1.00 | N/R | $1.75 | $1.94 |
| | 1831 | $0.65 | $0.87 | N/R | $1.32 | $1.56 |
| | 1832 | $0.80 | $0.94 | N/R | $1.35 | $1.62 |
| | 1833 | $0.80 | $0.75 | N/R | $1.18 | $1.44 |
| | 1834 | $1.15 | $1.03 | N/R | $1.35 | $1.48 |
| | 1835 | $1.12 | $1.03 | N/R | $1.39 | $1.52 |
| | 1836 | $1.12 | $1.03 | N/R | $1.42 | $1.50 |
| | 1837 | $1.15 | $1.05 | N/R | $1.42 | $1.55 |
| | 1838 | $1.22 | $1.04 | N/R | $1.40 | $1.56 |
| | 1839 | $1.24 | $1.25 | N/R | $1.60 | $2.00 |
| | 1840 | $1.25 | $1.03 | N/R | $1.55 | $1.68 |
| | 1841 | $0.92 | $1.03 | N/R | $1.38 | $1.56 |
| | 1842 | $0.98 | $0.70 | N/R | $1.12 | $1.51 |
| | 1843 | $0.88 | $0.88 | N/R | $1.08 | $1.38 |
| | 1844 | $0.85 | $0.80 | N/R | $1.08 | $1.18 |
| | 1845 | $0.80 | $0.70 | N/R | $1.00 | $1.15 |
| | 1846 | $0.78 | $0.58 | N/R | $0.95 | $1.20 |
| | 1847 | $0.86 | $0.75 | N/R | $0.95 | N/R |
| | 1848 | $0.72 | $0.62 | N/R | $0.95 | N/R |
| | 1849 | $0.78 | $0.68 | N/R | $0.95 | N/R |
| Iron - Bar, Per ton | 1825 | $97.50 | $117.50 | $4.88 | $102.50 | $125.00 |
| *(Charleston Per hundredweight)* | 1826 | $105.00 | $97.50 | $4.88 | $102.50 | $125.00 |
| | 1827 | $102.50 | $90.00 | $4.75 | $109.00 | $130.00 |
| | 1828 | $100.00 | $78.80 | $4.75 | $109.00 | $130.00 |
| | 1829 | $100.00 | $81.20 | $4.88 | $109.00 | $130.00 |
| | 1830 | $85.00 | $75.00 | $4.44 | $92.50 | $120.00 |

| Commodity | Year | Philadelphia Currency | New York Currency | Charleston Currency | New Orleans Currency | Cincinnati Currency |
|---|---|---|---|---|---|---|
| | 1831 | $81.00 | $71.20 | $4.31 | $100.00 | $106.00 |
| | 1832 | $84.00 | $73.50 | $4.12 | $85.00 | $120.00 |
| | 1833 | $82.80 | $75.00 | $4.06 | $85.00 | $120.00 |
| | 1834 | $85.00 | $73.80 | $4.00 | $95.00 | $100.00 |
| | 1835 | $80.00 | $68.80 | $4.06 | $96.50 | $106.40 |
| | 1836 | $102.50 | $102.50 | $4.06 | $96.50 | $140.00 |
| | 1837 | $102.50 | $105.00 | $5.00 | $96.50 | $156.80 |
| | 1838 | $87.50 | $92.50 | $5.00 | $96.50 | $128.80 |
| | 1839 | $97.50 | $90.00 | $5.00 | $101.50 | $128.80 |
| | 1840 | $77.50 | $73.80 | $5.00 | $100.00 | $89.60 |
| | 1841 | $73.80 | $73.80 | $5.00 | $97.50 | $100.80 |
| | 1842 | $73.80 | $55.00 | $5.00 | $97.50 | $100.80 |
| | 1843 | $73.80 | $56.20 | $5.00 | $97.50 | $100.80 |
| | 1844 | $76.20 | $58.80 | $5.00 | $97.50 | $84.00 |
| | 1845 | $87.50 | $82.50 | N/R | $100.00 | $89.60 |
| | 1846 | $82.50 | $78.80 | N/R | $100.00 | $70.00 |
| | 1847 | $82.50 | $71.20 | N/R | $100.00 | $70.00 |
| | 1848 | $87.20 | $60.00 | N/R | $100.00 | $70.00 |
| | 1849 | $62.50 | $55.00 | N/R | $95.00 | $70.00 |
| Iron-Pig, per ton | 1825 | $45.00 | $45.00 | N/R | $60.00 | N/R |
| | 1826 | $47.50 | $65.50 | N/R | $40.00 | N/R |
| | 1827 | $44.00 | $52.50 | N/R | $25.00 | N/R |
| | 1828 | $37.00 | $52.50 | N/R | $30.00 | N/R |
| | 1829 | $35.00 | $52.50 | N/R | $32.20 | N/R |
| | 1830 | $35.00 | $45.00 | N/R | $32.20 | N/R |
| | 1831 | $35.00 | $43.80 | N/R | $32.20 | N/R |
| | 1832 | $35.00 | $43.80 | N/R | $32.20 | N/R |
| | 1833 | $40.00 | $41.20 | N/R | $32.20 | N/R |
| | 1834 | $30.00 | $41.50 | N/R | $32.20 | N/R |
| | 1835 | $30.50 | $40.20 | N/R | $32.00 | N/R |
| | 1836 | $41.20 | $57.50 | N/R | $36.00 | N/R |
| | 1837 | $47.50 | $51.20 | N/R | $36.00 | N/R |
| | 1838 | $31.00 | $46.20 | N/R | $32.50 | N/R |

## Based Upon US Dollars

| Year | Value of 19th Century Dollar in 2002 US Dollars |
|---|---|
| 1825 | $18.00 |
| 1830 | $19.00 |
| 1835 | $20.00 |
| 1840 | $20.00 |
| 1845 | $23.00 |
| 1849 | $23.00 |

*Calculations are approximate values based upon economic historical data*

| Commodity | Year | Philadelphia Currency | New York Currency | Charleston Currency | New Orleans Currency | Cincinnati Currency |
|---|---|---|---|---|---|---|
| | 1839 | $34.00 | $41.50 | N/R | $32.50 | N/R |
| | 1840 | $30.50 | $33.80 | N/R | $31.50 | N/R |
| | 1841 | $29.00 | $36.20 | N/R | $25.00 | N/R |
| | 1842 | $28.50 | $27.50 | N/R | $27.50 | N/R |
| | 1843 | $25.00 | $26.00 | N/R | $23.50 | $19.00 |
| | 1844 | $28.00 | $30.80 | N/R | $23.50 | N/R |
| | 1845 | $38.00 | $51.20 | N/R | $40.00 | N/R |
| | 1846 | $31.50 | $41.20 | N/R | $22.00 | $31.50 |
| | 1847 | $30.20 | $35.00 | N/R | $31.50 | $32.50 |
| | 1848 | $29.50 | $28.80 | N/R | $31.50 | $34.00 |
| | 1849 | $24.80 | $26.80 | N/R | $25.50 | $26.50 |
| Lard, per pound | 1825 | $0.095 | $0.085 | $0.102 | $0.100 | $0.065 |
| | 1826 | $0.080 | $0.070 | $0.085 | $0.064 | $0.048 |
| | 1827 | $0.090 | $0.075 | $0.085 | $0.069 | $0.050 |
| | 1828 | $0.085 | $0.065 | $0.075 | $0.068 | $0.042 |
| | 1829 | $0.070 | $0.055 | $0.060 | $0.059 | $0.045 |
| | 1830 | $0.060 | $0.060 | $0.078 | $0.064 | $0.045 |
| | 1831 | $0.104 | $0.090 | $0.108 | $0.080 | $0.055 |
| | 1832 | $0.085 | $0.070 | $0.078 | $0.075 | $0.065 |
| | 1833 | $0.085 | $0.085 | $0.105 | $0.082 | $0.055 |
| | 1834 | $0.075 | $0.070 | $0.085 | $0.060 | $0.058 |
| | 1835 | $0.090 | $0.090 | $0.088 | $0.082 | $0.075 |
| | 1836 | $0.145 | $0.160 | $0.165 | $0.142 | $0.122 |
| | 1837 | $0.095 | $0.075 | $0.078 | $0.072 | $0.065 |
| | 1838 | $0.084 | $0.090 | $0.092 | $0.076 | $0.068 |
| | 1839 | $0.120 | $0.115 | $0.135 | $0.112 | $0.105 |
| | 1840 | $0.102 | $0.090 | $0.108 | $0.102 | $0.102 |
| | 1841 | $0.081 | $0.080 | $0.085 | $0.062 | $0.065 |
| | 1842 | $0.052 | $0.060 | $0.059 | $0.045 | $0.038 |
| | 1843 | $0.064 | $0.065 | $0.075 | $0.048 | $0.050 |
| | 1844 | $0.062 | $0.060 | $0.062 | $0.052 | $0.050 |
| | 1845 | $0.081 | $0.075 | $0.094 | $0.080 | $0.079 |
| | 1846 | $0.070 | $0.065 | $0.055 | $0.058 | $0.055 |
| | 1847 | $0.101 | $0.095 | $0.100 | $0.084 | $0.090 |
| | 1848 | $0.068 | $0.065 | $0.075 | $0.051 | $0.052 |
| | 1849 | $0.068 | $0.060 | $0.075 | $0.056 | $0.058 |
| Leather, Tanned, per pound | 1825 | $0.26 | $0.24 | N/R | $0.20 | $0.26 |
| | 1826 | $0.24 | $0.22 | N/R | $0.20 | $0.26 |
| | 1827 | $0.24 | $0.20 | N/R | $0.20 | $0.25 |
| | 1828 | $0.22 | $0.21 | N/R | $0.20 | $0.26 |
| | 1829 | $0.22 | $0.20 | N/R | $0.22 | $0.26 |
| | 1830 | $0.22 | $0.20 | N/R | $0.20 | $0.26 |
| | 1831 | $0.25 | $0.22 | N/R | $0.22 | $0.26 |
| | 1832 | $0.26 | $0.22 | N/R | $0.25 | $0.26 |
| | 1833 | $0.22 | $0.18 | N/R | $0.24 | $0.26 |
| | 1834 | $0.22 | $0.16 | N/R | $0.18 | $0.24 |
| | 1835 | $0.19 | $0.18 | N/R | $0.18 | $0.24 |
| | 1836 | $0.20 | $0.18 | N/R | $0.18 | $0.22 |

| Commodity | Year | Philadelphia Currency | New York Currency | Charleston Currency | New Orleans Currency | Cincinnati Currency |
|---|---|---|---|---|---|---|
| | 1837 | $0.22 | $0.20 | N/R | $0.21 | $0.24 |
| | 1838 | $0.22 | $0.18 | N/R | $0.21 | $0.24 |
| | 1839 | $0.22 | $0.22 | N/R | $0.21 | N/R |
| | 1840 | $0.21 | $0.18 | N/R | $0.20 | $0.23 |
| | 1841 | $0.21 | $0.20 | N/R | $0.21 | $0.24 |
| | 1842 | $0.19 | $0.18 | N/R | $0.21 | $0.24 |
| | 1843 | $0.18 | $0.16 | N/R | $0.21 | $0.20 |
| | 1844 | $0.18 | $0.16 | N/R | N/R | $0.20 |
| | 1845 | $0.18 | $0.14 | N/R | N/R | $0.18 |
| | 1846 | $0.18 | $0.14 | N/R | N/R | $0.18 |
| | 1847 | $0.17 | $0.16 | N/R | N/R | $0.16 |
| | 1848 | $0.18 | $0.14 | N/R | N/R | $0.19 |
| | 1849 | $0.16 | $0.16 | N/R | N/R | $0.22 |
| Linseed Oil, per gallon | 1825 | $0.96 | $1.00 | N/R | $0.75 | $0.74 |
| | 1826 | $0.71 | $0.78 | N/R | $0.64 | $0.59 |
| | 1827 | $0.71 | $0.77 | N/R | $0.64 | $0.60 |
| | 1828 | $0.62 | $0.67 | N/R | $0.62 | $0.53 |
| | 1829 | $0.81 | $0.85 | N/R | $0.75 | $0.64 |
| | 1830 | $0.72 | $0.74 | N/R | $0.85 | $0.61 |
| | 1831 | $0.96 | $0.99 | N/R | $0.88 | $0.66 |
| | 1832 | $0.96 | $0.94 | N/R | $1.25 | $1.06 |
| | 1833 | $0.94 | $0.96 | N/R | $1.18 | $1.00 |
| | 1834 | $0.84 | $0.87 | N/R | $0.85 | $0.82 |
| | 1835 | $1.20 | $1.28 | N/R | $1.22 | $1.18 |
| | 1836 | $1.08 | $1.14 | N/R | $1.50 | $1.10 |
| | 1837 | $0.82 | $1.00 | N/R | $1.18 | $1.10 |
| | 1838 | $0.74 | $0.76 | N/R | $1.00 | $0.90 |
| | 1839 | $0.85 | $0.88 | N/R | $0.98 | $1.25 |
| | 1840 | $0.60 | $0.59 | N/R | $0.88 | $0.70 |
| | 1841 | $0.78 | $0.83 | N/R | $0.92 | $0.78 |
| | 1842 | $0.82 | $0.82 | N/R | $1.12 | $0.92 |
| | 1843 | $0.82 | $0.89 | N/R | $0.78 | $0.75 |
| | 1844 | $0.76 | $0.71 | N/R | $0.79 | $0.74 |

## Based Upon US Dollars

| Year | Value of 19th Century Dollar in 2002 US Dollars |
|---|---|
| 1825 | $18.00 |
| 1830 | $19.00 |
| 1835 | $20.00 |
| 1840 | $20.00 |
| 1845 | $23.00 |
| 1849 | $23.00 |

*Calculations are approximate values based upon economic historical data*

| Commodity | Year | Philadelphia Currency | New York Currency | Charleston Currency | New Orleans Currency | Cincinnati Currency |
|---|---|---|---|---|---|---|
| | 1845 | $0.72 | $0.80 | N/R | $0.78 | $0.76 |
| | 1846 | $0.60 | $0.78 | N/R | $0.69 | $0.68 |
| | 1847 | $0.70 | $0.73 | N/R | $0.72 | $0.59 |
| | 1848 | $0.60 | $0.56 | N/R | $0.62 | $0.51 |
| | 1849 | $0.60 | $0.58 | N/R | $0.60 | $0.56 |
| Lumber Boards, per one hundred feet | 1825 | $27.50 | $15.00 | $20.00 | $17.50 | $15.00 |
| | 1826 | $30.00 | $17.00 | $28.00 | $21.50 | $17.50 |
| | 1827 | $30.00 | $15.50 | $27.00 | $15.00 | $17.50 |
| | 1828 | $24.00 | $16.00 | $21.00 | $19.00 | $17.50 |
| | 1829 | $21.50 | $15.00 | $20.00 | $19.00 | N/R |
| | 1830 | $19.00 | $15.00 | $22.00 | $19.00 | N/R |
| | 1831 | $26.00 | $15.00 | $27.50 | $19.00 | N/R |
| | 1832 | $25.00 | $15.00 | $27.00 | $19.00 | N/R |
| | 1833 | $25.00 | $15.00 | $27.00 | $15.50 | N/R |
| | 1834 | $22.50 | $16.50 | $27.00 | $14.00 | N/R |
| | 1835 | $22.50 | $16.50 | $32.00 | $14.00 | N/R |
| | 1836 | $26.50 | $16.50 | $35.00 | $16.00 | N/R |
| | 1837 | $26.50 | $37.50 | $40.00 | $35.00 | N/R |
| | 1838 | $20.00 | $37.50 | $28.00 | $25.00 | N/R |
| | 1839 | $20.00 | $37.50 | $38.00 | $22.50 | N/R |
| | 1840 | $17.50 | $32.50 | $30.00 | $20.00 | N/R |
| | 1841 | $19.50 | $35.00 | $25.00 | $20.00 | N/R |
| | 1842 | $16.50 | $35.00 | $24.00 | $14.50 | N/R |
| | 1843 | $16.20 | $32.50 | N/R | $11.50 | $27.50 |
| | 1844 | $16.00 | $32.50 | N/R | $11.50 | N/R |
| | 1845 | $20.00 | $32.50 | N/R | $11.50 | N/R |
| | 1846 | $20.50 | $37.50 | N/R | $13.00 | $27.50 |
| | 1847 | $17.00 | $32.50 | N/R | $13.00 | $30.00 |
| | 1848 | $14.00 | $37.50 | N/R | $13.00 | $20.00 |
| | 1849 | $13.80 | $36.50 | N/R | $13.00 | $30.00 |
| Molasses, per gallon | 1825 | $0.31 | $0.32 | $0.36 | $0.16 | $0.45 |
| | 1826 | $0.32 | $0.31 | $0.35 | $0.20 | $0.45 |
| | 1827 | $0.30 | $0.31 | $0.34 | $0.22 | $0.40 |
| | 1828 | $0.30 | $0.28 | $0.34 | $0.21 | $0.40 |
| | 1829 | $0.26 | $0.28 | $0.32 | $0.20 | $0.39 |
| | 1830 | $0.26 | $0.24 | $0.30 | $0.19 | $0.35 |
| | 1831 | $0.24 | $0.24 | $0.26 | $13.00 | $0.33 |
| | 1832 | $0.26 | $0.24 | $0.28 | $0.20 | $0.38 |
| | 1833 | $0.27 | $0.27 | $0.30 | $0.19 | $0.34 |
| | 1834 | $0.27 | $0.24 | $0.32 | $0.20 | $0.36 |
| | 1835 | $0.28 | $0.28 | $0.32 | $0.22 | $0.48 |
| | 1836 | $0.35 | $0.36 | $0.45 | $0.34 | $0.55 |
| | 1837 | $0.27 | $0.28 | $0.36 | $0.22 | $0.44 |
| | 1838 | $0.29 | $0.28 | $0.34 | $0.20 | $0.40 |
| | 1839 | $0.32 | $0.30 | $0.29 | $0.24 | $0.50 |
| | 1840 | $0.22 | $0.22 | $0.28 | $0.14 | $0.30 |
| | 1841 | $0.21 | $0.18 | $0.26 | $0.16 | $0.29 |
| | 1842 | $0.18 | $0.16 | $0.25 | $0.09 | $0.21 |

| Commodity | Year | Philadelphia Currency | New York Currency | Charleston Currency | New Orleans Currency | Cincinnati Currency |
|---|---|---|---|---|---|---|
| | 1843 | $0.19 | $0.18 | $0.22 | $0.16 | $0.19 |
| | 1844 | $0.24 | $0.24 | $0.20 | $0.26 | $0.33 |
| | 1845 | $0.26 | $0.29 | $0.30 | $0.26 | $0.35 |
| | 1846 | $0.20 | $0.20 | $0.32 | $0.23 | $0.32 |
| | 1847 | $0.20 | $0.20 | $0.36 | $0.28 | $0.34 |
| | 1848 | $0.18 | $0.19 | $0.27 | $0.14 | $0.25 |
| | 1849 | $0.21 | $0.20 | $0.28 | $0.15 | $0.24 |
| Nails, per pound | 1825 | $0.075 | N/R | N/R | $0.070 | $0.088 |
| | 1826 | $0.075 | N/R | N/R | $0.068 | $0.080 |
| | 1827 | $0.068 | N/R | N/R | $0.069 | $0.075 |
| | 1828 | $0.070 | $0.075 | N/R | $0.075 | $0.088 |
| | 1829 | $0.069 | $0.075 | $0.074 | $0.078 | $0.080 |
| | 1830 | $0.052 | $0.055 | $0.058 | $0.055 | $0.070 |
| | 1831 | $0.054 | $0.055 | $0.058 | $0.056 | $0.065 |
| | 1832 | $0.059 | $0.060 | $0.061 | $0.060 | $0.065 |
| | 1833 | $0.055 | $0.055 | $0.059 | $0.059 | $0.068 |
| | 1834 | $0.055 | $0.055 | $0.058 | $0.058 | $0.064 |
| | 1835 | $0.064 | $0.063 | $0.065 | $0.069 | $0.064 |
| | 1836 | $0.070 | $0.073 | $0.075 | $0.072 | $0.076 |
| | 1837 | $0.070 | $0.066 | $0.066 | $0.071 | $0.086 |
| | 1838 | $0.060 | $0.060 | $0.064 | $0.069 | $0.076 |
| | 1839 | $0.070 | $0.065 | $0.074 | $0.072 | $0.084 |
| | 1840 | $0.058 | $0.052 | $0.065 | $0.056 | $0.055 |
| | 1841 | $0.052 | $0.054 | $0.058 | $0.058 | $0.062 |
| | 1842 | $0.052 | $0.052 | $0.052 | $0.050 | $0.055 |
| | 1843 | $0.040 | $0.041 | $0.049 | $0.045 | $0.050 |
| | 1844 | $0.045 | $0.044 | $0.041 | $0.044 | $0.050 |
| | 1845 | $0.048 | $0.049 | $0.049 | $0.052 | $0.050 |
| | 1846 | $0.043 | $0.041 | $0.044 | $0.042 | $0.041 |
| | 1847 | $0.045 | $0.045 | $0.046 | $0.049 | $0.038 |
| | 1848 | $0.050 | $0.041 | $0.046 | $0.049 | $0.037 |
| | 1849 | $0.042 | $0.040 | $0.041 | $0.039 | $0.032 |

### Based Upon US Dollars

| Year | Value of 19th Century Dollar in 2002 US Dollars |
|---|---|
| 1825 | $18.00 |
| 1830 | $19.00 |
| 1835 | $20.00 |
| 1840 | $20.00 |
| 1845 | $23.00 |
| 1849 | $23.00 |

*Calculations are approximate values based upon economic historical data*

| Commodity | Year | Philadelphia Currency | New York Currency | Charleston Currency | New Orleans Currency | Cincinnati Currency |
|---|---|---|---|---|---|---|
| Pork, per barrel | 1825 | $13.75 | $14.50 | $14.50 | $14.50 | $9.50 |
| | 1826 | $11.25 | $11.22 | $12.50 | $10.20 | $9.00 |
| | 1827 | $11.88 | $11.75 | $11.50 | $8.40 | $8.00 |
| | 1828 | $14.00 | $13.17 | $14.20 | $11.80 | $9.00 |
| | 1829 | $13.25 | $12.96 | $13.50 | $11.00 | $8.75 |
| | 1830 | $13.00 | $13.12 | $13.50 | $13.00 | $10.50 |
| | 1831 | $14.75 | $15.11 | $15.80 | $12.50 | $11.00 |
| | 1832 | $13.38 | $13.57 | $14.80 | $11.50 | $9.75 |
| | 1833 | $14.25 | $14.25 | $13.20 | $13.50 | $10.75 |
| | 1834 | $13.38 | $14.25 | $14.00 | $12.20 | $10.12 |
| | 1835 | $17.25 | $17.66 | $17.80 | $16.50 | $12.88 |
| | 1836 | $24.25 | $21.75 | $23.50 | $22.20 | $21.00 |
| | 1837 | $17.30 | $19.17 | $17.50 | $16.80 | $16.25 |
| | 1838 | $18.50 | $20.50 | $17.50 | $19.80 | $15.25 |
| | 1839 | $21.75 | $22.33 | $20.50 | $21.80 | $19.50 |
| | 1840 | $15.63 | $15.19 | $16.00 | $15.90 | $13.75 |
| | 1841 | $12.13 | $12.03 | $12.20 | $11.90 | $10.25 |
| | 1842 | $7.75 | $9.00 | $8.10 | $7.00 | $5.75 |
| | 1843 | $9.56 | $9.58 | N/R | $8.60 | $7.25 |
| | 1844 | $9.19 | $9.38 | N/R | $9.10 | $7.88 |
| | 1845 | $13.13 | $13.52 | N/R | $13.80 | $13.00 |
| | 1846 | $11.38 | $10.95 | N/R | $10.10 | $9.12 |
| | 1847 | $16.25 | $10.26 | N/R | $16.00 | $15.00 |
| | 1848 | $10.38 | $10.40 | N/R | $8.40 | $7.50 |
| | 1849 | $10.50 | $10.05 | N/R | $9.40 | $9.00 |
| Pot Ashes, per hundredweight | 1825 | N/R | $111.20 | N/R | N/R | N/R |
| *(New York per ton 1825-1830)* | 1826 | $5.00 | $88.50 | N/R | N/R | N/R |
| | 1827 | $4.12 | $80.00 | N/R | N/R | N/R |
| | 1828 | $5.25 | $100.00 | N/R | N/R | N/R |
| | 1829 | $6.75 | $115.00 | N/R | N/R | N/R |
| | 1830 | $5.25 | $110.00 | N/R | N/R | N/R |
| | 1831 | $5.00 | $4.78 | N/R | N/R | N/R |
| | 1832 | $5.00 | $4.48 | N/R | N/R | N/R |
| | 1833 | $4.75 | $4.22 | N/R | N/R | N/R |
| | 1834 | $4.50 | $4.11 | N/R | N/R | N/R |
| | 1835 | $4.88 | $4.55 | N/R | N/R | N/R |
| | 1836 | $6.50 | $6.50 | N/R | N/R | N/R |
| | 1837 | $4.00 | $4.00 | N/R | N/R | N/R |
| | 1838 | $5.56 | $4.75 | N/R | N/R | N/R |
| | 1839 | $5.00 | $5.00 | N/R | N/R | N/R |
| | 1840 | $4.88 | $4.50 | N/R | N/R | $5.50 |
| | 1841 | $5.00 | $5.00 | N/R | N/R | $4.50 |
| | 1842 | $5.50 | $5.38 | N/R | N/R | $5.75 |
| | 1843 | $4.56 | $4.56 | N/R | N/R | $5.00 |
| | 1844 | $4.25 | $4.38 | N/R | N/R | $3.75 |
| | 1845 | $3.88 | $3.84 | N/R | N/R | $3.12 |
| | 1846 | $4.06 | $3.75 | N/R | N/R | $3.25 |
| | 1847 | $5.03 | $5.00 | N/R | N/R | $4.50 |
| | 1848 | $5.75 | $5.25 | N/R | N/R | $5.12 |
| | 1849 | $6.44 | $5.53 | N/R | N/R | $4.50 |

| Commodity | Year | Philadelphia Currency | New York Currency | Charleston Currency | New Orleans Currency | Cincinnati Currency |
|---|---|---|---|---|---|---|
| Rice, per hundredweight | 1825 | $3.88 | $3.50 | $3.88 | $3.75 | $5.90 |
| | 1826 | $3.12 | $3.00 | $2.88 | $3.75 | $6.25 |
| | 1827 | $3.38 | $3.06 | $3.00 | $3.12 | $5.50 |
| | 1828 | $3.25 | $3.00 | $3.12 | $3.00 | $4.00 |
| | 1829 | $3.00 | $2.44 | $3.00 | $3.38 | $6.00 |
| | 1830 | $2.38 | $2.37 | $2.62 | $2.61 | $4.50 |
| | 1831 | $3.31 | $3.12 | $3.25 | $2.88 | $5.50 |
| | 1832 | $2.88 | $3.00 | $3.00 | $3.12 | $5.00 |
| | 1833 | $3.25 | $3.13 | $2.88 | $3.25 | $5.25 |
| | 1834 | $3.00 | $2.63 | $2.88 | $3.00 | $4.75 |
| | 1835 | $3.37 | $3.19 | $3.56 | $4.12 | $5.75 |
| | 1836 | $3.88 | $3.75 | $3.62 | $4.38 | $5.00 |
| | 1837 | $3.88 | $3.37 | $2.75 | $3.75 | $5.75 |
| | 1838 | $4.06 | $3.81 | $4.62 | $4.62 | $5.25 |
| | 1839 | $4.88 | $4.62 | $4.81 | $5.12 | $7.75 |
| | 1840 | $3.62 | $3.12 | $3.12 | $3.69 | $5.00 |
| | 1841 | $3.56 | $3.19 | $3.25 | $3.88 | $4.25 |
| | 1842 | $3.06 | $2.91 | $3.00 | $3.50 | $4.50 |
| | 1843 | $2.37 | $2.62 | $2.50 | $2.88 | $3.38 |
| | 1844 | $2.88 | $3.06 | $3.00 | $3.38 | $3.88 |
| | 1845 | $3.79 | $3.66 | $3.25 | $3.56 | $4.75 |
| | 1846 | $4.19 | $3.56 | $3.75 | $4.75 | $5.25 |
| | 1847 | $4.62 | $3.50 | $4.50 | $4.75 | $5.25 |
| | 1848 | $3.44 | $3.13 | $3.12 | $3.69 | $4.62 |
| | 1849 | $3.19 | $2.94 | $3.25 | $3.31 | $3.88 |
| Rum, per gallon | 1825 | $0.38 | $0.95 | $0.39 | $0.31 | N/R |
| | 1826 | $0.38 | $0.97 | $0.36 | $0.35 | N/R |
| | 1827 | $0.40 | $1.06 | $0.39 | $0.36 | N/R |
| | 1828 | $0.37 | $1.23 | $0.34 | $0.38 | N/R |
| | 1829 | $0.35 | $1.26 | $0.33 | $0.32 | N/R |
| | 1830 | $0.30 | $1.18 | N/R | $0.31 | $0.26 |
| | 1831 | $0.36 | $1.08 | $0.36 | $0.30 | N/R |
| | 1832 | $0.34 | $1.08 | $0.34 | $0.35 | N/R |

## Based Upon US Dollars

| Year | Value of 19th Century Dollar in 2002 US Dollars |
|---|---|
| 1825 | $18.00 |
| 1830 | $19.00 |
| 1835 | $20.00 |
| 1840 | $20.00 |
| 1845 | $23.00 |
| 1849 | $23.00 |

*Calculations are approximate values based upon economic historical data*

| Commodity | Year | Philadelphia Currency | New York Currency | Charleston Currency | New Orleans Currency | Cincinnati Currency |
|---|---|---|---|---|---|---|
| | 1833 | $0.36 | $1.05 | $0.36 | $0.38 | N/R |
| | 1834 | $0.30 | $1.13 | $0.34 | $0.38 | N/R |
| | 1835 | $0.37 | $1.13 | $0.32 | $0.38 | N/R |
| | 1836 | $0.42 | $1.31 | $0.46 | $0.46 | N/R |
| | 1837 | $0.42 | $1.31 | $0.46 | $0.44 | N/R |
| | 1838 | $0.38 | $1.31 | $0.45 | $0.39 | N/R |
| | 1839 | $0.40 | $1.43 | $0.38 | $0.45 | N/R |
| | 1840 | $0.30 | $1.63 | $0.28 | $0.45 | N/R |
| | 1841 | $0.26 | $1.63 | $0.28 | $0.30 | N/R |
| | 1842 | $0.20 | $1.44 | $0.20 | $0.25 | N/R |
| | 1843 | $0.23 | $1.63 | $0.24 | $0.28 | N/R |
| | 1844 | $0.32 | $1.70 | $0.28 | $0.29 | N/R |
| | 1845 | $0.34 | $1.63 | $0.30 | $0.31 | N/R |
| | 1846 | $0.28 | $1.63 | N/R | $0.28 | $0.31 |
| | 1847 | $0.28 | $1.68 | $0.30 | $0.30 | N/R |
| | 1848 | $0.28 | $1.95 | $0.28 | $0.30 | N/R |
| | 1849 | $0.26 | $1.63 | $0.28 | $0.30 | N/R |
| Salt petre, per pound | 1825 | $0.09 | $0.09 | N/R | $0.11 | $0.11 |
| | 1826 | $0.08 | $0.08 | N/R | $0.11 | $0.11 |
| | 1827 | $0.08 | $0.08 | N/R | $0.10 | $0.10 |
| | 1828 | $0.09 | $0.08 | N/R | $0.08 | $0.10 |
| | 1829 | $0.10 | $0.10 | N/R | $0.08 | $0.10 |
| | 1830 | $0.09 | $0.10 | N/R | $0.10 | $0.10 |
| | 1831 | $0.12 | $0.11 | N/R | $0.11 | $0.10 |
| | 1832 | $0.10 | $0.09 | N/R | $0.09 | N/R |
| | 1833 | $0.09 | $0.09 | N/R | $0.09 | N/R |
| | 1834 | $0.08 | $0.08 | N/R | $0.08 | $0.11 |
| | 1835 | $0.08 | $0.08 | N/R | $0.10 | $0.11 |
| | 1836 | $0.08 | $0.08 | N/R | $0.10 | $0.11 |
| | 1837 | $0.08 | $0.08 | N/R | $0.09 | $0.11 |
| | 1838 | $0.08 | $0.08 | N/R | $0.09 | $0.12 |
| | 1839 | $0.08 | $0.09 | N/R | $0.09 | $0.10 |
| | 1840 | $0.08 | $0.08 | N/R | $0.09 | $0.10 |
| | 1841 | $0.08 | $0.07 | N/R | $0.09 | $0.08 |
| | 1842 | $0.08 | $0.08 | N/R | $0.09 | $0.08 |
| | 1843 | $0.08 | $0.06 | N/R | $0.09 | $0.08 |
| | 1844 | $0.08 | $0.08 | N/R | $0.09 | $0.08 |
| | 1845 | $0.08 | $0.07 | N/R | N/R | $0.08 |
| | 1846 | $0.08 | $0.07 | N/R | N/R | $0.08 |
| | 1847 | $0.08 | $0.07 | N/R | N/R | $0.08 |
| | 1848 | $0.08 | $0.07 | N/R | N/R | $0.08 |
| | 1849 | $0.08 | $0.07 | N/R | N/R | $0.08 |
| Salt, per bushel | 1825 | $0.530 | $2.500 | $2.380 | $2.500 | $0.325 |
| (New Orleans per sack) | 1826 | $0.480 | $2.430 | $2.120 | $2.500 | $0.280 |
| (Charleston - per four bushels) | 1827 | $0.475 | $2.250 | $2.440 | $2.188 | $0.440 |
| | 1828 | $0.450 | $2.550 | $2.190 | $2.125 | $0.500 |
| | 1829 | $0.480 | $2.500 | $1.750 | $2.375 | $0.500 |
| | 1830 | $0.425 | $2.050 | $1.910 | $2.750 | $0.500 |

| Commodity | Year | Philadelphia Currency | New York Currency | Charleston Currency | New Orleans Currency | Cincinnati Currency |
|---|---|---|---|---|---|---|
| | 1831 | $0.430 | $2.060 | $1.440 | $1.438 | $0.500 |
| | 1832 | $0.465 | $2.130 | $1.810 | $1.600 | $0.475 |
| | 1833 | $0.375 | $1.680 | $1.620 | $1.600 | $0.320 |
| | 1834 | $0.300 | $1.630 | $1.360 | $1.062 | $0.360 |
| | 1835 | $0.390 | $1.690 | $1.500 | $1.250 | $0.325 |
| | 1836 | $0.400 | $2.060 | $1.620 | $1.438 | $0.320 |
| | 1837 | $0.430 | $1.300 | $1.620 | $1.250 | $0.425 |
| | 1838 | $0.435 | $1.660 | $1.410 | $1.142 | $0.500 |
| | 1839 | $0.360 | $1.760 | $1.810 | $1.700 | $0.750 |
| | 1840 | $0.345 | $1.430 | $1.290 | $1.690 | $0.425 |
| | 1841 | $0.310 | $1.580 | $1.400 | $1.380 | $0.305 |
| | 1842 | $0.280 | $1.500 | $1.280 | $1.250 | $0.240 |
| | 1843 | $0.285 | $1.590 | $1.190 | $0.970 | $0.170 |
| | 1844 | $0.290 | $1.440 | $1.280 | $1.180 | $0.240 |
| | 1845 | $0.265 | $1.320 | $1.020 | $1.050 | $0.235 |
| | 1846 | $0.278 | $1.290 | $1.200 | $1.000 | $0.195 |
| | 1847 | $0.192 | $1.250 | $1.150 | $0.680 | $0.215 |
| | 1848 | $0.235 | $1.410 | $1.160 | $0.920 | $0.300 |
| | 1849 | $0.220 | $1.250 | $0.880 | $0.740 | $0.305 |
| Sheeting, per piece | 1825 | $10.75 | $11.50 | N/R | $0.14 | N/R |
| (Philadelphia per piece) | 1826 | $9.75 | $0.13 | N/R | $0.14 | N/R |
| | 1827 | $9.38 | $0.12 | N/R | $0.13 | N/R |
| | 1828 | $8.75 | $0.12 | N/R | $0.12 | N/R |
| | 1829 | $9.12 | $0.10 | N/R | $0.12 | N/R |
| | 1830 | $10.63 | $0.09 | N/R | $0.08 | N/R |
| | 1831 | $10.75 | $0.11 | N/R | $0.11 | N/R |
| | 1832 | $9.38 | $0.10 | N/R | $0.11 | N/R |
| | 1833 | $8.94 | $0.10 | N/R | $0.11 | N/R |
| | 1834 | $8.75 | $0.09 | N/R | $0.08 | N/R |
| | 1835 | $8.88 | $0.10 | N/R | $0.12 | N/R |
| | 1836 | $11.25 | $0.12 | N/R | $0.12 | N/R |
| | 1837 | $10.63 | $0.10 | N/R | $0.14 | N/R |
| | 1838 | $9.88 | $0.09 | N/R | $0.14 | N/R |

## Based Upon US Dollars

| Year | Value of 19th Century Dollar in 2002 US Dollars |
|---|---|
| 1825 | $18.00 |
| 1830 | $19.00 |
| 1835 | $20.00 |
| 1840 | $20.00 |
| 1845 | $23.00 |
| 1849 | $23.00 |

*Calculations are approximate values based upon economic historical data*

| Commodity | Year | Philadelphia Currency | New York Currency | Charleston Currency | New Orleans Currency | Cincinnati Currency |
|---|---|---|---|---|---|---|
| | 1839 | $9.00 | $0.10 | N/R | $0.12 | N/R |
| | 1840 | $9.38 | $0.08 | N/R | $0.09 | N/R |
| | 1841 | $8.88 | $0.08 | N/R | $0.09 | N/R |
| | 1842 | $8.50 | $0.07 | N/R | $0.10 | N/R |
| | 1843 | $8.50 | $0.06 | N/R | $0.10 | N/R |
| | 1844 | $7.50 | $0.08 | N/R | $0.10 | N/R |
| | 1845 | $8.00 | $0.07 | N/R | $0.08 | N/R |
| | 1846 | $8.38 | $0.08 | N/R | $0.08 | N/R |
| | 1847 | $8.50 | $0.08 | N/R | $0.08 | N/R |
| | 1848 | $8.50 | $0.07 | N/R | $0.09 | N/R |
| | 1849 | $8.50 | $0.06 | N/R | $0.10 | N/R |
| Staves, per 1200 units | 1825 | $37.50 | $43.00 | N/R | $16.50 | N/R |
| | 1826 | $37.00 | $42.00 | N/R | $18.00 | N/R |
| | 1827 | $36.00 | $33.50 | N/R | $20.00 | N/R |
| | 1828 | $40.00 | $35.00 | N/R | $25.00 | N/R |
| | 1829 | $38.00 | $32.00 | N/R | $25.00 | N/R |
| | 1830 | $31.00 | $33.50 | N/R | $22.40 | N/R |
| | 1831 | $31.00 | $38.00 | N/R | $21.00 | N/R |
| | 1832 | $37.50 | $38.00 | N/R | $24.50 | N/R |
| | 1833 | $33.00 | $38.00 | N/R | $25.00 | N/R |
| | 1834 | $35.50 | $38.50 | N/R | $30.00 | N/R |
| | 1835 | $32.50 | $46.00 | N/R | $30.00 | N/R |
| | 1836 | $36.50 | $43.00 | N/R | $30.00 | N/R |
| | 1837 | $34.00 | $57.00 | N/R | $30.00 | N/R |
| | 1838 | $33.50 | $42.50 | N/R | $30.00 | N/R |
| | 1839 | $34.00 | $41.50 | N/R | $37.50 | N/R |
| | 1840 | $34.00 | $43.50 | N/R | $35.00 | N/R |
| | 1841 | $35.00 | $43.50 | N/R | $25.00 | N/R |
| | 1842 | $32.50 | $46.50 | N/R | $25.00 | N/R |
| | 1843 | $27.50 | $30.00 | N/R | $25.20 | $11.00 |
| | 1844 | $23.00 | $34.00 | N/R | $26.30 | N/R |
| | 1845 | $19.50 | $40.00 | N/R | $27.30 | N/R |
| | 1846 | $24.00 | $40.00 | N/R | $27.50 | $15.00 |
| | 1847 | $16.50 | $40.00 | N/R | $27.50 | $20.00 |
| | 1848 | $20.00 | $45.00 | N/R | $27.50 | $14.00 |
| | 1849 | $22.50 | $45.50 | N/R | $27.50 | $15.00 |
| Steel, per pound | 1825 | $0.13 | $0.12 | N/R | $0.17 | $0.11 |
| | 1826 | $0.13 | $0.12 | N/R | $0.17 | $0.09 |
| | 1827 | $0.12 | $0.12 | N/R | $0.16 | $0.09 |
| | 1828 | $0.12 | $0.12 | N/R | $0.14 | $0.08 |
| | 1829 | $0.12 | $0.12 | N/R | $0.14 | $0.08 |
| | 1830 | $0.12 | $0.12 | N/R | $0.14 | $0.08 |
| | 1831 | $0.12 | $0.12 | N/R | $0.14 | $0.08 |
| | 1832 | $0.12 | $0.12 | N/R | $0.14 | N/R |
| | 1833 | $0.12 | $0.12 | N/R | $0.14 | N/R |
| | 1834 | $0.12 | $0.12 | N/R | $0.14 | $0.08 |
| | 1835 | $0.14 | $0.12 | N/R | $0.14 | $0.08 |
| | 1836 | $0.13 | $0.12 | N/R | $0.12 | $0.08 |

| Commodity | Year | Philadelphia Currency | New York Currency | Charleston Currency | New Orleans Currency | Cincinnati Currency |
|---|---|---|---|---|---|---|
| | 1837 | $0.13 | $0.12 | N/R | $0.12 | $0.08 |
| | 1838 | $0.13 | $0.12 | N/R | $0.12 | $0.08 |
| | 1839 | $0.13 | $0.12 | N/R | $0.12 | N/R |
| | 1840 | $0.13 | $0.12 | N/R | $0.12 | $0.12 |
| | 1841 | $0.13 | $0.12 | N/R | $0.12 | $0.10 |
| | 1842 | $0.13 | $0.12 | N/R | $0.12 | $0.10 |
| | 1843 | $0.13 | $0.12 | N/R | $0.12 | $0.10 |
| | 1844 | $0.13 | $0.12 | N/R | $0.11 | $0.06 |
| | 1845 | $0.13 | $0.12 | N/R | $0.10 | $0.06 |
| | 1846 | $0.12 | $0.12 | N/R | $0.10 | $0.06 |
| | 1847 | $0.12 | $0.12 | N/R | $0.11 | $0.06 |
| | 1848 | $0.12 | $0.12 | N/R | $0.10 | $0.06 |
| | 1849 | $0.12 | $0.12 | N/R | $0.10 | $0.06 |
| Sugar, per hundredweight | 1825 | $11.75 | $8.25 | $10.50 | $6.90 | $12.25 |
| | 1826 | $11.75 | $8.50 | $9.00 | $6.38 | $9.50 |
| | 1827 | $9.75 | $7.50 | $8.50 | $6.88 | $8.50 |
| | 1828 | $10.13 | $7.50 | $9.20 | $7.75 | $9.00 |
| | 1829 | $9.00 | $7.00 | $8.20 | $7.12 | $7.75 |
| | 1830 | $8.50 | $8.00 | $9.20 | $6.88 | $9.50 |
| | 1831 | $7.50 | $6.00 | $6.90 | $4.88 | $7.50 |
| | 1832 | $8.00 | $6.50 | $6.80 | $5.38 | $7.25 |
| | 1833 | $7.75 | $6.00 | $7.20 | $5.88 | $7.25 |
| | 1834 | $8.50 | $5.00 | $9.00 | $5.50 | $8.25 |
| | 1835 | $9.32 | $7.00 | $8.20 | $6.88 | $9.50 |
| | 1836 | $10.88 | $9.00 | $12.00 | $11.25 | $13.75 |
| | 1837 | $7.88 | $6.00 | $8.50 | $5.25 | $8.50 |
| | 1838 | $8.62 | $6.50 | $10.00 | $5.75 | $7.25 |
| | 1839 | $8.25 | $7.00 | $8.50 | $5.75 | $8.25 |
| | 1840 | $7.25 | $5.00 | $6.50 | $3.38 | $5.62 |
| | 1841 | $7.38 | $6.00 | $8.20 | $5.38 | $7.00 |
| | 1842 | $5.75 | $3.50 | $5.00 | $3.75 | $5.25 |
| | 1843 | $6.50 | $5.00 | $6.20 | $4.62 | $5.25 |
| | 1844 | $7.06 | $6.50 | $7.60 | $6.38 | $7.12 |

## Based Upon US Dollars

| Year | Value of 19th Century Dollar in 2002 US Dollars |
|---|---|
| 1825 | $18.00 |
| 1830 | $19.00 |
| 1835 | $20.00 |
| 1840 | $20.00 |
| 1845 | $23.00 |
| 1849 | $23.00 |

*Calculations are approximate values based upon economic historical data*

| Commodity | Year | Philadelphia Currency | New York Currency | Charleston Currency | New Orleans Currency | Cincinnati Currency |
|-----------|------|----------------------|-------------------|---------------------|----------------------|---------------------|
| | 1845 | $8.38 | $6.00 | $7.00 | $5.88 | $6.75 |
| | 1846 | $7.25 | $6.00 | $6.90 | $5.19 | $6.38 |
| | 1847 | $6.81 | $6.50 | $7.50 | $6.25 | $7.88 |
| | 1848 | $4.62 | $4.00 | $5.70 | $3.25 | $4.12 |
| | 1849 | $6.06 | $4.50 | $5.70 | $4.00 | $4.50 |
| Tallow, per pound | 1825 | $0.08 | $0.08 | $0.10 | $0.08 | $0.06 |
| | 1826 | $0.08 | $0.09 | $0.12 | $0.08 | $0.08 |
| | 1827 | $0.09 | $0.09 | $0.12 | $0.09 | $0.08 |
| | 1828 | $0.08 | $0.08 | $0.10 | $0.08 | $0.08 |
| | 1829 | $0.06 | $0.06 | $0.08 | $0.08 | $0.06 |
| | 1830 | $0.06 | $0.06 | $0.08 | $0.06 | $0.07 |
| | 1831 | $0.08 | $0.09 | $0.08 | $0.07 | $0.08 |
| | 1832 | $0.08 | $0.08 | $0.10 | $0.10 | $0.08 |
| | 1833 | $0.09 | $0.10 | $0.11 | $0.08 | $0.08 |
| | 1834 | $0.08 | $0.07 | $0.09 | $0.09 | $0.08 |
| | 1835 | $0.08 | $0.08 | $0.08 | $0.08 | $0.08 |
| | 1836 | $0.10 | $0.10 | $0.10 | $0.09 | $0.09 |
| | 1837 | $0.10 | $0.11 | $0.10 | $0.09 | $0.10 |
| | 1838 | $0.10 | $0.08 | $0.12 | $0.09 | $0.08 |
| | 1839 | $0.12 | $0.12 | $0.12 | $0.12 | $0.10 |
| | 1840 | $0.09 | $0.08 | $0.12 | $0.09 | $0.10 |
| | 1841 | $0.09 | $0.07 | $0.12 | $0.09 | $0.08 |
| | 1842 | $0.07 | $0.08 | $0.12 | $0.07 | $0.05 |
| | 1843 | $0.07 | $0.07 | $0.08 | $0.06 | $0.05 |
| | 1844 | $0.07 | $0.06 | $0.08 | $0.06 | $0.06 |
| | 1845 | $0.07 | $0.06 | $0.08 | $0.06 | $0.06 |
| | 1846 | $0.07 | $0.07 | $0.08 | $0.06 | $0.06 |
| | 1847 | $0.09 | $0.08 | $0.08 | $0.08 | $0.08 |
| | 1848 | $0.08 | $0.08 | N/R | $0.07 | $0.08 |
| | 1849 | $0.08 | $0.08 | N/R | $0.07 | $0.07 |
| Tea, per pound | 1825 | $0.32 | $1.13 | $1.15 | $1.05 | $1.16 |
| | 1826 | $0.95 | $0.96 | $1.12 | $1.05 | $0.98 |
| | 1827 | $1.10 | $1.00 | $1.08 | $1.05 | $0.92 |
| | 1828 | $1.00 | $0.92 | $1.05 | $1.05 | $0.98 |
| | 1829 | $0.90 | $0.96 | $1.02 | $1.05 | $0.95 |
| | 1830 | $0.88 | $0.88 | $0.92 | $1.05 | $0.90 |
| | 1831 | $0.90 | $0.90 | $1.00 | $1.05 | $0.98 |
| | 1832 | $0.75 | $0.88 | $0.84 | $1.00 | $0.90 |
| | 1833 | $0.68 | $0.70 | $0.84 | $0.89 | $0.92 |
| | 1834 | $0.64 | $0.61 | $0.76 | $0.84 | $0.72 |
| | 1835 | $0.52 | $0.68 | $0.65 | $0.65 | $0.70 |
| | 1836 | $0.55 | $0.64 | $0.65 | $0.70 | $0.55 |
| | 1837 | $0.56 | $0.64 | $0.65 | $0.62 | $0.52 |
| | 1838 | $0.54 | $0.57 | $0.68 | $0.61 | $0.50 |
| | 1839 | $0.46 | $0.62 | $0.78 | $0.61 | $0.50 |
| | 1840 | $0.49 | $0.62 | $0.78 | $0.61 | $0.62 |
| | 1841 | $0.78 | $0.68 | $0.78 | $0.70 | $0.70 |
| | 1842 | $0.60 | $0.58 | $0.90 | $0.70 | $0.65 |

| Commodity | Year | Philadelphia Currency | New York Currency | Charleston Currency | New Orleans Currency | Cincinnati Currency |
|---|---|---|---|---|---|---|
| | 1843 | $0.59 | $0.60 | $0.90 | $0.48 | $0.58 |
| | 1844 | $0.72 | $0.60 | $0.90 | $0.48 | $0.58 |
| | 1845 | $0.72 | $0.62 | $0.90 | $0.48 | $0.58 |
| | 1846 | $0.66 | $0.56 | $0.92 | $0.45 | $0.58 |
| | 1847 | $0.66 | $0.50 | $0.85 | $0.45 | N/R |
| | 1848 | $0.66 | $0.49 | $0.85 | $0.72 | $0.60 |
| | 1849 | $0.66 | $0.46 | N/R | $0.72 | $0.52 |
| Tobacco, per hundredweight | 1825 | $0.08 | $0.07 | $5.50 | $6.50 | $6.00 |
| *(Philadelphia & New York - per pound)* | 1826 | $0.07 | $0.06 | $5.00 | $3.62 | $8.50 |
| | 1827 | $0.06 | $0.04 | $4.00 | $3.75 | $6.00 |
| | 1828 | $0.05 | $0.04 | $4.00 | $4.62 | $6.50 |
| | 1829 | $0.06 | $0.06 | $4.50 | $4.50 | $6.50 |
| | 1830 | $0.05 | $0.06 | $4.75 | $4.12 | $6.50 |
| | 1831 | $0.04 | $0.04 | $4.75 | $3.75 | $5.00 |
| | 1832 | $0.05 | $0.04 | $4.75 | $4.25 | $5.00 |
| | 1833 | $0.06 | $0.04 | $5.50 | $5.00 | $5.50 |
| | 1834 | $0.08 | $0.06 | $5.50 | $5.50 | $7.00 |
| | 1835 | $0.08 | $0.08 | $5.50 | $7.62 | $9.25 |
| | 1836 | $0.10 | $0.08 | $8.75 | $8.00 | $11.75 |
| | 1837 | $0.06 | $0.06 | $5.50 | $4.00 | $8.25 |
| | 1838 | $0.06 | $0.07 | $4.50 | $7.50 | $7.50 |
| | 1839 | $0.14 | $0.13 | $9.50 | $13.50 | $13.75 |
| | 1840 | $0.08 | $0.08 | $9.50 | $7.50 | $8.88 |
| | 1841 | $0.08 | $0.10 | $9.75 | $9.50 | $7.50 |
| | 1842 | $0.05 | $0.04 | $7.75 | $5.38 | $6.00 |
| | 1843 | $0.05 | $0.05 | $6.75 | $3.50 | $4.50 |
| | 1844 | $0.05 | $0.04 | $6.75 | $3.20 | $4.50 |
| | 1845 | $0.05 | $0.04 | $6.75 | $3.80 | $5.75 |
| | 1846 | $0.08 | $0.05 | $6.25 | $4.20 | $5.75 |
| | 1847 | $0.06 | $0.05 | N/R | $3.50 | $6.00 |
| | 1848 | $0.07 | $0.06 | N/R | $4.10 | $5.75 |
| | 1849 | $0.05 | $0.06 | N/R | $5.50 | $6.25 |

## Based Upon US Dollars

| Year | Value of 19th Century Dollar in 2002 US Dollars |
|---|---|
| 1825 | $18.00 |
| 1830 | $19.00 |
| 1835 | $20.00 |
| 1840 | $20.00 |
| 1845 | $23.00 |
| 1849 | $23.00 |

*Calculations are approximate values based upon economic historical data*

| Commodity | Year | Philadelphia Currency | New York Currency | Charleston Currency | New Orleans Currency | Cincinnati Currency |
|---|---|---|---|---|---|---|
| Turpentine, per gallon | 1825 | $3.00 | N/R | $3.00 | $0.68 | $1.12 |
| *(Philadelphia and Charleston per barrel)* | 1826 | $2.15 | $0.31 | $2.00 | $0.52 | $1.00 |
| | 1827 | $2.62 | $0.43 | $2.38 | $0.42 | $0.88 |
| | 1828 | $2.50 | $0.44 | $2.25 | $0.42 | $1.12 |
| | 1829 | $2.50 | $0.39 | $2.75 | $0.42 | $0.84 |
| | 1830 | $2.12 | $0.31 | $2.25 | $0.42 | $1.00 |
| | 1831 | $2.25 | $0.29 | $2.19 | $0.33 | N/R |
| | 1832 | $2.25 | $0.39 | $2.25 | $0.48 | N/R |
| | 1833 | $2.31 | $0.40 | $2.25 | $0.45 | N/R |
| | 1834 | $2.25 | $0.50 | $2.75 | $0.60 | N/R |
| | 1835 | $2.94 | $0.49 | $3.00 | $0.63 | N/R |
| | 1836 | $4.12 | $0.65 | $5.00 | $0.85 | N/R |
| | 1837 | $2.50 | $0.40 | $2.88 | $0.66 | N/R |
| | 1838 | $2.19 | $0.30 | $2.12 | $0.48 | N/R |
| | 1839 | $3.03 | $0.35 | $2.12 | $0.55 | N/R |
| | 1840 | $2.56 | $0.27 | $2.12 | $0.42 | N/R |
| | 1841 | $2.75 | $0.29 | $2.12 | $0.44 | N/R |
| | 1842 | $2.88 | $0.30 | $2.12 | $0.42 | N/R |
| | 1843 | $2.75 | $0.36 | $2.00 | $0.39 | $0.69 |
| | 1844 | $2.62 | $0.34 | $2.00 | $0.36 | $0.62 |
| | 1845 | $3.00 | $0.42 | N/R | $0.52 | $0.61 |
| | 1846 | $4.25 | $0.53 | N/R | $0.67 | $0.82 |
| | 1847 | $3.25 | $0.43 | N/R | $0.52 | $0.65 |
| | 1848 | $2.44 | $0.35 | $2.55 | $0.40 | $0.55 |
| | 1849 | $2.13 | $0.34 | $2.25 | $0.40 | $0.50 |
| Whale Oil, per gallon | 1825 | $0.31 | $0.29 | N/R | $0.35 | N/R |
| | 1826 | $0.30 | $0.27 | N/R | $0.32 | N/R |
| | 1827 | $0.29 | $0.35 | N/R | $0.38 | N/R |
| | 1828 | $0.32 | $0.32 | N/R | $0.45 | N/R |
| | 1829 | $0.29 | $0.29 | N/R | $0.36 | N/R |
| | 1830 | $0.32 | $0.30 | N/R | $0.38 | N/R |
| | 1831 | $0.36 | $0.32 | N/R | $0.38 | N/R |
| | 1832 | $0.30 | $0.26 | N/R | $0.36 | N/R |
| | 1833 | $0.32 | $0.26 | N/R | $0.22 | N/R |
| | 1834 | $0.33 | $0.27 | N/R | $0.42 | N/R |
| | 1835 | $0.48 | $0.38 | N/R | $0.45 | N/R |
| | 1836 | $0.50 | $0.42 | N/R | $0.56 | N/R |
| | 1837 | $0.44 | $0.33 | N/R | $0.64 | N/R |
| | 1838 | $0.36 | $0.33 | N/R | $0.50 | N/R |
| | 1839 | $0.42 | $0.38 | N/R | $0.50 | N/R |
| | 1840 | $0.39 | $0.33 | N/R | $0.56 | N/R |
| | 1841 | $0.38 | $0.32 | N/R | $0.56 | N/R |
| | 1842 | $0.42 | $0.33 | N/R | $0.45 | N/R |
| | 1843 | $0.38 | $0.31 | N/R | $0.55 | $0.58 |
| | 1844 | $0.40 | $0.35 | N/R | $0.49 | $0.65 |
| | 1845 | $0.38 | $0.34 | N/R | $0.52 | $0.65 |
| | 1846 | $0.38 | $0.35 | N/R | $0.45 | N/R |
| | 1847 | $0.39 | $0.34 | N/R | $0.55 | N/R |
| | 1848 | $0.37 | $0.31 | N/R | $0.60 | $0.60 |
| | 1849 | $0.38 | $0.36 | N/R | $0.60 | $0.60 |

| Commodity | Year | Philadelphia Currency | New York Currency | Charleston Currency | New Orleans Currency | Cincinnati Currency |
|---|---|---|---|---|---|---|
| Wheat, per bushel | 1825 | $1.24 | $1.06 | N/R | N/R | $0.40 |
| | 1826 | $0.85 | $0.73 | N/R | N/R | $0.42 |
| | 1827 | $1.00 | $0.93 | N/R | N/R | $0.40 |
| | 1828 | $0.98 | $0.98 | N/R | N/R | $0.55 |
| | 1829 | $1.45 | $1.39 | N/R | N/R | $0.81 |
| | 1830 | $1.01 | $1.02 | N/R | N/R | $0.50 |
| | 1831 | $1.18 | $1.25 | N/R | N/R | $0.48 |
| | 1832 | $1.10 | $1.08 | N/R | N/R | $0.75 |
| | 1833 | $1.11 | $1.14 | N/R | N/R | $0.65 |
| | 1834 | $1.10 | $1.00 | N/R | N/R | $0.51 |
| | 1835 | $1.27 | $1.38 | N/R | N/R | $0.72 |
| | 1836 | $1.37 | $1.39 | N/R | N/R | $0.90 |
| | 1837 | $2.05 | $1.60 | N/R | N/R | $0.98 |
| | 1838 | $1.67 | $1.69 | N/R | N/R | $1.03 |
| | 1839 | $1.55 | $1.32 | N/R | N/R | $1.07 |
| | 1840 | $0.92 | $1.03 | $1.04 | $0.75 | $0.53 |
| | 1841 | $0.96 | $0.98 | N/R | $0.70 | $0.68 |
| | 1842 | $1.31 | $1.23 | N/R | $0.98 | $0.82 |
| | 1843 | $0.92 | $1.03 | N/R | $0.74 | $0.52 |
| | 1844 | $1.01 | $1.09 | N/R | $0.90 | $0.75 |
| | 1845 | $0.96 | $1.03 | N/R | $0.81 | $0.75 |
| | 1846 | $0.96 | $1.08 | N/R | $0.65 | $0.62 |
| | 1847 | $1.75 | $1.50 | N/R | $1.10 | $0.90 |
| | 1848 | $1.40 | $1.28 | N/R | $0.72 | $0.88 |
| | 1849 | $1.06 | $1.25 | N/R | $0.81 | $0.71 |
| Whisky, per gallon | 1825 | $0.26 | $0.26 | $0.29 | $0.24 | $0.16 |
| | 1826 | $0.28 | $0.28 | $0.34 | $0.31 | $0.24 |
| | 1827 | $0.29 | $0.30 | $0.33 | $0.26 | $0.20 |
| | 1828 | $0.21 | $0.22 | $0.23 | $0.21 | $0.16 |
| | 1829 | $0.22 | $0.22 | $0.25 | $0.25 | $0.20 |
| | 1830 | $0.21 | $0.22 | $0.24 | $0.24 | $0.17 |
| | 1831 | $0.30 | $0.28 | $0.34 | $0.31 | $0.28 |
| | 1832 | $0.29 | $0.26 | $0.30 | $0.34 | $0.28 |

## Based Upon US Dollars

| Year | Value of 19th Century Dollar in 2002 US Dollars |
|---|---|
| 1825 | $18.00 |
| 1830 | $19.00 |
| 1835 | $20.00 |
| 1840 | $20.00 |
| 1845 | $23.00 |
| 1849 | $23.00 |

*Calculations are approximate values based upon economic historical data*

| Commodity | Year | Philadelphia Currency | New York Currency | Charleston Currency | New Orleans Currency | Cincinnati Currency |
|---|---|---|---|---|---|---|
| | 1833 | $0.30 | $0.30 | $0.34 | $0.30 | $0.26 |
| | 1834 | $0.21 | $0.22 | $0.26 | $0.23 | $0.17 |
| | 1835 | $0.34 | $0.32 | $0.36 | $0.45 | $0.37 |
| | 1836 | $0.35 | $0.36 | $0.40 | $0.36 | $0.28 |
| | 1837 | $0.33 | $0.32 | $0.46 | $0.28 | $0.22 |
| | 1838 | $0.32 | $0.32 | $0.41 | $0.34 | $0.29 |
| | 1839 | $0.40 | $0.36 | $0.36 | $0.44 | $0.42 |
| | 1840 | $0.22 | $0.22 | $0.25 | $0.24 | $0.20 |
| | 1841 | $0.19 | $0.20 | $0.24 | $0.18 | $0.16 |
| | 1842 | $0.17 | $0.18 | $0.20 | $0.14 | $0.13 |
| | 1843 | $0.20 | $0.20 | $0.20 | $0.16 | $0.14 |
| | 1844 | $0.22 | $0.22 | $0.22 | $0.19 | $0.18 |
| | 1845 | $0.21 | $0.23 | $0.26 | $0.20 | $0.19 |
| | 1846 | $0.20 | $0.21 | $0.24 | $0.17 | $0.16 |
| | 1847 | $0.30 | $0.29 | $0.24 | $0.20 | $0.18 |
| | 1848 | $0.22 | $0.25 | $0.21 | $0.16 | $0.14 |
| | 1849 | $0.22 | $0.22 | $0.23 | $0.17 | $0.15 |
| Wine, per gallon | 1825 | $3.00 | $2.75 | N/R | $0.72 | $3.50 |
| | 1826 | $2.75 | $2.75 | N/R | $0.60 | $4.00 |
| | 1827 | $2.75 | $2.75 | N/R | $0.75 | $2.62 |
| | 1828 | $2.75 | $2.75 | N/R | $0.52 | $3.75 |
| | 1829 | $2.38 | $1.94 | N/R | $0.55 | $3.50 |
| | 1830 | $2.12 | $2.13 | N/R | $0.56 | $3.25 |
| | 1831 | $2.12 | $1.88 | N/R | $0.58 | $3.00 |
| | 1832 | $2.12 | $1.56 | N/R | $0.56 | $3.00 |
| | 1833 | $2.12 | $1.69 | $2.50 | $0.51 | $2.88 |
| | 1834 | $2.12 | $1.56 | $2.50 | $0.52 | $3.47 |
| | 1835 | $2.12 | $1.69 | $2.50 | $0.50 | $3.50 |
| | 1836 | $2.25 | $1.63 | $2.50 | $0.47 | $4.00 |
| | 1837 | $2.25 | $1.63 | $2.25 | $0.45 | $4.00 |
| | 1838 | $2.25 | $1.63 | $2.25 | $0.44 | $3.00 |
| | 1839 | $2.25 | $2.00 | $2.25 | $0.39 | N/R |
| | 1840 | $2.25 | $2.00 | $2.25 | $0.32 | $3.75 |
| | 1841 | $2.25 | $1.90 | $2.25 | $0.32 | $3.75 |
| | 1842 | $2.06 | $1.13 | $2.25 | $0.29 | $3.25 |
| | 1843 | $2.06 | $1.13 | $2.25 | $0.39 | $3.25 |
| | 1844 | $2.06 | $1.75 | $2.25 | $0.45 | $2.62 |
| | 1845 | $2.06 | $1.30 | N/R | $0.48 | $2.62 |
| | 1846 | $2.06 | $1.55 | N/R | $0.44 | $2.62 |
| | 1847 | $2.06 | $1.88 | N/R | $0.52 | N/R |
| | 1848 | $2.06 | $1.80 | N/R | $0.52 | $2.68 |
| | 1849 | $2.00 | $1.83 | N/R | $0.52 | $2.00 |
| Wool, per pound | 1825 | $0.52 | $0.34 | N/R | N/R | $0.38 |
| | 1826 | $0.52 | $0.29 | N/R | N/R | N/R |
| | 1827 | $0.32 | $0.25 | N/R | N/R | N/R |
| | 1828 | $0.28 | $0.25 | N/R | N/R | N/R |
| | 1829 | $0.38 | $0.22 | N/R | N/R | N/R |
| | 1830 | $0.38 | $0.19 | N/R | N/R | $0.25 |

| Commodity | Year | Philadelphia Currency | New York Currency | Charleston Currency | New Orleans Currency | Cincinnati Currency |
|---|---|---|---|---|---|---|
| | 1831 | $0.59 | $0.22 | N/R | N/R | N/R |
| | 1832 | $0.48 | $0.30 | N/R | N/R | N/R |
| | 1833 | $0.56 | $0.32 | N/R | N/R | N/R |
| | 1834 | $0.48 | $0.32 | N/R | N/R | $0.28 |
| | 1835 | $0.55 | $0.32 | N/R | N/R | $0.25 |
| | 1836 | $0.68 | $0.45 | N/R | N/R | $0.25 |
| | 1837 | $0.60 | $0.45 | N/R | N/R | $0.38 |
| | 1838 | $0.44 | $0.30 | N/R | N/R | $0.35 |
| | 1839 | $0.51 | $0.38 | N/R | N/R | N/R |
| | 1840 | $0.43 | $0.32 | N/R | N/R | $0.28 |
| | 1841 | $0.41 | $0.28 | N/R | N/R | $0.28 |
| | 1842 | $0.34 | $0.19 | N/R | N/R | $0.25 |
| | 1843 | $0.30 | $0.19 | N/R | N/R | $0.16 |
| | 1844 | $0.41 | $0.28 | N/R | N/R | $0.22 |
| | 1845 | $0.38 | $0.29 | N/R | N/R | $0.20 |
| | 1846 | $0.34 | $0.27 | N/R | N/R | $0.20 |
| | 1847 | $0.34 | $0.26 | N/R | N/R | $0.18 |
| | 1848 | $0.36 | $0.28 | N/R | N/R | $0.18 |
| | 1849 | $0.38 | $0.30 | N/R | N/R | $0.22 |

### Based Upon US Dollars

| Year | Value of 19th Century Dollar in 2002 US Dollars |
|---|---|
| 1825 | $18.00 |
| 1830 | $19.00 |
| 1835 | $20.00 |
| 1840 | $20.00 |
| 1845 | $23.00 |
| 1849 | $23.00 |

*Calculations are approximate values based upon economic historical data*

# SELECTED PRICES 1825-1849

| Item | Data Source | Description | Price |
|------|-------------|-------------|-------|
| **Alcohol** | | | |
| Brandy | Inventory of John Adair (1831) | Ten gallon cask of French brandy in Franklin County, Indiana, 1831 | $8.00 |
| Cordial | Inventory of Doctor Burwell Chick (1847) | Bottle of cordial in Greenville County, South Carolina, 1847 | $0.37 |
| Gin | Inventory of John Adair (1831) | Quart of gin in Franklin County, Indiana, 1831 | $0.50 |
| Port | Inventory of Doctor Burwell Chick (1847) | Bottle of port in Greenville County, South Carolina, 1847 | $0.11 |
| Rum | Inventory of John Adair (1831) | Quart of rum in Franklin County, Indiana, 1831 | $0.35 |
| Spirits | Pace & McGee, The life and Times of Ridgeway, Virginia. | Half pint of spirits charged in a tavern in Ridgeway, Virginia, 1849 | 6¼ cents |
| Whiskey | Geoffery Ward, The West (1996) | Pint of water downed whiskey sold in the South Pass, Wyoming 1837 | $4.00 |
| Wine | Inventory of Chilon Foster (1830) | Barrell of currant wine in Franklin County, Indiana, 1830 | $12.00 |
| **Apparel - Children** | | | |
| Hose | Humphery Clark & Co. Account Book (1838) | Pair of misses white cotton hose in Charleston, South Carolina, 1838 | $0.21 |
| Shoes | Inventory of William Servey (1836) | Pair cacks youths brogans in Uxbridge, Massachusetts, 1836 | $0.45 |
| **Apparel - Men** | | | |
| Boots | Inventory of Doane Atwood (1829) | Pair of calf skin boots in Sturbridge, Massachusetts, 1829 | $1.50 |
| Boots | Inventory of Coolidge Perry (1836) | Pair of thick boots in Milford, Massachusetts, 1836 | $4.00 |
| Coat | Inventory of Doane Atwood (1829) | Brown coat in Sturbridge, Massachusetts, 1829 | $3.00 |
| Coat | Inventory of John Morrision (1834) | Cloth blue dress coat in Franklin County, Indiana, 1834 | $5.00 |
| Collar | Humphery Clark & Co. Account Book (1838) | Men's shirt collar in Charleston, South Carolina, 1838 | $0.25 |
| Comforter | Inventory of Joseph Cloyes (1833) | Neck Comforter in Worcester, Massachusetts, 1833 | $0.25 |
| Cravat | Inventory of John Morrision (1834) | Cravet in Franklin County, Indiana, 1834 | 18¾ cents |
| Drawers | Inventory of Doane Atwood (1829) | Pair of red drawers in Sturbridge, Massachusetts, 1829 | $0.34 |
| Gloves | Humphery Clark & Co. Account Book (1838) | Pair of beaver gloves in Charleston, South Carolina, 1838 | $0.75 |
| Gloves | Humphery Clark & Co. Account Book (1838) | Pair of mens' buck gloves in Charleston, South Carolina, 1838 | $3.75 |
| Handkerchief | Inventory of Joseph Cloyes (1833) | White cotton handkerchief in Worcester, Massachusetts, 1833 | $0.50 |
| Hat | Inventory of Doane Atwood (1829) | Fur hat in Sturbridge, Massachusetts, 1829 | $1.50 |
| Pantaloons | Inventory of Joseph Cloyes (1833) | Pair checkered kerseymere pantaloons in Worcester, Massachusetts, 1833 | $4.00 |
| Pants | Humphery Clark & Co. Account Book (1838) | Pair of dark blue pants in Charleston, South Carolina, 1838 | $5.04 |

| Item | Data Source | Description | Price |
|---|---|---|---|
| Sash | Inventory of Doane Atwood (1829) | Woollen sash in Sturbridge, Massachusetts, 1829 | $0.16 |
| Shirt | Inventory of John Morrision (1834) | Shirt in Franklin County, Indiana, 1834 | $0.66 |
| Shoes | Inventory of William Servey (1836) | Pair mens narrow strapped black shoes in Uxbridge, Massachusetts, 1836 | $0.67 |
| Shoes | Inventory of William Servey (1836) | Pair thick mens brogans in Uxbridge, Massachusetts, 1836 | $0.75 |
| Spencer | Inventory of Doane Atwood (1829) | Spencer in Sturbridge, Massachusetts, 1829 | $0.33 |
| Stock | Inventory of Joseph Cloyes (1833) | Neck stock in Worcester, Massachusetts, 1833 | $0.33 |
| Stockings | Inventory of Joseph Cloyes (1833) | Short stockings in Worcester, Massachusetts, 1833 | 12½ cents |
| Suspenders | Humphery Clark & Co. Account Book (1838) | Pair of worsted suspenders in Charleston, South Carolina, 1838 | $0.30 |
| Vest | Inventory of Doane Atwood (1829) | Black wool vest in Sturbridge, Massachusetts, 1829 | $1.25 |
| Vest | Humphery Clark & Co. Account Book (1838) | Satin vest in Charleston, South Carolina, 1838 | $3.37 |

## Apparel - Women

| Item | Data Source | Description | Price |
|---|---|---|---|
| Bonnet | Humphery Clark & Co. Account Book (1838) | Bonnet in Charleston, South Carolina, 1838 | $3.00 |
| Cloak | Humphery Clark & Co. Account Book (1838) | Ladies cloak in Charleston, South Carolina, 1838 | $6.25 |
| Gloves | Humphery Clark & Co. Account Book (1838) | Pair of ladies white silk gloves in Charleston, South Carolina, 1838 | $0.42 |
| Handkerchief | Inventory of Joseph Cloyes (1833) | Silk handkerchief in Worcester, Massachusetts, 1833 | $0.33 |
| Hose | Humphery Clark & Co. Account Book (1838) | Pair of ladies Irish cotton hose in Charleston, South Carolina, 1838 | $0.20 |
| Hose | Humphery Clark & Co. Account Book (1838) | Pair of ladies China silk hose in Charleston, South Carolina, 1838 | $18.00 |
| Pocketbook | Inventory of Joseph Milholland (1830) | Pocketbook and purse in Franklin County, Indiana, 1830 | $0.25 |
| Shawl | Humphery Clark & Co. Account Book (1838) | Thick woolen shawl in Charleston, South Carolina, 1838 | $1.33 |

### Based Upon US Dollars

| Year | Value of 19th Century Dollar in 2002 US Dollars |
|---|---|
| 1825 | $18.00 |
| 1830 | $19.00 |
| 1835 | $20.00 |
| 1840 | $20.00 |
| 1845 | $23.00 |
| 1849 | $23.00 |

*Calculations are approximate values based upon economic historical data*

| Item | Data Source | Description | Price |
|------|-------------|-------------|-------|
| Shoes | Inventory of William Servey (1836) | Pair womens shutees black grain shoes in Uxbridge, Massachusetts, 1836 | $0.70 |
| Skirt | Humphery Clark & Co. Account Book (1838) | Cordide skirt in Charleston, South Carolina, 1838 | 37½ cents |
| Slippers | Inventory of William Servey (1836) | Womens slippers in Uxbridge, Massachusetts, 1836 | $0.33 |

**Commodities**

| Item | Data Source | Description | Price |
|------|-------------|-------------|-------|
| Bran | Inventory of Doctor Burwell Chick (1847) | Bushel of bran in Greenville County, South Carolina, 1847 | $0.08 |
| Corn | Inventory of Doane Atwood (1829) | Bushel of corn in the ear in Sturbridge, Massachusetts, 1829 | 62½ cents |
| Corn | Inventory of Doctor Burwell Chick (1847) | Barrel of corn in Greenville County, South Carolina, 1847 | $1.40 |
| Field Ashes | Herman Stickney's Ash Book (1825) | Cost for one bushel of wood ashes burned in the fields | $0.06 |
| Flour | Inventory of Doctor Burwell Chick (1847) | Hundred pounds of flower in Greenville County, South Carolina, 1847 | $2.37½ |
| Fodder | Inventory of George Spillers (1833) | 100 bundles of blade fodder in Greenville County, South Carolina, 1833 | $0.75 |
| Hay | Inventory of Doane Atwood (1829) | Stack of hay in Sturbridge, Massachusetts, 1829 | $5.00 |
| Iron | Inventory of Doctor Burwell Chick (1847) | Pound of iron in Greenville County, South Carolina, 1847 | $0.02 |
| Lead | Inventory of George Spillers (1833) | Pound of lead in Greenville County, South Carolina, 1833 | $0.10 |
| Malt | Inventory of Doctor Burwell Chick (1847) | Barrel of malt in Greenville County, South Carolina, 1847 | $1.25 |
| Molasses | Inventory of Doctor Burwell Chick (1847) | Gallon of molasses in Greenville County, South Carolina, 1847 | $0.58 |
| Peas | Inventory of William Blassingame (1846) | Bushel of peas in Greenville County, South Carolina, 1846 | $0.78 |
| Potatoes | Inventory of Doane Atwood (1829) | Bushel of potatoes in Sturbridge, Massachusetts, 1829 | 12½ cents |
| Rice | Inventory of Doctor Burwell Chick (1847) | Lot of rice in Greenville County, South Carolina, 1847 | $4.00 |
| Salt | Historical Gazette (1999) | Bushel of salt sold in the Pacific Northwest in 1846 | $2.00 |
| Sugar | Inventory of Doctor Burwell Chick (1847) | Pound of sugar in Greenville County, South Carolina, 1847 | $0.12 |
| Wheat | Historical Gazette (1999) | Bushel of wheat sold in the Pacific Northwest in 1846 | $0.60 |
| Wood | Inventory of John Adair (1831) | Cord of wood in Franklin County, Indiana, 1831 | $0.75 |
| Wool | Inventory of Doane Atwood (1829) | Pound of woolen rools in Sturbridge, Massachusetts, 1829 | $0.50 |

**Entertainment**

| Item | Data Source | Description | Price |
|------|-------------|-------------|-------|
| Backgammon | Inventory of William Blassingame (1846) | Back gammon box in Greenville County, South Carolina, 1846 | $0.75 |
| Billiards | Inventory of Doctor Burwell Chick (1847) | Billiard table in Greenville County, South Carolina, 1847 | $81.00 |
| Concert | McKearin, American Bottles & Flasks (1978) | Ticket for Jenny Lind's first performance in New York City, 1848 | $225.00 |
| Ticket | Laurence A. Johnson, Over The Counter and On The Shelf 1620-1920 (1961) | Cost for a box at the opera in New York City in 1835 | $1.00 |

| Item | Data Source | Description | Price |
|------|-------------|-------------|-------|
| Ticket | Laurence A. Johnson, Over The Counter and On The Shelf 1620-1920 (1961) | Cost for a gallery seat at the opera in New York City in 1835 | $0.25 |

### Fabrics & Sewing Materials

| Item | Data Source | Description | Price |
|------|-------------|-------------|-------|
| Buttons | Humphery Clark & Co. Account Book (1838) | Gross of pearl shirt buttons in Charleston, South Carolina, 1838 | $0.25 |
| Carpet | Inventory of Dr. William Baker (1838) | Yard of Venetian carpet in Wilmington, Delaware, 1838 | $0.50 |
| Fabric | Inventory of George Spillers (1833) | Yard of brown hollins in Greenville County, South Carolina, 1833 | 37½ cents |
| Fabric | Geoffery Ward, The West (1996) | Scarlet cloth sold to Indian woman in the South Pass, Wyoming, 1837 | $6.00 |
| Loom | Inventory of George Spillers (1833) | Loom in Greenville County, South Carolina, 1833 | $6.50 |
| Matting | Inventory of Aaron Bayard (1849) | Yard of matting in New Castle County, Delaware, 1849 | $0.10 |
| Quilting Frame | Inventory of John Adair (1831) | Pair of quilting frames in Franklin County, Indiana, 1831 | $0.50 |
| Ribbon | Humphery Clark & Co. Account Book (1838) | Piece of rich cap ribbon in Charleston, South Carolina, 1838 | $1.00 |
| Thread | Humphery Clark & Co. Account Book (1838) | Pound of linen thread in Charleston, South Carolina, 1838 | 1.37½ cents |

### Farm Equipment & Tools

| Item | Data Source | Description | Price |
|------|-------------|-------------|-------|
| Adz | Inventory of Chilon Foster (1830) | Foot adz in Franklin County, Indiana, 1830 | $1.50 |
| Auger | Inventory of William Blassingame (1846) | Auger in Greenville County, South Carolina, 1846 | $0.25 |
| Axe | Inventory of William Blassingame (1846) | Hand ax in Greenville County, South Carolina, 1846 | 62½ cents |
| Bailer | Inventory of Doane Atwood (1829) | Sheet iron bailer in Sturbridge, Massachusetts, 1829 | $0.50 |
| Bee gum | Inventory of George Spillers (1833) | Bee gum in Greenville County, South Carolina, 1833 | 6¼ cents |
| Bee Hive | Inventory of Royston Betts Jr (1841) | Bee hive in Fredericksburg County in Virginia, 1841 | $1.50 |

## Based Upon US Dollars

| Year | Value of 19th Century Dollar in 2002 US Dollars |
|------|------------------------------------------------|
| 1825 | $18.00 |
| 1830 | $19.00 |
| 1835 | $20.00 |
| 1840 | $20.00 |
| 1845 | $23.00 |
| 1849 | $23.00 |

*Calculations are approximate values based upon economic historical data*

| Item | Data Source | Description | Price |
|---|---|---|---|
| Bee Stand | Inventory of George Spillers (1833) | Bee stand in Greenville County, South Carolina, 1833 | $1.00 |
| Box | Inventory of Dr. William Baker (1838) | Cutting box in Wilmington, Delaware, 1838 | $1.00 |
| Bucket | Inventory of Chilon Foster (1830) | Slop bucket in Franklin County, Indiana, 1830 | $0.25 |
| Chain | Inventory of Royston Betts Jr (1841) | Ox chain in Fredericksburg County in Virginia, 1841 | $1.50 |
| Chain | Inventory of William Blassingame (1846) | Log chain in Greenville County, South Carolina, 1846 | $2.00 |
| Cheese Basket | Inventory of Doane Atwood (1829) | Cheese basket & hoops in Sturbridge, Massachusetts, 1829 | $0.25 |
| Cheese Hoop | Inventory of Doane Atwood (1829) | Cheese hoop and dippers in Sturbridge, Massachusetts, 1829 | $0.25 |
| Cheese Press | Inventory of Doane Atwood (1829) | Cheese press in Sturbridge, Massachusetts, 1829 | $0.50 |
| Cheese Tub | Inventory of Doane Atwood (1829) | Cheese tub in Sturbridge, Massachusetts, 1829 | $0.75 |
| Chisel | Inventory of Chilon Foster (1830) | Socket chisel in Franklin County, Indiana, 1830 | 12½ cents |
| Clovis | Inventory of Doane Atwood (1829) | Clovis & pin in Sturbridge, Massachusetts, 1829 | $25.00 |
| Crowbar | Inventory of Chilon Foster (1830) | Crobar in Franklin County, Indiana, 1830 | $1.00 |
| Cultivator | Inventory of Royston Betts Jr (1841) | Cultivator in Fredericksburg County in Virginia, 1841 | $2.00 |
| Fork | Inventory of Doane Atwood (1829) | Dung fork in Sturbridge, Massachusetts, 1829 | $0.34 |
| Grindstone | Inventory of Doane Atwood (1829) | Grindstone in Sturbridge, Massachusetts, 1829 | $0.75 |
| Grindstone | Inventory of William Blassingame (1846) | Grindstone in Greenville County, South Carolina, 1846 | $0.35 |
| Hammer | Inventory of John Adair (1831) | Claw hammer in Franklin County, Indiana, 1831 | 37½ cents |
| Harrow | Inventory of Thomas Roe (1848) | Harrow in Greenville County, South Carolina, 1848 | $0.75 |
| Hatchet | Inventory of Doane Atwood (1829) | Hatchet in Sturbridge, Massachusetts, 1829 | $0.06 |
| Hayfork | Inventory of Chilon Foster (1830) | Hayfork in Franklin County, Indiana, 1830 | 37½ cents |
| Hoe | Inventory of George Spillers (1833) | Weeding hoe in Greenville County, South Carolina, 1833 | 12½ cents |
| Hook | Inventory of David C. Coyle (1827) | Bramble hook in Fredericksburg County in Virginia, 1827 | $1.00 |
| Jack Screw | Inventory of Thomas Roe (1848) | Jack screw and iron in Greenville County, South Carolina, 1848 | $1.25 |
| Knife | Inventory of Billingsley Roberts (1831) | Drawing knife in Franklin County, Indiana, 1831 | 62½ cents |
| Nails | Inventory of William Blassingame (1846) | Pound of nails in Greenville County, South Carolina, 1846 | 6¾ cents |
| Pail | Inventory of Coolidge Perry (1836) | Milk pail in Milford, Massachusetts, 1836 | $0.25 |
| Pan | Inventory of Coolidge Perry (1836) | Tin milk pan in Milford, Massachusetts, 1836 | $0.16 |
| Pitchfork | Inventory of Isaac Hoar (1833) | Pitchfork in Worcester, Massachusetts, 1833 | $0.40 |

| Item | Data Source | Description | Price |
|------|-------------|-------------|-------|
| Plane | Inventory of Doctor Burwell Chick (1847) | Floor plain in Greenville County, South Carolina, 1847 | $1.00 |
| Plough | Inventory of Chilon Foster (1830) | Bull plough in Franklin County, Indiana, 1830 | $2.00 |
| Plow | Inventory of David C. Coyle (1827) | Free born plow in Fredericksburg County in Virginia, 1827 | $5.00 |
| Rake | Inventory of Isaac Hoar (1833) | Rake in Worcester, Massachusetts, 1833 | $0.17 |
| Rake | Inventory of Royston Betts Jr (1841) | Iron rake in Fredericksburg County in Virginia, 1841 | $0.35 |
| Riddle | Inventory of Chilon Foster (1830) | Riddle in Franklin County, Indiana, 1830 | 12½ cents |
| Saw | Inventory of David C. Coyle (1827) | Woodsaw in Fredericksburg County in Virginia, 1827 | $2.00 |
| Screw | Inventory of Chilon Foster (1830) | Jack screw in Franklin County, Indiana, 1830 | $3.00 |
| Scythe | Inventory of David C. Coyle (1827) | Scythe in Fredericksburg County in Virginia, 1827 | $1.00 |
| Sieve | Inventory of Doane Atwood (1829) | Wire sieve in Sturbridge, Massachusetts, 1829 | 12½ cents |
| Shovel | Inventory of Isaac Hoar (1833) | Iron shovel in Worcester, Massachusetts, 1833 | $0.50 |
| Shovel | Inventory of William Blassingame (1846) | Spade shovel in Greenville County, South Carolina, 1846 | $0.50 |
| Sickle | Inventory of Billingsley Roberts (1831) | Sickle in Franklin County, Indiana, 1831 | 6¼ cents |
| Spring Wheel | Inventory of Thomas Roe (1848) | Springwheel in Greenville County, South Carolina, 1848 | 87½ cents |
| Steelyard | Inventory of Chilon Foster (1830) | Steel yard in Franklin County, Indiana, 1830 | $1.25 |
| Stillyards | Inventory of George Spillers (1833) | Pair of stilyards in Greenville County, South Carolina, 1833 | $1.50 |
| Thrasher | Inventory of Doctor Burwell Chick (1847) | Thrasher in Greenville County, South Carolina, 1847 | $10.00 |
| Tub | Inventory of George Spillers (1833) | Pickling tub in Greenville County, South Carolina, 1833 | $0.75 |
| Wedge | Inventory of Chilon Foster (1830) | Iron wedge in Franklin County, Indiana, 1830 | 18¾ cents |

## Based Upon US Dollars

| Year | Value of 19th Century Dollar in 2002 US Dollars |
|------|-------------------------------------------------|
| 1825 | $18.00 |
| 1830 | $19.00 |
| 1835 | $20.00 |
| 1840 | $20.00 |
| 1845 | $23.00 |
| 1849 | $23.00 |

*Calculations are approximate values based upon economic historical data*

| Item | Data Source | Description | Price |
|------|-------------|-------------|-------|
| Wheelbarrow | Inventory of Chilon Foster (1830) | Wheel barrow in Franklin County, Indiana, 1830 | $0.25 |
| Work & Screw | Inventory of Royston Betts Jr (1841) | Work and screw in Fredericksburg County in Virginia, 1841 | $1.00 |

### Firearms & Supplies

| Item | Data Source | Description | Price |
|------|-------------|-------------|-------|
| Gun | Inventory of Royston Betts Jr (1841) | Small gun in Fredericksburg County in Virginia, 1841 | $8.00 |
| Gunpowder | William Dutton, Du Pont (1949) | Pound of gunpowder manufactured by Du Pont, 1827 | $0.16 |
| Musket | Arcadi Gluckman, Identifying Old U.S. Muskets, Rifles & Carbines (1965) | Price per stand of Daniel Nippes 1835 flintlock musket, Model 1835, for the US Government, 1842 | $14.75 |
| Musket Improvement | Arcadi Gluckman, Identifying Old U.S. Muskets, Rifles & Carbines (1965) | Price to convert one musket, the 1835 Model, to the Maynard precussion system - worked performed by Daniel Nippes, 1848 | $4.00 |
| Pouch | Inventory of William Blassingame (1846) | Shot pouch in Greenville County, South Carolina, 1846 | $0.55 |
| Rifle | Arcadi Gluckman, Identifying Old U.S. Muskets, Rifles & Carbines (1965) | Price per rifle, S North Contract Flintlock Rifle - Model 1819, manufactured by Simeon North, 1828 | $17.50 |
| Shotgun | Inventory of Chilon Foster (1830) | Shot gun in Franklin County, Indiana, 1830 | $4.00 |
| Shotgun | Inventory of George Spillers (1833) | Shot gun and powder horn in Greenville County, South Carolina, 1833 | $3.00 |

### Food Products

| Item | Data Source | Description | Price |
|------|-------------|-------------|-------|
| Bran | Inventory of Doctor Burwell Chick (1847) | Bushel of bran in Greenville County, South Carolina, 1847 | $0.08 |
| Cheese | Inventory of Doane Atwood (1829) | Pound of cheese in Sturbridge, Massachusetts, 1829 | $0.04 |
| Chicken | American Heritiage (1957) | One four pound chicken sold at retail in New York City, 1837 | $1.12½ |
| Coffee | Inventory of Doctor Burwell Chick (1847) | Pound of coffee in Greenville County, South Carolina, 1847 | 12½ cents |
| Corn | Inventory of George Spillers (1833) | Barrel of corn in Greenville County, South Carolina, 1833 | $2.00 |
| Dried Fruit | Inventory of John Adair (1831) | Bushel of dried fruit in Franklin County, Indiana, 1831 | $0.50 |
| Fish | American Heritiage (1957) | Bass weighing 14 pounds and sold retail in New York City, 1837 | $2.50 |
| Honey | Inventory of George Spillers (1833) | Jar of honey in Greenville County, South Carolina, 1833 | $1.50 |
| Lard | Inventory of John Adair (1831) | Pound of lard in Franklin County, Indiana, 1831 | $0.05 |
| Lard | Inventory of William Blassingame (1846) | Pound of lard in Greenville County, South Carolina, 1846 | $0.12 |
| Molasses | Inventory of Doctor Burwell Chick (1847) | Gallon of molasses in Greenville County, South Carolina, 1847 | $0.58 |
| Mutton | American Heritiage (1957) | Mutton-neck & breast, per pound, sold in New York City, 1837 | $0.12½ |
| Oil | Inventory of Doctor Burwell Chick (1847) | Gallon of oil in Greenville County, South Carolina, 1847 | $0.75 |
| Onions | Inventory of George Spillers (1833) | Lot of onions in Greenville County, South Carolina, 1833 | $0.37½ |
| Partridge | American Heritiage (1957) | A partridge sold at retail in New York City, 1837 | $1.00 |

| Item | Data Source | Description | Price |
|------|-------------|-------------|-------|
| Peas | Inventory of William Blassingame (1846) | Bushel of peas in Greenville County, South Carolina, 1846 | $0.78 |
| Pork | Inventory of John Adair (1831) | Pound of pickled pork in Franklin County, Indiana, 1831 | $0.05 |
| Potatoes | Inventory of George Spillers (1833) | Cask of potatoes in Greenville County, South Carolina, 1833 | $0.75 |
| Spice | Inventory of Doctor Burwell Chick (1847) | Bag of peper in Greenville County, South Carolina, 1847 | $0.95 |
| Sugar | Inventory of George Spillers (1833) | Gourd of sugar in Greenville County, South Carolina, 1833 | $2.00 |
| Sugar | Inventory of Doctor Burwell Chick (1847) | Pound of sugar in Greenville County, South Carolina, 1847 | $0.19 |
| Sweetbread | American Heritiage (1957) | Sweetbread sold in New York City, 1837 | $0.12½ |
| Tea | Inventory of Doctor Burwell Chick (1847) | Bundle of Hyson tea in Greenville County, South Carolina, 1847 | $0.65½ |
| Turkey | American Heritiage (1957) | One small turkey sold at retail in New York City, 1837 | $1.75 |
| Veal | American Heritiage (1957) | Hind-quarter of veal, per pound, sold in New York City, 1837 | $0.19 |
| Vinegar | Inventory of Casswell Barrett (1846) | Jar of vinegar in Greenville County, South Carolina, 1846 | $0.25 |
| Wheat | Inventory of Royston Betts Jr (1841) | Bushel of wheat in Fredericksburg County in Virginia, 1841 | $1.00 |
| Whiting | Inventory of Richard Johnston (1835) | Barrel Spanish whiting in Fredericksburg County in Virginia, 1835 | $3.00 |

## Household Furniture

| Item | Data Source | Description | Price |
|------|-------------|-------------|-------|
| Bed | Inventory of Billingsley Roberts (1831) | Curtain bedstead, bed and bedding in Franklin County, Indiana, 1831 | $12.00 |
| Bed | Inventory of Joseph Bailey (1843) | Feather bed in Wilmington, Delaware, 1843 | $12.00 |
| Bed set | Inventory of Colonel John Stanard (1834) | Bed, Bedstead & furniture in Fredericksburg County in Virginia, 1834 | $26.00 |
| Bedstead | Inventory of Richard Johnston (1835) | Mahogany carved post hedstead in Fredericksburg County in Virginia, 1835 | $15.00 |
| Bellows | Inventory of David C. Coyle (1827) | Hand bellows in Fredericksburg County in Virginia, 1827 | $3.00 |

## Based Upon US Dollars

| Year | Value of 19th Century Dollar in 2002 US Dollars |
|------|-------------------------------------------------|
| 1825 | $18.00 |
| 1830 | $19.00 |
| 1835 | $20.00 |
| 1840 | $20.00 |
| 1845 | $23.00 |
| 1849 | $23.00 |

*Calculations are approximate values based upon economic historical data*

| Item | Data Source | Description | Price |
|------|-------------|-------------|-------|
| Bookcase | Inventory of Dr. William Baker (1838) | Bookcase in Wilmington, Delaware, 1838 | $4.00 |
| Bureau | Inventory of Chilon Foster (1830) | Toy bureau in Franklin County, Indiana, 1830 | $5.00 |
| Bureau | Inventory of Mainville F. Lewis (1834) | Bureau, glass mounted in Greenville County, South Carolina, 1834 | $20.00 |
| Carpet | Inventory of George Spillers (1833) | Floor carpet in Greenville County, South Carolina, 1833 | $0.25 |
| Chair | Inventory of Joseph Bailey (1843) | Windsor chair, yellow in Wilmington, Delaware, 1843 | 37½ cents |
| Clock | Inventory of Chilon Foster (1830) | Clock and case in Franklin County, Indiana, 1830 | $25.00 |
| Clock | Inventory of Joseph Bailey (1843) | Eight day clock in Wilmington, Delaware, 1843 | $15.00 |
| Cot | Inventory of Dr. William Baker (1838) | Cot bedstead & sacking in Wilmington, Delaware, 1838 | $1.50 |
| Crib | Inventory of Colonel John Stanard (1834) | Crib in Fredericksburg County in Virginia, 1834 | $1.50 |
| Cricket | Inventory of Doane Atwood (1829) | Cricket in Sturbridge, Massachusetts, 1829 | 12½ cents |
| Cupboard | Inventory of George Spillers (1833) | Pine cupboard in Greenville County, South Carolina, 1833 | $0.50 |
| Desk | Inventory of Joseph Bailey (1843) | Desk & bookcase in Wilmington, Delaware, 1843 | $3.00 |
| Dressing Glass | Inventory of Royston Betts Jr (1841) | Dressing glass in Fredericksburg County in Virginia, 1841 | $0.75 |
| Dressing Table | Inventory of Colonel John Stanard (1834) | Dressing table in Fredericksburg County in Virginia, 1834 | $10.00 |
| Liquor Case | Inventory of Royston Betts Jr (1841) | Liquor case and bottles in Fredericksburg County in Virginia, 1841 | $1.50 |
| Mirror | Inventory of Dr. William Baker (1838) | Mantle mirror in Wilmington, Delaware, 1838 | $20.00 |
| Secretary | Inventory of Joseph Bailey (1843) | Secretary & bookcase in Wilmington, Delaware, 1843 | $10.00 |
| Settee | Inventory of Richard Johnston (1835) | Rush bottom settee in Fredericksburg County in Virginia, 1835 | $5.00 |
| Side Board | Inventory of Royston Betts Jr (1841) | Mahogany Side Board in Fredericksburg County in Virginia, 1841 | $30.00 |
| Sofa | Inventory of Royston Betts Jr (1841) | Mahogany sopha in Fredericksburg County in Virginia, 1841 | $20.00 |

| Item | Data Source | Description | Price |
|------|-------------|-------------|-------|
| Stand | Inventory of David C. Coyle (1827) | Cherry stand in Fredericksburg County in Virginia, 1827 | $2.00 |
| Table | Inventory of David C. Coyle (1827) | Small mehogany table in Fredericksburg County in Virginia, 1827 | $1.25 |
| Tables | Inventory of Aaron Bayard (1849) | Pair mahagony side tables in New Castle County, Delaware, 1849 | $10.00 |
| Waiter | Inventory of Joseph Bailey (1843) | Japan waiter in Wilmington, Delaware, 1843 | 12½ cents |

## Household Products

| Item | Data Source | Description | Price |
|------|-------------|-------------|-------|
| Andirons | Inventory of Joseph Bailey (1843) | Pair brass andirons in Wilmington, Delaware, 1843 | $2.00 |
| Bag | Inventory of Joseph Bailey (1843) | Bag in Wilmington, Delaware, 1843 | $0.05 |
| Basket | Inventory of Doane Atwood (1829) | Clothes basket in Sturbridge, Massachusetts, 1829 | $0.12 |
| Basket | Inventory of Doctor Burwell Chick (1847) | Silver basket in Greenville County, South Carolina, 1847 | $6.00 |
| Bed Stool | Inventory of Richard Johnston (1835) | Mahogany close bed stool in Fredericksburg County in Virginia, 1835 | $3.00 |
| Beeswax | Laurence A. Johnson, Over The Counter and On The Shelf 1620-1920 (1961) | Cost for one pound of beeswax | $0.18 |
| Bellows | Inventory of Coolidge Perry (1836) | Pair of bellows in Milford, Massachusetts, 1836 | $0.17 |
| Blanket | Humphery Clark & Co. Account Book (1838) | Rose blanket in Charleston, South Carolina, 1838 | $1.00 |
| Blinds | Inventory of Richard Johnston (1835) | Pair of venetian blinds in Fredericksburg County in Virginia, 1835 | $4.00 |
| Bottle | Inventory of Doane Atwood (1829) | Gallon bottle in Sturbridge, Massachusetts, 1829 | $0.25 |
| Bowl | Inventory of George Spillers (1833) | Earthen bole in Greenville County, South Carolina, 1833 | $0.25 |
| Bowl | Inventory of Colonel John Stanard (1834) | Glass bowl in Fredericksburg County in Virginia, 1834 | $3.00 |
| Broom | Inventory of Colonel John Stanard (1834) | Hearth broom in Fredericksburg County in Virginia, 1834 | $0.20 |

## Based Upon US Dollars

| Year | Value of 19th Century Dollar in 2002 US Dollars |
|------|--------------------------------------------------|
| 1825 | $18.00 |
| 1830 | $19.00 |
| 1835 | $20.00 |
| 1840 | $20.00 |
| 1845 | $23.00 |
| 1849 | $23.00 |

*Calculations are approximate values based upon economic historical data*

| Item | Data Source | Description | Price |
|------|-------------|-------------|-------|
| Broom | Laurence A. Johnson, Over The Counter and On The Shelf 1620-1920 (1961) | Homemade Indian brooms | $0.08 |
| Brush | Inventory of John Adair (1831) | Clothes brush in Franklin County, Indiana, 1831 | $0.25 |
| Brush | Inventory of John Morrision (1834) | Small hair brush in Franklin County, Indiana, 1834 | 12½ cents |
| Bucket | Inventory of Chilon Foster (1830) | Tin bucket in Franklin County, Indiana, 1830 | $0.50 |
| Can | Inventory of William Blassingame (1846) | Pair of steelyards in Greenville County, South Carolina, 1846 | $0.21 |
| Chandelier | Inventory of Richard Johnston (1835) | Candelier in Fredericksburg County in Virginia, 1835 | $5.00 |
| Candles | Inventory of John Adair (1831) | Pound of candles in Franklin County, Indiana, 1831 | 12½ cents |
| Candlestick | Inventory of John Adair (1831) | Brass candlestick in Franklin County, Indiana, 1831 | 12½ cents |
| Canister | Inventory of Doane Atwood (1829) | Tin tea cannister in Sturbridge, Massachusetts, 1829 | $0.06 |
| Canopy | Inventory of Colonel John Stanard (1834) | Danitz canopy in Fredericksburg County in Virginia, 1834 | $1.00 |
| Carpet | Inventory of Colonel John Stanard (1834) | Stair case carpet & rods in Fredericksburg County in Virginia, 1834 | $10.00 |
| Case | Inventory of David C. Coyle (1827) | Knife case in Fredericksburg County in Virginia, 1827 | $1.00 |
| Cask | Inventory of Aaron Bayard (1849) | Water cask in New Castle County, Delaware, 1849 | $0.25 |
| Caster | Inventory of Dr. William Baker (1838) | Plated caster in Wilmington, Delaware, 1838 | $1.50 |
| Chest | Inventory of Doctor Burwell Chick (1847) | Walnut chest in Greenville County, South Carolina, 1847 | $3.00 |
| China | Inventory of David C. Coyle (1827) | Set of blue china in Fredericksburg County in Virginia, 1827 | $8.00 |
| China set | Inventory of Dr. William Baker (1838) | Canton chinaware dinner set in Wilmington, Delaware, 1838 | $18.00 |
| Clothes Horse | Inventory of Dr. William Baker (1838) | Clothes horse in Wilmington, Delaware, 1838 | $0.50 |
| Coaster | Inventory of Colonel John Stanard (1834) | Coaster in Fredericksburg County in Virginia, 1834 | $0.75 |
| Coffee & Cream pots | Inventory of Royston Betts Jr (1841) | Britannia Coffee and Cream pot in Fredericksburg County in Virginia, 1841 | $6.00 |
| Comb | Laurence A. Johnson, Over The Counter and On The Shelf 1620-1920 (1961) | Cost of a horn comb sold on a peddling wagon in 1828 | $0.90 |
| Coverlid | Inventory of John Adair (1831) | Coverlid in Franklin County, Indiana, 1831 | $1.50 |
| Cream pot | Inventory of David C. Coyle (1827) | Cream pot in Fredericksburg County in Virginia, 1827 | $1.00 |
| Curtains | Inventory of Richard Johnston (1835) | Cotton window curtians in Fredericksburg County in Virginia, 1835 | $1.00 |
| Curtains | Inventory of Joseph Bailey (1843) | Paper window curtains in Wilmington, Delaware, 1843 | $0.01 |
| Decanter | Inventory of Doane Atwood (1829) | Decanter in Sturbridge, Massachusetts, 1829 | $0.25 |
| Demijohn | Inventory of Colonel John Stanard (1834) | Demijohn in Fredericksburg County in Virginia, 1834 | $0.10 |
| Desk | Inventory of Billingsley Roberts (1831) | Desk in Franklin County, Indiana, 1831 | $3.00 |

| Item | Data Source | Description | Price |
|---|---|---|---|
| Dining set | Inventory of Royston Betts Jr (1841) | Dining set of Liverpool china in Fredericksburg County in Virginia, 1841 | $12.00 |
| Dish | Inventory of Royston Betts Jr (1841) | Oyster dish in Fredericksburg County in Virginia, 1841 | $0.50 |
| Dish | Inventory of Doctor Burwell Chick (1847) | Silver sugar dish in Greenville County, South Carolina, 1847 | $25.00 |
| Dog Irons | Inventory of Billingsley Roberts (1831) | Dog irons in Franklin County, Indiana, 1831 | $1.25 |
| Fender | Inventory of Dr. William Baker (1838) | Fire fender in Wilmington, Delaware, 1838 | $1.00 |
| Fire dogs | Inventory of Thomas Roe (1848) | Fire dogs in Greenville County, South Carolina, 1848 | $1.00 |
| Fire set | Inventory of Doane Atwood (1829) | Brass fire set in Sturbridge, Massachusetts, 1829 | $2.25 |
| Flatware | Inventory of John Adair (1831) | Half dozen knives and forks in Franklin County, Indiana, 1831 | $1.00 |
| Flax Wheel | Inventory of Sarah McClimmons (1833) | Flax wheel in Greenville County, South Carolina, 1833 | $2.50 |
| Fork | Inventory of George Spillers (1833) | Flesh fork in Greenville County, South Carolina, 1833 | $0.25 |
| Freezer | Inventory of Colonel John Stanard (1834) | Tin freezer in Fredericksburg County in Virginia, 1834 | $0.25 |
| Furnace | Inventory of Doane Atwood (1829) | Iron Furnance in Sturbridge, Massachusetts, 1829 | $0.75 |
| Glass | Inventory of Joseph Bailey (1843) | Shaving glass in Wilmington, Delaware, 1843 | $0.25 |
| Glasses | Inventory of Colonel John Stanard (1834) | Dozen jelly glasses in Fredericksburg County in Virginia, 1834 | $1.00 |
| Hearth Items | Inventory of Colonel John Stanard (1834) | Grate, fender, shovel & tongs in Fredericksburg County in Virginia, 1834 | $6.00 |
| Jar | Inventory of Billingsley Roberts (1831) | Preserve jar in Franklin County, Indiana, 1831 | $0.50 |
| Jar | Inventory of George Spillers (1833) | Stone jar in Greenville County, South Carolina, 1833 | 62½ cents |

| Item | Data Source | Description | Price |
|---|---|---|---|
| Jug | Inventory of Chilon Foster (1830) | Gallon jug in Franklin County, Indiana, 1830 | 12½ cents |
| Kettle | Inventory of George Spillers (1833) | Tea kettle in Greenville County, South Carolina, 1833 | $1.00 |
| Knife | Inventory of George Cummings (1843) | Cutting knife in Marshall County, Tennessee, 1843 | 87½ cents |
| Knife case | Inventory of David C. Coyle (1827) | Knife case in Fredericksburg County in Virginia, 1827 | $4.00 |
| Ladle | Inventory of Billingsley Roberts (1831) | Silver ladle in Franklin County, Indiana, 1831 | $1.50 |
| Lamp | Inventory of Coolidge Perry (1836) | Glass lamp in Milford, Massachusetts, 1836 | $0.20 |
| Lantern | Inventory of Coolidge Perry (1836) | Glass lanthorn in Milford, Massachusetts, 1836 | $0.06 |
| Lining | Inventory of Doane Atwood (1829) | Comforter lining in Sturbridge, Massachusetts, 1829 | $0.37 |
| Looking Glass | Inventory of Colonel John Stanard (1834) | Looking glass in Fredericksburg County in Virginia, 1834 | $6.00 |
| Mantle Glass | Inventory of Royston Betts Jr (1841) | Mantle Glass in Fredericksburg County in Virginia, 1841 | $10.00 |
| Mop Stick | Laurence A. Johnson, Over The Counter and On The Shelf 1620-1920 (1961) | Mop made of cotton sold on a peddling wagon in 1828 | $0.20 |
| Mug | Inventory of John Adair (1831) | Chamber mug in Franklin County, Indiana, 1831 | $0.25 |
| Napkins | Inventory of Colonel John Stanard (1834) | Dozen napkins in Fredericksburg County in Virginia, 1834 | $2.00 |
| Ornament | Inventory of Colonel John Stanard (1834) | Alabaster ornament in Fredericksburg County in Virginia, 1834 | $0.44 |
| Ornaments | Inventory of David C. Coyle (1827) | Set charry mantle ornaments in Fredericksburg County in Virginia, 1827 | $1.75 |
| Pillow case | Inventory of Colonel John Stanard (1834) | Pillow case in Fredericksburg County in Virginia, 1834 | $0.15 |
| Pins | Inventory of Doane Atwood (1829) | Pair glass pins in Sturbridge, Massachusetts, 1829 | $0.12 |
| Pitcher | Inventory of George Spillers (1833) | Red earthen pitcher in Greenville County, South Carolina, 1833 | 37½ cents |
| Pitcher | Inventory of Colonel John Stanard (1834) | Stone pitcher in Fredericksburg County in Virginia, 1834 | $0.50 |

| Item | Data Source | Description | Price |
|------|-------------|-------------|-------|
| Plates | Inventory of Doane Atwood (1829) | Edged fish plate in Sturbridge, Massachusetts, 1829 | $0.17 |
| Plates | Inventory of Colonel John Stanard (1834) | Dozen large tea plates with gilt edge in Fredericksburg County in Virginia, 1834 | $3.00 |
| Platter | Inventory of Coolidge Perry (1836) | Printed oval platte in Milford, Massachusetts, 1836 | $0.25 |
| Pot | Inventory of Doctor Burwell Chick (1847) | Silver cream pot in Greenville County, South Carolina, 1847 | $13.00 |
| Print | Inventory of Colonel John Stanard (1834) | Declaration of Independence with gilt frame in Fredericksburg County in Virginia, 1834 | $2.50 |
| Quilt | Inventory of Dr. William Baker (1838) | Bed quilt in Wilmington, Delaware, 1838 | $1.00 |
| Razor | Inventory of John Adair (1831) | Raxor, strap & box in Franklin County, Indiana, 1831 | $2.00 |
| Rug | Inventory of Doane Atwood (1829) | Woolen rug in Sturbridge, Massachusetts, 1829 | $0.50 |
| Safe | Inventory of David C. Coyle (1827) | Tin safe in Fredericksburg County in Virginia, 1827 | $5.00 |
| Salt Cellar | Inventory of Joseph Bailey (1843) | Salt sellars in Wilmington, Delaware, 1843 | $0.06 |
| Sauce boat | Inventory of David C. Coyle (1827) | Plated Sauce boat & spoon in Fredericksburg County in Virginia, 1827 | $1.50 |
| Scales | Inventory of Dr. William Baker (1838) | Scales & weights iin Wilmington, Delaware, 1838 | $0.25 |
| Screen | Inventory of Colonel John Stanard (1834) | Chimney screen in Fredericksburg County in Virginia, 1834 | $0.50 |
| Scuttle | Inventory of Dr. William Baker (1838) | Copper coal scuttle in Wilmington, Delaware, 1838 | $1.25 |
| Sheet | Inventory of Doctor Burwell Chick (1847) | Linnen sheet in Greenville County, South Carolina, 1847 | $1.50 |
| Sheets | Inventory of Doane Atwood (1829) | Pair of woolen sheets in Sturbridge, Massachusetts, 1829 | $2.00 |
| Shovel & Tongs | Inventory of Joseph Bailey (1843) | Shovel & tongs in Wilmington, Delaware, 1843 | $1.00 |
| Spindle | Inventory of Chilon Foster (1830) | Hand mill spindle in Franklin County, Indiana, 1830 | $0.25 |
| Spinning Wheel | Inventory of William Blassingame (1846) | Spinning wheel in Greenville County, South Carolina, 1846 | 62½ cents |

## Based Upon US Dollars

| Year | Value of 19th Century Dollar in 2002 US Dollars |
|------|------------------------------------------------|
| 1825 | $18.00 |
| 1830 | $19.00 |
| 1835 | $20.00 |
| 1840 | $20.00 |
| 1845 | $23.00 |
| 1849 | $23.00 |

*Calculations are approximate values based upon economic historical data*

| Item | Data Source | Description | Price |
|---|---|---|---|
| Spoon | Inventory of John Adair (1831) | Large silver table spoon in Franklin County, Indiana, 1831 | $1.66 |
| Spoons | Inventory of Royston Betts Jr (1841) | Dozen silver tea spoons in Fredericksburg County in Virginia, 1841 | $10.00 |
| Stove | Inventory of Joseph Bailey (1843) | Coal stove & pipe in Wilmington, Delaware, 1843 | $8.00 |
| Sugar Box | Laurence A. Johnson, Over The Counter and On The Shelf 1620-1920 (1961) | Cost of a sugar box sold on a peddling wagon in 1828 | $0.80 |
| Table | Inventory of Richard Johnston (1835) | Small work table in Fredericksburg County in Virginia, 1835 | $3.00 |
| Table mats | Inventory of Colonel John Stanard (1834) | Parcel of table mats in Fredericksburg County in Virginia, 1834 | $1.00 |
| Tablecloth | Inventory of Richard Johnston (1835) | Diaper table cloth in Fredericksburg County in Virginia, 1835 | $2.00 |
| Tallow | Inventory of John Adair (1831) | Pound of tallow in Franklin County, Indiana, 1831 | $0.07 |
| Tea cups | Inventory of Billingsley Roberts (1831) | Dozen tea cups and saucers in Franklin County, Indiana, 1831 | $0.75 |
| Tea Kettle | Inventory of Billingsley Roberts (1831) | Iron tea kettle in Franklin County, Indiana, 1831 | $0.75 |
| Tea pot | Inventory of Coolidge Perry (1836) | Britannia tea pot in Milford, Massachusetts, 1836 | $0.50 |
| Tea set | Inventory of Dr. William Baker (1838) | Canton chinaware tea set in Wilmington, Delaware, 1838 | $18.00 |
| Tea set | Inventory of Dr. William Baker (1838) | Common tea set in Wilmington, Delaware, 1838 | $2.00 |
| Toilet cover | Inventory of Richard Johnston (1835) | Toilet cover in Fredericksburg County in Virginia, 1835 | $0.50 |
| Toilet Table | Inventory of Royston Betts Jr (1841) | Toilet table in Fredericksburg County in Virginia, 1841 | $2.00 |
| Tongs | Inventory of Royston Betts Jr (1841) | Pair Silver Sugar Tongs in Fredericksburg County in Virginia, 1841 | $3.00 |
| Towels | Inventory of Colonel John Stanard (1834) | Dozen towels in Fredericksburg County in Virginia, 1834 | $1.00 |
| Tray | Inventory of Doane Atwood (1829) | Mahogany tea tray in Sturbridge, Massachusetts, 1829 | $0.17 |
| Trunk | Inventory of Doane Atwood (1829) | Wooden trunk in Sturbridge, Massachusetts, 1829 | $0.50 |
| Tub | Inventory of Chilon Foster (1830) | Wash tub in Franklin County, Indiana, 1830 | 62½ cents |
| Tumbler | Inventory of Colonel John Stanard (1834) | Cut glass tumbler in Fredericksburg County in Virginia, 1834 | $0.25 |
| Utensils | Inventory of Colonel John Stanard (1834) | Set ivory handle knives & forks in Fredericksburg County in Virginia, 1834 | $7.00 |
| Vase | Inventory of Royston Betts Jr (1841) | Flower vase in Fredericksburg County in Virginia, 1841 | 16½ cents |
| Vise | Inventory of Doane Atwood (1829) | Vice in Sturbridge, Massachusetts, 1829 | $0.12 |
| Waiter | Inventory of Doane Atwood (1829) | Waiter in Sturbridge, Massachusetts, 1829 | $0.12 |
| Waiter | Inventory of Dr. William Baker (1838) | Waiter in Wilmington, Delaware, 1838 | $1.00 |
| Wash Bowl | Inventory of William Blassingame (1846) | Wash bowl & pitcher in Greenville County, South Carolina, 1846 | $0.25 |
| Washboard | Inventory of John Adair (1831) | Washboard in Franklin County, Indiana, 1831 | 7½ cents |

| Item | Data Source | Description | Price |
|------|-------------|-------------|-------|
| Wine safe | Inventory of Royston Betts Jr (1841) | Wine safe in Fredericksburg County in Virginia, 1841 | $3.00 |
| Woodware | Inventory of Colonel John Stanard (1834) | Piece of woodware in Fredericksburg County in Virginia, 1834 | $0.15 |

### Investment
| | | | |
|------|-------------|-------------|-------|
| Bond | Inventory of J. Earle (1845) | A $250 Georgia bond in Greenville County, South Carolina, 1845 | $74.00 |
| Stock | Inventory of Joseph Bailey (1843) | Share of the Bank of Delaware in Wilmington, Delaware, 1843 | $285.00 |
| Stock | Inventory of Joseph Bailey (1843) | Share of State Bank at Camden in Wilmington, Delaware, 1843 | $25.00 |
| Stock | Inventory of Joseph Bailey (1843) | Share of Delaware Coal Company in Wilmington, Delaware, 1843 | $5.00 |
| Stock | Inventory of Joseph Bailey (1843) | Share of Wilmington & Christiana Turnpike Co in Wilmington, Delaware, 1843 | $10.00 |
| Stock | Inventory of Joseph Bailey (1843) | Share of Wilmington Turnpike Company in Wilmington, Delaware, 1843 | $1.50 |
| Stock | Inventory of J. Earle (1845) | Share of Charleston Insurance & Trust Company, Charleston, South Carolina, 1845 | $55.00 |

### Jewelry
| | | | |
|------|-------------|-------------|-------|
| Watch | Inventory of John Morrision (1834) | Silver watch in Franklin County, Indiana, 1834 | $8.00 |
| Watch | Inventory of William Blassingame (1846) | Silver watch in Greenville County, South Carolina, 1846 | $13.50 |

### Kitchen Items
| | | | |
|------|-------------|-------------|-------|
| Baker | Inventory of Colonel John Stanard (1834) | Baker in Fredericksburg County in Virginia, 1834 | $0.50 |
| Boiler | Inventory of Richard Johnston (1835) | Tin coffee boiler in Fredericksburg County in Virginia, 1835 | $0.25 |
| Can | Inventory of Joseph Bailey (1843) | Oil can in Wilmington, Delaware, 1843 | $0.06 |
| Churn | Inventory of Coolidge Perry (1836) | Stone churn in Milford, Massachusetts, 1836 | $0.42 |
| Cloth | Inventory of Joseph Bailey (1843) | Carpet & crum cloth in Wilmington, Delaware, 1843 | $0.50 |

### Based Upon US Dollars

| Year | Value of 19th Century Dollar in 2002 US Dollars |
|------|-------------------------------------------------|
| 1825 | $18.00 |
| 1830 | $19.00 |
| 1835 | $20.00 |
| 1840 | $20.00 |
| 1845 | $23.00 |
| 1849 | $23.00 |

*Calculations are approximate values based upon economic historical data*

| Item | Data Source | Description | Price |
|---|---|---|---|
| Coffee Mill | Inventory of William Blassingame (1846) | Coffee mill in Greenville County, South Carolina, 1846 | $0.25 |
| Coffee toaster | Inventory of Colonel John Stanard (1834) | Patent coffee toaster in Fredericksburg County in Virginia, 1834 | $1.50 |
| Egg Breaker | Inventory of John Adair (1831) | Egg breaker in Franklin County, Indiana, 1831 | 37½ cents |
| Fork | Inventory of Royston Betts Jr (1841) | Flesh fork in Fredericksburg County in Virginia, 1841 | $0.19 |
| Griddle | Inventory of Joseph Bailey (1843) | Griddle in Wilmington, Delaware, 1843 | $0.25 |
| Gridiron | Inventory of Doane Atwood (1829) | Gridiron in Sturbridge, Massachusetts, 1829 | $0.50 |
| Iron | Inventory of Colonel John Stanard (1834) | Flat iron in Fredericksburg County in Virginia, 1834 | $0.25 |
| Iron Pot | Inventory of John Adair (1831) | Iron pot in Franklin County, Indiana, 1831 | $1.00 |
| Kettle | Inventory of Doane Atwood (1829) | Brass kettle in Sturbridge, Massachusetts, 1829 | $2.00 |
| Kettle | Inventory of Chilon Foster (1830) | Iron kettle in Franklin County, Indiana, 1830 | $1.12½ |
| Knife | Inventory of Doane Atwood (1829) | Chopping knife in Sturbridge, Massachusetts, 1829 | $0.16 |
| Ladle | Inventory of Doane Atwood (1829) | Brass ladle in Sturbridge, Massachusetts, 1829 | $0.04 |
| Measures | Inventory of Colonel John Stanard (1834) | Set of measures in Fredericksburg County in Virginia, 1834 | $0.40 |
| Mortar & Pestle | Inventory of Colonel John Stanard (1834) | Marble mortar & pestle in Fredericksburg County in Virginia, 1834 | $0.50 |
| Mould | Inventory of Richard Johnston (1835) | Tin cake mould in Fredericksburg County in Virginia, 1835 | $0.25 |
| Oven | Inventory of Richard Johnston (1835) | Iron oven in Fredericksburg County in Virginia, 1835 | $0.75 |
| Pan | Inventory of Doane Atwood (1829) | Bake pan in Sturbridge, Massachusetts, 1829 | $0.75 |
| Pot | Inventory of Billingsley Roberts (1831) | Small stew pot & hooks in Franklin County, Indiana, 1831 | $1.00 |
| Pot | Inventory of George Spillers (1833) | Large pot in Greenville County, South Carolina, 1833 | $2.00 |
| Pot rack | Inventory of Colonel John Stanard (1834) | Pot rack in Fredericksburg County in Virginia, 1834 | $0.25 |
| Rack | Inventory of William Blassingame (1846) | Pot rack in Greenville County, South Carolina, 1846 | $0.50 |
| Sifter | Inventory of Colonel John Stanard (1834) | Sifter in Fredericksburg County in Virginia, 1834 | 12½ cents |
| Skillet | Inventory of Colonel John Stanard (1834) | Bell mettle skillet in Fredericksburg County in Virginia, 1834 | $2.50 |
| Skimmer | Inventory of Coolidge Perry (1836) | Tin skimmer in Milford, Massachusetts, 1836 | $0.02 |
| Spider | Inventory of Richard Johnston (1835) | Spider in Fredericksburg County in Virginia, 1835 | $0.25 |
| Stove | Inventory of Coolidge Perry (1836) | Cooking stove & pipe in Milford, Massachusetts, 1836 | $18.00 |
| Stove | Inventory of Joseph Bailey (1843) | Stove with boiler in Wilmington, Delaware, 1843 | $2.00 |
| Toast Iron | Inventory of Coolidge Perry (1836) | Toast iron in Milford, Massachusetts, 1836 | $0.25 |
| Trough | Inventory of Joseph Bailey (1843) | Dough trough in Wilmington, Delaware, 1843 | $1.00 |

| Item | Data Source | Description | Price |
|------|-------------|-------------|-------|
| Tub | Inventory of Richard Johnston (1835) | Iron bound tub in Fredericksburg County in Virginia, 1835 | $0.50 |
| Wafer Iron | Inventory of Richard Johnston (1835) | Pair wafer irons in Fredericksburg County in Virginia, 1835 | |
| Water tub | Inventory of Royston Betts Jr (1841) | Water tub in Fredericksburg County in Virginia, 1841 | $0.50 |

## Livery Animals & Tools

| Item | Data Source | Description | Price |
|------|-------------|-------------|-------|
| Blanket | Humphery Clark & Co. Account Book (1838) | Saddle blanket in Charleston, South Carolina, 1838 | $0.62½ |
| Bucket | Inventory of John Adair (1831) | Wagon bucket in Franklin County, Indiana, 1831 | $0.50 |
| Carriage | Inventory of Royston Betts Jr (1841) | Carriage and Harness in Fredericksburg County in Virginia, 1841 | $300.00 |
| Cart | Inventory of William Blassingame (1846) | Ox cart & yoke in Greenville County, South Carolina, 1846 | $10.12½ |
| Cover | Inventory of Billingsley Roberts (1831) | Wagon cover in Franklin County, Indiana, 1831 | $1.00 |
| Feed | Pace & McGee, The life and Times of Ridgeway, Virginia. | Price for one serving of horse feed at a tavern in Ridgeway, Virginia, 1849 | $0.12 |
| Gig | Inventory of Dr. William Baker (1838) | Gig & harness in Wilmington, Delaware, 1838 | $50.00 |
| Harness | Inventory of William Servey (1836) | Harness in Uxbridge, Massachusetts, 1836 | $10.00 |
| Horse | Inventory of John Adair (1831) | Bay horse in Franklin County, Indiana, 1831 | $67.00 |
| Mare | Inventory of George Cummings (1843) | Sorrel mare in Marshall County, Tennessee, 1843 | $10.00 |
| Mule | Inventory of Doctor Burwell Chick (1847) | Mule in Greenville County, South Carolina, 1847 | $111.00 |
| Ox | Inventory of Royston Betts Jr (1841) | Yak ox in Fredericksburg County in Virginia, 1841 | $30.00 |
| Racehorse | Letter from Emily Sinkler (1843) | Price for racehorse after winning a $500 race in Charleston, 1843 | $3,000.00 |
| Saddle | Laurence A. Johnson, Over The Counter and On The Shelf 1620-1920 (1961) | Cost for a leather saddle in New Orleans (approximatly 1830) | $5.00 |

## Based Upon US Dollars

| Year | Value of 19th Century Dollar in 2002 US Dollars |
|------|-------------------------------------------------|
| 1825 | $18.00 |
| 1830 | $19.00 |
| 1835 | $20.00 |
| 1840 | $20.00 |
| 1845 | $23.00 |
| 1849 | $23.00 |

*Calculations are approximate values based upon economic historical data*

| Item | Data Source | Description | Price |
|------|-------------|-------------|-------|
| Saddle | Laurence A. Johnson, Over The Counter and On The Shelf 1620-1920 (1961) | Cost for a leather saddle in St Louis (approximately 1830) | $15.00 |
| Saddle wallets | Inventory of George Spillers (1833) | Pair of saddle wallets in Greenville County, South Carolina, 1833 | $3.00 |
| Sled | Inventory of Doane Atwood (1829) | Ox sled in Sturbridge, Massachusetts, 1829 | $1.00 |
| Sleigh | Inventory of William Servey (1836) | Sleigh in Uxbridge, Massachusetts, 1836 | $12.00 |
| Springs | Inventory of David C. Coyle (1827) | Set of carriage springs in Fredericksburg County in Virginia, 1827 | $4.00 |
| Spurs | Inventory of Joseph Milholland (1830) | Pair of spurs in Franklin County, Indiana, 1830 | $1.25 |
| Wagon | Inventory of Billingsley Roberts (1831) | Ox wagon in Franklin County, Indiana, 1831 | $27.50 |
| Whip | Inventory of George Spillers (1833) | Riding whip in Greenville County, South Carolina, 1833 | $0.50 |
| Yoke | Inventory of Doane Atwood (1829) | New ox yoke in Sturbridge, Massachusetts, 1829 | $1.00 |

## Livestock

| Item | Data Source | Description | Price |
|------|-------------|-------------|-------|
| Bull | Inventory of Royston Betts Jr (1841) | White bull in Fredericksburg County in Virginia, 1841 | $12.00 |
| Bull | Inventory of Royston Betts Jr (1841) | Bull yearling in Fredericksburg County in Virginia, 1841 | $3.00 |
| Cow | Inventory of Doane Atwood (1829) | Big horned cow in Sturbridge, Massachusetts, 1829 | $12.00 |
| Cow | Inventory of George Spillers (1833) | Red cow in Greenville County, South Carolina, 1833 | $7.50 |
| Duck | Inventory of George Spillers (1833) | Duck in Greenville County, South Carolina, 1833 | $0.14 |
| Goat | Inventory of William Blassingame (1846) | Goat in Greenville County, South Carolina, 1846 | $0.09 |
| Goose | Inventory of Chilon Foster (1830) | Goose in Franklin County, Indiana, 1830 | $0.06 |
| Goose | Inventory of George Cummings (1843) | Goose in Marshall County, Tennessee, 1843 | $0.04 |
| Heifer | Inventory of Doane Atwood (1829) | Yearling heifer in Sturbridge, Massachusetts, 1829 | $5.50 |
| Hog | Inventory of Chilon Foster (1830) | Hog in Franklin County, Indiana, 1830 | $1.33 |
| Hog | Inventory of Doctor Burwell Chick (1847) | Hog in Greenville County, South Carolina, 1847 | $5.62½ |
| Oxen | Inventory of Doane Atwood (1829) | A yoke of oxen in Sturbridge, Massachusetts, 1829 | $40.00 |
| Pig | Inventory of Chilon Foster (1830) | Small pig in Franklin County, Indiana, 1830 | $0.50 |
| Sheep | Inventory of Doane Atwood (1829) | Sheep in in Sturbridge, Massachusetts, 1829 | $1.00 |
| Shoat | Inventory of Thomas Roe (1848) | Shoat in Greenville County, South Carolina, 1848 | $2.25 |
| Sow | Inventory of Royston Betts Jr (1841) | Sow in Fredericksburg County in Virginia, 1841 | $4.00 |
| Turkey | Inventory of Billingsley Roberts (1831) | Turkey in Franklin County, Indiana, 1831 | $0.25 |

| Item | Data Source | Description | Price |
|------|-------------|-------------|-------|
| **Manufactured Products** | | | |
| Bottle | McKearin, American Bottles & Flasks (1978) | Per Gross - Porter Bottles, 1st Quality, 1 qt from the New-England Glass-Bottle Company, Boston, 1829 | $8.50 |
| Fruit Squares | McKearin, American Bottles & Flasks (1978) | Per Gross - Fruit Squares, 2 qt from the New-England Glass-Bottle Company, Boston, 1829 | $18.00 |
| Mold | McKearin, American Bottles & Flasks (1978) | Mold for a Square gin mold, 1 qt from France for manufacturing in the United States, 1834 | $25.00 |
| **Medical Equipment** | | | |
| Instruments | Inventory of Dr. William Baker (1838) | Box of amputating instruments in Wilmington, Delaware, 1838 | $2.00 |
| Instruments | Inventory of Dr. William Baker (1838) | Set obstetric instruments in Wilmington, Delaware, 1838 | $2.00 |
| Thermometer | Inventory of William Blassingame (1846) | Thermometer in Greenville County, South Carolina, 1846 | $2.37½ |
| **Medicine** | | | |
| Medicine | Smith, Early American Home Remedies (1968) | Bottle of Tinctura Assafoetide Composita Tincture, a moderate stimulant, powerful antispasmodic, efficient expectorant and a mild laxative, 1847 | $0.25 |
| Medicine | Smith, Early American Home Remedies (1968) | Bottle to Cure Drunkenness - Sulphate of iron, pepermint water and nutmeg to be taken twice a day in does of about a wine-glassful or less, with or without water, 1848 | $1.00 |
| Tonic | McKearin, American Bottles & Flasks (1978) | *Dr Jayne's Hair Tonic New England, 1840* | $1.00 |
| **Music** | | | |
| Fiddle | Inventory of David C. Coyle (1827) | Fiddle & case in Fredericksburg County in Virginia, 1827 | $5.00 |
| Guitar | Inventory of David C. Coyle (1827) | Gettar in Fredericksburg County in Virginia, 1827 | $3.00 |
| Piano | Inventory of Colonel John Stanard (1834) | Piano forte, music stool and metronome in Fredericksburg County in Virginia, 1834 | $100.00 |
| Piano | Inventory of Doctor Burwell Chick (1847) | Piano in Greenville County, South Carolina, 1847 | $195.00 |
| Trumpet | Inventory of Chilon Foster (1830) | Tin trumpet in Franklin County, Indiana, 1830 | $0.75 |

### Based Upon US Dollars

| Year | Value of 19th Century Dollar in 2002 US Dollars |
|------|-------------------------------------------------|
| 1825 | $18.00 |
| 1830 | $19.00 |
| 1835 | $20.00 |
| 1840 | $20.00 |
| 1845 | $23.00 |
| 1849 | $23.00 |

*Calculations are approximate values based upon economic historical data*

| Item | Data Source | Description | Price |
|------|-------------|-------------|-------|
| **Other** | | | |
| Admission | American Heritiage (1958) | Admission to the Trumbull Gallery of Painting at Yale College, New Haven, Connecticut, 1845 | $0.25 |
| Beaver Fur | Geoffery Ward, The West (1996) | Pound of Beaver fur in Missouri, 1837 | $4.00 |
| Book | Inventory of Isaac Hoar (1833) | Account book in Worcester, Massachusetts, 1833 | $0.30 |
| Bust | Inventory of Colonel John Stanard (1834) | Bust of General Jackson in Fredericksburg County in Virginia, 1834 | $1.00 |
| Canteen | Inventory of Doane Atwood (1829) | Canteen in Sturbridge, Massachusetts, 1829 | $0.08 |
| Dog House | Inventory of Aaron Bayard (1849) | Dog house in New Castle County, Delaware, 1849 | $0.06 |
| Door Frame | Inventory of Royston Betts Jr (1841) | Door frame in Fredericksburg County in Virginia, 1841 | $1.00 |
| Garden Tools | Inventory of Colonel John Stanard (1834) | Lot of garden tools in Fredericksburg County in Virginia, 1834 | $0.50 |
| Hobby horse | Inventory of Colonel John Stanard (1834) | Hobby horse in Fredericksburg County in Virginia, 1834 | $1.00 |
| Ink Stand | Inventory of Casswell Barrett (1846) | Ink stand in Greenville County, South Carolina, 1846 | $0.25 |
| Initiation Fee | Will of Major John Row, Sr. (1800) | Initiation fee for entrance into the Society for the Promotion of Internal Improvements, ca 1825 | $33.66 |
| Map | Inventory of William Blassingame (1846) | Map of the state of South Carolina in Greenville County, South Carolina, 1846 | $1.00 |
| Paper | Humphery Clark & Co. Account Book (1838) | Rheme Writting paper in Charleston, South Carolina, 1838 | $4.50 |
| Patent Rights | Arcadi Gluckman, Identifying Old U.S. Muskets, Rifles & Carbines (1965) | Sum paid to Dr Edward Maynard by the US Government to apply his tape primer device for 4,000 muskets, 1845 | $4,000.00 |
| Pocketbook | Inventory of Joseph Cloyes (1833) | Calfskin pocketbook in Worcester, Massachusetts, 1833 | $0.50 |
| Portrait | Inventory of Richard Johnston (1835) | Portrait of Jas Madison in Fredericksburg County in Virginia, 1835 | $5.00 |
| Portrait | Inventory of Richard Johnston (1835) | Portrait of Thos Jefferson in Fredericksburg County in Virginia, 1835 | $5.00 |
| Postage | Geoffery Ward, The West (1996) | Postage paid for letter from Fort Laramie, Wyoming to Sutter's Fort, California, 1849 | $0.25 |
| Refrigerator | Inventory of Richard Johnston (1835) | Refrigerator in Fredericksburg County in Virginia, 1835 | $10.00 |
| Slate | Inventory of Isaac Hoar (1833) | Slate in Worcester, Massachusetts, 1833 | $0.06 |
| Spectacles | Inventory of John Morrision (1834) | Pair of spectacles and case in Franklin County, Indiana, 1834 | $4.00 |
| Speech | Inventory of Richard Johnston (1835) | Speech of Rob Emmet in a frame in Fredericksburg County in Virginia, 1835 | $2.00 |
| Spice press | Inventory of Colonel John Stanard (1834) | Spice press in Fredericksburg County in Virginia, 1834 | $4.00 |
| Trap | Inventory of David C. Coyle (1827) | Wire rat trap in Fredericksburg County in Virginia, 1827 | $0.16 |
| Trap | Laurence A. Johnson, Over The Counter and On The Shelf 1620-1920 (1961) | Cost to purchase an animal trap produced by Sewall Newhouse in Oneida, New York | $0.62 |
| Umbrella | Humphery Clark & Co. Account Book (1838) | Silk umbrella in Charleston, South Carolina, 1838 | $4.50 |

| Item | Data Source | Description | Price |
|------|-------------|-------------|-------|
| Wallet | Inventory of Joseph Cloyes (1833) | Calfskin wallet in Worcester, Massachusetts, 1833 | $0.40 |
| Washing Machine | Inventory of Colonel John Stanard (1834) | Washing machine in Fredericksburg County in Virginia, 1834 | 12½ cents |

### Publication

| Item | Data Source | Description | Price |
|------|-------------|-------------|-------|
| Bible | Inventory of Colonel John Stanard (1834) | Family Bible in Fredericksburg County in Virginia, 1834 | $3.50 |
| Book | Inventory of Chilon Foster (1830) | Geography atlas in Franklin County, Indiana, 1830 | $1.00 |
| Book | Inventory of Dr. William Baker (1838) | Darwin's Zoonemia - 2 vol in Wilmington, Delaware, 1838 | $0.75 |
| Journal | Inventory of Dr. William Baker (1838) | American Journal of Medical Science -11 vol, Wilmington, Delaware, 1838 | $3.00 |
| Magazine | Inventory of Chilon Foster (1830) | Methodist magazine in Franklin County, Indiana, 1830 | $1.25 |
| Weekly | Inventory of Dr. William Baker (1838) | Nile's Weekly Register - 50 vols in Wilmington, Delaware, 1838 | $25.00 |

### Real Estate

| Item | Data Source | Description | Price |
|------|-------------|-------------|-------|
| Building Lease | San Francisco Chamber (2004) | A lease on a single story building at Kearny & Washington in San Francisco in 1847 | $6,000.00 |
| Cabin | Inventory of Doctor Burwell Chick (1847) | Acre of land and cabbin in Greenville County, South Carolina, 1847 | $75.00 |
| Farm | Inventory of Doane Atwood (1829) | Farm with buildings containing about 98½ acres in Sturbridge, Massachusetts, 1829 | $985.00 |
| Grocer | Laurence A. Johnson, Over The Counter and On The Shelf 1620-1920 (1961) | Cost to acquire property of a merchant store in Onondaga County, New York in 1839 by Henry Graves | $2,400.00 |
| Grocer | Laurence A. Johnson, Over The Counter and On The Shelf 1620-1920 (1961) | Cost to acquire property of a merchant store in Onondaga County, New York in 1839 by Richard Pomeroy | $2,400.00 |
| Insurance | Statutes at Large of South Carolina (1836) | Insurance on building of South Carolina College, 1836 | $500.00 |
| Land | Inventory of Coolidge Perry (1836) | Seventy eight rods of land with a dwelling house in Milford, Massachusetts, 1836 | $550.00 |

### Based Upon US Dollars

| Year | Value of 19th Century Dollar in 2002 US Dollars |
|------|-------------------------------------------------|
| 1825 | $18.00 |
| 1830 | $19.00 |
| 1835 | $20.00 |
| 1840 | $20.00 |
| 1845 | $23.00 |
| 1849 | $23.00 |

*Calculations are approximate values based upon economic historical data*

| Item | Data Source | Description | Price |
|------|-------------|-------------|-------|
| Land | Inventory of Doctor Burwell Chick (1847) | Seventy-five arces of land in Greenville County, South Carolina, 1847 | $261.00 |
| Lot | San Francisco Chamber (2004) | Value of a lot facing Portsmouth Plaza in San Francisco in 1847 | $16.50 |
| Lot | San Francisco Chamber (2004) | Value of a lot facing Portsmouth Plaza in San Francisco in early 1848 | $6,000.00 |
| Lot | San Francisco Chamber (2004) | Value of a lot facing Portsmouth Plaza in San Francisco in late 1848 | $45,000.00 |
| Pew | Inventory of Joseph Cloyes (1833) | Pew in First Cong Meeting House in Grafton, Massachusetts, 1833 | $20.00 |

## Servant

| Item | Data Source | Description | Price |
|------|-------------|-------------|-------|
| Slave | Inventory of George Spillers (1833) | Boy, Andrew in Greenville County, South Carolina, 1833 | $387.50 |
| Slave | Inventory of Mainville F. Lewis (1833) | Henry, a negro man in Greenville County, South Carolina, 1834 | $500.00 |
| Slave | Inventory of Mainville F. Lewis (1833) | Caty, a woman in Greenville County, South Carolina, 1834 | $425.00 |
| Slave | Inventory of Doctor Burwell Chick (1847) | Negro child Nancy Caroline Hodges in Greenville County, South Carolina, 1847 | $125.00 |

## Tobacco Products

| Item | Data Source | Description | Price |
|------|-------------|-------------|-------|
| Cigars | Inventory of Dr. William Baker (1838) | Box of segars in Wilmington, Delaware, 1838 | $0.50 |
| Cigars | Inventory of Doctor Burwell Chick (1847) | Box of sigars in Greenville County, South Carolina, 1847 | $6.00 |
| Spittoon | Laurence A. Johnson, Over The Counter and On The Shelf 1620-1920 (1961) | Cost for a wooden spittoon sold on a peddling wagon in 1828 | $0.25 |

## Trade Equipment & Tools

| Item | Data Source | Description | Price |
|------|-------------|-------------|-------|
| Apron | Inventory of Isaac Hoar (1833) | Leather apron in Worcester, Massachusetts, 1833 | $0.25 |
| Auger | Inventory of Coolidge Perry (1836) | One inch auger in Milford, Massachusetts, 1836 | $0.25 |
| Awl | Inventory of Joseph Milholland (1830) | Scribe awl in Franklin County, Indiana, 1830 | 12½ cents |
| Bammer | Inventory of William Servey (1836) | Shoe bammer in Uxbridge, Massachusetts, 1836 | $0.50 |
| Bench | Inventory of Isaac Hoar (1833) | Shoemakers bench in Worcester, Massachusetts, 1833 | $1.50 |
| Blacksmith Tools | Inventory of Doctor Burwell Chick (1847) | Set of blacksmith tools in Greenville County, South Carolina, 1847 | $33.75 |
| Carpenter tools | Inventory of Doctor Burwell Chick (1847) | Set of carpenters tools in Greenville County, South Carolina, 1847 | $7.00 |
| Chisel | Inventory of Joseph Milholland (1830) | Chisel in Franklin County, Indiana, 1830 | $0.20 |
| Compass | Inventory of Joseph Milholland (1830) | Pair of compasses in Franklin County, Indiana, 1830 | 18¼ cents |
| Cutters | Inventory of Amos Ainsworth (1837) | Peg cutter in Brookfield, Massachusetts, 1837 | 12½ cents |
| Diamond | Inventory of Doane Atwood (1829) | Diamond in Sturbridge, Massachusetts, 1829 | $2.00 |
| Fork | Inventory of Coolidge Perry (1836) | Peet fork in Milford, Massachusetts, 1836 | $0.75 |
| Gimlet | Inventory of Doane Atwood (1829) | Gimblet in Sturbridge, Massachusetts, 1829 | $0.04 |

| Item | Data Source | Description | Price |
|------|-------------|-------------|-------|
| Gouge | Inventory of Joseph Milholland (1830) | Gouge in Franklin County, Indiana, 1830 | 37½ cents |
| Hammer | Inventory of Isaac Hoar (1833) | Shoe hammer in Worcester, Massachusetts, 1833 | 62½ cents |
| Hammer | Inventory of Amos Ainsworth (1837) | Pegging hammer in Brookfield, Massachusetts, 1837 | $0.33 |
| Hide | Inventory of William Blassingame (1846) | Raw hide in Greenville County, South Carolina, 1846 | $1.60 |
| Horse | Inventory of Chilon Foster (1830) | Coopers horse in Franklin County, Indiana, 1830 | $0.25 |
| Jointer | Inventory of Doane Atwood (1829) | Coopers jointer in Sturbridge, Massachusetts, 1829 | $0.17 |
| Kit | Inventory of Coolidge Perry (1836) | Shoemakers kit in Milford, Massachusetts, 1836 | $5.00 |
| Knife | Inventory of Amos Ainsworth (1837) | Shoe knife in Brookfield, Massachusetts, 1837 | $0.06 |
| Leather | Inventory of Joseph Cloyes (1833) | Buffalo skin in Worcester, Massachusetts, 1833 | $4.00 |
| Leather | Inventory of William Servey (1836) | Foot of black grain leather in Uxbridge, Massachusetts, 1836 | $0.12 |
| Nails | Inventory of William Servey (1836) | Pound of shoe nails in Uxbridge, Massachusetts, 1836 | $0.10 |
| Nippers | Inventory of Amos Ainsworth (1837) | Pair of nippers in Brookfield, Massachusetts, 1837 | $0.34 |
| Patterns | Inventory of Coolidge Perry (1836) | Set sole leather patterns in Milford, Massachusetts, 1836 | $0.42 |
| Pincers | Inventory of Amos Ainsworth (1837) | Pair of pincers in Brookfield, Massachusetts, 1837 | $0.30 |
| Pinch | Inventory of Joseph Milholland (1830) | Pinch in Franklin County, Indiana, 1830 | 6¼ cents |
| Rule | Inventory of William Servey (1836) | Box rule in Uxbridge, Massachusetts, 1836 | $0.25 |
| Saw | Inventory of Joseph Milholland (1830) | Tenon saw in Franklin County, Indiana, 1830 | $1.12½ |
| Shave | Inventory of Doane Atwood (1829) | Crooked tray shave in Sturbridge, Massachusetts, 1829 | $0.06 |
| Spokes | Inventory of Joseph Milholland (1830) | Set of spokes in Franklin County, Indiana, 1830 | $0.25 |

## Based Upon US Dollars

| Year | Value of 19th Century Dollar in 2002 US Dollars |
|------|--------------------------------------------------|
| 1825 | $18.00 |
| 1830 | $19.00 |
| 1835 | $20.00 |
| 1840 | $20.00 |
| 1845 | $23.00 |
| 1849 | $23.00 |

*Calculations are approximate values based upon economic historical data*

| Item | Data Source | Description | Price |
|------|-------------|-------------|-------|
| Stamp | Inventory of Amos Ainsworth (1837) | Shoe stamp and marker in Brookfield, Massachusetts, 1837 | $0.08 |
| Steam Box | Inventory of Joseph Milholland (1830) | Steam box in Franklin County, Indiana, 1830 | $0.25 |
| Tallow & Sponge | Inventory of Isaac Hoar (1833) | Heel ball bayberry tallow & sponge in Worcester, Massachusetts, 1833 | $0.08 |
| Thread | Inventory of Coolidge Perry (1836) | Pound shoemaker's thread in Milford, Massachusetts, 1836 | $0.38 |
| Whetstones | Inventory of Isaac Hoar (1833) | Three whetstones and hone in Worcester, Massachusetts, 1833 | $0.50 |

### Travel & Transportation

| Item | Data Source | Description | Price |
|------|-------------|-------------|-------|
| Breakfast | Pace & McGee, The life and Times of Ridgeway, Virginia. | Price for breakfast at a tavern in Ridgeway, Virginia, 1849 | $0.25 |
| Coach | American Heritage (1960) | Fee advertized to American travelers in Europe for a four-horse a roundtrip coach ride from Brussels to Waterloo, 1848 | 5 Francs |
| Dinner | Pace & McGee, The life and Times of Ridgeway, Virginia. | Price for dinner at a tavern in Ridgeway, Virginia, 1849 | 37½ cents |
| Freight Expense | Milner, Oxford History of the American West | Cost per ounce for letters delivered from New York to California in 1848 | $0.80 |
| Hotel | Charleston Courier (1847) | One day at the Merchant's Hotel - Ladies' Ordinary - Corner of King and Society Streets, Charleston, South Carolina, 1847 | $1.50 |
| Lodging | Pace & McGee, The life and Times of Ridgeway, Virginia. | Price for a one night lodging at a tavern in Ridgeway, Virginia, 1849 | $0.25 |
| Lunch | Pace & McGee, The life and Times of Ridgeway, Virginia. | Price for lunch at a tavern in Ridgeway, Virgnia, 1849 | $0.25 |
| Ship | American Heritage (1960) | Approximate price for the whaling ship Wiscasset from New England with fittings and other expenses 1833 | $80,000.00 |
| Subsidy | American Heritiage (1957) | Subsidy, by British Post Office, to Samuel Cunard for shipment of mail from Liverpool to Boston, 1840 | $60,000.00 |
| Train Fare | Whitten, These were the Women | Fare from Lockport to Niagara in 1849 | $0.94 |
| Yacht | American Heritiage (1958) | Yacht of 102 feet in length and carry 140 tons, 1849 | $30,000.00 |
| Freight Rate | William Dutton, Du Pont (1949) | One ton of freight between New York and Buffalo on the Erie Canal, 1825 | $8.00 |

# MISCELLANY 1825-1849

## Account on Hiring Slaves from Owners, 1832

I have been going all day and have not hired a hand. The sale of Minors Negroes took place to day. The men sold from $500 to $700 the Women from 4 to $520. I had the promis of some hand here to day but in consequence of the prices they have been hired to others. Mr. Wayt hired his 200 to Mr. Clark for $105. Doct Masse has hired his hands to Clark also. I have not found a hand in this neighborhood that is willing to go Back or there masters to send them at $60. I shal leave here in the morning.

*Source: Letter written on January 2, 1832 by Jos. Wimm to Col. John Jordan, Lexington, Va concerning his attempts to hire slaves*

## Freedom of a Slave in Bourbon, Kentucky, 1843

Know all men by these presents that I Hugh Campbell of the County of Monroe and State of Indiana, for and in consideration of the faithfulness to me and for other consideration received of my negro Sam. Now in the County of Bourbon and State of Kentucky; doth hereby manumit and set free for life my said negro Sam. The Bourbon County court is hereby authorized to allow said negro man Sam the necessary freedom papers, upon his complying with the requisitions of the law in such case.

*Source: Letter of Hugh Campbell, Monroe County, Indiana, 1843*

## Diary of Christopher Columbus Baldwin, Templeton, Massachusetts

### January, 1830.

**1.** A very beautiful day. I am at Templeton, and spend the whole day in hunting. In the evening, the neighbors call at my father's and the time is spent in talking about former days and those who are now dead. Play whist.

**2.** Pleasant as before and warm. I read Gill Blas in the morning, and then take gun and dog, in company with brother Jonathan, and we go a hunting. Just at sunset we find a red squirrel upon the top of a very high dead pine and we fire at him seven times before we bring him down; adjudge to be twelve rods high and nothing in sight but his tail and ears! Neighbors come in at evening and we spent the time in pleasant conversation, Wm. Brown & Henry Newton.

**4.** Rise early, the day being pleasant & go a hunting all day. Have Asa Hosmer with me, who is a hunter by profession having done nothing else for several years. He informs me that during the last fall he caught eight hundred and thirty dozens of pigeons, and the story is confirmed by his father. We hunt foxes all day and have no luck. Some of the neighbors come in at night & we talk about old times, and how Templeton looked formerly.

**5.** Very pleasant, tho' it rained during Sunday night, which rendered the travelling very bad. At eleven, take the stage and return to Worcester. Have Isaac Bassett for a companion. There was a small boy in the stage whom we leave at Holden, believing him to be runaway; his name was Skiff, ten years old. Reach Worcester at sunset.

**12.** Very cold. We have venison today for dinner and have six gentlemen to dine with me. Dr. Butler & T[hornton] A. Merrick invite other gentlemen and we have a very pleasant time of it indeed. We drank temperately, yet did not go away dry, nor suffer our friends to, either. In the evening attend a party at Geo. T. Rice's.

### February, 1830.

**4.** Warmer and looks like a storm. The sleighing is perfect. Many parties of pleasure are formed to enjoy it.

**5.** Very pleasant, and very cold. A sleigh ride is got up to go to Westboro. Mr. Newcomb induces me to attend. Ride with him and Mary and Catherine Robinson in a 4-horse sleigh. Leave Worcester at 3 and return at 10. Between 20 & 30 in the party. Most all married people. Mulled wine was prepared for the ladies and flip for the gentlemen, but by *mistake* the flip is carried to the ladies and they do not find their error until our flip is mostly gone, when they pronounce it very unpleasant stuff !! I find that I have been very dissipated this week; and form a resolution to be more sober.

**6.** Thermometer this morning at 8 o'clock stands 10° below zero. It is very cold all day, and is said to be as cold as it was last Saturday. The Debating Club, composed of law students generally, hold a public debate...

**9.** Warmer and pleasant. In evening attend a geographical lecture from Mr. Evans.

**12.** Very cold. Study law all day, and in the evening attend Mr. Evans' lecture on geography. Go with Miss Elizabeth Green.

**22.** Washington's birthday. Ball in evening. I do not attend. It has been the invariable practice in this town for many years on the 22nd of February, the birthday of Washington, to have a public ball. I have been here seven years and a like observance of the day has not been omitted. During my residence here, I have, until now, at every ball with the exception of three, taken part as one of the managers. This year I did not attend. I am told by those who did that the occasion was very pleasant tho' the number was small, being only about twenty couples. The expense to each has always been three dollars. The music generally consists of two fiddles, a clarionet or bugle and base viol. The entertainer furnishes this under direction of the managers, and also carriages to collect & distribute the ladies. Two coaches are employed with a manager in each, who commence soon after sunset to carry the ladies to the hall, and it is a part of their duties to wait upon them home in the same way. The party retired about one o'clock, sometimes earlier and sometimes later.

*Source: "Diary of Christopher Columbus Baldwin, 1829-1835"*
*in* Transactions and Collections of
the American Antiquarian Society

## A record book of and dishonorable discharges from work, Lowell, Massachusetts, 1838-1839:

1838, *Dec.* 31. Ann ———. No. 4, weaving room; discharged for altering her looms and thinning her cloth.

1839, *Jan.* 2. Lydia ———. No. 1, spinning room; obtained an honorable discharge by false pretences. Her name has been sent round to the other Corporations as a thief and a liar.

*Jan.* 3. Harriet ——— and Judith ———. From No. 4, spinning room, and No. 5, weaving room; discharged as worthless characters.

*Jan.* 9. Lydia ———. From No. 2, spinning room; left irregularly; name sent round.

*Feb.* 15. Hadassah ———. From No. 3, lower weaving room; discharged for improper conduct—stealing from Mrs. ———.

*March* 8. Abby ———. No. 2, spinning room; discharged for improper conduct.

*March* 14. Ann ———, No. 2, spinning room; discharged for reading in the mill; gave her a line stating the facts.

*March* 26. Harriet ———, No. 4, carding room; Laura ———, No. 4, spinning room; Ellen ———, No.

1, carding room; George ———, repair shop—all discharged for improper conduct.

*March* 29. Martha ———, No. 2, spinning room; Apphia ———, No. 2, spinning room; left irregularly, and names sent round.

*April* 3. Emily ———. No. 5, carding room; discharged for profanity, and sundry other misdemeanors. Name sent round.

*Source: Rev. Henry A. Miles,* Lowell, As It Was, and As It *Is, 1845*

## Children's Story Book Excerpt, 1845

An old man found a rude boy upon one of his trees stealing apples, and desired him to come down; but the young sauce—box* told him plainly he would not. Won't you? said the old Man, then I will fetch you down; so he pulled up some tufts of grass, and threw at him; but this only made the Youngster laugh, to think the old Man should pretend to beat him down from the tree with grass only.

Well, well, said the old Man, if neither words nor grass will do, I must try what virtue there is in Stones; so the old man pelted him heartily with stones; which soon made the young chap haste down from the tree and beg the old man's pardon.

**MORAL.**

If good words and gentle means will not reclaim the wicked, they must be dealt with in a more severe manner.

*Source: Noah Webster,* The Pictorial Elementary
Spelling Book, *1845*

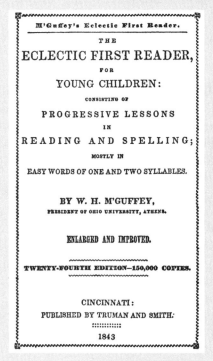

## The Occupation of Wagoner, *The Book of Trades, 1830*

Some wagons come a great distance to market, over high hills and wide plains. When this is the case the wagoner has a fine opportunity of becoming acquainted with different places, and also of improving his mind. As his wagon travels slowly, he has plenty of time to examine every important object that may be along the road; and should the day be warm, he can creep into his wagon, and read or lean back while his horses trudge along in the well-known road. Many wagon horses are furnished with bells, which are necessary in dark nights, both to warn people to get out of the wagon road, and to afford individuals an opportunity of purchasing articles along the way.

There are several other kinds of wagons beside the one we have mentioned, but they are all used in carrying some sort of provisions, either from the country to the city, or from one part of a town to another.

The occupation of the wagoner is a very healthy one. He is continually in the open air, and in constant exercise, either on horseback, or while walking beside his wagon; and when his labour is over, and he has received an ample reward for his trouble, he can spend many hours of quiet recreation at home.

Like all other employments, however, it has some disadvantages connected with it. The wagon is liable to be attacked by robbers when returning home at night, among solitary roads . . . . Besides this they suffer much in the winter, while exposed all day, and are often obliged to remain two or three weeks from their homes and families.

*Source:* The Book of Trades, *1830*

## Excerpts from the diary of Edward Jenner Carpenter, 1844:

**Tuesday March 5th, 1844**   It has been pleasant today but rather cold. I went down to the Literary Club tonight held in the Fellenburg Schoolhouse and listened to a debate on the question Which is productive of the most happiness Married life or Single life, it was decided by the President in the negative. As I came up from the Club I called at the Cotillion party held at Mr. Keith's & see them dance about an hour.

**Monday March 11th**   Very pleasant, the robins begin to appear to charm us with their songs.

After 9 this evening I went over to the Town Hall to see the Aristocracy of this village dance or make an attempt to dance. The music by

Mr. Temple Charles Lyons & Isaac Harkness was good I staid till nearly 11 o'clock I think I shall feel rather sleepy tomorrow therefore I will stop my scribbling and go to bed.

**Wednesday Sept 11th**   Rather pleasant but it looks a little like rain this evening. The Mechanics have a dance tonight down to Keiths. I went down and staid till 11 o'clock, therefore I think it would be well enough to retire if I want to feel right tomorrow.

**Friday, Oct 11th**   A pleasant day but cool morning & evening. There is a Cotillion Party down to Heath's this, Charles Lyons & Temple played for them.

**Monday Dec 16th**   Considerable cold.

Horatio Rockwood talks of starting a dancing school here if he can get scholars enough. I think I shall go, if I have to go alone. Terms $4.00 per couple.

**Thursday Dec 19th**   Rather milder than it was yesterday.

I put my name on to a paper, this evening, to go to the dancing school.

**Thursday Dec 26th**   I slept off my headache last night but I had a stiff neck in place of it. We had the first dancing school tonight, there was about 18 couples there, it went off first rate, we had a livery team to go around & pick up the girls. I had Frances Wells for a partner.

**Monday Dec 30th**   . . . . We had another dancing school this evening, we began to dance with the ladies a little, did not get along very well, but as well as could be expected for new beginners, we have another next Friday night. The "big bugs" have a dance tonight in opposition to ours.

*Source: "The Diary of an Apprentice Cabinetmaker: Edward Jenner Carpenter's 'Journal' 1844-45," edited by Christopher Clark in the* Proceedings of the American Antiquarian Society, *Vol. 98, Part 2 (Worcester, Mass.: 1988), 322-323, 356, 362, 371-378, 380-383, 385, 387, 394, by permission of the publisher. Selected entries. Edited by Old Sturbridge Village*

## Accepting a Marriage Proposal via Mail

[Postmarked Boston, May, 1840]

Mr. Freeman Dear Sir

I did not receive your letter until the 23rd of may and was happy to hear that your bodily health was good. My health is as good as it was when I left. I am sorry to hear that Augusta is so unwell. It makes it unpleasant for you but hope her Thomsonian medercine will relieve her.

You have give me an Invitation to your castle for a home and am happy of the Invitation as I know you are a man of honour. I shall throw myself upon your care and protection and according to your Invitation I will meet you at Brookfield the 5th day of June.

My respects to Augusta and except the same yourself.

Your sincere friend and well-wisher Mary Pease

*Source: Mary Pease to Pliny Freeman, Sr., May, 1840, Freeman Family Papers, Old Sturbridge Village Research Library*

## Choosing a Good Wife

**William Alcott's book of advice, *The Young Man's Guide,* regarding choosing a wife**

### Female Qualifications for Marriage.

1. *Moral Excellence.*

The highest as well as noblest trait in female character, is love to God . . . Indeed there are very few men to be found . . . who do not prefer pious companions of the other sex . . .

2. *Common Sense.*

Next on the list of particular qualifications in a female, for matrimonial life, I place COMMON SENSE . . . By *common sense,* as used in this place, I mean the faculty by means of which we see things *as they* really are. It implies judgement and discrimination, and a proper sense in regard to the common concerns of life . . . It is very different from genius or talent, as they are commonly defined; but much better than either. It never blazes forth with the splendor of noon, but shines with a constant and useful light. To the housewife—but, above all, to the mother—it is indispensible . . .

3. *Desire for Improvement.*

Whatever other recommendations a lady may possess, she should have an inextinguishable thirst for improvement. No sensible person can be truly happy in the world, without this; much less qualified to make others happy. But the genuine spirit of improvement, wherever it exists, atones for the absence of many qualities which would

otherwise be indispensable . . . with it, every thing else is rendered doubly valuable . . . *With* the fond, the ardent, the never failing desire to improve, physically, intellectually, and morally, there are few females who may not make tolerable companions for a man of sense;— *without* it, though a young lady were beautiful and otherwise lovely beyond comparison, wealthy as the Indies, surrounded by thousands of the most worthy friends, and even talented, let him beware! . . .

4. *Fondness for Children.*

Few traits of female character are more important than this . . . A dislike of children, even in men, is an unfavorable omen; in woman it is insupportable; for it is grossly unnatural . . . Wo[e] to the female who is doomed to drag out a miserable existence with a husband who 'can't bear children;' but thrice miserable is the doom of him who has a wife and a family of children, but whose children have no *mother!* . . .

No home can ever be a happy one to any of its inmates, where there is no maternal love, nor any desire for mental or moral improvement. But where these exist, in any considerable degree, and the original attachment was founded on correct principles, there is always hope of brighter days, even though clouds at present obscure the horizon. No woman who loves her husband, and desires to make continual improvement, will long consent to render those around her unhappy.

5. *Love of Domestic Concerns.*

Without the knowledge and the love of domestic concerns, even the wife of a peer, is but a poor affair . . . I am, however, addressing myself, in this work, to persons in the middle ranks of life; and here a knowledge of domestic affairs is so necessary in every wife, that the lover ought to have it continually in his eye. Not only a knowledge of these affairs—not only to know how things *ought to be done,* but how to *do them;* not only to know what ingredients ought to be put into a pie or a pudding, but to be able *to make* the pie or the pudding . . .

If a young farmer or mechanic *marry* a girl, who has been brought up only to 'play music;' to *draw,* to *sing,* to waste paper, pen and ink in writing long and half romantic letters, and to see shows, and plays, and read novels—if a young man do marry such an unfortunate young creature, let him bear the consequences with temper . . .

It is cold comfort for a hungry man, to tell him how delightfully his wife plays and sings. *Lovers* may live on very aerial diet, but husbands stand in need of something more solid; and young women may take my word for it, that a constantly clean table, well cooked victuals, a house in order, and a cheerful fire will do more towards preserving a husband's heart, than all the 'accomplishments' taught in all the 'establishments' in the world without them.

6. *Sobriety.*

. . . By *sobriety,* I do not mean a habit which is opposed to *intoxication,* for if that be hateful in a man, what must it be in a woman? . . . By the word SOBRIETY in a young woman, I mean a great deal more than even a rigid abstinence from a love of drink...I mean sobriety of conduct. The word *sober* and its derivatives mean *steadiness, seriousness, carefulness, scrupulous propriety of conduct* .

Now this kind of sobriety is of great importance in the person with whom we are to live constant-ly...When they [girls] are arrived at an age which turns their thoughts toward a situation for life; when they begin to think of having the command of a house, however small or poor, it is time to cast away, not the cheerfulness or the simplicity, but the *levity* of a child . . .

This sobriety is a title to trustworthiness; and this, young man, is the treasure that you ought to prize above all others. Miserable is the husband who, when he crosses the threshold of his house, carries with him doubts, and fears, and suspicions. I do not mean suspicions of the *fidelity* of his wife; but of her care, frugality, attention to his interests, and to the health and morals of his children . . . He is the happy husband who can go away at a moment's warning . . . no more fearing to find, on his return, any thing wrong, than he would fear a dis-continuance of the rising and setting of the sun . . .

But in order to possess this precious *trustworthi-ness,* you must, if you can, exercise your reason in the choice of your partner . . .

7. *Industry.*

Let not the individual whose eye catches the word *industry,* at the beginning of this division of my subject, condemn me as degrading females to the condition of mere wheels in a machine for money-making; for I mean no such thing . . .

Still if woman is intended to be a 'help meet,' for the other sex, I know of no reason why she should not be so in physical concerns, as well as mental and moral . . . The woman who does not actually prefer action to inaction—industry to idleness—labor to ease—and who does not resolve to labor moderately as long as she lives, whatever her

circumstances, is unfit for life, social or domestic . . . It is not for me to say, in what *form* her labor shall be applied, except in rearing the young . . .

But, who is to tell whether a girl will make an industrious woman? . . . There are . . . certain *rules,* which, if attended to with care, will serve as pretty sure guides.

And, first, if you find the tongue lazy, you may be nearly certain that the hands and feet are not very industrious . . . The pronunciation of an industrious person is generally *quick,* and *distinct;* the voice, if not strong, *firm* at the least . . .

Another mark of industry is, *a quick step,* and a somewhat *heavy tread,* showing that the foot comes down with a *hearty good will.* If the body lean a little forward, and the eyes keep steadily in the same direction, while the feet are going, so much the better, for these discover earnestness to arrive at the intended point . . .

8. *Early Rising.*

*Early rising* is another mark of industry . . . Where a living and a provision for children is to be sought by labor of some sort or other, late rising in the wife is certain ruin; and rarely will you find an early-rising wife, who had been a late-rising girl . . .

9. *Frugality.*

This means the contrary of extravagance. It does not mean *stinginess;* it does not mean *pinch-ing;* but it means an abstaining from all unneces-sary expenditure, and all unnecessary use of goods of any and of every sort. It is a quality of great importance, whether the rank in life be high or low . . . Some of the indications of extravagance in a lady are ear-rings, broaches, bracelets, buck-les, necklaces, diamonds, (real or mock,) and nearly all the ornaments which women put upon their persons . . . To marry a girl of this disposi-tion is really self-destruction. You never can have either property or peace . . .

10. *Personal Neatness.*

. . . There never can exist, for any length of time, ardent *affection,* in any man towards a woman who neglects neatness, either in her person, or in her house affairs . . .

How much do women lose by inattention to these matters! . . . Beauty is valuable; it is one of the *ties,* and a *strong* one too; but it cannot last to old age; whereas the charm of cleanliness never ends but with life itself . . . So the most beautiful woman, if found with an uncleansed skin, is, in my estimation, the most disagreeable.

11. *A Good Temper*

. . . By 'good temper,' I do not mean an easy temper, a serenity which nothing disturbs; for that is a mark of laziness. Sullenness, if you be not too blind to perceive it, is a temper to be avoided by all means . . .

*Querulousness* is a great fault . . . An everlasting complaining, without rhyme or reason, is a bad sign. It shows want of patience, and indeed, want of sense. But the contrary of this, a cold *indifference,* is still worse . . .

*Pertinacity* is a very bad thing in anybody, and especially in a young woman; and it is sure to increase in force with the age of the party. To have the last word, is a poor triumph; but with some people it is a species of disease of the mind . . . A fierce *disputer* is a most disagreeable companion . . .

Still, of all the faults as to *temper,* your melancholy ladies have the worst, unless you have the same mental disease yourself . . .

12. *Accomplishments.*

By accomplishments, I mean those things, which are usually comprehended in what is termed a useful and polite education . . .

Mental cultivation, and even what is called *polite* learning . . . are a most valuable acquisition, and make every female, as well as all her associates, doubly happy. It is only when books, and music, and a taste for the fire arts are substituted for other and more important things, that they should be allowed to change love or respect to disgust . . .

*Source: William A. Alcott,* The Young Man's Guide, *Fourteenth Edition, 1839*

### Cooking Ice, 1831

*To produce ice for culinary purposes.* Fill a gallon stone bottle with hot spring water, leaving about a pint vacant, and put in 2 oz. of fined nitre; the bottle must then be stopped very close, and let down into a deep well. After three or four hours it will be completely frozen; but the bottle must be broken to procure the ice. If the bottle is moved up and down so as to be sometimes in and sometime out of the water, the consequent evaporation will hasten the process. The heating of the water assists the subsequent congelation; and experience has proved, that hot water in winter will freeze more rapidly than cold water just drawn from a spring.

*Source:* Secrets of All Trades and Arts, *1831*

# 1850-1865

# Railroads, Slavery and a Nation at War with Itself

## PRESIDENTS

| | |
|---|---|
| Millard Fillmore | 1850-1853 |
| Franklin Pierce | 1853-1857 |
| James Buchanan | 1857-1861 |
| Abraham Lincoln | 1861-1865 *(Assassinated)* |
| Andrew Johnson | 1865-1869 |

By the turn of the half-century mark, two distinct, dissimilar social structures had developed within the United States-one in the South and the other in the North. The agricultural South was focused on crops such as cotton, tobacco, sugar and rice, often grown with slave labor. The North, while still tied to farming, had diversified its economy with commerce and manufacturing, fueled by low wage labor. Many came to believe that the two regions were so divergent in their economies and views concerning the morality of slavery that holding the Union together might prove impossible. The politics of fear invaded nearly every issue.

Fittingly, the period began with the Compromise of 1850, brokered by Henry Clay in a futile attempt to end sectional controversy and preserve the nation's unity. To Southerners he offered the enactment of a drastic fugitive slave law mandating the return of runaways, plus the organization of the New Mexico and Utah territories. To the North, Clay called for the admission of California as a free state and abolition of the slave trade in Washington, DC, the nation's capital. It proved to be a measure that merely delayed the actual outbreak of the Civil War for a decade.

At the same time the national economy was growing in a variety of ways. As a result of natural increase, immigration and the absorption of people living in the acquired territories, there were six times as many people-31.4 million-in the United States in 1860 as in 1800. Similarly, labor productivity rose impressively. In 1860, one person could produce twice as much wheat as in 1800, twice as much pig iron and more than four times as much cotton cloth. Between 1840 and 1860, the nation's agricultural output more than

doubled in value, and its mining and manufacturing industries tripled.

In the North, the economy was aided by the swell of the wage-earner class, even during the midst of the Civil War, when millions of foreigners from Ireland, Germany and Britain made their way to industrial America. Thanks to this massive influx, foreign-born workers represented about 15 percent of employees in the 1850s. Industrial production increased 50 percent from 1850 to 1860, and another 65 percent in the war-torn decade of the 1860s. But this dependence on manufacturing had its downside. When the nation's economy dipped in 1857, cotton-textile employment for the state of Rhode Island, for example, fell by 68 percent, jewelry by 78 percent and iron works employment by 43 percent. Wages shrank at the same rate. Skilled workers accustomed to $1.25 a day found their pay plummet to $0.60 per day. Yet, remittances by immigrants to relatives and friends in the Old World-often used to pay the cost of passage to discover America themselves-grew during this period.

The decade before the Civil War also saw the expansion of slavery as Southern planters fanned west to Louisiana, Tennessee, Arkansas and Texas. In the 1850s, the American South produced five million bales of cotton annually, or two-thirds of all the cotton grown in the world. Most was sold to the British, whose textile mills clothed Europe, America, East Asia and parts of Africa. This made the South highly dependent on English manufacturing needs and thus made small, single-crop cotton planters highly vulnerable to fluctuations in cotton prices. By 1850, 31 percent of the Southern white population owned slaves; by 1860, the percentage was down to 26 percent.

At the top of the slaveholding pyramid was the planter aristocracy, representing less than three percent of all slaveholders, but possessing one-fourth of all slaves. Their slave plantations of sugar cane, rice, tobacco or cotton produced enormous wealth and concentrated power in the hands of a few. The wealthy actively discouraged the creation of factories, the immigration of foreign-born workers, and even the building of major cities to control competition.

During the period, too, ambition and discovery were populating the frontier West, unleashing an army of eager fortune hunters willing to leave the past behind, often on a whim. The discovery of gold in California in 1849 touched off a dramatic migration west by boat, by horse and by rail. In a similar fashion, earlier discoveries had dispersed the national population when the discovery of salt mining deposits in Michigan drew workers from Cape Cod and copper mining drew unprecedented settlers to Colorado. This westward expansion also accelerated the building of railroads nationwide. Ironically, the dramatic rise in railroad construction, which drove the economy of this period, was largely funded by foreign investors, primarily the Germans and the British.

By 1850, schools were also undergoing a revolutionary change. Based on a reform movement begun in the 1830s, most Northern and Western communities endorsed and supported free education, including compulsory attendance for students and training of teachers, along with a curriculum suitable for the changing workplace of the times. At the outbreak of the Civil War, the United States could justly boast of the most complete and highly developed public school system in the world.

The dominant event of the period was the Civil War, America's second revolution. When new President Abraham Lincoln took the oath of office in 1861, seven Southern states had already departed the Union and more were teetering on the edge. Lincoln believed secession was impractical. How would the national debt be divided? What portion of the territories would each claim? How would fugitive slaves be dealt with? In addition, a divided United States of America was far more susceptible to foreign imperialism from the major powers in Europe.

But the rebellious Confederacy did possess the advantage of geography. To reunite the nation, the Union Army was required to invade the South and drag it back-a daunting task, indeed. However, the North was blessed with size and wealth. The more prosperous North boasted a population of 32 million, capable of mobilizing 2.5 million soldiers; the South claimed 9 million people, 3.5 million of them slaves. Largely because of the availability of slave labor, the South was able to mobilize one million men. Many southerners believed they were defending a fundamental way of life. As one South Carolina planter wrote, "Slavery with us is no abstraction but a great and vital fact. Without it our every comfort would be taken from us. Our wives, our children made unhappy-education, the light of knowledge-all, all lost and our people ruined forever."

To finance the battle of state against state and brother against brother, the North substantially increased the taxes on tobacco and alcohol, while also imposing the first income tax in the nation's history. Customs receipts also proved to be an important revenue source. The Treasury issued paper money called Greenbacks, the value of which, while backed by gold, fluctuated widely during the war years. The South used its printing presses to keep the war financed, issuing nearly $1 billion in inadequately backed treasury notes. The resulting inflation rendered Confederate money virtually worthless. The physical devastation, primarily in the South, was enormous: burned or plundered homes, pillaged farms, destroyed railway lines, ruined buildings, bridges and dams, devastated college campuses, and neglected roads all left the South in economic ruin. The direct monetary costs of the conflict were recorded at $15 billion, a figure that does not include the lost potential of the more than one million men and women who died on the battlefield or from disease. The approximately 10,455 Civil War military engagements, accidents, suicides, sicknesses, murders, and executions resulted in total casualties of 1,094,453. Estimates of wounded Union army personnel top 275,000; Confederate records indicate 194,000 were wounded.

# HISTORICAL SNAPSHOTS
## 1850-1865

### 1850–1859

**1850**

- President Zachary Taylor died after serving only 16 months; he was succeeded by Vice President Millard Fillmore
- Ninety-eight percent of the population died before age 65
- The Compromise Bill of 1850 on slavery was passed to preserve the fragile union of states
- The Allan Pinkerton Agency was founded
- Folger's Coffee was established in San Francisco to sell coffee to miners
- Ninety percent of the black population of 3.6 million was native-American born
- Baking powder was invented
- Thirteen states stopped the practice of committing women to mental institutions based solely on the word of their husbands
- Book publishers began switching to cheaper paper based on wood pulp instead of rags and linen
- Nathaniel Hawthorne's *The Scarlet Letter* was published
- California was admitted as the thiry-first state

**1851**

- Abolitionist Sojourner Truth delivered her "Ain't I a Woman?" speech at a women's rights conference in Akron, Ohio
- The Dakota Indians agreed to sell 24 million acres in Minnesota
- Photography advanced with the development of a new emulsion called collodion
- Maine became the first state to prohibit the sale of alcohol
- Harriet Beecher Stow published the first installment of *Uncle Tom's Cabin* in *The National Era*
- *The New York Times* was founded as a counterpoint to Horace Greeley's *Tribune*

- The Sioux pledged not to harass the wagon trains traveling the Oregon Trail in exchange for a $50,000 annuity
- Isaac Singer was granted a patent on a sewing machine
- Louis Napoleon, the nephew of Napoleon Bonaparte, staged a coup and took power in France
- Herman Melville's novel *Moby Dick* was first published in the United States
- Fire swept the Library of Congress in Washington, DC, destroying about 35,000 volumes
- The Great Exhibition in London was the first World's Fair

**1852**

- Gun manufacturer Smith & Wesson was founded in Springfield, Massachusetts
- The first Holstein cow was shipped to North America on a Dutch ship on which sailors requested milk
- Dog tags were introduced
- Emma Snodgrass was arrested in Boston for wearing pants
- The number of Chinese in California reached 25,000
- Uncle Sam made his debut as a cartoon character in the *New York Lantern*
- Henry C. Wells founded Wells, Fargo & Co. with William C. Fargo in San Francisco
- The first edition of Peter Mark Roget's *Thesaurus* was published
- Louis Napoleon established the Second Empire in France and called himself Napoleon III

**1853**

- Heinrich Steinweg founded a piano company called Steinway & Sons three years after moving to America from Germany
- The United States acquired 45,000 square miles of land from Mexico in the Gadsden Purchase

- The 22-acre island of Alcatraz was fortified to protect San Francisco from attack
- Levi Strauss and Co. started selling tough pants to California gold miners
- The New Haven Clock Company was founded
- The hypodermic needle was invented for morphine injection
- Karl Gerhardt discovered aspirin
- Elisha Graves Otis invented the safety elevator powered by steam
- The Territory of Washington was organized
- Cincinnati became the first city to pay its firefighters a regular salary
- Gail Borden applied for a patent for condensed milk
- Japan opened its ports to trade with the West after 250 years of isolation
- Verdi's opera *Il Trovatore* premiered in Rome

**1854**

- The Knights of the Golden Circle was organized in the Midwest to promote the extension of slavery
- Yosemite Valley was granted to California as a public trust
- The New England Emigrant Aid Society was created to colonize Kansas with northern abolitionists
- Phillip Morris began making cigarettes in London
- Florence Nightingale nursed wounded soldiers at Scutari Hospital in Turkey during the Crimean War
- Anthony Foss patented an accordion
- Approximately 50 slavery opponents met to call for the creation of a new political group, which became the Republican Party
- The territories of Nebraska and Kansas were established

- The U.S. Naval Academy in Annapolis, Maryland, held its first graduation
- Henry David Thoreau published *Walden*
- Henry Meyer patented a sleeping rail car
- Alfred, Lord Tennyson's poem, "The Charge of the Light Brigade," was published in England

## 1855

- President Millard Fillmore declined an honorary degree from the University of Oxford, saying, "I had not the advantage of a classical education, and no man should, in my judgment, accept a degree he cannot read"
- The Makah tribe of Washington secured the right to continue hunting whales
- Conical innersprings came into use in furniture seats
- The first train crossed Niagara Falls on a suspension bridge
- Abraham Gesner patented kerosene
- Walt Whitman published *Leaves of Grass,* a collection of 12 poems
- The calliope was patented by Joshua Stoddard of Worcester, Massachusetts
- The Bessemer steel-making process was patented
- P.T. Barnum wrote *The Life of P.T. Barnum, Written by Himself*
- Henry Wadsworth Longfellow composed his poem "Hiawatha"
- The Point Bonita lighthouse was built for ships approaching the Golden Gate of San Francisco

## 1856

- Mifflin W. Gibbs founded California's first African-American newspaper
- Democrat James Buchanan was elected president
- Fly-tackle manufacturer Orvis began operations in Manchester, Vermont
- A Neanderthal skeleton was found in a limestone cave in Germany

- Borax was discovered in Tuscan Springs, California
- Lawrence, Kansas, was captured and sacked by pro-slavery forces
- Massachusetts Senator Charles Sumner was assaulted on the senate floor by South Carolina's Preston Brooks
- The Republican Party nominated John C. Fremont at its first national convention
- Cyrus Chambers Jr. patented a machine that folded books and newspapers

## 1857

- Frederick Law Olmstead and Calvert Vaux won the competition to develop Central Park in New York City
- Laclede Gas Light Co. was formed in St. Louis to provide gas-powered street lamps
- The Supreme Court ruled in the Dred Scott case that black people were not citizens and could not expect federal protection
- A horse-drawn potato planter was patented in America
- Moses G. Farmer and William Francis Channing were granted the patent for an electric fire alarm system
- A nationwide financial crunch was ignited by the failure of the New York branch of the Ohio Life Insurance and Trust Company
- Timothy Alder patented a typesetting machine
- The American Chess Association was formed
- *The Atlantic Monthly* magazine was first published
- John Mohler Studebaker's South Bend, Indiana, firm began producing wagons and carriages

## 1858

- Eleazer A. Gardner of Philadelphia patented a cable street car run on overhead cables
- The pencil with an eraser attached on one end was patented by Hyman L. Lipman of Philadelphia
- Minnesota became the thirty-second state

- U.S. Senate candidate Abraham Lincoln declared that the slavery issue had to be resolved, declaring, "A house divided against itself cannot stand"
- Darwin's theory of evolution was unveiled at a meeting of the Linnean Society of London
- An admission of $0.50 was charged at the All Star baseball game between New York and Brooklyn
- The first transatlantic cable was completed
- The Butterfield Overland Mail Company began delivering mail from St. Louis to San Francisco
- Hamilton Smith patented a rotary washing machine
- RH Macy and Company opened its first store at 6th Avenue, New York City
- The New York Symphony Orchestra held its first performance

## 1859

- Ground was broken in Egypt for the Suez Canal
- French acrobat Blondin crossed Niagara Falls on a tightrope as 5,000 spectators watched
- Florence Nightingale authored *Notes on Hospitals,* which addressed hospital management
- A report relating tobacco to cancer was published in France
- Alfred Nobel built a factory to manufacture nitroglycerin in Sweden
- Oregon was admitted to the Union as the thirty-third state
- Former army officer Colonel Edwin L. Drake drilled the first oil well in Titusville, Pennsylvania
- Harriot E. Wilson became the first African-American woman to publish a novel in the United States
- Abolitionist John Brown led a group of about 20 men in a raid on the Federal Arsenal at Harper's Ferry
- Evangelist Phoebe Palmer published *Promise of the Father* on a woman's right to preach
- Charles Darwin published *On the Origin of Species*
- South Carolina declared itself an "independent commonwealth"

## 1860–1869

### 1860

- Former Illinois congressman Abraham Lincoln was elected president
- The U.S. Secret Service was created to arrest counterfeiters and protect the president.
- The nation's first successful silver mill began operations near Virginia City, Nevada
- The Great Lakes Brewing Co. was established in Cleveland
- Mass production of watches began
- Quicksilver was discovered in the Mayacamas Range of Calistoga, California
- A New England-based strike of shoemakers that involved 20,000 workers resulted in higher wages for all workers, including women workers
- The First Pony Express rider arrived in San Francisco with mail originating in St. Joseph, Missouri
- Mary Ann Evans, under the name George Eliot, wrote her novel *The Mill on the Floss*
- English inventor Frederick Walton made "linoleum" out of linseed oil
- The martini drink cocktail was invented
- South Carolina became the first state to secede from the Union

### 1861

- The Civil War was ignited when South Carolina forces fired on federal troops housed at Fort Sumter in Charleston Harbor, South Carolina
- President Abraham Lincoln declared a state of insurrection and called for 75,000 Union volunteers
- New York City's mayor proposed that it become a free city so it might continue trading with the North and the South during the conflict
- Mississippi and Florida became the second and third states to secede from the Union
- Delegates from six Southern states met to form the Confederate States of America
- The population of the Northern states was approximately 22 million; the total Southern population was about 9 million including 3.5 million slaves
- General Winfield Scott offered Robert E. Lee command of the Union army, but Lee declined, deciding to support the Confederacy
- The federal government levied an income tax for the first time to finance the war
- In the first major battle of the Civil War, Confederate forces repelled the Union Army; the battle became known by the Confederates as Manassas, while the Union called it Bull Run
- Matthew Brady began a quest to make a complete photographic record of the Civil War

- Camels were brought to Virginia City, Nevada, to carry supplies and salt for miners at the Comstock Lode
- Kansas was admitted as the thirty-fourth state of the Union

### 1862

- The Homestead Act officially opened the Nebraska territory for settlement
- The Morrill Act granted large tracts of public land to the states with the directive to sell for the support of institutions teaching the mechanical and agricultural arts
- "The Battle Hymn of the Republic" by Julia Ward Howe was first published in *The Atlantic Monthly* as an anonymous poem
- The five-hour battle of ironclads between the *Merrimac* of the South and the *Monitor* resulted in a draw at Hampton Roads, Virginia
- Slavery was abolished in Washington, DC
- The Battle of Shiloh in Tennessee resulted in the death of 9,000 soldiers
- The bugle call known as "Taps" was introduced in the Union Army
- The U.S. Army Ambulance Corps was established
- The Sioux Uprising erupted in Minnesota
- Union forces were defeated by the Confederates at the Second Battle of Bull Run in Manassas, Virginia

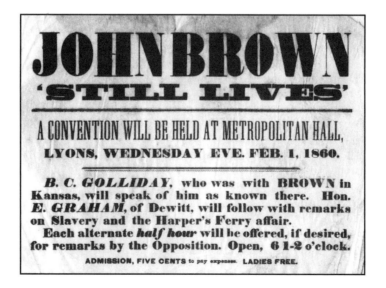

## 1863

- Abraham Lincoln signed the Emancipation Proclamation
- The National Bank Act was passed to create a market in government bonds needed to finance the Civil War
- President Lincoln signed the Conscription Act compelling U.S. citizens to report for duty in the Civil War or pay $300
- Rioting against the military draft erupted in New York City, resulting in the death of about 1,000 people over three days
- The three-day Battle of Gettysburg in Pennsylvania ended in a major victory for the North
- General U.S. Grant's Union Army captured the Confederate town of Vicksburg after a long siege
- President Lincoln delivered the Gettysburg Address
- Roller skates with four wheels were patented by James Plimpton of New York
- Construction began on the Central Pacific Railroad from Sacramento, California, heading east
- Lewis Carroll published *Alice's Adventures in Wonderland*
- Free city delivery of mail was authorized by the U.S. Postal Service
- Confederate General Stonewall Jackson was killed by friendly fire as he returned to his lines during the Battle of Chancellorsville in Virginia
- West Virginia was admitted as the thirty-fifth state
- President Lincoln declared the last Thursday in November Thanksgiving Day
- The Worldwide Red Cross was organized in Geneva

## 1864

- President Lincoln was reelected with Andrew Johnson as his vice president
- Both the Union and the Confederate armies suffered significant losses during the Battle of Spotsylvania, Virginia
- The Confederate submarine *H.L. Hunley* attacked the *USS Housatonic* in Charleston Harbor, South Carolina, killing five Union soldiers and all nine crewmembers of the *Hunley*
- Union Major General William T. Sherman's troops set fires that destroyed much of Atlanta during their march through the South
- General Ulysses S. Grant banned the trading of prisoners
- The first travel accident policy was issued to James Batterson by the Travelers Insurance Company
- Congress authorized the use of the phrase "In God We Trust" for the first time on a $0.02 coin
- Congress created the Montana Territory
- Secretary of War Edwin M. Stanton signed an order establishing a military burial ground at Confederate General Robert E. Lee's home estate in Arlington, Virginia
- Maryland voters adopted a new constitution that included the abolition of slavery
- Nevada became the thirty-sixth state

## 1865

- Union General William T. Sherman conducted a "scorched earth" march through the Carolinas, where he called for 40 acres and a mule to be given to freed slaves' families
- The South Carolina capital city, Columbia, was half-destroyed by fire as Union forces marched through
- Confederate President Davis and most of his Cabinet fled to Danville, Virginia, when its previous capital, Richmond, was engulfed in flames
- Confederate General Robert E. Lee surrendered to General Ulysses S. Grant at Appomattox Court House, Virginia, ending the Civil War
- President Lincoln was shot and mortally wounded by John Wilkes Booth
- Vice President Andrew Johnson became the seventeenth president
- The Thirteenth Amendment to the Constitution, abolishing slavery, was adopted by Congress
- Approximately 12,000 Chinese workers were brought to America to help complete the transcontinental railroad
- E.L. Godkin announced the start of a new magazine called *The Nation*
- The auction house of Butterfield & Butterfield was established
- The first known baseball card was issued featuring the Brooklyn Atlantics
- Machine-made left and right shoes replaced the "straights" that fit on either foot
- Jules Verne published his book *From the Earth to the Moon*

# Currency Issues and War

In the beginning of the 1850s, the banking and currency markets within the United States were stable. In the previous years, the government debated how to resolve the nation's banking and currency issues, but was unable to arrive at a unified resolution. As a result, many state legislatures enacted banking guidelines and regulations that supported commercial activity while upholding the federal constitution. Many of the conditions required sound investments with liquid collateral in the event of a default and provisions mandating the publication of reports on a bank's condition to remove any questions regarding operations. Even with the protections in place, the only currencies typically permitted would be ones backed by gold or silver specie.

It was not until 1851 that the use of paper checks became more acceptable as a form of paper currency. Checks initially appeared in New York City as a necessity for commerce and trade. The city established a clearinghouse that enabled the business community to use paper checks. Banks imposed restrictions on their clients as to the proper use of writing checks on their accounts. Once a bank received a check from an associated bank, it would daily send the checks it collected to the clearinghouse. Under the clearinghouse, interbank transactions would be accounted for and recorded, permitting a check to be accepted and returned to the origin of the account. Through regulation, reporting and required deposits against liabilities, checks would work through the clearinghouse with little difficulty. The system diminished the use of actual cash in the market and maintained the required gold and silver currency needed within the banks. Banks in other cities rapidly established their own clearinghouses.

The economic growth of the1850s saw an increase in imports over exports, resulting in a diminished amount of gold and silver specie available within the nation's banks. Railway construction grew rapidly during this period, but many foreign lenders lacked interest in a large number of American investments. This resulted in many banks in the United States absorbing a large number of railroad loans. The strong economy further limited the amount of gold and silver specie. When the Ohio Life Insurance and Trust Company failed to process notes from Eastern banks in 1857, a national financial crisis occurred, known as the Panic of 1857.

Banks that provided large loans on railroad construction and speculative transactions were unable to call in debt obligations and failed to raise the necessary gold and silver specie. The nation experienced thousands of business failures and inflation during the Panic of 1857. To resolve the matter, the federal government issued over $20 million in treasury notes to resupply the necessary gold and silver within the economy. President Buchanan attacked the banks for the negative impact they provided on the nation's economy, depreciation of property and national debt. By the time the economy turned toward recovery with resumed railroad construction, manufacturing and trade, the nation was inching closer to war.

The election results of 1860 provided a fiscal and political change as Southern banks withdrew funds from Northern banks and states talked of secession. The pending action created another fiscal downturn by November of 1860. The government issued treasury notes at extremely high rates because the nation's credit was poor. With the country at war, its fiscal stability became more of a priority.

In 1862, the United States Government suspended payment with gold and silver specie throughout the country. As a substitute for gold and silver for debt payment, the government issued legal tender notes called Greenbacks. The government promised to pay the holder of the Greenbacks in gold within 5 years at a rate of 6 percent. The financial community realized that the Greenbacks would be paid upon the success of the Union Army and the political results of the war. Throughout the Civil War, speculation occurred with individuals trading Greenbacks for gold dollars.

With the end of the Civil War, currency depreciated greatly and impacted the entire nation. Many supporters of the Confederacy invested in Southern bonds and banks; this resulted in a large number of losses in a worthless Confederate debt. The government amassed substantial debt to finance its war efforts at a significant cost. The debt obligation on the unified country had to be repaid and was an issue addressed during the nation's postwar reconstruction.

# SELECTED INCOMES 1850-1865

| Occupation | Data Source | Description | Price |
|---|---|---|---|
| Appraisal | Inventory of Wm. Phillips | For appraising property of Wm Phillips of Collin County Texas, 1857 | $9.00 |
| Attorney General | The Texas Almanac (1857) | Annual salary of the Attorney General of Texas | $1,800.00 |
| Blacksmith | US Census (1976) | Daily wage of a blacksmith in the United States, 1860 | $1.62 |
| Blacksmith | The Congressional Globe (1863) | Monthly pay of blacksmiths in the United States Army, 1863 | $18.00 |
| Blacksmith | US Census (1976) | Daily wage of a blacksmith in the United States, 1865 | $2.50 |
| Bottle Maker | McKearin, American Bottles & Flasks (1978) | Salary paid per dozen quart bottles made at McCully's Sligo Glass Works in Stoddard, New Hampshire, 1856 | $0.09 |
| Bottle Maker | McKearin, American Bottles & Flasks (1978) | Daily earnings from a worker at a bottle factory for manufacturing 28 dozen quart wine bottles in Stoddard, New Hampshire, 1856 | $2.66 |
| Bugler | The Congressional Globe (1863) | Monthly pay of buglers in the United States Army, 1863 | $15.00 |
| Carpenter | US Census (1976) | Daily wage for a carpenter on the Erie Canal, 1851 | $1.50 |
| Carpenter | Wells, The Origins of the South Middle Class (2004) | Daily wages for a Georgia carpenter in 1853 | $2.00 |
| Carpenter | US Census (1976) | Daily wage for a carpenter on the Erie Canal, 1855 | $1.75 |
| Carpenter | Eliot Lord, History of the Comstock Lode (1959) | Daily wage of a carpenter in Virginia City, Nevada, 1860 | $6.00 |
| Carpenter | US Census (1976) | Daily wage for a carpenter on the Erie Canal, 1860 | $1.75 |
| Carpenter | US Census (1976) | Daily wage of a carpenter in the United States, 1860 | $1.65 |
| Carpenter | US Census (1976) | Daily wage for a carpenter on the Erie Canal, 1863 | $2.00 |
| Carpenter | US Census (1976) | Daily wage for a carpenter on the Erie Canal, 1865 | $2.50 |
| Carpenter | US Census (1976) | Daily wage of a carpenter in the United States, 1865 | $2.68 |
| Carriage maker | Wells, The Origins of the South Middle Class (2004) | Average annual wage for white male at Hodgson Carriage in Georgia in 1853 | $780.00 |
| Chief Justice | The Texas Almanac (1857) | Annual salary of the Chief Justice of the Supreme Court of Texas | $3,000.00 |
| Commissioner | The Texas Almanac (1857) | Annual Salary of the Commissioner of General Land Office in Texas | $2,000.00 |
| Comptroller | The Texas Almanac (1857) | Annual salary of the Comptroller of Texas | $1,800.00 |
| Cook | Eliot Lord, History of the Comstock Lode (1959) | Monthly wage of a cook in Virginia City, Nevada, 1860 | $60.00 |
| Corporal | The Congressional Globe (1863) | Monthly pay of corporals in the United States Army, 1863 | $20.00 |
| Farm Laborer | US Census (1976) | Average monthly earnings for a farm laborer in New England, 1850 | $14.73 |
| Farm Laborer | US Census (1976) | Average monthly earnings for a farm laborer in Middle Atlantic United States, 1850 | $11.17 |
| Farm Laborer | US Census (1976) | Average monthly earnings for a farm laborer in South Atlantic United States, 1850 | $8.20 |
| Farm Laborer | US Census (1976) | Average monthly earnings for a farm laborer in Pacific Coast, 1850 | $68.00 |
| Farm Laborer | US Census (1976) | Average monthly earnings for a farm laborer in Pacific Coast, 1860 | $34.16 |

| Occupation | Data Source | Description | Price |
|---|---|---|---|
| Farm Laborer | US Census (1976) | Average monthly earnings for a farm laborer in New England, 1860 | $12.98 |
| Farm Laborer | US Census (1976) | Average monthly earnings for a farm laborer in Middle Atlantic United States, 1860 | $12.75 |
| Farm Laborer | US Census (1976) | Average monthly earnings for a farm laborer in South Atlantic United States, 1860 | $11.08 |
| Governor | The Texas Almanac (1857) | Annual salary of the Governor of Texas | $3,000.00 |
| Governor | Statutes at Large of South Carolina (1863) | Annual income of the Governor of South Carolina, within the Confederate States of America, 1863 | $3,500.00 |
| House-painters | Eliot Lord, History of the Comstock Lode (1959) | Daily wage of a house-painter in Virginia City, Nevada, 1860 | $4.00 |
| Judge | The Congressional Globe (1864) | Annual salary of military appointed judges in New Orleans, 1864 | $5,000.00 |
| Laborer | US Census (1976) | Daily wage for a laborer on the Erie Canal, 1851 | $0.88 |
| Laborer | US Census (1976) | Daily wage for a laborer on the Erie Canal, 1855 | $1.00 |
| Laborer | Eliot Lord, History of the Comstock Lode (1959) | Daily wage of a laborer in Virginia City, Nevada, 1860 | $4.00 |
| Laborer | US Census (1976) | Daily wage for a laborer on the Erie Canal, 1860 | $1.00 |
| Laborer | US Census (1976) | Daily wage for a laborer on the Erie Canal, 1863 | $1.25 |
| Laborer | The Congressional Globe (1864) | Monthly pay of a freed man in Memphis, Tennessee, 1864 | $10.00 |
| Laborer | US Census (1976) | Daily wage for a laborer on the Erie Canal, 1865 | $1.50 |
| Machinist | US Census (1976) | Daily wage of a machinist in the United States, 1860 | $1.61 |
| Machinist | US Census (1976) | Daily wage of a machinist in the United States, 1865 | $2.56 |
| Mason | US Census (1976) | Daily wage for a mason on the Erie Canal, 1855 | $2.00 |
| Mason | Eliot Lord, History of the Comstock Lode (1959) | Daily wage of a mason in Virginia City, Nevada, 1860 | $8.00 |
| Mason | US Census (1976) | Daily wage for a mason on the Erie Canal, 1860 | $2.00 |
| Mason | US Census (1976) | Daily wage for a mason on the Erie Canal, 1863 | $2.00 |
| Mason | US Census (1976) | Daily wage for a mason on the Erie Canal, 1865 | $2.50 |
| Master-at-arms | Francis Lord, Civil War Collector's Encyclopedia (1989) | Monthly income for Master-at-arms in the US Navy, 1862 | $25.00 |
| Master's Mate | Francis Lord, Civil War Collector's Encyclopedia (1989) | Monthly income for master's mate in the US Navy, 1862 | $40.00 |

## Based Upon US Dollars

| Year | Value of 19th Century Dollar in 2002 US Dollars |
|---|---|
| 1850 | $22.00 |
| 1855 | $20.00 |
| 1860 | $21.00 |
| 1865 | $11.00 |

*Calculations are approximate values based upon economic historical data*

| Occupation | Data Source | Description | Price |
|---|---|---|---|
| Miner | Eliot Lord, History of the Comstock Lode (1959) | Daily wage of a miner in Virginia City, Nevada, 1860 | $4.00 |
| Mining | Geoffrey Ward, The West (1996) | Daily income from seven men hiring fifty Indians in the California to mine gold, 1850 | $20.00 |
| Officer | The Congressional Globe (1863) | Second Assistant Secretary of War in the United States government, 1863 | $3,000.00 |
| Private | The Congressional Globe (1864) | Monthly pay of a private in the United States military, 1864 | $13.00 |
| Sergeant Major | The Congressional Globe (1863) | Monthly pay of sergeant majors of cavalry in the United States Army, 1863 | $23.00 |
| Secretary of State | The Texas Almanac (1857) | Annual salary of the Secretary of State of Texas | $1,800.00 |
| Servant | Harper's Magazine (1865) | Servant, monthly income, in New York City, 1865 | $8.00 |
| Slave Artisan | Wells, The Origins of the South Middle Class (2004) | Cost to hire slave labor at Hodgson Carriage in Georgia in 1853 | $280.00 |
| Squaw Hunter | Geoffrey Ward, The West (1996) | Bounty offered by Shasta City government for every Indian head brought to city hall, California, 1857 | $5.00 |
| Tailoring | Inventory of Wm. Phillips | Cutting and making one coat in Collin County, Texas in 1857 | $1.50 |
| Teacher | Eliot Lord, History of the Comstock Lode (1959) | Annual salary of a grammar teacher in Virginia City, Nevada, 1865 | $1,800.00 |
| Teacher | Eliot Lord, History of the Comstock Lode (1959) | Annual salary of a music teacher in Virginia City, Nevada, 1865 | $900.00 |
| Teamworker | US Census (1976) | Daily rate for a driver of horses on the Erie Canal in 1851 | $2.25 |
| Teamworker | US Census (1976) | Daily rate for a driver of horses on the Erie Canal in 1855 | $2.50 |
| Teamworker | US Census (1976) | Daily rate for a driver of horses on the Erie Canal in 1860 | $3.00 |
| Teamworker | US Census (1976) | Daily rate for a driver of horses on the Erie Canal in 1863 | $3.50 |
| Teamworker | US Census (1976) | Daily rate for a driver of horses on the Erie Canal in 1865 | $4.00 |
| Tinsmith | Eliot Lord, History of the Comstock Lode (1959) | Daily wage of a tinsmith in Virginia City, Nevada, 1860 | $5.00 |
| Typesetter | Wells, The Origins of the South Middle Class (2004) | Daily wages for male typesetter at a Mobile newspaper in 1854 | $2.60 |

# SERVICES & FEES 1850-1865

| Service/Fee | Data Source | Description | Price |
|---|---|---|---|
| Advertising | Invoice from L. Surimdell (1856) | Payment for adverstising in the Dallas Herald in 1856 | $25.00 |
| Amputations | Julian P. Price, Brief Historical Sketch of the Pee Dee Medical Association | Cost to do an uncomplicated amputation in South Carolina, 1853 | $25.00 |
| Amputations | Julian P. Price, Brief Historical Sketch of the Pee Dee Medical Association | Cost to provide a difficult amputation in South Carolina, 1853 | $50.00 |
| Bed | Eliot Lord, History of the Comstock Lode (1959) | Nightly rate for a bunk with hay in Virginia City, Nevada, 1860 | $1.00 |
| Bed | Eliot Lord, History of the Comstock Lode (1959) | Weekly rate for a bunk with hay in Virginia City, Nevada, 1860 | $4.50 |
| Chartered Vessels | "The Vanderbilts", by Jerry E. Patterson (1989) | Daily price asked by Cornelius Vanderbilt for chartering two of his vessels for use in the Civil War | $2,000.00 |
| Delivery Fee | Geoffrey Ward, The West (1996) | Fee charged by expressman for single letter brought to San Francisco, 1850 | $2.00 |
| Doctor's Visit | Pace & McGee, The life and Times of Ridgeway, Virginia. | Payment by county to Dr Jr. Bishop for attending 8 cases of smallpox at Lacy's Hospital in Henry County, Virginia, 1863 | $400.00 |
| Doctor's Visit | Julian P. Price, Brief Historical Sketch of the Pee Dee Medical Association | Cost for a doctor's visit in Chesterfield, South Carolina during the day, 1853 | $1.00 |
| Doctor's Visit | Julian P. Price, Brief Historical Sketch of the Pee Dee Medical Association | Cost for a doctors's visit at night in Chesterfield, South Carolina, 1853 | $2.00 |
| Doctor's Visit | Maud Carter Clement, History of Pittsylvania County Virginia | Cost for a Virginia physician to prescribe a sick member of a detachment of Federal soldiers | $0.50 |

## Based Upon US Dollars

| Year | Value of 19th Century Dollar in 2002 US Dollars |
|---|---|
| 1850 | $22.00 |
| 1855 | $20.00 |
| 1860 | $21.00 |
| 1865 | $11.00 |

*Calculations are approximate values based upon economic historical data*

| Service/Fee | Data Source | Description | Price |
|---|---|---|---|
| Embalmer | Francis Lord, Civil War Collector's Encyclopedia (1989) | Fee charged to embalm an officer in the Union army , 1862 | $50.00 |
| Embalmer | Francis Lord, Civil War Collector's Encyclopedia (1989) | Fee charged to embalm an enlisted man in the Union army, 1862 | $35.00 |
| Library Subscription | Harper's Magazine (1865) | Annual library subscription in New York City, 1865 | $3.00 |
| Mileage | Julian P. Price, Brief Historical Sketch of the Pee Dee Medical Association | Cost per mile added to the cost of a doctor's visit in good weather in South Carolina, 1853 | $0.50 |
| Mileage | Julian P. Price, Brief Historical Sketch of the Pee Dee Medical Association | Cost per mile added to doctor's visit in bad weather in South Carolina | $1.50 |
| Operation | Julian P. Price, Brief Historical Sketch of the Pee Dee Medical Association | Cost for trephining a cranium, South Carolina, 1853 | $50.00 |
| Recruiter | The Congressional Globe (1863) | Bonus paid to recruiter enlistinging a non-veteran in the United States Army, 1863 | $25.00 |
| Recruiter | The Congressional Globe (1863) | Bonus paid to recruiter enlistinging a veteran in the United States Army, 1863 | $15.00 |
| Reward | War Department Reward Poster (1865) | Reward for the capture of John H Surratt or David C Harold, accomplices of John Wilkes Booth in Lincoln's assassination of President Lincoln, 1865 | $25,000.00 |
| Reward | Geoffrey Ward, The West (1996) | Reward offered by California governor for Joaquin Murietta, a Mexican bandit, 1851 | $1,000.00 |
| Reward | American Heritage (1959) | Reward offered by the Queen Victoria to each sailor on the American crew that rescued the British ship The Resolute from the Arctic Ice, 1856 | 100 pounds |
| Salt Fee | Heritage of Russell County, Virginia, Vol. 1.1786-1986, (1985) | Per barrel cost for a salt agent in Russell County, Virginia, 1862 | $1.00 |
| Tariff | Dewey, Early Financial History of the United States (1934) | Per square yard tariff on carpets imported into the United States, 1857 | $0.24 |
| Tariff | Dewey, Early Financial History of the United States (1934) | Per square yard tariff on carpets imported into the United States, 1861 | $0.40 |
| Tax | The Congressional Globe (1864) | Tax on one gallon of whiskey in the United States, 1864 | $0.60 |
| Tax | Geoffery Ward, The West (1996) | Monthly tax by California Legislature on miners who were non-United States citizens, 1850 | $20.00 |
| Tooth Pull | Julian P. Price, Brief Historical Sketch of the Pee Dee Medical Association | Cost to extract one tooth from a doctor in South Carolina, 1853 | $1.00 |
| Treatment | Julian P. Price, Brief Historical Sketch of the Pee Dee Medical Association | Cost to treat a South Carolina patient for syphilis, 1853 | $30.00 |

| Service/Fee | Data Source | Description | Price |
|---|---|---|---|
| Treatment | Suzanne C. Linder, Medicinein Marlboro County, 1736 to 1980 | Cost to treat a child for diarrhea in South Carolina, 1860 | $0.50 |
| Snake Bite | Suzanne C. Linder, Medicine in Marlboro County, 1980 | Treatment for a snake bite, 1860 | $1.00 |

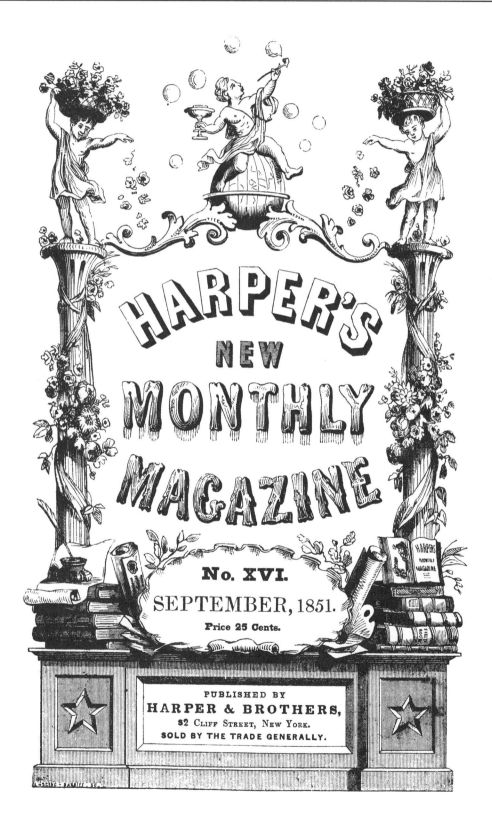

# FINANCIAL RATES & EXCHANGES
## 1850-1865

| Year | United States Official Price of Gold (per Ounce) | Inflation Rate in the United States | United States Exchange Rate for One British Pound | US Federal Government High Grade Bond Yields - New Issue | US Federal Government High Grade Bond Yields - Select Market | New England Municipal Bond Yields |
|------|------|------|------|------|------|------|
| 1850 | $20.67 | 2.17% | $4.87 | N/R | 4.58% | 5.13% |
| 1851 | $20.67 | −2.13% | $4.91 | N/R | 4.47% | 5.08% |
| 1852 | $20.67 | 1.09% | $4.90 | N/R | 4.39% | 4.98% |
| 1853 | $20.67 | 0.00% | $4.89 | N/R | 4.02% | 4.99% |
| 1854 | $20.67 | 8.60% | $4.88 | N/R | 4.14% | 5.13% |
| 1855 | $20.67 | 2.97% | $4.89 | N/R | 4.18% | 5.16% |
| 1856 | $20.67 | −1.92% | $4.91 | N/R | 4.11% | 5.10% |
| 1857 | $20.67 | 2.94% | $4.89 | N/R | 4.30% | 5.19% |
| 1858 | $20.67 | −5.71% | $4.86 | 4.70% | 4.32% | 5.03% |
| 1859 | $20.67 | 1.01% | $4.90 | N/R | 4.72% | 4.81% |
| 1860 | $20.67 | 0.00% | $4.85 | 4.92% | 5.57% | 4.79% |
| 1861 | $20.67 | 6.00% | $4.77 | 6.73% | 6.45% | 5.04% |
| 1862 | $20.67 | 14.15% | $5.56 | 6.00% | 6.25% | 4.91% |
| 1863 | $20.67 | 24.79% | $7.08 | 6.00% | 6.00% | 4.37% |
| 1864 | $20.67 | 25.17% | $9.97 | 5.60% | 5.10% | 4.80% |
| 1865 | $20.67 | 3.70% | $7.69 | 5.42% | 5.19% | 5.51% |

Books are a substantial world.—WORDSWORTH.

## HARPER AND BROTHERS' ISSUES FOR AUGUST.

### MEMOIR OF REV. E. BICKERSTETH.

A MEMOIR OF THE LATE REV. EDWARD BICKERSTETH, RECTOR OF WATTON.
BY REV. T. R. BIRKS, M.A. WITH A PREFACE, ETC.,
BY REV. STEPHEN H. TYNG, D.D.

2 vols. 12mo, Muslin, $1 75.

**A MANUAL OF ROMAN ANTIQUITIES.**
From the most recent German Works. With a Description of the City of Rome, &c.
By CHARLES ANTHON, LL.D.
With numerous Illustrations. 12mo, Sheep, 87½ cents.

**ELEMENTS OF ALGEBRA,**
Designed for Beginners. By Professor ELIAS LOOMIS of the New York University, Author of "A Course of Mathematics," "The Recent Progress of Astronomy, &c. 12mo, Sheep, 62½ cents.

### HISTORY OF THE RESTORATION
#### of Monarchy in France.
**Being a Sequel to the "History of the Girondists."**
BY ALPHONSE DE LAMARTINE.

Vol. I., 12mo, neatly bound in Paper or Muslin.

**THE STONE-MASON**
Of Saint Point. A Village Tale. By A. DE LAMARTINE, Author of "Raphael," "Genevieve," &c. 12mo, Paper, 25 cents; Muslin, 37½ cents.

**THE FATE:**
A Tale of Stirring Times. By G. P. R. JAMES, Author of "The Commissioner," "Henry Smeaton," &c. 8vo, Paper, 50 cents.

**ARTHUR CONWAY;**
Or, Scenes in the Tropics. By Captain E. H. MILMAN, late H. M. 33d Regiment, Author of "The Wayside Cross." 8vo, Paper, 25 cents.

### THE LITERATURE AND THE LITERARY MEN
#### of Great Britain and Ireland.
BY ABRAHAM MILLS, A.M.

2 vols. 8vo, Muslin.

**TRAVELS IN THE UNITED STATES, ETC.**
During 1849 and 1850. By the Lady EMMELINE STUART WORTLEY. 12mo, Paper, 60 cents; Muslin, 75 cents.

**TRAVELS AND ADVENTURES IN MEXICO:**
in the Course of Journeys of 2500 Miles, performed on Foot. By WILLIAM W. CARPENTER, late of the U. S. Army. 12mo, Paper, 60 cents; Muslin, 75 cents.

### HISTORY OF THE UNITED STATES.
BY RICHARD HILDRETH.

*First Series.*—From the First Settlement of the Country to the Adoption of the Federal Constitution. 3 vols. 8vo, Muslin, $6 00; Sheep, $6 75; half Calf, $7 50.

*Second Series.*—From the Adoption of the Federal Constitution to the End of the Sixteenth Congress. 3 vols. 8vo, Muslin, $6 00; Sheep, $6 75; half Calf, $7 50. Vols. I. and II. now ready.

**THE NILE-BOAT;**
Or, Glimpses of the Land of Egypt. By W. H. BARTLETT. With numerous Illustrations. 8vo, Muslin.

**GODFREY MALVERN;**
Or, the Life of an Author. By THOMAS MILLER. With 24 Illustrations by Phiz. 8vo, Paper, 75 cents.

**STUART OF DUNLEATH.**
A Story of the Present Time. By Hon. CAROLINE NORTON. 8vo, Paper, 25 cents.

Leisure without books is the sepulchre of the living soul.—SENECA.

# COMMODITIES 1850-1861

Currency expressed in US dollars.

| Commodity | Year | Philadelphia Currency | New York Currency | Charleston Currency | New Orleans Currency | Cincinnati Currency |
|---|---|---|---|---|---|---|
| Bacon, per pound | 1850 | $0.085 | $0.048 | $0.059 | $0.034 | $0.049 |
| | 1851 | $0.102 | $0.051 | $0.101 | $0.068 | $0.083 |
| | 1852 | $0.116 | $0.095 | $0.118 | $0.077 | $0.092 |
| | 1853 | $0.110 | $0.090 | $0.088 | $0.062 | $0.074 |
| | 1854 | $0.115 | $0.075 | $0.078 | $0.052 | $0.063 |
| | 1855 | $0.118 | $0.090 | $0.101 | $0.072 | $0.085 |
| | 1856 | $0.120 | $0.085 | $0.112 | $0.072 | $0.085 |
| | 1857 | $0.128 | $0.105 | $0.136 | $0.098 | $0.120 |
| | 1858 | $0.120 | $0.095 | $0.106 | $0.069 | $0.084 |
| | 1859 | $0.110 | $0.085 | $0.104 | $0.079 | $0.099 |
| | 1860 | $0.115 | $0.090 | $0.108 | $0.071 | $0.094 |
| | 1861 | $0.110 | $0.080 | $0.160 | $0.078 | N/R |
| Beef, per barrel | 1850 | $12.25 | $8.56 | N/R | $11.20 | N/R |
| | 1851 | $12.75 | $10.16 | N/R | $12.00 | N/R |
| | 1852 | $16.25 | $9.66 | N/R | $13.20 | N/R |
| | 1853 | $16.25 | $11.44 | N/R | $13.50 | N/R |
| | 1854 | $17.25 | $12.50 | N/R | $14.50 | N/R |
| | 1855 | $18.75 | $13.17 | N/R | $16.50 | N/R |
| | 1856 | $17.25 | $11.00 | N/R | $13.50 | N/R |
| | 1857 | $18.25 | $16.08 | N/R | $18.50 | N/R |
| | 1858 | $16.00 | $12.75 | N/R | $15.20 | N/R |
| | 1859 | $13.00 | $11.69 | N/R | $15.00 | N/R |
| | 1860 | $15.25 | $5.00 | N/R | $14.00 | N/R |
| | 1861 | $12.50 | $5.75 | N/R | $12.00 | N/R |
| Bread, per hundredweight | 1850 | $3.38 | $2.75 | N/R | $3.50 | N/R |
| *(Cincinnati per barrel)* | 1851 | $3.12 | $2.75 | N/R | $3.50 | $2.25 |
| | 1852 | $2.88 | $2.75 | N/R | N/R | $2.25 |
| | 1853 | $3.50 | $3.25 | N/R | N/R | $2.25 |
| | 1854 | $5.50 | $4.50 | N/R | N/R | $2.25 |
| | 1855 | $6.00 | $5.50 | N/R | N/R | $2.50 |
| | 1856 | $3.00 | $3.00 | N/R | N/R | $2.50 |
| | 1857 | $3.12 | $3.25 | N/R | N/R | $2.50 |
| | 1858 | $3.12 | $2.75 | N/R | $3.75 | N/R |
| | 1859 | $4.00 | $3.75 | N/R | $3.75 | N/R |
| | 1860 | $2.88 | $3.25 | N/R | $5.00 | N/R |
| | 1861 | $3.00 | $3.25 | N/R | $5.00 | N/R |
| Butter, per pound | 1850 | $0.078 | $0.150 | $0.200 | $0.250 | $0.180 |
| | 1851 | $0.096 | $0.155 | $0.205 | $0.230 | $0.160 |
| | 1852 | $0.150 | $0.250 | $0.205 | $0.325 | $0.180 |
| | 1853 | $0.130 | $0.185 | $0.260 | $0.235 | $0.150 |

| Commodity | Year | Philadelphia Currency | New York Currency | Charleston Currency | New Orleans Currency | Cincinnati Currency |
|---|---|---|---|---|---|---|
| | 1854 | $0.120 | $0.225 | $0.255 | $0.215 | $0.160 |
| | 1855 | $0.150 | $0.225 | $0.250 | $0.375 | $0.250 |
| | 1856 | $0.170 | $0.195 | $0.250 | $0.290 | $0.180 |
| | 1857 | $0.145 | $0.250 | $0.250 | $0.270 | $0.200 |
| | 1858 | $0.115 | $0.210 | $0.250 | $0.270 | $0.165 |
| | 1859 | $0.095 | $0.170 | $0.250 | $0.270 | $0.155 |
| | 1860 | $0.095 | $0.150 | N/R | $0.245 | $0.135 |
| | 1861 | $0.095 | $0.175 | $0.450 | $0.400 | N/R |
| Candles, per pound | 1850 | $0.100 | $0.420 | N/R | $0.405 | $0.100 |
| | 1851 | $0.100 | $0.440 | N/R | $0.415 | $0.110 |
| | 1852 | $0.100 | $0.425 | N/R | $0.385 | $0.100 |
| | 1853 | $0.120 | $0.325 | N/R | $0.340 | $0.110 |
| | 1854 | $0.140 | $0.290 | N/R | $0.315 | $0.140 |
| | 1855 | $0.150 | $0.295 | N/R | $0.315 | $0.140 |
| | 1856 | $0.145 | $0.390 | N/R | $0.430 | $0.120 |
| | 1857 | $0.140 | $0.420 | N/R | $0.430 | $0.140 |
| | 1858 | $0.140 | $0.395 | N/R | $0.435 | $0.115 |
| | 1859 | $0.125 | $0.405 | N/R | $0.425 | $0.125 |
| | 1860 | $0.128 | $0.390 | N/R | $0.390 | $0.125 |
| | 1861 | $0.118 | $0.335 | N/R | $0.370 | N/R |
| Coal, per bushel | 1850 | $0.158 | $0.055 | N/R | $0.450 | $0.129 |
| (New York per ton) | 1851 | $0.175 | $0.049 | N/R | $0.450 | $0.108 |
| (New Orleans per barrel) | 1852 | $0.190 | $0.058 | N/R | $0.450 | $0.120 |
| | 1853 | $0.195 | $0.052 | N/R | $0.550 | $0.140 |
| | 1854 | $0.210 | $0.062 | N/R | $0.450 | $0.160 |
| | 1855 | $0.160 | $0.078 | $0.062 | $0.400 | $0.140 |
| | 1856 | $0.200 | $0.058 | N/R | $0.425 | $0.140 |
| | 1857 | $0.204 | $0.060 | N/R | $0.625 | $0.160 |
| | 1858 | $0.167 | $0.051 | N/R | $0.550 | $0.120 |
| | 1859 | $0.194 | $0.075 | $0.052 | $0.550 | $0.120 |
| | 1860 | $0.161 | $0.055 | N/R | $0.550 | $0.115 |
| | 1861 | $0.167 | $0.058 | N/R | $0.375 | N/R |

### Based Upon US Dollars

| Year | Value of 19th Century Dollar in 2002 US Dollars |
|---|---|
| 1850 | $22.00 |
| 1855 | $20.00 |
| 1860 | $21.00 |
| 1865 | $11.00 |

*Calculations are approximate values based upon economic historical data*

| Commodity | Year | Philadelphia Currency | New York Currency | Charleston Currency | New Orleans Currency | Cincinnati Currency |
|---|---|---|---|---|---|---|
| Coffee, per pound | 1850 | $0.080 | $0.080 | $0.102 | $0.079 | $0.100 |
| | 1851 | $0.090 | $0.095 | $0.102 | $0.094 | $0.110 |
| | 1852 | $0.084 | $0.090 | $0.095 | $0.092 | $0.105 |
| | 1853 | $0.084 | $0.090 | $0.095 | $0.091 | $0.102 |
| | 1854 | $0.099 | $0.100 | $0.122 | $0.091 | $0.120 |
| | 1855 | $0.094 | $0.100 | $0.111 | $0.095 | $0.115 |
| | 1856 | $0.104 | $0.110 | $0.119 | $0.096 | $0.122 |
| | 1857 | $0.108 | $0.110 | $0.116 | $0.105 | $0.112 |
| | 1858 | $0.106 | $0.105 | $0.115 | $0.110 | $0.115 |
| | 1859 | $0.099 | $0.115 | $0.120 | $0.111 | $0.125 |
| | 1860 | $0.128 | $0.135 | $0.138 | $0.132 | $0.148 |
| | 1861 | $0.124 | $0.130 | $0.155 | $0.132 | N/R |
| Copper, per pound | 1850 | $0.22 | $0.22 | N/R | N/R | N/R |
| | 1851 | $0.21 | $0.20 | N/R | N/R | $0.28 |
| | 1852 | $0.22 | $0.22 | N/R | N/R | $0.28 |
| | 1853 | $0.30 | $0.31 | N/R | N/R | $0.40 |
| | 1854 | $0.33 | $0.30 | N/R | N/R | $0.35 |
| | 1855 | $0.32 | $0.28 | N/R | N/R | $0.35 |
| | 1856 | $0.32 | $0.32 | N/R | N/R | $0.35 |
| | 1857 | $0.32 | $0.33 | N/R | N/R | $0.35 |
| | 1858 | $0.28 | $0.26 | N/R | N/R | N/R |
| | 1859 | $0.27 | $0.27 | N/R | N/R | N/R |
| | 1860 | $0.28 | $0.26 | N/R | N/R | N/R |
| | 1861 | $0.25 | $0.24 | N/R | N/R | N/R |
| Corn meal, per barrel | 1850 | $2.88 | $2.84 | N/R | N/R | N/R |
| | 1851 | $2.75 | $3.06 | N/R | N/R | N/R |
| | 1852 | $3.12 | $3.38 | N/R | N/R | N/R |
| | 1853 | $2.75 | $3.06 | N/R | N/R | N/R |
| | 1854 | $3.62 | $3.75 | N/R | N/R | N/R |
| | 1855 | $5.00 | $5.18 | N/R | N/R | N/R |
| | 1856 | $2.50 | $3.28 | N/R | N/R | N/R |
| | 1857 | $3.56 | $3.30 | N/R | N/R | N/R |
| | 1858 | $3.25 | $3.43 | N/R | N/R | N/R |
| | 1859 | $4.12 | $3.93 | N/R | N/R | N/R |
| | 1860 | $3.62 | $3.83 | N/R | N/R | N/R |
| | 1861 | $2.88 | $2.83 | N/R | N/R | N/R |
| Corn, per bushel | 1850 | $0.610 | $0.610 | $0.645 | $0.700 | $0.455 |
| | 1851 | $0.620 | $0.635 | $0.725 | $0.475 | $0.355 |
| | 1852 | $0.640 | $0.625 | $0.665 | $0.460 | $0.280 |
| | 1853 | $0.628 | $0.675 | $0.650 | $0.460 | $0.475 |
| | 1854 | $0.810 | $0.850 | $0.890 | $0.605 | $0.510 |
| | 1855 | $1.125 | $1.125 | $1.190 | $1.085 | $0.760 |
| | 1856 | $0.520 | $0.610 | $0.590 | $0.465 | $0.340 |
| | 1857 | $0.820 | $0.790 | $0.830 | $0.800 | $0.775 |
| | 1858 | $0.705 | $0.745 | $0.700 | $0.530 | $0.400 |
| | 1859 | $0.980 | $0.870 | $0.950 | $1.025 | $0.900 |

| Commodity | Year | Philadelphia Currency | New York Currency | Charleston Currency | New Orleans Currency | Cincinnati Currency |
|---|---|---|---|---|---|---|
| | 1860 | $0.755 | $0.820 | $0.855 | $0.840 | $0.490 |
| | 1861 | $0.620 | $0.670 | $0.750 | $0.540 | N/R |
| Cotton yarn, per pound | 1850 | N/R | N/R | N/R | N/R | $0.195 |
| | 1851 | N/R | N/R | N/R | N/R | $0.190 |
| | 1852 | N/R | N/R | N/R | N/R | $0.145 |
| | 1853 | N/R | N/R | N/R | N/R | $0.148 |
| | 1854 | N/R | N/R | N/R | N/R | $0.175 |
| | 1855 | N/R | N/R | N/R | N/R | $0.175 |
| | 1856 | N/R | N/R | N/R | N/R | $0.205 |
| | 1857 | N/R | N/R | N/R | N/R | $0.235 |
| | 1858 | N/R | N/R | N/R | N/R | $0.215 |
| | 1859 | N/R | N/R | N/R | N/R | $0.205 |
| | 1860 | N/R | N/R | N/R | N/R | $0.200 |
| Cotton, per pound | 1850 | $0.13 | $0.13 | $0.12 | $0.12 | $0.12 |
| | 1851 | $0.11 | $0.11 | $0.10 | $0.09 | $0.09 |
| | 1852 | $0.10 | $0.10 | $0.09 | $0.08 | $0.07 |
| | 1853 | $0.11 | $0.11 | $0.10 | $0.09 | $0.10 |
| | 1854 | $0.10 | $0.11 | $0.09 | $0.07 | $0.08 |
| | 1855 | $0.09 | $0.11 | $0.11 | $0.09 | $0.09 |
| | 1856 | $0.12 | $0.11 | $0.11 | $0.10 | $0.11 |
| | 1857 | $0.14 | $0.14 | $0.14 | $0.13 | $0.14 |
| | 1858 | $0.13 | $0.12 | $0.13 | $0.11 | $0.12 |
| | 1859 | $0.13 | $0.11 | $0.12 | $0.10 | $0.13 |
| | 1860 | $0.10 | $0.11 | $0.12 | $0.10 | $0.11 |
| | 1861 | $0.12 | $0.14 | $0.11 | $0.10 | N/R |
| Duck Cloth, per bolt | 1850 | $6.38 | N/R | N/R | $15.75 | N/R |
| | 1851 | $6.38 | N/R | N/R | $15.75 | N/R |
| | 1852 | $6.38 | N/R | N/R | $15.75 | N/R |
| | 1853 | $6.38 | N/R | N/R | $15.75 | N/R |
| | 1854 | $6.38 | N/R | N/R | $15.75 | N/R |
| | 1855 | $7.50 | N/R | N/R | N/R | N/R |

## Based Upon US Dollars

| Year | Value of 19th Century Dollar in 2002 US Dollars |
|---|---|
| 1850 | $22.00 |
| 1855 | $20.00 |
| 1860 | $21.00 |
| 1865 | $11.00 |

*Calculations are approximate values based upon economic historical data*

| Commodity | Year | Philadelphia Currency | New York Currency | Charleston Currency | New Orleans Currency | Cincinnati Currency |
|---|---|---|---|---|---|---|
| | 1856 | $7.50 | N/R | N/R | N/R | N/R |
| | 1857 | $7.25 | N/R | N/R | N/R | N/R |
| | 1858 | $7.25 | N/R | N/R | N/R | N/R |
| | 1859 | $7.25 | N/R | N/R | N/R | N/R |
| | 1860 | $7.25 | N/R | N/R | N/R | N/R |
| | 1861 | $7.25 | N/R | N/R | N/R | N/R |
| Fish, per hundredweight | 1850 | $2.62 | $2.81 | N/R | $0.88 | $14.75 |
| *(Cincinnati per barrel)* | 1851 | $2.88 | $2.63 | N/R | $0.78 | $12.75 |
| *(New Orleans per box)* | 1852 | $4.38 | $4.19 | N/R | $0.75 | $12.50 |
| | 1853 | $3.25 | $3.38 | N/R | $0.88 | $15.50 |
| | 1854 | $3.13 | $3.50 | N/R | $0.98 | $20.00 |
| | 1855 | $3.69 | $3.94 | N/R | $0.98 | $24.00 |
| | 1856 | $3.75 | $4.16 | N/R | $1.08 | $23.00 |
| | 1857 | $3.50 | $3.44 | N/R | $0.88 | $22.00 |
| | 1858 | $3.00 | $3.25 | N/R | $1.00 | $22.00 |
| | 1859 | $3.31 | $3.91 | N/R | $0.85 | $24.50 |
| | 1860 | $3.38 | $4.00 | N/R | $0.90 | $23.50 |
| | 1861 | $2.88 | $3.19 | N/R | $0.95 | N/R |
| Flour, per barrel | 1850 | $6.18 | $5.81 | $5.62 | $5.75 | $5.05 |
| | 1851 | $4.26 | $4.62 | $5.25 | $3.88 | $3.56 |
| | 1852 | $4.20 | $4.91 | $4.94 | $3.60 | $3.25 |
| | 1853 | $4.68 | $5.05 | $5.50 | $4.44 | $3.72 |
| | 1854 | $8.69 | $9.13 | $8.00 | $7.31 | $7.78 |
| | 1855 | $10.75 | $9.72 | $11.81 | $9.88 | $9.52 |
| | 1856 | $6.06 | $5.78 | $6.70 | $5.99 | $5.20 |
| | 1857 | $7.19 | $5.98 | $7.62 | $6.94 | $6.82 |
| | 1858 | $4.44 | $4.19 | $5.88 | $4.11 | $3.62 |
| | 1859 | $7.25 | $5.43 | $7.88 | $7.50 | $7.28 |
| | 1860 | $5.94 | $5.43 | $6.25 | $5.75 | $5.55 |
| | 1861 | $5.56 | $5.18 | N/R | N/R | N/R |
| Gin, per gallon | 1850 | $1.23 | $1.12 | N/R | $0.38 | N/R |
| | 1851 | $1.22 | $0.98 | N/R | $0.28 | N/R |
| | 1852 | $1.22 | $0.86 | N/R | $0.26 | N/R |
| | 1853 | $1.22 | $1.13 | N/R | $0.28 | N/R |
| | 1854 | $1.33 | $1.35 | N/R | $0.32 | N/R |
| | 1855 | $1.51 | $1.25 | N/R | $0.40 | N/R |
| | 1856 | $1.45 | $1.55 | N/R | $0.40 | N/R |
| | 1857 | $1.45 | $1.48 | N/R | $0.40 | N/R |
| | 1858 | $1.12 | $1.00 | N/R | $0.40 | N/R |
| | 1859 | $1.03 | $0.95 | N/R | $0.40 | N/R |
| | 1860 | $1.03 | $0.90 | N/R | $0.40 | N/R |
| | 1861 | $1.15 | $1.13 | N/R | $0.40 | N/R |
| Hides, per pound | 1850 | N/R | N/R | N/R | $0.06 | N/R |
| | 1851 | N/R | N/R | N/R | $0.08 | N/R |
| | 1852 | N/R | N/R | N/R | $0.07 | N/R |
| | 1853 | N/R | N/R | N/R | $0.09 | N/R |

| Commodity | Year | Philadelphia Currency | New York Currency | Charleston Currency | New Orleans Currency | Cincinnati Currency |
|-----------|------|----------------------|-------------------|---------------------|----------------------|---------------------|
| | 1854 | N/R | N/R | N/R | $0.10 | N/R |
| | 1855 | N/R | N/R | N/R | $0.11 | N/R |
| | 1856 | N/R | N/R | N/R | $0.12 | N/R |
| | 1857 | N/R | N/R | N/R | $0.16 | N/R |
| | 1858 | N/R | N/R | N/R | $0.13 | N/R |
| | 1859 | N/R | N/R | N/R | $0.13 | N/R |
| | 1860 | N/R | N/R | N/R | $0.12 | N/R |
| | 1861 | N/R | N/R | N/R | $0.06 | N/R |
| Hops, per pound | 1850 | $0.17 | $0.17 | N/R | N/R | $0.20 |
| | 1851 | $0.40 | $0.27 | N/R | N/R | $0.40 |
| | 1852 | $0.28 | $0.28 | N/R | N/R | $0.30 |
| | 1853 | $0.18 | $0.20 | N/R | N/R | $0.22 |
| | 1854 | $0.27 | $0.32 | N/R | N/R | $0.35 |
| | 1855 | $0.23 | $0.18 | N/R | N/R | $0.22 |
| | 1856 | $0.09 | $0.08 | N/R | N/R | $0.10 |
| | 1857 | $0.08 | $0.08 | N/R | N/R | $0.11 |
| | 1858 | $0.08 | $0.06 | N/R | N/R | $0.08 |
| | 1859 | $0.14 | $0.12 | N/R | N/R | $0.13 |
| | 1860 | $0.12 | $0.10 | N/R | N/R | $0.14 |
| | 1861 | $0.17 | $0.19 | N/R | N/R | N/R |
| Indigo, per pound | 1850 | $0.79 | $0.70 | N/R | $0.95 | N/R |
| | 1851 | $0.85 | $0.70 | N/R | $0.82 | N/R |
| | 1852 | $0.75 | $0.70 | N/R | $0.80 | N/R |
| | 1853 | $0.89 | $0.75 | N/R | $0.85 | N/R |
| | 1854 | $0.78 | $0.78 | N/R | $0.85 | N/R |
| | 1855 | $0.65 | $0.80 | N/R | N/R | N/R |
| | 1856 | $0.58 | $0.83 | N/R | N/R | N/R |
| | 1857 | $0.85 | $0.80 | N/R | N/R | N/R |
| | 1858 | $0.82 | $0.65 | N/R | N/R | N/R |
| | 1859 | $0.78 | $0.90 | N/R | N/R | N/R |
| | 1860 | $0.50 | $0.85 | N/R | N/R | N/R |
| | 1861 | $0.75 | $0.80 | N/R | N/R | N/R |

### Based Upon US Dollars

| Year | Value of 19th Century Dollar in 2002 US Dollars |
|------|--------------------------------------------------|
| 1850 | $22.00 |
| 1855 | $20.00 |
| 1860 | $21.00 |
| 1865 | $11.00 |

*Calculations are approximate values based upon economic historical data*

| Commodity | Year | Philadelphia Currency | New York Currency | Charleston Currency | New Orleans Currency | Cincinnati Currency |
|-----------|------|----------------------|-------------------|---------------------|----------------------|---------------------|
| Iron - Bar, per ton | 1850 | $70.00 | $43.80 | N/R | $95.00 | $70.00 |
| | 1851 | $66.20 | $36.50 | N/R | $95.00 | $52.00 |
| | 1852 | $53.80 | $34.50 | N/R | $97.50 | $48.00 |
| | 1853 | $92.50 | $67.50 | N/R | $106.00 | $78.00 |
| | 1854 | $87.50 | $76.20 | N/R | $108.50 | $78.00 |
| | 1855 | $92.50 | $57.50 | N/R | $108.50 | $58.00 |
| | 1856 | $72.50 | $63.50 | N/R | $108.50 | $58.00 |
| | 1857 | $67.50 | $61.80 | N/R | $108.50 | $60.00 |
| | 1858 | $52.50 | $46.20 | N/R | $123.00 | $52.00 |
| | 1859 | $57.50 | $47.20 | N/R | $123.00 | $56.00 |
| | 1860 | $56.20 | $41.80 | N/R | $123.00 | $50.00 |
| | 1861 | $51.50 | $44.50 | N/R | $123.00 | N/R |
| Iron-Pig, per ton | 1850 | $23.80 | $23.50 | N/R | $25.50 | $25.00 |
| | 1851 | $23.00 | $21.20 | N/R | $23.80 | $25.00 |
| | 1852 | $22.00 | $20.50 | N/R | $21.50 | $24.50 |
| | 1853 | $34.50 | $33.50 | N/R | $33.50 | $43.50 |
| | 1854 | $37.00 | $39.50 | N/R | $41.00 | $44.00 |
| | 1855 | $28.00 | $28.00 | N/R | $33.50 | $30.50 |
| | 1856 | $28.50 | $32.50 | N/R | $39.00 | $34.50 |
| | 1857 | $28.00 | $36.20 | N/R | $39.00 | $30.50 |
| | 1858 | $23.50 | $26.00 | N/R | $35.00 | $27.50 |
| | 1859 | $24.00 | $24.20 | N/R | $29.00 | $33.00 |
| | 1860 | $24.50 | $24.20 | N/R | $29.00 | $25.50 |
| | 1861 | $22.00 | $21.00 | N/R | $29.00 | N/R |
| Lard, per pound | 1850 | $0.07 | $0.07 | $0.07 | $0.06 | $0.06 |
| | 1851 | $0.11 | $0.10 | $0.10 | $0.10 | $0.09 |
| | 1852 | $0.11 | $0.10 | $0.11 | $0.09 | $0.09 |
| | 1853 | $0.11 | $0.11 | $0.10 | $0.10 | $0.10 |
| | 1854 | $0.11 | $0.09 | $0.11 | $0.10 | $0.09 |
| | 1855 | $0.11 | $0.10 | $0.12 | $0.11 | $0.10 |
| | 1856 | $0.12 | $0.10 | $0.10 | $0.10 | $0.10 |
| | 1857 | $0.15 | $0.14 | $0.16 | $0.14 | $0.14 |
| | 1858 | $0.13 | $0.12 | $0.12 | $0.12 | $0.11 |
| | 1859 | $0.13 | $0.11 | $0.12 | $0.12 | $0.12 |
| | 1860 | $0.12 | $0.11 | $0.12 | $0.12 | $0.11 |
| | 1861 | $0.11 | $0.10 | $0.16 | $0.10 | N/R |
| Leather, Tanned, per pound | 1850 | $0.18 | $0.16 | N/R | N/R | $0.17 |
| | 1851 | $0.18 | $0.14 | N/R | N/R | $0.17 |
| | 1852 | $0.18 | $0.15 | N/R | N/R | $0.19 |
| | 1853 | $0.20 | $0.18 | N/R | N/R | $0.22 |
| | 1854 | $0.26 | $0.23 | N/R | N/R | $0.27 |
| | 1855 | $0.24 | $0.22 | N/R | N/R | $0.26 |
| | 1856 | $0.30 | $0.26 | N/R | N/R | $0.30 |
| | 1857 | $0.36 | $0.30 | N/R | N/R | $0.37 |
| | 1858 | $0.28 | $0.24 | N/R | N/R | $0.25 |
| | 1859 | $0.32 | $0.26 | N/R | N/R | $0.33 |

| Commodity | Year | Philadelphia Currency | New York Currency | Charleston Currency | New Orleans Currency | Cincinnati Currency |
|---|---|---|---|---|---|---|
| | 1860 | $0.30 | $0.22 | N/R | N/R | $0.28 |
| | 1861 | $0.26 | $0.20 | N/R | N/R | N/R |
| Linseed Oil, per gallon | 1850 | $0.79 | $0.79 | N/R | $1.00 | $1.02 |
| | 1851 | $0.77 | $0.73 | N/R | $0.82 | $0.92 |
| | 1852 | $0.62 | $0.63 | N/R | $0.64 | $0.62 |
| | 1853 | $0.64 | $0.61 | N/R | $0.75 | $0.64 |
| | 1854 | $0.99 | $0.90 | N/R | $1.05 | $0.86 |
| | 1855 | $0.84 | $0.86 | N/R | $1.05 | $0.98 |
| | 1856 | $0.82 | $0.77 | N/R | $1.04 | $0.92 |
| | 1857 | $0.76 | $0.85 | N/R | $0.98 | $0.91 |
| | 1858 | $0.60 | $0.69 | N/R | $0.76 | $0.66 |
| | 1859 | $0.62 | $0.63 | N/R | $0.72 | $0.73 |
| | 1860 | $0.60 | $0.61 | N/R | $0.70 | $0.64 |
| | 1861 | $0.59 | $0.58 | N/R | $0.88 | N/R |
| Lumber Boards, per one hundred feet | 1850 | $18.50 | $40.00 | N/R | $13.00 | $21.50 |
| | 1851 | $21.00 | $36.20 | N/R | $13.00 | $22.00 |
| | 1852 | $17.50 | $38.80 | N/R | $13.00 | $35.00 |
| | 1853 | $19.00 | $39.80 | N/R | $13.00 | $35.00 |
| | 1854 | $24.00 | $38.80 | N/R | $13.00 | $35.00 |
| | 1855 | $23.20 | $38.80 | N/R | $13.00 | $40.00 |
| | 1856 | $17.50 | $42.50 | N/R | $13.00 | $40.00 |
| | 1857 | $18.00 | $43.80 | N/R | $13.00 | N/R |
| | 1858 | $16.50 | $42.50 | N/R | $17.50 | N/R |
| | 1859 | $19.00 | $33.00 | N/R | $13.50 | N/R |
| | 1860 | $18.00 | $36.20 | N/R | $15.50 | N/R |
| | 1861 | $18.50 | $36.20 | N/R | $21.50 | N/R |
| Molasses, per gallon | 1850 | $0.18 | $0.18 | $0.25 | $0.16 | $0.25 |
| | 1851 | $0.20 | $0.20 | $0.35 | $0.28 | $0.34 |
| | 1852 | $0.20 | $0.18 | $0.34 | $0.24 | $0.33 |
| | 1853 | $0.22 | $0.22 | $0.30 | $0.18 | $0.26 |
| | 1854 | $0.20 | $0.20 | $0.27 | $0.11 | $0.21 |

### Based Upon US Dollars

| Year | Value of 19th Century Dollar in 2002 US Dollars |
|---|---|
| 1850 | $22.00 |
| 1855 | $20.00 |
| 1860 | $21.00 |
| 1865 | $11.00 |

*Calculations are approximate values based upon economic historical data*

| Commodity | Year | Philadelphia Currency | New York Currency | Charleston Currency | New Orleans Currency | Cincinnati Currency |
|---|---|---|---|---|---|---|
| | 1855 | $0.25 | $0.22 | $0.32 | $0.26 | $0.34 |
| | 1856 | $0.32 | $0.30 | $0.48 | $0.34 | $0.44 |
| | 1857 | $0.51 | $0.51 | $0.70 | $0.56 | $0.71 |
| | 1858 | $0.22 | $0.22 | $0.40 | $0.29 | $0.36 |
| | 1859 | $0.28 | $0.24 | $0.41 | $0.37 | $0.38 |
| | 1860 | $0.25 | $0.24 | $0.49 | $0.34 | $0.46 |
| | 1861 | $0.18 | $0.16 | $0.40 | $0.12 | N/R |
| Nails, per pound | 1850 | $0.038 | $0.036 | $0.041 | $0.044 | $0.031 |
| | 1851 | $0.033 | $0.031 | $0.031 | $0.036 | $0.029 |
| | 1852 | $0.028 | $0.029 | $0.031 | $0.034 | $0.026 |
| | 1853 | $0.048 | $0.040 | $0.054 | $0.052 | $0.044 |
| | 1854 | $0.045 | $0.046 | $0.049 | $0.048 | $0.045 |
| | 1855 | $0.046 | $0.038 | $0.044 | $0.045 | $0.038 |
| | 1856 | $0.040 | $0.048 | $0.041 | $0.042 | $0.036 |
| | 1857 | $0.036 | $0.039 | $0.039 | $0.041 | $0.035 |
| | 1858 | $0.034 | $0.035 | $0.034 | $0.041 | $0.034 |
| | 1859 | $0.036 | $0.036 | $0.040 | $0.039 | $0.031 |
| | 1860 | $0.036 | $0.035 | $0.034 | $0.034 | $0.029 |
| | 1861 | $0.029 | N/R | $0.032 | $0.039 | N/R |
| Pork, per barrel | 1850 | $10.88 | $10.49 | N/R | $10.00 | $10.00 |
| | 1851 | $16.75 | $15.40 | N/R | $14.90 | $14.44 |
| | 1852 | $19.63 | $18.43 | N/R | $16.90 | $16.44 |
| | 1853 | $15.94 | $15.57 | N/R | $15.60 | $14.62 |
| | 1854 | $15.00 | $12.98 | N/R | $13.00 | $12.00 |
| | 1855 | $17.88 | $17.63 | N/R | $16.80 | $15.50 |
| | 1856 | $19.25 | $18.59 | N/R | $16.00 | $16.00 |
| | 1857 | $24.00 | $23.59 | N/R | $23.90 | $23.25 |
| | 1858 | $18.00 | $17.90 | N/R | $17.50 | $16.50 |
| | 1859 | $18.00 | $17.26 | N/R | $19.20 | $18.81 |
| | 1860 | $18.38 | $17.82 | N/R | $18.10 | $17.50 |
| | 1861 | $18.00 | $17.00 | N/R | $19.20 | N/R |
| Pot Ashes, per hundredweight | 1850 | $5.12 | $5.53 | N/R | N/R | $5.00 |
| | 1851 | $4.81 | $4.75 | N/R | N/R | $4.62 |
| | 1852 | $5.03 | $5.03 | N/R | N/R | $3.88 |
| | 1853 | $4.94 | $5.00 | N/R | N/R | $4.00 |
| | 1854 | $5.94 | $5.78 | N/R | N/R | $5.12 |
| | 1855 | $5.90 | $5.81 | N/R | N/R | $5.25 |
| | 1856 | $6.38 | $6.00 | N/R | N/R | $5.88 |
| | 1857 | $7.50 | $7.69 | N/R | N/R | $5.62 |
| | 1858 | $6.00 | $6.00 | N/R | N/R | $5.50 |
| | 1859 | $5.88 | $5.38 | N/R | N/R | $5.38 |
| | 1860 | $5.25 | N/R | N/R | N/R | $4.75 |
| | 1861 | $5.12 | N/R | N/R | N/R | N/R |
| Rice, per hundredweight | 1850 | $3.56 | $3.00 | $3.38 | $3.75 | $4.38 |
| | 1851 | $3.41 | $3.06 | $3.12 | $3.94 | $4.19 |

| Commodity | Year | Philadelphia Currency | New York Currency | Charleston Currency | New Orleans Currency | Cincinnati Currency |
|---|---|---|---|---|---|---|
| | 1852 | $4.06 | $3.13 | $3.75 | $4.12 | $4.50 |
| | 1853 | $4.25 | $4.13 | $4.25 | $4.12 | $5.19 |
| | 1854 | $4.06 | $4.31 | $4.00 | $4.50 | $5.38 |
| | 1855 | $6.38 | $5.19 | $6.12 | $7.12 | $7.38 |
| | 1856 | $4.06 | $3.88 | $4.25 | $4.19 | $5.12 |
| | 1857 | $4.88 | $4.63 | $4.62 | $5.50 | $5.88 |
| | 1858 | $3.81 | $3.59 | $3.62 | $3.75 | $4.62 |
| | 1859 | $3.81 | $3.50 | $4.50 | $4.38 | $5.12 |
| | 1860 | $4.23 | $3.94 | $4.12 | $4.62 | $4.88 |
| | 1861 | $5.75 | $5.00 | $4.00 | $5.75 | N/R |
| Rum, per gallon | 1850 | $0.28 | $1.63 | $0.28 | $0.30 | N/R |
| | 1851 | $0.28 | $1.44 | $0.29 | $0.30 | N/R |
| | 1852 | $0.26 | $1.63 | $0.26 | $0.38 | N/R |
| | 1853 | $0.30 | $1.38 | $0.26 | $0.38 | N/R |
| | 1854 | $0.34 | $1.75 | $0.34 | $0.34 | N/R |
| | 1855 | $0.42 | $1.88 | $0.42 | $0.42 | N/R |
| | 1856 | $0.44 | $1.75 | $0.44 | $0.42 | N/R |
| | 1857 | $0.49 | $2.05 | $0.44 | $0.78 | N/R |
| | 1858 | $0.36 | $1.63 | $0.31 | $0.78 | N/R |
| | 1859 | $0.38 | $1.38 | $0.34 | $0.48 | N/R |
| | 1860 | $0.36 | $1.38 | $0.31 | $0.48 | N/R |
| | 1861 | $0.32 | $1.38 | $0.37 | $0.48 | N/R |
| Salt petre, per pound | 1850 | $0.08 | $0.07 | N/R | N/R | $0.08 |
| | 1851 | $0.08 | $0.08 | N/R | N/R | $0.07 |
| | 1852 | $0.09 | $0.07 | N/R | N/R | $0.09 |
| | 1853 | $0.07 | $0.07 | N/R | N/R | $0.08 |
| | 1854 | $0.09 | $0.09 | N/R | N/R | $0.09 |
| | 1855 | $0.09 | $0.08 | N/R | $0.08 | $0.09 |
| | 1856 | $0.14 | $0.12 | N/R | N/R | $0.19 |
| | 1857 | $0.12 | $0.09 | N/R | $0.19 | $0.10 |
| | 1858 | $0.10 | $0.10 | N/R | $0.16 | $0.10 |

### Based Upon US Dollars

| Year | Value of 19th Century Dollar in 2002 US Dollars |
|---|---|
| 1850 | $22.00 |
| 1855 | $20.00 |
| 1860 | $21.00 |
| 1865 | $11.00 |

*Calculations are approximate values based upon economic historical data*

| Commodity | Year | Philadelphia Currency | New York Currency | Charleston Currency | New Orleans Currency | Cincinnati Currency |
|---|---|---|---|---|---|---|
| | 1859 | $0.12 | $0.13 | N/R | $0.16 | $0.10 |
| | 1860 | $0.14 | N/R | N/R | $0.16 | $0.10 |
| | 1861 | $0.12 | N/R | N/R | $0.14 | N/R |
| Salt, per bushel | 1850 | $0.210 | $1.380 | $0.780 | $0.790 | $0.300 |
| *(New Orleans per sack)* | 1851 | $0.210 | $1.380 | $0.730 | $0.770 | $0.220 |
| *(Charleston - per four bushels)* | 1852 | $0.215 | $1.150 | $0.700 | $0.750 | $0.250 |
| | 1853 | $0.350 | $1.580 | $0.880 | $0.980 | $0.260 |
| | 1854 | $0.445 | $1.630 | $1.050 | $1.000 | $0.350 |
| | 1855 | $0.445 | $0.960 | $1.080 | $0.940 | $0.420 |
| | 1856 | $0.410 | $0.930 | $0.910 | $0.900 | $0.380 |
| | 1857 | $0.250 | $0.800 | $0.740 | $0.880 | $0.200 |
| | 1858 | $0.250 | $0.740 | $0.650 | $0.740 | $0.160 |
| | 1859 | $0.220 | $0.760 | $0.720 | $0.800 | $0.220 |
| | 1860 | $0.210 | $0.690 | $0.720 | $0.580 | $0.270 |
| | 1861 | $0.225 | $0.530 | $2.000 | $0.540 | N/R |
| Sheeting, per yard | 1850 | $8.50 | $0.07 | N/R | $0.10 | N/R |
| *(Philadelphia per piece)* | 1851 | $8.50 | $0.07 | N/R | $0.10 | N/R |
| | 1852 | $8.50 | $0.06 | N/R | $0.10 | N/R |
| | 1853 | $8.50 | $0.06 | N/R | $0.10 | N/R |
| | 1854 | $8.50 | $0.07 | N/R | $0.10 | N/R |
| | 1855 | $8.50 | $0.07 | N/R | $0.10 | N/R |
| | 1856 | $8.50 | $0.08 | N/R | $0.10 | N/R |
| | 1857 | $8.50 | $0.09 | N/R | $0.10 | N/R |
| | 1858 | $9.25 | $0.08 | N/R | $0.10 | N/R |
| | 1859 | $9.25 | $0.07 | N/R | $0.10 | N/R |
| | 1860 | $9.25 | N/R | N/R | $0.10 | N/R |
| | 1861 | $9.25 | N/R | N/R | $0.24 | N/R |
| Staves, per 1200 units | 1850 | $31.20 | $45.50 | N/R | $38.50 | $12.00 |
| | 1851 | $37.50 | $46.00 | N/R | $38.50 | $15.00 |
| | 1852 | $36.00 | $46.00 | N/R | $38.50 | $18.00 |
| | 1853 | $36.00 | $47.00 | N/R | $41.00 | $14.00 |
| | 1854 | $36.00 | $60.00 | N/R | $41.00 | $12.50 |
| | 1855 | $33.40 | $63.00 | N/R | $41.00 | $13.50 |
| | 1856 | $33.40 | $65.00 | N/R | $60.00 | $20.00 |
| | 1857 | $50.00 | $65.00 | N/R | $95.00 | $20.00 |
| | 1858 | $45.00 | $52.50 | N/R | $65.00 | N/R |
| | 1859 | $42.50 | $52.50 | N/R | $65.00 | N/R |
| | 1860 | $42.50 | $47.50 | N/R | $70.00 | $11.00 |
| | 1861 | $42.50 | $70.00 | N/R | $70.00 | N/R |
| Steel, per pound | 1850 | $0.12 | $0.12 | N/R | $0.10 | $0.06 |
| | 1851 | $0.12 | $0.12 | N/R | $0.10 | $0.05 |
| | 1852 | $0.12 | $0.14 | N/R | $0.10 | $0.05 |
| | 1853 | $0.12 | $0.14 | N/R | $0.10 | $0.06 |
| | 1854 | $0.12 | $0.14 | N/R | $0.10 | $0.06 |
| | 1855 | $0.12 | $0.14 | N/R | $0.11 | $0.06 |

| Commodity | Year | Philadelphia Currency | New York Currency | Charleston Currency | New Orleans Currency | Cincinnati Currency |
|---|---|---|---|---|---|---|
| | 1856 | $0.11 | $0.14 | N/R | $0.11 | $0.06 |
| | 1857 | $0.10 | $0.11 | N/R | $0.11 | $0.06 |
| | 1858 | $0.10 | $0.11 | N/R | $0.12 | $0.06 |
| | 1859 | $0.10 | $0.08 | N/R | $0.11 | $0.06 |
| | 1860 | $0.10 | N/R | N/R | $0.11 | $0.06 |
| | 1861 | $0.10 | N/R | N/R | $0.11 | N/R |
| Sugar, per hundredweight | 1850 | $5.75 | $4.50 | $5.00 | $3.75 | $4.88 |
| | 1851 | $6.25 | $5.00 | $5.60 | $4.62 | $6.38 |
| | 1852 | $5.75 | $4.50 | $4.70 | $4.00 | $5.75 |
| | 1853 | $6.25 | $4.50 | $5.60 | $3.94 | $4.38 |
| | 1854 | $5.75 | $4.00 | $5.00 | $2.88 | $5.00 |
| | 1855 | $6.25 | $5.00 | $5.10 | $5.00 | $6.25 |
| | 1856 | $8.00 | $7.00 | $7.50 | $6.12 | $8.25 |
| | 1857 | $11.00 | $10.00 | $11.40 | $9.88 | $12.00 |
| | 1858 | $7.12 | $6.00 | $6.50 | $5.38 | $7.00 |
| | 1859 | $7.62 | $6.50 | $6.80 | $5.62 | $7.25 |
| | 1860 | $7.00 | $7.00 | $6.40 | $5.88 | $8.00 |
| | 1861 | $5.50 | $4.50 | $7.50 | $4.12 | N/R |
| Tallow, per pound | 1850 | $0.08 | $0.06 | N/R | $0.06 | $0.07 |
| | 1851 | $0.08 | $0.07 | N/R | $0.07 | $0.08 |
| | 1852 | $0.08 | $0.08 | N/R | $0.07 | $0.08 |
| | 1853 | $0.09 | $0.09 | N/R | $0.08 | $0.09 |
| | 1854 | $0.12 | $0.12 | N/R | $0.11 | $0.11 |
| | 1855 | $0.12 | $0.11 | N/R | $0.11 | $0.11 |
| | 1856 | $0.10 | $0.10 | N/R | $0.09 | $0.09 |
| | 1857 | $0.12 | $0.11 | N/R | $0.10 | $0.11 |
| | 1858 | $0.10 | $0.10 | N/R | $0.10 | $0.10 |
| | 1859 | $0.11 | $0.10 | N/R | $0.10 | $0.10 |
| | 1860 | $0.10 | $0.10 | N/R | $0.10 | $0.10 |
| | 1861 | $0.09 | $0.08 | N/R | $0.10 | N/R |

### Based Upon US Dollars

| Year | Value of 19th Century Dollar in 2002 US Dollars |
|---|---|
| 1850 | $22.00 |
| 1855 | $20.00 |
| 1860 | $21.00 |
| 1865 | $11.00 |

*Calculations are approximate values based upon economic historical data*

| Commodity | Year | Philadelphia Currency | New York Currency | Charleston Currency | New Orleans Currency | Cincinnati Currency |
|---|---|---|---|---|---|---|
| Tea, per pound | 1850 | $0.65 | $0.50 | N/R | $0.72 | N/R |
| | 1851 | $0.60 | $0.51 | N/R | $0.72 | $0.44 |
| | 1852 | $0.54 | $0.50 | N/R | $0.72 | $0.55 |
| | 1853 | $0.52 | $0.50 | N/R | $0.72 | $0.55 |
| | 1854 | $0.58 | $0.42 | N/R | $0.72 | $0.55 |
| | 1855 | $0.58 | $0.36 | N/R | $0.72 | $0.55 |
| | 1856 | $0.58 | $0.38 | N/R | $0.72 | $0.55 |
| | 1857 | $0.58 | $0.42 | N/R | $0.72 | $0.55 |
| | 1858 | $0.62 | $0.36 | N/R | $0.72 | N/R |
| | 1859 | $0.60 | $0.21 | N/R | $0.72 | N/R |
| | 1860 | $0.45 | $0.28 | N/R | $0.72 | N/R |
| | 1861 | $0.52 | $0.41 | N/R | $0.72 | N/R |
| Tobacco, per hundredweight | 1850 | $0.06 | $0.08 | N/R | $7.50 | $8.00 |
| (Philadelphia & New York - per pound) | 1851 | $0.09 | $0.10 | N/R | $8.50 | $12.50 |
| | 1852 | $0.06 | $0.06 | N/R | $5.00 | $7.00 |
| | 1853 | $0.08 | $0.07 | N/R | $6.40 | $8.75 |
| | 1854 | $0.08 | $0.08 | N/R | $6.60 | $9.25 |
| | 1855 | $0.08 | $0.10 | N/R | $8.40 | $8.50 |
| | 1856 | $0.08 | $0.11 | N/R | $8.00 | $12.00 |
| | 1857 | $0.08 | $0.16 | N/R | $13.20 | $12.00 |
| | 1858 | $0.06 | $0.11 | N/R | $8.00 | $8.50 |
| | 1859 | $0.06 | $0.10 | N/R | $6.80 | $10.50 |
| | 1860 | $0.06 | $0.08 | N/R | $6.00 | $8.00 |
| | 1861 | $0.08 | $0.08 | N/R | $0.07 | N/R |
| Turpentine, per gallon | 1850 | $2.33 | $0.33 | $1.88 | $0.33 | $0.39 |
| (Philadelphia and Charleston per barrel) | 1851 | $2.21 | $0.37 | $1.90 | $0.48 | $0.44 |
| | 1852 | $2.66 | $0.50 | $2.24 | $0.52 | $0.60 |
| | 1853 | $3.62 | $0.66 | N/R | $0.55 | $0.69 |
| | 1854 | $5.25 | $0.62 | N/R | $0.68 | $0.77 |
| | 1855 | $3.62 | $0.44 | N/R | $0.45 | $0.57 |
| | 1856 | $3.62 | $0.41 | $3.31 | $0.46 | $0.52 |
| | 1857 | $3.62 | $0.48 | $2.75 | $0.55 | $0.59 |
| | 1858 | $6.25 | $0.49 | N/R | $0.50 | $0.56 |
| | 1859 | $3.25 | $0.53 | N/R | $0.52 | $0.59 |
| | 1860 | $3.25 | $0.47 | N/R | $0.40 | $0.53 |
| | 1861 | $4.25 | $0.81 | N/R | $0.30 | N/R |
| Whale Oil, per gallon | 1850 | $0.54 | $0.44 | N/R | $0.60 | N/R |
| | 1851 | $0.46 | $0.43 | N/R | $0.70 | $0.75 |
| | 1852 | $0.79 | $0.76 | N/R | $0.85 | $0.90 |
| | 1853 | $0.62 | $0.52 | N/R | $0.90 | $0.90 |
| | 1854 | $0.62 | $0.56 | N/R | $0.90 | $0.90 |
| | 1855 | $0.69 | $0.66 | N/R | $0.95 | $0.90 |
| | 1856 | $0.84 | $0.78 | N/R | $0.95 | $0.90 |
| | 1857 | $0.78 | $0.74 | N/R | $0.92 | $1.09 |
| | 1858 | $0.60 | $0.55 | N/R | $0.82 | $0.88 |
| | 1859 | $0.59 | $0.51 | N/R | $0.80 | $0.98 |

| Commodity | Year | Philadelphia Currency | New York Currency | Charleston Currency | New Orleans Currency | Cincinnati Currency |
|---|---|---|---|---|---|---|
| | 1860 | $0.50 | $0.43 | N/R | $0.75 | N/R |
| | 1861 | $0.48 | $0.41 | N/R | $0.75 | N/R |
| Wheat, per bushel | 1850 | $1.12 | $1.34 | N/R | $0.94 | $1.17 |
| | 1851 | $0.92 | $1.14 | N/R | $0.82 | $0.70 |
| | 1852 | $0.94 | $1.10 | N/R | $0.66 | $0.61 |
| | 1853 | $1.10 | $1.32 | N/R | $0.85 | $0.76 |
| | 1854 | $2.02 | $2.25 | N/R | $1.58 | $1.65 |
| | 1855 | $2.48 | $2.78 | N/R | $2.00 | $2.00 |
| | 1856 | $1.34 | $1.78 | N/R | $1.19 | $1.10 |
| | 1857 | $1.78 | $1.88 | N/R | $1.39 | $1.50 |
| | 1858 | $1.05 | $1.33 | N/R | $0.91 | $0.75 |
| | 1859 | $1.82 | $1.48 | N/R | $1.25 | $1.70 |
| | 1860 | $1.40 | $1.65 | N/R | $1.50 | $1.34 |
| | 1861 | $1.36 | $1.55 | N/R | $1.30 | N/R |
| Whisky, per gallon | 1850 | $0.22 | $0.24 | $0.24 | $0.21 | $0.21 |
| | 1851 | $0.22 | $0.23 | $0.24 | $0.19 | $0.17 |
| | 1852 | $0.21 | $0.21 | $0.22 | $0.17 | $0.15 |
| | 1853 | $0.22 | $0.22 | $0.26 | $0.19 | $0.18 |
| | 1854 | $0.26 | $0.26 | $0.28 | $0.22 | $0.21 |
| | 1855 | $0.39 | $0.36 | $0.42 | $0.36 | $0.33 |
| | 1856 | $0.26 | $0.28 | $0.28 | $0.23 | $0.21 |
| | 1857 | $0.32 | $0.29 | $0.33 | $0.30 | $0.30 |
| | 1858 | $0.21 | $0.21 | $0.25 | $0.18 | $0.17 |
| | 1859 | $0.28 | $0.26 | $0.30 | $0.28 | $0.28 |
| | 1860 | $0.21 | $0.22 | $0.31 | $0.19 | $0.18 |
| | 1861 | $0.17 | $0.18 | $0.32 | $0.22 | N/R |
| Wine, per gallon | 1850 | $2.12 | $1.93 | N/R | $0.52 | N/R |
| | 1851 | $2.12 | $1.90 | N/R | $0.32 | $2.00 |
| | 1852 | $2.12 | $1.90 | N/R | $0.41 | $2.00 |
| | 1853 | $1.95 | $1.93 | N/R | $0.49 | $2.00 |

## Based Upon US Dollars

| Year | Value of 19th Century Dollar in 2002 US Dollars |
|---|---|
| 1850 | $22.00 |
| 1855 | $20.00 |
| 1860 | $21.00 |
| 1865 | $11.00 |

*Calculations are approximate values based upon economic historical data*

| Commodity | Year | Philadelphia Currency | New York Currency | Charleston Currency | New Orleans Currency | Cincinnati Currency |
|---|---|---|---|---|---|---|
| | 1854 | $2.38 | $2.25 | N/R | $0.66 | $1.62 |
| | 1855 | $2.75 | $2.25 | N/R | $0.75 | $2.25 |
| | 1856 | $2.75 | $2.50 | N/R | $0.75 | $2.25 |
| | 1857 | $2.75 | $3.38 | N/R | $1.05 | $2.25 |
| | 1858 | $2.75 | $3.25 | N/R | $1.05 | $2.25 |
| | 1859 | $2.38 | $3.50 | N/R | $1.05 | $1.68 |
| | 1860 | $2.75 | $3.50 | N/R | $1.05 | N/R |
| | 1861 | $2.75 | $4.25 | N/R | $1.05 | N/R |
| Wool, per pound | 1850 | $0.41 | $0.32 | N/R | N/R | $0.23 |
| | 1851 | $0.50 | $0.40 | N/R | N/R | $0.29 |
| | 1852 | $0.41 | $0.26 | N/R | N/R | $0.20 |
| | 1853 | $0.58 | $0.42 | N/R | N/R | $0.35 |
| | 1854 | $0.46 | $0.37 | N/R | N/R | $0.25 |
| | 1855 | $0.44 | $0.32 | N/R | N/R | $0.23 |
| | 1856 | $0.56 | $0.36 | N/R | N/R | $0.26 |
| | 1857 | $0.58 | $0.40 | N/R | N/R | $0.34 |
| | 1858 | $0.39 | $0.30 | N/R | $0.25 | N/R |
| | 1859 | $0.54 | $0.44 | N/R | N/R | $0.31 |
| | 1860 | $0.54 | $0.36 | N/R | N/R | $0.31 |
| | 1861 | $0.45 | $0.34 | N/R | N/R | N/R |

# SELECTED PRICES 1850-1865

| Item | Data Source | Description | Price |
|---|---|---|---|
| **Alcohol** | | | |
| Brandy | Inventory of John Haggard (1859) | One keg of brandy in Collin County, Texas in 1859 | $3.00 |
| Drink | Eliot Lord, History of the Comstock Lode (1959) | Glass of whiskey in Virginia City, Nevada, 1860 | $0.50 |
| Rum | Geoffery Ward, The West (1996) | Bottle of rum in California, 1850 | $20.00 |
| Still | Inventory of William Hite (1860) | Copper still, cap and worm in Franklin County, Indiana, 1860 | $25.00 |
| Whiskey | Eliot Lord, History of the Comstock Lode (1959) | Gallon of whiskey in Virginia City, Nevada, 1860 | $16.00 |
| Whiskey | The Congressional Globe (1864) | Wholesale price of whiskey in Illinois, 1864 | $1.00 |
| **Apparel - Children** | | | |
| Shoes | Inventory of Austin Taylor (1853) | Pair of children's shoes in Greenville, South Carolina, 1853 | $0.26 |
| **Apparel - Men** | | | |
| Boots | Inventory of Austin Taylor (1853) | Pair of fine boots in Greenville, South Carolina, 1853 | $2.51 |
| Britches | Inventory of John Haggard (1859) | One Pair of britches in Collin County, Texas in 1859 | $3.00 |
| Collar | Invoice to D. Malley (1855) | Cost for a men's linen collar in Dallas, Texas in 1855 | $0.35 |
| Gloves | Inventory of Austin Taylor (1853) | Pair wool gloves in Greenville, South Carolina, 1853 | $0.14 |
| Gloves | Invoice to D. Malley (1855) | Cost for one pair of kid gloves in Dallas, Texas in 1858 | $1.25 |
| Hat | Inventory of Austin Taylor (1853) | Palm hat in Greenville, South Carolina, 1853 | $0.10 |
| Hat | Inventory of Samuel Bourne (1860) | Fine hat in Franklin County, Indiana, 1860 | $2.00 |
| Hose | Account of John C. Evans (1859) | Cost for a pair of hose in Dallas, Texas in 1859 | $0.20 |
| Hose | Inventory of Austin Taylor (1853) | Pair of hose in Greenville, South Carolina, 1853 | 12½ cents |

## Based Upon US Dollars

| Year | Value of 19th Century Dollar in 2002 US Dollars |
|---|---|
| 1850 | $22.00 |
| 1855 | $20.00 |
| 1860 | $21.00 |
| 1865 | $11.00 |

*Calculations are approximate values based upon economic historical data*

| Item | Data Source | Description | Price |
|------|-------------|-------------|-------|
| Mitts | Inventory of Austin Taylor (1853) | Pair of mitts in Greenville, South Carolina, 1853 | $0.11 |
| Overcoat | Inventory of Austin Taylor (1853) | Overcoat in Greenville, South Carolina, 1853 | $4.00 |
| Pants | Invoice to D. Malley (1855) | Cost for a pair of men's pants in Dallas, Texas in 1855 | $3.50 |
| Robe | Inventory of Rev. Joseph Barr (1854) | Buffalo robe in New Castle County, Delaware, 1854 | $3.00 |
| Shirt | Invoice to D. Malley (1855) | Cost for a men's shirt in Dallas, Texas in 1855 | $0.75 |
| Shoes | Inventory of Austin Taylor (1853) | Pair of brogans in Greenville, South Carolina, 1853 | $0.61 |
| Suspenders | Inventory of Austin Taylor (1853) | Pair of suspenders in Greenville, South Carolina, 1853 | $0.25 |
| Vest | Inventory of Austin Taylor (1853) | Vest in Greenville, South Carolina, 1853 | $0.50 |

**Apparel - Women**

| Item | Data Source | Description | Price |
|------|-------------|-------------|-------|
| Bonnet | Inventory of Austin Taylor (1853) | Pink bonnet in Greenville, South Carolina, 1853 | $0.15 |
| Gloves | Inventory of Austin Taylor (1853) | Pair silk gloves in Greenville, South Carolina, 1853 | $0.20 |
| Handkerchief | Inventory of Austin Taylor (1853) | Fine handkerchief in Greenville, South Carolina, 1853 | $0.26 |
| Hat | Receipt of John Coit (1859) | Cost for one fine black ladies hat in Dallas, Texas in 1859 | $4.50 |
| Hose | Account of John C. Evans (1859) | Cost for a pair of misses hose in Dallas, Texas in 1859 | $0.15 |
| Mitts | Inventory of Austin Taylor (1853) | Pair of white mitts in Greenville, South Carolina, 1853 | 12½ cents |
| Shawl | Inventory of Austin Taylor (1853) | Shawl in Greenville, South Carolina, 1853 | $0.20 |
| Shoes | Inventory of Austin Taylor (1853) | Pair of ladies shoes in Greenville, South Carolina, 1853 | $0.87 |
| Shoes | Invoice to D. Malley (1859) | One pair of ladies walking shoes in Dallas, Texas, 1859 | $1.75 |
| Slippers | Invoice to D. Malley (1859) | Cost for one pair of women's slippers in Dallas, Texas, 1859 | $1.00 |

| Item | Data Source | Description | Price |
|---|---|---|---|
| **Commodity** | | | |
| Buckwheat | Inventory of Anson Buckley (1860) | Bushel of buckwheat in Franklin County, Indiana, 1860 | 62½ cents |
| Coal | Inventory of Miss Sarah Black (1862) | Ton of coal in New Castle County, Delaware, 1862 | $2.00 |
| Coal | Harper's Magazine (1865) | Coal, one ton, for kitchen range, New York City, 1865 | $8.50 |
| Corn | Inventory of Brice B. Moore (1851) | Bushel of corn in Franklin County, Indiana, 1851 | $0.25 |
| Corn | Inventory of Samuel Alsop, Jr. (1859) | Barrel of corn in Spotsylvania County, Virginia, 1859 | $13.50 |
| Hay | Inventory of Shubal Wardner (1859) | Ton of hay in Windsor, Vermont, 1859 | $9.00 |
| Hay | Inventory of Samuel Alsop, Jr. (1859) | Stack of hay in Spotsylvania County, Virginia, 1859 | $6.00 |
| Iron | William Dutton, Du Pont (1949) | Ton of pig iron in New York City, 1860 | $22.00 |
| Iron | William Dutton, Du Pont (1949) | Ton of pig iron in New York City, 1864 | $70.00 |
| Lumber | Apprasial of Daniel Herring (1859) | 200 feet of walnut plank in Collin County, Texas in 1858 | $8.00 |
| Lumber | Eliot Lord, History of the Comstock Lode (1959) | Price for one thousand foot of board in Virginia City, Nevada, March 1860 | $300.00 |
| Lumber | Inventory of Adanijah Wiley (1862) | One hundred foot of cherry lumber in Franklin County, Indiana, 1862 | $1.43 |
| Oats | Inventory of Warren A. Wiglesworth (1853) | Bushel of oats in Fredericksburg, Virginia, 1853 | $0.47 |
| Oats | Inventory of Peter Updike (1862) | Bushel of oats in Franklin County, Indiana, 1862 | $0.20 |
| Ore | Milner, Oxford History of the American West | Value per ton of silver and gold of the Comstock Lode's Ophir mine in 1859 | $3,876.00 |
| Pork | Inventory of Isaac Benedict (1856) | Pound of salted pork in Greenville, South Carolina, 1856 | $0.07 |
| Pork | The Congressional Globe (1864) | Barrel of mess pork in Chicago, 1864 | $19.50 |
| Rye | Inventory of Shubal Wardner (1859) | Bushel of rye in Windsor, Vermont, 1859 | $0.55 |
| Salt | Inventory of Joseph McCafferty (1852) | Bushel of salt in Franklin County, Indiana, 1852 | 37½ cents |
| Seed | Inventory of George Hubble (1854) | Bushel of timothy seed in Franklin County, Indiana, 1854 | $2.00 |

### Based Upon US Dollars

| Year | Value of 19th Century Dollar in 2002 US Dollars |
|---|---|
| 1850 | $22.00 |
| 1855 | $20.00 |
| 1860 | $21.00 |
| 1865 | $11.00 |

*Calculations are approximate values based upon economic historical data*

| Item | Data Source | Description | Price |
|---|---|---|---|
| Seed | Inventory of Anson Buckley (1860) | Bushel of clover seed in Franklin County, Indiana, 1860 | $3.12½ |
| Straw | Inventory of Samuel Alsop, Jr. (1859) | Stack of wheat straw in Spotsylvania County, Virginia, 1859 | $3.00 |
| Sugar | Receipt of T.H. Tomlinson (1858) | Cost for one pound of crushed sugar in Dallas, Texas | $0.17 |
| Wheat | Inventory of Lydia Montgomery (1854) | Bushel of wheat in Franklin County, Indiana, 1854 | $0.50 |
| Wheat | Inventory of Isaac Benedict (1856) | Bushel of wheat in Greenville, South Carolina, 1856 | $1.00 |
| Wood | Inventory of Shubal Wardner (1859) | Cord of wood in Windsor, Vermont, 1859 | $60.00 |
| Wood | Eliot Lord, History of the Comstock Lode (1959) | Cord of wood in Virginia City, Nevada, 1864 | $17.50 |
| Wool | Inventory of Caleb Phillip (1859) | One pound for lot of wool in Collin County, Texas in 1859 | $2.50 |

### Education

| Item | Data Source | Description | Price |
|---|---|---|---|
| Doctor's Qualification | Suzanne C. Linder, Medicine in Marlboro County, 1736 to 1980 | Cost for a individual to qualify as a "steam doctor" by purchasing the book Samuel Thomson's textbook-autobiograpy, including fill-in diploma-license, 1861 | $20.00 |
| Tuition | American Heritage (1960) | Yearly private education cost for a Grand Tour of Europe for an American visiting Europe, 1854 | $6,000.00 |

### Entertainment

| Item | Data Source | Description | Price |
|---|---|---|---|
| Admission | Ford's Theater Advertisement (1865) | Orchestra seating to Our American Cousin at Ford's Theater in Washington DC, 1865 | $1.00 |
| Admission | Ford's Theater Advertisement (1865) | Family circle seating to Our American Cousin at Ford's Theater in Washington DC, 1865 | $0.25 |
| Admission | Ford's Theater Advertisement (1865) | Private Box seating to Our American Cousin at Ford's Theater in Washington DC, 1865 | $10.00 |
| Stereoscope Views | American Heritage (1960) | Dozen stereoscopic pictures advertized by Henry T Anthony in the United States (1860) | $3.00 |

### Fabrics & Sewing Materials

| Item | Data Source | Description | Price |
|---|---|---|---|
| Buttons | Account of John C. Evans (1859) | Cost for a dozen buttons in Dallas, Texas in 1859 | $0.10 |
| Carpet | Inventory of George Hubble (1854) | Yard of carpeting in Franklin County, Indiana, 1854 | $0.10 |
| Fabric | Inventory of Austin Taylor (1853) | Yard of calico in Greenville, South Carolina, 1853 | $0.09 |
| Fabric | Inventory of Austin Taylor (1853) | Yard of casimer in Greenville, South Carolina, 1853 | $0.81 |
| Muslin | Inventory of Austin Taylor (1853) | Yard of swiss muslin in Greenville, South Carolina, 1853 | $0.32 |
| Needles | Inventory of Austin Taylor (1853) | Lot of needles in Greenville, South Carolina, 1853 | $0.25 |
| Pattern | Inventory of Austin Taylor (1853) | Black vest pattern in Greenville, South Carolina, 1853 | $0.50 |
| Quilting Frame | Inventory of Shubal Wardner (1859) | Quilting frame in Windsor, Vermont, 1859 | $0.10 |
| Ribbon | Inventory of Austin Taylor (1853) | Yard of ribbon in Greenville, South Carolina, 1853 | $0.06 |
| Thimble | Inventory of Isaac Benedict (1856) | Silver thimble in Greenville, South Carolina, 1856 | $0.25 |

| Item | Data Source | Description | Price |
|------|-------------|-------------|-------|
| Thimble | Inventory of Isaac Benedict (1856) | Gold thimble in Greenville, South Carolina, 1856 | $2.00 |
| Thread | Inventory of Austin Taylor (1853) | Lot of silk thread in Greenville, South Carolina, 1853 | $0.32 |
| Ticking | Inventory of Austin Taylor (1853) | Yard of bed ticking in Greenville, South Carolina, 1853 | 13½ cents |

## Farm Equipment & Tools

| Item | Data Source | Description | Price |
|------|-------------|-------------|-------|
| Axe | Inventory of Caleb Phillip (1859) | Band axe in Collin County, Texas in 1859 | $2.00 |
| Barrel | Inventory of Thomas F. Boren (1858) | Price of a barrel in Collin County, Texas in 1858 | $0.50 |
| Bee Hive | Inventory of George Hubble (1854) | Bee hive & bees in Franklin County, Indiana, 1854 | $1.50 |
| Blade | Inventory of Samuel Alsop, Jr. (1859) | Bramble blade in Spotsylvania County, Virginia, 1859 | $0.50 |
| Box | Inventory of Samuel Alsop, Jr. (1859) | Cutting box in Spotsylvania County, Virginia, 1859 | $1.66 |
| Brush | Inventory of Austin Taylor (1853) | Paint brush in Greenville, South Carolina, 1853 | $0.25 |
| Bucket | Inventory of Lydia Montgomery (1854) | Tar bucket & strap in Franklin County, Indiana, 1854 | $0.10 |
| Bucket | Inventory of Thomas F. Boren (1858) | One well bucket with rope in Collin County, Texas in 1858 | $0.50 |
| Can | Inventory of William Hite (1860) | Water can in Franklin County, Indiana, 1860 | $0.25 |
| Chain | Inventory of Thomas F. Boren (1858) | Log Chain in Collin County, Texas in 1858 | $2.00 |

| Item | Data Source | Description | Price |
|------|-------------|-------------|-------|
| Chisel | Inventory of Austin Taylor (1853) | Chisel in Greenville, South Carolina, 1853 | $0.20 |
| Churn | Inventory of John Miller (1851) | Butter churn in Franklin County, Indiana, 1851 | $0.75 |
| Coop | Inventory of Miss Sarah Black (1862) | Chicken coop in New Castle County, Delaware, 1862 | $2.00 |
| Crowbar | Inventory of George Hubble (1854) | Crow bar in Franklin County, Indiana, 1854 | $0.75 |
| Cultivator | Inventory of George Hubble (1854) | Cultivator in Franklin County, Indiana, 1854 | $1.00 |
| Cultivator Teeth | Apprasial of Daniel Herring (1859) | Set of 12 cultivator teeth in Collin County, Texas in 1858 | $10.00 |
| Files | Inventory of Austin Taylor (1853) | Saw file in Greenville, South Carolina, 1853 | $0.26 |
| Fork | Inventory of Brice B. Moore (1851) | Manure fork in Franklin County, Indiana, 1851 | $1.00 |
| Fork | Inventory of George Hubble (1854) | Pitch fork in Franklin County, Indiana, 1854 | $0.25 |
| Gear | Inventory of John Haggard (1859) | Pair of Gears in Collin County, Texas in 1859 | $5.00 |
| Grain Cradle | Inventory of Shubal Wardner (1859) | Grain craddle in Windsor, Vermont, 1859 | $0.50 |
| Grind Stone | Inventory of John Haggard (1859) | Grind Stone in Collin County, Texas in 1859 | $0.50 |
| Hammer | Inventory of Joseph McCafferty (1852) | Hammer in Franklin County, Indiana, 1852 | $0.25 |
| Harrow | Inventory of Isaac Benedict (1856) | Harrow in Greenville, South Carolina, 1856 | $1.00 |
| Hatchet | Inventory of John Haggard (1859) | Hatchet in Collin County, Texas in 1858 | $0.25 |
| Haw & Auger | Inventory of John Haggard (1859) | Haw & Auger in Collin County, Texas in 1859 | $0.75 |
| Hoe | Inventory of Brice B. Moore (1851) | Hoe in Franklin County, Indiana, 1851 | $0.25 |
| Hog Cutter | Inventory of Shubal Wardner (1859) | Hog Cutter in Windsor, Vermont, 1859 | $1.00 |
| Hook | Inventory of Samuel Alsop, Jr. (1859) | Three ice hooks in Spotsylvania County, Virginia, 1859 | $0.50 |
| Ladder | Inventory of Isaac Benedict (1856) | Ladder in Greenville, South Carolina, 1856 | $1.00 |
| Lumber | Inventory of John Haggard (1859) | Fencing lumber per board in Collin County, Texas in 1859 | $0.05 |
| Mill | Inventory of Mary Shirk (1857) | Fanning mill in Franklin County, Indiana, 1857 | $3.00 |
| Molds | Inventory of Elizabeth Newnam (1853) | Candle moulds in Franklin County, Indiana, 1853 | $0.25 |
| Nails | Inventory of Wm. Phillips (1957) | One pound of nails in Collin County, Texas in 1857 | $0.10 |
| Nails | Eliot Lord, History of the Comstock Lode (1959) | Pound of nails in Virginia City, Nevada, 1860 | $1.00 |
| Ox Yoke | Inventory of John Haggard (1859) | Ox Yoke in Collin County, Texas in 1859 | $0.25 |
| Pan | Inventory of Peter Updike (1862) | Milk pan in Franklin County, Indiana, 1862 | $0.05 |
| Plough | Inventory of Austin Taylor (1853) | Scoop plough in Greenville, South Carolina, 1853 | $0.65 |
| Plough | Inventory of Samuel Alsop, Jr. (1859) | Shovel plough in Spotsylvania County, Virginia, 1859 | $2.00 |

| Item | Data Source | Description | Price |
|------|-------------|-------------|-------|
| Rake | Inventory of William Hite (1860) | Iron tooth rake in Franklin County, Indiana, 1860 | $0.25 |
| Saw | Inventory of Samuel Alsop, Jr. (1859) | Cross cut saw in Spotsylvania County, Virginia, 1859 | $0.50 |
| Screw | Inventory of Joseph McCafferty (1852) | Iron screw in Franklin County, Indiana, 1852 | $0.25 |
| Scythe | Inventory of Samuel Alsop, Jr. (1859) | Scythe and cradle in Spotsylvania County, Virginia, 1859 | $2.50 |
| Shears | Inventory of Austin Taylor (1853) | Pair of shears in Greenville, South Carolina, 1853 | $0.78 |
| Shovel | Apprasial of Daniel Herring (1859) | Shovel in Collin County, Texas in 1858 | $1.50 |
| Shovel | Inventory of Samuel Alsop, Jr. (1859) | Shovel in Spotsylvania County, Virginia, 1859 | $0.25 |
| Spade | Inventory of Catharine Feighan (1861) | Spade in Franklin County, Indiana, 1861 | $0.25 |
| Steelyards | Inventory of Elizabeth Newnam (1853) | Steelyards in Franklin County, Indiana, 1853 | $0.37 |
| Scythe | Inventory of Samuel Bourne (1860) | Mowing sythe in Franklin County, Indiana, 1860 | $1.00 |
| Teeth | Inventory of Joseph McCafferty (1852) | Ten harrow teeth in Franklin County, Indiana, 1852 | $0.50 |
| Threshing Machine | Inventory of Warren A. Wiglesworth (1853) | Threshing machine in Fredericksburg, Virginia, 1853 | $80.00 |
| Vise | Inventory of Isaac Benedict (1856) | Bench vice in Greenville, South Carolina, 1856 | $2.50 |
| Wheelbarrow | Inventory of Isaac Benedict (1856) | Wheel barrow in Greenville, South Carolina, 1856 | $4.00 |
| Windmill | Inventory of George Hubble (1854) | Windmill in Franklin County, Indiana, 1854 | $10.00 |
| Wrench | Inventory of Shubal Wardner (1859) | Monkey wrench in Windsor, Vermont, 1859 | $0.25 |

## Firearms & Supplies

| Item | Data Source | Description | Price |
|------|-------------|-------------|-------|
| Buckshot | Inventory of Austin Taylor (1853) | Pound of buckshot in Greenville, South Carolina, 1853 | $0.09 |
| Buckshot | Invoice of White, Smith & Daldwin (1859) | Cost for one bag of buck shot bought in Shreveport, Louisania in 1859 | $2.60 |
| Gunpowder | William Dutton, Du Pont (1949) | Pound of gunpowder smuggled by blockade runners for the Confederacy, 1861 | $3.00 |

### Based Upon US Dollars

| Year | Value of 19th Century Dollar in 2002 US Dollars |
|------|--------------------------------------------------|
| 1850 | $22.00 |
| 1855 | $20.00 |
| 1860 | $21.00 |
| 1865 | $11.00 |

*Calculations are approximate values based upon economic historical data*

| Item | Data Source | Description | Price |
|------|-------------|-------------|-------|
| Gunpowder | William Dutton, Du Pont (1949) | Pound of gunpowder sold by Du Pont to the US Government, 1861 | $0.18 |
| Musket | Francis Lord, Civil War Collector's Encyclopedia (1989) | Manufacturer's price of a Springfield musket, 1861 | $14.93 |
| Pistol | Inventory of John Haggard (1859) | Pistol in Collin County, Texas in 1859 | $17.50 |
| Rifle | Arcadi Gluckman, Identifying Old U.S. Muskets, Rifles & Carbines (1965) | Price per rifle, Remington, Rifle 1841 Model, for the US Government, 1851 | $11.00 |
| Rifle | Francis Lord, Civil War Collector's Encyclopedia (1989) | Colt Revolving Rifle purchased by the US Navy, 1863 | $50.00 |
| Shotgun | Inventory of Brice B. Moore (1851) | Shotgun in Franklin County, Indiana, 1851 | $2.00 |
| Shotgun | Inventory of John Haggard (1859) | Shotgun in Collin County, Texas, in 1859 | $15.00 |

### Food Products

| Item | Data Source | Description | Price |
|------|-------------|-------------|-------|
| Apples | Inventory of Catharine Feighan (1861) | Lot of dried apples in Franklin County, Indiana, 1861 | $1.25 |
| Bacon | Inventory of Austin Taylor (1853) | Pound of bacon in Greenville, South Carolina, 1853 | 11½ cents |
| Bacon | Eliot Lord, History of the Comstock Lode (1959) | Pound of bacon in Virginia City, Nevada, 1860 | $0.40 |
| Beef | Inventory of Warren A. Wiglesworth (1853) | Pound of beef in Fredericksburg, Virginia, 1853 | $0.04 |
| Beef | Harper's Magazine (1865) | Beef Steak, per pound, in New York City, 1865 | $0.35 |
| Bread | Harper's Magazine (1865) | Bread, per loaf, in New York City, 1865 | $0.04 |
| Butter | Eliot Lord, History of the Comstock Lode (1959) | Pound of butter in Virginia City, Nevada, 1860 | $1.00 |
| Candy | Inventory of Austin Taylor (1853) | Pound of candy in Greenville, South Carolina, 1853 | $0.10 |
| Cheese | John D. Billings, Hardtack and Coffee (1888) | Cost for one pound of cheese from a sutler in the Union Army | $0.50 |
| Coffee | Inventory of Austin Taylor (1853) | Pound of coffee in Greenville, South Carolina, 1853 | $0.13 |
| Coffee | Harper's Magazine (1865) | Coffee, one pound, in New York City, 1865 | $0.40 |
| Cookies | Francis Lord, Civil War Collector's Encyclopedia (1989) | Ten Molasses cookies purchased by a sutler, 1864 | $0.25 |
| Corn | Inventory of Austin Taylor (1853) | Bushel of corn in Greenville, South Carolina, 1853 | 37½ cents |
| Corn | Inventory of Warren A. Wiglesworth (1853) | Bushel of corn in Fredericksburg, Virginia, 1853 | $3.00 |
| Egg | Geoffery Ward, The West (1996) | Single egg in California, 1850 | $0.50 |
| Fish | Harper's Magazine (1865) | Mackerel, per pound, in New York City, 1865 | $0.15 |
| Flour | Inventory of Lydia Montgomery (1854) | Pound of flour in Franklin County, Indiana, 1854 | 1½ cent |
| Flour | Invoice to D. Malley (1859) | One sack of flour in Dallas, Texas in 1858 | $3.50 |
| Fruit | Francis Lord, Civil War Collector's Encyclopedia (1989) | Can of fruit purchased from a sutler in City Point, Virginia 1864 | $1.25 |
| Honey | Inventory of Isaac Benedict (1856) | Jar of honey in Greenville, South Carolina, 1856 | $0.50 |
| Lard | Inventory of Isaac Benedict (1856) | Pound of lard in Greenville, South Carolina, 1856 | $0.10 |
| Milk | John D. Billings, Hardtack and Coffee (1888) | Cost for a can of Borden condensed milk from a sutler in the Union Army | $0.75 |

| Item | Data Source | Description | Price |
|------|-------------|-------------|-------|
| Milk | Harper's Magazine (1865) | Milk, one quart, in New York City, 1865 | $0.10 |
| Molasses | Invoice of White, Smith & Daldwin (1859) | Cost for one gallon of molasses bought in Shreveport, Louisania in 1859 | 35½ cents |
| Onions | Francis Lord, Civil War Collector's Encyclopedia (1989) | Pound of onions purchased from a sutler in City Point, Virginia, 1864 | $0.15 |
| Onions | Harper's Magazine (1865) | Onions, per pound, in New York City, 1865 | $0.03 |
| Peaches | Graves Account Book (1857) | Cost per pound of dried peaches sold at South Butler, New York in 1857 | 12½ cents |
| Peas | Inventory of Isaac Benedict (1856) | Bushel of peas in Greenville, South Carolina, 1856 | $0.71 |
| Pork | Inventory of Isaac Benedict (1856) | Pound of salted pork in Greenville, South Carolina, 1856 | $0.07 |
| Pork | The Congressional Globe (1864) | Barrel of mess pork in Chicago, 1864 | $20.00 |
| Potatoes | Geoffery Ward, The West (1996) | Pound of potatoes in California, 1850 | $1.00 |
| Potatoes | Francis Lord, Civil War Collector's Encyclopedia (1989) | Pound of sweet potatoes purchased from a sutler in City Point, Virginia 1864 | $0.15 |
| Rice | Receipt of John Coit (1859) | Cost for one pound of rice in Dallas, Texas in 1859 | $0.10 |
| Rice | Eliot Lord, History of the Comstock Lode (1959) | Pound of rice in Virginia City, Nevada, 1860 | $0.45 |
| Saleratus | Inventory of Wm. Phillips (1957) | A pound of Saleratus in Collin County, Texas in 1857 | $0.35 |
| Salt | Inventory of Wm. Phillips (1957) | One pound of salt in Collin County, Texas in 1857 | $0.04 |
| Soda | Receipt of John Coit (1859) | Cost of soda powder in Dallas, Texas in 1859 | $0.20 |
| Spice | Inventory of Austin Taylor (1853) | Pound of pepper in Greenville, South Carolina, 1853 | $0.11 |
| Sugar | Receipt of T. Levit (1858) | Cost for one pound of sugar sold in Texas | $0.15 |
| Sugar | Eliot Lord, History of the Comstock Lode (1959) | Pound of brown sugar in Virginia City, Nevada, 1860 | $0.50 |
| Syrup | Inventory of Austin Taylor (1853) | Bottle of lemon syrup in Greenville, South Carolina, 1853 | $0.06 |
| Turnips | Inventory of Catharine Feighan (1861) | Bushel of turnips in Franklin County, Indiana, 1861 | $0.25 |
| Vinegar | Inventory of John Haggard (1859) | Vinegar with Barrel in Collin County, Texas in 1859 | $2.35 |
| Wheat | Inventory of Lydia Montgomery (1854) | Bushel of wheat in Franklin County, Indiana, 1854 | $0.50 |

**Based Upon US Dollars**

| Year | Value of 19th Century Dollar in 2002 US Dollars |
|------|------|
| 1850 | $22.00 |
| 1855 | $20.00 |
| 1860 | $21.00 |
| 1865 | $11.00 |

*Calculations are approximate values based upon economic historical data*

| Item | Data Source | Description | Price |
|------|-------------|-------------|-------|
| **Household Furniture** | | | |
| Bed | Inventory of Revd. Joseph Barr (1854) | 1 featherbed, bolster & 2 pillows in New Castle County, Delaware, 1854 | $18.00 |
| Bedstead | Inventory of Catharine Feighan (1861) | Trundle bedstead in Franklin County, Indiana, 1861 | $0.10 |
| Bookcase | Inventory of Joseph McCafferty (1852) | Book case in Franklin County, Indiana, 1852 | $0.50 |
| Bookcase | Inventory of Elizabeth Newnam (1853) | Book case in Franklin County, Indiana, 1853 | $5.00 |
| Bookcase | Inventory of Isaac Benedict (1856) | Bookcase in Greenville, South Carolina, 1856 | $15.00 |
| Bureau | Inventory of Miss Sarah Black (1862) | Cedar bureau in New Castle County, Delaware, 1862 | $0.25 |
| Bureau | Inventory of Joseph McCafferty (1852) | Bureau in Franklin County, Indiana, 1852 | $9.00 |
| Chair | Inventory of Isaac Benedict (1856) | High chair in Greenville, South Carolina, 1856 | $0.25 |
| Chair | Inventory of Samuel Alsop, Jr. (1859) | Cane seat rocking chair in Spotsylvania County, Virginia, 1859 | $4.00 |
| Clock | Inventory of Isaac Benedict (1856) | High clock in Greenville, South Carolina, 1856 | $10.00 |
| Clock | Inventory of Caleb Phillip (1859) | Clock in Collin County, Texas in 1859 | $50.00 |
| Cot | Inventory of Miss Sarah Black (1862) | Cot in New Castle County, Delaware, 1862 | $1.00 |
| Cupboard | Inventory of Joseph McCafferty (1852) | Cupboard in Franklin County, Indiana, 1853 | $1.50 |
| Desk | Inventory of Peter Updike (1862) | Small desk in Franklin County, Indiana, 1862 | $1.00 |
| Divan | Inventory of Thomas C. Alrich (1865) | Divan in Wilmington, Delaware, 1865 | $5.00 |
| Footstool | Inventory of Miss Sarah Black (1862) | Footstool in New Castle County, Delaware, 1862 | $1.00 |
| Hat rack | Inventory of Thomas C. Alrich (1865) | Hat rack in Wilmington, Delaware, 1865 | $5.00 |
| Hat stand | Inventory of Miss Sarah Black (1862) | Hat stand in New Castle County, Delaware, 1862 | $2.50 |
| Looking Glass | Inventory of John Haggard (1859) | Looking glass in Collin County, Texas in 1859 | $1.00 |
| Mattress | Inventory of Miss Sarah Black (1862) | Straw mattress in New Castle County, Delaware, 1862 | $1.00 |
| Ottoman | Inventory of Miss Sarah Black (1862) | Ottoman in New Castle County, Delaware, 1862 | $1.00 |
| Secretary | Inventory of George Hubble (1854) | Secretary in Franklin County, Indiana, 1854 | $9.00 |
| Secretary | Inventory of Miss Sarah Black (1862) | Secretary bookcase in New Castle County, Delaware, 1862 | $20.00 |
| Settee | Inventory of Elizabeth Newnam (1853) | Settee in Franklin County, Indiana, 1853 | $3.00 |
| Sideboard | Inventory of Samuel Alsop, Jr. (1859) | Sideboard in Spotsylvania County, Virginia, 1859 | $6.00 |
| Sofa | Inventory of Samuel Alsop, Jr. (1859) | Mahogany sofa in Spotsylvania County, Virginia, 1859 | $15.00 |
| Stand | Inventory of Anson Buckley (1860) | Plain stand in Franklin County, Indiana, 1860 | $0.50 |

| Item | Data Source | Description | Price |
|------|-------------|-------------|-------|
| Stool | Inventory of Miss Sarah Black (1862) | Stool in New Castle County, Delaware, 1862 | $0.25 |
| Sugar Chest | Inventory of Alexander Carouth (1859) | Sugar Chest in Collin County, Texas in 1859 | $5.00 |
| Table | Inventory of Revd. Joseph Barr (1854) | Mahagony breakfast table in New Castle County, Delaware, 1854 | $2.50 |
| Table | Inventory of George Hubble (1854) | Walnut table in Franklin County, Indiana, 1854 | 87½ cents |
| Table | Inventory of Thomas C. Alrich (1865) | Marble top table in Wilmington, Delaware, 1865 | $15.00 |
| Table Set | Inventory of Thomas F. Boren (1858) | One table and six chairs, Collin County, Texas, 1858 | $6.00 |
| Towel rack | Inventory of Miss Sarah Black (1862) | Towel rack in New Castle County, Delaware, 1862 | $0.25 |
| Washstand | Inventory of Miss Sarah Black (1862) | Wash stand in New Castle County, Delaware, 1862 | $6.00 |
| Workstand | Inventory of Miss Sarah Black (1862) | Workstand in New Castle County, Delaware, 1862 | $2.00 |

## Household Products

| Item | Data Source | Description | Price |
|------|-------------|-------------|-------|
| Bag | Inventory of Isaac Benedict (1856) | Indian bag in Greenville, South Carolina, 1856 | $0.25 |
| Barrel | Inventory of Lydia Montgomery (1854) | Rain barrel in Franklin County, Indiana, 1854 | $0.20 |
| Basin | Inventory of Miss Sarah Black (1862) | Basin, mug & pitcher in New Castle County, Delaware, 1862 | $1.00 |
| Basket | Inventory of Samuel Alsop, Jr. (1859) | Plated cake basket in Spotsylvania County, Virginia, 1859 | $10.00 |
| Basket | Inventory of Miss Sarah Black (1862) | Cloths basket in New Castle County, Delaware, 1862 | $0.50 |
| Bed cord | Inventory of Mary Shirk (1857) | Bed cord in Franklin County, Indiana, 1857 | $0.10 |
| Bed Curtains | Inventory of Rev. Joseph Barr (1854) | Set of white bed curtains in New Castle County, Delaware, 1854 | $1.00 |
| Bed Sheets | Inventory of John Haggard (1859) | Old set of bed sheets in Collin County, Texas in 1859 | $0.50 |
| Bedpan | Inventory of Rev. Joseph Barr (1854) | Bed pan in New Castle County, Delaware, 1854 | $0.50 |
| Bedspread | Inventory of Rev. Joseph Barr (1854) | Calico bedspread in New Castle County, Delaware, 1854 | $0.50 |

## Based Upon US Dollars

| Year | Value of 19th Century Dollar in 2002 US Dollars |
|------|-------------------------------------------------|
| 1850 | $22.00 |
| 1855 | $20.00 |
| 1860 | $21.00 |
| 1865 | $11.00 |

*Calculations are approximate values based upon economic historical data*

| Item | Data Source | Description | Price |
|------|-------------|-------------|-------|
| Bedstead | Inventory of Joseph McCafferty (1852) | Bedstead, bed, bedding in Franklin County, Indiana, 1852 | $4.00 |
| Bell | Inventory of Miss Sarah Black (1862) | Table bell in New Castle County, Delaware, 1862 | $0.50 |
| Blanket | Inventory of Austin Taylor (1853) | Blanket in Greenville, South Carolina, 1853 | $0.95 |
| Blind | Inventory of Joseph McCafferty (1852) | Boat window blind in Franklin County, Indiana, 1852 | $0.20 |
| Bottle | Inventory of Jacob Otto (1861) | Bottle in Franklin County, Indiana, 1861 | $0.03 |
| Bowl | Inventory of Isaac Benedict (1856) | Glass bowl in Greenville, South Carolina, 1856 | $1.50 |
| Bowl | Inventory of Mary Shirk (1857) | Bread bowl in Franklin County, Indiana, 1857 | $0.10 |
| Box | Inventory of Austin Taylor (1853) | Shoe box in Greenville, South Carolina, 1853 | $0.10 |
| Box | Inventory of Isaac Benedict (1856) | Walnut box in Greenville, South Carolina, 1856 | $0.20 |
| Broom | Inventory of Peter Updike (1862) | Fire broom in Franklin County, Indiana, 1862 | $0.75 |
| Brush | Inventory of Mary Shirk (1857) | Clothes brush in Franklin County, Indiana, 1857 | $0.10 |
| Brushes | Inventory of Austin Taylor (1853) | Pair of blacking brushes in Greenville, South Carolina, 1853 | $0.16 |
| Bucket | Receipt of John Coit (1859) | Cost of a wooden bucket in Dallas, Texas in 1859 | $0.50 |
| Candelabra | Inventory of Thomas C. Alrich (1865) | Candelabra in Wilmington, Delaware, 1865 | $0.50 |
| Candles | Eliot Lord, History of the Comstock Lode (1959) | Pound of candles in Virginia City, Nevada, 1860 | $1.00 |
| Candlestick | Invoice of T. Holmes (1859) | Cost for one candlestick in Dallas, Texas in 1858 | $0.15 |
| Canister | Inventory of Isaac Benedict (1856) | Tea canister in Greenville, South Carolina, 1856 | $0.10 |
| Carpet | Inventory of Elizabeth Newnam (1853) | Carpet in large room in Franklin County, Indiana, 1853 | $2.00 |
| Carpet | Inventory of Shubal Wardner (1859) | Hall carpet in Windsor, Vermont, 1859 | $0.50 |
| Castor | Inventory of George Hubble (1854) | Castor in Franklin County, Indiana, 1854 | $0.25 |
| Chamber bucket | Inventory of Miss Sarah Black (1862) | Chamber bucket in New Castle County, Delaware, 1862 | $0.50 |
| Chest | Inventory of George Hubble (1854) | Chest in Franklin County, Indiana, 1854 | $0.25 |
| Cloth | Inventory of Miss Sarah Black (1862) | Oil cloth in New Castle County, Delaware, 1862 | $0.50 |
| Clothes line | Inventory of George Hubble (1854) | Clothes line and basket in Franklin County, Indiana, 1854 | $0.10 |
| Comforter and Blanket | Inventory of John Haggard (1859) | Comforter and blanket in Collin County, Texas in 1859 | $2.50 |
| Commode | Inventory of Miss Sarah Black (1862) | Commode in New Castle County, Delaware, 1862 | $1.00 |
| Counterpane | Inventory of Miss Sarah Black (1862) | Counterpanes in New Castle County, Delaware, 1862 | $4.00 |
| Cover | Inventory of Benjamin M. Barron (1865) | Muslin bureau cover in New Castle County, Delaware, 1865 | $0.50 |
| Coverlet | Inventory of Elizabeth Newnam (1853) | New double coverlet, Franklin County, Indiana, 1853 | $7.00 |

| Item | Data Source | Description | Price |
|------|-------------|-------------|-------|
| Cup | Inventory of Miss Sarah Black (1862) | China cup in New Castle County, Delaware, 1862 | $0.25 |
| Cup & tumbler | Inventory of Miss Sarah Black (1862) | Silver cream cup & tumbler in New Castle County, Delaware, 1862 | $5.00 |
| Curtains | Inventory of Miss Sarah Black (1862) | White curtains in New Castle County, Delaware, 1862 | $1.00 |
| Demijohn | Inventory of Miss Sarah Black (1862) | Demijohn in New Castle County, Delaware, 1862 | $0.25 |
| Desk | Inventory of Austin Taylor (1853) | Writing desk in Greenville, South Carolina, 1853 | $0.50 |
| Dish | Inventory of Isaac Benedict (1856) | Preserve dish in Greenville, South Carolina, 1856 | $0.25 |
| Dish | Inventory of Miss Sarah Black (1862) | Covered dish in New Castle County, Delaware, 1862 | $0.50 |
| Engraving | Lincoln Magazine (2005) | A 2 foot by 3 foot plain proof engraving of Death of Lincoln signed by Alexander Hay Ritchie, 1865 | $30.00 |
| Fender | Inventory of Isaac Benedict (1856) | Wire fender in Greenville, South Carolina, 1856 | $2.00 |
| Fire dogs | Inventory of Austin Taylor (1853) | Fire dogs and shovel in Greenville, South Carolina, 1853 | $1.30 |
| Fire Iron | Apprasial of Daniel Herring (1859) | One pair of fire irons in Collin County, Texas in 1858 | $2.50 |
| Fly Brush | Inventory of Isaac Benedict (1856) | Fly brush in Greenville, South Carolina, 1856 | 12½ cents |
| Forks | Inventory of Miss Sarah Black (1862) | Dozen silver forks in New Castle County, Delaware, 1862 | $36.00 |
| Glasses | Inventory of Isaac Benedict (1856) | Dozen wine glasses in Greenville, South Carolina, 1856 | $1.00 |
| Jug | Inventory of Lydia Montgomery (1854) | Stone jug in Franklin County, Indiana, 1854 | $0.10 |
| Knife | Inventory of Isaac Benedict (1856) | Fruit knife in Greenville, South Carolina, 1856 | $1.25 |
| Knife | Inventory of Miss Sarah Black (1862) | Silver knife in New Castle County, Delaware, 1862 | $1.00 |
| Ladder | Inventory of Miss Sarah Black (1862) | Step ladder in New Castle County, Delaware, 1862 | $0.50 |
| Ladle | Inventory of Miss Sarah Black (1862) | Silver ladle in New Castle County, Delaware, 1862 | $10.00 |
| Lamp | Inventory of Jacob Otto (1861) | Fluid lamp & can in Franklin County, Indiana, 1861 | $0.25 |

### Based Upon US Dollars

| Year | Value of 19th Century Dollar in 2002 US Dollars |
|------|------------------------------------------------|
| 1850 | $22.00 |
| 1855 | $20.00 |
| 1860 | $21.00 |
| 1865 | $11.00 |

*Calculations are approximate values based upon economic historical data*

| Item | Data Source | Description | Price |
|------|-------------|-------------|-------|
| Lantern | Inventory of John Haggard (1859) | Latern in Collin County, Texas in 1859 | $0.80 |
| Looking glass | Inventory of Elizabeth Newnam (1853) | Looking glass in Franklin County, Indiana, 1853 | $1.50 |
| Loom | Inventory of Samuel Alsop, Jr. (1859) | Loom & spinning wheel in Spotsylvania County, Virginia, 1859 | $10.00 |
| Lounge | Inventory of Shubal Wardner (1859) | Lounge in Windsor, Vermont, 1859 | $1.00 |
| Mats | Inventory of Miss Sarah Black (1862) | Dozen tea mats in New Castle County, Delaware, 1862 | $0.25 |
| Mill | Inventory of Peter Updike (1862) | Coffey mill in Franklin County, Indiana, 1862 | $0.25 |
| Music Box | Inventory of Isaac Benedict (1856) | Music box in Greenville, South Carolina, 1856 | $2.10 |
| Napkin | Inventory of Miss Sarah Black (1862) | Napkin in New Castle County, Delaware, 1862 | $0.02 |
| Ornament | Inventory of Benjamin M. Barron (1865) | Mantle ornament in New Castle County, Delaware, 1865 | 12½ cents |
| Pail | Inventory of Shubal Wardner (1859) | Ash pail in Windsor, Vermont, 1859 | $0.25 |
| Painting | Inventory of Isaac Benedict (1856) | Painting referencing View of Falls - Greenville, South Carolina, 1856 | $5.00 |
| Pan | Invoice of T. Holmes (1859) | Cost for one wash pan in Dallas, Texas in 1859 | $0.50 |
| Parlor screen | Inventory of Miss Sarah Black (1862) | Parlor screen in New Castle County, Delaware, 1862 | $1.00 |
| Picture | Inventory of Elizabeth Newnam (1853) | Picture of James Madison in Franklin County, Indiana, 1853 | $0.10 |
| Picture | Inventory of Benjamin M. Barron (1865) | Picture of steam boat in New Castle County, Delaware, 1865 | $1.50 |
| Pillowcase | Inventory of Miss Sarah Black (1862) | Pair of muslin pillow cases in New Castle County, Delaware, 1862 | $0.25 |
| Pitcher | Inventory of Miss Sarah Black (1862) | Plated pitcher in New Castle County, Delaware, 1862 | $4.00 |
| Pitcher | Inventory of Miss Sarah Black (1862) | Pitcher in New Castle County, Delaware, 1862 | $0.50 |
| Pitcher & Cruet | Inventory of William Hite (1860) | Pitcher & cruet in Franklin County, Indiana, 1860 | $0.25 |
| Plate | Inventory of Isaac Benedict (1856) | Glass plate in Greenville, South Carolina, 1856 | $0.05 |
| Plate | Eliot Lord, History of the Comstock Lode (1959) | Tin plate in Virginia City, Nevada, 1860 | $0.75 |
| Poker | Inventory of Miss Sarah Black (1862) | Poker in New Castle County, Delaware, 1862 | $0.20 |
| Polish | Laurence A. Johnson, Over The Counter and On The Shelf 1620-1920 (1961) | *Bath Brick*, a commerical scouring polish, 1856 | $0.10 |
| Pot | Inventory of Isaac Benedict (1856) | Wash pot in Greenville, South Carolina, 1856 | $2.00 |
| Press | Inventory of Isaac Benedict (1856) | Clothes press in Greenville, South Carolina, 1856 | $1.00 |
| Quilt | Inventory of Isaac Benedict (1856) | Marsailles quilt in Greenville, South Carolina, 1856 | $2.00 |
| Razor | Inventory of Jacob Otto (1861) | Rasor & strap in Franklin County, Indiana, 1861 | $0.10 |
| Reflector | Inventory of Elizabeth Newnam (1853) | Reflector in Franklin County, Indiana, 1853 | $0.05 |

| Item | Data Source | Description | Price |
|------|-------------|-------------|-------|
| Rug | Invoice of John C. Cherw (1859) | Cost for a Dining Hall Carpet in Texas in 1858 | $2.00 |
| Rug | Inventory of Miss Sarah Black (1862) | Sheep skin rug in New Castle County, Delaware, 1862 | $0.75 |
| Safe | Inventory of Benjamin M. Barron (1865) | Safe in New Castle County, Delaware, 1865 | $1.00 |
| Salt cellar | Inventory of Miss Sarah Black (1862) | Salt sellar in New Castle County, Delaware, 1862 | $0.25 |
| Scales | Inventory of Isaac Benedict (1856) | Pair of small scales in Greenville, South Carolina, 1856 | $0.50 |
| Scuttle | Inventory of Miss Sarah Black (1862) | Scuttle in New Castle County, Delaware, 1862 | $0.31 |
| Shade | Inventory of Miss Sarah Black (1862) | Window shade in New Castle County, Delaware, 1862 | $0.12 |
| Shades | Inventory of Benjamin M. Barron (1865) | Pair window shades in New Castle County, Delaware, 1865 | $1.00 |
| Sheets | Inventory of Revd. Joseph Barr (1854) | Pair of new muslin sheets in New Castle County, Delaware, 1854 | $1.00 |
| Shovel | Inventory of Benjamin M. Barron (1865) | Coal shovel in New Castle County, Delaware, 1865 | $0.05 |
| Shovel & tongs | Inventory of Miss Sarah Black (1862) | Shovel & tongs in New Castle County, Delaware, 1862 | $0.50 |
| Soap | Laurence A. Johnson, Over The Counter and On The Shelf 1620-1920 (1961) | *Fuller's Earth* soap like substance used to clean woolens, perton, 1855 | $35.00 |
| Soap | Inventory of Isaac Benedict (1856) | Keg of soft soap in Greenville, South Carolina, 1856 | $1.00 |
| Spinning wheel | Inventory of Caleb Phillip (1859) | Home spinning wheel in Collin County, Texas in 1859 | $40.00 |
| Spittoon | Inventory of Shubal Wardner (1859) | Spittoon in Windsor, Vermont, 1859 | $0.10 |
| Spoon | Inventory of Revd. Joseph Barr (1854) | Large silver tablespoon in New Castle County, Delaware, 1854 | $1.75 |
| Spoons | Inventory of Miss Sarah Black (1862) | Dozen tablespoons in New Castle County, Delaware, 1862 | $40.00 |
| Spread | Inventory of Miss Sarah Black (1862) | White spreads in New Castle County, Delaware, 1862 | $1.00 |
| Stand | Inventory of Isaac Benedict (1856) | Candlestand in Greenville, South Carolina, 1856 | $0.50 |

## Based Upon US Dollars

| Year | Value of 19th Century Dollar in 2002 US Dollars |
|------|--------------------------------------------------|
| 1850 | $22.00 |
| 1855 | $20.00 |
| 1860 | $21.00 |
| 1865 | $11.00 |

*Calculations are approximate values based upon economic historical data*

| Item | Data Source | Description | Price |
|------|-------------|-------------|-------|
| Stool | Inventory of Shubal Wardner (1859) | Stool in Windsor, Vermont, 1859 | $0.05 |
| Stove | Inventory of Revd. Joseph Barr (1854) | Airtight stove in New Castle County, Delaware, 1854 | $4.00 |
| Table cover | Inventory of Miss Sarah Black (1862) | Woolen table cover in New Castle County, Delaware, 1862 | $1.00 |
| Tablecloth | Inventory of Miss Sarah Black (1862) | Linen table cloths in New Castle County, Delaware, 1862 | $1.00 |
| Tablespread | Inventory of Shubal Wardner (1859) | *Table Spread* in Windsor, Vermont, 1859 | $0.25 |
| Tallow | Inventory of Isaac Benedict (1856) | Pound of tallow in Greenville, South Carolina, 1856 | $0.10 |
| Ticking | Inventory of Revd. Joseph Barr (1854) | Yard of bed ticking in New Castle County, Delaware, 1854 | $0.16 |
| Tong | Inventory of Revd. Joseph Barr (1854) | Silver sugar tong in New Castle County, Delaware, 1854 | $1.25 |
| Towel | Inventory of Miss Sarah Black (1862) | Linen towel in New Castle County, Delaware, 1862 | $0.12 |
| Trunk | Apprasial of Daniel Herring (1859) | Trunk in Collin County, Texas in 1858 | $2.50 |
| Trunk | Account of John C. Evans (1859) | Cost for a trunk in Dallas, Texas in 1859 | $15.00 |
| Tumbler | Inventory of Isaac Benedict (1856) | Tumbler in Greenville, South Carolina, 1856 | $0.10 |
| Utensils | Inventory of Samuel Alsop, Jr. (1859) | Dozen knives & forks with buckhorn handles in Spotsylvania County, Virginia, 1859 | $5.00 |
| Varnish | Inventory of Austin Taylor (1853) | Bottle of varnish in Greenville, South Carolina, 1853 | $0.17 |
| Vase | Inventory of Miss Sarah Black (1862) | Mantle vase in New Castle County, Delaware, 1862 | $0.50 |
| Waiter | Inventory of George Hubble (1854) | Tea waiter in Franklin County, Indiana, 1854 | $0.10 |
| Ware | Inventory of John Miller (1851) | Lot of cupboard ware in Franklin County, Indiana, 1851 | $1.50 |
| Wash board | Inventory of Lydia Montgomery (1854) | Wash board in Franklin County, Indiana, 1854 | $0.20 |
| Washing machine | Inventory of George Hubble (1854) | Washing machine in Franklin County, Indiana, 1854 | $3.00 |
| Washstand | Inventory of Shubal Wardner (1859) | Washstand & Pitcher in Windsor, Vermont, 1859 | $0.20 |
| Wax | Inventory of Austin Taylor (1853) | Pound of bee's wax in Greenville, South Carolina, 1853 | $0.14 |
| Wheel | Inventory of Elizabeth Newnam (1853) | Big wheel and reel in Franklin County, Indiana, 1853 | $1.25 |
| Window blind | Inventory of Miss Sarah Black (1862) | Window blind, back & front in New Castle County, Delaware, 1862 | $2.50 |
| Window Sash | Inventory of Shubal Wardner (1859) | Window sash and glass in Windsor, Vermont, 1859 | $3.00 |
| Wood | Inventory of Caleb Phillip (1859) | Firewood per pound in Collin County, Texas in 1859 | $0.25 |

## Investment

| Item | Data Source | Description | Price |
|------|-------------|-------------|-------|
| Certificate | Inventory of Miss Sarah Black (1862) | Certificate in the Wilmington City Sinking Fund, Delaware, 1862 | $1,200.00 |
| Stock | Inventory of George Hubble (1854) | Share in Colerain Oxford and Brookville Tur Co - Franklin County, Indiana, 1854 | $40.00 |

| Item | Data Source | Description | Price |
|------|-------------|-------------|-------|
| Stock | Inventory of Isaac Benedict (1856) | Share of Greenville & Columbia Rail Road stock, South Carolina, 1856 | $14.00 |
| Stock | Inventory of Miss Sarah Black (1862) | Share in the Bank of Delaware in 1862 | $400.00 |
| Stock | Inventory of Benjamin M. Barron (1865) | Share of stock Wilmington & New Castle Railroad in New Castle County, Delaware, 1865 | $50.00 |

Jewelry

| Item | Data Source | Description | Price |
|------|-------------|-------------|-------|
| Bracelet | Inventory of Isaac Benedict (1856) | Gold bracelot in Greenville, South Carolina, 1856 | $4.50 |
| Broach | Inventory of Isaac Benedict (1856) | Brooch in Greenville, South Carolina, 1856 | $1.25 |
| Buttons | Inventory of Isaac Benedict (1856) | Pair gold sleeve buttons in Greenville, South Carolina, 1856 | $1.50 |
| Case | Inventory of Isaac Benedict (1856) | Watch case in Greenville, South Carolina, 1856 | $0.16 |
| Chain | Inventory of Isaac Benedict (1856) | Gold vest chain in Greenville, South Carolina, 1856 | $5.00 |
| Diamond | Inventory of Isaac Benedict (1856) | Diamond in Greenville, South Carolina, 1856 | $2.00 |
| Earrings | Inventory of Isaac Benedict (1856) | Pair gold earrings in Greenville, South Carolina, 1856 | $0.60 |
| Fob | Inventory of Isaac Benedict (1856) | Gold fob chain and seal in Greenville, South Carolina, 1856 | $15.00 |
| Locket | Inventory of Isaac Benedict (1856) | Gold double locket in Greenville, South Carolina, 1856 | $4.50 |
| Necklace | Inventory of Isaac Benedict (1856) | Coral necklace in Greenville, South Carolina, 1856 | $1.15 |
| Pin | Inventory of Isaac Benedict (1856) | Gold scarf pin in Greenville, South Carolina, 1856 | $2.00 |
| Ring | Inventory of Isaac Benedict (1856) | Plain gold ring in Greenville, South Carolina, 1856 | $0.50 |
| Studs | Inventory of Isaac Benedict (1856) | Pair gold shirt studs in Greenville, South Carolina, 1856 | $0.40 |
| Watch | Inventory of Isaac Benedict (1856) | Gold pocket watch in Greenville, South Carolina, 1856 | $46.00 |
| Watch | Inventory of Isaac Benedict (1856) | Brass watch in Greenville, South Carolina, 1856 | $5.00 |

### Based Upon US Dollars

| Year | Value of 19th Century Dollar in 2002 US Dollars |
|------|--------------------------------------------------|
| 1850 | $22.00 |
| 1855 | $20.00 |
| 1860 | $21.00 |
| 1865 | $11.00 |

*Calculations are approximate values based upon economic historical data*

| Item | Data Source | Description | Price |
|---|---|---|---|
| **Kitchen Item** | | | |
| Barrel | Inventory of Elizabeth Newnam (1853) | Meat barrel in Franklin County, Indiana, 1853 | $0.25 |
| Bucket | Inventory of Benjamin M. Barron (1865) | Flour bucket in New Castle County, Delaware, 1865 | $0.10 |
| Can | Inventory of Mary Shirk (1857) | Fruit can in Franklin County, Indiana, 1857 | $0.08 |
| Can | Inventory of Peter Updike (1862) | Lard can in Franklin County, Indiana, 1862 | $1.00 |
| Churn | Inventory of Elizabeth Newnam (1853) | Churn in Franklin County, Indiana, 1853 | $0.25 |
| Churn | Inventory of Shubal Wardner (1859) | Churn in Windsor, Vermont, 1859 | $1.00 |
| Cleaver | Inventory of Samuel Bourne (1860) | Beef cleaver in Franklin County, Indiana, 1860 | $0.50 |
| Crock | Inventory of Joseph McCafferty (1852) | Crock in Franklin County, Indiana, 1852 | $0.04 |
| Cupboard Ware | Inventory of John Haggard (1859) | Various cupboard ware in Collin County, Texas in 1859 | $5.00 |
| Grinder | Inventory of Adanijah Wiley (1862) | Sausage grinder in Franklin County, Indiana, 1862 | $2.00 |
| Iron | Inventory of Elizabeth Newnam (1853) | Waful iron in Franklin County, Indiana, 1853 | $0.05 |
| Irons | Inventory of Miss Sarah Black (1862) | Flat irons in New Castle County, Delaware, 1862 | $0.25 |
| Jug | Inventory of John Haggard (1859) | Jug in Collin County, Texas in 1859 | $0.80 |
| Kettle | Inventory of Revd. Joseph Barr (1854) | Bell metal tea kettle in New Castle County, Delaware, 1854 | $1.75 |
| Kitchen | Apprasial of Daniel Herring (1859) | Stove, cupboard ware and utensils in Collin County, Texas in 1858 | $80.00 |
| Oven | Inventory of Mary Shirk (1857) | Dutch oven in Franklin County, Indiana, 1857 | $0.10 |
| Oven | Inventory of John Haggard (1859) | Oven with lid in Collin County, Texas in 1859 | $1.10 |
| Pan | Inventory of Joseph McCafferty (1852) | Wash pan in Franklin County, Indiana, 1852 | $0.05 |
| Pan | Inventory of Isaac Benedict (1856) | Bake pan in Greenville, South Carolina, 1856 | $0.15 |
| Pie dish | Inventory of Miss Sarah Black (1862) | Pie dish in New Castle County, Delaware, 1862 | $0.15 |
| Plate | Invoice of T. Holmes (1859) | Cost for one tin plate in Dallas, Texas in 1858 | $0.10 |
| Pot | Inventory of Benjamin M. Barron (1865) | Dinner pot in New Castle County, Delaware, 1865 | $0.25 |
| Sieve | Inventory of Peter Updike (1862) | Meal sive in Franklin County, Indiana, 1862 | $0.10 |
| Skillet | Inventory of John Haggard (1859) | Skillet in Collin County, Texas in 1859 | $1.50 |
| Stuffer | Inventory of Isaac Benedict (1856) | Sausage stuffer in Greenville, South Carolina, 1856 | $1.00 |
| Tub | Inventory of George Hubble (1854) | Wash tub in Franklin County, Indiana, 1854 | $0.25 |
| Utensils | Account of John C. Evans (1859) | Cost for one set of knives and forks in Dallas, Texas in 1859 | $1.25 |

| Item | Data Source | Description | Price |
|------|-------------|-------------|-------|
| **Livery Animals & Tools** | | | |
| Bell | Inventory of Thomas F. Boren (1858) | Cow bell in Collin County, Texas in 1858 | $1.25 |
| Blanket | Inventory of Austin Taylor (1853) | Saddle blanket in Greenville, South Carolina, 1853 | $0.50 |
| Colt | Inventory of George Hubble (1854) | Two year old colt in Franklin County, Indiana, 1854 | $16.00 |
| Corn | Apprasial of Daniel Herring (1859) | Bushel of corn for livestock in Collin County, Texas in 1858 | $0.60 |
| Grain Box | Inventory of Shubal Wardner (1859) | Grain Box in Windsor, Vermont, 1859 | $1.00 |
| Halter | Inventory of John Haggard (1859) | Lines and Halter in Collin County, Texas in 1859 | $1.40 |
| Harness | Inventory of Alexander Carouth (1859) | Harness in Collin County, Texas in 1859 | $4.00 |
| Horse | Inventory of Thomas F. Boren (1858) | Bay Horse in Collin County, Texas in 1858 | $70.00 |
| Mare | Inventory of Thomas F. Boren (1858) | Bay Mare in Collin County, Texas in 1858 | $95.00 |
| Mule | Inventory of Warren A. Wiglesworth (1853) | Young mule in Fredericksburg, Virginia, 1853 | $50.00 |
| Mule | Inventory of Samuel Alsop, Jr. (1859) | Dark mare mule called Marth in Spotsylvania County, Virginia, 1859 | $150.00 |
| Oats | Apprasial of Daniel Herring (1859) | Sheaf Oats for livestock in Collin County, Texas in 1858 | $20.00 |
| Oxen | Inventory of Samuel Alsop, Jr. (1859) | Yoke of oxen called Buck & Lion in Spotsylvania County, Virginia, 1859 | $40.00 |
| Pitch Fork | Inventory of Shubal Wardner (1859) | Pitch Fork in Windsor, Vermont, 1859 | $0.25 |
| Pony | Apprasial of Daniel Herring (1859) | Sorrel Pony, Mare, in Collin County, Texas in 1858 | $45.00 |
| Rack | Inventory of Miss Sarah Black (1862) | Carriage rack in New Castle County, Delaware, 1862 | $0.25 |
| Saddle | Inventory of Thomas F. Boren (1858) | Man's Saddle in Collin County, Texas in 1858 | $6.00 |
| Saddle | Apprasial of Daniel Herring (1859) | Side Saddle in Collin County, Texas in 1858 | $15.00 |
| Saddle bag | Inventory of John Haggard (1859) | Saddlebag in Collin County, Texas in 1859 | $3.00 |

## Based Upon US Dollars

| Year | Value of 19th Century Dollar in 2002 US Dollars |
|------|--------------------------------------------------|
| 1850 | $22.00 |
| 1855 | $20.00 |
| 1860 | $21.00 |
| 1865 | $11.00 |

*Calculations are approximate values based upon economic historical data*

| Item | Data Source | Description | Price |
| --- | --- | --- | --- |
| Saddle wallets | Inventory of Thomas F. Boren (1858) | One pair of Saddle Wallets in Collin County, Texas in 1858 | $0.50 |
| Salt Box | Inventory of Shubal Wardner (1859) | Salt Box in Windsor, Vermont, 1859 | $0.25 |
| Shovel | Inventory of Shubal Wardner (1859) | Grain Shovel in Windsor, Vermont, 1859 | $0.25 |
| Sleigh | Inventory of Josiah Lowes (1861) | Sleigh in Franklin County, Indiana, 1861 | $2.00 |
| Steer | Inventory of Thomas F. Boren (1858) | A steer in Collin County, Texas in 1858 | $20.00 |

### Livestock

| Item | Data Source | Description | Price |
| --- | --- | --- | --- |
| Bull | Apprasial of Daniel Herring (1859) | A bull in Collin County, Texas in 1858 | $12.00 |
| Bull | Inventory of Josiah Lowes (1861) | Bull calf in Franklin County, Indiana, 1861 | $5.00 |
| Calf | Inventory of Lydia Montgomery (1854) | Calf in Franklin County, Indiana, 1854 | $2.75 |
| Chickens | Inventory of John Miller (1851) | Dozen chickens in Franklin County, Indiana, 1851 | $1.00 |
| Cow | Inventory of Brice B. Moore (1851) | Cow in Franklin County, Indiana, 1851 | $9.00 |
| Cow & calf | Inventory of John Haggard (1859) | Pair of cattle in Collin County, Texas in 1859 | $15.00 |
| Goose | Inventory of Lydia Montgomery (1854) | Goose in Franklin County, Indiana, 1854 | $0.10 |
| Heifer | Inventory of Joseph McCafferty (1852) | Red heifer in Franklin County, Indiana, 1852 | $5.00 |
| Heifer | Inventory of Anson Buckley (1860) | Spotted heifer in Franklin County, Indiana, 1860 | $12.00 |
| Hog | Inventory of Thomas F. Boren (1858) | Value of a hog in Collin County, Texas in 1858 | $4.00 |
| Hog | Apprasial of Daniel Herring (1859) | Fat hog in Collin County, Texas in 1858 | $24.00 |
| Lambs | Apprasial of Daniel Herring (1859) | Value per head of lamb in Collin County, Texas in 1858 | $1.50 |
| Ox | Inventory of John Haggard (1859) | Ox in Collin County, Texas in 1859 | $24.00 |
| Oxen | Apprasial of Daniel Herring (1859) | One yoke of oxen in Collin County, Texas in 1858 | $60.00 |
| Pig | Inventory of Thomas F. Boren (1858) | A pig in Collin County, Texas in 1858 | $0.50 |
| Sheep | Inventory of Joseph McCafferty (1852) | Sheep in Franklin County, Indiana, 1852 | $0.60 |
| Sheep | Inventory of Warren A. Wiglesworth (1853) | Sheep in Fredericksburg, Virginia, 1853 | $2.00 |
| Shoat | Inventory of Lydia Montgomery (1854) | Shoat in Franklin County, Indiana, 1854 | $1.10 |
| Sow | Inventory of Lydia Montgomery (1854) | Large white sow in Franklin County, Indiana, 1854 | $7.00 |
| Steer | Inventory of Brice B. Moore (1851) | Steer in Franklin County, Indiana, 1851 | $4.00 |
| Turkey | Inventory of Adanijah Wiley (1862) | Turkey in Franklin County, Indiana, 1862 | $0.28 |

| Item | Data Source | Description | Price |
|------|-------------|-------------|-------|
| **Manufacturing Equipment** | | | |
| Mandrill | The Texas Almanac (1857) | HL Perry's patent adjustable stop or Mandril for dressing the teeth of circular saws | $15.00 |
| Mill Stone | The Texas Almanac (1857) | Cost for Coleman's Corn and Flouring French Burr Stones - 14 inch Burr capable of milling 2½ -6 bushels an hour | $100.00 |
| Mill Stone | The Texas Almanac (1857) | Cost for Coleman's Corn and Flouring French Burr Stones - 36 inch Burr capable of milling 50 -75 bushels an hour, Jefferson, Louisiana, 1857 | $500.00 |
| Press | The Texas Almanac (1857) | Cost for Star Cotton Press - Can pack in the very best style 40 bags per day Galveston, Texas, 1857 | $400.00 |
| Pump | The Texas Almanac (1857) | Cost for Lindsey's Double Acting Rotary Lift & Force Pump - 1½ inch pump pipe and 50 feet of pipe - Boxed and shipped free of Expense, New York, 1857 | $54.00 |
| Saw Mill | Albertson & Mudge Advertisement (1860) | Albertson & Mudge Portable Steam Engine and Saw Mill with 25 Horse Power with 12 inch face wrought iron crank, Governor, Pump and every fixture required to raise steam | $2,500.00 |
| Steam Engine | Albertson & Mudge Advertisement (1860) | Albertson & Mudge Portable Steam Engine with 12 Horse Power that can drive four seventy saw gins, Galveston, Texas, 1860 | $1,150.00 |
| **Medical Equipment** | | | |
| Microscope | Francis Lord, Civil War Collector's Encyclopedia (1989) | Craig Microscope - 5 ¾ in high, 2 ½ base, tube 1 in hard rubber, 1862 | $2.00 |
| **Medicine** | | | |
| Bitters | McKearin, American Bottles & Flasks (1978) | Bottle of Phoenix Bitters , 1850 | $0.75 |

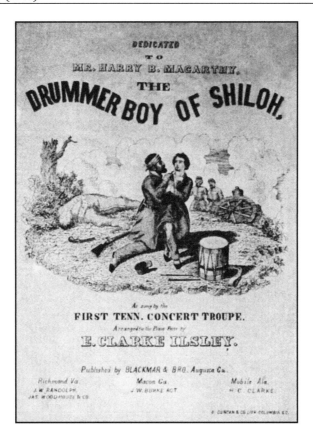

| Item | Data Source | Description | Price |
|------|-------------|-------------|-------|
| Castor Oil | Inventory of Austin Taylor (1853) | Bottle of castor oil in Greenville, South Carolina, 1853 | $0.15 |
| Drops | Inventory of Austin Taylor (1853) | Vial of tooth drops in Greenville, South Carolina, 1853 | $0.21 |
| Morphine | Joye E. Jordan, Civil War Medicine 1861-1865 | Cost of one spoonful of morphine in Southern states, 1865 | $0.30 |
| Pain Reliever | Suzanne C. Linder, Medicine in Marlboro County, 1736 to 1980 | Cost for cherry pectoral to relieve pain, 1860 | $0.16 |
| Powder | Inventory of Isaac Benedict (1856) | Tooth powder in Greenville, South Carolina, 1856 | $1.00 |
| Quinine | Joye E. Jordan, Civil War Medicine 1861-1865 | Cost of one ounce of quinine in Southern states, 1865 | $10.00 |
| Salts | Inventory of Austin Taylor (1853) | Vial of smelling salts in Greenville, South Carolina, 1853 | $2.50 |

## Music

| Item | Data Source | Description | Price |
|------|-------------|-------------|-------|
| Accordion | Inventory of William Hite (1860) | Acordeon in Franklin County, Indiana, 1860 | $0.25 |
| Clarinet | Inventory of Austin Taylor (1853) | Clarinet in Greenville, South Carolina, 1853 | $2.25 |
| Fiddle | Inventory of Caleb Phillip (1859) | Fiddle and box in Collin County, Texas in 1859 | $1.50 |
| Flute | Inventory of Shubal Wardner (1859) | Flute in Windsor, Vermont, 1859 | $2.00 |
| Music Book | Inventory of Shubal Wardner (1859) | Music book and music in Windsor, Vermont, 1859 | $2.00 |
| Piano | Inventory of Thomas C. Alrich (1865) | Piano in Wilmington, Delaware, 1865 | $50.00 |

## Other

| Item | Data Source | Description | Price |
|------|-------------|-------------|-------|
| Cologne | Inventory of Austin Taylor (1853) | Bottle of cologne in Greenville, South Carolina, 1853 | $0.13 |
| Comb | Invoice to D. Malley (1855) | Cost for a comb in Dallas, Texas in 1855 | $0.20 |
| Cooler | Inventory of Benjamin M. Barron (1865) | Water cooler in New Castle County, Delaware, 1865 | $1.00 |
| Daguerreotype | Inventory of Shubal Wardner (1859) | Daguerreotype in Windsor, Vermont, 1859 | $0.20 |
| Flag | Francis Lord, Civil War Collector's Encyclopedia (1989) | State Flag of the 10th Massachusetts Infantry trimmed with yellow silk fringe, gold cord & tassels | $275.00 |
| Flowers | Inventory of Austin Taylor (1853) | Tinsel flowers in Greenville, South Carolina, 1853 | $0.02 |
| Gift | The Congressional Globe (1864) | Gift of a steamship to the United States government for the war effort, 1862 | $800,000.00 |
| Glue | Inventory of Austin Taylor (1853) | Pound of glue in Greenville, South Carolina, 1853 | $0.10 |
| Gold Nugget | Geoffery Ward, The West (1996) | Eight-pound gold nugget photographed with James W Woolsey, 1851, | $1,900.00 |
| Knife | Inventory of Austin Taylor (1853) | Pocket knife in Greenville, South Carolina, 1853 | $0.10 |
| Knife and Folk | Francis Lord, Civil War Collector's Encyclopedia (1989) | Army Knife and Fork, JP Snow & Company Camp Knife and Fork, 1862 | $0.60 |
| Life Preserver | Inventory of Rev. Joseph Barr (1854) | Life preservers in New Castle County, Delaware, 1854 | $0.50 |
| Lock | Invoice to D. Malley (1859) | Cost for one pad lock in Dallas, Texas in 1858 | $0.37 |
| Map | Inventory of Miss Sarah Black (1862) | Map of the United States in New Castle County, Delaware, 1862 | $2.00 |

| Item | Data Source | Description | Price |
|------|-------------|-------------|-------|
| Matches | Inventory of Austin Taylor (1853) | Half dozen box of matches in Greenville, South Carolina, 1853 | $0.09 |
| Mold | Receipt of John Coit (1859) | Cost for a candle mold in Dallas, Texas in 1859 | $0.12 |
| Net | Inventory of Jacob Otto (1861) | Set of fly nets in Franklin County, Indiana, 1861 | $1.00 |
| Padlock | Inventory of Mary Shirk (1857) | Padlock in Franklin County, Indiana, 1857 | $0.12 |
| Parasol | Inventory of Austin Taylor (1853) | Parasol in Greenville, South Carolina, 1853 | $0.20 |
| Perfume | Inventory of Austin Taylor (1853) | Vial of perfumery in Greenville, South Carolina, 1853 | $0.06 |
| Photograph | Francis Lord, Civil War Collector's Encyclopedia (1989) | Tintype photograph, dime size image | $0.25 |
| Pin | Francis Lord, Civil War Collector's Encyclopedia (1989) | Solid 18K gold soilder's company pin Handsomely engraved with name and regiment, 1863 | $3.50 |
| Postage | Harper's New Montly Weekly (1851) | Postage for Harper's New Monthly Magazine when sent under 500 miles of New York | $0.04 |
| Refrigerator | Inventory of Miss Sarah Black (1862) | Refrigerator in New Castle County, Delaware, 1862 | $2.00 |
| Spectacles | Inventory of Isaac Benedict (1856) | Pair gold spectacles in Greenville, South Carolina, 1856 | $4.25 |
| Spectacles | Inventory of Isaac Benedict (1856) | Pair iron spectacles in Greenville, South Carolina, 1856 | 12½ cents |
| Stain Glass | C. Nicholes, Historical Sketches of Sumter County (1975) | Cost for stain galss windows from Munich, Bavaria and placed into Church of the Holy Cross in Sumter, South Carolina, 1851 | $1,003.00 |
| Syringe | Inventory of Revd. Joseph Barr (1854) | Syringe in New Castle County, Delaware, 1854 | $1.50 |
| Tent | Francis Lord, Civil War Collector's Encyclopedia (1989) | Price of a poncho tent, waterproofed with rubber, 1862 | $10.00 |
| Tools | Inventory of Adanijah Wiley (1862) | Dental tools in Franklin County, Indiana, 1862 | $0.75 |
| Toothbrush | Inventory of Austin Taylor (1853) | Tooth brush in Greenville, South Carolina, 1853 | $0.10 |
| Toothpick | Inventory of Isaac Benedict (1856) | Gold tooth pick in Greenville, South Carolina, 1856 | $1.33 |
| Umbrella | Inventory of Jacob Otto (1861) | Umbrella in Franklin County, Indiana, 1861 | $0.25 |

**Publications**

| Item | Data Source | Description | Price |
|------|-------------|-------------|-------|
| Bible | Inventory of Elizabeth Newnam (1853) | Bible in Franklin County, Indiana, 1853 | $1.00 |

**Based Upon US Dollars**

| Year | Value of 19th Century Dollar in 2002 US Dollars |
|------|--------------------------------------------------|
| 1850 | $22.00 |
| 1855 | $20.00 |
| 1860 | $21.00 |
| 1865 | $11.00 |

*Calculations are approximate values based upon economic historical data*

| Item | Data Source | Description | Price |
|---|---|---|---|
| Book | Harper's New Montly Weekly (1851) | Memoir of Rev E Bickersteth A memoir of the Late Rev Edward Bickerstegh, Rector of Watton by Rev TR Birks 2 Volumes in Muslin | $1.75 |
| Book | Harper's New Montly Weekly (1851) | Elements of Algebra by Professor Elias Loomis of New York University | $0.63 |
| Guide Book | Eastin, Emigrants' guide to Pike's Peak (1859) | Promotional guide for Leavenworth City; printed in newspaper format for gold prospectors Sold in lots of 100 | $0.10 |
| Magazine | Harper's Magazine (1865) | *Harper's Magazine, annual subscription, 1865* | $4.00 |
| Newspaper | The Texas Almanac (1857) | Cost for annual subscription to the *Democrat and Planter,* a weekly Politica, Agricultural and Family Newspaper | $3.00 |
| Newspaper | Receipt of John Coit (1859) | Cost for an annual subscription to the Tri-Weekly *Charleston Mercury* South Carolina in 1859 | $5.00 |

## Real Estate

| Item | Data Source | Description | Price |
|---|---|---|---|
| Church | C. Nicholes, Historical Sketches of Sumter County (1975) | Construction of the Church of the Holy Cross in Sumter, South Carolina, 1851 | $11,358.00 |
| Cigarstand | Eliot Lord, History of the Comstock Lode (1959) | Monthly rate for the privilege of a cigarstand in a store's corner, Virginia City, Nevada 1860 | $125.00 |
| College | C. Nicholes, Historical Sketches of Sumter County (1975) | Purchase price of 519 acres of land, buildings, furnishings and chattle to establish the Harmony Female College in Sumter, South Carolina, 1853 | $10,000.00 |
| Home | Harper's Magazine (1865) | New home, wood built, in Brooklyn, New York, 1865 | $2,500.00 |
| House | Inventory of Isaac Benedict (1856) | Wooden store house on P Cauble's lot on Main St in Greenville, South Carolina, 1856 | $140.00 |
| House | Inventory of Thomas C. Alrich (1865) | Dwelling house corner 7th & French in Wilmington, Delaware, 1865 | $7,260.00 |
| Insurance | Harper's Magazine (1865) | Insurance, on $2500 home, in Brooklyn, New York, 1865 | $12.50 |
| Land | Inventory of Warren A. Wiglesworth (1853) | Home tract of land, 650 acres in Fredericksburg, Virginia, 1853 | $4,500.00 |
| Lot | Harper's Magazine (1865) | Price of a lot 25x100 feet in Brooklyn, New York, 1865 | $500.00 |
| Property | The Texas Almanac (1857) | Average value of land per acre in Haris County in 1854 | $1.14 |
| Rent | Invoice to S.S. Mills (1863) | Lease of space to quarter Confederate troops in Charleston, SC, 1863 | $75.00 |
| Rent | Harper's Magazine (1865) | Church pew rent for two persons in New York City, 1865 | $2.50 |

| Item | Data Source | Description | Price |
|------|-------------|-------------|-------|
| **Servant** | | | |
| Slave | Inventory of Isaac Benedict (1856) | Negro woman, Patty 50 years old in Greenville, South Carolina, 1856 | $125.00 |
| Slave | Inventory of Isaac Benedict (1856) | Negro woman, Lucy, 12 years old in Greenville, South Carolina, 1856 | $650.00 |
| Slave | Inventory of John Haggard (1859) | Negro - Barnet supposed age 30 years in Collin County, Texas, 1859 | $250.00 |
| Slave | Inventory of John Haggard (1859) | Negro - Milly supposed age 40 years with 1 year child Harrison in Collin County, Texas, 1859 | $600.00 |
| Slave | Inventory of John Haggard (1859) | Negro - Arch supposed age 14 years in Collin County, Texas, 1859 | $800.00 |
| **Tobacco Products** | | | |
| Spittoon | Inventory of Miss Sarah Black (1862) | Spitoon in New Castle County, Delaware, 1862 | $0.15 |
| Tobacco | Francis Lord, Civil War Collector's Encyclopedia (1989) | One pound of *Kinikinic* tobacco, 1864 | $1.00 |
| **Trade Equipment & Tools** | | | |
| Adze | Inventory of Joseph McCafferty (1852) | Carpenter adze in Franklin County, Indiana, 1852 | $2.00 |
| Auger | Inventory of Joseph McCafferty (1852) | ¾ auger in Franklin County, Indiana, 1852 | $0.25 |
| Blacksmith Tools | Inventory of Austin Taylor (1853) | Set of blacksmith tools in Greenville, South Carolina, 1853 | $5.60 |
| Blacksmith Tools | Inventory of William Hite (1860) | Set of blacksmith tools in Franklin County, Indiana, 1860 | $40.00 |
| Chisel | Inventory of Joseph McCafferty (1852) | Framing chisel in Franklin County, Indiana, 1852 | $0.75 |
| Hammer | Inventory of Joseph McCafferty (1852) | Hammer in Franklin County, Indiana, 1852 | $0.25 |
| Knife | Inventory of Joseph McCafferty (1852) | Drawing knife in Franklin County, Indiana, 1852 | $0.75 |
| Leather | Inventory of Adanijah Wiley (1862) | Pound of sole leather in Franklin County, Indiana, 1862 | $0.30 |
| Loom | Inventory of Caleb Phillip (1859) | House loom in Collin County, Texas in 1859 | $8.00 |
| Mallet | Inventory of Joseph McCafferty (1852) | Mallet in Franklin County, Indiana, 1852 | $0.25 |

### Based Upon US Dollars

| Year | Value of 19th Century Dollar in 2002 US Dollars |
|------|-------------------------------------------------|
| 1850 | $22.00 |
| 1855 | $20.00 |
| 1860 | $21.00 |
| 1865 | $11.00 |

*Calculations are approximate values based upon economic historical data*

| Item | Data Source | Description | Price |
|------|-------------|-------------|-------|
| Pick | Geoffery Ward, The West (1996) | Pick (without handle) sold in California to individual miner, 1850 | $6.50 |
| Plane | Inventory of Joseph McCafferty (1852) | Match plane in Franklin County, Indiana, 1852 | $0.75 |
| Plane | Inventory of Joseph McCafferty (1852) | Sash plane in Franklin County, Indiana, 1852 | $0.62 |
| Saw | Inventory of Joseph McCafferty (1852) | Sash saw in Franklin County, Indiana, 1852 | $0.50 |
| Skin | Inventory of Austin Taylor (1853) | Sheep skin in Greenville, South Carolina, 1853 | $0.35 |
| Snick | Inventory of Joseph McCafferty (1852) | Carpenter snick in Franklin County, Indiana, 1852 | $0.75 |
| Trowel | Inventory of Adanijah Wiley (1862) | Trowell in Franklin County, Indiana, 1862 | $0.50 |
| Wood Handle | Geoffery Ward, The West (1996) | Wood handle for pick sold in California to individual miner, 1850 | $0.50 |
| Work Bench | Inventory of John Haggard (1859) | Work Bench in Collin County, Texas in 1859 | $5.00 |

### Travel & Transportation

| Item | Data Source | Description | Price |
|------|-------------|-------------|-------|
| Coach | Concord Coach Gallery (2004) | Cost to build Concord Coach built by Abbot-Downing Company | $1,050.00 |
| Afternoon Tea | American Heritage (1960) | Fee charged to an American visitor in Britain for tea and strawberries, 1854 | 2 Shillings |
| Breakfast | American Heritage (1960) | Fee charged to an American visitor in Britian for breakfast, 1854 | 4 Shillings |
| Fare | Milner, Oxford History of the American West | Cost to travel to San Francisco from New York utilizing railroad across Panama in 1855 | $500.00 |
| Fare | American Heritiage (1957) | Throughfare, from St Louis to San Francisco, on Butterfield Stagecoach Twenty-Five day journey, 1859 | $200.00 |
| Fare | American Heritiage (1957) | Local & wayfare, per mile, on Butterfield Stagecoach, 1859 | $0.10 |
| First-class boat fare | "The Vanderbilts", by Jerry E. Patterson (1989) | First-class fare for passage from New York to California via Nicaragua in 1851 | $150.00 |
| Freight | American Heritiage (1957) | Freight, one head of cattle, from New York to Chicago, 1860 | $1.00 |
| Hotel | Laurence A. Johnson, Over The Counter and On The Shelf 1620-1920 (1961) | Cost for a stay in hotel in New Orleans, Louisiana, 1857 with meals | $1.00 |
| Passage | American Heritage (1960) | Fee for a low level cabin on the Cunard Line from Boston, Massachusetts to Liverpool, England 1854 | $80.00 |
| Passage | American Heritage (1960) | Fee for a high level cabin on the Cunard Line from Boston, Massachusetts to Liverpool, England 1854 | $130.00 |
| Rail Fare | Wells, The Origins of the South Middle Class (2004) | New York to Baltimore, Maryland on the Great South Rail Line in 1859 | $6.00 |
| Rail Fare | Wells, The Origins of the South Middle Class (2004) | New York to Raleigh, North Carolina on the Great South Rail Line in 1859 | $18.50 |
| Rail Freight | Wells, The Origins of the South Middle Class (2004) | Cost of Second Class per 100 pounds - New York to Knoxville in 1858 | $1.44 |
| Rail Freight | Wells, The Origins of the South Middle Class (2004) | Cost of First Class per 100 pounds - New York to Memphis in 1858 | $2.16 |
| Ship | American Heritiage (1957) | Schooner, price at auction for the Indian, 1865 | $3,345.00 |

| Item | Data Source | Description | Price |
|------|-------------|-------------|-------|
| Steerage-class boat fare | "The Vanderbilts", by Jerry E. Patterson (1989) | Steerage-class boat fare from New York to California via Nicaragua in 1851 | $45.00 |
| *Vanderbilt* | "The Vanderbilts", by Jerry E. Patterson (1989) | Approximate cost of steamship built by Cornelius Vanderbilt in 1856 | $500,000.00 |

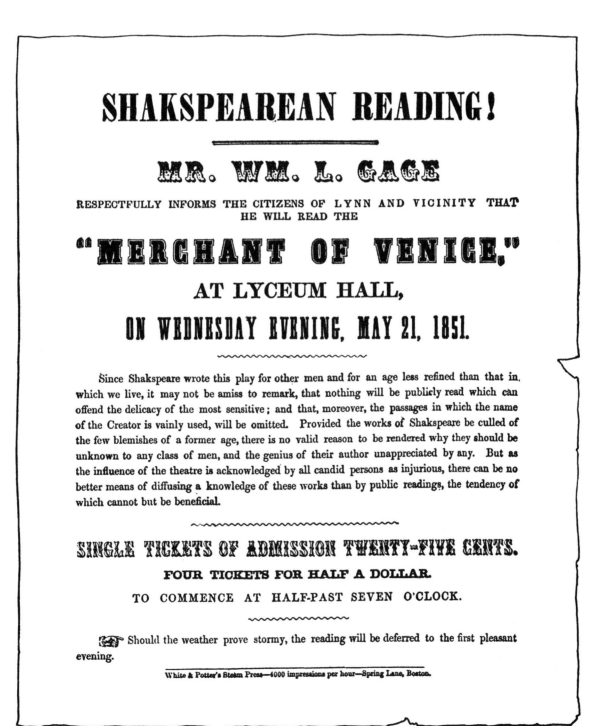

# SHAKSPEAREAN READING!

## MR. WM. L. GAGE

RESPECTFULLY INFORMS THE CITIZENS OF LYNN AND VICINITY THAT HE WILL READ THE

## "MERCHANT OF VENICE,"

### AT LYCEUM HALL,

## ON WEDNESDAY EVENING, MAY 21, 1851.

Since Shakspeare wrote this play for other men and for an age less refined than that in which we live, it may not be amiss to remark, that nothing will be publicly read which can offend the delicacy of the most sensitive; and that, moreover, the passages in which the name of the Creator is vainly used, will be omitted. Provided the works of Shakspeare be culled of the few blemishes of a former age, there is no valid reason to be rendered why they should be unknown to any class of men, and the genius of their author unappreciated by any. But as the influence of the theatre is acknowledged by all candid persons as injurious, there can be no better means of diffusing a knowledge of these works than by public readings, the tendency of which cannot but be beneficial.

## SINGLE TICKETS OF ADMISSION TWENTY-FIVE CENTS.

### FOUR TICKETS FOR HALF A DOLLAR.

TO COMMENCE AT HALF-PAST SEVEN O'CLOCK.

Should the weather prove stormy, the reading will be deferred to the first pleasant evening.

White & Potter's Steam Press—4000 impressions per hour—Spring Lane, Boston.

# MISCELLANY 1850-1865

## Letter Requesting Dresses from Philadelphia

The pattern gave great satisfaction, so much so, that Charles was keen for my getting four dresses of the sort but I think that rather too much of one good thing, and am contented with getting one. Will you therefore get me 10 yards of the blue and Anna 10 yards of the brown? Please get me some patterns of whatever they have pretty at Levys in the way of Spring and Summer best dresses, and send them on in your next letter. You know the Spring begins here so soon that one wants thin dresses in April, and I have actually nothing to begin on. I enclose this Ten dollars; after paying for my dress and Anna's there will be a remainder of $4.66.

*Source: Letter from Emily Wharton Sinkler of Charleston, S.C. to her sister Mary in Philadelphia, May 15, 1852*

## Cost of a Home, 1865

Giving our observations…let us assume $2000 to be the income of a man desirous of enjoying life in the true sense of the word…the proprietor will experience no difficulty in finding persons willing to advance $2500 on a mortgage upon the lot and upon the house which to be built. Along some of the car routes of Brooklyn, within an hour's ride of the city of New York, lots of 25x100 feet can be purchased for the cash price of $500 per lot; and granting the house owner to spend $1500 on furniture (such as is denominated "cottage furniture"), the following statement would be an exhibit of the outlay of his $2000 and of the money raised for building purposes:

Cash paid for building lot...........................$500
Cash paid for furniture............................$1500
Mortgage on house and
lot for 5 years, renewable for 3 years......$2500

*Source: Harper's New Monthly Magazine*

## Mining Claim in Nevada, 1859

July 4th 1859
Recorded this day
V.A. Houseworth
Recorder
The Bowers Company had located their claim in May, 1859, as they alleged, and recorded it on July 2, 1859.

## Notice

That we the undersign claim Six hundred feet two claims commencing South line of Gould & Curry liying west of Curry & Co Including Quarts & Surface two hundred feet square running up the hill from Curry claim.
21st May 1859

J. F. ROGERS
T.S. BOWERS
JOS WEBB
G.A. HAMMACK

Recorded July 2, 1859
V A HOUSEWORTH Recorder

*Source: Eliot Lord, Comstock Mining and Minders (1959)*

## Brady Photographs the Dead, 1853

Having spent most of the past year in Europe, in examining the Celebrated Galleries and works of art, especially in France and Italy, Mr. [Mathew] Brady has introduced into his establishment all the improvements and discoveries of those countries, and is prepared to execute every description of work pertaining to his business, in the highest style of the art.

Portraits of *Sick* or *Deceased* persons taken at their residence by a skilful and experienced artist.

*Source: A.D. Jones,* The Illustrated American Biography containing Correct Portraits and Brief Notices of the Principal Actors in American History *(1853)*

## Letter to Abraham Lincoln from a Supporter in 1860

It has been several months since I heard from you, almost a year. Last Spring I took a trip to Canada, came back by Niagara Falls...I crossed Lake Ontario in a steamboat there was a Negro aboard from Virginia. He came through the underground railroad. He had been concealed in Oberlin Ohio some four weeks, was well dressed and quite intelligent. Had a pass to Toronto, Ca. You are aware that Oberlin Ohio is the greatest abolitionist town in the States. Just at present we have great political excitement, on the ninth of this month our state election comes off. Republicans are in great hopes that the will elect their man...

I believe that every letter I have wrote you in the last four years I have complained of the crops, this year we have an abundance. Wheat was good. Twenty five and thirty bushels was a common average to the acre.

Corn, our main dependence, is good. It will average some fifty bushels. There has been great excitement about hogs at four and five cents a pound. I have two hundred that I am feeding. I fence off eight or ten acres at a time (and) turn them in — they waste but little. It saves a great deal of work. I have eighty five head of four year old cattle that I expect I will have to stall feed this winter. Cattle at present are dull sale. I have bought ninety acres of corn at twenty cents a bushel. Should I have to feed I will be prepared.

Tho. Scott rents his farm at $500 a year, he lives in Iowa. He is shipping flour to Kansas, two hundred barrels a week—he makes about fifty cents on the barrel.

The wheat being so good this season has put people in the notion sowing—there is a great amount growing now. There is to be one thousand wide awakes in Attica tonight. I am going down this afternoon, Douglas was in Lafayette on Monday the first of this month, several of the liners from this neighborhood went up.

We are all in good health. I brought a girl from Canada sixteen years old to live with us. She proves to be good my wife likes her uncommon well. Wages in Canada are low $10.00 a month for good hands to work on a farm and 75 cents a week for girls.

*Source: Letter written on October 3, 1860, by Abraham Lincoln supporter John Gass, mayor of Attica, Indiana, to Charles Moon of Bucks County, Pennsylvania*

## The Fort Pillow massacre, north of Memphis, Tennessee, 1864

Hdqrs. US Colored Troops in Tennessee Memphis, Tenn., April 14, 1864
Hon. E. B. Washburne
Washington, DC:

My Dear Sir: Before this letter reaches you you will have learned of the capture of Fort Pillow and of the slaughter of our troops after the place was captured. This is the most infernal outrage that has been committed since the war began. Three weeks ago I sent up four companies of colored troops to that place under Major Booth, a most brave and efficient [officer], who took command of the post. Forrest and Chalmers, with about 3,000 devils , attacked the place on the 12th at 9 a.m. and succeeded after three assaults, and when both Major Boothe and Major Bradford, of the Thirteenth Tennessee Cavalry, had been killed, in capturing the place at 4 p.m. We had, in all, less then 500 effective men, and one-third of whom were colored.

The colored troops fought with desperation throughout. After the capture our colored men were literally butchered. Chalmers was present and saw it all. Out of over 300 colored men, not 25 were taken prisoners, and they may have been killed long before this.

There is a great deal of excitement in town in consequence of this affair, especially among our colored troops. If this is to be the game of the enemy they will soon learn that it is one at which two can play.

The Government will no doubt take cognizance of this matter immediately and take such measures as will prevent a recurrence.

It is reported that Forrest will move on this place in a few days. I do not believe it. I am hurried and can write no more to-day. I am feeling dreadfully over the fate of my brave officers and men. Like all others, I feel that the blood of these heroes must be avenged. Forrest will probably try to get out of West Tennessee as soon as he can. We have re-enforcements coming in, and we shall soon be on his track. In haste, sincerely, your friend,

Chetlain
Brigadier-General.
*Source: The War of the Rebellion: a Compilation of the Official Records of the Union and Confederate Armies*

## Life under Union occupation, the Diary of Alice Williamson, Gallatin, Tennessee, 1864

**Feb. 19th 1864** What a negligent creature I am I should have been keeping a journal all this time to show to my rebel brothers. I have been studying all the morning and talking all the evening seeking & sighing for rebels. Our king (Union General Eleazer A. Paine) has just passed. I suppose he has killed every rebel in twenty miles of Gallatin and burned every town. Poor fellow! you had better be praying old Sinner! His Lordship left Tuesday. Wednesday three wagons loaded with furniture came over. I do not pretend to say that he sent them. No! I indeed, I would not. I would not slander our king. Any old citizen can see by going to his (Payne's) palace that his furniture was not taken from Archie Miller's house & other places near by. He always goes for rebels but-invariably brings furniture. I suppose his task is to furnish the contrabad camp, i.e. the camp of his angels (colored).

**March 2d** Snow four inches deep, no winds and the air is quite pleasant, just cold enough to skate. Our king left Monday with a few soldiers in the direction of Hartsville. All the stores are closed by his order and no passes given till his return. Mr. D. has come to get Pa to go and hear what he says to his negroes as he is going to drive them off & he has been so ill used by old Payne that he is afraid to speak without a witness to prove what he said.

**March 3d** Snow all melted and weather fine. Gen. Payne rode out this evening to look at the stock, in his last trip he killed only one man (citizen, he always kills citizens when he cant find soldiers) swears he will kill every man in Gallatin and Hartsville if bush whacking isn't stopped shortly.

**March 11th** Yesterday was the day of elections and as only the union men were allowed to vote nobody knows how it turned out nor do they care. Sallie Montgomery rode out this evening, the pickets would not let her pass, so she slipped them as many do. I suppose they are scared again. Perhaps that scamp John Morgan is about. I only hope he is, for we have not seen a rebel for more than a year and our day must come soon

**March 12th** Old Payne dined at Mrs. Hales today: every one despises him but are afraid to show it. Yesterday he went up the country a few miles to a Mr. Dalton's whose son came home from the Southern Army the day before and had the same day taken the Amnesty Oath. Riding up to the door he enquired of Mr. Dalton if his son was at home but before he answered his son came to the door. Old Nick then told him to get his horse and go with him. After insulting the father he carried his son a half mile away and shot him six times. One of Payne's escort hearing the young man groan with pain placed a pistol to his temple and remarked, I will stop that, sir, he shot him again. But this is nothing new this is the fifth man that has been shot in this way, besides numbers that have been carried off by scouts and never return.

**March 11th** I learn today that Gen. Payne had no charge against Mr. Dalton, so he told his (Dalton's) father. After killing him he rode back to the house and told Mr. D. that his son was in sight - he could bury him if he wished. Today a gentleman (Col. E____) was in Paynes office when he was trying a young man about sixteen years old and the only support of an aged father who was with him. His crime was being a rebel. Payne sent the young man to jail telling the guard to bring him out a seven o'clo. The father actually fell upon his knees before the heartless tyrant but was heartlessly bidden to rise and go home, the young man has never been heard of since.

**March 12th** Weather moderate; so is old Payne, but as weather is changeable our general is too.

*Source: Special Collections at Duke University*

# Index

# Bibliography

## A

A. Barton Hepburn, *A History of Currency in the United States* (Honolulu, HI: University Press of the Pacific, 2002).

A.J. Langguth, Patriots *The Men Who Started the American Revolution* (New York, NY: Simon & Schuster, 1988).

Alan D. Watson, editor, *Society in Early North Carolina* (Raleigh, N.C.: Division of Archives and History, North Carolina Department of Cultural Resources, 2000).

*American Heritage*, April 1958, Volume IX, Number 3 (1958).

*American Heritage*, April 1961, Volume XII, No. 3.

*American Heritage*, December 1959, Volume XI, No. 1.

*American Heritage*, December 1960, Vol. XII, No 1.

*American Heritage*, February 1960, Vol. XI, No 3.

*American Heritage*, January 1961, Vol. XII, No. 2.

*American Heritage*, October 1957, Vol. VIII No. 6.

*American Heritage*, October 1959, Volume X, No. 6.

*American Heritage*, September 1959, Vol. X, No 5.

*American Heritage*, August 1957, Volume VIII, No. 5.

*American Heritage*, August 1958, Volume IX, No. 4.

*American Heritage*, August 1958, Volume IX, No. 5.

*American Heritage*, December 1956, Volume VIII, No.1.

*American Heritage*, February 1957, Volume VIII, No. 2.

*American Heritage*, June 1957, Volume VII, No. 4.

*American Heritage*, October 1958, Volume IX, No. 6.

Anne Sinkler Fishburne, Belvidere, *A Plantation Memory* (Columbia, S.C.: University of South Carolina Press, 1949).

Annie Lash Jester, *Domestic Life in Virginia in the Seventeenth Century* (Charlottesville: University Press of Virginia, 1957).

*Antiques: The Magazine*, July 1982.

Arcadi Gluckman, *Identifying Old U.S. Muskets, Rifles & Carbines* (Harrisburg, PA: Stackpole Books, 1965).

Arthur Cecil Bining, *The Rise of American Economic Life* (New York, NY: Charles Scribner's Son, 1955).

Arthur Harrison Cole, *Wholesale Commodity Prices in the United States 1700-1861* (Cambridge, MA: Harvard University Press, 1938).

Asa Earl Martin, *History of the United States, 1492-1865* (Boston, MA: Ginn and Company, 1946).

*Aurora General Advertiser*, Philadelphia, Pennsylvania, 1810-182

## B

Benjamin Hillman, Editor, *Executive Journal of the Council of Colonial Virginia, Vol VI.* (Richmond, VA: Virginia State Library, 1966).

Bernard Grun, *The Timetables of History* (New York, NY: Simon & Schuster, 1979).

Bridget Smith, editor, *Historical Gazette –Vol. 4 No. 6, 1999.*

Brock Jobe, *New England Furniture: The Colonial Era* (Boston, MA: Houghton Mifflin, 1984).

## C

Cassie Nichols, *Historical Sketches of Sumter County: Its Birth and Growth* (Columbia, S.C.: The R.L. Bryan Company, 1975).

Charles Peterson, annotator, *The Carpenters' Company 1786 Rule Book* (Philadelphia, PA: The Carpenters' Company of the City and County of Philadelphia, 1992).

Charles Peterson, editor, *Building Early America* (Mendham, NJ: Astragal Press, 1976).

Charles W. Arnade, *The Siege of St. Augustine in 1702* (University of Florida Press, 1959).

*Charleston Courier*, 1847.

*Cheraw Intelligencer and Southern Register*, 1823.

Clyde A., II Milner, editor, *The Oxford History of the American West* (Oxford University Press, 1996).

Concord Coach Gallery

## D

D. Bottom, *Executive Journals of the Council of Colonial Virginia, Vol. I-IV* (Richmond, VA: Virginia State Library, 1966).

Dallas Historical Society

David Cressy, *Coming Over: Migration and Communication Between England and New England in the Seventeenth Century* (Cambridge University Press, 1987).

David McCord, editor, *The Statutes At Large of South Carolina, Volumes 1-6* (Columbia, SC: A.S. Johnston, 1839).

Davis Rich Dewey, *Early Financial History of the United States* (Washington D.C.: BeardBooks, 1934).

Denver Public Library, Western History Department

Don Taxay, *Money of the American Indians and Other Primitive Currencies of the Americas* (New York, NY: Nummus Press, 1970).

Douglas T. Miller, editor, *The Nature of Jacksonian America* (New York, NY: Wiley, 1972).

Dr. Samuel Davis McGill, *Narrative of Reminiscences in Williamsburg County* (1894).

## E

Economic History Association

EH.Net

Eliot Lord, *Comstock Mining and Miners* (Berkeley, CA: Howell-North, 1959).

Elmer L. Smith, *Early American Home Remedies*, (Lebanon, PA: Applied arts Publishers, 1968).

## F

Francis Lord, *Civil War Collector's Encyclopedia: Volumes I & II* (Blue & Grey Press, 1989).

## G

George L. Jackson, *The Development of School Support in Colonial Massachusetts* (Teachers College, Columbia University 1909).

George Leroy Jackson, *The Development of School Support in Colonial Massachusetts* (New York, NY: Arno Press, 1969).

*Gunston Hall Probate Inventory Database* (Mason Neck, VA: Gunston Hall Plantation, 2005).

# H

H.R. McIlwaine, editor, *Executive Journals of the Council of Colonial Virginia, Vol. IV* (Richmond, VA: Virginia State Library, 1930).

*Harper's Magazine*, October 1866, Vol. 22, No. 197.

*Harper's New Monthly Weekly, No XVI*, September, 1851.

Helen McKearin, *American Bottles and Flasks and Their Ancestry* (New York, NY: Random House Value Publishing, 1988).

Henry J. Kauffman, *The Pennsylvania-Kentucky Rifle* (Harrisburg, PA :1960).

Herbert G. Gutman, *Who Built America?* (New York, NY: Pantheon Books, 1989).

*Heritage of Russell County, Virginia, 1786-1986, Vol. 1* (Maceline, MO: Walsworth Publishing 1985).

*Historical Statistics of the United States, Colonial Times to 1970 - Bicentennial Edition* (U.S. Department of Commerce, Bureau of the Census, Basic Books, 1976).

Howard Zinn, *A People's History of the United States* (New York, NY: HarperPerennial, 1980).

J. H. Easterby, editor, *The Colonial Records of South Carolina - The Journal of the Commons House of Assembly February 20, 1744-May 25, 1745* (Columbia, SC: South Carolina Archives Department, 1955).

# J

J. Thomas Scharf, *History of Western Maryland* (Baltimore, MD: Clearfield Co. AND Family Life Publications, 1995).

J.C. Furnas, *The Americans, A Social History of the United States* (New York, NY: G. P. Putnam's Sons, 1969).

Jeffery Ward, *The West: An Illustrated History* (Pub Overstock Unlimited Inc, 1996).

Jerry E. Patterson, *The Vanderbilts* (New York, NY: Harry N Abrams, 1989).

Jim O'Donoghue, *Consumer Price Inflation Since 1750* (Britain's Office of National Statistics, March, 2004).

John C. Rives, editor, *The Congressional Globe: Containing The Debates and Proceedings of the First Session of the Thirty-Eighth Congress*, (Washington, D.C.: Congressional Globe, 1864).

John D. Morse, *Country Cabinetwork and Simple City Furniture* (Charlottesville, VA: The University of Virginia, 1970).

John Duffy, The Healers: *The Rise of the Medical Establishment* (University of Illinois Press, 1979).

John McCuster & Russell Menard, *The Economy of British America 1607-1789* (Chapel Hill, NC: University of North Carolina Press, 1991).

John William Ward, *Andrew Jackson - Symbol for an Age* (New York, NY: Oxford University Press, 1962).

Jonathan Daniel Wells, *The Origins of the Southern Middle Class, 1800-1861* (Chapel Hill, N.C.: The University of North Carolina Press, 2004).

Joseph I. Waring, *A History of Medicine in South Carolina, 1670-1825* (Columbia, SC: South Carolina Medical Association, 1967).

Judity M. Brimelow, *Accounts Audited of Claims Growing out of the Revolution in South Carolina* (Columbia, SC: Department of Archives and History, 1985).

Judy Jones and William Wilson, *An Incomplete Education* (New York, NY: Ballantine Books, 1987).

Julian P. Price, *Brief Historical Sketch of the Pee Dee Medical Association Commemorating its One Hundredth Anniversary*, 1848-1948 (1948).


**K**

Karen Greenspan, *The Timetables of Women's History* (New York, NY: Simon & Schuster, 1996).


**L**

L. A. Johnson & Marcia Ray, editors, *Over the Counter and on the Shelf: Country Storekeeping in America, 1620-1920* (New York, NY: Charles E Tuttle Co, 1970).
Leslie V. Brock, *The Colonial Currency, Prices and Exchange Rates, Essays in History* (Charlottesville: Corcoran Department of History at the University of Virginia, 1992).
*Lincoln* Magazine (2005).
Linda Kerber, *Women of the Republic* (Chapel Hill, NC: University of North Carolina Press, 1980).
Louis Jordan, *The Coins of Colonial and Early America*, A Project of the Robert H. Gore, Jr. Numismatic Endowment, University of Notre Dame, Department of Special Collections, 2005.
Lucian Johnston Eastin, *Emigrants' Guide to Pike's Peak* (1859).


**M**

Marie Goegel Kimball, *Thomas Jefferson's Cook Book* (Charlottesville: University Press of Virginia, 1977).
Marvin Kitman, *George Washington's Expense Account* (New York, NY: Harper & Row, 1970).
Mary W. Strange, *The Revolutionary Soldiers of Catholic Presbyterian Church* (York-Clover Printing Co., 1978).
Massachusetts Archives
Maud Carter Clement, *History of Pittsylvania County Virginia* (Clearfield Co; Reprint edition, 1987).


**P**

Patricia Scott Deetz, Christopher Fennell and J. Eric Deetz, *The Plymouth Colony Archive Project, 1998-2005*.
Paulette Carpenter, editor, USGenNet, 2004.


**R**

Ray Billington, *America's Frontier Heritage* (Univ. of New Mexico Press, 1966).
Rhode Island Historical Society, Manuscripts Division
Richard E. Stevens, *New Castle County Probate Inventories* (Borough of Wilmington, University of Delaware, 2004).
Richard Middleton, *Colonial America, A History, 1565-1776* (Oxford, UK: Blackwell Publishers, 2002).
Richland County Public Library, South Carolina.
Robert Bray & Paul Bushnell, editors, *Diary of a Common Soldier in the American Revolution, 1775-1883* (DeKalb, IL: Northern Illinois University Press, 1978).
Robert E. Wright, *Commercial Banking in Colonial America*, Archiving Early America, Online, 2005.
Ron Michener, *Money in the American Colonies*, EH. Net Encyclopedia, edited by Robert Whaples, 2003.

Rootsweb.com

Ruth Pace, Mary P. McGee, Mary Pace McGee, *The Life and Times of* Ridgeway Virginia 1728-1990 (Pocahontas Press, 2001).

## S

Samuel Shepherd, *The Statutes at Large of Virginia, 1792-1806* (Richmond, VA: Printed by Samuel Shepherd, 1836).

San Francisco Chamber of Commerce

Seymour E. Harris, *American Economic History* (New York, NY: McGraw-Hill Book Company, Inc., 1961).

Sidney Homer and Richard Sylla, *A History of Interest Rates, Third Edition* (Rutgers University Press, 1996).

South Carolina Department of Archives and History

South Carolina State Library

Stanley Engerman and Eugene Genovese, editors, *Race and Slavery in the Western Hemisphere: Quantitative Studies* (Princeton University Press).

Sue Patterson, *Collin County, Texas Genealogical and Historical Records* (2002).

Suzanne C. Linder, *Medicine in Marlboro County 1736 to 1980* (Baltimore, MD: Gateway Press, 1980).

## T

Terry W. Lipscomb, editor, *South Carolina Journal of the Commons House of Assembly, October 6, 1757-January 24, 1761* (South Carolina Department of Archives and History, 1996).

Terry W. Lipscomb, editor, *The Colonial Records of South Carolina - Journal of the Commons House of Assembly, October 6, 1757-January 24, 1761* (South Carolina Department of Archives and History, 1996).

*Texas Almanac for 1857* (Facsimile Reproduction by A.H. Belo Corporation, Dallas, 1966).

The Avalon Project at Yale Law School, The Lillian Goldman Law Library

*The Cincinnati Inquisitor and Advertiser* (1819)

The Free Library of Philadelphia

The Library of Virginia

The Old Sturbridge Village, Online Archive Collection, 2005

*The Pennsylvania Gazette 1728-1815*, Hall & Sellers, Philadelphia, Pennsylvania,

*The Statutes At Large of South Carolina, Acts From 1838, Volumes I-XI* (Columbia, SC: Republican Printing Company, 1873).

Thomas Bailey & David Kennedy, *The American Pageant: A History of the Republic* (Lexington: D.C. Heath and Company, 1983).

Thomas Cooper, editor, *The Statutes at Large of South Carolina 1786-1837* (Columbia, S.C.: A.S. Johnston, 1839).

Thomas L. Connelly and Michael D. Senecal, editors, *Almanac of American Presidents, Facts On File* (New York, 1991).

## U

University of Mary Washington, Department of Historic Preservation

# V

Virginia Historical Society

# W

Warren B. Smith, *White Servitude in Colonial America* (Columbia, SC: University of South Carolina Press, 1961).

Warren M Billings, *The Old Dominion in the Seventeenth Century: A Documentary History of Virginia, 1606-1689* (University of North Carolina Press, 1975).

William A. Degregorio, *The Complete Book of U.S. Presidents, Fourth Edition* (New York,NY: Wing Books1993).

William Dutton, *Du Pont* (New York, NY: Scribner, 1949).

William Weeden, *Economic and Social History of New England 1620-1789* (Williamstown: Corner House Publications, 1978).

# Y

Yale University Library, Kaplanoff Librarian for American History. Research Services and Collections

Yanis Varoufakis, *Foundations of Economics: A Beginner's Companion* (Routledge, 1998).

# Mackenzie & Harris
## General Reference Titles

## The Value of a Dollar 1860-2004, Third Edition

A guide to practical economy, *The Value of a Dollar* records the actual prices of thousands of items that consumers purchased from the Civil War to the present, along with facts about investment options and income opportunities. This brand new Third Edition boasts a brand new addition to each five-year chapter, a section on Trends. This informative section charts the change in price over time and provides added detail on the reasons prices changed within the time period, including industry developments, changes in consumer attitudes and important historical facts. Plus, a brand new chapter for 2000-2004 has been added. Each 5-year chapter includes a Historical Snapshot, Consumer Expenditures, Investments, Selected Income, Income/Standard Jobs, Food Basket, Standard Prices and Miscellany. This interesting and useful publication will be widely used in any reference collection.

*"Recommended for high school, college and public libraries." –ARBA*

600 pages; Hardcover ISBN 1-59237-074-8, $135.00

## Working Americans 1880-1999
## Volume I: The Working Class, Volume II: The Middle Class, Volume III: The Upper Class

Each of the volumes in the *Working Americans 1880-1999* series focuses on a particular class of Americans, The Working Class, The Middle Class and The Upper Class over the last 120 years. Chapters in each volume focus on one decade and profile three to five families. Family Profiles include real data on Income & Job Descriptions, Selected Prices of the Times, Annual Income, Annual Budgets, Family Finances, Life at Work, Life at Home, Life in the Community, Working Conditions, Cost of Living, Amusements and much more. Each chapter also contains an Economic Profile with Average Wages of other Professions, a selection of Typical Pricing, Key Events & Inventions, News Profiles, Articles from Local Media and Illustrations. The *Working Americans* series captures the lifestyles of each of the classes from the last twelve decades, covers a vast array of occupations and ethnic backgrounds and travels the entire nation. These interesting and useful compilations of portraits of the American Working, Middle and Upper Classes during the last 120 years will be an important addition to any high school, public or academic library reference collection.

*"These interesting, unique compilations of economic and social facts, figures and graphs will support multiple research needs. They will engage and enlighten patrons in high school, public and academic library collections." –Booklist*

Volume I: The Working Class ◆ 558 pages; Hardcover ISBN 1-891482-81-5, $145.00
Volume II: The Middle Class ◆ 591 pages; Hardcover ISBN 1-891482-72-6; $145.00
Volume III: The Upper Class ◆ 567 pages; Hardcover ISBN 1-930956-38-X, $145.00

## Working Americans 1880-1999  Volume IV: Their Children

This Fourth Volume in the highly successful *Working Americans 1880-1999* series focuses on American children, decade by decade from 1880 to 1999. This interesting and useful volume introduces the reader to three children in each decade, one from each of the Working, Middle and Upper classes. Like the first three volumes in the series, the individual profiles are created from interviews, diaries, statistical studies, biographies and news reports. Profiles cover a broad range of ethnic backgrounds, geographic area and lifestyles – everything from an orphan in Memphis in 1882, following the Yellow Fever epidemic of 1878 to an eleven-year-old nephew of a beer baron and owner of the New York Yankees in New York City in 1921. Chapters also contain important supplementary materials including News Features as well as information on everything from Schools to Parks, Infectious Diseases to Childhood Fears along with Entertainment, Family Life and much more to provide an informative overview of the lifestyles of children from each decade. This interesting account of what life was like for Children in the Working, Middle and Upper Classes will be a welcome addition to the reference collection of any high school, public or academic library.

600 pages; Hardcover ISBN 1-930956-35-5, $145.00

To preview any of our Directories Risk-Free for 30 days, call (800) 562-2139 or fax to (518) 789-0556

## Working Americans 1880-2003 Volume V: Americans At War

*Working Americans 1880-2003 Volume V: Americans At War* is divided into 11 chapters, each covering a decade from 1880-2003 and examines the lives of Americans during the time of war, including declared conflicts, one-time military actions, protests, and preparations for war. Each decade includes several personal profiles, whether on the battlefield or on the homefront, that tell the stories of civilians, soldiers, and officers during the decade. The profiles examine: Life at Home; Life at Work; and Life in the Community. Each decade also includes an Economic Profile with statistical comparisons, a Historical Snapshot, News Profiles, local News Articles, and Illustrations that provide a solid historical background to the decade being examined. Profiles range widely not only geographically, but also emotionally, from that of a girl whose leg was torn off in a blast during WWI, to the boredom of being stationed in the Dakotas as the Indian Wars were drawing to a close. As in previous volumes of the *Working Americans* series, information is presented in narrative form, but hard facts and real-life situations back up each story. The basis of the profiles come from diaries, private print books, personal interviews, family histories, estate documents and magazine articles. For easy reference, *Working Americans 1880-2003 Volume V: Americans At War* includes an in-depth Subject Index. The *Working Americans* series has become an important reference for public libraries, academic libraries and high school libraries. This fifth volume will be a welcome addition to all of these types of reference collections.

600 pages; Hardcover ISBN 1-59237-024-1; $145.00
Five Volume Set (Volumes I-V), Hardcover ISBN 1-59237-034-9, $675.00

## Working Americans 1880-2005 Volume VI: Women at Work

Unlike any other volume in the *Working Americans* series, this Sixth Volume, is the first to focus on a particular gender of Americans. *Volume VI: Women at Work*, traces what life was like for working women from the 1860's to the present time. Beginning with the life of a maid in 1890 and a store clerk in 1900 and ending with the life and times of the modern working women, this text captures the struggle, strengths and changing perception of the American woman at work. Each chapter focuses on one decade and profiles three to five women with real data on Income & Job Descriptions, Selected Prices of the Times, Annual Income, Annual Budgets, Family Finances, Life at Work, Life at Home, Life in the Community, Working Conditions, Cost of Living, Amusements and much more. For even broader access to the events, economics and attitude towards women throughout the past 130 years, each chapter is supplemented with News Profiles, Articles from Local Media, Illustrations, Economic Profiles, Typical Pricing, Key Events, Inventions and more. This important volume illustrates what life was like for working women over time and allows the reader to develop an understanding of the changing role of women at work. These interesting and useful compilations of portraits of women at work will be an important addition to any high school, public or academic library reference collection.

600 pages; Hardcover ISBN 1-59237-063-2; $145.00

## Working Americans 1880-2005 Volume VII: Social Movements

The newest addition to the widely-successful *Working Americans* series, *Volume VII: Social Movements* explores how Americans sought and fought for change from the 1880s to the present time. Following the format of previous volumes in the Working Americans series, the text examines the lives of 34 individuals who have worked -- often behind the scenes --- to bring about change. Issues include topics as diverse as the Anti-smoking movement of 1901 to efforts by Native Americans to reassert their long lost rights. Along the way, the book will profile individuals brave enough to demand suffrage for Kansas women in 1912 or demand an end to lynching during a March on Washington in 1923. Each profile is enriched with real data on Income & Job Descriptions, Selected Prices of the Times, Annual Incomes & Budgets, Life at Work, Life at Home, Life in the Community, along with News Features, Key Events, and Illustrations. The depth of information contained in each profile allow the user to explore the private, financial and public lives of these subjects, deepening our understanding of how calls for change took place in our society. A must-purchase for the reference collections of high school libraries, public libraries and academic libraries.

600 pages; Hardcover ISBN 1-59237-101-9; $145.00
Seven Volume Set (Volumes I-VII), Hardcover ISBN 1-59237-133-7, $945.00

## The Encyclopedia of Warrior Peoples & Fighting Groups

Many military groups throughout the world have excelled in their craft either by fortuitous circumstances, outstanding leadership, or intense training. This new second edition of The Encyclopedia of Warrior Peoples and Fighting Groups explores the origins and leadership of these outstanding combat forces, chronicles their conquests and accomplishments, examines the circumstances surrounding their decline or disbanding, and assesses their influence on the groups and methods of warfare that followed. This edition has been completely updated with information through 2005 and contains over 20 new entries. Readers will encounter ferocious tribes, charismatic leaders, and daring militias, from ancient times to the present, including Amazons, Buffalo Soldiers, Green Berets, Iron Brigade, Kamikazes, Peoples of the Sea, Polish Winged Hussars, Sacred Band of Thebes, Teutonic Knights, and Texas Rangers. With over 100 alphabetical entries, numerous cross-references and illustrations, a comprehensive bibliography, and index, the Encyclopedia of Warrior Peoples and Fighting Groups is a valuable resource for readers seeking insight into the bold history of distinguished fighting forces.

*"This work is especially useful for high school students, undergraduates, and general readers with an interest in military history."* –Library Journal

Pub. Date: May 2006; Hardcover ISBN 1-59237-116-7; $95.00

## To preview any of our Directories Risk-Free for 30 days, call (800) 562-2139 or fax to (518) 789-0556

## The Encyclopedia of Invasions & Conquests, From the Ancient Times to the Present

Throughout history, invasions and conquests have played a remarkable role in shaping our world and defining our boundaries, both physically and culturally. This second edition of the popular Encyclopedia of Invasions & Conquests, a comprehensive guide to over 150 invasions, conquests, battles and occupations from ancient times to the present, takes readers on a journey that includes the Roman conquest of Britain, the Portuguese colonization of Brazil, and the Iraqi invasion of Kuwait, to name a few. New articles will explore the late 20th and 21st centuries, with a specific focus on recent conflicts in Afghanistan, Kuwait, Iraq, Yugoslavia, Grenada and Chechnya. Categories of entries include countries, invasions and conquests, and individuals. In addition to covering the military aspects of invasions and conquests, entries cover some of the political, economic, and cultural aspects, for example, the effects of a conquest on the invade country's political and monetary system and in its language and religion. The entries on leaders – among them Sargon, Alexander the Great, William the Conqueror, and Adolf Hitler – deal with the people who sought to gain control, expand power, or exert religious or political influence over others through military means. Revised and updated for this second edition, entries are arranged alphabetically within historical periods. Each chapter provides a map to help readers locate key areas and geographical features, and bibliographical references appear at the end of each entry. Other useful features include cross-references, a cumulative bibliography and a comprehensive subject index. This authoritative, well-organized, lucidly written volume will prove invaluable for a variety of readers, including high school students, military historians, members of the armed forces, history buffs and hobbyists.

*"Engaging writing, sensible organization, nice illustrations, interesting and obscure facts, and useful maps make this book a pleasure to read." –ARBA*

Pub. Date: March 2006; Hardcover ISBN 1-59237-114-0; $95.00

## Encyclopedia of Prisoners of War & Internment

This authoritative second edition provides a valuable overview of the history of prisoners of war and interned civilians, from earliest times to the present. Written by an international team of experts in the field of POW studies, this fascinating and thought-provoking volume includes entries on a wide range of subjects including the Crusades, Plains Indian Warfare, concentration camps, the two world wars, and famous POWs throughout history, as well as atrocities, escapes, and much more. Written in a clear and easily understandable style, this informative reference details over 350 entries, 30% larger than the first edition, that survey the history of prisoners of war and interned civilians from the earliest times to the present, with emphasis on the 19th and 20th centuries. Medical conditions, international law, exchanges of prisoners, organizations working on behalf of POWs, and trials associated with the treatment of captives are just some of the themes explored. Entries range from the Ardeatine Caves Massacre to Kurt Vonnegut. Entries are arranged alphabetically, plus illustrations and maps are provided for easy reference. The text also includes an introduction, bibliography, appendix of selected documents, and end-of-entry reading suggestions. This one-of-a-kind reference will be a helpful addition to the reference collections of all public libraries, high schools, and university libraries and will prove invaluable to historians and military enthusiasts.

*"Thorough and detailed yet accessible to the lay reader. Of special interest to subject specialists and historians; recommended for public and academic libraries." - Library Journal*

Pub. Date: March 2006; Hardcover ISBN 1-59237-120-5; $95.00

## The Religious Right, A Reference Handbook

Timely and unbiased, this third edition updates and expands its examination of the religious right and its influence on our government, citizens, society, and politics. From the fight to outlaw the teaching of Darwin's theory of evolution to the struggle to outlaw abortion, the religious right is continually exerting an influence on public policy. This text explores the influence of religion on legislation and society, while examining the alignment of the religious right with the political right. A historical survey of the movement highlights the shift to "hands-on" approach to politics and the struggle to present a unified front. The coverage offers a critical historical survey of the religious right movement, focusing on its increased involvement in the political arena, attempts to forge coalitions, and notable successes and failures. The text offers complete coverage of biographies of the men and women who have advanced the cause and an up to date chronology illuminate the movement's goals, including their accomplishments and failures. This edition offers an extensive update to all sections along with several brand new entries. Two new sections complement this third edition, a chapter on legal issues and court decisions and a chapter on demographic statistics and electoral patterns. To aid in further research, The Religious Right, offers an entire section of annotated listings of print and non-print resources, as well as of organizations affiliated with the religious right, and those opposing it. Comprehensive in its scope, this work offers easy-to-read, pertinent information for those seeking to understand the religious right and its evolving role in American society. A must for libraries of all sizes, university religion departments, activists, high schools and for those interested in the evolving role of the religious right.

*" Recommended for all public and academic libraries." - Library Journal*

Pub. Date: November 2006; Hardcover ISBN 1-59237-113-2; $95.00

To preview any of our Directories Risk-Free for 30 days, call (800) 562-2139 or fax to (518) 789-0556

## From Suffrage to the Senate, An Encyclopedia of American Women in Politics

From Suffrage to the Senate is a comprehensive and valuable compendium of biographies of leading women in U.S. politics, past and present, and an examination of the wide range of women's movements. Up to date through 2006, this dynamically illustrated reference work explores American women's path to political power and social equality from the struggle for the right to vote and the abolition of slavery to the first African American woman in the U.S. Senate and beyond. This new edition includes over 150 new entries and a brand new section on trends and demographics of women in politics. The in-depth coverage also traces the political heritage of the abolition, labor, suffrage, temperance, and reproductive rights movements. The alphabetically arranged entries include biographies of every woman from across the political spectrum who has served in the U.S. House and Senate, along with women in the Judiciary and the U.S. Cabinet and, new to this edition, biographies of activists and political consultants. Bibliographical references follow each entry. For easy reference, a handy chronology is provided detailing 150 years of women's history. This up-to-date reference will be a must-purchase for women's studies departments, high schools and public libraries and will be a handy resource for those researching the key players in women's politics, past and present.

*"An engaging tool that would be useful in high school, public, and academic libraries looking for an overview of the political history of women in the US." –Booklist*

Pub. Date: March 2006; Two Volume Set; Hardcover ISBN 1-59237-117-5; $195.00

## An African Biographical Dictionary

This landmark second edition is the only biographical dictionary to bring together, in one volume, cultural, social and political leaders – both historical and contemporary – of the sub-Saharan region. Over 800 biographical sketches of prominent Africans, as well as foreigners who have affected the continent's history, are featured, 150 more than the previous edition. The wide spectrum of leaders includes religious figures, writers, politicians, scientists, entertainers, sports personalities and more. Access to these fascinating individuals is provided in a user-friendly format. The biographies are arranged alphabetically, cross-referenced and indexed. Entries include the country or countries in which the person was significant and the commonly accepted dates of birth and death. Each biographical sketch is chronologically written; entries for cultural personalities add an evaluation of their work. This information is followed by a selection of references often found in university and public libraries, including autobiographies and principal biographical works. Appendixes list each individual by country and by field of accomplishment – rulers, musicians, explorers, missionaries, businessmen, physicists – nearly thirty categories in all. Another convenient appendix lists heads of state since independence by country. Up-to-date and representative of African societies as a whole, An African Biographical Dictionary provides a wealth of vital information for students of African culture and is an indispensable reference guide for anyone interested in African affairs.

*"An unquestionable convenience to have these concise, informative biographies gathered into one source, indexed, and analyzed by appendixes listing entrants by nation and occupational field." –Wilson Library Bulletin*

Pub. Date: July 2006; Hardcover ISBN 1-59237-112-4; $125.00

## American Environmental Leaders, From Colonial Times to the Present

A comprehensive and diverse award winning collection of biographies of the most important figures in American environmentalism. Few subjects arouse the passions the way the environment does. How will we feed an ever-increasing population and how can that food be made safe for consumption? Who decides how land is developed? How can environmental policies be made fair for everyone, including multiethnic groups, women, children, and the poor? American Environmental Leaders presents more than 350 biographies of men and women who have devoted their lives to studying, debating, and organizing these and other controversial issues over the last 200 years. In addition to the scientists who have analyzed how human actions affect nature, we are introduced to poets, landscape architects, presidents, painters, activists, even sanitation engineers, and others who have forever altered how we think about the environment. The easy to use A–Z format provides instant access to these fascinating individuals, and frequent cross references indicate others with whom individuals worked (and sometimes clashed). End of entry references provide users with a starting point for further research.

*"Highly recommended for high school, academic, and public libraries needing environmental biographical information." –Library Journal/Starred Review*

Two Volume Set; Hardcover ISBN 1-57607-385-8 $175.00

## World Cultural Leaders of the Twentieth Century

An expansive two volume set that covers 450 worldwide cultural icons, World Cultural Leaders of the Twentieth Century includes each person's works, achievements, and professional careers in a thorough essay. Who was the originator of the term "documentary"? Which poet married the daughter of the famed novelist Thomas Mann in order to help her escape Nazi Germany? Which British writer served as an agent in Russia against the Bolsheviks before the 1917 revolution? These and many more questions are answered in this illuminating text. A handy two volume set that makes it easy to look up 450 worldwide cultural icons: novelists, poets, playwrights, painters, sculptors, architects, dancers, choreographers, actors, directors, filmmakers, singers, composers, and musicians. World Cultural Leaders of the Twentieth Century provides entries (many of them illustrated) covering the person's works, achievements, and professional career in a thorough essay and offers interesting facts and statistics. Entries are fully cross-referenced so that readers can learn how various individuals influenced others. A thorough general index completes the coverage.

*"Fills a need for handy, concise information on a wide array of international cultural figures."-ARBA*

Two Volume Set; Hardcover ISBN 1-57607-038-7 $175.00

To preview any of our Directories Risk-Free for 30 days, call (800) 562-2139 or fax to (518) 789-0556

# Universal Reference Publications
## Statistical & Demographic Reference Books

## The Asian Databook: Statistics for all US Counties & Cities with Over 10,000 Population

This is the first-ever resource that compiles statistics and rankings on the US Asian population. *The Asian Databook* presents over 20 statistical data points for each city and county, arranged alphabetically by state, then alphabetically by place name. Data reported for each place includes Population, Languages Spoken at Home, Foreign-Born, Educational Attainment, Income Figures, Poverty Status, Homeownership, Home Values & Rent, and more. Next, in the Rankings Section, the top 75 places are listed for each data element. These easy-to-access ranking tables allow the user to quickly determine trends and population characteristics. This kind of comparative data can not be found elsewhere, in print or on the web, in a format that's as easy-to-use or more concise. A useful resource for those searching for demographics data, career search and relocation information and also for market research. With data ranging from Ancestry to Education, *The Asian Databook* presents a useful compilation of information that will be a much-needed resource in the reference collection of any public or academic library along with the marketing collection of any company whose primary focus in on the Asian population.

1,000 pages; Softcover ISBN 1-59237-044-6 $150.00

## The Hispanic Databook: Statistics for all US Counties & Cities with Over 10,000 Population

Previously published by Toucan Valley Publications, this second edition has been completely updated with figures from the latest census and has been broadly expanded to include dozens of new data elements and a brand new Rankings section. The Hispanic population in the United States has increased over 42% in the last 10 years and accounts for 12.5% of the total US population. For ease-of-use, *The Hispanic Databook* presents over 20 statistical data points for each city and county, arranged alphabetically by state, then alphabetically by place name. Data reported for each place includes Population, Languages Spoken at Home, Foreign-Born, Educational Attainment, Income Figures, Poverty Status, Homeownership, Home Values & Rent, and more. Next, in the Rankings Section, the top 75 places are listed for each data element. These easy-to-access ranking tables allow the user to quickly determine trends and population characteristics. This kind of comparative data can not be found elsewhere, in print or on the web, in a format that's as easy-to-use or more concise. A useful resource for those searching for demographics data, career search and relocation information and also for market research. With data ranging from Ancestry to Education, *The Hispanic Databook* presents a useful compilation of information that will be a much-needed resource in the reference collection of any public or academic library along with the marketing collection of any company whose primary focus in on the Hispanic population.

*"This accurate, clearly presented volume of selected Hispanic demographics is recommended for large public libraries and research collections."-Library Journal*

1,000 pages; Softcover ISBN 1-59237-008-X, $150.00

## Ancestry in America: A Comparative Guide to Over 200 Ethnic Backgrounds

This brand new reference work pulls together thousands of comparative statistics on the Ethnic Backgrounds of all populated places in the United States with populations over 10,000. Never before has this kind of information been reported in a single volume. Section One, Statistics by Place, is made up of a list of over 200 ancestry and race categories arranged alphabetically by each of the 5,000 different places with populations over 10,000. The population number of the ancestry group in that city or town is provided along with the percent that group represents of the total population. This informative city-by-city section allows the user to quickly and easily explore the ethnic makeup of all major population bases in the United States. Section Two, Comparative Rankings, contains three tables for each ethnicity and race. In the first table, the top 150 populated places are ranked by population number for that particular ancestry group, regardless of population. In the second table, the top 150 populated places are ranked by the percent of the total population for that ancestry group. In the third table, those top 150 populated places with 10,000 population are ranked by population number for each ancestry group. These easy-to-navigate tables allow users to see ancestry population patterns and make city-by-city comparisons as well. Plus, as an added bonus with the purchase of *Ancestry in America*, a free companion CD-ROM is available that lists statistics and rankings for all of the 35,000 populated places in the United States. This brand new, information-packed resource will serve a wide-range or research requests for demographics, population characteristics, relocation information and much more. *Ancestry in America: A Comparative Guide to Over 200 Ethnic Backgrounds* will be an important acquisition to all reference collections.

*"This compilation will serve a wide range of research requests for population characteristics ... it offers much more detail than other sources." –Booklist*

1,500 pages; Softcover ISBN 1-59237-029-2, $225.00

To preview any of our Directories Risk-Free for 30 days, call (800) 562-2139 or fax to (518) 789-0556

## Weather America, A Thirty-Year Summary of Statistical Weather Data and Rankings

This valuable resource provides extensive climatological data for over 4,000 National and Cooperative Weather Stations throughout the United States. *Weather America* begins with a new Major Storms section that details major storm events of the nation and a National Rankings section that details rankings for several data elements, such as Maximum Temperature and Precipitation. The main body of *Weather America* is organized into 50 state sections. Each section provides a Data Table on each Weather Station, organized alphabetically, that provides statistics on Maximum and Minimum Temperatures, Precipitation, Snowfall, Extreme Temperatures, Foggy Days, Humidity and more. State sections contain two brand new features in this edition – a City Index and a narrative Description of the climatic conditions of the state. Each section also includes a revised Map of the State that includes not only weather stations, but cities and towns.

*"Best Reference Book of the Year." –Library Journal*

2,013 pages; Softcover ISBN 1-891482-29-7, $175.00

## Profiles of America: Facts, Figures & Statistics for Every Populated Place in the United States

*Profiles of America* is the only source that pulls together, in one place, statistical, historical and descriptive information about every place in the United States in an easy-to-use format. This award winning reference set, now in its second edition, compiles statistics and data from over 20 different sources – the latest census information has been included along with more than nine brand new statistical topics. This Four-Volume Set details over 40,000 places, from the biggest metropolis to the smallest unincorporated hamlet, and provides statistical details and information on over 50 different topics including Geography, Climate, Population, Vital Statistics, Economy, Income, Taxes, Education, Housing, Health & Environment, Public Safety, Newspapers, Transportation, Presidential Election Results and Information Contacts or Chambers of Commerce. Profiles are arranged, for ease-of-use, by state and then by county. Each county begins with a County-Wide Overview and is followed by information for each Community in that particular county. The Community Profiles within the county are arranged alphabetically. *Profiles of America* is a virtual snapshot of America at your fingertips and a unique compilation of information that will be widely used in any reference collection.

*A Library Journal Best Reference Book "An outstanding compilation." –Library Journal*

10,000 pages; Four Volume Set; Softcover ISBN 1-891482-80-7, $595.00

## The Comparative Guide to American Suburbs, 2005

*The Comparative Guide to American Suburbs* is a one-stop source for Statistics on the 2,000+ suburban communities surrounding the 50 largest metropolitan areas – their population characteristics, income levels, economy, school system and important data on how they compare to one another. Organized into 50 Metropolitan Area chapters, each chapter contains an overview of the Metropolitan Area, a detailed Map followed by a comprehensive Statistical Profile of each Suburban Community, including Contact Information, Physical Characteristics, Population Characteristics, Income, Economy, Unemployment Rate, Cost of Living, Education, Chambers of Commerce and more. Next, statistical data is sorted into Ranking Tables that rank the suburbs by twenty different criteria, including Population, Per Capita Income, Unemployment Rate, Crime Rate, Cost of Living and more. *The Comparative Guide to American Suburbs* is the best source for locating data on suburbs. Those looking to relocate, as well as those doing preliminary market research, will find this an invaluable timesaving resource.

*"Public and academic libraries will find this compilation useful…The work draws together figures from many sources and will be especially helpful for job relocation decisions." – Booklist*

1,700 pages; Softcover ISBN 1-59237-004-7, $130.00

## The Environmental Resource Handbook, 2005/06

*The Environmental Resource Handbook* is the most up-to-date and comprehensive source for Environmental Resources and Statistics. Section I: Resources provides detailed contact information for thousands of information sources, including Associations & Organizations, Awards & Honors, Conferences, Foundations & Grants, Environmental Health, Government Agencies, National Parks & Wildlife Refuges, Publications, Research Centers, Educational Programs, Green Product Catalogs, Consultants and much more. Section II: Statistics, provides statistics and rankings on hundreds of important topics, including Children's Environmental Index, Municipal Finances, Toxic Chemicals, Recycling, Climate, Air & Water Quality and more. This kind of up-to-date environmental data, all in one place, is not available anywhere else on the market place today. This vast compilation of resources and statistics is a must-have for all public and academic libraries as well as any organization with a primary focus on the environment.

*"…the intrinsic value of the information make it worth consideration by libraries with environmental collections and environmentally concerned users." –Booklist*

1,000 pages; Softcover ISBN 1-59237-090-X, $155.00 ♦ Online Database $300.00

## America's Top-Rated Cities, 2005

*America's Top-Rated Cities* provides current, comprehensive statistical information and other essential data in one easy-to-use source on the 100 "top" cities that have been cited as the best for business and living in the U.S. This handbook allows readers to see, at a glance, a concise social, business, economic, demographic and environmental profile of each city, including brief evaluative comments. In addition to detailed data on Cost of Living, Finances, Real Estate, Education, Major Employers, Media, Crime and Climate, city reports now include Housing Vacancies, Tax Audits, Bankruptcy, Presidential Election Results and more. This outstanding source of information will be widely used in any reference collection.

> *"The only source of its kind that brings together all of this information into one easy-to-use source. It will be beneficial to many business and public libraries." –ARBA*

2,500 pages, 4 Volume Set; Softcover ISBN 1-59237-076-4, $195.00

## America's Top-Rated Smaller Cities, 2004/05

A perfect companion to *America's Top-Rated Cities*, *America's Top-Rated Smaller Cities* provides current, comprehensive business and living profiles of smaller cities (population 25,000-99,999) that have been cited as the best for business and living in the United States. Sixty cities make up this 2004 edition of *America's Top-Rated Smaller Cities*, all are top-ranked by Population Growth, Median Income, Unemployment Rate and Crime Rate. City reports reflect the most current data available on a wide-range of statistics, including Employment & Earnings, Household Income, Unemployment Rate, Population Characteristics, Taxes, Cost of Living, Education, Health Care, Public Safety, Recreation, Media, Air & Water Quality and much more. Plus, each city report contains a Background of the City, and an Overview of the State Finances. *America's Top-Rated Smaller Cities* offers a reliable, one-stop source for statistical data that, before now, could only be found scattered in hundreds of sources. This volume is designed for a wide range of readers: individuals considering relocating a residence or business; professionals considering expanding their business or changing careers; general and market researchers; real estate consultants; human resource personnel; urban planners and investors.

> *"Provides current, comprehensive statistical information in one easy-to-use source... Recommended for public and academic libraries and specialized collections." –Library Journal*

1,100 pages; Softcover ISBN 1-59237-043-8, $160.00

## Crime in America's Top-Rated Cities, 2000

This volume includes over 20 years of crime statistics in all major crime categories: violent crimes, property crimes and total crime. *Crime in America's Top-Rated Cities* is conveniently arranged by city and covers 76 top-rated cities. *Crime in America's Top-Rated Cities* offers details that compare the number of crimes and crime rates for the city, suburbs and metro area along with national crime trends for violent, property and total crimes. Also, this handbook contains important information and statistics on Anti-Crime Programs, Crime Risk, Hate Crimes, Illegal Drugs, Law Enforcement, Correctional Facilities, Death Penalty Laws and much more. A much-needed resource for people who are relocating, business professionals, general researchers, the press, law enforcement officials and students of criminal justice.

> *"Data is easy to access and will save hours of searching." –Global Enforcement Review*

832 pages; Softcover ISBN 1-891482-84-X, $155.00

## The American Tally: Statistics & Comparative Rankings for U.S. Cities with Populations over 10,000

This important statistical handbook compiles, all in one place, comparative statistics on all U.S. cities and towns with a 10,000+ population. *The American Tally* provides statistical details on over 4,000 cities and towns and profiles how they compare with one another in Population Characteristics, Education, Language & Immigration, Income & Employment and Housing. Each section begins with an alphabetical listing of cities by state, allowing for quick access to both the statistics and relative rankings of any city. Next, the highest and lowest cities are listed in each statistic. These important, informative lists provide quick reference to which cities are at both extremes of the spectrum for each statistic. Unlike any other reference, *The American Tally* provides quick, easy access to comparative statistics – a must-have for any reference collection.

> *"A solid library reference." –Bookwatch*

500 pages; Softcover ISBN 1-930956-29-0, $125.00

To preview any of our Directories Risk-Free for 30 days, call (800) 562-2139 or fax to (518) 789-0556

# Sedgwick Press
## Health Directories

## The Complete Directory for People with Disabilities, 2005

A wealth of information, now in one comprehensive sourcebook. Completely updated for 2005, this edition contains more information than ever before, including thousands of new entries and enhancements to existing entries and thousands of additional web sites and e-mail addresses. This up-to-date directory is the most comprehensive resource available for people with disabilities, detailing Independent Living Centers, Rehabilitation Facilities, State & Federal Agencies, Associations, Support Groups, Periodicals & Books, Assistive Devices, Employment & Education Programs, Camps and Travel Groups. Each year, more libraries, schools, colleges, hospitals, rehabilitation centers and individuals add *The Complete Directory for People with Disabilities* to their collections, making sure that this information is readily available to the families, individuals and professionals who can benefit most from the amazing wealth of resources cataloged here.

*"No other reference tool exists to meet the special needs of the disabled in one convenient resource for information." –Library Journal*

1,200 pages; Softcover ISBN 1-59237-054-3, $165.00 ◆ Online Database $215.00 ◆ Online Database & Directory Combo $300.00

## The Complete Directory for People with Chronic Illness, 2005/06

Thousands of hours of research have gone into this completely updated 2005/06 edition – several new chapters have been added along with thousands of new entries and enhancements to existing entries. Plus, each chronic illness chapter has been reviewed by an medical expert in the field. This widely-hailed directory is structured around the 90 most prevalent chronic illnesses – from Asthma to Cancer to Wilson's Disease – and provides a comprehensive overview of the support services and information resources available for people diagnosed with a chronic illness. Each chronic illness has its own chapter and contains a brief description in layman's language, followed by important resources for National & Local Organizations, State Agencies, Newsletters, Books & Periodicals, Libraries & Research Centers, Support Groups & Hotlines, Web Sites and much more. This directory is an important resource for health care professionals, the collections of hospital and health care libraries, as well as an invaluable tool for people with a chronic illness and their support network.

*"A must purchase for all hospital and health care libraries and is strongly recommended for all public library reference departments." –ARBA*

1,200 pages; Softcover ISBN 1-59237-081-0, $165.00 ◆ Online Database $215.00 ◆ Online Database & Directory Combo $300.00

## The Complete Learning Disabilities Directory, 2005

*The Complete Learning Disabilities Directory* is the most comprehensive database of Programs, Services, Curriculum Materials, Professional Meetings & Resources, Camps, Newsletters and Support Groups for teachers, students and families concerned with learning disabilities. This information-packed directory includes information about Associations & Organizations, Schools, Colleges & Testing Materials, Government Agencies, Legal Resources and much more. For quick, easy access to information, this directory contains four indexes: Entry Name Index, Subject Index and Geographic Index. With every passing year, the field of learning disabilities attracts more attention and the network of caring, committed and knowledgeable professionals grows every day. This directory is an invaluable research tool for these parents, students and professionals.

*"Due to its wealth and depth of coverage, parents, teachers and others… should find this an invaluable resource." -Booklist*

900 pages; Softcover ISBN 1-59237-092-6, $145.00 ◆ Online Database $195.00 ◆ Online Database & Directory Combo $280.00

## The Complete Mental Health Directory, 2004/05

This is the most comprehensive resource covering the field of behavioral health, with critical information for both the layman and the mental health professional. For the layman, this directory offers understandable descriptions of 25 Mental Health Disorders as well as detailed information on Associations, Media, Support Groups and Mental Health Facilities. For the professional, *The Complete Mental Health Directory* offers critical and comprehensive information on Managed Care Organizations, Information Systems, Government Agencies and Provider Organizations. This comprehensive volume of needed information will be widely used in any reference collection.

*"… the strength of this directory is that it consolidates widely dispersed information into a single volume." –Booklist*

800 pages; Softcover ISBN 1-59237-046-2, $165.00 ◆ Online Database $215.00 ◆ Online & Directory Combo $300.00

To preview any of our Directories Risk-Free for 30 days, call (800) 562-2139 or fax to (518) 789-0556

## Older Americans Information Directory, 2004/05

Completely updated for 2004/05, this Fifth Edition has been completely revised and now contains 1,000 new listings, over 8,000 updates to existing listings and over 3,000 brand new e-mail addresses and web sites. You'll find important resources for Older Americans including National, Regional, State & Local Organizations, Government Agencies, Research Centers, Libraries & Information Centers, Legal Resources, Discount Travel Information, Continuing Education Programs, Disability Aids & Assistive Devices, Health, Print Media and Electronic Media. Three indexes: Entry Index, Subject Index and Geographic Index make it easy to find just the right source of information. This comprehensive guide to resources for Older Americans will be a welcome addition to any reference collection.

*"Highly recommended for academic, public, health science and consumer libraries..."* –Choice

1,200 pages; Softcover ISBN 1-59237-037-3, $165.00 ◆ Online Database $215.00 ◆ Online Database & Directory Combo $300.00

## The Complete Directory for Pediatric Disorders, 2004/05

This important directory provides parents and caregivers with information about Pediatric Conditions, Disorders, Diseases and Disabilities, including Blood Disorders, Bone & Spinal Disorders, Brain Defects & Abnormalities, Chromosomal Disorders, Congenital Heart Defects, Movement Disorders, Neuromuscular Disorders and Pediatric Tumors & Cancers. This carefully written directory offers: understandable Descriptions of 15 major bodily systems; Descriptions of more than 200 Disorders and a Resources Section, detailing National Agencies & Associations, State Associations, Online Services, Libraries & Resource Centers, Research Centers, Support Groups & Hotlines, Camps, Books and Periodicals. This resource will provide immediate access to information crucial to families and caregivers when coping with children's illnesses.

*"Recommended for public and consumer health libraries."* –Library Journal

1,200 pages; Softcover ISBN 1-59237-045-4, $165.00 ◆ Online Database $215.00 ◆ Online Database & Directory Combo $300.00

## The Complete Directory for People with Rare Disorders

This outstanding reference is produced in conjunction with the National Organization for Rare Disorders to provide comprehensive and needed access to important information on over 1,000 rare disorders, including Cancers and Muscular, Genetic and Blood Disorders. An informative Disorder Description is provided for each of the 1,100 disorders (rare Cancers and Muscular, Genetic and Blood Disorders) followed by information on National and State Organizations dealing with a particular disorder, Umbrella Organizations that cover a wide range of disorders, the Publications that can be useful when researching a disorder and the Government Agencies to contact. Detailed and up-to-date listings contain mailing address, phone and fax numbers, web sites and e-mail addresses along with a description. For quick, easy access to information, this directory contains two indexes: Entry Name Index and Acronym/Keyword Index along with an informative Guide for Rare Disorder Advocates. The Complete Directory for People with Rare Disorders will be an invaluable tool for the thousands of families that have been struck with a rare or "orphan" disease, who feel that they have no place to turn and will be a much-used addition to the reference collection of any public or academic library.

*"Quick access to information... public libraries and hospital patient libraries will find this a useful resource in directing users to support groups or agencies dealing with a rare disorder."* –Booklist

726 pages; Softcover ISBN 1-891482-18-1, $165.00

## The Directory of Drug & Alcohol Residential Rehabilitation Facilities

This brand new directory is the first-ever resource to bring together, all in one place, data on the thousands of drug and alcohol residential rehabilitation facilities in the United States. *The Directory of Drug & Alcohol Residential Rehabilitation Facilities* covers over 1,000 facilities, with detailed contact information for each one, including mailing address, phone and fax numbers, email addresses and web sites, mission statement, type of treatment programs, cost, average length of stay, numbers of residents and counselors, accreditation, insurance plans accepted, type of environment, religious affiliation, education components and much more. It also contains a helpful chapter on General Resources that provides contact information for Associations, Print & Electronic Media, Support Groups and Conferences. Multiple indexes allow the user to pinpoint the facilities that meet very specific criteria. This time-saving tool is what so many counselors, parents and medical professionals have been asking for. *The Directory of Drug & Alcohol Residential Rehabilitation Facilities* will be a helpful tool in locating the right source for treatment for a wide range of individuals. This comprehensive directory will be an important acquisition for all reference collections: public and academic libraries, case managers, social workers, state agencies and many more.

*"This is an excellent, much needed directory that fills an important gap..."* –Booklist

300 pages; Softcover ISBN 1-59237-031-4, $135.00

To preview any of our Directories Risk-Free for 30 days, call (800) 562-2139 or fax to (518) 789-0556

# Sedgwick Press
## Education Directories

### The Comparative Guide to American Elementary & Secondary Schools, 2004/05

The only guide of its kind, this award winning compilation offers a snapshot profile of every public school district in the United States serving 1,500 or more students – more than 5,900 districts are covered. Organized alphabetically by district within state, each chapter begins with a Statistical Overview of the state. Each district listing includes contact information (name, address, phone number and web site) plus Grades Served, the Numbers of Students and Teachers and the Number of Regular, Special Education, Alternative and Vocational Schools in the district along with statistics on Student/Classroom Teacher Ratios, Drop Out Rates, Ethnicity, the Numbers of Librarians and Guidance Counselors and District Expenditures per student. As an added bonus, *The Comparative Guide to American Elementary and Secondary Schools* provides important ranking tables, both by state and nationally, for each data element. For easy navigation through this wealth of information, this handbook contains a useful City Index that lists all districts that operate schools within a city. These important comparative statistics are necessary for anyone considering relocation or doing comparative research on their own district and would be a perfect acquisition for any public library or school district library.

*"This straightforward guide is an easy way to find general information. Valuable for academic and large public library collections." –ARBA*

2,400 pages; Softcover ISBN 1-59237-047-0, $125.00

### Educators Resource Directory, 2005/06

*Educators Resource Directory* is a comprehensive resource that provides the educational professional with thousands of resources and statistical data for professional development. This directory saves hours of research time by providing immediate access to Associations & Organizations, Conferences & Trade Shows, Educational Research Centers, Employment Opportunities & Teaching Abroad, School Library Services, Scholarships, Financial Resources, Professional Consultants, Computer Software & Testing Resources and much more. Plus, this comprehensive directory also includes a section on Statistics and Rankings with over 100 tables, including statistics on Average Teacher Salaries, SAT/ACT scores, Revenues & Expenditures and more. These important statistics will allow the user to see how their school rates among others, make relocation decisions and so much more. For quick access to information, this directory contains four indexes: Entry & Publisher Index, Geographic Index, a Subject & Grade Index and Web Sites Index. *Educators Resource Directory* will be a well-used addition to the reference collection of any school district, education department or public library.

*"Recommended for all collections that serve elementary and secondary school professionals." –Choice*

1,000 pages; Softcover ISBN 1-59237-080-2, $145.00 ◆ Online Database $195.00 ◆ Online Database & Directory Combo $280.00

# Sedgwick Press
## Hospital & Health Plan Directories

### The Comparative Guide to American Hospitals

This brand new title is the first ever resource to compare all of the nation's hospitals by 17 measures of quality in the treatment of heart attack, heart failure and pneumonia. This data is based on the recently announced Hospital Compare, produced by Medicare, and is available in print and in a unique and user-friendly format from Grey House Publishing, along with extra contact information from Grey House's *Directory of Hospital Personnel. The Comparative Guide to American Hospitals* provides a snapshot profile of each of the nations 6,000 hospitals. These informative profiles illustrate how the hospital rates in 17 important areas: Heart Attack Care (% who receive Aspirin at Arrival, Aspirin at Discharge, ACE Inhibitor for LVSD, Beta Blocker at Arrival, Beta Blocker at Discharge, Thrombolytic Agent Received, PTCA Received and Adult Smoking Cessation Advice); Heart Failure (% who receive LVF Assessment, ACE Inhibitor for LVSD, Discharge Instructions, Adult Smoking Cessation Advice); and Pneumonia (% who receive Initial Antibiotic Timing, Pneumococcal Vaccination, Oxygenation Assessment, Blood Culture Performed and Adult Smoking Cessation Advice). Each profile includes the raw percentage for that hospital, the state average, the US average and data on the top hospital. For easy access to contact information, each profile includes the hospitals address, phone and fax numbers, email and web addresses, type and accreditation along with 5 top key administrations. These profiles will allow the user to quickly identify the quality of the hospital and have the necessary information at their fingertips to make contact with that hospital. Most importantly, *The Comparative Guide to American Hospitals* provides an easy-to-use Ranking Table for each of the data elements to allow the user to quickly locate the hospitals with the best level of service. This brand new title will be a must for the reference collection at all public, medical and academic libraries.

2,500 pages; Softcover ISBN 1-59237-109-4 $175.00

To preview any of our Directories Risk-Free for 30 days, call (800) 562-2139 or fax to (518) 789-0556

# The Directory of Hospital Personnel, 2005

*The Directory of Hospital Personnel* is the best resource you can have at your fingertips when researching or marketing a product or service to the hospital market. A "Who's Who" of the hospital universe, this directory puts you in touch with over 150,000 key decision-makers. With 100% verification of data you can rest assured that you will reach the right person with just one call. Every hospital in the U.S. is profiled, listed alphabetically by city within state. Plus, three easy-to-use, cross-referenced indexes put the facts at your fingertips faster and more easily than any other directory: Hospital Name Index, Bed Size Index and Personnel Index. *The Directory of Hospital Personnel* is the only complete source for key hospital decision-makers by name. Whether you want to define or restructure sales territories... locate hospitals with the purchasing power to accept your proposals... keep track of important contacts or colleagues... or find information on which insurance plans are accepted, *The Directory of Hospital Personnel* gives you the information you need – easily, efficiently, effectively and accurately.

*"Recommended for college, university and medical libraries." -ARBA*

2,500 pages; Softcover ISBN 1-59237-065-9 $275.00 ◆ Online Database $545.00 ◆ Online Database & Directory Combo, $650.00

## The Directory of Health Care Group Purchasing Organizations

This comprehensive directory provides the important data you need to get in touch with over 800 Group Purchasing Organizations. By providing in-depth information on this growing market and its members, *The Directory of Health Care Group Purchasing Organizations* fills a major need for the most accurate and comprehensive information on over 800 GPOs – Mailing Address, Phone & Fax Numbers, E-mail Addresses, Key Contacts, Purchasing Agents, Group Descriptions, Membership Categorization, Standard Vendor Proposal Requirements, Membership Fees & Terms, Expanded Services, Total Member Beds & Outpatient Visits represented and more. Five Indexes provide a number of ways to locate the right GPO: Alphabetical Index, Expanded Services Index, Organization Type Index, Geographic Index and Member Institution Index. With its comprehensive and detailed information on each purchasing organization, *The Directory of Health Care Group Purchasing Organizations* is the go-to source for anyone looking to target this market.

*"The information is clearly arranged and easy to access...recommended for those needing this very specialized information." –ARBA*

1,000 pages; Softcover ISBN 1-59237-036-5, $325.00 ◆ Online Database, $650.00 ◆ Online Database & Directory Combo, $750.00

## The HMO/PPO Directory, 2005

*The HMO/PPO Directory* is a comprehensive source that provides detailed information about Health Maintenance Organizations and Preferred Provider Organizations nationwide. This comprehensive directory details more information about more managed health care organizations than ever before. Over 1,100 HMOs, PPOs and affiliated companies are listed, arranged alphabetically by state. Detailed listings include Key Contact Information, Prescription Drug Benefits, Enrollment, Geographical Areas served, Affiliated Physicians & Hospitals, Federal Qualifications, Status, Year Founded, Managed Care Partners, Employer References, Fees & Payment Information and more. Plus, five years of historical information is included related to Revenues, Net Income, Medical Loss Ratios, Membership Enrollment and Number of Patient Complaints. Five easy-to-use, cross-referenced indexes will put this vast array of information at your fingertips immediately: HMO Index, PPO Index, Other Providers Index, Personnel Index and Enrollment Index. *The HMO/PPO Directory* provides the most comprehensive information on the most companies available on the market place today.

*"Helpful to individuals requesting certain HMO/PPO issues such as co-payment costs, subscription costs and patient complaints. Individuals concerned (or those with questions) about their insurance may find this text to be of use to them." -ARBA*

600 pages; Softcover ISBN 1-59237-057-8, $275.00 ◆ Online Database, $495.00 ◆ Online Database & Directory Combo, $600.00

## The Directory of Independent Ambulatory Care Centers

This first edition of *The Directory of Independent Ambulatory Care Centers* provides access to detailed information that, before now, could only be found scattered in hundreds of different sources. This comprehensive and up-to-date directory pulls together a vast array of contact information for over 7,200 Ambulatory Surgery Centers, Ambulatory General and Urgent Care Clinics, and Diagnostic Imaging Centers that are not affiliated with a hospital or major medical center. Detailed listings include Mailing Address, Phone & Fax Numbers, E-mail and Web Site addresses, Contact Name and Phone Numbers of the Medical Director and other Key Executives and Purchasing Agents, Specialties & Services Offered, Year Founded, Numbers of Employees and Surgeons, Number of Operating Rooms, Number of Cases seen per year, Overnight Options, Contracted Services and much more. Listings are arranged by State, by Center Category and then alphabetically by Organization Name. Two indexes provide quick and easy access to this wealth of information: Entry Name Index and Specialty/Service Index. *The Directory of Independent Ambulatory Care Centers* is a must-have resource for anyone marketing a product or service to this important industry and will be an invaluable tool for those searching for a local care center that will meet their specific needs.

*"Among the numerous hospital directories, no other provides information on independent ambulatory centers. A handy, well-organized resource that would be useful in medical center libraries and public libraries." –Choice*

986 pages; Softcover ISBN 1-930956-90-8, $185.00 ◆ Online Database, $365.00 ◆ Online Database & Directory Combo, $450.00

To preview any of our Directories Risk-Free for 30 days, call (800) 562-2139 or fax to (518) 789-0556

# Grey House Publishing
## Business Directories

## The Directory of Business Information Resources, 2006

With 100% verification, over 1,000 new listings and more than 12,000 updates, this 2006 edition of *The Directory of Business Information Resources* is the most up-to-date source for contacts in over 98 business areas – from advertising and agriculture to utilities and wholesalers. This carefully researched volume details: the Associations representing each industry; the Newsletters that keep members current; the Magazines and Journals - with their "Special Issues" - that are important to the trade, the Conventions that are "must attends," Databases, Directories and Industry Web Sites that provide access to must-have marketing resources. Includes contact names, phone & fax numbers, web sites and e-mail addresses. This one-volume resource is a gold mine of information and would be a welcome addition to any reference collection.

*"This is a most useful and easy-to-use addition to any researcher's library." –The Information Professionals Institute*

2,500 pages; Softcover ISBN 1-59237-078-0, $195.00 ◆ Online Database $495.00

## Nations of the World, 2005  A Political, Economic and Business Handbook

This completely revised edition covers all the nations of the world in an easy-to-use, single volume. Each nation is profiled in a single chapter that includes Key Facts, Political & Economic Issues, a Country Profile and Business Information. In this fast-changing world, it is extremely important to make sure that the most up-to-date information is included in your reference collection. This 2005 edition is just the answer. Each of the 200+ country chapters have been carefully reviewed by a political expert to make sure that the text reflects the most current information on Politics, Travel Advisories, Economics and more. You'll find such vital information as a Country Map, Population Characteristics, Inflation, Agricultural Production, Foreign Debt, Political History, Foreign Policy, Regional Insecurity, Economics, Trade & Tourism, Historical Profile, Political Systems, Ethnicity, Languages, Media, Climate, Hotels, Chambers of Commerce, Banking, Travel Information and more. Five Regional Chapters follow the main text and include a Regional Map, an Introductory Article, Key Indicators and Currencies for the Region. New for 2004, an all-inclusive CD-ROM is available as a companion to the printed text. Noted for its sophisticated, up-to-date and reliable compilation of political, economic and business information, this brand new edition will be an important acquisition to any public, academic or special library reference collection.

*"A useful addition to both general reference collections and business collections." –RUSQ*

1,700 pages; Print Version Only Softcover ISBN 1-59237-051-9, $145.00 ◆ Print Version and CD-ROM $180.00

## The Grey House Performing Arts Directory, 2005

*The Grey House Performing Arts Directory* is the most comprehensive resource covering the Performing Arts. This important directory provides current information on over 8,500 Dance Companies, Instrumental Music Programs, Opera Companies, Choral Groups, Theater Companies, Performing Arts Series and Performing Arts Facilities. Plus, this edition now contains a brand new section on Artist Management Groups. In addition to mailing address, phone & fax numbers, e-mail addresses and web sites, dozens of other fields of available information include mission statement, key contacts, facilities, seating capacity, season, attendance and more. This directory also provides an important Information Resources section that covers hundreds of Performing Arts Associations, Magazines, Newsletters, Trade Shows, Directories, Databases and Industry Web Sites. Five indexes provide immediate access to this wealth of information: Entry Name, Executive Name, Performance Facilities, Geographic and Information Resources. *The Grey House Performing Arts Directory* pulls together thousands of Performing Arts Organizations, Facilities and Information Resources into an easy-to-use source – this kind of comprehensiveness and extensive detail is not available in any resource on the market place today.

*"Immensely useful and user-friendly … recommended for public, academic and certain special library reference collections." –Booklist*

1,500 pages; Softcover ISBN 1-59237-023-3, $185.00 ◆ Online Database $335.00

## Research Services Directory:  Commercial & Corporate Research Centers

This Ninth Edition provides access to well over 8,000 independent Commercial Research Firms, Corporate Research Centers and Laboratories offering contract services for hands-on, basic or applied research. *Research Services Directory* covers the thousands of types of research companies, including Biotechnology & Pharmaceutical Developers, Consumer Product Research, Defense Contractors, Electronics & Software Engineers, Think Tanks, Forensic Investigators, Independent Commercial Laboratories, Information Brokers, Market & Survey Research Companies, Medical Diagnostic Facilities, Product Research & Development Firms and more. Each entry provides the company's name, mailing address, phone & fax numbers, key contacts, web site, e-mail address, as well as a company description and research and technical fields served. Four indexes provide immediate access to this wealth of information: Research Firms Index, Geographic Index, Personnel Name Index and Subject Index.

*"An important source for organizations in need of information about laboratories, individuals and other facilities." –ARBA*

1,400 pages; Softcover ISBN 1-59237-003-9, $395.00 ◆ Online Database (includes a free copy of the directory) $850.00

To preview any of our Directories Risk-Free for 30 days, call (800) 562-2139 or fax to (518) 789-0556

## The Directory of Venture Capital & Private Equity Firms, 2005

This edition has been extensively updated and broadly expanded to offer direct access to over 2,800 Domestic and International Venture Capital Firms, including address, phone & fax numbers, e-mail addresses and web sites for both primary and branch locations. Entries include details on the firm's Mission Statement, Industry Group Preferences, Geographic Preferences, Average and Minimum Investments and Investment Criteria. You'll also find details that are available nowhere else, including the Firm's Portfolio Companies and extensive information on each of the firm's Managing Partners, such as Education, Professional Background and Directorships held, along with the Partner's E-mail Address. *The Directory of Venture Capital & Private Equity Firms* offers five important indexes: Geographic Index, Executive Name Index, Portfolio Company Index, Industry Preference Index and College & University Index. With its comprehensive coverage and detailed, extensive information on each company, *The Directory of Venture Capital & Private Equity Firms* is an important addition to any finance collection.

*"The sheer number of listings, the descriptive information provided and the outstanding indexing make this directory a better value than its principal competitor, Pratt's Guide to Venture Capital Sources. Recommended for business collections in large public, academic and business libraries." –Choice*

1,300 pages; Softcover ISBN 1-59237-062-4, $450.00 ♦ Online Database (includes a free copy of the directory) $889.00

## The Directory of Mail Order Catalogs, 2005

Published since 1981, this 2005 edition features 100% verification of data and is the premier source of information on the mail order catalog industry. Details over 12,000 consumer catalog companies with 44 different product chapters from Animals to Toys & Games. Contains detailed contact information including e-mail addresses and web sites along with important business details such as employee size, years in business, sales volume, catalog size, number of catalogs mailed and more. Four indexes provide quick access to information: Catalog & Company Name Index, Geographic Index, Product Index and Web Sites Index.

*"This is a godsend for those looking for information." –Reference Book Review*

1,700 pages; Softcover ISBN 1-59237-066-7 $250.00 ♦ Online Database (includes a free copy of the directory) $495.00

## The Directory of Business to Business Catalogs, 2005

The completely updated 2005 *Directory of Business to Business Catalogs*, provides details on over 6,000 suppliers of everything from computers to laboratory supplies… office products to office design… marketing resources to safety equipment… landscaping to maintenance suppliers… building construction and much more. Detailed entries offer mailing address, phone & fax numbers, e-mail addresses, web sites, key contacts, sales volume, employee size, catalog printing information and more. Jut about every kind of product a business needs in its day-to-day operations is covered in this carefully-researched volume. Three indexes are provided for at-a-glance access to information: Catalog & Company Name Index, Geographic Index and Web Sites Index.

*"An excellent choice for libraries… wishing to supplement their business supplier resources." –Booklist*

800 pages; Softcover ISBN 1-59237-064-0, $165.00 ♦ Online Database (includes a free copy of the directory) $325.00

## Thomas Food and Beverage Market Place, 2005

*Thomas Food and Beverage Market Place* is bigger and better than ever with thousands of new companies, thousands of updates to existing companies and two revised and enhanced product category indexes. This comprehensive directory profiles over 18,000 Food & Beverage Manufacturers, 12,000 Equipment & Supply Companies, 2,200 Transportation & Warehouse Companies, 2,000 Brokers & Wholesalers, 8,000 Importers & Exporters, 900 Industry Resources and hundreds of Mail Order Catalogs. Listings include detailed Contact Information, Sales Volumes, Key Contacts, Brand & Product Information, Packaging Details and much more. *Thomas Food and Beverage Market Place* is available as a three-volume printed set, a subscription-based Online Database via the Internet, on CD-ROM, as well as mailing lists and a licensable database.

*"An essential purchase for those in the food industry but will also be useful in public libraries where needed. Much of the information will be difficult and time consuming to locate without this handy three-volume ready-reference source." –ARBA*

8,500 pages, 3 Volume Set; Softcover ISBN 1-59237-058-6, $495.00 ♦ CD-ROM $695.00 ♦
CD-ROM & 3 Volume Set Combo $895.00 ♦ Online Database $695.00 ♦ Online Database & 3 Volume Set Combo, $895.00

To preview any of our Directories Risk-Free for 30 days, call (800) 562-2139 or fax to (518) 789-0556

## The Grey House Safety & Security Directory, 2005

*The Grey House Safety & Security Directory* is the most comprehensive reference tool and buyer's guide for the safety and security industry. Arranged by safety topic, each chapter begins with OSHA regulations for the topic, followed by Training Articles written by top professionals in the field and Self-Inspection Checklists. Next, each topic contains Buyer's Guide sections that feature related products and services. Topics include Administration, Insurance, Loss Control & Consulting, Protective Equipment & Apparel, Noise & Vibration, Facilities Monitoring & Maintenance, Employee Health Maintenance & Ergonomics, Retail Food Services, Machine Guards, Process Guidelines & Tool Handling, Ordinary Materials Handling, Hazardous Materials Handling, Workplace Preparation & Maintenance, Electrical Lighting & Safety, Fire & Rescue and Security. The Buyer's Guide sections are carefully indexed within each topic area to ensure that you can find the supplies needed to meet OSHA's regulations. Six important indexes make finding information and product manufacturers quick and easy: Geographical Index of Manufacturers and Distributors, Company Profile Index, Brand Name Index, Product Index, Index of Web Sites and Index of Advertisers. This comprehensive, up-to-date reference will provide every tool necessary to make sure a business is in compliance with OSHA regulations and locate the products and services needed to meet those regulations.

*"Presents industrial safety information for engineers, plant managers, risk managers, and construction site supervisors..." —Choice*

1,500 pages, 2 Volume Set; Softcover ISBN 1-59237-067-5, $225.00

## The Grey House Homeland Security Directory, 2005

This updated edition features the latest contact information for government and private organizations involved with Homeland Security along with the latest product information and provides detailed profiles of nearly 1,000 Federal & State Organizations & Agencies and over 3,000 Officials and Key Executives involved with Homeland Security. These listings are incredibly detailed and include Mailing Address, Phone & Fax Numbers, Email Addresses & Web Sites, a complete Description of the Agency and a complete list of the Officials and Key Executives associated with the Agency. Next, *The Grey House Homeland Security Directory* provides the go-to source for Homeland Security Products & Services. This section features over 2,000 Companies that provide Consulting, Products or Services. With this Buyer's Guide at their fingertips, users can locate suppliers of everything from Training Materials to Access Controls, from Perimeter Security to BioTerrorism Countermeasures and everything in between – complete with contact information and product descriptions. A handy Product Locator Index is provided to quickly and easily locate suppliers of a particular product. Lastly, an Information Resources Section provides immediate access to contact information for hundreds of Associations, Newsletters, Magazines, Trade Shows, Databases and Directories that focus on Homeland Security. This comprehensive, information-packed resource will be a welcome tool for any company or agency that is in need of Homeland Security information and will be a necessary acquisition for the reference collection of all public libraries and large school districts.

*"Compiles this information in one place and is discerning in content. A useful purchase for public and academic libraries." —Booklist*

800 pages; Softcover ISBN 1-59237-057-8, $195.00 ◆ Online Database (includes a free copy of the directory) $385.00

## The Grey House Transportation Security Directory & Handbook, 2005

This brand new title is the only reference of its kind that brings together current data on Transportation Security. With information on everything from Regulatory Authorities to Security Equipment, this top-flight database brings together the relevant information necessary for creating and maintaining a security plan for a wide range of transportation facilities. With this current, comprehensive directory at the ready you'll have immediate access to: Regulatory Authorities & Legislation; Information Resources; Sample Security Plans & Checklists; Contact Data for Major Airports, Seaports, Railroads, Trucking Companies and Oil Pipelines; Security Service Providers; Recommended Equipment & Product Information and more. Using the *Grey House Transportation Security Directory & Handbook*, managers will be able to quickly and easily assess their current security plans; develop contacts to create and maintain new security procedures; and source the products and services necessary to adequately maintain a secure environment. This valuable resource is a must for all Security Managers at Airports, Seaports, Railroads, Trucking Companies and Oil Pipelines.

800 pages; Softcover ISBN 1-59237-075-6, $195

To preview any of our Directories Risk-Free for 30 days, call (800) 562-2139 or fax to (518) 789-0556

## The Grey House Biometric Information Directory, 2006

*The Biometric Information Directory* is the only comprehensive source for current biometric industry information. This 2006 edition is the first published by Grey House. With 100% updated information, this latest edition offers a complete, current look, in both print and online form, of biometric companies and products – one of the fastest growing industries in today's economy. Detailed profiles of manufacturers of the latest biometric technology, including Finger, Voice, Face, Hand, Signature, Iris, Vein and Palm Identification systems. Data on the companies include key executives, company size and a detailed, indexed description of their product line. Plus, the Directory also includes valuable business resources, and current editorial make this edition the easiest way for the business community and consumers alike to access the largest, most current compilation of biometric industry information available on the market today. The new edition boasts increased numbers of companies, contact names and company data, with over 700 manufacturers and service providers. Information in the directory includes: Editorial on Advancements in Biometrics; Profiles of 700+ companies listed with contact information; Organizations, Trade & Educational Associations, Publications, Conferences, Trade Shows and Expositions Worldwide; Web Site Index; Biometric & Vendors Services Index by Types of Biometrics; and a Glossary of Biometric Terms. This resource will be an important source for anyone who is considering the use of a biometric product, investing in the development of biometric technology, support existing marketing and sales efforts and will be an important acquisition for the business reference collection for large public and business libraries.

800 pages; Softcover ISBN 1-59237-121-3, $295

## Sports Market Place Directory, 2005

For over 20 years, this comprehensive, up-to-date directory has offered direct access to the Who, What, When & Where of the Sports Industry. With over 20,000 updates and enhancements, the *Sports Market Place Directory* is the most detailed, comprehensive and current sports business reference source available. In 1,800 information-packed pages, *Sports Market Place Directory* profiles contact information and key executives for: Single Sport Organizations, Professional Leagues, Multi-Sport Organizations, Disabled Sports, High School & Youth Sports, Military Sports, Olympic Organizations, Media, Sponsors, Sponsorship & Marketing Event Agencies, Event & Meeting Calendars, Professional Services, College Sports, Manufacturers & Retailers, Facilities and much more. *The Sports Market Place Directory* provides organization's contact information with detailed descriptions including: Key Contacts, physical, mailing, email and web addresses plus phone and fax numbers. Plus, nine important indexes make sure that you can find the information you're looking for quickly and easily: Entry Index, Single Sport Index, Media Index, Sponsor Index, Agency Index, Manufacturers Index, Brand Name Index, Facilities Index and Executive/Geographic Index. For over twenty years, *The Sports Market Place Directory* has assisted thousands of individuals in their pursuit of a career in the sports industry. Why not use "THE SOURCE" that top recruiters, headhunters and career placement centers use to find information on or about sports organizations and key hiring contacts.

1,800 pages; Softcover ISBN 1-59237-077-2, $225.00 ♦ CD-ROM $479.00

## New York State Directory, 2005/06

*The New York State Directory*, published annually since 1983, is a comprehensive and easy-to-use guide to accessing public officials and private sector organizations and individuals who influence public policy in the state of New York. *The New York State Directory* includes important information on all New York state legislators and congressional representatives, including biographies and key committee assignments. It also includes staff rosters for all branches of New York state government and for federal agencies and departments that impact the state policy process. Following the state government section are 25 chapters covering policy areas from agriculture through veterans' affairs. Each chapter identifies the state, local and federal agencies and officials that formulate or implement policy. In addition, each chapter contains a roster of private sector experts and advocates who influence the policy process. The directory also offers appendices that include statewide party officials; chambers of commerce; lobbying organizations; public and private universities and colleges; television, radio and print media; and local government agencies and officials.

New York State Directory - 800 pages; Softcover ISBN 1-59237-093-4; $129.00
New York State Directory with Profiles of New York – 2 volumes; 1,600 pages; Softcover ISBN 1-59237-095-0; $195

To preview any of our Directories Risk-Free for 30 days, call (800) 562-2139 or fax to (518) 789-0556

## Profiles of New York, 2005/06 ♦ Profiles of Florida, 2005/06 ♦ Profiles of Texas, 2005/06

Packed with over 50 pieces of data that make up a complete, user-friendly profile of each state, these directories go even further by then pulling selected data and providing it in ranking list form for even easier comparisons between the 100 largest towns and cities! The careful layout gives the user an easy-to-read snapshot of every single place and county in the state, from the biggest metropolis to the smallest unincorporated hamlet. The richness of each place or county profile is astounding in its depth, from history to weather, all packed in an easy-to-navigate, compact format. No need for piles of multiple sources with this volume on your desk. Here is a look at just a few of the data sets you'll find in each profile: History, Geography, Climate, Population, Vital Statistics, Economy, Income, Taxes, Education, Housing, Health & Environment, Public Safety, Newspapers, Transportation, Presidential Election Results, Information Contacts and Chambers of Commerce. As an added bonus, there is a section on Selected Statistics, where data from the 100 largest towns and cities is arranged into easy-to-use charts. Each of 22 different data points has its own two-page spread with the cities listed in alpha order so researchers can easily compare and rank cities. A remarkable compilation that offers overviews and insights into each corner of the state, *Profiles of New York, Profiles of Florida* and *Profiles of Texas* go beyond Census statistics, beyond metro area coverage, beyond the 100 best places to live. Drawn from official census information, other government statistics and original research, you will have at your fingertips data that's available nowhere else in one single source. Data will be published on additional states in 2006 and 2007.

Profiles of New York, 2005/06: 800 pages; Softcover ISBN 1-59237-108-6; $129.00
Profiles of Florida, 2005/06: 800 pages; Softcover ISBN 1-59237-110-8; $129.00
Profies of Texas, 2005/06: 800 pages; Softcover ISBN 1-59237-111-6; $129.00

## International Business and Trade Directories

Completely updated, the Third Edition of *International Business and Trade Directories* now contains more than 10,000 entries, over 2,000 more than the last edition, making this directory the most comprehensive resource of the worlds business and trade directories. Entries include content descriptions, price, publisher's name and address, web site and e-mail addresses, phone and fax numbers and editorial staff. Organized by industry group, and then by region, this resource puts over 10,000 industry-specific business and trade directories at the reader's fingertips. Three indexes are included for quick access to information: Geographic Index, Publisher Index and Title Index. Public, college and corporate libraries, as well as individuals and corporations seeking critical market information will want to add this directory to their marketing collection.

*"Reasonably priced for a work of this type, this directory should appeal to larger academic, public and corporate libraries with an international focus." –Library Journal*

1,800 pages; Softcover ISBN 1-930956-63-0, $225.00 ♦ Online Database (includes a free copy of the directory) $450.00

To preview any of our Directories Risk-Free for 30 days, call (800) 562-2139 or fax to (518) 789-0556